Encyclopedia of Caribbean Literature

Advisory Board

VOLUME 1, A–L

Encyclopedia of Caribbean Literature

Edited by

D. H. FIGUEREDO

Greenwood Press
Westport, Connecticut • London

Library of Congress Cataloging-in-Publication Data

Encyclopedia of Caribbean literature / edited by D.H. Figueredo.
   p. cm.
   Includes bibliographical references and index.
   ISBN 0-313-32742-4 (set : alk. paper) — ISBN 0-313-32743-2 (v. 1: alk. paper) — ISBN 0-313-32744-0 (v. 2 : alk. paper)
   1. Caribbean literature—Encyclopedias.   2. Authors, Caribbean—Biography—Encyclopedias.
I. Figueredo, D.H., 1951– .
   PN849.C3E53   2006
   809'.89729—dc22   2005025483

British Library Cataloguing in Publication Data is available.

This book is included in the *African American Experience*
database from Greenwood Electronic Media. For more
information, visit: www.africanamericanexperience.com.

Library of Congress Catalog Card Number: 2005025483
ISBN: 0-313-32742-4 (set)
     0-313-32743-2 (vol. 1)
     0-313-32744-0 (vol. 2)

First published in 2006

Greenwood Press, 88 Post Road West, Westport, CT 06881
An imprint of Greenwood Publishing Group, Inc.
www.greenwood.com

Printed in the United States of America

The paper used in this book complies with the
Permanent Paper Standard issued by the National
Information Standards Organization (Z39.48-1984).

10 9 8 7 6 5 4 3 2 1

Contents

List of Entries

Guide to Related Topics

In addition to biographical entries, the *Encyclopedia* includes entries on numerous special topics. The following list conveniently groups these topical entries in broad categories.

Drama:
Carreta, La

Fiction:
Brown Girl, Brownstones
Cecilia Valdés o La Loma del Àngel; novela de costumbres cubanas
Charca, La
Compère Général Soleil
Farming of Bones, The
Gouverneurs de la rosée
Hills Were Joyful Together, The
House for Mr. Biswas, A
In the Castle of My Skin
New Day
Palace of the Peacock, The
Paradiso
"Viaje a la semilla"
Wide Sargasso Sea

Genres *and* Types of Literature:
Abolitionist Literature
Anancy Stories
Anti-Castro Literature
Barrack Yard Literature
Barroco/Baroque
Children's Literature in the English-Speaking Caribbean
Children Literature in the Hispanic Caribbean
Costumbrismo
Detective Fiction
Dub Poetry

Exile Literature
Gay and Lesbian Literature
Historical Novel
Immigrant Literature
Indianist Literature
Literatura Comprometida/Socially Engaged Literature
Magical Realism
Negrista Literature
Noismo
Nuyorican Literature
Peasant Novel, The
Performance Poetry
Plantation Society in Caribbean Literature, The
Slave Narratives
Testimonio
Trujillo Era

Cultural or National Identity:
Ainsi parla l'oncle
Bovaryism
Caliban
Code Switching
Créolité
Indigènisme
Insularismo
Negrista Literature
Négritude

Journals:
Asomante
Beacon, The

Preface

Arranged alphabetically, this encyclopedia provides general information on the literature of the Caribbean. It is in many ways unique: for the contributors are presenting the readers the many universes that make up the Caribbean. In this reference volume, the literature of the anglophone, the Dutch, the francophone, and the Hispanic Caribbean is housed under one roof, as it were. Other reference sources have approached the topic from a single perspective, usually arranged by language. In such a scheme, the norm has been to favor the Hispanic Caribbean, probably the best known and most popular. In other endeavors where the larger Caribbean was targeted, the editors and the contributors provided valuable bibliographic information but sketchy details of the lives of the authors. This encyclopedia aims to draw a biographical profile of a writer, a summary of themes, brief analyses of major works, and a list of each writer's most important works. Other entries include major works, genres, movements, historical events, national literatures, and the like.

The authors and the topics selected were recommended by the members of the editorial board. The members of the board also suggested the countries and territories for inclusion: Antigua, Barbados, Cuba, Dominican Republic, Grenada, Guadeloupe, Haiti, Jamaica, Martinique, Netherlands Antilles, Puerto Rico, St. Lucia, and Trinidad-Tobago. Three countries or territories from South America are also included: French Guiana, Guyana, and Suriname. French Guiana and Suriname are often neglected from studies of Latin American literature, thus members of the board supported their inclusion in this project. Guyana has been the home or birthplace of numerous writers of global significance, of which Wilson Harris is the best known, and the Guyanese people feel as if they live on an island, since the country is flanked by an impenetrable forest on one side and the Atlantic on the other. Guyanese seldom travel through the forest, and their communications with the rest of the world is through and from the Atlantic Coast. Because space is limited, other countries from Central and South America facing the Caribbean were not included. But often these nations, such as Colombia and Venezuela, are well represented in literary surveys and reference volumes.

The members of the board and the contributors, nearly forty, are experts and published authors themselves. Collectively, they represent such universities as City University of New York, Columbia University, Hunter College, Notre Dame University, Princeton University, University of California–Davis, University of Havana, University of Puerto Rico, University of the West Indies, and Vanderbilt University, as well as such prestigious institutions as the Americas Society and such publications as the *Miami Herald* and the *Multicultural Review*, among others. As a group, they speak several languages, including English, Dutch, French, Kreyòl, Spanish, and Papiamentu.

Scope

Individual board members compiled a list of authors and topics he or she felt was crucial for any knowledge of the literature of a particular country. After all the entries were gathered, I, as editor, shared the list with the entire board. Once they nodded their collective approval, came the next more difficult step: which entries would stay and which entries would be dismissed? Again, the members of the board recommended deletions based on several criteria:

1. How important is this author to the development of a national literature?
2. How is the author regarded within the Caribbean at large?
3. Is the author currently in the canon?
4. Should this author be incorporated into the canon?
5. If the author is considered by critics a literary figure of little importance, is the author nevertheless a popular figure at home and therefore deserving of inclusion?
6. Would this be the very first time the author appears in a reference volume, and by including him or her, are we providing an important service to the dissemination of the national literature and to the general knowledge?
7. Would this author be significant in a generation hence?

But there were also other considerations. Normally, a literary sourcebook might not include historians, social scientists, and politicians who dabble in writing. But often these individuals produce works that are both highly readable and influential; thus, a number of such individuals found a spot in this reference volume. There were also discoveries of emerging authors not yet tested by time and the canon but whose writings clearly exhibit the makings of a literary legacy or who themselves, at the very least, are important cultural figures. These promising newcomers are therefore included.

There are omissions, to be sure. Those are my errors. Whatever is good in this reference source comes from the editorial board. Whatever is missing is attributable to my own deficiency.

How to Use the Encyclopedia

The encyclopedia is arranged from A to Z, following the Library of Congress cataloguing rule. For example, for Spanish surnames, the first surname dictated position in the encyclopedia, thus Gustavo Pérez Firmat is listed as **Pérez Firmat, Gustavo.** When an author used a pen name, a cross reference appears: **Fernandes, Carlos M. See Lauffer, Pierre A.** This encyclopedia also includes information on several selected major literary works. In such cases, the title known in English directs the reader to the original title, where the entry then appears: **Masters of Dew. See *Gouverneurs de la rosée.*** General or popular literary expressions are referred to the entry: **Literature of Local Color. See Costumbrismo.** Literary terms that are similar in two languages appear together: **Naturalism/Naturalismo.** Within the entry, cross-references are presented in bold: **peasant novel.** Special emphasis was given to identifying families of writers, and in such cases several entries are placed within a general category. For example, **Césaire Family, The** includes the entries for father, Aimé Césaire; mother, Suzanne Césaire; and daughter, Ina Césaire, all important writers.

At the end of each entry, books, articles, and Web sites are listed. In cases wherein a contemporary author was interviewed by the contributor, the interview date is indicated. At the end of the volume is a bibliography of general sources. For clarity's sake, members of the editorial board advised against translating foreign-language titles into English. We arrived at this conclusion when in an earlier draft we realized it was easy to confuse the reader into thinking that an English translation of a title implied availability of that work in English. At the end of the entry, there are, as needed, "see also" notes: *See also* Literary Journals.

Although every attempt has been made to remain current, some authors have produced new works, received new honors, or passed away since the completion of this encyclopedia.

Acknowledgments

Above all, I must acknowledge my wife, Yvonne, my son, Daniel, and my daughter, Gabriela. They walked gently with me as I took this exciting journey. As an academic administrator, I received neither funding nor time off for researching and writing, so the intrepid trio accompanied me on trips and excused me for chores. They did so with a smile.

I must thank several authors who were eager to provide me with information, refer me to friends, and even rally contributors: Emilio Bejel, Belkis Cuza Malé, Barbara Flanagan, Kwame Dawes, Margarita Mateo Palmer, Pablo Medina, Himilce Novas, Philip Nourbese and Rolando Pérez. I visited many libraries, but there were a handful that served as second base for my research, and I must thank the unknown librarians there: the Alexander and the Kilmer Libraries at Rutgers University, New Brunswick and Piscataway, respectively; the Center for Puerto Rican Studies Library at Hunter College; the Firestone Library at Princeton University; the Davidson Library at the University of California–Santa Barbara; and the Schomburg Center for Research in Black Culture, New York Public Library.

Heartfelt gracias to Daniel Shapiro, Americas Society, Salvador Guereña, Multicultural Archives at the University of California–Santa Barbara, Nelida Pérez, Center for Puerto Rican Studies, David Tambo and Edward C. Fields, from rare books and archives at the University of California–Santa Barbara, and Fernando Acosta and Peter Johnson, Princeton University, for sharing archives and rare journals; and Margaret Rouse-Jones, University of the West Indies–Trinidad, for providing contacts and scholars. My warm thanks to Lisa Finder, Hunter College, for tracking down photographs and conducting research at the Schomburg Center for Research in Black Culture; Sandra Stelts of The Pennsylvania State University, Special Collections Library, Rare Books and Manuscripts; Roberto González Echevarría, Yale University; Lesbia Orta Varona, Cuban Heritage Collection, the Otto C. Richter Library at the University of Miami; cartographer Armando H. Portela, Miami Herald; and Elsa M. Ruiz, photographer.

And thanks to the dedicated editors from Greenwood Press: Anne Thompson, who introduced me to this project, and George Butler, who guided me, encouraged me, and demonstrated patience and faith; and to Carol Singer and Juliann Barbato of GGS Book Services.

Introduction

"The Caribbean is unending."

The tweed-jacketed gentleman who made the observation while we were sipping coffee at a conference did not know that he was echoing a sentiment that had been expressed a few years earlier by Cuban writer Antonio Benítez-Rojo in his classic *La isla que se repite* (1989). Benítez-Rojo himself knew that his own assertion was neither new nor original. Decades before, great writers such as Aimé Césaire, Edward Kamau Brathwaite, and Derek Walcott had come to a similar realization. For their own growth as individuals, their development as authors and their psychological and philosophical explorations of the region had been challenged and constrained, energized and frustrated by the ever-changing, never-ending evolutionary nature of the Caribbean.

It is an evasive, elusive nature, seen and not seen, always present. The coquí comes to mind. This Puerto Rican frog, as small as a thumbnail and as delicate as the breeze, sings a beautiful song—*co-quí, co-quí, co-quí*—from which its name is derived. When emitting this delightful sound, the tiny frog projects its voice in such a manner that the sound bounces back from any object, conjuring the illusion that the minuscule amphibian sits on a spot opposite its actual location. The echo the listener hears is a reflection of the source away from the source.

Thus it is with Caribbean writers. Consider, for example, Puerto Rican José Luis González crossing an avenue in Mexico City, writing in his heart about Puerto Rico, and the Trinidadian V. S. Naipaul in the British countryside, seeing not pines and oak trees but a Caribbean landscape a continent away. These writers were projecting their souls across the ocean, from the New World to the Old, from the Old to the New. But it doesn't end there. For their longing was an exercise in longing and not an actual wish for a literal return to the source. For González and Naipaul, and scores of other writers, could not and did not want to lead lives in the very source of their lives: their respective native country. They longed to escape, and desperately so.

The Caribbean, however, did not escape from them, did not desert these writers. Whether they journeyed to Montreal or Nigeria, Liverpool or Mexico, the Caribbean lingered in the souls of these writers, giving substance to their writings—informing their writings, as critics like to say. No matter how British or Spanish or French they became, these writers remained—with some exceptions—Caribbean to the core: a Haitian from Miami, a Puerto Rican of the San Juan suburb of El Barrio, located in Manhattan.

The cue for questions surfaces now. If these writers who live in Europe and the United States write about the Caribbean and often not in the language of the host country, are they producing a Caribbean literature? Do they belong in other literary canons? Paule Marshall, for example, doesn't always identify herself as Barbadian. Are her novels, therefore, representative of contemporary Barbadian literature or of American literature? Is the Haitian American novelist Edwidge Danticat a writer of Haitian literature or of fiction written in English but dealing with Haiti? It is a dual existence that multiplies itself from writer to writer, country to country, century to century. A student might hear a professor assert that if an author, such as Julia alvarez, writes in English even though she was born in the Dominican Republic, she is not creating literature of her native country but rather American literature, in the same way the Polish writer Joseph Conrad crafted British novels.

For that professor, that's where the classification ends. But then, poets like Miguel Algarín and novelists like Nicholasa Mohr grab their Puerto Ricanness, shake up their Americanness, and throw in their experiences in New York to form Nuyorican literature, which was once rejected by Spanish-language purists in Puerto Rico but is now praised as another Puerto Rican experience—as well as a unique experience of American literature.

The variations on this theme play loudly. Take Andrew York, a spy novelist who dashes up exciting thrillers with a James Bond–like protagonist—who is far more human and complex. Yet, York is the pseudonym of Christopher R. Nicholson, who was born in Guyana and studied in the Caribbean before sailing to the English Channel Islands, where he lives. Does he not want to be identified as Guyanese? Is this why he uses a half dozen pen names? Maybe. Maybe not. It might just be a scheme for success, not much different than writers from Haiti—such as Gary Klang—who get published in France and Canada, gathering francs—or Eurodollars—along the way. It might not be an issue of ethnic and national pride but rather one of economic reality. After all, with the exception of Cuba, where authors draw government checks, opportunities in the Caribbean are just not there.

But far from the native country, the doors to opportunity do not readily yield to all who knock: the legendary Puerto Rican poet Julia de Burgos died in poverty in Manhattan, and her body decomposed at a morgue before friends claimed her. And in the land of milk and honey, Caribbean writers must contend with grievances endemic to their national, political, and ethnic conditions. If you're a Cuban exile and dislike Fidel Castro, as novelist Guillermo Cabrera Infante had learned, many publishers might not publish you. If you're black and from the anglophone Caribbean and suggest assimilation and understanding, as Guyanese E. R. Braithwaite does in his best-seller *To Sir, With Love* (1959), colleagues and critics might dismiss you. If you're from Martinique, like Eduoard Glissant, and oppose Négritude, you might encounter the wrath of such giants as Aimé Césaire, one of the fathers of Négritude. On the other hand, writers like Maryse Condé, who warmed up slowly to those who opposed Césaire and was not so ready to dismiss the importance of Négritude and its emphasis on the creation of black consciousness, were considered immature by the likes of Patrick Chamoiseau, who also belittled Condé's feminist viewpoints.

Do these writers protest too much? Surely, but protest, social and political, has been a genuine enterprise of Caribbean writers; protest, in fact, serves as genre, "literatura comprometida," and as an inspiration, and as a theme. There are other themes as well: colonialism, discrimination, life in exile, the pains of immigration, identity crisis, uses of the host country language versus the native country's language, political oppression, racism, and sexual identity. Scholar Belinda J. Edmonson, in the essay "The Caribbean: Myths, Tropes, Discourse," which appears in the anthology *Caribbean Romances: The Politics of Regional Representation* (1999), prefers key words over themes, key words and phrases that prompt instantaneous discourses in and out of the Caribbean.

The discourses shape up in a diversity of styles, from realism to experimental to the fantastic, which in turn prompt writers to visit genres not of their own specialization such as with the poet who writes novels, the dramatist who ventures into literary criticism, and the critic who cultivates fiction and poetry. Their willingness to try out a variety of genres also indicates a willingness to extend beyond the written page, thus transforming themselves into other entities. Caribbean authors, for example, often double up as politicians: Aimé Césaire, Juan Bosch, and Eric Williams, to name a few. And Caribbean politicians often double up as writers: Joaquín Balaguer, Debrot Cola, François Duvalier, and Albert Gomes. Whether they're good writers or good politicians, that's another story. But some writers do become legendary in both spheres, the political and the creative: José Martí, Pachín Marín, and Jean Stephen Alexis.

It is no accident that these legendary figures did not die in their beds. As Veloz Maggioli points out in *Cultura, teatro y relatos en Santo Domingo* (1972), writing in the Caribbean can be dangerous. Novelist Roger Mais was arrested in Jamaica during the 1940s for expressing anti-British views. Ramon Marrero Aristy, from the Dominican Republic, was murdered by Trujillo henchmen for criticizing the dictatorship. And many ended their own lives, protesting against oppression: the Cuban Reinaldo Arenas, for one.

In Cuba, Arenas's opposition to the Castro regime resulted in silence: during his lifetime pro-Castro Cuban intellectuals maintained that on the island there was no such writer as Arenas. After his death, it seemed that a final, complete silence would be the end of his career. But that was not so. His autobiography, *Antes que anochezca* (1992), written on his deathbed, became a best-seller and a movie, and then, as if writing from his grave, all the manuscripts he had written but had not had published, were published, not only in Spanish but in English and Italian as well. Two decades after his death, his life as a writer had not come to an end, but to a beginning.

Arenas fits well with this Caribbean experience, with this literature, for it has no ending and it is always beginning. Caribbean writers are constantly reinventing words, reinventing genres, reinventing themselves. In *Defining Jamaican Fiction* (1996), Barbara Lalla writes: "The definition of Caribbean literature is . . . incomplete." Echos of Césaire, Benítez-Rojo, Brathwaite, and Walcott.

This unending universe makes by its very existence this encyclopedia unending. Thus, my excuse for the errors I have made in this adventure: not all writers who should be here are here. But this encyclopedia had to pause to meet *the* publisher's deadlines. This encyclopedia had to be "finished." Now, the writing is done, the volumes are printed, the tomes are in your hands. Yet the project is *not* over: it will *never* be over.

"This Caribbean encyclopedia is unending," I will tell the tweed-jacketed gentleman the next time we sip coffee together.

—D. H. Figueredo
Editor

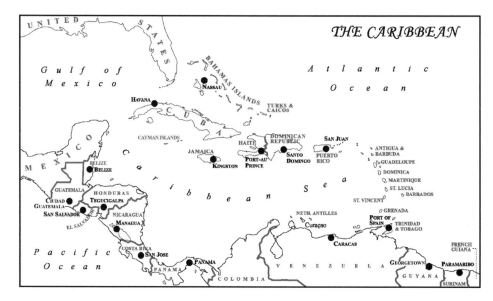

Map by Armando H. Portela.

A

Abella, Alex (1950–)

Alex Abella is a Cuban American novelist who has created a new twist within the detective-story genre: a Sam Spade–type of investigator who specializes in cult crimes related to Santería, an Afro-Cuban religion. Abella is an also a court reporter, a journalist, and a playwright.

Born on November 8, 1950, in Havana, Cuba, Abella and his parents emigrated to Miami, Florida, in 1961. In 1972, Abella graduated from Columbia University. He worked for several entertainment journals and public relations firms before moving to California in 1975. He wrote for the *San Francisco Chronicle* and was a broadcast journalist for a Spanish radio station. In the meantime, Abella doubled up as a court interpreter, translating for Spanish-speaking defendants.

His contact with the legal system and familiarity with criminal trials served as the foundation for his mystery novels, which feature Charlie Morell, a Cuban attorney, as protagonist. Abella's knowledge of Santería and cult crimes that occurred in Cuba at the turn of the twentieth century provided him with materials for the plot of *The Killing of the Saints* (1997), *Dead of Night* (1998), and *Final Acts* (2000). The first of the trio is the most well known; it tells the story of two Cuban criminals who claim to be possessed by spirits during a killing spree.

Abella also wrote *The Great American* (1997), a historical romance of the Cuban revolution centered on the life of an American rebel named William Morgan (1928–61), an actual participant in the revolutionary struggle who was executed by the Castro regime. Though the work falls within the genre of the **anti-Castro literature**, it offers a sympathetic portrayal of many of the early leaders, including Ernesto "Che" Guevara (1928–67).

Abella writes in a style referred to as **magical realism**, which involve the appearance of spirits and bizarre phenomenons of nature (a windstorm occurring in a courtroom, for example). He often employs a technique called **code switching**, in which characters speak in English peppered with Spanish words and phrases. His sex scenes are graphic and erotic, perhaps influenced by **naturalismo**. *See also* Cuban American Literature; Detective Fiction; Santería in Literature.

Further Reading

Figueredo, Danilo H. "The Stuff Dreams Are Made Of: The Latino Detective Novel." *Multicultural Review* 8, no. 3 (September 1999): 22–29.

—D. H. Figueredo

Abolitionist Literature
■

Abolitionist literature was a body of work produced with the political objective of ending slavery. The abolitionist movement began toward the end of the eighteenth century England and the Northeast of the United States and spread throughout the Caribbean, reaching its summit in the nineteenth century with the abolition of slavery in Cuba in 1880. Abolitionist literature, also called antislavery literature, was printed in newspapers and broadsides.

Probably the best known work from the Caribbean is the autobiography *The Interesting Narratives of the Life of Olaudah Equiano, or Gustavus Vassa, The African, written by himself* (1787). In 1833, former slave **Mary Prince** told her story to Thomas Pringle, who edited the narrative into *The History of Mary Prince, a West Indian Slave, Related by Herself*. The volume, published as an antislavery tract, depicts the horrors of slavery from a very personal view and serves also as a document of resistance.

In the 1800s, according to Gwen Kirkpatrick, in *Modern Latin American Culture* (2004), Cuba played a central role in the production of antislavery novels: *Francisco: el ingenio o las delicias del campo* (1839) by **Anselmo Suárez y Romero**; *Sab* by **Gertrudis Gómez de Avellaneda**; and *Cecilia Valdés o La Loma del Ángel: novela de costumbres cubanas* (1839, expanded in 1879, published 1882) by **Cirilo Villaverde**. In 1867, Puerto Rican **Alejandro Tapia y Rivera** wrote an abolitionist drama, *La cuarterona*. That same year, Segundo Ruíz Belvis, also from Puerto Rico, wrote a brilliant argument against slavery: *Proyecto para la abolición de la esclavitud en Puerto Rico*.

Supporters of abolition turned as well to the **slave narratives**, autobiographical accounts of the evils of slavery, as documentation for editorials and debates. *See also* Equiano, Olaudah.

Further Reading

Butler, Kim D. "Abolition and the Politics of Identity in the Afro-Atlantic Diaspora: Toward a Comparative Approach." In *Crossing Boundaries: Comparative History of Black People in Diaspora*, edited by Marlene Clark Hine and Jacqueline McLeod, 121–33. Bloomington: Indiana University Press, 1999.

Kirkpatrick, Gwen. "Spanish American Narrative, 1810–1920." In *The Cambridge Companion to Modern Latin American Culture*, edited by John King, 74–75. Cambridge: Cambridge University Press, 2004.

—D. H. Figueredo

Acosta, Agustín (1886–1979)

Cuba's National Poet Agustín Acosta was a poet of social protest whose most famous work, *La zafra* (1926), decried Cubans' willingness to allow American capitalism to grow unchecked on the island. He was also a public official and promoter of Cuban literature and culture.

Agustín Acosta y Bello was born on November 12, 1886, in Matanzas. He attended secondary school at the Instituto Provincial de Matanzas and became an attorney in 1918. Along with poets Regino Boti and José Manuel Poveda, Acosta inspired poetic activities and a cultural renaissance in the provinces rather than the capital, the usual center of literary enterprise. During the 1920s, Acosta worked as an attorney at a sugar plantation, witnessing firsthand the exploitation of the sugar laborers and the expansion of American interests in the Cuban sugar industry. From this experience came the basis for his most famous book of poetry, *La zafra*.

Two poems in the collection, published in 1926, became widely known: "Las carretas de la noche" and "Mediodía en el campo." The poems, using words that evoke the sounds made by carts and the sugar mill, re-create the look and feel of a sugar plantation. The sugar plantation itself becomes a symbol of the oppressed farmers. *La zafra* was viewed as a cry of protest and a cry for nationalism.

In the early 1930s, Acosta was arrested during the regime of Gerardo Machado (1871–1939). Upon his release in 1933, after the fall of Machado's dictatorship, Acosta was appointed governor of Matanzas province. From 1936 to 1944 he served as a senator. In 1955, the Cuban congress conferred upon Acosta the title of Cuba's National Poet. In 1973, he left Cuba for Miami, where he passed away in 1979.

His other works include *Los camellos distantes* (1941), *Las islas desoladas* (1943), *Caminos de hierro* (1963), and, published after his death, *Poemas escojidos* (1988). The influential scholar **Max Henríquez Ureña**, in his *Panorama histórico de la literatura cubana* (1979), described Acosta's poetry as "lofty and dignified. It occupies in Cuban poetry a prominent place: it is poetry of . . . combat" (350). *See also* Cuban Literature, History of; Literatura Comprometida/Socially Engaged Literature.

Further Reading

Capote, María. *Agustín Acosta: el modernista y su isla*. Miami: Ediciones Universal, 1990.

Henríquez Ureña, Max. *Panorama histórico de la literatura cubana, Tomo II*. Habana: Editorial Arte y Literatura, 1979.

—Wilfredo Cancio Isla

Acosta, Iván (1943–)

The author of one of the most popular plays written in Spanish in the United States about Latino immigration, Iván Acosta is a Cuban dramatist, performer, and producer. The play, entitled *El super*, made into a successful film in 1979, attracted thousands of Cuban exiles, who lined up outside movie theaters in Florida, New Jersey, and New York to watch a production that for the first time portrayed Cuban Americans without resorting to the fervent anti-Castro or criminal stereotype so popular in the media.

Acosta was born in the city Santiago de Cuba, Cuba, and arrived in the United States in 1961. Settling in New York City, he founded the Centro Cultural Cubano, where he produced plays written by Latino authors. In 1971, he wrote a musical, *Grito 71*, which received several prizes, including the Thalia and Ariel Awards. He also produced two albums of his own songs, which he performed himself: *Iván Acosta: canciones de la vida, de la patria, del amor* (1978) and *Iván Acosta, Cantautor* (1981).

During the 1980s, Acosta worked for a Spanish television network in Chicago and directed the Spanish-language drama department at the Henry Street Playhouse in New York City. In 1986, he wrote and produced the film *Amigos*, about a Cuban refugee who participated in the Mariel Boatlift of 1980 and the difficulties he encountered in Miami when older Cubans, who considered themselves economically and socially superior, discriminated against him. In 1989, he published a collection of three plays, *Un cubiche en la luna: tres obras teatrales*, and in 2001 wrote and produced the documentary *Como se forma una rumba*, about the evolution of modern Cuban music. It is *El super*, however, that remains his most important contribution: its study of a man who longs for his country but cannot return, and thus feels trapped in the United States, appeals to immigrants from all over the world. The film won the Main Award at the Mannheim-Heidelberg Filmfestival, in West Germany; was a popular art-house feature in New York City; and introduced Cuban actress Elizabeth Peña. *See also* Cuban American Literature; Immigrant Literature.

Further Reading

Kanellos, Nicolás. "Iván Acosta (1943–)" in *Herencia: The Anthology of Hispanic Literature of the United States,* edited by Nicolás Kanellos, 411–14. Oxford: Oxford University Press, 2002.

—*D. H. Figueredo*

Ada, Alma Flor (1938–)

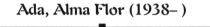

Cuban American Alma Flor Ada is a prolific author of children's books and educational texts, as well as an editor and translator. Like many other children's writers from the Caribbean, such as Puerto Rican **Pura Belpré** and Jamaican **James Berry**, Ada is inspired by her childhood memories and by Latin American customs and folklore.

Alma Flor Ada was born on January 3, 1938, in Camagüey, Cuba. She grew up in a comfortable environment—her father was a professor and her mother an accountant—surrounded by aunts, uncles, and grandparents. Her grandmother taught young Ada how to read before she was three years old, and her relatives would spend many evenings telling stories about their lives. There were also in her neighborhood memorable and colorful people, such as the ballet teacher who literally danced until the day she died and the shy girl with the flaming red hair who was a Holocaust survivor.

In the late 1950s, Ada went to Spain to study. She graduated from the Universidad Complutense de Madrid in 1959, then returned to Latin America to attend the Pontificia Universidad Católica del Perú, earning a master and a doctorate. She then conducted postdoctoral work at Harvard University. A fellow at Radcliffe Institute and a Fulbright scholar, she first taught at Emory University (Atlanta) and Mercy College of Detroit before moving in 1976 to the University of San Francisco, where she is an education professor and the director of the Center for Multicultural Literature for Children and Young Adults.

Despite her professional commitments, Ada began to write children's stories in the mid-1970s. As a young child in Cuba, she had promised herself that one day she would write children's books that were entertaining and not as monotonous and pedantic as the texts she had read in school. Thus, she set out to write tales that were humorous and told in down-to-earth language, with a repetitive pattern that made reading easier. Her first children's books were written in Spanish and published in Peru. But in the 1980s, she wrote bilingual stories—in Spanish and English—and picture books in English that were published in the United States. Her stories can be divided into three groups: (1) retelling of folktales from Latin America, such as *The Rooster Who Went to His Uncle's Wedding* (1993); (2) original stories, such as *The Gold Coin* (1992), about a thief whose life is changed by a gentle old woman; and (3) memoirs, such as *Under the Royal Palms: A Childhood in Cuba* (1998).

Alma Flor Ada has won numerous awards, including the Parents' Choice Honor Book (1995), the Simon Wiesenthal Museum of Tolerance Award (1998), and the Pura Belpré Award from the American Library Association (2000). She has written many books with her daughter Rosalma Zubizarreta. At conferences and book readings, she encourages participants, often children, to write their own stories. One of her aims as a writer, according to the *Multicultural Review*, is "to encourage her readers to write about their experiences and their relatives," reminding everyone that "life is filled with wonder and we all have a story to tell." *See also* Children's Literature in the Hispanic Caribbean.

Further Reading

Ada, Alma Flor. *Under the Royal Palms: A Childhood in Cuba*. New York: Simon & Schuster, 1998.

Figueredo, Danilo H. "Review of Under Royal Palms." *Multicultural Review* 8, no. 3 (September 1999): 95–96.

D. H. Figueredo

Adisa, Opal Palmer (1954–)

Opal Palmer Adisa belongs to a group of Caribbean women writers and scholars, that includes Jamaican **Erna Brodber**, **Jamaica Kincaid**, from Antigua, and **Paule Marshall**, from Barbados, each of whom first achieved prominence in the mid-1980s, presenting the literary world with a feminist view of life and culture in the Caribbean. Adisa is a poet, a children's writer, a literary critic, and an artist.

Born on November 6, 1954, in Kingston, Jamaica, Opal Palmer Adisa emigrated to the United States in 1970. She earned a BA at Hunter College and an MA in English at San Francisco State University. In 1992, she earned a PhD from the University of California–Berkeley. In 1985, she wrote the children's book *Pina, the Many-Eyed Fruit*. In 1989, she wrote the book of poetry, *Traveling Women*; in 1992, she published the collection of poems *Tamarind and Mango Women*. Critical notice came with the publication of her novel *It Begins with Tears*, published in 1997. The novel recounts two separate stories: one about a former prostitute and the destruction she causes in her hometown when she returns and engages in sexual relations with married men; the other about a mythical village where a couple is planning their son's wedding. By the end of the novel, the two stories come together.

In her writings, Adisa explores Jamaican culture, celebrating the land's natural beauty and the people's ability to survive despite hardship. Her academic publications include essays on Caribbean literature and pedagogical texts aimed at the teaching of reading and writing. In 1992, she recorded *Fierce Love*, a poetry and jazz composition. *See also* Jamaican Literature, History of.

Further Reading

Feng, Pin-chia. "Rituals of Rememory: Afro-Caribbean religions in Myal and It Begins with Tears." *Melus* 27, no. 1 (Spring 2002): 149–76.

—*D. H. Figueredo*

Agard, John (1949–)

A prolific writer of children's books and performer and promoter of Caribbean culture, John Agard is a Guyanese poet and short-story writer. Although he lives in England, he writes about his native Guyana and about Afro-Caribbean traditions, customs, and legends.

John Agard was born on June 21, 1949, in the former British Guiana, now Guyana. A journalist, he was an editor of the *Guyana Sunday Chronicle*. Like many other Anglophone Caribbean writers before him, Agard moved to London in 1977 to search for better publishing opportunities. He was hired by the

Commonwealth Institute to visit schools throughout the United Kingdom to promote Caribbean culture. In 1993, he became writer in residence at the South Bank Center, in London, and poet in residence at the British Broadcasting Corporation (BBC).

Agard's children's poetry is playful, and he uses it with a pedagogical objective in mind: to teach all children that they can learn anything they want to and to reaffirm the heritage of children from the Caribbean. His *Man to Pan* (1982) is about the steel drums used to play Calypso. *Limbo Dancer in Dark Glasses* (1983) is a history and celebration of the limbo. And *Einstein: The Girl Who Hated Math* (2002) teaches children how to enjoy math rather than regard it as a boring subject. His adult poetry, such as *Mango and Bullets* (1985) and *From the Devil's Pulpit* (1997), examines racism in British society.

Agard has won numerous awards and grants, including a **Casa de las Américas** literary prize for *Man to Pan*, the Nestlé Smarties Book Prize in 1987 and 1995, the Arts Council Bursary in 1989, and the Paul Hamlyn Award for Poetry in 1997. *See also* Guyanese Literature, History of.

Further Reading

Donnell, Alison, and Sarah Lawson Welsh. *The Routledge Reader in Caribbean Literature.* London: Routledge, 1996.

—*D. H. Figueredo*

Agostini de del Río, Amelia (1896–1996)

Author, poet, critic, and professor, Agostini de del Río wrote over forty-five books in a wide range of genres—poetry, drama, short story, literary criticism, grammar texts, art histories, manuals on good manners, and instructional manuals for improving the use and knowledge of the Spanish language. In collaboration with her husband, the well-known and influential Spanish professor and critic Dr. Ángel del Río (1900–1962), she published *Antología de la literatura española* (1954), which remains a classic.

She was born in Yauco, Puerto Rico, and studied there until she enrolled in Vassar College, where she earned her bachelor's degree in 1922 with distinction as a member of Phi Beta Kappa. At Columbia University Agostini de del Río completed her master's degree and then earned a doctorate at the University of Madrid. During her long teaching career, she taught at different institutions, including Barnard College, where she was chair of the Spanish Department; Vassar; City College; Middlebury; and Denver University. With Laura de los Ríos de García and Margarita Ucelay she promoted and produced the first Spanish plays performed in Spanish in the Minor Latham Playhouse at Barnard, in New York City, during the 1940s.

She was a prolific critic who wrote on Spanish authors such as Cervantes, Lope de Vega, Quevedo, Rosalía de Castro, and many others. Her scholarly productions include works inspired by her interest in the Spanish romances, *Flores del romance* (1970), and extend to the appreciation and examination of Spanish American and Puerto Rican authors, as exhibited in her books *Por viejos y nuevos senderos: Ensayos y reseñas* (1980) and *Rosa de los vientos* (1980).

As a writer, it is difficult to situate Agostini de del Río within the traditional historiography of Puerto Rican literature. As a founding member of **Generación del 30**, she shared many the beliefs and national struggles of its members. By 1926, she had coauthored with playwright **Emilio S. Belaval** a play entitled *La romanticona*, but afterward she devoted herself to the pursuit of a fascinating career as a university professor: she was immersed in presenting scholarly productions, promoting Spanish theater, establishing literary relations with famous figures, and contributing to the dissemination of Hispanic literature and culture in the United States. It was not until the death of her husband, and later, of her son, that she returned to Puerto Rico and commenced, in the 1960s and at age sixty-four, when most of her contemporaries were gone or inactive, two decades of fiction writings.

In 1964, she published *Insomios*, her first poetry book, followed by *A la sombra del arce* (1965), *Hasta que el sol se muera* (1969), *Canto a San Juan de Puerto Rico y otros poemas* (1974), *Duerme, hijo*, dedicated to her son (1978), and *Quiero irme gozoza* (1981). As a prose writer she wrote short stories and novels: *Viñetas de Puerto Rico* (1965); *Puertorriqueños en Nueva York* (1974), about the life experiences of Puerto Ricans in the island and New York City; and *Nuestras vidas son los ríos* (1974). Her poetry and narrative deal with love, death, nostalgia for childhood, the historical past, and nationalism; all framed stylistically within the traditional mode of writing.

Agostini de del Río was very active in the intellectual life of the cities of New York and San Juan, where she performed important services in various capacities for such institutions as La Real Academia de la Lengua, the Academia Norteamericana de la Lengua, the Sociedad de Autores Puertorriqueños, and the Instituto de Cultura Puertorriqueña. The last decades of her life were devoted to painting and to the Museo de Reproducciones Artísticas de Bayamón, which she founded in Puerto Rico in 1985. She died on December 11, 1996, in New Jersey.

During her lifetime she received many awards, such as the keys to the city of New York from Mayor Robert Wagner (1910–91); a recognition from King Juan Carlos I (1938–), king of Spain; and the Citizen of the Year Award by the Institute of Puerto Rican Culture in San Juan, Puerto Rico. *See also* Puerto Rican Literature, History of.

Further Reading

Agostini de del Río, Amelia. *Nuestras vidas son los ríos*. San Juan De Puerto Rico: Parcelan, España: Medinaceli, 1974.

Toro-Sugrañes, José A. *Nueva enciclopedia de Puerto Rico: biografías*. Hato Rey, Puerto Rico: Editorial Lector, 1994.

—Asela R. Laguna

Aguinaldo puertorriqueño (1843)

The first book credited with inaugurating Puerto Rican literature, *Aguinaldo puertorriqueño* was the product of six Puerto Rican students, two Venezuelan students, and four Spanish students who were living Spain and attending the Universidad de Barcelona. Homesick, the Puerto Rican students decided to publish a volume that would contain poems and prose celebrating the island's beauty. Of a romantic and sentimental nature, the book was nevertheless received with great acclaim by the general Puerto Rican populace. Poet **Francisco Matos Paoli**, however, considered the publication trite and lacking in aesthetic value. Nevertheless, *Aguinaldo puertorriqueño* was an important introduction to **Romanticismo** on the island.

The contributors include Francisco Pastrana, Carlos Cabrera, Martín J. Travieso, Benicia Aguayo, Mateo Cavailhon, **Alejandrina Benítez de Gautier**, Ignacio Guasp, Juan Manuel Echavarría, Eduardo González Pedroso, Fernando Roig, and **Francisco Vasallo y Cabrera**. *See also* Puerto Rican Literature, History of.

Further Reading

Aguinaldo puertorriqueño de 1843. Edición conmemorativa del centenario Río Piedras, Puerto Rico: Junta Editora de la Universidad de Puerto Rico, 1946.

"Poesía" in *La Gran enciclopedia de Puerto Rico*. San Juan: Puerto Rico en la Mano and La Gran Enciclopedia de Puerto Rico, Inc. 1980.

—*D. H. Figueredo*

Ainsi parla l'oncle (1928)

The major work of Haitian author Dr. **Jean Price-Mars**, *Ainsi parla l'oncle*—translated as *So Spoke the Uncle*—focuses on African cultural traditions and the development of popular culture and folklore in Haiti. In this book, Price-Mars gives the lie to prejudices about a lack of culture in Haiti. He studied vodou as a religion with its own belief in divinity and moral values, arguing against the idea that religious ecstasy or possession is a form of "racial psycho-neurosis." The book was arranged in five sections: (1) Popular Beliefs, (2) Africa, Her Races and Civilizations, (3) African Societies and the Outside World, (4) African Animism, and (5) Religious Sentiments Among Haitian Masses.

The volume, a response to the growing American presence as result of the invasion of 1915 and a rejection of Haitians' desires to identify with France rather than Africa, shook the nation to its foundation. The author criticized his compatriots for practicing a sort of **"bovaryism"** (an allusion to Emma Bovary's isolation in the world of her own romantic dreams), which denied their blackness. According to author Jacques C. Antoine, in his 1981 volume *Jean Price-Mars and Haiti*, the book "caused a literary, spiritual and social revolution" (188) in Haiti. The volume was one of the seeds that flowered in the **Négritude** movement of the 1930s and that influenced the radicalism of such activist as Stokely Carmichael (1941–98) during the 1960s. *See also* American Occupation of Haiti, Literature of the (1915–34).

Further Reading

Antoine, Jacques C. *Jean Price-Mars and Haiti*. Washington, DC and Boulder: Three Continents Press and Lynne Rienner Publishers, 1981.

Price-Mars, Jean. *Ainsi parla l'oncle*. Paris: Imp. De Compiègne, 1928.

Price-Mars, Jean. *So spoke the uncle—Ainsi parla l'oncle*. Translated by Magdaline W. Shannon. Washington, DC: Three Continents 1983.

—Carrol F. Coates and D. H. Figueredo

Alcántara Almánzar, José (1946–)

∎

Alcántara Almánzar is the foremost contemporary writer of short stories in the Dominican Republic. Maturing as a writer during the 1960s, he was influenced by **the Latin American Boom,** especially the experimental stories of the Argentine Julio Cortázar (1914–84).

Alcántara Almánzar was born in Santo Domingo, Dominican Republic, on February 5, 1946. He started to write as a teenager but did not submit his stories for publication until he was about twenty-five years old. In the meantime, he attended elementary school at the Colegio **Eugenio María de Hostos** and then enrolled at the Universidad Autónoma de Santo Domingo, earning a masters in sociology. In 1971, he was awarded a scholarship to study at the International Centre of French Studies in Guadeloupe. From 1974 to 1984 he taught social science at the Universidad Nacional **Pedro Henríquez Ureña** and the Instituto Technológico de Santo Domingo. In the late 1980s, he started to work as an editorial consultant for several publishers in the Dominican Republic.

The need to support his family limited his time for creative output, which was one reason why short stories proved an attractive genre. His stories, appearing initially in journals and then collected in several volumes, have made him a controversial figure because of the themes they address: social hypocrisy, sexuality, and transvestism. His first collections of stories, *Viaje al otro mundo* (1973) and *Callejón sin salida* (1975), proved popular. He has been twice awarded the National Prize for Short Stories—in 1983 for the volume *Las máscaras de la seducción*, and in 1989 for *La carne estremecida*. Alcántara Almánzar is a rare literary experience in the Dominican Republic, where publishing opportunities are limited: his books have never gone out of print and are often reissued in several editions.

This short-story writer is equally respected for his scholarly production. He has written a critical volume—*Imagenes de Hector Incháustegui Cabral* (1980)—on his favorite author, **Hector Incháustegui Cabral,** a work on the development of poetry in the republic—*Medio siglo de poesía dominicana* (1983)—and a volume on Latin American literature—*Narrativa y sociedad en Hispanoamerica* (1984). His recognition as a scholar resulted in a Fulbright Award at Stillman College in Tuscaloosa, Alabama (1987–88).

Further Reading

Manzari, J. H. "An Afternoon with José Alcántara Almánzar." *Callaloo* 23, no. 3 (Summer 2000): 953–60.

—*D. H. Figueredo*

Alexis, Jacques Stephen (1922–61)

Physician, writer, political activist, Alexis is one of the most widely read and influential francophone novelists from the Caribbean. A descendant of Jean-Jacques Dessalines, Alexis was born on April 22 in Gonaïves, on the Gulf of Gonâve, and lived in Paris with his mother from 1926 to 1929 while his father was serving as Haiti's ambassador to France and Belgium. His secondary education was at the well-known Institut de Saint-Louis de Gonzague, from which he received his *baccalauréat* in 1940. He began his study of medicine in Port-au-Prince during World War II and thereafter specialized in neurology in France.

Along with **René Depestre** and other students, Alexis was instrumental in organizing a revolt against President Élie Lescot (1883–1974) in late 1945. Lescot, who had maintained the wartime powers he imposed in 1942, was forced to resign in January 1946. The military junta that assumed power gave Alexis and Depestre scholarships to study in Paris. In 1947, Alexis returned to Haiti to help found the Parti Ouvrier Progressiste (Progressive Workers' Party). Representing Haiti, Alexis spoke on "The Marvellous Realism of the Haitians" at the first international "Congress of Negro Writers and Artists," held at the Sorbonne in September 1956. In the spring of 1961, he went to Cuba and, with a small group of revolutionaries, sailed for the northern coast of Haiti, intending to unseat President **François Duvalier.** The prevalent but unconfirmed assumption is that Duvalier's militia—the Tonton Makout—had been tipped off and were waiting for Alexis and his party. He disappeared on or about April 22, 1961.

Alexis is known primarily as a fiction writer, with three novels and a volume of short stories published before his death. His best-known novel is *Compère Général Soleil* (1955), which depicts the tribulations of workers and peasants in their struggle to survive in an undeveloped economy. Following the destruction of their small grocery store by a disastrous fire, Hilarion and Claire-Heureuse, his pregnant companion, flee Haiti for the northwestern Dominican Republic, where Hilarion will work as a cane cutter. Caught in the massacre of immigrant Haitians ordered by

President Rafael Leónidas Trujillo in late September 1937, the couple flee with their baby, who later dies of malnutrition. As they cross the Massacre River back into Haiti, a Dominican solider wounds Hilarion. He dies urging his companion to find another man and bear more children to carry on the fight for the survival and dignity of the people.

The novel *Les arbres musiciens* (1957) is set in wartime Haiti,1941–42, during the presidency of Élie Lescot, who under pressure from the United States allowed peasant lands to be seized by SHADA—the Haitian American Society for Agricultural Development—for purposes of cultivating *cryptostegia grandiflora*, an Australian weed, intended for the production of rubber to use in the American war effort. The Catholic Church is in collusion with this expropriation in the interest of combating the peasant belief in vodou, the popular religion. The plot focuses on the struggle between the entrenched power of church and state, embodied by Léonie Osmin's three sons—priest, military officer, lawyer—and the peasants, holding to their land and their traditional faith.

The scene of *L'espace d'un cillement* (1959), Alexis's third novel, is the spring of 1948, under the regime of President Dumarsais Estimé (1900–1953). In a period of international worker unrest, a Cuban laborer and Communist organizer, El Caucho, working in Port-au-Prince, is instinctively drawn to La Niña Estrellita, an attractive young prostitute at the Sensation Bar. Carefully observing each other during Holy Week, they realize on Good Friday that they had met and fallen in love as teenagers in Oriente, the eastern province of Cuba. El Caucho senses a strong mission to defend workers' rights against the exploitative system. La Niña, who has persisted in maintaining a sense of self in her degrading career as a prostitute, discovers that she is still capable of true love. At the end, she abruptly leaves El Caucho in order to regain her own integrity and to prove that even a prostitute is capable of a life change. An uncompleted novel (*L'Églantine*) was intended to recount the Cuban couple meeting once more in pursuit of love.

Alexis's last published book was *Le romancero aux étoiles* (1960), a volume of nine narratives that are framed as an oral storytelling contest between the mythological figure Old Caribbean Wind and his young, human "nephew." The *Romancero* includes a wide variety of narratives, beginning with the "Dit de Bouqui et de Malice," a tale in which Bouqui, the eternal victim, allows his mother to undergo "medical" treatment by his hungry companion, who places her in a pot of boiling water with aromatic herbs. Closer to the realm of literary fiction, there is the short story of "Le sous-lieutenant enchanté," in which a former American soldier falls under the enchantment of a beautiful young Caribbean Indian early in the period of the first U.S. occupation of Haiti (1915–34). This volume of tales derives its unity from its absolute inscription in "marvelous realism" and the oral traditions of Haiti. This concept was partially inspired by the Cuban novelist and musicologist, **Alejo Carpentier**, whom Alexis had heard speak in Haiti in 1943. Moved by his visit to Haiti, Carpentier wrote the novel *El reino de este mundo* (1949), in which he gives an overview of Haitian history from colonial times to the mid-nineteenth century.

Each of Alexis's three published novels highlights a love theme involving workers or peasants, but the novelist gives a very precise historical setting to each story: the Dominican Vespers of October 1937, the dispossession of Haitian peasants in 1942, and the rumblings of workers' revolt in 1948. References to popular culture—religion, music, folk wisdom, plant lore—abound, along with allusions to contemporary history and European culture. The use of terms and fragments of dialogue from Haitian Kreyòl or Creole, Spanish, and English are characteristic of Alexis's French prose.

The most important literary influences on Alexis were Émile Zola (1840–1902) and his unusual combination of mythical vision and realistic description and **Jacques Roumain**'s hopeful view of peasant dignity and agricultural renewal in his novel, *Gouverneurs de la rosée*. In turn, Alexis has exercised an avowed influence on many younger Haitian writers, including **Dany Laferrière** and **Edwidge Danticat**. *See also* Haitian Literature, History of; Magical Realism; Naturalismo/Naturalism; Négritude; Vodouism in Literature.

Further Reading

Alexis, Jacques Stephen. *General Sun, My Brother*. Translated by Carrol F. Coates. Charlottesville: University Press of Virginia, 1999.

———. *In the Flicker of an Eyelid*. Translated by Carrol F. Coates and Edwidge Danticat. Charlottesville: University Press of Virginia, 2002.

Antoine, Yves. *Sémiologie et personnage romanesque chez Jacques Stéphen Alexis*. Montréal: Editions Balzac, 1993.

—*Carrol F. Coates*

Alfau Galván de Solalinde, Jesusa (1890–1943)

Novelist, painter, and educator Jesusa Alfau Galván was the daughter of Antonio Abad Alfau Baralt and Eugenia Galván Velázquez. Born in Galicia, Spain, in 1890, she spent much of her life in the shadows of her illustrious maternal grandfather, the Dominican **Manuel de Jesús Galván**, author of *Enriquillo*, one of the better known and best regarded *indianista*—idealized-Indian-themed—novels in the Spanish Caribbean and Latin America. Alfau's husband was the distinguished *hispanista*—Hispanic studies professor—Antonio G. Solalinde (1892–1937). Alfau spent a considerable number of years living in her native Spain and in the Dominican Republic, land of her ancestors. She received her formal education in Spain and later on worked with her husband in the field of research on philology and education. At the age of eighteen, Jesusa Alfau Galván authored the novel *Los débiles*, published four years later (1912) in Spain.

She lived in the United States on and off from 1916 onward. While in the United States, Alfau Galván de Solalinde was a regular contributor to the weekly *Las Novedades*, edited between 1916 and 1918 by her father. Her essays published in *Las Novedades* are meant to interpret for many in the Latino communities, within and outside the United States, customs and values of North American culture, much as **José Martí** and **Pachín Marín**, among many, had done before her. Her articles published in *Las Novedades* include "Sábado" (Saturday), "Thanksgiving," and "Visiones del Norte" (Visions of the North).

For several decades most Dominican literary histories have indicated that *Los débiles* had been translated into English in the United States. There is a 1930 edition of *Los débiles* that was published by Prentice Hall, with a prologue and notes by Professor J. Horace Nunmaker of the Department of Foreign Languages at State College of Washington. This edition was prepared for use as a textbook in intermediate to advanced Spanish-language courses. The brief prologue is the only section written in English. The text features a glossary and a series of exercises. A copy of this second edition of *Los débiles* was found by **Daisy Cocco De Filippis** on the shelves of the Queens College library, one of the colleges of the City University of New York. Professor Cocco de Filippis edited the novel and published it in a slim volume entitled *Como los crisantemos lila, Obra escogida de Jesusa Alfau Galván de Solalinde*. Eight of the articles written by Galván de Solalinde for *Las Novedades* are included in the volume.

Jesusa Alfau Galván de Solalinde began writing her thesis *Nomenclatura de los tejidos españoles del siglo XIII* in English for the master of arts degree at the University of Wisconsin. Sadly, she died in Mexico in 1941 before completing the project. Her unfinished thesis was translated into Spanish by her nephew Antonio Gobernado de García and published in 1969 by the Real Academia de la Lengua Española. Her life and work are early precursors of what would become the diasporic Dominican-Hispanic family in the twentieth century. *See also* Dominican Literature, History of; Indianist Literature.

Further Reading

Alfau Galván de Solalinde, Jesusa. *Los débiles*. Madrid: Imprenta Artística José Blas, 1912.

———. *Los débiles*. Prologue and annotations by J. Horace Nunemaker. New York: Prentice Hall, 1930.

———. *Como los crisantemos lila, obra escogida*. Selection and prologue by Daisy Cocco De Filippis. New York: Alcance, Colección Tertuliando, 2000.

—*Daisy Cocco de Filippis*

Alfonseca, Miguel (1942–94)

Miguel Alfonseca was a political poet from the Dominican Republic. His poetry, inspired by the American invasion of the country in 1965, was a typical example of socially engaged writings or **literatura comprometida**.

Alfonseca was born in 1942 into a family that openly opposed the dictatorship of Rafael Trujillo: his grandfather was deported in 1940 and his was father was denied employment and forced into house arrest. In 1960, Alfonseca was arrested and sent to prison for conspiring against the regime.

The oppression that the young Alfonseca experienced informed his first book of poetry, *Arribo de la luz* (1965). The civil war that rocked the nation in 1965 and the subsequent landing of American troops enraged Alfonseca, who responded with

La guerra y los cantos (1966) and *El enemigo* (1970), encouraging his compatriots to fight with lines such as the following:

> Morirán sin los abetos de Vermont
> Morirán sin los grandes pastos rizados por el viento
> . . . Porque son invasores.

(They will die without their Vermont evergreens / They will die without fields of hay combed by the wind / . . . Because they're invaders).

But Alfonseca also rallied Dominicans to create a democratic regime and to oppose all dictatorships, regardless of political ideology. His compatriot **Marcio Veloz Maggiolo** described him, in *Cultura, teatro y relatos en Santo Domingo* (1972), as "the son of bullets and mortars . . . of the constant fighting movement that mingles with poems of protest" (249). *See also* Trujillo Era.

Further Reading

Piña Contreras, Guillermo. *Doce en la literatura dominicana*. Santiago, República Dominicana: Universidad Católica Madre y Maestra, 1982.

Veloz Maggiolo, Marcio. *Cultura, teatro y relatos en Santo Domingo*. Santiago, República Dominicana: Universidad Católica Madre y Maestra, 1972.

—*D. H. Figueredo*

Algarín, Miguel (1941–)

One of the best known Puerto Rican authors living in New York City, Algarín is one of the creators of the Nuyorican movement, a combination of a Puerto Rican and New Yorker literary identity, and the founder, with playwright **Miguel Piñero**, of the Nuyorican Poets Café in Manhattan. His poetry combines both English and Spanish to create an idiom called **Spanglish**. Algarín's poetry ranges from the political to the romantic and erotic.

Algarín was born in Santurce, Puerto Rico, on September 11, 1941. Seeking the promise of a better life, his parents moved to New York City when Algarín was nine years old. After attending public schools in Manhattan, he went to the University of Wisconsin, earning a BA in 1963. Two years later he received an MA from Pennsylvania State University. While pursuing a career as a writer, he achieved success as an academician, teaching at several colleges and universities followed by his appointment as assistant professor of English at Rutgers University in 1971. He retired in 2001.

Algarín's first book of poetry, *Mongo Affair* (1977), might be his best known. The book is critical of the American government's treatment of Puerto Ricans, both on the island and on the mainland. The poems develop as a conversation between a dark-skinned Puerto Rican and the poetic "I." The poet criticizes the events surrounding Operation Bootstraps—planned by governor **Luis Muñoz Marín** in the

1950s to attract American corporations to the island—which gave way to the large migration of Puerto Ricans to New York and perpetuated the myth that Puerto Ricans would be better off living in the United States. The poems in the collection are sexually explicit and filled with anger, but by the end of the volume, the poet progresses from anger to optimism, climaxing with a metaphorical call to arms to end oppression and discrimination.

With his second book, *On Call* (1980), Algarín begins to branch out and look for common ground among different cultures. In poems such as "Buddha" and "Balance" he evokes aspects of Asian culture and religion. *Body Bee Calling From the Twenty-first Century* (1980) is concerned with sex, and *Time's Now* (1985) explores the theme of love.

In 1975, Algarín, with Piñero, edited the first anthology of Nuyorican poetry, *Nuyorican Poetry: An Anthology of Puerto Rican Words and Feelings*. In the 1990s, he edited two more anthologies, *Aloud! Voices from the Nuyorican Poets' Café* (1994) and *Action: The Nuyorican Poets Café Theater Festival* (1997). He has also written several plays, including *Apartment 6-D* (1974) and *The Murder of Pito* (1976). *See also* Code Switching; Nuyorican Literature.

Further Reading

Kanellos, Nicolás. *Hispanic Literature of the United States*. Westport, CT: Greenwood Press, 2003.

Luis, William. *Dance Between Two Cultures: Latino Caribbean Literature Written in the United States*. Nashville: Vanderbilt University Press, 1997.

—*William Luis*

Alix, Juan Antonio (1833–1917?)

Still controversial almost a century after his death, Dominican Republic poet Alix is a popular writer who often changed political allegiances and who is seen by many contemporary readers as racist. Nevertheless, his ability to replicate the vernacular of the peasants and farmers and his depictions of Dominican characteristics and personality traits endeared him to his compatriots. He was one of a handful of writers who actually earned money from what he wrote.

Born in the town of Moca, Alix was raised in Santo Domingo. Poetry attracted him from a very young age, and he soon mastered a form he would use all his life: the décima. The décima is a rhyming poem with ten-line stanzas. Easy to memorize, this type of poetry was favored by most nineteenth-century readers and was often published in local newspapers.

Alix was involved in the political conflicts going on in the Dominican Republic. When Spain annexed the nation after Dominicans had gained their independence from Haiti in 1842, Alix joined the anti-Spanish movement in 1863, fighting against Spanish forces. Then he switched sides and betrayed his comrades. For a while, Alix had to seek shelter in Santo Domingo to avoid potential avengers.

When the Spanish left the country, Alix supported the presidency of Ulíses Heureaux (1845–99), who had opposed the Spanish presence. Then, in 1899, when Heureaux was assassinated, Alix's poetry celebrated the slain leader's death and called him a tyrant. Somehow, Alix survived his political maneuvering and managed to become a popular poet.

Alix's poetry tended to be humorous and descriptive of the events that were occurring throughout the country. He did not write much about the flora and the fauna, as nationalist and romantic poets were bound to do, but rather about individuals. In some instances, his poems narrated events as if he were a reporter covering a story for a newspaper. He printed these poems as leaflets and sold them throughout the Dominican Republic. Probably his best-known poem is "Diálogo cantado entre un guajiro dominicano y un papa boc haitiano en un fandango en Dajabón." The dialogue is a verbal contest between a Dominican peasant and a Haitian vodou priest. The Dominican embodies his nation's best qualities and patriotism, which includes fear of Haitian invaders. The Haitian is depicted in a derogatory and stereotypical manner. As the poem progresses, the contest turns into an argument and then a fight, which ends with the Dominican killing the Haitian. "Diálogo" celebrates the killing as a way of maintaining the Dominican Republic for all Dominicans.

There are critics who do not consider the poem racist and indicate that the Dominican Republic was still recovering after two decades of living under Haitian rule. However, the action in the poem takes place in the town of Dajabón, where in 1937, dictator Rafael Leónidas Trujillo (1891–1961) ordered the massacre of more than twenty-thousand Haitians living in the Dominican Republic. Some scholars suggest that the poem served as an inspiration for Trujillo.

Alix was a mysterious, enigmatic figure. Not much is written about his personal life. His poetry appeared in several volumes decades after his death, *Décimas* (1953), *Décimas políticas* (1977), and *Décimas inéditas* (1982). Many of his poems are included in several anthologies, including *Poesía popular dominicana* (1938), edited by Emilio Rodríguez Demorizi, and *Antología literaria dominicana* (1981), edited by Margarita Vallejo de Paredes.

Further Reading

Balaguer, Joaquín. *Azul en los charcos.* Bogotá, Colombia: Editorial Selecta, 1941.

"Biografia de Juan Antonio Alix." http://www.los-poetas.com/n/bioalix.htm (accessed 8/29/05).

—*D. H. Figueredo*

Allen, Lillian (1951–)

Allen is a dub poet, lecturer, and activist from Jamaica. Influenced by performance artist **Louise Bennet**, Allen uses Jamaican vernacular in her poetry. Through her work, she affirms the African heritage of the people of the Caribbean.

Allen was born in Spanish Town, Jamaica. Involved in church and school activities, she started writing plays and songs for schoolmates and friends before she was ten years old. When she was a teenager she left for Canada but also spent some time in New York City, where she studied African American literature at New York University. She then returned to Canada, graduating from York University. In 1979, she met dub poet Oku Onuora in Cuba and he encouraged her to write **dub poetry**, a type of poetry that is meant to be performed and not written. Upon her return to Canada, she decided to invest her creative energy in the creation and performance of dub poetry. She toured Canada and Europe, gaining recognition for her dramatic performances.

Though at times Allen has refused to commit her poems to the printed page, she has published a few titles, *The Teeth of the Whirlwind* (1984), *Women Do This Every Day: Selected Poems* (1993), and *Psychic Unrest* (1999). These poems, according to **Kwame Dawes** in *Talk Yuh Talk* (2001), "have very strong feminist/womanist overtones—a strong articulation of the experience of women, black women and minority women" (152). She has also written children's books: *Nothing But a Hero Dub* (1987) and *Why Me?* (1991). Her fame, however, rests on her many sound recordings of her performances, including *Rhythm an' Hardtimes* (1982), *Revolutionary Tea Party* (1986), *From Barrooms to Bayous* (1989), and *Our Freedom & Dance* (1999).

Allen has received numerous awards, including, in 1986, the Juno Award and the Canadian Academy of Recording and Sciences Award, and, in 1989, the Margo Binghard Award.

Further Reading

Dawes, Kwame. *Talk Yuh Talk: Interviews with Anglophone Caribbean Poets.* Charlottesville: University Press of Virginia, 2001.

—*D. H. Figueredo*

Allfrey, Phyllis Shand (1908–)

∎

Born into a prominent Dominican family of European ancestry in 1908, Phyllis Shand Allfrey could trace her paternal lineage back to English nobility, supposedly to a knight of King Arthur's Round Table, and her maternal lineage to Empress Josephine of France. Her earliest ancestor in the West Indies, William Byam, was governor of both Surinam and Antigua in the mid-seventeenth century as well as the owner of vast sugar and tobacco plantations. During Allfrey's childhood, her family's wealth was largely gone; nonetheless, the family remained relatively affluent for Dominican society. Her father, Francis Byam Berkeley Shand, held the official position of the island's Crown Attorney.

Allfrey grew up in a family known for both its involvement in political affairs and its politically conservative positions. At an early age, however, Allfrey espoused liberal sympathies, particularly in relation to issues of racism. The Afro-Caribbean culture of Dominica had a strong influence on her, particularly in the form of two household servants: her nurse, Lally, and the family cook, Julia. For instance, although her father belonged to the League for the Suppression of French-Patois, Allfrey defied his mandate against learning and speaking it.

Francis Shand's absence due to service in World War I, and his resulting shell shock, marked the childhood of his daughter as a time of emotional and financial instability. He was able to maintain his position as Crown Attorney with the support of his wife and daughters; he did not, however, participate significantly in Dominican political affairs. This lack of political activism was a break in family tradition, a break that Allfrey herself seemed intent to remedy in her own involvement in Dominican politics once she reached adulthood.

After leaving Dominica in 1927, first for the United States and then eventually England, Allfrey met and married Robert Edward Allfrey, a young Englishman with an engineering degree from Oxford. They became interested in socialist causes; while in England, Allfrey joined the British Labour Party and campaigned for various liberal candidates. Upon returning to Dominica, after an absence of twenty-six years, she applied her experience with leftist politics to the island's reactionary political system. Although many conservative families were shocked at her flouting of racial and social conventions, she agitated for equal treatment of people, in both a legal and social sense, regardless of gender, race, or class. In 1955, she founded the Labour Party of Dominica, and in 1958, she became Minister of Labour and Social Affairs in the federal government of the West Indies. After the failure of this West Indian Federation, Allfrey and her husband took to the newspaper business, first running *The Dominica Herald*, and then founding their own newspaper, *The Star*.

During the early part of her political career, Allfrey also found time for a literary career. In the 1940s, she began publishing short pieces of fiction in the literary pages of the leftist London newspaper *Tribune*. She published her first collection of poetry, *In Circles*, in 1940, and her second collection, *Palm and Oak*, in 1950. Her literary career reached its peak in 1953 with the publication of her novel, *The Orchid House*, although she continued to write short pieces, as well as drafts of two unfinished novels in the later years of her life. *The Orchid House* is an autobiographical novel, which clearly draws on such early aspects of her life as growing up in a family of girls in Dominica with an unstable, yet beloved, father and the strong impact of the servants on the children in the family. In fact, Allfrey closely patterns the narrator of the story after her own nurse, Lally, providing her with the same name, employment, and close relationship with her charges.

Despite Allfrey's seeming abandonment of her literary career for a more active role in the politics in Dominica, she remained interested in the reception of her literary creations, at one point enlisting fellow native Dominican **Jean Rhys**'s support in the publication of a new edition of *The Orchid House* in the 1970s. Her ultimate devotion to social causes, though, is evident in her acceptance of a life of obscurity and poverty in her homeland of Dominica, and both her literary themes and her political activism attest to her dedication to the welfare of the Dominican people.

Further Reading

Campbell, Elaine. Introduction. *In The Orchid House*, by Phyllis Shand Allfrey. London: Virago Press, 1982.

Paravisini-Gebert, Lizabeth. *Phyllis Shand Allfrey: A Caribbean Life*. New Brunswick, NJ: Rutgers University Press, 1996.

—Paula Makris

Alonso, Dora (1910–2001)

∎

Dora Alonso was an award-winning Cuban writer whose prose celebrated the people of the countryside and Cuba's natural beauty. She was a children's book author, a script writer, and a novelist.

Dora Alonso was born on December 22, 1910, in the province of Matanzas, Cuba. She was raised in the countryside—her family were cattle ranchers—and had only a primary school education. She started to write at a young age, and by the time she was twenty years old, she was writing for a local newspaper. In 1936, she won a short-story prize offered by the influential weekly *Bohemia*. In 1944, the Ministry of Education gave her a national literature award for her novel *Tierra adentro*. In 1946, she received the Enrique José Varona journalism award. In 1947, she won first prize in the prestigious Hernández Cata literary contest. That same year her play *La hora de estar ciegos* won her the Luis de Soto drama award.

During the 1940s and 50s, she wrote radio scripts for programs in Cuba and in Latin America. In 1959, she embraced the triumph of the Cuban revolution. In 1961, she traveled to the Bay of Pigs battlefront—when CIA-backed Cuban exiles had tried to invade the island to overthrow **Fidel Castro**—to write about the war; the result was the volume *El año 61*. In 1969, she wrote what is considered the first young-adult novel written in Cuba, *Las aventuras de Guille*. A writer of realistic prose and realistic characters, in 1970 she stepped in a new direction with a novel set in the Havana Zoo; entitled *Once caballos*, the animals were the main characters and the humans were marginal figures.

In 1988, Alonso was named Cuba's National Writer. Two years later, the **Unión de Escritores y Artistas de Cuba** awarded her the **Rosa Blanca** literary prize for her work as a children's writer. Alonso proved a popular author within the former Soviet Bloc. Her works were translated into Russian, Romanian, Lithuanian, and Ukrainian. She died on March 21, 2001, in Havana, Cuba.

Further Reading

Cuatrogatos: revista de literatura infantil, no. 6 (abril-junio 2001). http://www.cuatrogatos.org/6dossier.html (accessed 8/29/05).

Martínez, Julio A., ed. *Dictionary of Twentieth-Century Cuban Literature*. Westport, CT: Greenwood Press, 1990.

—D. H. Figueredo

Alonso, Manuel A. (1822–89)

Described as one the fathers of Puerto Rican literature and the first Puerto Rican author to express concern with a Puerto Rican identity and to write about the island at a time when the Spanish crown was suspicious of any expressions of nationalism, Alonso was the author of a collection of stories and local sketches titled *El gíbaro* (1849), a term used to describe a Puerto Rican farmer, and one of the creators of the classic *Album puertorriqueño* (1844). He was a journalist and a patriot who sought independence from Spain.

Manuel Antonio Alonso was born in San Juan on October 6, 1822, but spent his childhood in the countryside. After graduation from the seminary (Seminario Conciliar), he sailed to Spain in 1842 and studied medicine at the Universidad de Barcelona. It was at the university that with a group of compatriots a homesick Alonso collaborated in the creation and publication of *Album puertorriqueño*. In 1849, Alonso returned to Puerto Rico, setting up a medical office in the town of Caguas. That same year, he published *El gíbaro*, a book consisting of verses and stories. A good illustration of the genre of **costumbrismo**—literature of local color—the poems mimicked the vernacular and diction of Puerto Rican farmers, and the stories depicted local events and scenery.

During the late 1850s and throughout of the most 1860s, Alonso spent time in Spain, working as a physician but also studying Spanish politics and developing a political vision of Puerto Rico. In 1871, he returned to Puerto Rico and was appointed director of the Asilo de Beneficencia, a shelter and poorhouse; he also continued his medical practice. Much of the poetry he wrote addressed such themes as love and patriotism. His essays revealed a preoccupation with the island's future. Comments Ribes Tiber: "Alonso was a man of prophetic vision, precursor . . . of the painful gestation of the idea of political autonomy" (80). *See also* Puerto Rican Literature, History of.

Further Reading

Ribes Tover, Federico. *100 Outstanding Puerto Ricans*. New York: Plus Ultra Educational Publishers, 1976.

Rivera Rivera, Modesto. *Manuel A. Alonso: su vida y su obra*. San Juan, Puerto Rico: Editorial Caqui, 1966.

—*D. H. Figueredo*

Alvarez, Julia (1950–)

With the publication of *How the García Girls Lost Their Accents* in 1991, Alvarez emerged as a new voice in Latino literature, one with roots in the Dominican Republic rather than the more familiar Mexico, Puerto Rico, or Cuba. The loosely autobiographical novel follows the lives of four sisters who emigrate as children to New York City from their island nation as a result of their wealthy father's failed efforts to topple brutal dictator Rafael Leónidas Trujillo (1891–1961).

Like her fictional persona, Yolanda García, Alvarez came to the United States in 1960 at the age of ten, along with her father, mother, and three sisters. She unwittingly traded her wealthy, privileged life for the harsh, unfamiliar existence of an immigrant while her father, on the run from Trujillo's secret police, struggled to achieve a semblance of the prosperity he enjoyed in their former homeland. Her first novel reflects the dilemmas of the transitional generation often referred to as the "1.5 generation," people raised partly in their country of origin and partly in the United States. The four García sisters confront economic hardship, language barriers, the prejudice of their Anglo peers, repressive Catholic schools, and the conflict between parents' traditional values regarding sex and gender roles and the frankness and freedom of late 1960s youth culture in the United States. Alvarez's first novel addressed these themes through an innovative chronology, beginning the story with Yolanda's trip to the Dominican Republic, where she realizes she can never return to what she had as a child, and moving backward to end with a vignette of her as a three-year-old living in her family's lush compound.

In addition to *Yo!* (1996), a sequel to *How the García Girls Lost Their Accents*, Alvarez is the author of two historical novels that explore her country of origin and the Spanish Caribbean as a whole. *In the Time of the Butterflies* (1994) portrays the three Mirabal sisters, regarded as martyrs after their 1960 deaths in a car crash ruled accidental but later determined to be the work of Trujillo's security forces. From the third-person perspective of the surviving sister and the first-person voices of the dead, Alvarez explores how each came through separate paths to take part in the underground resistance against the corrupt and megalomaniacal dictator, who also appears as a character in the novel. An even more ambitious work of historical fiction, *In the Name of Salomé* depicts the late-nineteenth-century Dominican political poet **Salomé Ureña** (1850–97) and her daughter, Camila. Camila, who moved to the United States and in 1960 retired from college teaching, attempts to learn about her long-dead mother through Salomé's papers. The novel explores not only Dominican history but also that of Cuba, where the family lived after American occupation forces deposed Camila's father, Dominican president Francisco Henríquez y Carvajal. Like her earlier historical novel, *In the Name of Salomé* reclaims the voice of women in the narration of history.

Before her first novel appeared, Alvarez published several collections of poetry. She is more recently the author of the bilingual poetry collection *The Other Side/El otro lado* (1995); *Something to Declare* (1998), a collection of essays focusing on the immigrant experience; and several books for children and young adults. *See also* Literature of the Dominican Republic, History of; Dominican American Literature; Exile Literature; Immigrant Literature; Henríquez Ureña Family.

Further Reading

Castells, Ricardo. "The silence of exile in *How the García Girls Lost Their Accents.*" *Bilingual Review* 26, no. 1 (2001): 34–42.

Contemporary Authors. 101: 22–26. Detroit, MI: Gale, 2002.

Rich, Charlotte. "Talking back to *El Jefe*: genre, polyphony, and dialogic resistance in Julia Alvarez's *In the Time of Butterflies.*" *MELUS* 27, no. 4 (2002): 165–83.

Sirias, Silvio. *Julia Alvarez: A Critical Companion.* Westport, CT.: Greenwood, 2001.

—Lyn Miller Lachman

Álvarez Nazario, Manuel (1924–2001)

Álvarez Nazario was a Puerto Rican scholar and linguist who dedicated his life to the study of the use of Spanish on the island and the development of a Puerto Rican identity as expressed in the local vernacular.

A native of Aibonito, Álvarez Nazario earned a BA in education in 1948 and an MA in literature in 1950, both from the Universidad de Puerto Rico. He then traveled to Spain, where he received a PhD in philosophy and literature from the Universidad de Madrid in 1954. In the 1950s, he began to pursue his interest in the use of the Spanish language in Puerto Rico, publishing articles and essays in journals such as *Revista de estudios hispánicos* and *Revista de ciencias sociales.*

Álvarez Nazario taught Spanish at his alma mater, at the Mayagüez campus. In 1957, he published a major study, *El arcaísmo vulgar en el español de Puerto Rico,* an exploration of popular language on the island, and, in 1961, *El elemento afronegroide en el español de Puerto Rico,* an in-depth analysis of the African roots of Puerto Rican vernacular. This latter volume was awarded a scholarly prize by the Instituto de Literatura Puertorriqueña.

While writing numerous studies for academic presses and journals, he also contributed articles on the subject, written in more accessible language, to such popular newspapers as *El Mundo* and *La Prensa.* His other works include *Introducción al estudio de la lengua española* (1981), *El habla campesina del país* (1990), and *Arqueología lingüística* (1996). For his contribution to the study of the Spanish language in Puerto Rico, he received an award from the Academia Española de la Lengua.

Further Reading

Enciclopedia puertorriqueña: siglo XXI. Santurce, Puerto Rico: Caribe Grolier, 1998.

—D. H. Figueredo

American Occupation of Haiti, Literature of the (1915–34)

The American occupation of Haiti lasted from 1915 to 1934. The occupation humiliated all Haitians who until that time had taken pride in being a country that had defeated Napoleon's forces during its war of independence, had supported the liberation wars of Simon Bolivar (1783–1830) in South America, and had been the second independent republic in the Americas, after the United States. All along, Haitians had acknowledged the political strife within their nation but had not succumbed to a foreign power. The American occupation meant that for the first time in nearly a century and a half, Haitians were ruled by foreigners who were whites. The occupation prompted such an intellectual and creative reaction by Haitian writers that it served as a catalyst for the renaissance of Haitian letters. Many of the internationally renowned works of literature from Haiti emerged during this period.

The events that led to the occupation were rooted in economic and political interests. Early in the decade, the New York National City Bank and the American National Railroad had been pressuring the American government for intervention to help obtain payments the Haitian government had refused to remit as a result of a labor dispute between the National Railroad and the government. Also, according to historian Hans Schmidt, in *The United States Occupation of Haiti, 1915–1934* (1971), President Woodrow Wilson had expressed a desire for the United States to control the national banks in the Caribbean, thus making intervention of Haiti an attractive enterprise.

From 1911 to 1915, the scenario for the invasion grew more feasible, as internal unrest and chaos beset the island. During those years the following events unfolded: one president was blown up in the Presidential Palace, another was poisoned, and three others were overthrown. The final crisis was the assassination on July 27, 1915, of President Vilbrun Guillaume Sam. Sam, a despot, had ordered the summary execution of 173 of his political rivals. The subsequent revolt forced him to seek asylum in the French embassy, but an angry mob discovered his location, broke into the embassy, murdered him, and mutilated his body. The following day, American forces disembarked.

Haitian writers reacted immediately to the occupation. The poet **Edmund Laforest** committed suicide to protest. Journalist **Georges Sylvain** founded the newspaper *La Patrie* and the organization L'Union patriotique to affirm Haitian nationalism and to challenge U.S. authority over his country. The writer **Leon Laleau**, began to work on the novel *Le choc* which depicted the occupation—*Le choc* was eventually published in 1932.

The well-respected Dr. **Jean Price-Mars**, who was serving in the Haitian embassy in Washington, returned home to rally discouraged intellectuals. In 1928, he published *Ainsi parla l'oncle*, in which he examined the events and social attitudes that led to the occupation. In the book, Price-Mars accused his countrymen of practicing collective "**bovaryism**," which is the practice of pretending to be colored French men and women in order to deny one's African heritage. He also accused Haitian aristocrats of neglecting the rest of the population, especially the black peasants. In response to Price-Mars's call, younger writers turned to their origins and celebrated their blackness. The journal *La Revue Indigène*, (1927) was founded by **Normil Sylvain**. The journal attempted to foster a national culture in Haiti and the rejection of American influences, as well as the imitation, then in vogue, of French literature by Haitian writers. One genre that proved popular was the **peasant novel**, which sympathetically portrayed the struggles of the Haitian peasants. The most famous work to emerge from this genre is *Gouverneurs de la rosée* (1944) by **Jacques Roumain**.

The American forces left Haiti in 1934, leaving behind a stable but repressive Haitian government. The occupation stimulated writers to develop a distinct national identity and an affirmation of **Négritude**, or black consciousness. For decades, reaction against the occupation influenced and shaped the works of such post-occupation writers as the novelist **Jacques Stephen Alexis**. *See also* Haitian Literature, History of.

Further Reading

Bellegarde-Smith, Patrick. *Haiti: The Breached Citadel*. Boulder: Westview Profiles, 1990.

Hoffmann, Léon-François. *Essays on Haitian Literature*. Washington, DC: Three Continents Press, 1984.

Renda, Mary A. *Taking Haiti: Military Occupation and the Culture of U.S. Imperialism 1915–1940*. Chapel Hill: University of North Carolina Press, 2001.

Schmidt, Hans. *The United States Occupation of Haiti, 1915–1934*. New Brunswick, NJ: Rutgers University Press, 1971.

—Carrol F. Coates and D. H. Figueredo

Anancy Stories

Generally, Caribbean Anancy stories are folktales derived predominantly from the African oral tradition, although the occasional influence from European fairy tales or beast fables may also be evident. More specifically, however, the Anancy story is a tale detailing the exploits of Anancy, a part human, part spider figure who has both positive and negative qualities. Anancy is a clever trickster figure: ambitious, manipulative, greedy, and often distinctly immoral.

The Caribbean, typically Jamaican, Anancy has his origins in a West African deity, Ananse, or Anansi, a creator in the figure of a spider weaving the fate of the world. Ghanaian oral and print literature today still includes stories of the trickster figure who takes the form of a spider but has human concerns. This figure survived the middle passage to take root in the cultural consciousness of the Caribbean slave who could appreciate the need of the trickster to take advantage of any situation presented to him and not be constrained by society's codes of conduct and morality.

Early Jamaican Anancy stories were often first recorded by writers of European ancestry who would attempt to replicate Afro-Caribbean pronunciation and vocabulary in a manner similar to the methods of Joel Chandler Harris (1848–1908), who collected the B'rer Rabbit stories of the American South. In the past century, however, Anancy stories have permeated many areas of Caribbean cultural expression, from **Louise Bennet**'s collections of Caribbean folktales to **James Berry**'s children's book *Anancy Spiderman* (1988). Poets are also attracted to the archetypal image of the Anancy figure; for instance both **Edward Kamau Brathwaite** and **John Agard** refer to the trickster in the their respective poems, "Ananse" and "Limbo Dancer at Immigration" (1983). Anancy also makes an appearance in twentieth-century dramatic performances, such as the Little Theatre Movement of Jamaica's National Pantomime, an annual performance at Christmastime that first introduced Anancy in 1949. He has continued to appear in various performances throughout the sixty-plus-year span of the Pantomime. The storyteller who recounts an Anancy tale routinely includes the question "Is Anancy meck it?" to indicate the scope of Anancy's creative power, as well as the phrase "Jack Mandora, me noh choose none" to disclaim any accountability for Anancy's immoral behavior. *See also* Children's Literature in the English-Speaking Caribbean.

Further Reading

Abrahams, Roger, and John Szwed, eds. *After Africa: Extracts from British Travel Accounts and Journals of the Seventeenth, Eighteenth, and Nineteenth Centuries Concerning the Slaves, their Manners, and Customs in the British West Indies.* New Haven, CT: Yale University Press, 1983.

Cummings, Pat. *Ananse and the Lizard: A West African Tale.* New York: Henry Holt and Co, 2002.

Egglestone, Ruth Minott. *A Philosophy of Survival: Anancyism in Jamaican Pantomime.* (2001) Online Proceedings of the Society for Caribbean Studies 2. Edited by Sandra Courtman. http://www.scsonline.freeserve.co.uk/olvol2.html (accessed 8/29/05).

Joyce, Jonas. *Anancy in the Great House: Ways of Reading West Indian Fiction.* Westport, CT: Greenwood Press, 1990.

Lalla, Barbara. "Black Laughter: Foundations of Irony in the Earliest Jamaican Literature." *Journal of Black Studies* 20, no. 4: The African Literary Imagination (June 1990): 14–425.

Okpewho, Isidore. *African Oral Literature: Backgrounds, Character, and Continuity.* Bloomington, IN: Indiana University Press, 1992.

—Paula Makris

Andreu Iglesias, César (1915–76)

■

Andreu Iglesias was a major Puerto Rican intellectual, novelist, journalist, and political activist. He is best known for his political novel, *Los derrocatos* (1956), and for his role as the editor of the memoirs of Puerto Rican writer **Bernardo Vega**. He was also president of Puerto Rico's Communist Party during the McCarthy era in the 1950s.

Andreu Iglesias was born in Ponce, Puerto Rico, on July 31, 1915. After attending elementary and secondary schools in his hometown, he was drafted into the U.S. Army. In 1946, he was one of the founders of the Partido Independista Puertorriqueño. In 1949, he graduated from the Universidad de Puerto Rico with a BA in Social Sciences.

In 1950, Andreu Iglesias became the editorial director of the Communist journal *Verdad* and wrote weekly columns for several newspapers. A year later, he published as a book a series of essays entitled *Independecia y socialismo*, a Marxist interpretation of Puerto Rican politics since 1898. During this time he also served as secretary and chairman of the Puerto Rican Communist Party.

Elected president of the island's Communist Party at a time when the McCarthy era was at its height in the early 1950s, Andreu Iglesias, fearing arrest, sought refuge in the Puerto Rican countryside. There he wrote the novel *Los derrocados*, about Puerto Rican nationalists plotting to sabotage American interests; the narrative also served as a platform for the author's exploration of the island's failure at achieving full independence.

In 1960, as the political climate changed and Andreu Iglesias gained recognition as a writer, he returned to San Juan, where he continued his political involvement and his work as a political essayist and columnist. During this decade, Andreu Iglesias cemented his friendship with journalist Bernardo Vega, whom he had met in 1948. Both were members of the Socialist Party and they toured Puerto Rico together. Vega asked Andreu Iglesias to help him edit an autobiographical novel, which the latter suggested should remain a memoir. The process took over a decade, and in 1977, the famous *Memoria de Bernardo Vega* was published, which has become a classic of **immigrant literature** as well as a controversial topic about which scholars attempt to understand how much Andreu Iglesias actually wrote. Since Vega passed away in 1965 and Andreu Iglesias in 1976, there is very little known about the editing of the text. However, scholars point out that without Andreu Iglesias's involvement, the book would never have been published.

Andreu Iglesias's reputation as a writer continues to grow. *Los derrocados* was translated into English, in 2002, as *The Vanquished*, and *Memoria de Bernardo Vega* has become part of the Latino canon in American universities and colleges. Andreu Iglesias's other writings include *Luis Muñoz Marín, un hombre acorralado por la historia* (1972), *Cosas de aquí: una visión de la década del '60 en Puerto Rico* (1975), and *El derrumbe* (1981).

Further Reading

Fromm, Georg H. *César Andreu Iglesias: aproximación a su vida y obra*. Río Piedras, Puerto Rico: Ediciones Huracán, 1977.

Luis, William. *Dance Between Two Cultures: Latino Caribbean Literature Written in the United States*. Nashville: Vanderbilt University Press, 1997.

—*D. H. Figueredo*

Anglophone Caribbean Literature, History of

This term refers to the literature written in the islands where English is the official and the dominant language; often these islands are referred to as the West Indies, though the term can be misleading, since it also refers to the Hispanic and

Francophone islands. Anglophone Caribbean literature has also been called Commonwealth literature and West Indian literature.

The English-speaking islands are Anguilla, Antigua, Barbados, Barbuda, Dominica, Grenada, Jamaica, Montserrat, St. Kitts-Nevis, St. Lucia, St. Vincent, Trinidad-Tobago, and the Virgin Islands. Guyana, though located in South America, is regarded as a Caribbean nation. These islands were under British rule, beginning with colonization in the seventeenth and eighteenth centuries and terminating with the independence movements of the late twentieth century.

The early literature consisted of travelogues written by British colonialists visiting or stopping by on their way somewhere else. A pioneer Jamaican poet was **Francis Williams** who during the 1720s wrote poetry, including a famous ode in Latin, commemorating the arrival to the island of a new governor. One of the earliest descriptions of the Caribbean and an exposition of the horrors of the slavery was *The Interesting Narrative of the Life of Olaudah Equiano, or Gustavus Vassa, the African* written by **Olaudah Equiano**, a freed slave, in 1789. In the 1800s, several **slave narratives** and literature protesting the oppression of blacks appeared, including *Free Mulatto* (1824) by **Jean Baptiste Philippe** and *Emmanuel Appadocca: A Tale of the Boucaneers* (1854) by Maxwell Phillips. In 1887, Guyanese poet **"Leo" Martin Egbert** achieved notoriety with his writings of two additional stanzas to "God Save the Queen." Inherent in these writings were protests against slavery and racism, as well as a growing sense of nationalism.

Pride in the natural beauty of the region, which can be interpreted as an evolving pride of nationhood, if not nationalism, is evident in the novel *Becka's Buckra Baby* (1903), written by Jamaican **Tom Redcam**. His poetry also reveals a deep love for Jamaica:

> I sing of the island I love
> Jamaica, the land of my birth
> Of summer-lit heavens above
> An island the fairest on earth . . .

The early twentieth century begins with literary productivity manifested in the historical and realistic novels, such as *Jane's Career* (1913) by G. H. de Lisser, nationalist poetry by **Claude McKay** and **Vivian Virtue**—all from Jamaica—and the foundation of the Jamaica Poetry League in 1923. The 1930s saw the appearance of works by authors who would become major figures in world literature, such as the Trinidadian **CRL James**, who in 1936 published his novel *Minty Alley* and two years later his seminal history of the Haitian revolution, *The Black Jacobins*.

The 1940s was dominated by the appearance of three extraordinary literary reviews—*Bim*, in Barbados; *Kyk-Over-Al*, in Guyana; *Focus*, in Jamaica, and a radio program that helped to internationalize Anglophone Caribbean writers: *Caribbean Voices*. Combined, the journals and the radio program, which broadcast from London, introduced emerging talents to Caribbean readers and listeners and promoted a need for a national culture. The 1950s can be described as the era when Caribbean writers left their homes and relocated to London to look for better publishing opportunity, initiating a trend that has yet to subside; some of the transplanted writers were the Jamaican **Roger Mais**, the Trinidadian **Samuel Selvon**, and **Edward Kamau Brathwaite**, from Barbados. Their stay in Europe allowed them to cultivate solidarity with other writers from the Caribbean through the foundation in London of such organization as the **Caribbean Artists Movement (CAM)**.

The 1950s and 1960s were decades of political change and revolutionary fervor, as the islands achieved independences. **Vic Reid** celebrated Jamaica's self-rule with the historical novel *New Day* (1949), **Martin Carter**, from Guyana, published *Poems of Resistance* (1952), rallying his compatriots to rebel against the British, Roger Mais wrote *The Hills Were Joyful Together*, (1953) a classic example of **Barrack Yard Literature**, which celebrated the common people, and would-be Nobel laureate **V. S. Naipul** wrote three novels, *The Mystic Masseur* (1957), *The Suffrage of Elvira* (1958) and *A House for Mr. Biswas*. (1961), considered one of the best works of fiction written in English. These two decades also saw the continued the migration to England and, later on, Canada, an experience explored by Samuel Selvon and **Andrew Salkey**, among others.

The 1960s were characterized by the works of two authors considered the most important in Anglophone Caribbean literature as well as influential participants in world literature: Edward Kamau Brathwaite and **Wilson Harris**. The first is a poet, critic, and historian who uses dialect, which was usually not accepted by most publishers, and questions African heritage and identity in the Caribbean. The latter is a Guyanese novelist whose erudite texts and multilayered stories place the universal over the local, expressing concern over the potential danger of nationalism and racial pride.

The 1970s saw the institutionalization of Anglophone Caribbean literature as the writers assumed teaching positions at prestigious universities throughout the world, literary critics engaged in serious studies of the literature, literary works were accepted into the curriculum, and conferences, such as the **Conference of the Association for Commonwealth Literature and Language Studies (1971)** promoted and studied the region's literature at public gatherings. True excitement flourished in the 1980s with the appearance of women writers who brought feminist perspective to the exploration of colonialism, sexual relationships, and gender roles, exemplified by the work of such novelists as **Jamaica Kincaid**, with her novel *Annie John* (1983), **Valerie Belgrave** with *Ti Marie* (1988), and poet **Grace Nichols** with *The Flat Black Woman's Poems* (1984).

The end of the twentieth century and the beginning of the twenty-first revealed the continued popularity of Anglophone Caribbean writers, with the literary torch being passed from one generation to the next. Thus the demise of such crucial figures as Vic Reid and Martin Carter did not translate into a vacuum: new voices, such as those of **James Berry** and **Jinta "Binta" Breeze**, filled the void with children's literature crafted to foster pride in the Caribbean and experimental poetic techniques, such as **dub poetry**, meant to promote activism. Transnationalism emerged in the writings of authors who lived on several islands at different times as well as maintaining residence either in the United States or in Canada; one of the best known in the early 2000s was **Dionne Brand**, a filmmaker and a writer. *See also* Children's Literature in the English-Speaking Caribbean; Literary Journals.

Further Reading

Breiner, Laurence A. *An Introduction to West Indian Poetry*. Cambridge: Cambridge University Press, 1998.

Cudjoe, Selwyn R. *Caribbean Women Writers: Essays From the First International Conference*. Wellesley, MA: Calaloux Publications, 1990.

Dathorne, O. R. *Caribbean Narrative: An Anthology of West Indian Writing*. London: Heinemann Educational Books, 1966, 1973.

Ramchand, Kenneth. *An Introduction to the Study of West Indian Literature*. Kenya and Jamaica: Nelson Caribbean, 1976.

Walmsley, Anne. *The Caribbean Artists Movement 1966–1972*. London: New Beacon Books, 1992.

—*D. H. Figueredo*

Angulo Guridi, Alejandro (1822–1906)

Born in Cuba, where his parents had settled after the Haitian invasion of the Dominican Republic in 1822, Angulo Guridi studied law at the Universidad de la Habana, and was brother to Javier Angulo Guridi. Upon graduation, he traveled to the United States. In Cuba in 1843, Angulo Guridi wrote the novel *Los amores indios*, an indianist novel, regarded as the first novel written by a Dominican. In 1852, after the Dominican Republic was reestablished, he returned to Santo Domingo. For the next twenty years, Angulo Guridi wrote for several newspapers, worked as an attorney, was appointed to several government positions, and taught literature at the Colegio de San Buenaventura and law at the Colegio Seminario de Santo Domingo. During this period he introduced the emerging Cuban literature to readers in the Dominican Republic through a series of articles and lectures.

In 1878, tired of political turmoil in the Dominican Republic and the rule of several dictatorial presidents, Angulo Guridi left his country for good, touring Latin America once more before settling in El Salvador. He edited several newspapers in Cuba and in Central America.

In Chile he published in 1891, *Temas políticos*, which discusses the nature of freedom and judicial power. His novel *La joven Carmela* (1841) has yet to be published.

Angulo Guridi, Francisco Javier (1816–85)

Francisco Javier was one of the earliest writers of **Romanticismo** in the Dominican Republic, was one of the first to introduce indianist literature, with his novel *Iguaniona* (1867), and was the first playwright to use Dominican dialect in literature.

Born in Santo Domingo, in the Dominican Republic, Francisco Javier relocated with his parents to Cuba at the age of six. He was brother to Alejandro Angulo Guridi. During the three decades he lived on the island, he wrote for several publications and founded the newspaper *La Prensa*. In Cuba in 1843, he wrote the book of poetry *Ensayos poéticos*.

Returning to the Dominican Republic, he explored indianist themes and was attracted by local legends, which he recounted in two books: *La fantasma de Higuey* (1857) and *La ciguapa* (1866). In the 1860s, he began to write plays that captured the ways in which people from the countryside expressed themselves: *Cacharros y manigüeros* (1867), *Don Junípero* (1868), and *Los apuros de un destierro* (1868). *See also* Indianismo.

Further Reading

Montelego, Alfonso. "Dominican Republic." In *Encyclopedia of Latin American Theater*, edited by Eladio Cortés and Mirta Barrea-Marlys, 201–15. Westport, CT: Greenwood Press, 2003.

—*D. H. Figueredo*

Anthony, Michael (1932–)

∎

Michael Anthony is a novelist and short-story writer from Trinidad. He is known for writing stories with realistic characters and settings that capture the psychological experience of children or young people growing up. He is also known as a Caribbean historian.

Michael Anthony was born on February 10, 1932, in Mayaro, Trinidad. When Anthony was ten years old his father died, which caused him to grow closer to his mother. He attended primary school in Mayaro, then went to the Junior Technical School of San Fernando so that he could earn a living as a tradesman and support his mother. He became a molder in an iron foundry but left at the age of twenty to migrate to England, where he worked as a telegraph operator. In 1968, he went to Brazil, and from there he returned to Trinidad in 1970.

Anthony wrote poetry while working at different jobs. Realizing that as a poet his talented was limited, he switched to short stories. Some of his pieces were accepted for inclusion in the famous radio program *Caribbean Voices*, produced by the BBC and broadcast from London to the Caribbean. In 1960, an editor encouraged Anthony to write a novel.

The Games Were Coming, probably his best-known work, was published in 1963. It is a story of a father-and-son relationship, a major theme in Anthony's works. Two years later, Anthony published *The Year in San Fernando*, a coming-of-age novel about a young boy living away from home while working for a rich family. Both works established a pattern that Anthony would continue to follow: stories based on people he knew well, realistic depiction of everyday events, and exploration of family conflicts. Critic Daryl Cumber Dance comments that Anthony's predilection for psychological studies rather than social and political commentary, as practiced by many writers from the Caribbean, have prompted some critics to dismiss his work. But, Dance observes in *Fifty Caribbean Writers*, "The genius of Anthony . . . is that despite the apparent simplicity of his plot, his stories are narrated with such power that not only does the reader never doubt the significance of whatever . . . experience the protagonist is undergoing . . . he is also irresistibility caught up in it" (21).

As a historian, Anthony's nonfiction works include *Glimpses of Trinidad and Tobago: With a Glance at the West Indies* (1974), *The Making of Port of Spain* (1978), and *Bright Road to El Dorado* (1981).

Further Reading

Dance, Daryl Cumber, ed. *Fifty Caribbean Writers: A Bio-Bibliographical Critical Sourcebook*. CT: Greenwood Press 1986.

—*Paula Morgan and D. H. Figueredo*

Anti-Castro Drama. See Anti-Castro Literature.

Anti-Castro Literature

Though hundreds of poems and dozens of plays have been written since 1959 criticizing Cuban leader **Fidel Castro**, it is the genre of the novel that has proven the most prolific in this regard. Published outside the island, for to do so in Cuba meant immediate imprisonment, the very first such novel to appear was *Enterrado Vivo*, by Andrés Rivera Collado. Printed in Mexico in 1960, it tells of the author's disillusionment with the revolution. Soon, score of similarly themed novels followed, and by the end of the decade over thirty titles had been published in Spain, Mexico, and the United States.

The novels bear certain characteristics: (1) chronicling Castro's transformation from liberator to dictator, (2) exposing to the world Castro's dictatorial regime, (3) recounting major historical events, such as the Bay of Pigs invasion, (4) portraying Castro supporters as villains, (5) exploring life in exile, and (6) longing for a return to pre-1959 Cuba. The initial novels were written by amateurs: professors and physicians who did not intend to create literary works of lasting value but who were eager to tell the world about the failures of the Cuban Revolution. As such, according to critic Seymour Menton, most of the novels were much closer to political pamphlets than literary attempts.

During the 1970s and '80s, a more serious literature emerged. These novels were the products of established authors, like **Guillermo Cabrera Infante** and **Calvert Casey**, who had achieved a certain reputation on the island and initially had supported the revolutionary government. However, as the regime grew less tolerant of dissenting views and demanded literary works that promoted the aims of the revolution as expressed by Fidel Castro—who in 1968 defined the culturally accepted borders as **"within the Revolution everything; outside the Revolution nothing"**—these writers felt ostracized and chose to go into exile.

In the 1980s, a younger generation of little known writers produced a new wave of anti-Castro novels. These authors were members of the so-called **Mariel Generation**, referring to the boatlift that took place in the summer of 1980 when 110,000 refugees sailed across the Florida straits from the port of Mariel to Key West, Florida. As a group, these authors had not been published in Cuba. Once in the United States, they penned autobiographical novels that documented human rights violations on the island. The most famous member of this generation was the novelist and poet **Reinaldo Arenas**.

Of the first group of anti-Castro novels, those written by the exiles who came in the 1960s, the best examples are *No hay aceras* (1969) by Pedro Estanza, about an anti-Castro cell planning sabotages, and *Obrero de vanguardia* (1972) by Francisco Chao, the story of a worker falsely accused of plotting against the government. Of the second group, writers Reinaldo Arenas and **Zoé Valdés** might be the most notables. In novels such as *Arturo, la estrella más brillante* (1984) and *El color del verano, o, Nuevo "Jardín de las delicias"* (1999), Arenas inventories the ills of the revolution and satirizes Fidel Castro. Valdés, on the other hand, in works such as *La nada cotidiana* (1995), describes the intense poverty plaguing the island, which is blamed on Castro's administrative style and poor planning, and the frustrations experienced by artists and intellectuals censured for expressing views critical of the government.

Most of the anti-Castro novels are written in Spanish for a Spanish-speaking audience. As such, authors like Arenas and Cabrera Infante considered their works as belonging within the canon of Latin American belles lettres. To this list may be added the works of **Severo Sarduy**, who in 1993 published his last piece, *Pájaros de la playa*, a novel dealing with the Castro regime's inhumane treatment of homosexuals infected with the AIDS virus.

Some novels, however, such **Virgil Suárez**'s *The Cutter* (1991), about a labor camp on the island, were penned in English for English-language readers. One such recent work written directly in English is Teresa de la Caridad Doval's novel *A Girl Like Che Guevara* (2004), which takes on the social and economic injustices of the present-day Castro dictatorship from the perspective of a teenager who was born into it.

Anti-Castro poetry, however, was written primarily in Spanish. Thematically linked to the novel, hundreds of poems were published in little journals and "periodiquitos," weeklies subsidized by ads and distributed free of charge in Cuban grocery stores in the New York area and in Florida in the 1960s and '70s. The poems lament the Cuban condition and paint Castro as an ogre or Antichrist figure; most are written in a traditional rhyming scheme.

A better anti-Castro poetry was produced on the island where, because of the elusive nature of the genre, anti-revolutionary criticism sometimes went unnoticed.

The prototype was the collection of poems *Fuera del juego* by **Heberto Padilla**. Published in 1969, the poems didn't directly criticize Castro but questioned, on a philosophical level, the accomplishments of the revolutionary regime. A few months after the work came out, it was deemed anti-revolutionary, leading to the eventual arrest of its author. The regime humiliated Padilla by forcing him to publicly ask the State for forgiveness. A similar fate awaited poet **María Elena Cruz Valera**, who in the 1990s wrote poems critical of the government and was forced to eat part of her manuscript, according to a Human Rights Watch/Americas Report in November 1991.

Anti-Castro drama flourished in Miami in the 1960s. The pieces were primarily satirical, lampooning economic conditions on the island; a comic actor usually dressed up as Fidel Castro, aping his mannerism and speech patterns. In the 1980s, there were attempts in New York at presenting a more serious drama. The play *Los perros jíbaros* (1979), written by political prisoner Jorge Valls while still incarcerated on the island—written on bits of paper and smuggled out piece by piece—was a surrealist exploration of the psychological tortures practiced by Castro's secret service. The experimental production *Sparrows*, written in English by Manuel Martin Jr. in 1980, purposely offered contradictory and conflicting views of the Cuban Revolution. *See also* Cuban American Literature; Exile Literature; Mariel Generation.

Further Reading

Figueredo, Danilo H. "Ser Cubano: To Be Cuban. The Evolution of Cuban-American Literature." *Multicultural Review* 6, no. 1 (March 1997): 18–28.

Gutiérrez de la Solana, Alberto. "La novela cubana escrita fuera de Cuba." *Anales De Literatura Hispanoamericana* 2–3 (1973–74): 767–89.

Menton, Seymour. *Prose Fiction of the Cuban Revolution*. Austin, TX: University of Texas Press, 1975.

—*Rolando Pérez and D. H. Figueredo*

Anti-Castro Novel. See Anti-Castro Literature.

Anti-Castro Poetry. See Anti-Castro Literature.

Anti-slavery Literature. See Abolionist Literature.

Apollon, Marlène Rigaud (1945–)

Marlène Rigaud Apollon is a Haitian American poet who writes in English, French, and Creole or Kreyòl. Her poems address political conditions in Haiti and the impact the United States has had on the island nation.

Apollon was born on May 23, 1945, in Cap-Haitien, Haiti, grew up in Port-au-Prince, and migrated to the United States in 1964, with the intention of eventually returning home. She graduated from the University of Maryland and earned a master of science degree from Towson University. She taught elementary school in Maryland, worked for the Voice of America, and contributed numerous essays to Haitian publications. Though as a poet she writes in English and in French, her subject is always Haiti and Haitians. Her poems, which have been published in several anthologies, are political in nature, as expressed in this 1996 piece:

> Tiers est monde
> Où les enfants vont nus
> Pansae en avant

(My world is the third / where are naked / bellies swollen).

Apollon often lectures on the generational conflict between Haitian parents, who are bound by Haitian traditions, and their Haitian American children, intent on pursuing materialism and wealth. She is the author of two books of poems, *Cris de colère, Chants d'espoir* (1992) and *I Want to Dance* (1996). She has also written several works of children's literature, including *The Moon's a Banana, I Am Me* (*la lune est une banane, je suis moi*) (1998) and *A Land Called Darling-Une terre nommée Chérie* (1998). According to Bob Corbett of Western University, Apollon's children books serve as an introduction to Haiti for foreign adult readers. *Haiti Trivia, Questions et Réponses sur Haïti* (1998) and *Haitian Art Trivia* (1998) are small multilingual volumes that share a similar structure, providing information, questions, and answers on Haiti.

Further Reading

Fenwick, M. J., ed. *Sisters of Caliban: Contemporary Women Writers of the Caribbean; a Multicultural Anthology.* Falls Church, Virginia: Azul Editions, 1996.

—*Jayne R. Boisvert and D. H. Figueredo*

Arce de Vázquez, Margot (1904–90)

A leading Puerto Rican scholar and literary critic, Arce de Vázquez advocated for the maintenance of a Puerto Rican cultural identity and for the preservation of the Spanish language on the island. She mentored numerous young poets and critics, the likes of which include **Luis M. Arrigoitia**.

Arce de Vázquez was born in Caguas on March 10, 1904. She attended the Universidad de Puerto Rico and from there went to Spain to study at the Universidad de Madrid. She finished her thesis on the Spanish writer Garcilaso de la Vega

(1503–36) in 1930; the work was published the following year in the prestigious journal *Revista de filología española*. The thesis received immediate attention from scholars who claimed Arce de Vázquez had written a fundamental reference work on the Spanish soldier and poet. As her scholarly reputation grew, Arce de Vázquez returned to Puerto Rico, where she soon turned her attention to Puerto Rican themes and writers.

Arce de Vázquez was visiting professor at Middlebury College from 1932 to 1938. After she befriended Chilean poet Gabriela Mistral (1889–1957), the two traveled together throughout Europe during the 1930s. In the meantime, she wrote dozens of essays that were published in such major Puerto Rican journals as *Asomante, Revista del Ateneo Puertorriqueño*, and *Revista de cultura puertor-riqueña*. In 1950, she published the book *Impresiones*, a collection of essays on Puerto Rican culture and on poets such as **Luis Palés Matos** and **Luis Llorens Torres**; above all, the author demonstrated a concern with American influence on the island and the potential for Puerto Rico to lose its Hispanic identity. In 1958, she published *Gabriela Mistral, persona y poesía*, a reflection on her friendship with mistral as well as an academic study on her poetry; the volume is considered one of the best ever written about the Chilean poet. In 1967, she published *La obra literaria de José de Diego*, a major study on her compatriot. In 1968, she edited the anthology *Lecturas puertorriqueñas: poesía*, which has since become a standard text in American universities.

Further Reading

Arrigoitia, Luis de. *La ejemplaridad en Margot Arce de Vázquez*. San Juan, Puerto Rico: Fundación Felisa Rincón de Gautier, 1992.

—*D. H. Figueredo*

Archibald, (Rupert) Douglas (1919–)

■

Archibald is a playwright from Trinidad-Tobago. He is a journalist and promoter of the performing arts.

(Rupert) Douglas Archibald was born in Port of Spain, Trinidad, on April 25, 1919. He grew up in a comfortable middle-class home and during World War II served in the Trinidadian army and the Canadian Army Reserve. He graduated with a BS in engineering from McGill University, Canada, in 1946. For the next thirty years, he worked at a variety of government posts involved in either transportations or communications.

Though he had contemplated writing as a youth, he did not begin his dramatist career until 1958 with the play *Junction Village*, produced by University of West Indies in 1958. Trinidad-Tobago and the Caribbean became the major themes of his plays, of which the best known are *Ann-Marie* (1967), *Defeat with Honour* (1977), and *Tobago: "Melancholy Isle"* (1987). In 1977, he wrote the novel *Isidore and the*

Turtle, which he adapted to the stage. During the 1970s, he was a tutor at the University of West Indies.

His works, which consist of short acts with well-drawn characters and engaging dialogue, reflect an upper-class perspective of life in the Anglophone Caribbean as well as a sense of cultural isolation. The isolation leads to a melancholic and sometimes lethargic existence.

Archibald's plays have been staged in his native country and in Jamaica. He awaits recognition outside the Anglophone Caribbean.

Further Reading

(Rupert) Douglas Archibald. *Contemporary Authors Online.* http://www.galenet.galegroup. com (accessed 8/29/05).

—D. H. Figueredo

Ardouin Brothers

These three brothers—Beaubrun, Céligni, and Coriolan—from Haiti were writers and politicians during the nineteenth century. Despite personal loss and tragedy, and political upheavals, they produced literary works that promoted a Haitian identity and nationalism.

Ardouin, Beaubrun (1796–1865). Ardouin was one of Haiti's first historians. At a time of passion and political agendas, this historian, according to Joan Dayan, in *Haiti, History and the Gods* (1998) "represented exactitude and verifiability" (28).

The son of a black mother and a white father, Beaubrun was born in Petit-Trou-des-Baradères in 1796. His studies were interrupted as a result of the Haitian revolution (1791–1804), yet he acquired a solid education on his own, favoring the writings of such French philosophers as Voltaire (1694–1778) and Rousseau (1712–78). As a teenager, he found employment at Haiti's National Printing Office, progressing from typesetting to book publishing.

In 1832, he was elected senator. Despite his political activities he managed to write the first book on Haitian geography, *Géographie de l'Île d'Haïti* (1832) and to found in 1837, with his brother Céligni, the Cénacle, a salon where literature and politics were discussed. During this period, he was elected president of the Haitian Senate, but in 1843, when revolution broke out against the regime of President Jean Pierre Boyer (1776–1850), Ardouin sought exile in Jamaica. Upon his return to Haiti, he was appointed to several government posts and, working behind the scenes with a group of politicians, helped General Faustin-Élie Soulouque (1782–1867) become president in 1847. The following year, Ardouin served in Paris as minister of Haiti. He remained in France after learning that President Soulouque had executed his brother Céligny.

In Paris, Ardouin researched the national archives and read the letters of General Charles Leclerc (1772–1802), who had been sent to Haiti during the revolution to defeat leader Toussaint Louverture, as well as numerous army reports on the revolution. The result was the volume *Études sur l'histoire d'Haïti*. This history depicts intimate details of the revolution, describing how women fought, commenting on the bravery of Dessaline's wife, Claire Heureuse (1758–1858), who protected many whites her husband had sentenced to death, and narrating the assassination of **Jean-Jacques Dessalines**. But throughout the volume, as Dayan points out, Ardouin was preoccupied with what it meant to be Haitian, wanting to promote a Caribbean identity distinct from French characteristics. *Études sur l'histoire d'Haïti* was published between 1853 and 1860. It consisted of eleven volumes.

Ardouin passed away in 1865.

Ardouin, Céligni (1806–49). Historian and politician Céligni Ardouin was the author of the volume *Essais sur l'histoire d'Haiti* (1865).

Céligni Ardouin was born in Petit-Trou-de-Nippes in 1806. In 1837, he co-founded with Beaubrun and the **Nau brothers** the Cénacle. Though literature attracted Céligni, politics was his passion. He was a senator and served as minister of the interior in 1847. A year later, his opposition to President Soulouque resulted in his arrest and execution. After his death, his brother collected the manuscript for his history of Haiti. The volume was published twenty years later.

Essais sur l'histoire d'Haiti is notable for its depiction of the private lives of major Haitian figures of the revolution and for the account of such incidents as the betrayal and arrest of Toussaint L'Overture in 1802. It was one of the first documents toward the creation of a national history of Haiti.

Ardouin, Coriolan (1812–36). This doomed Haitian poet is regarded, according to Naomi Garret in *The Renaissance of Haitian Poetry* (1963), as one of the inaugurators of romantic expression in Haitian poetry. He set the stage for the development of the romantic movement in Haiti.

Ardouin was born in Port-au-Prince on December 11, 1812. He was exposed to death at very early age. The day he was born, an older brother died. At the age of twelve, he lost his mother, father, and an older sister.

His life was marked by sorrow, and he found comfort in poetry and in his studies at the L'Institution Jonathan Granville—where he befriended another would-be writer and equally tragic figure, **Ignace Nau**. He experienced a respite from suffering when he met a young woman named Amelia Sterlin; they were married in 1835. But this happiness was short-lived when his wife passed away five months after their marriage.

The young poet never recovered from the loss of his wife. He passed away a year after her death. In such poems as "Mon âme" and "La Brise au tombeau d'Emma" he lamented his fate, claiming "Le coeur de l'homme juste est un vase de pleurs" (the heart of man is a vase of tears). *See also* Haitian Literature, History of; Romanticismo/Romanticism.

Further Reading

Dayan, Joan. *Haiti, History and the Gods*. Berkeley: University of California Press, 1998.

Berrou, Raphaël and Pompilus, Pradel. *Histoire de la Littérature Haïtienne.* Tome 1. Port-au-Prince: Éditions Caraëbes.

Trouillot, Hénock. *Beaubrun Ardouin, l'homme politique et l'historien.* Port-au-Prince, 1950.

—*D. H. Figueredo*

Areito. See Areyto.

Arenas, Reinaldo (1943–90)

∎

Reinaldo Arenas was one of Cuba's and Latin America's most important writers of the post-**Boom** generation. After receiving early recognition for his writing from the Cuban cultural establishment, Arenas faced censorship, as well as persecution for his homosexuality, from **Fidel Castro**'s regime. Most of his oeuvre was published outside his country. Arenas's literature, much of which is experimental in form, encompasses nearly all the major genres: novels, short stories, poetry, drama, and memoir. His work explores the theme of freedom in a repressive world.

Arenas was born on July 16, 1943, into dire poverty, near Holguín, in Oriente Province. Soon after his birth, his father abandoned his mother, and she returned with Arenas to her parents' home. Arenas experienced deprivation and loneliness growing up in his grandparents' household, but it also allowed him close contact with nature—in various books, he describes eating dirt and climbing trees. In 1958, he left home to join the rebels fighting the Fulgencio Batista dictatorship (1901–73).

After the triumph of the revolution, he went to Havana to study agricultural accounting. A few years later, he began working in the National Library. During this time, he met the writers **José Lezama Lima** and **Virgilio Piñera**, both of whom became his mentors. He completed his first novel, *Celestino antes el alba* (1967), which although awarded honorable mention in the **Cirilo Villaverde** competition, was published in a limited edition that received little circulation. In 1967, friends visiting Havana smuggled the manuscripts of that novel and another, *El mundo alucinante* (1969), out of the country. They were subsequently published to great acclaim in France and Mexico, a development that helped launch the author's international reputation.

Meanwhile, Arenas was experiencing growing marginalization by the Cuban government. Over the next few years, he had to rewrite his novel *Otra vez el mar* three times: the first version was confiscated by the police; the second disappeared mysteriously; and the third—again, with the help of friends—was smuggled out of Cuba and published abroad in 1982. In the early 1970s, he was sent to cut cane at a sugar mill, where he wrote the long poem *El Central* (1970). After being arrested, in 1973, for lewd and counterrevolutionary behavior, he spent the next few years serving time in El Morro Castle and other state prisons in Havana; ultimately, he was forced to sign a confession and sent to a rehabilitation camp.

Arenas escaped Cuba in 1980 during the Mariel exodus. He lived briefly in Miami but, disillusioned with the exile community there, soon moved to New York. He received a Guggenheim fellowship and lectured in the United States and Europe. During this time, authorized editions of his most important novels appeared. Throughout his years in exile, he remained an outspoken critic of the Castro regime and denounced it unapologetically. Toward the end of his life, he coauthored an open letter entitled *Un plebiscito a Fidel Castro* (1990), which was signed by ten Nobel laureates and hundreds of writers worldwide.

He was diagnosed with AIDS in 1987. He completed a memoir, *Antes de que anochezca*, in August 1990. Four months later, his body ravaged by illness, he committed suicide. Arenas's posthumous publications include *Antes de que anochezca* and the novels *El color del verano* (1991), a carnivalesque, parodic vision of Cuba, and *El asalto* (1991), a utopian work that depicts a totalitarian society of the future. These novels, together with *Cantando en el pozo* (1982), *El palacio de las blanquísimas mofetas* (1980), and *Otra vez el mar*, compose what Arenas called his "Pentagonía" cycle, which he described as autobiographical and a metaphor of Cuban history.

Many of Arenas's novels and other works explore the world of childhood and are narrated, in whole or in part, from the point of view of a child, a writer, or some other oppressed individual. In *Cantando en el pozo*, the nameless speaker is trapped in the confining world of his family and attempts to escape it through fantasy, in particular by inventing an imaginary cousin who writes poems on trees that are subsequently cut down by the protagonist's enraged grandfather. Fortunato, the hero of *El palacio de las blanquísimas mofetas*, literally escapes home by going off, as the young Reinaldo did, to fight with the rebels.

The quest for freedom from an oppressive world, whether through resistance, art, or sexuality, is the major theme in Arenas's work. In *El mundo alucinante*, Fray Servando is imprisoned in a dungeon, encased from head to toe in chains, but his mind is free. *El Central* equates the enslavement of blacks by the Spaniards with the oppression of sugarcane workers in modern-day Cuba; the act of writing the poem embodies transcendence. Finally, in *Antes de que anochezca*, Arenas presents many of his sexual escapades as both statements of defiance and as metaphors for liberation in a homophobic system.

Subversion is a theme as well as a formal strategy in Arenas's texts. The notion of time and reality are often subverted by the presentation of multiple versions of events, as in the opening of *El mundo alucinante*, and by the invention of multiple, protean, or even vanishing characters, as at the end of *Otra vez el mar*, when the reader learns that the character of the wife—the narrator of the first half of the novel—never existed. Arenas employs parodic humor, hyperbole, and fantasy to undercut both the seriousness and authenticity of events. The cast of characters in *El color del verano* brings together historical figures such as **Gertrudis Gómez de Avellaneda** and **José Martí** with contemporary ones like **Nicolás Guillén** and

Alicia Alonso (1921–). In *El portero* (1989), a motley assortment of animals— dogs, fleas, fish, and even a Russian bear—meet in the basement of a New York apartment building to conspire against their masters. In the story "Mona," the figure in the *Mona Lisa* slips away each evening to have adventures with night watchmen and pimps while the painting is on loan to the Metropolitan Museum of Art.

Arenas's use of stream of consciousness, shifting points of view, and nontraditional narrative structure reflects the influence of authors such as William Faulkner (1897–1962), James Joyce (1882–1941), Marcel Proust (1871–1922), and Virginia Woolf (1882–1941). Yet Reinaldo Arenas's oeuvre is the sum of its parts and something more: its formal experimentation, autobiographical content, directness in relating experience, and irreverence all combine to produce a body of work that is wholly original and distinctly Cuban.

In 2005, *Antes de que anochezca* was adapted as an opera by musician and librettist Jorge Martin. Selections from this opera were staged at Lincoln Center. *See also* Anti-Castro Literature; Cuban Literature, History of; Gay and Lesbian Literature; Mariel Generation; *Mariel*, Journal.

Further Reading

Hernández Miyares, Julio, and Perla Rozencvaig, eds. *Reinaldo Arenas: alucinaciones, fantasía, y realidad*. Glenview, IL: Scott, Foresman, 1990.

Rozencvaig, Perla. "Reinaldo Arenas's Last Interview." *Review: Latin American Literature and Arts*, no. 44 (January-June 1991).

Soto, Francisco. *Reinaldo Arenas: The Pentagonia*. Gainesville: University of Florida Press, 1994.

———. *Reinaldo Arenas*. Twayne's World Authors Series: Cuban Literature. New York: Twayne, 1998.

—Daniel Shapiro

Areyto

This was an early type of entertainment used by the Taínos, the Amerindians who lived in Puerto Rico before the conquest and colonization of the island. Areyto was a combination of narration, poetry, singing, and dancing used to relate events from the past, comment on local developments, such as a birth or a death, and even rally Taínos into battle with rival tribes. In essence, the areyto was a form of theatrical performance and precursor of Caribbean theater.

Areytos were also present in Cuba and in Central America. Over the years, the term has been associated with singing or certain types of songs. Symbolically, the term is currently used in Puerto Rico to affirm a Puerto Rican cultural identity. The term is also spelled areito.

Further Reading

Yin, Philippa Brown. "Puerto Rico." In *Encyclopedia of Latin American Theater*, edited by Eladio Cortés and Mirta Barrea Marlys. Westport, CT: Greenwood Press, 2003.

—D. H. Figueredo

Arias, Aurora (1962–)

Aurora Arias is a short story writer and journalist from the Dominican Republic.

Arias was born in Santo Domingo, Dominican Republic, on April 22, 1962. During the mid-1970s she attended the Escuela Nacional de Artes, concentrating on public relations. In 1982, she graduated from Universidad Mundial de Santo Domingo with a graduate degree in clinical psychology. She is a member of the Unión de Escritores Dominicanos and of the Centro de Investigación para la Acción Femenina. She is a columnist for several national publications, including the journal *Quehaceres*.

She started to write as an adolescent, publishing her first poems at the age of twenty-one in the journal *Revista Ahora*. In 1987, she published her first book of poetry, *Vivienda de pàjaro*. In 1993, she wrote a second collection, titled *Piano lila*. In 1998, she wrote her first book of short stories, *Fin de mundo*. In her poetry and stories Arias exhibits a playful sense of reality, toying with words. In the story "Inesperado encuentro con la Cosa," the narrator meets a personification of the word *cosa*—thing—a common expression in Spanish used to explain any circumstance in life, such as "Como va la cosa?" or "Las cosas pasan," meaning "How are things going?" or "Stuff happens."

In 1994, Arias received the short-story award from the Casa de Teatro. Her stories have been anthologized in collections in the United States and in Europe. Critic Catharenia Vallejo, in *Mujeres como islas* (2002), observes that in Arias's there is a "masterful presentation of the humorous which also applies to tragedy." Vallejo further describes Arias' style as "elegant, rich in its voluptuousness" (101).

Further Reading

Vallejo, Catharina. "Innovación, calidad y riqueza en la cuentística dominicana femenina contemporánea." In *Mujeres como islas*. Habana: Ediciones UNIÓN; Santo Domingo: Ediciones FERILIBRO, 2002.

—D. H. Figueredo

Arlen, Leslie. See Nicholson, Christopher R.
Armeth, Auguste. See Macouba, Auguste.

Arozarena, Marcelino (1912–96)

Poet Marcelino Arozarena was born on March 13, 1912, in a Havana tenement to a working class family—his father was a construction worker and his mother a washerwoman. He attended public school, where he caught the attention of the principal, who asked Professor Salvador García Agüero to coach him for the admission exam to Havana's teachers school, Escuela Normal de Maestros. García Agüero introduced Arozarena to poetry and politics. During his years at Havana's teachers school, Arozarena began to write poetry and joined a Marxist student organization.

In the 1920s, many Cuban poets wrote what has been called Poesia Negrista, based on and inspired by the life, customs, and speech patterns of the Afro-Cuban masses, and Arozarena became one of the most outstanding cultivators of the genre. Though as a young man his poems were published in Havana periodicals, turning him into something of a celebrity within literary circles, his first book of poetry, *Canción negra sin color I*, was not published out until 1966. In 1983, he published *Canción negra sin color II*, containing selections from his first collection plus forty-one new poems. He also published the collection *Habra que esperar*.

His Negrista poems have a distinguishing thrust and zest. In "Amalia" the meter is the rhythm of a *son*, a Cuban musical and dance form, with the repetition of certain verses. This erotic song vibrates with splendid onomatopoeias, alliterations, and *jitanjaforas* (repeated sounds without meaning). In "Evohe," a political poem, he combines the ritual evocation of an African deity with a call to action to exploited Afro-Cubans, concluding it with the verse "piensa un poco en Scottboro y no en Ogun.": think more about the consequences of the Scottoboro trial than about the African god Ogun. Arozarena's poetry is apparently simple, primal, and rhythmic, but as he explained in the prologue to *Canción negra sin color I*, he "sings while speaking his mind." This is perhaps what makes significant the poetry of Arozarena, which has been translated into several languages, including English, French, and German.

Arozarena founded the radio station Emisora Mil Diez, and later on worked for *Hoy*, the newspaper of the Cuban Communist Party. When *Hoy* was banned by Cuban president Fulgencio Batista (1901–1973) in 1953, Arozarena taught in primary school. After the triumph of the Cuban Revolution, he went to work at the editorial board of *La Gaceta de Cuba*. He died at Havana in 1996. *See also* Negrista Literature; Négritude.

Further Reading

Guirao, Ramón, ed. *Órbita de la poesía afrocubana, 1928–37 (antología)*. Habana: Talleres de Ucar, García y cía., 1938.

Jackson, Richard L. *The Black Image in Latin American Literature*. Albuquerque: University of New Mexico Press, 1976.

—Rafael E. Tarrago

Arrigoitia, Luis M. (1933–)

Arrigoitia is a poet and literary critic from Puerto Rico. Born in Santurce, he attended the Universidad de Puerto Rico, where he studied under the literary critic **Margot Arce de Vázquez**, who mentored him. From this university he earned both a BA and an MA in arts. In 1963, he received a PhD in philosophy and literature from the Universidad Central de Madrid. While teaching literature at the Universidad de Puerto Rico, he wrote poetry and published literary criticism in such important journals as *Sin Nombre*.

In 1961, he cowrote, with Margot Arce de Vázquez, the anthology and critical study *Lecturas puertorriqueñas: poesía*, an authoritative text that proved popular in universities and colleges in the United States. In 1968, he published *Cuarzo*, a book of his poetry. In 1989, he published *Pensamiento y forma en la prosa de Gabriela Mistral*, on the life and work of the Chilean Nobel Prize recipient. *La ejemplaridad en Margot Arce de Vázquez*, a critical evaluation of his mentor and colleague, was published in 1992. In 1997, he published *Manatí y Enrique Zorrilla, 1880–1928, un poeta en la Atenas de Puerto Rico*. Through these works, he promoted the importance of Puerto Rican literature on the island and its significance within the Latin American literary canon.

Arrigoitia retired from the Universidad de Puerto in 1998.

Further Reading

Enciclopedia puertorriqueña. siglo XXI. Santurce, Puerto Rico: Caribe Grolier, 1998.

—*D. H. Figueredo*

Arrillaga, María (1940–)

Born in Mayagüez, Puerto Rico, María Arrillaga, the offspring of a very distinguished family, is a poet and writer of short stories, novels, and autobiographical narratives. She has also exceled as a translator, critic, and professor.

Arrillaga came to the Unites States in 1957 and graduated in 1961 from the University of St. Louis, where she studied French and English literature but nothing about the history of Puerto Rico or Puerto Rican identity. After graduation, she moved to New York City, where she went through several maturing experiences—discrimination as a divorced Puerto Rican woman and the tribulations of single motherhood—and became active in the social and civic struggles of the sixties. Deciding to learn more about Puerto Rico and to become Puerto Rican, as well as to seek a Puerto Rican companion, she moved back to the island in 1973.

Arrillaga is the author of numerous poetry books, including *Vida en el tiempo*, winner of the first-place prize in the poetry contest of the **Ateneo**

Puertorriqueño in 1972 and published in 1974; *New York in the Sixties* (1976); *Poemas 747* (1977); *Cascada de sol* (1977); *Frescura* (1981); and *Yo soy Filí Melé: obra poética* (1999). She has translated into English the poems of **Evaristo Ribera Chevremont, Julia de Burgos**, Marina Arzola, and Angelamaría Dávila for the anthology *The Puerto Rican Poets* (1972). In addition, in the decades of the nineties, she published two important anthologies, one of twentieth-century Spanish poets, *Voces nuevas: IX selección de poetisas* (1992), and *Concierto de voces insurgentes: tres autoras puertorriqueñas* (1998), an important contribution in which she showcases and examines the writings of three neglected Puerto Rican poets: Edelmira González Maldonado, Violeta López Suria and **Anagilda Garrastegui**.

As a critic, her pioneering study *Los silencios de María Bibiana Benítez* (1985), about the nineteenth-century first Puerto Rican female poet, still stands as the first full-scale examination of Bibiana Benítez's poetry. She also has written about Puerto Rican women writers from a feminist perspective in several literary publications.

Her short story "Una cuestión de tamaño" (1980), with its sharp criticism of the male role in heterosexual relations, stirred controversy among Puerto Rican intellectual and literary circles when it was first published. Her novel *Mañana Valentina*, a finalist of the Award Letras de Oro in 1994, enriches the Puerto Rican tradition of fine and eclectic narratives by women writers. It incorporates themes and obsessions already dealt with in her poetry and stories, such as the search for identity (whether political or personal); the centrality of women's experience in denouncing patriarchal society; solitude; discrimination; eroticism; sexual liberation; and nostalgia, while also celebrating life and the right of the self to be. Structurally, the novel incorporates the story "Una cuestión de tamaño" to come up with a hybrid narrative text that mixes numerous genres—micro-story, novel, letter, chronicle, children, music, gastronomy, and topics and so on—and in which she narrates and critically decodes the historical, social, and moral decline of an upper-class Puerto Rican family from the nineteenth century to its demise after 1898. The text is also revealing of the passionate and irreverent style of the writer. *See also* Feminism in Caribbean Literature; Nuyorican Literature.

Further Reading

"End of Ideologies." *El mundo* (November 25, 1989): 4–5.

—*Asela R. Laguna*

Arriví, Francisco (1915–)

■

A major figure in the development of contemporary Puerto Rican theater, Arriví is a Puerto Rican dramatist, poet, and essayist. Director of the experimental company Tinglado Puertorriqueño from 1940 to 1948, he not only promoted

Puerto Rican writers but brought an awareness of international drama to the island.

Born in San Juan, he was attracted to theater as a young man. After graduating from the Universidad de Puerto Rico in 1937, he pursued graduate studies on drama at Columbia University. In 1940, he wrote the farce *Club de solteros*, followed by an experimental drama, *El diablo se humaniza*, in 1941. During this period, he managed a radio station in Puerto Rico. In 1951, he produced the first television program in Puerto Rico.

After writing several plays, Arriví began to write poetry in the 1950s and 1960s. His poems addressed issues of a Puerto Rican identity as well as celebration of the island's history and natural beauty. His collections include *Tríptico* (1956), *Isla y nada* (1958), *Frontera* (1960), and *Ciclo de lo ausente* (1962). His theoretical and practical knowledge of the writing of drama and production of plays resulted in the publication of books on the subject, including *La generación del treinta: el teatro* (1960) and *Conciencia puertorriqueña del teatro contemporaneo* (1967).

Arriví was the director of the Oficina de Fomento Teatral del Instituto de Cultura Puertorriqueña. He also directed and produced historic drama for radio and was director of the national festival of the theater. *See also* Puerto Rican Literature, History of.

Further Reading

Enciclopedia puertorriqueña: siglo XXI. Vol 1. Santurce, Puerto Rico: Caribe Grolier, 1998.

Morfi, Angelina. *Historia crítica de un siglo de teatro puertorriqueño*. San Juan, Puerto Rico: Instituto de Cultura Puertorriqueña, 1980.

—D. H. Figueredo

Arrufat, Antón (1935–)

The recipient of Cuba's 2000 National Literary Prize, Arrufat is a critic, novelist, playwright, and poet. He attracted international attention in 1968 when his play *Los siete contra Tebas*, a retelling of a Greek tragedy by Aeschylus (526–456 B.C.E.), was criticized by militants within the revolutionary government as counter-revolutionary. The work, however, was not only published but received an award from the **Unión de Escritores y Artistas de Cuba (UNEAC)**, Cuba's writers and artists guild.

Born in Santiago de Cuba on August 14, 1935, Arrufat attended the city's prestigious Jesuit elementary school during the 1940s, finished his secondary education at the Instituto de la Habana in 1955, and earned a degree in philology from the Universidad de la Habana in 1979. He also lived in the United States during the mid-1950s. He wrote for the influential journal *Ciclón* and befriended writer and playwright **Virgilio Piñera**. He served on the staff of the periodical *Lunes de Revolución*, was editor of the journals *Casa de las Américas* and *Revolución y Cultura*.

Though *Los siete contra Tebas* was published, the play, which hinted criticism of the revolutionary process, was not staged for nearly twenty-five years. While many of his colleagues and friends, such as the poet **Heberto Padilla** and the novelist and critic **Antonio Benítez Rojo** sought exile, Arrufat has chosen to remain in Cuba. His most important books include *La caja está cerrada* (1984), *Las pequeñas cosas* (1988), *De las pequeñas cosas* (1997), *Lirios sobre un fondo de espadas* (1995), and *La huella en la arena: antología poética* (2000).

Further Reading

Arrufat, Antón. *Antología personal*. Barcelona: Mondadori, 2001.

Avila, Leopoldo. *Cuba: letteratura e rivoluzione. Le correnti della critica della letteratura cubana*. Milano: Libreria Feltrinelli, 1969.

Barquet, Jesús J. *Teatro y Revolución Cubana: subversión y utopía en Los siete contra Tebas de Antón Arrufat—Theater and the Cuban Revolution: subversion and utopia in Seven against Thebes by Antón Arrufat*. Lewiston, NY: E. Mellen Press, 2002.

—*Peter T. Johnson*

Arzola, Marina (1939–76)

Arzola was a Puerto Rican poet whose literary work was affected by mental illness and tragedy. She was also an editor and a journalist.

Born in Guayanilla, Puerto Rico, on July 12, 1939, Marina Arzola Porcell received her elementary and secondary education in her hometown before attending the Universidad de Puerto Rico in 1957. In 1961, she earned a BA and was also introduced at the **Ateneo Puertorriqueño** as an emerging poet.

Arzola began to write for the journal *Guajana* in 1962. Six years later, she won a literary contest sponsored by the Ateneo for the collection of unpublished poems *El niño de cristal y los olvidados*, about a younger brother who suffers from schizophrenia. In 1968, *Palabras vivas*, the only book published during her lifetime was released and won a literary prize from the Club Cívico de Damas. In 1976, Arzola, deeply affected by the death of her father, suffered from depression and other mental disorders. An asthmatic, Arzola's death is believed to be the result of either an asthma attack or accidental overdose of medication. A year after her death, *El niño de cristal y los olvidados* was published by the Instituto de Cultura Puertorriqueña.

Arzola's poetry was experimental and free-flowing, often reflecting the mercurial nature of her emotions. Her themes were the political and social issues of the 1970s as well as childhood, mortality, and language. She filled nearly a dozen notebooks with poems that have yet to be published. She also wrote essays and travelogues that have been published in numerous journals and newspapers.

Further Reading

Vázquez, Lourdes. *Aterrada de cuernos y cuervos: Marina Arzola, el testimonio.* San Juan, Puerto Rico: Ediciones El Gallo Rojo, 1990.

—*D. H. Figueredo*

Asomante (1945–70)

A Puerto Rican journal founded in San Juan by **Nilita Vientós Gastón** with the objective of "establishing a dialogue with Spanish-speaking countries, encouraging literature production in Puerto Rico, evaluating the past, and promoting contemporary literature in Spanish, English, and French," as Vientós Gastón recalled decades later in a 1984 issue of *Sin Nombre* (11). The journal attempted to affirm a Puerto Rican identity and advocated the knowledge of the universal through the national, that is, from the local to the universal. The journal published works by major authors from Spain, such as Jorge Guillén (1893–1984), and Puerto Rican writers such as **Francisco Matos Paoli**.

The journal was funded by the Asociación de Graduadas de la Universidad de Puerto Rico—the Alumni Association of the University of Puerto Rico—and during its first two decades, the association did not intervene with the editorial choices made by Vientós Gastón. In 1970, however, the members of the association considered the journal to be promoting leftist ideas and anti-American sentiments. When the association began to question submissions accepted for publication and suggested the creation of a committee to oversee the publication, Vientós Gastón broke away from the association. However, when she tried to publish *Asomante* independently, the alumni association sued, claiming that the association owned the intellectual rights and title of the journal. In 1970, Vientós Gastón was not allowed to publish the journal. Three days after publication ceased, Vientós Gastón issued a new literary journal with the same objectives and in the same style but without the title, thus the name of the new publication *Sin Nombre*, meaning "nameless." *See also* Literary Journals; Puerto Rican Literature, History of.

Further Reading

Vientós Gastón, Nilita. "Biografía de una revista *Asomante-Sin Nombre* (1945–1980)." *Sin Nombre* 15, no. 1. (Octubre-Diciembre 1984): 9–21.

—*Fernando Acosta-Rodríguez and D. H. Figueredo*

Association for Commonwealth Literature and Language Studies.
See Conference of the Association for Commonwealth Literature and Language
Studies (1971).

Astol Bussatti, Eugenio (1868–1948)

Self-educated poet and journalist Eugenio Astol was dubbed the "Poet of the Puerto
Rican Masonry" due to his involvement and identification with the Masonic order.
He was also a well-known orator and activist within the Puerto Rican community
in New York City.

Astol was born in Caguas. Attracted to theater, he was an actor. But he also felt a
passion for literature and language: to appreciate international literature, he taught
himself English, French, Italian, and Portuguese. He wrote for numerous newspapers,
including *El Diario Popular, El Imparcial*, and *La Luz*. He directed the publication *El
Día*. Many of his articles explore Puerto Rican nationalism and identity.

Astol became a Mason in 1919, and in that capacity he founded and directed
several Masonic journals; he also presented conferences at lodges. His books include *Noche de fiesta* (1897), *Cuentos y fantasías* (1904), *En torno a Cristo* (1931),
and *Tres banderas* (1912).

Further Reading

Enciclopedia puertorriqueña: siglo XXI. Vol 1. Santurce, Puerto Rico: Caribe Grolier, 1998.

—*D. H. Figueredo*

Atalaya de los dioses. See Atalayismo.

Atalayismo

A literary movement founded in 1928 by **Graciany Miranda Archilla,
Alfredo Margenat,** Francisco González Alberty and **Clemente Soto Vélez.** Atalaya
de los dioses, or Atalayismo, as it came to be known, one of the most
debated of the vanguard movements in Puerto Rico, became also one of the most
prolific. Its members, basically young men, kept their hair long, wore wild
clothes, and adopted strange pseudonyms. Though these authors didn't write a
manifesto explaining their aesthetics, their intent was to revolutionize
Puerto Rican poetry by breaking with decades of **Romanticismo,** both in content
and form. Theirs was to be a different kind of lyric poetry using new themes,

imagery, and rhythms, as illustrated in the poem "Abrazo interno" (1954) by Soto Vélez:

> Y aquí, donde lo caduco
> Quema el aire sin fuego
> El estremecimiento de lo Nuevo:
> Lo Nuevo estremecido
> Abre de par en par sus puertas

(Here, where I place it / the air burns without flames, / the novelty that trembles: / the trembling novelty / opens its doors wide.)

Several of the island's magazines and newspapers opened their pages to the works of the Atalayistas. The magazine *Gráfico* allowed them a weekly page to publish their poetry. *El Diluvio, La Linterna*, and *Índice* also were receptive to their works. Miranda Archilla became director of the poetry section of *Alma Latina*, where the Atalayistas gave voice to their literary theories. They quickly attracted numerous poets to their group, including Antonio Cruz y Nieves, **Luis Hernández Aquino**, and Pedro Carrasquillo, among others. The Atalayistas established a press called Atalaya de los dioses and published a book of poetry by Miranda Archilla entitled *Responso a mis poemas náufragos* (1931), considered the classic Atalayista text.

The Grupo Atalaya expressed a need for a more socially conscious and politicized poetry. During the 1930s, under the influence of the charis-matic leader of the Nationalist Party, Pedro Albizu Campos (1893–1965), the Atalayistas' writings began to manifest nationalistic tendencies and to incorporate the Nationalists' ideology. A number of them became followers of Albizu and in fact suffered imprisonment and persecution for their political convictions.

The Atalaya movement manifested itself through poetry and remained a Puerto Rican experience and experiment. *See also* Puerto Rican Literature, History of.

Further Reading

Puebla, Manuel de la, ed. *Historia y significado del atalayismo*. San Juan, Puerto Rico: Ediciones Mairena, 1994.

—Nélida Pérez and Nelly Cruz

Ateneo Puertorriqueño

■

First suggested by writer **Alejandro Tapia y Rivera,** this Puerto Rican institution was founded in 1876 by **Manuel de Elzaburu y Vizcarrondo** with the objective of raising educational levels on the island, enriching cultural awareness, and affirming a Puerto Rican identity. Ateneo has served as a center for **tertulias**, literary salons, where new writers have gathered together with established authors to discuss literature, politics, and cultural trends. The majority of the island's great writers have belonged to the Ateneo, served on its board, and offered lectures or courses within its confines. In 1972, the Ateneo established the Honor del Ateneo Puertorriqueño to award individuals who have promoted Puerto Rican culture. An integral part of Puerto Rican cultural life, the Ateneo is lovingly known as the "Docta Casa."

Further Reading

Rodríguez Otero, Eladio. "Ateneo Puertorriqueño." *La Gran enciclopedia de Puerto Rico: educación, fauna, economía.* San Juan, Puerto Rico: Puerto Rico en la Mano, La Gran Enciclopedia de Puerto Rico, Inc. 1976.

Ateneo Puertorriqueño is a major cultural center in Puerto Rico that actively promotes a national literature. During the last 200 years, most major Puerto Rican writers have been members of the Ateneo. *Source: D. H. Figueredo*

—*D. H. Figueredo*

Avelino, Andrés (1900–74)

A poet from the Dominican Republic, Avelino was one of the founders of **Postumismo**, a literary movement that looked toward the country's history, geography, and traditions for inspiration, rejecting European influences. He was a prolific writer, publishing over fifteen volumes of poetry.

Avelino was born in Monte Cristi, Dominican Republic, on December 13, 1900. Believing that poetry in the Dominican Republic needed to avoid the exuberances of **Modernismo**, with its complex allusion to the plastic arts and French culture, and to emphasize the national rather than the foreign, Avelino, with poets **Domingo Moreno Jimenes** and Rafael Augusto Zorrilla, founded Postumismo— meaning beyond Modernismo—in 1921. A philosopher, he soon assumed the role of the theoretician of the movement, writing its manifesto and collecting its poetry in the volume *Pequeña antología postumista* (1922).

During the late 1920s and during the 1930s, Avelino applied mathematical concepts to his poetry, developing a more abstract style, as illustrated in the poem "Poema 32," wherein he describes nature thusly:

> . . . el solo hizo piruetas sobre las frias ventanillas
> de los monstruos devoradores de gasolina y llanto.

(. . . the sun pirouetted over the cold windows / of the monstrous devourers of gas and tears.)

Avelino experimented with literature throughout his life, always attempting to distance himself from any poetry that evoked realism. He passed away in 1974. His other works include *Esencia y existencia del ser y de la nada* (1942), *Filosofía de conocimiento* (1948–50), *La relatividad de Einsten y la relatividad de García de la Concha* (1970).

Further Reading

Ross, Waldo. *El mundo metafísico de Andrés Avelino*. Ciudad Trujillo: Sociedad Dominicana de Filosofía, 1956.

Veloz Maggiolo, Marcio. *Cultura, teatro y relatos in Santo Domingo*. Santiago de los Caballeros, Republica Dominicana: Universidad Católica Madre y Maestra, 1972.

—*D. H. Figueredo*

Avilés Blonda, Máximo (1931–88)

Avilés Blonda was a dramatist, actor, educator, and poet from the Dominican Republic. In his plays, he explored the social and political conflicts faced by the upper classes during the period known as the **Trujillo Era**.

Avilés Blonda was born on May 16, 1931, in Santo Domingo, Dominican Republic. He attended elementary and secondary school in Santo Domingo, then graduated from the Universidad de Santo Domingo in 1953 with a BA in literature and philosophy; later on, he obtained a law degree from the same university. While teaching literature at the university, he published his first book of poetry, and probably his most famous, *Centro del mundo* (1952), followed by *Trío* (1957). Two years later, he wrote the play *Las manos vacías*, which was staged in the capital. His other plays include *La otra estrella en el cielo* (1963), *Yo, Bertolt Brecht* (1966), and *Pirámide 179* (1966); the latter is a study of conflicting and uneasy political relationship between Haiti and the Dominican Republic.

Avilés Blonda combined prolific writing and successful administrative careers. He was the director of the Teatro Experimental Universitario, the university's Department of Cultural Outreach, and the Public Relations Department. He was twice awarded the National Poetry Award—in 1977 for the volumes *Los profetas*, and in 1983 for *Viacrucis*.

Further Reading

"Máximo Avilés Blonda." http://www.escritoresdomicanos.com (accessed 8/29/05).

Veloz Maggiolo, Marcio. *Cultura, teatro y relatos in Santo Domingo*. Santiago de los Caballeros, República Dominicana: Universidad Católica Madre y Maestra, 1972.

—*D. H. Figueredo*

Aybar o Rodríguez, Manuela. See Deana, La.

Ayerra Santa María, Francisco de (1630–1708)

Ayerra Santa María is recognized as Puerto Rico's first poet. A priest, he was also a theologian and a jurist.

Ayerra Santa María was born in San Juan, Puerto Rico, where he conducted his early studies before moving to Mexico to attend the Pontifical University. He earned a degree in canon law and held several important positions within the Catholic Church, including dean of the Tridentino Seminary. A philosopher and a well-known orator, he also wrote poetry, which he submitted to literary contests sponsored by the Universidad de México. In 1691, he won a literary award for a sonnet describing a battle that took place in the Dominican Republic between French and Spanish forces when France was trying to take over the isle of Hispaniola. In 1683, his poetry was included in the anthology *Triunpho Parthénicoa: Palestra Literaria*, edited by the Mexican writer and humanist **Carlos de Sigüenza y Góngora**. In 1695, he wrote a sonnet to honor the memory of the Mexican poet and nun, Sor Juana Inés de la Cruz (1651–95). According to scholar **Josefina Rivera de Álvarez**, in *Diccionario de literatura puertorriqueña* (1970), the sonnet was the poet's best work, balancing the contrast of life and death in verses that were controlled, formal, yet moving.

Ayerra Santa María did not return to Puerto Rico but died in Mexico City, where he was buried. There are some scholars, such as José A. Toros-Sugrañes, writing in the *Nueva enciclopedia de Puerto Rico* (1994), who do not consider Ayerra Santa María a Puerto Rican poet, since he spent his life in Mexico and did not address Puerto Rican themes in his writings.

Further Reading

Ribes Tovar, Federico. *100 Outstanding Puerto Ricans*. New York: Plus Ultra Educational Publishers, 1976.

Rivera de Álvarez, Josefina. *Diccionario de literatura puertorriqueña*. San Juan, Puerto Rico: Instituto de Cultura Puertorriqueña, 1970.

Toros-Sugrañes, José A. *Nueva enciclopedia de Puerto Rico: geografía, historia y cultura*. Vol. 4. Hato Rey, Puerto Rico: Editorial Lector, 1994.

—*D. H. Figueredo*

B

Babín Cortes, María Teresa (1910–89)

Award-winning scholar, Babín is much admired in Puerto Rico for her contribution to the dissemination of the study of Puerto Rican literature in the United States and in Latin America. She was also an active promoter of Puerto Rican culture, founding the Department of Puerto Rican studies at Lehman College, New York, in the 1960s, a time when many universities favored the study of Iberian and Latin American culture, deeming Puerto Rican scholarship an aggregate rather than a subject worthy of independent study. Babín was a prolific essayist and poet as well.

Born in San Juan on May 31, 1910, she attended elementary and secondary schools in the towns of Yauco and Ponce. In 1931, she graduated from the Universidad de Puerto Rico with a BA in Spanish literature, and in 1939 she completed her MA from the same university. That same year she published an authoritative study of the poetry of Federico García Lorca (1898–1936): *Federico García Lorca y su obra*. The book placed her within the circle of international experts on the Spanish poet. She wrote several other major studies on the poet: *García Lorca: vida y obra* (1955) and *Estudios lorquianos* (1962).

In 1954, she earned a PhD from Columbia University. While teaching literature at Hunter College, she wrote one of her most popular studies, *Fantasía boricua* (1956), which was translated into French. In the mid-1960s, she returned to Puerto Rico, where she was a professor at the Universidad de Puerto Rico. During this period she wrote two plays, *La hora colmada* (1960) and *La gesta de Puerto Rico* (1967), and published a book of poetry, *Las voces de tu voz* (1962).

In 1969, Babín accepted a position at Lehman College, where she remained for over ten years. Her scholarly attention was completely focused on Puerto Rico, coupled with her desire to promote knowledge of Puerto Rican literature. With that objective, she wrote several seminal and popular volumes: *La crítica literaria en Puerto Rico* (1968), *The Puerto Ricans' Spirit* (1971), and *Borinquen: An Anthology of Puerto Rican Literature* (1974). After her retirement, she wrote a book of poetry called *La barca varada* (1982).

Babín received numerous awards, including two from the Instituto de Literatura Puertorriqueña (1955, 1982), a prize from Unión de Mujeres Americanas (1964), the Instituto de Puerto Rico en Nueva York (1970), and a honorary doctorate from the Universidad de Puerto Rico (1984). She passed away in San Juan on December 19, 1989. Her literary texts remain crucial readings in colleges and universities in the United States and in Latin America.

Further Reading

Fernández, Ronald, et al., ed. *Puerto Rico: Past Presente, an Encyclopedia.*Westport, CT.: Greenwood Press, 1998.

—*D. H. Figueredo*

Bacardí Moreau, Emilio (1844–1922)

A member of the prominent family who created and manufactured the famous Bacardí rum, this Cuban writer was a patriot who suffered imprisonment during the war of independence and who opposed the American occupation of the island after 1898. His novel *Vía Crucis* (1910, 1914) was a two-volume chronicle of the 1868–78 war against Spain that offered a precise account—from a Cuban perspective—of the conflict.

Born on June 5, 1844, in Santiago de Cuba, Emilio Bacardí Moreau read extensively during his youth and began to write before he was an adolescent. The independence movement stirred his patriotic sentiments, and he joined the cause during his early twenties. He was arrested and sent to prison in Africa and in Spain.

Back in Cuba, during the 1890s he again participated in the independence movement. When the Spanish lost the Spanish-Cuban-American War in 1898, Bacardí opposed the American presence. In 1901, he was elected mayor of Santiago. In 1905, he was elected senator. While involved in political matters and helping to administer the family's business, he wrote a ten-volume history of Santiago, *Crónicas de Santiago de Cuba*, published between 1908 and 1925. In 1910, he wrote *Vía Crucis*, and in 1915 the historical novel *Doña Guiomar*, which takes place during the colonization of the island. He also wrote several novels and plays that have not been published. His children's book *Cuentos para todas las noches* was published posthumously in 1950.

Bacardí died in Santiago on August 28, 1922. While there is great interest in his work as an entrepreneur, his literary work has not been critically studied.

Further Reading

Foster, Peter. *Family Spirits: The Bacardi Saga.* Toronto: McFarlane Walter & Ross, 1990.

—*D. H. Figueredo*

Baghio'o, Jean-Louis (1910–)

Baghio'o is a writer from Guadeloupe whose novel *Le flamboyant à fluers bleues* tells of the complexities of race and class in the Caribbean. He has been praised for his depiction of the upper-class mulatto families.

Because Baghio'o is a private man, not much is written about his life. He was born in Guadeloupe and during the 1930s went to study in France. There he befriended the **Négritude** writers **Leon-Gontran Damas**, from Guyana, and the future president of Senegal, Léopold Sédar Senghor (1906–2001). When World War II broke out, he chose to remain in Paris, joining the underground and setting up a clandestine radio station. This experience served as the basis for his first work, *Fugue mineure*. After the war, he became the technical director of French broadcasting overseas.

Critical of France's colonial practices and interested in writing the history of Guadeloupe and of his ancestors, he published *Le flamboyant à fluers bleues* in 1973. The work won him recognition and earned him the Prix des Caraibes in France. In 1980, he wrote the novel *Le colibric blanc*. Then, in 1995 he wrote the sequel to the *Le flamboyant*. Titled *Choutoumounou*, the novel picks up the story of twins, the novel's protagonists, as they leave Guadeloupe for Paris during the 1920s.

Le flamboyant à fluers bleues is his most famous work. It is realistic novel with instances of the fantastic; for example, during a wedding, the leaves on a tree turn blue. Magical elements aside, though, the novel is a serious look at matters of race and class in Guadeloupe and the Caribbean. In the afterword to the English edition of the novel, writer **Maryse Condé** describes Baghio'o as a "poet and storyteller, placing his characters in mystical but natural settings . . . feeding on the musical and lyrical tradition that gives his story its unique atmosphere" (139).

Baghio'o has been criticized for promoting the exotic nature of the Caribbean. Overall, though, his work has received little academic attention.

Further Reading

Conde, Maryse. Afterword. In *The Blue-Flame-Tree*, by Jean-Louis Baghio'o. Manchester, UK: Carcanet Press, 1984, 139–42.

Wylie, Hal. "Guadeloupe—*Choutoumounou* by Jean-Louis Baghio'o with a preface by Mireille Sacotte." *World Literature Today* 70, no. 1 (Winter 1996): 223–30.

—*D. H. Figueredo*

Bahr, Aida (1958–)

Aida Bahr is a Cuban short-story writer who challenges the notion of gender equality in a revolutionary society that promotes sexual equality. Her characters are women who are used and abused by supposedly liberated men.

Aida Bahr was born in Holguín, Cuba, in 1958. Unlike most writers and artists who relocate to Havana, where they socialize with other Cuban writers and intellectuals visiting from abroad, Bahr has chosen to stay away from the capital. In 1976, she attended the Universidad de Oriente, on the other end of the island, concentrating on literature and writing. She was mentored by author **José Soler Puig**, who read her works and helped to shape her writing career. She also attended numerous writing workshops. Bahr is the director of the publishing house Ediciones Oriente and has written several collections of short stories: *Hay un gato en la ventana* (1984), *Ellas de noche* (1989), *Espejismos* (1998), and a novel entitled *Las voces y los ecos* (2003).

The short-story genre held an initial fascination for Bahr because it fitted her work schedule and her responsibilities as a mother raising a family. Her prose is contemplative, poetic, gentle, and sometimes repetitive, as illustrated in the story "Absences," anthologized in *Open Your Eyes and Soar* (2003):

> Sheets of rain are falling on the patio as before, but the flagstones are paler, not so lustrous, sunk deeper into the ground. Sheets of rain are falling on the patio and my skin forms goosebumps, for the skin has memory. (103)

Her narrative, usually written in the first-person singular, explores the narrator's emotions as she contemplates her relationships with men, who are usually not concerned with the narrator's feelings, and her friendship with other women, who are victimized by men. Though concentrating specifically on interpersonal matters, Bahr's stories also depict the ills plaguing contemporary Cuba: shortage of goods, limited employment, and rampant prostitution. Bahr is representative of the woman writer who was affected by the island's economic crisis of the 1990s, the reversal of women's achievement during the revolution, and "subsequent strategies with which women have risen to this challenge," as critic Luisa Campuaza points out in *Open Your Eyes and Soar* (11). *See also* Cuban Literature, History of; Feminism in Caribbean Literature.

Further Reading

Berg, Mary C., ed. *Open Your Eyes and Soar: Cuban Women Writing Now*. Buffalo, N.Y.: White Pine Press, 2003.

—D. H. Figueredo

Balaguer Ricardo, Joaquín (1906–2002)

Elected president of his country on eight occasions, Joaquin Balaguer is better known outside the Dominican Republic as a controversial political figure than as a writer. Yet, Balaguer managed to write books of poetry and literary criticism throughout his long political life. While the poetry might be essentially of local interest, his books of literary criticism have been studied and even used as textbooks in Latin America. Interestingly enough, his principal political rival, **Juan Bosch**, was also a writer.

Balaguer was born in Villa Bisono, Dominican Republic, on September 1, 1906. At the age of twenty-three, he earned a law degree from the Universidad Autónoma de Santo Domingo. He continued his studies in Paris, receiving in 1934 a doctorate in law and in economics from the Sorbonne. While studying, he wrote for several newspapers, including *La Información*. During the 1920s, he published three books of poetry: *Salmos paganos* (1920), *Claro de luna* (1920), and *Tebaida lírica* (1924). These volumes explored such themes as patriotism and the accomplishments of national heroes.

A supporter of dictator Rafael Leónidas Trujillo (1891–1961), whom he helped to attain power in 1930, Balaguer was assigned to the Dominican Republic embassy in Spain in 1932 and then as the council's secretary in Paris in 1934. These were the first of numerous posts he held during the **Trujillo Era**, including that of Minister of Foreign Relations, several ambassadorships in Latin American, vice president and president of the republic. During this period the ever energetic Balaguer not only wrote speeches for Trujillo but also penned several tomes on the literature and history of the Dominican Republic, of which the most famous are *Historia de la literatura dominicana* (1944), *Semblanzas literarias* (1948), and *El Cristo de la libertad* (1950).

After Trujillo's assassination in 1961, Balaguer, seen as Trujillo's puppet, attempted to maintain control of the nation, but social unrest and the onset of civil war resulted in his exile to New York City. Returning to the Dominican Republic in 1966 and favored by the United States, he was elected president. His opponent was the aforementioned Juan Bosch. Between 1966 and 1994, Balaguer was elected to office seven more times. On each occasion, there were suspicions of foul play, including harassing candidates—including Bosch—preventing voters from casting their votes, and delaying the counting of the ballots. In office, Balaguer, who was not married and was something of a hermit, wrote prodigiously: six books of poetry and over ten volumes of literary and political essays. Even when he was an octogenarian, a blind Balaguer was still writing and was still able to deliver political speeches.

Balaguer died of complications due to a bleeding ulcer on July 14, 2002. As a president, he is perceived as dictatorial and dishonest. As a writer, his histories of the literature of the Dominican Republic are still used by scholars. He belonged to a generation of politicians—the likes of which include **Luis Muñoz Marín** in Puerto Rico, **Eric Williams** in Trinidad, and **Aimé Césaire** in Martinique—who viewed themselves essentially as thinkers and writers. *See also* Dominican Republic Literature, History of; Trujillo Era.

Further Reading

Gerón, Cándido *Hacia una interpretación de la poesía de Joaquín Balaguer*. Santo Domingo, República Dominicana: C. Gerón, 1991.

Ramírez Morillo, Belarminio. *Joaquín Balaguer: la escuela del poder: su biografía, su pensamiento, su obra*. República Dominicana: Ediciones del Instituto de Formación, 1999.

—Frank Argote-Freyre and D. H. Figueredo

Balboa Troya y Quesada, Silvestre de (1563–1634?)

Creator of the first positive portrayal of an African slave in the Spanish-speaking Caribbean, and therefore Latin America, Balboa Troya y Quesada was a colonial administrator from the Canary Islands who arrived in Cuba sometime at the end of the sixteenth century and became fascinated with the tropical beauty of his new home. He lived in the town of Puerto Principe, in the province of Camagüey.

His poem "Espejo de paciencia," written in 1608, narrates the kidnapping of Bishop Juan de las Cabezas Altamirano (1565?–1615) by a French pirate, the bishop's release, and the death of the pirate at the hands of Salvador, a slave. At a time when colonialists didn't assign human traits to slaves, Salvador is drawn as faithful, intelligent, and brave, the equal of a white man. The poem is considered the first Cuban poem. *See also* Cuban Literature, History of.

Further Reading

Saínz, Enrique. *Silvestre de Balboa y la literatura cubana*. Habana: Editorial Letras Cubanas, 1982.

—*D. H. Figueredo*

Ballagas, Emilio (1908–54)

Emilio Ballagas was a Cuban poet who wrote metaphysical poetry and, along with **Nicolás Guillén**, was a pioneer in the writing of Afro-Cuban poetry.

Emilio Ballagas y Cubeñas was born on November 7, 1908, in the province of Camagüey, Cuba. Of humble background, he was able to attend the Universidad de la Habana in 1928 after winning the first prize in a writing contest sponsored by a literary journal. In 1933, he earned a doctorate in education from the same university. That year, he was appointed professor at the Escuela Normal Para Maestros de Santa Clara—Normal School for Teachers. In 1937, Ballagas was commissioned by the Cuban government to conduct research on aboriginal languages in Paris. In 1946, he earned a second doctorate, in philosophy, and visited Mexico, where he taught Afro-Cuban culture. A year later, he was awarded a fellowship to teach at the New York Institute for the Education of the Blind. He also taught at Columbia University. While in New York City, he met and married a Cuban professor, Antonia López y Villaverde; both returned to Cuba in 1948. While studying and working, Ballagas wrote several books of poetry: *Júbilo y fuga* (1931), *Cuaderno de poesía negra* (1934), *Nocturno y elegía* (1938), *Nuestra Señora del Mar* (1943), and *Cielo en rehenes* (1951), the last published after his death.

His most famous book of poetry is *Cuaderno de poesía negra*, in which he uses Afro-Cuban vernacular and diction. Since Ballagas was white, some critics believed his black poetry to be superficial, yet the book, which consisted only of fourteen poems, achieved fame throughout Latin America. The reason might be that Ballagas used black poetry to protest against the social oppression of Cuban blacks. The representative poem, and the best known, is "Elegía de María Belén Chacón," in which the poet, celebrating the physical beauty of a black woman, entices the reader into believing he or she would be reading an erotic poem only to discover that María Belén Chacón has died as a result of poor social conditions.

Ballagas was a mild-mannered, timid man. He said of himself in the poem "Nocturno y eligía" (1938):

> No soy el que traiciona a las palomas,
> a los niños, a las constelaciones . . .
> Soy una verde voz desamparada
> que su inocencia busca y solicita
> con dulce silbo de pastor herido

(I'm not one who betrays doves, / children, constellations . . . / I'm a new voice without a home / looking and asking for innocence / with the sweet breath of a wounded shepherd).

Ballagas died on September 11, 1954, of a heart ailment. *See also* Negrista Literature.

Further Reading

Henríquez Ureña, Max. *Panorama histórico de la literatura cubana*. Tomo II. Habana: Editorial Arte y Literatura, 1979.

Pallás, Rosa. *La poesía de Emilio Ballagas*. Madrid: Playor, 1973.

—*D. H. Figueredo*

Balsamo, José. See Morales Cabrera, Pablo.

Balseiro, José Agustín (1900–91)

Known primarily as a professor and literary critic of Hispanic literature, José A. Balseiro was a Puerto Rican poet and novelist. Though Balseiro spent most of his life outside Puerto Rico, either in Spain or in the United States, where he died in 1991, the island and its people, history, and culture were an integral part of his lifestyle and work.

Balseiro taught at such prominent universities as the University of Illinois, and from 1933 to 1936 was a visiting professor at the Department of Hispanic Studies at the Universidad de Puerto Rico. Since his first visit to Spain during the early

1920s he became a well-known lecturer at home and abroad who spoke on subjects ranging from the art of poetry, the Don Juan theme in literature, and Shakespeare and the musicians to Latin American poets such as Rubén Darío (1867–1916) and the Puerto Rican **José Gautier Benítez.**

As a literary critic he established a solid academic reputation throughout Spain, Latin America, and the United States with such studies as *El vigía: ensayos de crítica literaria y musical* (4 vols.: 1925, 1928, 1942, 1956), *Novelistas españoles modernos* (1933), *El Quijote de la España contemporánea: Miguel de Unamuno* (1935), *Blasco Ibáñez, Unamuno, Valle Inclán, Baroja: cuatro individualistas de España* (1949), *Expresión de Hispanoamérica* (1960), *Seis estudios sobre Rubén Darío* (1967) and *Recuerdos literarios y reminiscencias personales* (1981). Besides editing works by Spanish dramatist Alejandro Casona (1903–65), he published in Spanish and in English the long essay *The Hispanic Presence in Florida: Yesterday and Today, 1513–1973* (1976, 1977).

Balseiro also wrote poetry and narrative. As a poet he published *La copa de Anacreonte* (1924), *Saudades de Puerto Rico* (1957), *Vísperas de sombra y otros poemas* (1959) and *El ala y el beso* (1983). His first novels, *El sueño de Manón* (1922) and *La ruta eterna* (1923), are traditional lyric and romantic stories. His third and most important novel, *En vela mientras el mundo duerme*, was written in 1937 but printed in 1953. It is a text that best represents his ideological position with respect to the political status of Puerto Rico and reflects his pedagogical and political experience at the Universidad de Puerto Rico. It depicts the story of a young university student from the countryside, Juan de Jesús Rivera, who returns to his home disillusioned after having experienced unreciprocated love, class inequality, expulsion from the university, and an inability to defend his separatist ideals from those who profess the conviction that the island should remain united to the United States in order to enjoy a stable political life, with a respectable and respected constitution and without revolutions and dictatorships.

His last novel, *La gratitud humana* (1969), is a well-written and intense text about the life of a noble and gentle composer engaged in the composition of a unique work devoted to world peace.

Further Reading

Balseiro, José Agustín. *Obra selecta de José Agustín Balseiro*. Prólogo de María Teresa Babín; epílogo de Angel Encarnación. Río Piedras, Puerto Rico: Editorial de la Universidad de Puerto Rico, 1990.

—*Asela R. Laguna*

Baquero, Gastón (1918–97)

A poet, essayist, and journalist, Gastón Baquero was one of the founding members of the literary journal **Orígenes.** His poetry explored everyday life yet found philosophical significance in the simplest gesture; it was a way of celebrating the extraordinary in the ordinary. During his lifetime, his works were often anthologized and celebrated by such eminent critics as **Cintio Vitier**, from Cuba, and **Max Henríquez Ureña**, from the Dominican Republic.

Of humble origins, Baquero was born on May 4, 1918, in the province of Oriente, Cuba. At the age of eighteen, he gave up his agronomy studies at the Universidad de la Habana to purse a career in writing. He worked as a journalist for the prestigious Havana daily *Diario de la Marina*, where he became one of its most influential editors. He also wrote for several literary journals, including *Verbum*, and *Espuela de Plata*.

The author of many books of essays and articles, his *Indios, blancos y negros en el caldero de América* (1991) is his best-known work of nonfiction. His books of poetry include *Memorial de un testigo* (1966), *Magias e invenciones* (1984), *Poemas invisibles* (1991) and *Poesía completa* (1998). Baquero was a modest man who shied away from labels: he didn't make much of his connection with the legendary journal *Orígenes*, the launching pad for writers like **José Lezama Lima** and **Virgilio Piñera**, and wanted to be known simply as a poet rather than as an Afro-Cuban poet. He even made light of his poetry, saying that everything had already been written.

In 1959, Baquero left Cuba for Spain where he remained for the rest of his life. In 1987, King Juan Carlos honored him with the Order of Civil Merit. Toward the end of his life, a stroke left him paralyzed and unable to speak. He passed away on May 15, 1997. *See also* Negrista Literature.

Further Reading

Dorta, Walfrido. *Gastón Baquero: el testigo y su lámpara: para un relato de la poesía como conocimiento en Gastón Baquero*. Habana: Ediciones Unión, 2001.

Ortega, Alfonso C., and Alfredo Pérez Alecant. *Celebración de la existencia: Homenaje al poeta cubano Gastón Baquero*. Salamanca: Universidad Pontificia de Salamanca, 1994.

D. H. Figueredo

Barnet, Miguel (1940–)

∎

Internationally renowned novelist, poet, and ethnographer, Miguel Barnet is a pioneer in the creation of the genre known as **testimonio,** or testimonial novel. He is considered Cuba's most celebrated contemporary author.

Barnet was born in Havana on January 28, 1940. He studied social sciences at the Universidad de la Habana and at the Seminario de Etnología y Folklore, where he has taught folklore. He is a researcher at the Instituto de Etnología and president of the Fundación **Fernando Ortiz** in Havana.

Author of numerous volumes of poetry, much of it collected in the book *Con pies de gato* (1994), he is best known for his testimonial work *Biografía de un cimarrón* (1966). The work has no traditional plot: it consists of spoken monologues arranged in three parts, covering slavery, abolition, and the 1895 Cuban war of independence. The narrator is centenarian Esteban Montejo, a runaway slave whom Barnet had met and interviewed. *Biografía* advanced the study of black ethnography in Cuba and the Caribbean; the book served as the basis for the opera *Cimarrón* by German composer Hans Werner Henze (1926–).

Barnet's second testimonial novel was *Canción de Rachel* (1969), which was adapted for the screen as *La bella del Alhambra* (1989). *Gallego*, published in 1981 and the third in the trilogy of testimonial novels initiated with *Cimarrón*, chronicles the life of one of the many Spanish immigrants who settled in Cuba; this work was also adapted for the screen in 1987 under the same title. Barnet's most recent novel, *La vida real* (1986), researched in New York City with a Guggenheim Award, follows the life of a Cuban labor migrant who arrived in Manhattan in the 1940s. Barnet's short story "Miosvatis" was the central fiction piece in the 1998 *New Yorker* magazine's special issue on Cuba. Some of his ethnographic writings include *La fuente viva* (1983) and *Cultos afrocubanos: la regla de Ocha, la regla de Palo Monte* (1995).

Further Reading

Azougarh, Abdeslam, and Ángel Luis Fernández Guerra. *Acerca de Miguel Barnet*. Habana, Cuba: Editorial Letras Cubanas, 2000.

—*Pamela María Smorkaloff*

Barrack Yard Literature

Barrack Yard, or "literature of the yard," refers to a genre of Anglophone Caribbean writing that is set in shanty towns or ghetto-type surroundings. Slaves were housed in huts or barracks built of wood, wattle, and thatch. The term *barrack yard* recalls the area in front of the slaves' huts that was used for cooking and other household chores that could not be performed in the cramped space within the huts. This yard served as an extension of the barracks and was a gathering place where a great deal of social interaction took place.

In some parts of the Caribbean, notably Jamaica and Guyana, the Barrack Yard was called the Nigger Yard. Guyanese poet **Martin Carter** gave a vivid description of life in the yard in his poem entitled, "I come from the Nigger Yard." It was a place of want, where blacks lived in hunger and squalor, a place where the inhabitants never forgot the grievous wrongs committed by the perpetrators of slavery. Ironically, it was a place with a tradition of and love for music, where the bugle and the drum accompanied the voices of women who sang tales of torture and agony. It was a place of drunken and dying men, often visited by judges "full of scorn" and "priests and parsons fooling gods with words," as Carter phrases it.

In the novels, poems, and plays set in barrack yards, blacks form a majority group at the foot of the socioeconomic ladder. In literature, the yard is portrayed as the preserver of African culture. The yard's influence is exerted not only on the yard's inhabitants but also on outsiders and observers. It created its own language and code of conduct. It cultivated stereotypes in character and setting. In general, barrack yard literature also encapsulated an optimistic philosophy that stressed the need for self-determination and advancement rather than reliance on the help and charity offered by others.

One of the acclaimed exponents of this genre was Trinidadian-born writer **CLR James**. In his short story "Triumph" he describes the yard: "In one corner of the yard is the hopelessly inadequate water-closet, unmistakable to the nose if not to the eye; sometimes there is a structure with the title of bathroom: a courtesy title, for he or she who would wash in it with decent privacy must cover the person as if bathing on the Lido; the kitchen happily presents no difficulty; never is there one and each barrack-yarder cooks before her door." This short story and his novel *Minty Alley* (1936) are pioneering examples of barrack yard literature.

During the 1930s and 1940s, literary stalwarts such as **Alfred Mendes, Errol John, Albert Gomes**, Carlton Comma, and Frank Evans used the yard as the setting for plays and stories about life among the lower working class. This group met regularly for readings and discussions. They published short stories and articles with local flavor in *The Beacon* magazine, which began publishing in the 1930s in Trinidad. *The Beacon* aimed to provide a publishing venue for Caribbean writers and artists of materials relevant to Caribbean history, culture, and "total specificity," that is, materials authored by and dealing with black people but that the Caribbean public, along with anybody else, had not had access to. In the early 1950s, Jamaican **Roger Mais** wrote two novels that took place in the yard, *The Hills Were Joyful Together* (1953) and *Brother Man* (1954).

In the Spanish-speaking Caribbean, the equivalent of the barrack yard is the "solar," though the literary output from the region does not equal the number of works written in the Anglophone islands.

Further Reading

Archibald, Douglas. *The Rose Slip*. Port of Spain: Extra Mural Department, University of the West Indies, 1967.

Brathwaite, Edward, "Wings of a Dove." In *Rights of Passage*. London: Oxford University Press, 1967.

Campbell, George. "In the Slums." In *First Poems*. Kingston: City Printery Ltd., 1945.

Carter, Martin, "I Come from the Nigger Yard." In *Poems of Succession*. London: New Beacon Books Ltd., 1977.

Heath, Roy A. K. *A Man Come Home*. London: Longmans, 1974.

James, C. L. R. "Triumph." In *Stories from the Caribbean*, edited by Andrew Salkey. London: Elek Books, 1965.

John, Errol. *Moon on a Rainbow Shawl*. London: Faber and Faber, 1958.

Markham, E.A., ed. *The Penguin Book of Caribbean Short Stories*. London: Penguin, 1996.

Mendes, Alfred H. *Black Fauns*. Nendeln: Kraus, 1970.

Patterson, H. Orlando. *The Children of Sisyphus*. Kingston: Bolivar Press, 1971.

Walcott, Derek. "Laventille." In *The Castaway*. London: Cape, 1965.

—Reginald Eustace Clarke

Barrett, "Eseoghene" Lindsay (1941–)

Lindsay Barrett is a Jamaican novelist and poet committed to the advancement and promotion of African and Caribbean culture. His best-known work is the novel *Song for Mumu* (1967).

Lindsay Barrett was born in Lucea, Jamaica. After graduating from high school, he worked for the popular and influential newspapers *The Daily Gleaner* and *The Star*. In 1961, he became an editor for the Jamaica Broadcasting Corporation. He moved to England that same year to freelance for the British Broadcasting Corporation (BBC). From England, he traveled to France and then to Africa, settling in Nigeria, where he married an actress. He has taught at the University of Ibadan, in Nigeria, and has worked in radio and television in that country.

He is the author of two collections of poems, *State of Black Desire* (1966), which he self-published, and *The Conflict Eye* (1973), and the author of several plays and radio dramas. *Song for Mumu* is his only published novel. It is the episodic story of a youth from the countryside who moves to Jamaica and becomes fascinated with the city night life. When he contracts a venereal disease, he returns to the countryside, where he befriends an old farmer and falls in love with his daughter. Tragedy pursues the young man, who grows mad and murders one of his children and blinds the old farmer. After the young man is taken away to an asylum, the novel continues with the narration of the equally tragic story of his daughter, Mumu, who has several doomed relationships with several men and, like her father, finally grows mad. Scholar Norval "Nadi" Edwards, writing in *Fifty Caribbean Writers*, describes the novel as a "fable of black desire, of the search for identity."

Further Reading

Edwards, Norval "Nadi." "Lindsay Barrett (1941–)." *Fifty Caribbean Writers. A Bio-bibliographical Critical Sourcebook*, edited by Daryl Cumber Dance. Westport, CT: Greenwood Press, 1986.

—*D. H. Figueredo*

Barroco/Baroque

Everything about the Latin American Barroco—*baroque*, in English—is complicated by its history. Joan Corominas in his *Diccionario crítico etimológico de la lengua castellana* cites two possibilities for the Spanish acceptation of barroco. On the one hand, Corominas tells us, the word seems to come from the French *baroque*, signifying "extravagance" in architectural style, and on the other, from the Portuguese *barrôco* or *barrueco*, as applied to an "irregular pearl" (415). To complicate matters, its linguistic indeterminacy carries over into the aesthetic realm. Originally a European artistic style, and particularly a Spanish aesthetic of the seventeenth century with literary representatives like Calderón de la Barca (1600–1681), and Góngora y Argote (1561–1627), the movement—seen by critics likes José Antonio Maravall (1911–86) as exemplar of a society in social and economic decline—took roots almost immediately in the American soil. "Distinctive, even original, lyric poetry really began in the New World at the end of the sixteenth century and beginning of the seventeenth, in what has been called the 'Barroso de Indias' " observed scholar **Roberto González Echevarría** in *The Cambridge History of Latin America* (203). Writers like Bernardo de Balbuena (1627–52), author of *Grandeza mexicana*; **Carlos de Sigüenza y Góngora**, native of Mexico, nephew of Góngora y Argote, and author of *Infortunios de Alonso Ramírez*; and Sor Juana Inés de la Cruz (1651–95) with her poem "Primero sueño," were instrumental in establishing the style we today associate with the Latin American baroque.

The twentieth century has seen a reconceptualization of the **barroco**, through contemporary writers like **Alejo Carpentier, José Lezama Lima**, and **Severo Sarduy**. If implicit in the baroque style is a certain level of kitsch—artificiality—we are also reminded of its French etymological association with a style of exuberance, extravagance, and excessive ornateness. For **Lezama Lima**, the "American" baroque differentiated itself from its European counterpart in its cultural *tension* and *explosiveness*, as he wrote in *La expresión americana* (80). Though he never defined what he meant by either of these terms, one can surmise that the tension alluded to by the Cuban writer was historical in nature, that is to say, between the old Spain and the New Spain. The volcanic explosiveness—*plutonismo*—of the American **barroco** was simultaneously destructive and creative: giving way to new conceptions and forms of expression, e.g., "la expresión Americana." And to this new formulation of the baroque Lezama Lima gave the name "señor barroco," or Mr. Baroque (81).

Severo Sarduy, then, starting where Lezama Lima had left off, returned to its original meanings to develop his own theory of the neo-barroco—neo-baroque. For Sarduy the kitschiness of the baroque was not an argument against it, but quite literally, exactly what recommended it as an artistic movement. The artificial is what made for literature and art, and the more artificial, the more artistic. *Artifice*, claimed Sarduy, is art. But Sarduy did not stop there. While he agreed with Lezama Lima on the cosmically explosive quality of the *barroco de Indias*, it was at this point that Sarduy's theory of the barroco parted ways from that of his compatriot. For Sarduy, it was not unity, but cultural dispersal and heterogeneity that defined what he named the "neo-barroco" (131). In recent years, theorists like César Augusto Salgado have elaborated theories of the baroque, like Sarduy's, in conjunction with Homi Bhabha's postmodern theory of *hybridity*. Salgado has written in the *Journal of American Folklore*: "the baroque functions as a trope or adjective for the region's complex ethnic and artistic *mestizaje* (racial mixture) rather than as a reference to exclusively Western cultural forms" (316). And not without some controversy, other critics have refused to employ the European term to define Latin American aesthetics. Problematic in this, and constitutive of its tension, is the historical fact that any post-colonial expression, regardless of its degree of originality and break from the colonial power, can only refer, even if superficially, to the imperialist power which initially colonized it. As Lezama Lima seems to suggest, the break is significant primarily in terms of a unique artistic *expression*: enriched by indigenous and African cultures that have little to do with Europe. *See also* Post-Colonialism.

Further Reading

Corominas, Joan. *Diccionario crítico etimológico de la lengua castellana*. Vol. I: A-C. Madrid: Editorial Gredos, 1954.

González Echevarría, Roberto. "Colonial Lyric." *The Cambridge History of Latin America*. Eds. Roberto González Echevarría and Enrique Pupo-Walker. Vol. I: Discovery to Modernism. New York: Cambridge University Press, 1996.

Lezama, Lima, José. "La curiosidad barroca" *La expresión americana*. México: Fondo de Cultura Económica, 1993. pp. 79–105.

Maravall, José Antonio. *Culture of the Baroque: Analysis of a Historical Structure*. Trans. Terry Cochran. Foreword. Wlad Godzich and Nicholas Spadaccini. Minneapolis: University of Minnesota Press, 1986.

Pérez, Rolando. "Severo Sarduy." *The Review of Contemporary Fiction* 24 (Spring 2004): 94–138.

Salgado, César Augusto. "Hybridity in New World Baroque Theory." *Journal of American Folklore* 112, no. 445 (Summer 1999): 316–331.

Sarduy, Severo. "The Baroque and the Neobaroque." *Latin America in Its Literature*. Trans. Mary G. Berg. Eds. César Fernández Moreno, Julio Ortega, and Ivan. A. Schulman. New York: Holmes & Meir, 1980. pp. 115–132.

—*Rolando Pérez*

Baugh, Edward (1936–)

■

A respected critic and scholar of West Indian literature, Baugh is the author of one book of poetry, numerous academic texts and is a literary mentor as well.

Edward Baugh was born in Port Antonio, Jamaica, in 1936. He graduated from Titchfield High School and won a scholarship to attend the University College of the West Indies. After earning a BA in English literature, he was awarded a scholarship to conduct graduate studies Queen's University in Ontario. In 1964, he earned a PhD from the University of Manchester.

Influenced by British romantic poetry, Baugh started to write poetry as a young man. Initially writing in verses that rhymed, he switched to free verse in college, where he was attracted to the writings of T. S. Eliot (1888–1965) and Dylan Thomas (1914–53), among others. However, his responsibilities as a professor and administrator at the University of West Indies in Mona and his role as visiting professor at numerous institutions in the United States, including the University of California—Los Angeles, the University of Miami, and Howard University have limited his output. His only book of poetry, *A Tale from the Rainforest*, was published in 1988.

Baugh's reputation emerges from his scholarly works and books of criticism, which include *West Indian Poetry 1900–1970* (1971), *Derek Walcott: Memory as Vision* (1978), and a critical edition of Derek Walcott's *Another Life* (2004). As a critic, he has been responsible for introducing Anglophone Caribbean literature to readers in the United States. As a poet, he is described by poet and scholar **Kwame Dawes**, in *Talk Yuh Talk* (2001), as "a writer with an intensely dogged wit who is constantly aware of the masking and pretense that characterizes the art of making poems" (38). *See also* Romanticismo/Romanticism.

Further Reading

Dawes, Kwame. *Talk Yuh Talk: Interviews with Anglophone Caribbean Poets.* Charlottesville: University Press of Virginia, 2001. pp. 38–46.

—*D. H. Figueredo*

Beacon, The

Founded in March 1931, *The Beacon* was dedicated to changing the condition of Trinidadian society. Its editor and financier was **Albert Gomes**. From the start the monthly paper was anti-establishment and was under constant attack from the merchant and planter–controlled press. Its existence was uneven, with two issues published as one, some with more pages than others. It struggled on until November 1933. In November 1939 it made a brief reappearance, but World War II put an end to its attempt to continue publication.

The Beacon's purpose was to encourage the development of a West Indian literature. It sponsored a short-story competition in 1932, and the writing of poetry was encouraged. With a view to stimulating a love of reading, there were regular reviews of literary works such as those of Pushkin (1799–1837), Sinclair Lewis (1885–1951), Pearl Buck (1892–1973), **Claude McKay** and C. F. Andrews (1871–1940). The creative writing of the journal's contributors grew out of and reflected their concern for the poor and disadvantaged and the contorted, sometimes illicit, relations between the white Creoles and the "natives." Their subject matter opened the way for Geoffrey Drayton, **Ian MacDonald, Jean Rhys** and **Phyllis Allfrey, Ralph De Boissière** and **CLR James,** whose works reflect the same desire to portray social realism. For future politicians, *The Beacon* was a means of political expression for these talented and articulate young men. C. A. Thomasos was an early contributor, as was Albert Gomes, both of who were later to become members of the Legislative Council. CLR James was to become a spokesman for international socialism. For young Trinidadians, such as Adrian Cola Rienzi, the journal was a timely forum for the expression of socialist views. This, in a society in which Communist literature was not allowed free entry. Another topic that exercised the journal was the place of the Afro–West Indian in the society and the role of African survivals, such as drumming, which, according to an April 1932 article, required of the drummer as much sophistication as that of a player in a symphony orchestra.

The Beacon tried to portray the aspirations and conditions of all Afro–West Indians, black, brown, and mulatto. From the March 1932 issue there appeared a regular "India Section," which carried informed commentaries on politics in the subcontinent, including the state of the independence struggle, reviews of publications about India, interviews with visiting Indians, and accounts of leaders and sympathizers with the nationalist movement. At the same time *The Beacon* endeavored to cover the local Indian situation, continuing a tradition that had begun with the *The Indian Kohinoor Gazette*, the first of short-lived journals published between 1898 and 1928. Unlike the daily newspapers, *The Beacon* carried a pro-Indian and anti-British point of view; this encouraged Indians to write for the journal and had the interesting result of producing some exciting studies of East Indian life and culture by non-Indians, such as CLR James and **Alfred Mendes.**

Although *The Beacon* denied any political ambition, as the sole mouthpiece for protest and expression, it was inevitable that political issues would be taken up. These included the persecution of the Spiritual Baptists; shorter working hours and better working conditions for shop girls; the rise in the price of gasoline, with its consequent rise in the cost of living; and advocacy of unemployment insurance. The paper also reported on conditions in the rest of the Caribbean, giving warning of growing dissatisfaction felt throughout the British Caribbean. This dissatisfaction was to culminate in the disturbances of 1935, 1937, and 1938.

A most important part of the journal's content was its emphasis on historical writing about West Indian history. These include a series by Mrs. Eleanor Waby entitled, "Trinidad—then and now," articles on the West India Regiment, and travelogues by Jean De Boissiere. Although the journal did not last long, it made a difference to the literary and political scene in Trinidad. It was a testing ground for young people to write and to learn from the criticism of their fellows. It was a forum for progressive ideas. *See also* Anglophone Caribbean Literature, History of; Literary Journals

Further Reading

Breiner, Laurence A. *An Introduction to West Indian Poetry*. New York: Cambridge University Press, 1998. pp. 70–75.

Gomes, Albert. *Through a Maze of Colour*. Port of Spain, Trinidad : Key Caribbean Publications, 1974.

Paget, Henry and Paul Buhle. *C.L.R. James's Caribbean*. Durham, N.C.: Duke University Press, 1992.

—Reginald Eustace Clarke

Bébel-Gisler, Dany (1935–2003)

■

A writer from Guadeloupe, Bébel-Gisler often wrote in Creole to express her Caribbean identity and to challenge scholars' favoritism for works written in French. She was an educator and a promoter of literacy in her country.

Bébel-Gisler was born in Pointe-à-Pitre, Guadeloupe, on April 7, 1935. An intelligent student, she attended high school at the Lycée Carnot, where she won a scholarship to study in France in 1953. She earned a BA from the University of

Paris with concentration in sociolinguistics and ethnology. In 1974, she was appointed to the National Center for Scientific Research in France, where she studied Caribbean immigration to France. Conducting research in Martinique, Trinidad, and Guadeloupe, she published, with coauthor Laenec Hurbon, *Cultures et pouvoir dans la Caraïbe* (1975), a study on the use of Creole, vodou practices and other religions in Guadeloupe and Haiti.

Becoming interested in Creole, which she saw as a language that affirmed her Caribbean heritage, she wrote *La langue créole, force jugulée* (1976). During the 1980s, Bébel-Gisler founded in Guadeloupe a center, Centre Bwadoubout, to teach children how to read French and Creole. Her desire to increase literacy on the island and to help children perform better in schools led to her book *Les enfants de la Guadeloupe* (1985).

In 1985, she published her first literary work *Léonora: L'histoire enfouie dela Guadeloupe*. The work, which she described as a novel, was the result of hours of interviews with a Guadeloupean woman who recalled her life on the island during the twentieth century. This was the first **testimonial** novel published in Guadeloupe, and as such its reception was mixed: readers did not know whether to approach the volume as a work of fiction or nonfiction. Of a more philosophical nature was *Le defi culturel guadeloupeen* (1989).

In 1996, UNESCO placed her in charge of an international project known as The Road of the Slave, an attempt at identifying crucial locations of the middle passage, when slaves were brought to the Caribbean from Africa, and designating the sites as worthy of preservation. Part of this work resulted in 1998 in the volume *Grand'mère, ça commence où la Route de l'esclave?*

Bébel-Gisler died suddenly on September 28, 2003. Through her writings she rejected the concept that for a writer from the Francophone Caribbean to demonstrate talent and achieve success, such writer had to write in French. Today, many schools in Guadeloupe use *Léonora* as a textbook. *See also* Créolité; Haitian Literature in Kreyòl (the Haitian Language).

Further Reading

Bébel-Gisler, Dany. *Leonora: The Buried Story of Guadeloupe*. Translated by Andrea Leskes. Charlottesville: University Press of Virginia, 1994.

—*D. H. Figueredo*

Bec, Marie. See Colimon-Hall, Marie-Thérèse.

Bejel, Emilio (1944–)

Poet, essayist, and literary critic, Emilio Bejel is a foremost figure in Latino Gay writing. A Cuban by birth, Emilio Bejel left the island in 1962 and has lived in the United States ever since. Although exiled together with many fierce "anticastristas,"

he has been able to maintain both political and aesthetic distance from this rift throughout his career. Bejel, therefore, is not identified as either pro- or anti-Castro, which is one of the main divides in Cuban and Cuban American cultural fields. This ability to maintain a critical distance with both contenders in the post-1959 landscape has informed Bejel's literary work as well as his professional and personal choices.

This does not mean that Bejel has distanced himself from the historical reality surrounding him. He has participated in some of the most important political events in Cuban and Cuban American history of the last forty-odd years: the initial struggles for definition, Communist or otherwise, that the Cuban Revolution would take; the massive exodus from Cuba to Florida and New York; the "Diál-ogo" of the late seventies between exiles and the Cuban government; and the heated—sometimes vicious—debates within the Cuban American community, which reached particular intensity during the Reagan administration. The story surrounding his tenure process at the University of Florida–Gainesville, where sectors of the Cuban American community objected to his promotion to full professor because he failed to enlist himself in the ranks of furious anti-Castro militants, is of particular interest, since it reminds us—just like the Elián González story did a few years ago—of the intensity of passions surrounding the Cuban American experience.

Having emigrated as a destitute youngster, Bejel ultimately pursued an accomplished academic career. He earned a BA from the University of Miami and a PhD from Florida State University. Bejel is currently full professor and chair at the University of California–Davis, after holding teaching positions at Fairfield University, University of Florida–Gainesville, and University of Colorado–Boulder.

Emilio Bejel's oeuvre comprises several books of poetry and criticism, as well as many articles on Latin American literature and culture. All of them are remarkably loyal to the "foundational experience" of their author: being a small-town Cuban boy who had to work through his sexual, political, and personal riddles on both sides of the Florida Strait. Thus, his work embodies and challenges the many contradictions as well as the unresolved searches essential to Cuban and Cuban American identity: the intersection between politics and family life (his mother and his childhood on the island are constant motifs in his poetry); the collision between sexual preference and radical politics; fatherhood; friendship; and national solidarity. As a literary critic, he evolved from a more traditional approach to Hispanic texts—his doctoral dissertation on the Spanish writer Buero Vallejo (1916–2000), written in 1972—to a semiotic-driven approach, to a poststructuralist one—his 1994 book on poet **José Lezama Lima**, *José Lezama Lima, Poet of the Image* (1990)—to a wide-encompassing approach to Cuban culture from the point of view of queer studies and cultural criticism. However, as in the best tradition of the Latin American national essay, this evolution underlines a consistency: the pursuit of an investigation of the relationship between literary practice and the many lines of force—social, ethical, sexual, epistemological, semiotic—that cross it, and their identity-making effects.

His poetry followed a similar path. In his many books, the topics of memory and travel, both literal and metaphorical, permeate his writing, as does a continued exploration of ethical and political choices and the gains and losses involved in them. Thus, his poetry, as well as his recent autobiography *The Write Way*

Home—a unique blend of personal narrative, poetry, and essay in the tradition of the great Latin American essay—stand out among other representatives of Latino writing because it avoids the two main pitfalls that endanger it: either the triumphal narrative of "becoming American," à la Richard Rodriguez (1944–), or the (falsely) nostalgic and dismissive narratives, à la Gloria Anzaldua (1942–2004). Bejel addresses the paradoxes of being a Cuban American in a way that never betrays the meaning of politics when it comes to writing: to propose questions without giving the answers, or to give the reader the opportunity to look for answers in her or his own life experiences. Also, his work never forgets one basic truth, much forgotten among academics, that there is nothing more political than a zest for life, love, and liberty.

His books of poetry include *Del aire y la piedra* (1974), *Ese viaje único* (1977), *Direcciones y paraísos* (1977), *Huellas / Footprints* —bilingual volume of poetry with English re-creations by Marie Panico—(1982); *Casas deshabitadas* (1989), and *El libro regalado* (1994). His critical works include *Buero Vallejo: lo moral, lo social y lo metafísico* (1972), *Literatura de nuestra América: Estudios de literatura cubana e hispanoamericana* (1983), *La subversión de la semiótica: Análisis estructural de textos hispánicos* (1988); *Escribir en Cuba. Entrevistas con escritores cubanos, 1979–1989* (1991); and *Gay Cuban Nation* (2001). *See also* Anti-Castro Literature; Cuban American Literature; Gay and Lesbian Literature.

Further Reading

Clark, Stephen. "Entrevista a Emilio Bejel." *La Habana elegante* 15 (2001). http://www.habanaelegante.com/Fall2001/Agosto2001.html (accessed 8/31/05).

Fernández, Ramiro. "Aunciaciones y ocultamientos: Relectura de Del aire y la piedra de Emilio Bejel." *Cuadernos Americanos* 225 (1979): 230–34.

Panico, Marie J. "An Interview with Emilio Bejel." *Contemporary Poetry: A Journal of Criticism* 3 (1978): 1–9.

—*Juan Pablo Dabove*

Bélance, René (1915–2004)

■

A Haitian poet, Bélance used poetry as a tool for social change. But unlike writers of politically engaged literature, who sometimes rail at society, Bélance broadcast a message of hope and ultimate victory over social evils.

Bélance was born in Corail, Haiti, on June 8, 1915. Growing up during the American occupation of Haiti, he nurtured a mistrust of the United States and developed a sense of identification with people he saw as oppressed. He started to write poetry by the time he was in the sixth grade. Though he considered a career in medicine, he studied philosophy at Alexandre Pétion College in Port-au-Prince. Upon graduation, Bélance returned to his hometown to work as a teacher. In 1940, he published his first volume of poetry, *Rythme de mon coeur*. The poems in the collection revealed his concerns for the suffering of the black race, yet the overall message was the poet's hope in a world where social justice would triumph. In 1944, he published *Survivances*, followed a year later by *Épaule d'ombre*. These volumes again echoed his social commitment.

During the 1950s, Bélance worked for UNESCO. From 1956 to 1959, he was a researcher at the Universidad de Puerto Rico. In 1962, Bélance accepted a teaching position at the University of California–Berkeley. He spent the next twenty years teaching Caribbean literature at such universities as Brown, Whitman College, and Williams College. In 1983, he published *Nul ailleurs*.

In the 1980s, Bélance retired to Haiti, where he passed away on January 11, 2004. To honor his work, a public library in Haiti carries his name. *See also* Literatura Comprometida/Socially Engaged Literature.

Further Reading

Saussy, Haun. "A Note on René Bélance." *Callaloo* 22, no. 2(Spring 1999): 351–67

—*D. H. Figueredo*

Belaval, Emilio S. (1903–72)

One of Puerto Rico's major authors, Belaval was a member of the **Generación del 30**, a group of writers who were preoccupied with the development of a national identity. Though he led a successful life as an attorney, he devoted much of his creative energy and time to the creation and promotion of Puerto Rican culture. Noting his accomplishments as an attorney, a promoter of Puerto Rican letters, a dramatist, and a short-story writer is the best way to understand his genius.

In 1927, Belaval became an attorney, graduating from the Universidad de Puerto Rico. From 1928 to 1931, he was chief of Legal Department of the Puerto Rico Telephone Company. In the 1930s, he set up his own firm, and in 1952, he was appointed to Puerto Rico's Supreme Court. A member of the Council of Higher Education, he advocated for the use of Spanish as the language of instruction at a time when many political leaders, influenced by the United States, favored English. While pursuing his legal career, Belaval promoted his cultural agenda for the island. In 1939, he founded and was the first president of Sociedad Teatro **Areyto**, which signaled the beginning of modern theater on the island. He was president of the **Ateneo Puertorriqueño** (1941), member of the Instituto de Literatura Puertorriqueña (1941–45), and founder of Academia Puertorriqueña de la Lengua Española (1955). His concern for a lack of national Puerto Rican identity—a topic also addressed by other members of the Generation of 1930, including **Antonio Pedreira**—resulted in the essay "Los problemas de la cultura puertorriqueña" (1935). Aware that there was also a need for a national theater, he wrote in 1939 the essay "Lo que podría ser un teatro puertorriqueño." This manifesto, which promoted the creation of a nationalistic theater, led to his founding of the Teatro Areyto.

His dedication to the theater manifested itself in his work as an actor, director, and playwright. In 1953, he wrote the drama *La muerte*, and in 1959, *Hacienda de los cuatros vientos*. In 1963, he wrote *Circe o el amor*. These plays, which were staged throughout the 1960s, were philosophical and explored such themes as generational conflicts and the effects of industrialism on agrarian societies.

It is as a short-story writer, however, that Belaval is best known outside the island. In 1935, he published his first collection of stories, *Cuentos de la universidad*, written during the late 1920s and first appearing in journals and newspapers. The collection recalled his years as a college student but also revealed the growing American influence on intellectuals and the middle class. During the late 1930s and early 1940s he wrote a series of short stories that examined poverty on the island. The stories betrayed a sarcastic tone, where in the author contrasted the commercial promotion of the island as a paradise with the exploitation and suffering of the underclass. The collection of these stories, which might be Belaval's best work, was published in 1946 under the title of *Cuentos para fomentar el turismo*. Twenty years later he published *Cuentos de la plaza fuerte* (1963), a study of decline of Spanish power in the Americas and an attempt at reproducing the look and feel of colonial San Juan.

Toward the end of his life, Belaval started to lose his sight. He passed away in San Juan at the age of sixty-nine. Observes critic Flavia Lugo de Marichel, in *Spanish American Authors: The Twentieth Century* (1992): "Belaval, a writer of extraordinary merit as an essayist, short story writer, critic, and dramatist can be considered for his focus on stylistic, cultural, philosophical, and sociological matters one of the principal exponents . . . of the many problems of the Puerto Rican homeland" (89).

Further Reading

De Mariche, Flavia Lugo. "Emilio S. Belaval." In *Spanish American Authors: The Twentieth Century*, edited by Angel Flores, 86–89. New York: Wilson, 1992.

Sánchez, Luis Rafael. *Fabulación e ideología en la cuentística de Emilio S. Belaval*. San Juan de Puerto Rico: Instituto de Cultura Puertorriqueña, 1979.

—*D. H. Figueredo*

Belgrave, Valerie (1949–)

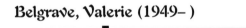

Valerie Belgrave is a Trinidadian novelist and artist who uses the genre of romance novels to address such social and political issues as racial discrimination and feminism while also portraying a positive and nonstereotypical image of the West Indies.

Belgrave was born in San Juan, Trinidad, where she currently lives and works. She combines the crafts of novel writing and batik production, using the traditional method of wax resist-and-submerge dying. Since the 1990s, Belgrave has returned to painting, working in both oils and watercolors. She has exhibited her batik artistry throughout the Caribbean as well as in the United Kingdom, the United States, and Canada.

Belgrave studied painting at the Sir George Williams University (Concordia) Montreal in the 1970s. The student uprising at that university, the U.S. civil rights movement, and the Black Power Uprising in Trinidad during that period left a lasting impact on Belgrave's sensibility and work. She pursues fine arts and fiction writing with a common intent, as she expressed in the volume *Caribbean Women Writers: Essays from the First International Conference* (1990):

> My artistic purpose in both writing and doing Batik is a deliberate attempt to ennoble my country and its people, to promote racial tolerance, not so much by condemning racism as by promoting positive images of West Indians, and to challenge the corrosion of our psyche and culture caused by foreign mass media, not so much by condemning it but by creating a greater self-appreciation. (317)

Belgrave's literary works include *Ti Marie* (1988); *Sun Valley Romance* (1993), which she wrote for the Heinemann Caribbean caresses series; *Tigress* (1996); and *Dance the Water* (2002), which has also been produced as a CD. She works in the romance genre because of its appeal to a young popular readership. In crafting her formulaic romances, Belgrave fuses social issues with the love theme. *Sun Valley Romance* and *Tigress* feature gutsy, independent, and socially aware protagonists. The resolution of *Sun Valley Romance* is contingent on environmental preservation and concern for the well-being of impoverished villagers. The lover is a wealthy businessman who must make good the environmental degradation caused by his firm before he can win his beautiful and creative village bride. Moreover, the grandmother, reminiscent of the Caribbean matriarchal figure, plays a significant role in the resolution.

Belgrave's literary romance *Ti Marie* joins the ranks of highly significant evocations of Caribbean social life and culture. Set in the Trinidad of the late eighteenth century, the text reconstructs a facet of the nation's history through characters that, were it not for explorations like this book, would otherwise remain one-dimensional figures on a page. Moreover, the panoramic canvas surveys the complex melee of peoples, ideologies, languages, and social and historical forces that intertwined to make Trinidad the unique place that it is.

The historical romance certainly captures the fairy-tale elements that appeal to the consumer of popular fiction—the vibrant, velvet-skinned mulatto beauty is pursued by the young son of an English earl. The series of obstacles to be overcome arise not only in the form of a rival but also in the stringent race and class prejudices that militate against the union. Suspense mounts when Elena marries another to give a name to the child, conceived unknown to her lover, Barry, during their single sexual encounter. The estranged lover is alerted by a portrait in which Elena, despite her marriage, wears his gift, a pair of macaws that function as their symbol of constancy and enduring love. He returns to Trinidad and assists Elena and her ailing husband in their ongoing struggle against the harsh and repressive British regime. The husband dies, and Barry claims his prize. A parallel narrative tells the life of the slave girl Tessa, whose desire to marry and to set up a humble home with her lover is flouted. The maelstrom of social and racial and gender antipathy envelops her, and fate casts her instead as the sacrificial lamb. For the slave couple there can be no romance, and certainly no happy ending.

Belgrave claims that the romance element is liberating, lending an "enhanced quality . . . engaging the emotions of the reader," with the result being the capacity "to stir people's emotions—romantically, ideologically, idealistically and patriotically." She also argues, in a letter written to scholar Paula Morgan on June 30, 1995, that idealized reality serves to project positive images of the island of Trinidad and to counteract "too much promotion of negativity in the world and an insufficiency of examples of goodness, niceness, decency."

Ti Marie simultaneously assigns value and deconstructs the fairy-tale model. While the fiction is about romance, it is also about the intrusion of grim reality; about the base inhumanity that can underlie human interactions within collective groupings—the family, the community, the nation. It is about the steady encroachment of disillusionment and impotence on an intelligent and patriotic young girl; and it is about the entrenchment of an unjust social and political order within an Edenic geographic and psychic space. Above all, it is about defining the limits of the romantic trope, within a romance which deconstructs itself. *See also* Historical Novel; Mulata in Caribbean Literature; Slave Narratives.

Further Reading

Belgrave, Valerie "On Combining Batik Art and Novel Writing" and "Thoughts on the Choice and Theme and Approach in Writing *Ti Marie*." In *Caribbean Women Writers: Essays from the First International Conference*, edited by Selwyn Cudjoe, 317–25. Wellesley: Callaloux Publishers, 1990.

Morgan, Paula. "Correspondence with Valerie Belgrave." June 30, 1995.

—Paula Morgan

Belpré (White), Pura (1899?–1982)

■

Pura Belpré, a bilingual author of children's literature and pioneer librarian, was an active participant in the Harlem Renaissance. A black Puerto Rican who moved to New York in 1920 and became the first Latina hired by the New York Public Library system, Belpré has been a role model for Latino librarians in the United States.

Belpré was born in Cidra, Puerto Rico. She attended secondary school on the island, then studied library science at the New York Public Library and Columbia University. Belpré first worked at the New York Public Library branch in Harlem, overlapping in time with the legendary Afro–Puerto Rican curator **Arthur Schomburg**. This branch, known as the 135th Street Library, became the cultural center of the Harlem Renaissance due to its central location in Harlem and sponsorship of a plethora of educational and cultural programs for adults and children, including dramatic productions, exhibitions, lectures, and public readings. Aware of a growing presence of Puerto Ricans in Manhattan and a shortage of children books on Puerto Rican culture and folklore, Belpré became a bilingual storyteller at the library and later worked at other New York Public Library branches. She often used puppets to reenact legends and stories from her native Puerto Rico, drawing crowds of children and adults alike. Belpré's first children's book, *Perez and Martina: A Portorican Folk Tale* (1932), was published as a result of its successful reception by library patrons and staff, which impressed the publisher.

In 1943, Belpré married African American composer, teacher, and violinist Clarence Cameron White (1880–1960). Though she resigned from the library a year later to accompany him on a concert

Pura Belpré was a pioneer of bilingual children's literature and the first Latina librarian in the United States. *Centro de Estudios Puertorriqueños.*

tour, he was instrumental in encouraging her to continue writing folktales and stories along with doing editorial work and translations. After White's death in 1960, Belpré returned to the New York Public Library system as the Spanish Children's Specialist for the next seven years. Following her retirement in 1968, Belpré continued her involvement within the Spanish-speaking neighborhoods of the Bronx by working for the South Bronx Library Project.

Belpré's bibliography is extensive, including *The Tiger and the Rabbit and Other Tales*—published in two editions, one in 1946 and in 1965, the latter illustrated by the well-known artist Tomie dePaola—*Juan Bobo and the Queen's Necklace: A Puerto Rican Folk Tale* (1962); and *Once in Puerto Rico: Six Folk Tales from Puerto Rico* (1973). Her *Firefly Summer*, a costumbrista work, a novel that emphasizes local color and traditions, was published posthumously in 1996. Belpre also translated several children books into Spanish, including *El cuento de Ferdinand* (*The Story of Ferdinand* by Munro Leaf) in 1962; *Danielito y el dinosaurio* (*Danny and the Dinosaur* by Syd Hoff), *Osito* (*Little Bear* by Else Holmelund Minarik), *El caso del forastero hambriento* (*The Case of the Hungry Stranger* by Crosby N. Bonsall), all in 1969; and *Ningún lugar para jugar* (*No Place to Play* by Paul Newman) in 1971.

In 1973, Belpré was awarded the Brooklyn Art Books for Children Citation for her book *Once in Puerto Rico* and was honored by the Bay Area Bilingual Education League and the University of San Francisco for her distinguished contribution to Spanish literature. In 1996, REFORMA, a national organization for librarians serving the Spanish-speaking community, created the Pura Belpré Award, which is presented to the Latino author and illustrator whose work celebrates the Latino cultural experience. Pura Belpré's oral history was recorded and transcribed at Columbia University in 1976, and her personal papers were a gift to the Centro de

Estudios Puertorriqueños, Hunter College in New York. *See also* Children's Literature, Hispanic; Costumbrismo; Puerto Rican Literature, History of.

Further Reading

Kanellos, Nicolás. *Hispanic Literature in the United States.* Westport, CT: Greenwood Press, 2003.

Meisner, Sylvia V. "Firefly Summer." *School Library Journal* 43 (February 1997): 100.

The Pura Belpré Papers. Centro de Estudio Puertorriqueños, Hunter College, CUNY. http://www.centropr.org/lib-arc/belpre.html (accessed 8/31/05).

The Reminiscences of Pura Belpré (1976). In the Oral History Collection of Columbia University.

—Gladys Markoff-Sotomayor and Claudia Hill

Benítez Family

This was an illustrious nineteenth-century Puerto Rican family whose members—an aunt, a niece, and a grandnephew—were pioneers in the development of a national literature. The aunt, María Bibiana Benítez, and the niece, Alejandrina Benítez y Gautier de Arce, were the first two published women poets on the island. The niece's son, José Gautier Benítez, is Puerto Rico's best romantic poet.

Benítez y Gautier de Arce, Alejandrina (1819–70). The mother of the romantic poet **José Gautier Benítez**, Benítez de Arce was the second published woman poet in Puerto Rico.

Benítez de Arce was born in Mayagüez on February 26, 1819. When her mother died, the young girl was brought to the home of **Maria Bibiana Benítez**, her aunt who raised her as a daughter. Her aunt homeschooled her and taught her the aesthetics of poetry.

In 1843, Benítez de Arce contributed, with her aunt, poems to the anthology *Aguinaldo puertorriqueño*. The poems were celebratory of the island's beauty but also expressed a romantic melancholia. Benítez de Arce contributed more poems to the 1846 edition of *Aguinaldo*.

She married Pedro José Gautier in 1851. They had four children, and one of them, José Gautier Benítez, became the island's best-known romantic poet. While raising a family, she did not write, but upon her husband's death, Benítez de Arce turned to poetry to alleviate her mourning and sense of loss.

In 1862, she received a literary prize for her poem "La patria del genio," about Puerto Rican artist José Campeche (1752–1809). The poems that she wrote during this decade expressed two sentiments: civic responsibility and contemplative, religious expression. Most of these poems were published in the anthologies *Nuevo cancionero de Borinquen* (1872) and *Antología de los poetas puertorriqueños* (1879), both published posthumously.

Benítez y Constanza, María Bibiana (1783–1873). The first woman poet in Puerto Rico, Bibiana Benítez was also a dramatist.

Bibiana Benítez was born in Aguadilla on December 10, 1783, the daughter of a Spanish officer. There was a library in her home, and she spent much time reading the works of such Spanish poets as Garcilaso de la Vega (1503–36) and Meléndez Valdés (1754–1817). Around the 1820s, Benítez brought into her home her niece Alejandrina Benítez de Arce, who was an orphan. She raised her niece as if she were her own daughter.

During the 1830s, Benítez wrote articles for local papers, and in 1833 she published "La ninfa de Puerto Rico," the first published poem by a woman on the island. The poem celebrated, in a heroic and joyful mood, the natural beauty of the island. Published in the journal *La Gaceta de Puerto Rico*, the poem proved so popular that a copy was framed and hung at the entrance of the court Real Audiencia Territorial in San Juan.

Along with her niece in 1843, she contributed poems to the anthology *Aguinaldo puertorriqueño*, the first book credited with inaugurating Puerto Rican literature. In 1858, she published "Diálogo en obsequio de deseado nacimiento de S.A.R, príncipe de Asturias." As she grew older, she contemplated her own aging process and wrote the powerfully bitter poem "A la vejez," in which she lamented the passing of the years and questioned God's decision to create life and then take it away. The poem was published posthumously in 1926.

In 1862, Benítez ventured into drama with *La Cruz del Morro*, about the defeat of Dutch invaders at the gates of the Morro Castle in 1625. By the time Benítez wrote this play, which was staged twenty years after her death, she was nearly blind.

Gautier Benítez, José (1848 or 1851–80). Considered one of Puerto Rico's best romantic poets, the island was the primary source of inspiration for Gautier Benítez. In what might be his most famous poem, "Canto a Puerto Rico" (1879), the poet, sensing an early death, declaims:

> Antes que llegue mi postrero día
> y mi cantar se extinga con aliento
> ¡toma Patria! Mi última poesía . . .

(Before the arrival of my last day and my song flickers off in a sigh / take Motherland! my last poem.) He was one of the founders of the **Ateneo Puertorriqueño**, a cultural center responsible for the dissemination of Puerto Rican culture on the island.

José Gautier Benítez was born in Caguas, Puerto Rico, either on April 12, 1848, or November 12, 1851. As a youth, he was sent to Spain to attend military school in Toledo. Returning to Puerto Rico in the 1870s, he became interested in developing a national literature. In 1876, he helped to found the Ateneo, and in 1878, he founded the journal *La Revista Puertorriqueña*. He published his poems in this journal and in *El Progreso* as well. Gautier Benítez was influenced by Spain's romantic poet Gustavo Adolfo Becquer (1836–70) and signed some of his poems under the name of Gustavo. He preferred rhyming verse and his themes often centered on love, friendship, religion, and his country.

Gautier Benítez died young, at the age of either thirty or thirty-two. His poems were collected in the volume *Poesías*, published posthumously. *See also* Puerto Rican Literature, History of; Romanticismo/Romanticism.

Further Reading

Arrillaga, María. *Los silencios de María Bibiana Benítez*. San Juan, Puerto Rico: Instituto de Cultura Puertorriqueña, 1985.

Girón, Socorro. *Vida y obra de José Gautier Benítez* San Juan, Puerto Rico: Instituto de Cultura Puertorriqueña, 1980.

Rivera de Álvarez, Josefina. *Diccionario de literatura puertorriqueña*. Río Piedras, Puerto Rico: Universidad de Puerto Rico, 1955.

—*D. H. Figueredo*

Benítez Rojo, Antonio (1931–2005)

Antonio Benítez Rojo was one of the most important Cuban writers to appear after the triumph of the Cuban Revolution. Benítez Rojo distinguished himself as a short-story writer, essayist, and novelist. He was particularly known for his historical novels. While most of his works were traditional in style and structure, some employ formal innovations. Benítez Rojo's overarching theme was the interplay of the historical and other forces that have shaped Caribbean identity.

Apart from the fact that Benítez Rojo was born on March 14, 1931, in Havana, his early life is not well documented. In 1955, he earned degrees in accounting, finance, and economics from the Universidad de la Habana and American University, in Washington, D.C. In 1959, after the triumph of the revolution, he began working in the Ministry of Labor but left after a few years to devote more time to writing—both journalism and fiction. He subsequently conducted research for **Casa de las Américas**, the Cuban government's cultural institution, and, from 1965 to 1966, served as vice director of theater and dance at the Cuban Council on Culture. From 1975 to 1980, he served as director of the publishing department of Casa de las Américas. During this time, Benítez Rojo began to receive critical acclaim outside Cuba for his writing. In 1980, while attending a conference in Paris, he defected, eventually moving to the United States. Beginning in 1983, he taught at Amherst College, where he was the Thomas B. Walton Memorial Professor of Romance Languages.

Benítez Rojo's books published in Cuba include the short-story collections *Tutee de reyes* (1967), winner of the Casa de las Américas literary prize, and *El escudo de hojas secas* (1969), recipient of

Short-story writer, novelist, and essayist Antonio Benítez Rojo explored the historical and cultural development of a Caribbean identity. *Source: Americas Society. Courtesy of Elsa M. Ruiz.*

the **Unión de Escritores y Artistas Cubans** literary prize, the screenplay *Los sobre-vivientes*, subsequently produced by Tomás Gutiérrez Alea (1928–96), and the novel *El mar de las lentejas* (both 1979). In the United States, he published several impor-tant works—the acclaimed *Sea of Lentils* (1990), translated by James Maraniss from his earlier novel; the seminal nonfiction work *The Repeating Island: The Caribbean and the Postmodern Perspective*; and two short-story collections, *The Magic Dog* (1990), a compilation from his earlier collections, and *A View from the Mangrove* (1998). In 2001, he published the novel *Mujer en traje de batalla*. At the time of his death on January 9, 2005, he was completing a memoir.

Much of Antonio Benítez Rojo's oeuvre has been influenced by seminal figures of Cuban literature such as **Fernando Ortiz, José Lezama Lima**, and **Alejo Carpentier**. His writing considers the historical, social, and economic forces that have shaped, and continue to shape, the Caribbean—including the European conquest, the Planta-tion, and language and religion—and how their inter-relationships are reflected in the region's literatures. On a formal level, he experimented with novelistic structure through the use of unexpected or multiple points of view and parallel plots.

In *Sea of Lentils*, for example, the author weaves together four separate narratives—King Philip II lying on his deathbed; the misadventures of Anton Babtista, a common soldier who accompanied Columbus on his second voyage; the massacre of French Huguenots at the colony of St. Augustine; and the seduction of John Hawkins, the English adventurer, into the triangular trade. Together these narratives present, in jewellike prose, a complex picture of the European enterprise in the Americas and its consequences for the conquerors as well as for the Indians and Africans they enslaved.

Benítez Rojo's *Repeating Island* brilliantly explores Caribbean identity as it relates to the Chaos Theory, viewing the region's history and culture through the lens of its polyrhythms, particularly as manifested through music, dance, and the phenomenon of carnival. The author postulates that throughout the Caribbean's long, turbulent history since the arrival of the Europeans, such rhythms have served to mediate the violence of slavery and the Plantation system and its aftermath, cul-minating in a mestizo, or racially mixed, culture that is continually in flux. In this context, he analyzes key texts of major Caribbean authors, among them, **Bartolomé de las Casas**, Ortiz, Carpentier, **Nicolás Guillén**, and **Wilson Harris**.

Mujer en traje de batalla exemplifies Benítez Rojo's mastery of the **historical novel**. The novel is based on the true story of Henriette Faber (1791–?), a French-woman who disguised herself as a man in order to attend medical school and who served as a doctor in Napoleon's army; she later emigrated to Cuba and married a woman before her true gender was exposed. Through its memorable protagonist, its rich language, and its picaresque plot, the novel brings history alive as well as addresses larger issues such as the marginalization of women. While it explores the various dimensions of identity, class, and exile, its main theme is the human yearn-ing for liberation and self-expression. *Mujer en traje de batalla* is also a perform-ance—by both protagonist and author—whereby Benítez Rojo returned to a subject he had explored in *The Repeating Island*.

Whether through his novels, short stories, or nonfiction, Antonio Benítez Rojo strove to understand what makes the Caribbean "Caribbean" while simultaneously celebrating it through its history, literature, and culture. *See also* Cuban Literature, History of.

Further Reading

Corticelli, María Rita, "Entrevista con Antonio Benítez Rojo." *Literate World* (June 2002). http://www.literateworld.com/spanish/2002/escritormes/june/w01/box1.html (accessed 4/05).

Ortega, Julio, "Una mujer (vestida de hombre) trasatlántica." *Literate World* (June 2002). http://www.literateworld.com/spanish/2002/escritormes/june/w01/box2.html (accessed 4/05).

Updike, John, "Books: Glasnost, Honne, and Conquistadores," *The New Yorker* (April 29, 1991): 100–104.

—*Daniel Shapiro*

Bennett, Louise (1919–)

■

As a pioneer who used Jamaican dialect in her poetry rather than standard English, Louise Bennett was initially shunned by literary critics and members of Jamaica's upper class, who considered her writing too commonplace and vulgar. Despite the brush-off, Bennett became popular with the average person, who appreciated her identification with common folks, her affirmation of blackness—at a time when the British and white Jamaicans considered anything black inferior and ugly—and her sense of humor. Her popularity was the result of her performance of her poetry at local festivals and the national Carnival as well as appearances on radio and television.

Bennett, who is affectionately called "Miss Lou," was born on September 7, 1919, in Kingston. As a child, she listened intently to the way Jamaicans spoke and was fascinated by the rhythm of the diction and the use of proverbs to pronounce moral statements and to laugh at adversities. While attending Excelsior High School in Kingston, Bennett started to reproduce in verse the speech patterns she heard on the streets, afterward reading the verses to her classmates.

Upon graduation from high school in 1938, Bennett took a journalism course via correspondence school and enrolled at Friends' College, where she studied social work and folklore. In 1945, she received a scholarship to study at the Royal Academy of Dramatic Art in London. In 1947, she returned to Jamaica; three years later she was in London again, working as a writer for the BBC program *West Indian Night*. In 1953, she traveled to New York City, working on radio and performing throughout the region as an actress and singer of Jamaica folk songs. In 1955, she went home to Jamaica, where she expanded on her studies of folklore and was appointed lecturer at the University College of the West Indies. She wrote for radio and hosted a television show for children.

In 1942, Bennett wrote *Dialect Verses*, published in Kingston. This work was followed by a dozen books, including *Jamaica Humour in Dialect* (1943), *Anancy Stories and Poems in Dialect* (1944), *Miss Lulu sez* (1949), *Laugh with Louise* (1961), *Jamaica Labrish* (1966), and *Selected Poems* (1982). She recorded over a half-dozen performances of her poetry, including *Jamaican Folk Songs* and *Jamaican Singing Songs*, both in 1954, and *The Honourable Miss Lou*, in 1981. Of these works, *Jamaica Labrish* is her most famous.

Bennett's poems are monologues meant for performance. Though the poems tend to be humorous, her message expresses concerns for social issues such as bigotry, inadequate public education in Jamaica, political corruption, and women's liberation. In "Jamaica Oman" (1982), she cunningly illustrates how women manipulate sexist men:

> Jamaica oman, cunny, sah!
> Is how dem jinnal so?
> Look how long dem liberated
> An de man dem never know.

(Jamaican women are clever, sir! / How can they be so happy? / Just look how long they've been liberated / And the men never knew it.)

Bennett's choice of the local vernacular for her artistic expression celebrates Jamaicans' commitment to their own identity and acceptance of the native culture over British-imposed values. It is a sentiment that has made her one of the most popular artists in the Anglophone Caribbean. She has been awarded several honors, including the Norman Manley Award for Excellence in the Arts (1972), the Order of Jamaica (1974), and the Musgrave Gold Medal of the Institute of Jamaica (1978). Influential throughout the Caribbean, Bennett's poetic style is regarded as a precursor of **dub poetry**, the improvised political rap that is played on sound systems throughout Jamaica. *See also* Anancy Stories; Performance Poetry.

Further Reading

Cooper, Carolyn. *Noises in the Blood*. Durham, NC: Duke University Press, 1995.

Donnell, Alison, and Sarah Lawson Welsh. *The Routledge Reader in Caribbean Literature*. London: Routledge, 1996.

—*D. H. Figueredo*

Bergeaud, Emeric (1818–58)

Bergeaud was the author of the first Haitian novel, *Stella* (1859). This is a patriotic novel that takes place during the Haitian revolution (1791–1806).

Bergeaud was born in Cayes in 1818. He was the personal secretary of General Jerome Maximilia Borgella, his uncle, who was the commander of the district of Cayes and chief of the army of the south of Haiti. In 1848, Bergeaud was implicated in the plot to oust President Faustin Élie Soulouque, (1785–1867), and he was forced to seek exile in St. Thomas. Nostalgic and homesick, Bergeaud wrote *Stella*, his only published work. Bergeaud gave the manuscript of the novel to his cousin **Beaubrun Ardouin**, who then edited the work. The novel was published in Paris by the highly respected publisher Edmund Dentu a year after Bergeaud's death in St. Thomas.

Stella is a historical novel that chronicles the revolution and the civil war that occurred after independence. The protagonist, Stella, is a symbol of Haiti, and the novel is the author's hope for the future of the emerging nation. According to scholar Léon-François Hoffmann, in *Essays on Haitian Literature, Stella* "eloquently articulates the basic obsession of all Haitian writers: a passionate affirmation of Haiti's originality and dignity." (122)

Further Reading

Hoffmann, Léon-François. *Essays on Haitian Literature*. Washington, DC: Three Continents Press, 1984.

—*D. H. Figueredo*

Bernard, Regnor Charles (1915–?)

■

Bernard is a Haitian poet and member of the 1946 generation, a political group that advocated and implemented social programs for the nation.

Bernard was born in Jérémie, Haiti, on October 18, 1915. He attended primary school in his hometown and then went to Port-au-Prince to attend high school at the prestigious Lycée Pétion. After graduation, he matriculated at the Normal School, where he earned a teacher's degree when he was in early twenties.

He wrote for the newspaper *La Nation* and also for the biweekly *Parti Socialiste Populaire*, where he expressed his socialist ideals. In 1940, he published the book of poetry *Le souvenir demeure*. In 1943, he published his second collection, *Pêche d'étoiles*. During this period, he became actively involved in politics and the generation of 1946, a revolutionary group of students and intellectuals who supported president Dumarsais Estimé (1900–1953), a leader who implemented labor reforms and established a social security program for Haiti.

In 1945, Bernard published *Nègres!!!* and received in 1953 the first poetry prize in a contest commemorating the creation of the Haitian republic in 1804. The poem, entitled "C'étail à l'Arcahaie," is one of his best known. In 1953, he published *Au milieu des flammes*. His poetry was revolutionary, though not optimistic: it often questioned man's ability to help one another. Anti-Catholic, Bernard criticized the Church, which he presented in his poems as an agent of repression.

Further Reading

Ferdinand, Joseph. *Regnor C. Bernard au naturel: sa vie, son oeuvre (de la perspective de l'exil)*. Montreal: Editions du CIDIHCA, 2000.

Herdeck, Donald E. *Caribbean Writers. A Bio-Bibliographical-Critical Encyclopedia*. Washington, DC: Three Continents Press, 1979.

—*D. H. Figueredo*

Bernardo, José Raul (1938–)

■

Cuban-American novelist whose historical romances portray strong women characters rebelling against stereotypical roles assigned to them by a male-dominated society. Like many writers from the Hispanic and Francophone Caribbean, José Raul Bernardo writes in English about life and events in the Caribbean.

José Raul Bernardo was born in Havana on October 3, 1938. His father was a well-known publisher, and his mother introduced him to music and art at a young age. As a child he surprised his parents by sitting at a piano and playing music without the benefit of music lessons. In 1958, he graduated from Havana Music Conservatory. Opposing **Fidel Castro**'s regime, Bernardo left Cuba in 1960 and moved to Florida, where he worked as tomato picker while attending University of Miami in 1969, earning a masters in music from the same university. He relocated to New York, where he received a PhD in architecture from Columbia University in 1972.

Bernardo worked as an architect in Manhattan. The death of his mother affected him deeply, and as part of the grieving process, he began to write the stories she had told him as a child about her parents and their courtship and romance in Cuba during the 1920s. The result was the novel *The Secret of the Bulls* (1966), a family saga in which the author studies and challenges the culture of machismo: when a wife cheats on her husband, he forgives her instead of murdering her, as mandated by the culture of the time. In 1998, he wrote *Silent Wing*, about an unconsummated love affair between the Cuban poet **José Martí** and the daughter of a president in Guatemala during the nineteenth century. Romantic and lyrical, Bernardo wrote a sensuous story in which the would-be lovers, sensitive to nineteenth-century mores, did not touch at all. As a fictional biography of José Martí, *Silent Wing* offers one of the more credible depictions of the Cuban poet and patriot. In 2002, Bernardo wrote *The Wise Women of Havana*, a family drama that confronts the theme of machismo once again.

Bernardo's syntax is influenced by the Spanish language: verbs are sometimes located at the end of a sentence, affording a certain lightness and musicality to the narrative. His paragraphs contain poetic allusions and repetitive patterns suggestive of musical verses. Bernardo's novels have been translated into several languages, including German and Polish. *The Wise Women of Havana* was adapted to the stage by Bernardo and was presented in New York City in 2003. Bernardo is also a composer; his classical compositions have been presented in Europe and the United States. *See also* Cuban American Literature; Historical Novel.

Further Reading

Figueredo, Danilo H. "Ser Cubano (To Be Cuban): The Evolution of Cuban-American Literature." *Multicultural Review* 6, no. 1 (March 1997): 18–28.

—*D. H. Figueredo*

Berry, James (1924–)

■

James Berry is a prolific Jamaican poet and author of children's books, young-adult stories, and novels. His writing is characterized by a light, lilting, and musical Jamaican diction, and his stories are inspired by Jamaica's culture, folklore, and history. Even while writing about the horrors of slavery, Berry manages to imbue his books with a sense of hope and victory.

James Berry was born in the countryside of Jamaica. Learning to read at the age of four, he spent hours reading the Bible. He also listened intently to folktales about the trickster **Anancy**, a mythological spider from West Africa. Decades later, both the Bible and Anancy would figure in his writings.

During World War II, Berry went to the United States but was disillusioned by the treatment of blacks there. He returned to Jamaica in 1948, but eager to find better economic opportunities, he migrated to London, where he met and married his wife. In London, Berry studied telegraphy. While working for the Telegraphs Department of the British Post Office, he started to write stories and poems. An early retirement and a grant from the C. Day Lewis Foundation afforded him the opportunity to write full-time.

Like poet **Una Marson** in the 1930s and **E. R. Braithwaite**, the author of the popular autobiography *To Sir, With Love*, Berry felt alienated in England. In 1976, he observed in his introduction to the anthology *Bluefoot Traveler: An Anthology of Westindian Poets in Britain* "British society . . . excludes blacks . . . wishing their non-existence" (9). In 1979, Berry published a book of poetry, *Fractured Circles*. In 1982, he wrote *Lucy's Letter and Loving*, epistolary poems about the alienation experienced by a Jamaican woman in London. A residency at an elementary school as a visiting scholar made him aware of the absence of children's books depicting black youngsters. For inspiration, he turned to the memories of his Jamaican childhood. The young-adult books *A Thief in the Village and Other Stories* (1988) and *The Future Telling Lady: Six Stories* (1993) take place in Jamaica. His *Anancy-Spiderman* (1988) retells West African stories. The novel *Ajeemah and His Son* (1992) falls within the genre of the **slave narrative**. Inspired by an ancient sugar mill where Berry played as a child, the novel tells of the enslavement of a father and his son, the son's eventual death, and the father's determination to survive.

Berry's engaging style, use of Jamaican dialect, poetic descriptions, and credible characters have made him popular with young readers, librarians, and teachers. Berry has received numerous awards, including the Signal Poetry Award (1989), Order of the British Empire (1990), the Coretta Scott King Award (twice, in 1988 and 1993), and the Boston Globe Horn Book Award (1993). *See also* Children's Literature in the English-Speaking Caribbean.

Further Reading

Berry, James, ed. *Bluefoot Traveller: an Anthology of Westindian Poets in Britain*. London: Limestone Publications, 1976.

"Popular Paperbacks for Young Adults: 1998." *School Library Journal* 44, no. 3 (March 1998): 113–16.

—*D. H. Figueredo*

Betances, Ramón Emeterio (1827–98)

∎

Abolitionist and leader of Puerto Rico's independence movement, Betances is one of the most beloved patriotic figures in Puerto Rico. Because he was an advocate for the creation of a federation of the Spanish Antilles, he is called "El Antillano." Betances wrote in Spanish and in French.

Betances was born on April 8, 1827, to a well-to-do family. Motherless at an early age, his father sent him to France when he was ten years old. In Paris he studied medicine and wrote a work descriptive of Parisian society, *Las cortesanas de Paris* (1853). In 1855, he graduated from medical school.

He returned to Puerto Rico in 1856 just as an epidemic of cholera was ravaging the island. For a year, he provided his medical services to all the afflicted, especially the poor people. Known as the "doctor of the poor," his reputation began to grow on the island. While practicing his profession, he wrote an account of the epidemic, *El cólera*, which earned him a Legion of Honor medal from the French government.

During this period, Betances founded an abolitionist society. Through the society, he and other wealthy members would purchase newborn slaves and would then free them. Betances also wrote antislavery tracts that resulted in the Spanish authorities sending him to exile. Before leaving the island, he fell in love with a young woman. Her early death inspired his drama *La Virgen de Borinquen* (1859).

During the 1860s, Betances was involved in several revolutionary movements, supporting the Dominican Republic's attempts to secede from Spain and Cuba's independence movement. He founded the Revolutionary Committee of Puerto Rico and plotted an insurrection that became known as El Grito de Lares (1868), the first military attempt in Puerto Rico to overthrow the Spanish government. By this point, Betances was promoting the union of Cuba, the Dominican Republic, and Puerto Rico as a confederation.

When the Puerto Rican insurrection failed, Betances first traveled to Venezuela, then New York, where he helped the Cuban exiles planning the independence war, and eventually Europe. In 1895, the Cuban government named him their diplomatic representative in Paris. He died three years later in that city.

The spiritual leader of his island's independence movement, as Kal Wagenheim and Olga Jiménez de Wagenheim described him in *The Puerto Ricans: A Documentary History* (2002), Betances's poetry and essays were of a patriotic nature. His intent was not aesthetics but more of a call to arms. *See also* Abolitionist Literature; Puerto Rican Literature, History of.

Further Reading

Betances, poeta. Edited by Luis Hernández Aquino. Bayamón, Puerto Rico: Ediciones Sarobei, 1986.

Suárez Diaz, Ada. *El doctor Ramón Emeterio Betances y la abolición de la esclavitud*. San Juan de Puerto Rico: Instituto de Cultura Puertorriqueña, 1980.

—*D. H. Figueredo*

Betancourt Family

The Betancourts were father and son writers and patriots from Cuba known for their costumbrista writings, sketches on local customs and traditions, and patriotic activities during the nineteenth century. Both were poets and journalists who published extensively in newspapers; of the two, the son Luis Victoriano was the more famous.

Betancourt, José Victoriano (1813–75). José Victoriano penned stylistic and humorous depictions of life both in cities and on the countryside, attempting to capture on the page the richness and complexities of a given moment and allowing the protagonists to speak for themselves, thus duplicating reality. Though his sketches lacked plot and character development, many critics feel that José Victoriano helped to make a literary form out of the practice of **costumbrismo**. His articles were collected by the Cuban government and published in 1941 under the title of *Artículos de costumbres*.

Betancourt, Luis Victoriano (1843–85). Luis Victoriano wrote costumbrista sketches meant to teach moral lessons. As a poet, he wrote poetry that expressed patriotism. In his most famous poem, "Simpatías del destino," written sometime in the 1870s, he praises the courage of the Cuban insurgents fighting against the Spanish troops in the Cuban jungles. Luis Victoriano was the second secretary and president of the House of Representatives of Cuba's provisional government during the first phase of the war of insurrection, lasting from 1868 to 1878. He published a collection of his poems and articles in 1867, *Artículos de costumbres y poesías*. He was also a gifted orator.

In their writings, the Betancourts affirmed nationalism and what it meant to be Cuban. *See also* Cuban Literature, History of.

Further Reading

Córdova, Federico. *Luis Victoriano Betancourt (1843–1885) Discurso leído por el académico de número dr. Federico de Córdova en la sesión solemne celebrada el 7 de mayo de 1943, en conmemoración del primer centenario del nacimiento de Luis Victoriano Betancourt.* Imprenta El Siglo XX. Habana: A. Muñiz y hno., 1943.

Santovenia y Echaide, Emeterio Santiago. *José Victoriano Betancourt: estudio biográfico.* Imprenta La Universal. Habana: de Ruiz y Comp., 1912.

—*D. H. Figueredo*

Beville, Albert. See Níger, Paul.

Bim (1942–73; 1992)

Dubbed the "literary journal of Barbados," *Bim* was the first major serial of this type in the West Indies. Published from 1942 to 1973, *Bim* was financed by the Young Men's Progressive Club and edited by short-story writer and poet **Frank Collymore.** From a somewhat whimsical beginning, featuring trivial quizzes, trite poetry, and prizes for the best ghost story of the year, *Bim* evolved into an important avenue for the promotion of contemporary West Indian literature, nurturing the early talent of writers such as the Barbadian **George Lamming** and Guyanan **Edgar Mittelhölzer**. The journal avoided political debates, favoring instead the belles letters. Always seeking new writers, the journal often printed poems and stories read over the air in the BBC production *Caribbean Voices*, which broadcast to the West Indies from London. By the mid-1940s, *Bim* had become, according to scholar Laurence A. Breiner, the "journal of record for the region . . . [an] open rostrum" for the written word. In 1992, there was a special issue published to honor the fiftieth anniversary of the founding of the journal. See also *Beacon, The*; Literary Journals.

Further Reading

Breiner, Laurence A. *An Introduction to West Indian Poetry*. New York: Cambridge University Press, 1998.

Collymore, Frank. *The Man Who Loved Attending Funerals and Other Stories*. Portsmouth, NH: Heinemann, 1993.

Peter T. Johnson and D. H. Figueredo

Bissoondath, Neil (1955–)

A novelist from Trinidad, Bissoondath is also a social critic and observer. His views on Canada's approaches to diversity have made him a controversial figure in his adopted country.

Bissoondath was born in Arima, Trinidad. His uncle is the writer **V. S. Naipul**, and as a child Bissoondath was impressed with the fact that Naipul made a living from writing. Therefore, it was not surprising that Bissoondath would follow in his uncle's footsteps rather than become a teacher, as expected by his family.

Bissoondath attended St. Mary's College and York University, where he studied English, French, and Spanish. In 1973, he migrated to London. He taught languages while pursuing a career in writing. In 1988, the publication of his collection of short stories, *Digging Up the Mountains*, was well received by the critics. In 1989, *A Casual Brutality*, his best-known work, was published. Through the story of a successful Indian who returns to his home island—unnamed but modeled after Trinidad—Bissoondath explores racism as practiced by those on the margins of society: people of color discriminating against each other. His next book, *Selling Illusions: The Cult of Multi-Culturalism in Canada* (1994), proved his most controversial. In the volume he criticizes Canada's official support of multiculturalism, claiming that it reinforces stereotypical images and limits the potential assimilation of immigrants. As if to reaffirm his stance, Bissoondath wrote *Doing the Heart Good* (2002), wherein the character is neither an Indian nor an immigrant but a white man from Quebec who is examining the meaning of his life after the loss of his wife and the destruction of his house in a fire.

Bissoondath's other works include *On the Eve of Uncertain Tomorrows* (1990), *The Innocence of Age* (1992), *The Worlds Within Her* (1998). Overall, his work, both fiction and nonfiction, are characterized by a sense of isolation and cultural misplacement. *See also* Naipual Family.

Further Reading

Kruk, Laurie. "All Voices Belong to Me: An Interview with Neil Bissoondath." *Canadian Literature*, no. 180 (Spring 2004) 53–70.

Mehrotra, Arvind Krishna. *A History of Indian Literature in English*. New York: Columbia University Press, 2003.

—D. H. Figueredo

Black, Clinton (1918–95?)

A popular Jamaican historian and archivist, Black dedicated his life to the gathering of legends and folklore from his island. He promoted Jamaican literature and arts.

Born in Kingston, Jamaica, on August 26, 1918, Clinton Vane de Brosse Black attended Kingston College and the University of London, graduating with a degree in archival studies in the early 1940s. In 1945, he was hired as the first government archivist of Jamaica, a post that brought him respect and recognition for his labor in researching and documenting Jamaican history. From 1949 to 1989, he was the archivist of Spanish Town, Jamaica, and represented his country at numerous international conferences on the retrieval and preservation of archives. His interest in history, local legends, and the pirates who roamed the Caribbean resulted in his most famous work, *Tales of Old Jamaica*. The book was published in 1952 and was an immediate success; it was reprinted several times.

Several volumes followed his initial success: *History of Jamaica* (1958), *Spanish Town: The Old Capital* (1960), *Port Royal: A History and Guide* (1970), *Jamaica Guide* (1973), and *The Pirates of the West Indies* (1989). Each of these volumes proved popular in schools and were reprinted several times. As popular was his column, for the newspaper *The Gleaner*, on words and usage. He is credited with revitalizing the study of Jamaican folklore art and legends.

Black was also an archivist in British Guiana, publishing the study "Archives of British Guiana" (1955), and in Trinidad Tobago. The research library at Jamaica's National Archives is named the Clinton Black Room in honor Black.

Further Reading

"Clinton V(ane De Brosse) Black." *Contemporary Authors Online*. Gale, 2002. http://www.galenet.galegroup.com (accessed 8/31/05).

Porter, Stephen D. "Jamaican Records." *Society of Genealogists, London, on Saturday, 21 June 1997*. http://www.rootsweb.com (accessed 5/19/05).

—D. H. Figueredo

Blanco, Oscar. See Miranda Archilla, Graciany.

Blanco, Tomás (1897–1975)

A member of Puerto Rico's **Generación del 30**, the writers who were born and raised after the arrival of American forces on the island as a result of the Spanish-Cuban-American War of 1898, Blanco was a historian, an essayist, and a creative writer.

Born in San Juan, Puerto Rico, on December 9, 1897, Blanco attended primary and secondary schools in that city. After high school, his parents sent him to the United States, where he studied at Georgetown University. In the early 1920s, he earned a medical degree from Georgetown.

Of affluent means, Banco traveled throughout out Europe. He began to write towards the end of the 1920s, first on the subject of literature and then writing his own poetry. In 1930, he published *Prontuario histórico de Puerto Rico*, an analysis of Puerto Rican culture. In 1942, he turned his attention to racial tension and racism on that island with the volume *El prejucio racial en Puerto Rico*. These two books established his fame in Puerto Rico as a scholar and social commentator.

In 1964, he made his literary debut as a poet with *Letras para música*. In 1968, he published *Los cinco sentidos*, in which he used the senses as an avenue to describe Puerto Rico and the island's traditions and history. In 1970, he published a collection of short stories, *Cuentos sin ton ni son*. Collectively, his works revealed the preoccupation typical of the generation of 1930: an affirmation of Puerto Rican and Hispanic culture in the presence of the growing American influence.

Tomás Blanco died on April 12, 1975, in the city of San Juan.

Further Reading

Montserrat Gámiz, María del Carmen. *Tomás Blanco y "Los vates."* San Juan, Puerto Rico: Instituto de Cultura Puertorriqueña, 1986.

—D. H. Figueredo

Bloom, Valerie (1956–)

A Jamaican poet who uses dialect in her writings, Valerie Bloom is a popular **dub poet**—a poet who performs poetry on a stage—as well as an educator. Her work appears in over eighty anthologies.

Bloom was born in Clarendon, Jamaica, in 1956 and relocated to England at the age of twenty-three. In 1983, she published her first book of poetry, *Touch Mi, Tell Mi*. She then attended the University of Kent, graduating with an honors degree in English in 1995. In 1997, her most popular book, *Fruits: Caribbean Counting Poems*, was published in England and the United States. The children's book tells the story of a youngster and her sister putting away tropical fruits and counting as they do so. The younger sister, however, eats the fruits, one by one, and the book ends with the younger girl suffering from indigestion.

Valerie Bloom performs her poems at schools all over Great Britain, where her poems are part of the curriculum. Though she is very popular with children who come from the Caribbean, her poetry appeals to all listeners who enjoy her performance and the cadence of poems such as "Language Barrier" (2002):

> Jamaica language sweet yuh know bwoy
> An yuh know mi nebba notice I'
> Till tarra day one foreign frien'
> Come spen some time wid mi.

Bloom uses dialect for artistic effect but also as an affirmation of her heritage. She told an interviewer in the periodical *The Voice:* "It's my language. I can write in English . . . but there is no reason why I shouldn't write in my own language" (35). *See also* Dub Poetry; Performance Poetry.

Further Reading

Bloom, Valerie. "Welcome to the Official Valerie Bloom Website." http://www.valbloom.co. uk (accessed 5/05).

Pinkerton, Lee. "Universal Medium: Valerie Bloom's award winning poems are a hit with school children all over Britain, even though they are written in a language most are not familiar with, Jamaican patois." *The Voice*, December 15, 1997.

—*D. H. Figueredo*

Bobes León, Marilyn (1955–)

■

Marilyn Bobes is a feminist poet and short-story writer who examines women's oppression in the Caribbean in general and in Cuba in particular. She is the recipient of the 1995 **Casa de las Américas** Award for fiction.

Born in Havana, Cuba, in 1955, Bobes attended the Universidad de la Habana with the intentions of becoming a historian. Instead, she chose journalism, working for the Cuban press service, Prensa Latina, and writing for the journal *Revolución y Cultura*. During the 1990s, she served as president of the **Unión de Escritores y Artistas de Cuba.**

Attracted to poetry, in 1978, she wrote *Alguien está escribiendo su ternura,* poems that celebrate the lives of feminist writers of previous eras, including Sor Juana Inés de la Cruz (1648–95), **Gertrudis Gómez de Avellaneda,** and Gabriela Mistral (1889–1957). In 1979, she won the Cuban literary award "David"—for unpublished manuscripts—for the poetry collection *La aguja en el pajar.* Ten years later she wrote her third book of poetry, *Hallar el modo.* But it was her fiction that brought her international recognition. In 1995, she received a Casa de las Américas literary prize for the collection of short stories *Alguien tiene que llorar.*

The volume presents Bobes's feminist perspective. The most famous piece is the short story that carries the collection's title. In an accessible narrative, shifting narrators comment on the enigmatic life of a beautiful, unattached woman who commits suicide. Through the narrators, Bobes comments on women's oppression in modern society, even in such a revolutionary society as Cuba's. The author maintains that feminine beauty is still defined by men and that even women accept and apply such a definition. She also suggests that women are trapped: those who assert themselves encounter tragic endings and those who yield to men are equally doomed.

Bobes has edited two anthologies of short stories by Cuban women, *Estatuas de sal* (1996) and *Cuentistas cubanas de hoy* (2001). She has also written books of criticism from a feminist perspective: *Fina García Marruz: elogio de la serena perfección* (1985), *Intervalos* (1992), *El esperado homenaje: Revolución y Cultura* (1998). *See also* Feminism in Caribbean Literature.

Further Reading

Pérez, Olga Marta. "Consideraciones sobre una muestra." *Mujeres como islas*. Habana: Ediciones Unión; Santo Domingo: Ediciones Ferilibro, 2002.

—*D. H. Figueredo*

Boisrond Tonnerre, Louis (1776–1806)

A rebel and officer during the Haitian revolution (1791–1804), Boisrond Tonnerre is known for having stated, according to Berrou and Pompilus in *Histoire de la littérature haïtienne*, "For our declaration of independence, we should have the skin of a white man for parchment, his skull for an inkwell, his blood for ink, and a bayonet for a pen!" (55). Secretary and advisor to Haitian Emperor Jean Jacques Dessalines (1758–1806), Boisrond Tonnerre is called the father of the Act of Independence.

Boisrond Tonnerre was born in Torbeck, Haiti, in 1776, the son of a carpenter. During his birth, there was a violent thunderstorm and, supposedly, lightning stuck his cradle; thus his father added the appellation Tonnerre, "thunder," to the child's surname. When Boisrond was an adolescent, a relative took him to Paris, where he attended secondary school at the College de la Marche. Upon his return to Haiti in 1798, he joined the revolution that had begun in 1791. He soon served under Jean Jacques Dessalines. Of impulsive and violent dispositions, both men shared a hatred of whites.

On January 1, 1804, Boisrond Tonnerre wrote the proclamation of independence, *Acte d'indépendence*. During this period, he also he wrote his memoirs, *Mémoires pour servir à l'histoire d'Haïti*. Published posthumously in 1852, it was the first volume to document the revolution and the fight against colonial France. Today, numerous schools in Haiti bear Boisrond Tonnerre's name.

Further Reading

Berrou, Raphaël and Pompilus, Pradel. *Histoire de la littérature haïtienne.* Tome 1. Port-au-Prince: Editions Caraëbes, 1975.

—*D. H. Figueredo*

Bonafoux Quintero, Luis (1855–1918)

This nineteenth-century Puerto Rican essayist and journalist spent much of his life in Europe. He was also a short-story writer and novelist.

A native of Saint Lubetz, France, he grew up in Puerto Rico, where he attended school. When he was in his early twenties, he studied law at the Universidad de Madrid and the Universidad de Salamanca. Upon his return to the island, he began to write for local publications, including *El Buscapié.* His criticism of the colonial government resulted in his banishment from the island during the 1870s.

In 1877, he published the novel *El asesinato de Victor Noir* as well as a collection of articles and essays, *Literatura de Bonafoux.* During the 1880s and 90s he traveled throughout Europe, writing several volumes consisting of chronicles, social commentaries, and stories: *Mosquetazos de Aramis* (1881), *Huellas literarias* (1894), and *Paris al día* (1900). He also wrote two biographies *Emilio Zola* (1901) and *Betances* (1910), about the Puerto Rican patriot and writer. His observation of the manners and behavior of Spanish travelers, *Los españoles en Paris,* was published in 1912. Bonafoux was noted for his sharp satire and negative depiction of colonial society, lampooning the stereotypical personalities of the era: the gluttonous priest, the avaricious official, and the pseudo-intellectual, among others.

Further Reading

Enciclopedia puertorriqueña. siglo XXI. Santurce, Puerto Rico: Caribe Grolier, 1998.

Girón, Socorro. *Bonafoux y su época.* Ponce, Puerto Rico: S. Girón, 1987.

—*D. H. Figueredo*

Boom, The Latin American

This expression describes the sudden appearance in world literature of a series of highly experimental and innovative novels written by a group of young men from Latin America. Their abrupt entrance into the literary scene was likened to an explosion, thus "boom." The use of the term also referred to the brisk sales stirred by the novels. Though *boom* is an English word, it was readily accepted and used by the readers and scholars from Latin America. The group of writers included **Guillermo Cabrera Infante,** from Cuba; Julio Cortázar (1914–84), from Argentina; José Donoso (1924–96), from Chile; Carlos Fuentes (1928–), from Mexico; Colombian Gabriel

García Márquez (1928–); and Peruvian Mario Vargas Llosa (1936–). Collectively, these authors wrote a half-dozen novels that were published in the mid-1960s and were quickly translated into several languages.

The most famous Boom novels are, in alphabetical order, *Cien años de soledad* by Gabriel García Márquez (1967); *La ciudad y los perros* by Mario Vargas Llosa (1963); *La muerte de Artemio Cruz* by Carlos Fuentes (1962); *El obsceno pájaro de la noche* by José Donoso (1970); *Rayuela* by Julio Cortázar (1963); and *Tres tristes tigres* by Guillermo Cabrera Infante (1965). The combined characteristics of these novels are: (1) multiple narrators and shifting viewpoints; (2) use of nonlinear time; (3) obscure allusions and references; (4) use of magical realism or the presence of the ordinary with the supernatural; (5) shifting tenses; (6) support of the Cuban revolution; and (7) the belief that literature could bring about peaceful political change. These characteristics influenced scores of emerging writers from Latin America and the United States, including Isabel Allende (1946–), from Chile; Laura Esquivel (1950–), from Mexico; **Luis Rafael Sánchez**, from Puerto Rico; and Toni Morrison, from the United States.

During the 1960s, the Boom writers became fast friends and promoted each other's work. They, like the members of the initial **Négritude** movement in the Francophone Caribbean, have been criticized for not including women within their group. Cuban novelist **Reinaldo Arenas** complained, in his autobiography *Antes que anochezca* (1992), that he was not included in the group because of his opposition to **Fidel Castro**. Chilean author Ernesto Sábato (1911–) is sometimes regarded as a Boom writer.

Though the Boom was not a literary movement, it clearly defined a moment in the history of Latin American literature. Many of the writers who matured after the 1960s are described as post-Boom writers.

Further Reading

Sacoto, Antonio. *Siete novelas maestras del boom hispanoamericano*. Quito, Ecuador: Casa de la Cultura Ecuatoriana, 2003.

Swanson, Philip. *The New Novel in Latin America: Politics and Popular Culture after the Boom*. New York: Manchester University Press, 1995.

—*D. H. Figueredo*

Borrero Family

The Borreros were father and daughter writers and promoters of Cuban culture during the nineteenth-century. Favoring independence, they participated in the struggle against Spain.

Borrero, Juana (1877–96). Juana was a painter and poet whose writings appeared in such well-known journals as *La Habana Elegante*, *El Figaro*, and *Gris y Azul*. With her father, she hosted **tertulias**, literary salons, in her home, where she and other writers, including **Julián del Casal**, read their works to each other, discussed European literature, and criticized the Spanish colonial system. As the activities for independence intensified and the Spanish colonial authorities grew more repressive, she and her family migrated to Tampa in 1895. Her ill fated engagement to poet Carlos Pío Uhrbach (1872–97) ended with her death from consumption in 1896. Uhrbach, who had joined the Cuban insurgents, was killed in combat the following year. When his compatriots retrieved his body, he was carrying a love poem written to him by Juana. Their love letters were published in 1996 under the title of *Epistolario*.

Borrero Echevarria, Esteban (1849–1906). Esteban was Juana's father. He was a physician and teacher. He edited several pedagogical and scientific journals, including *Revista cubana* and *Revista de ciencias médicas de la Habana*; his essays covered such topics as medicine, scientific progress, and teaching. As a poet, he published a book in 1878, *Poesía*. Influenced by the Romantic movement, his carefully constructed poems explored the pangs of love and separation. His short stories, which appeared in diverse journals, were gathered in the anthology *Narraciones*, published in Cuba in 1979.

As a result of his involvement in the struggle for independence, he was once jailed by the colonial authorities. In the mid-1890s, he relocated to the United States, returning to Cuba in 1902 when the island became a republic. *See also* Romanticismo/Romanticism.

Further Reading

Cuza Malé, Belkis. *El clavel y la rosa: biografía de Juana Borrero*. Madrid: Ediciones Cultura Hispánica, 1984.

Garrandes, Alberto. *Tres Cuentistas Cubanos*. Habana: Editorial Letras Cubanas, 1993.

—*D. H. Figueredo*

Bosch, Juan (1909–2001)

Novelist, short-story writer, essayist, and politician, Bosch is probably the most famous writer from the Dominican Republic. He is considered one of Latin America's greatest short-story writers. Like his compatriot **Pedro Henríquez Ureña**, and many other writers from the Caribbean, Bosch spent many years of his life in exile. His lifetime political rival was another writer, though of lesser talent, **Joaquín Balaguer.**

Juan Bosch was born in La Vega, Dominican Republic, on June 30, 1909. As a child he was surrounded by books and often watched his father writing poetry. Bosch himself began writing at the age of nine and was first published in a local newspaper when he was twelve years old. Moving to Santo Domingo as a young man, he joined a literary group called La Cueva. In 1929, his short stories were regularly featured in newspapers and journals. In 1933, his first collection of short stories was published under the title of *Camino real*. In 1936, he wrote his first novel, *La Mañosa*.

In 1937, protesting against the dictatorship of Rafael Leónidas Trujillo (1891–1961), Bosch left for Cuba, where two years later he founded the Partido Revolucionario Dominicano. While in Cuba he met the Puerto Rican poet **Julia de Burgos,** to whom he dictated—he was sick in bed—one of his most famous short stories "La bella alma de don Damián," an experimental exercise where the protagonist's soul leaves its infirm body to study the surroundings and contemplate its life. From Cuba, Bosch traveled to other Latin American countries, spending twenty-four years away from the Dominican Republic and earning a living performing a variety of jobs, from editing the works of Puerto Rican author **Eugenio María Hostos** and writing for Cuban journals to selling medicine and working in a factory. His years in exile would offer him the inspiration and materials for his most famous volumes, *Cuentos escritos en el exilio* (1962), *Más cuentos escritos en el exilio* (1964), and *Cuentos escritos antes del exilio* (1975).

Bust of Juan Bosch in San Juan, Puerto Rico. One of Latin America's great short-story writers, Bosch was the first democratically elected president of the Dominican Republic after the death of dictator Rafael L. Trujillo. *Source: D. H. Figueredo.*

When Trujillo was assassinated in 1961, Bosch returned to the Dominican Republic and was the first democratically elected president since the 1930s. Taking office in 1963, he was overthrown seven months later by the military; he sought exile in Costa Rica, where he taught at the Institute of Political Science. He then turned his creative energy into political writings: *Crisis de la democracia de América en la República Dominicana* (1966), *El próximo paso: Dictadura con respaldo popular* (1967), and *El pentagonismo, sustituto del imperialismo* (1968). These treatises provided an insider's view of the political process in Latin America. These works were also praised for Bosch's in-depth profiles of such political figures as **François Duvalier,** from neighboring Haiti.

In 1989, Bosch returned to the Dominican Republic, seeking reelection and losing to archrival Joaquin Balaguer. Overall, Bosch ran unsuccessfully for office in 1978, 1982, 1986, 1990, and 1994.

The political situation on the island informed Bosch's writings. His first novel, *La Mañosa,* depicted the poverty in the countryside. His second novel, *El oro y la paz* (1975), about miners searching for gold in a jungle, can be read as the author's elusive search for political justice in the Dominican Republic. Bosch was also a literary critic, and his essay "Apuntes sobre el arte de escribir cuentos" (1958) has served as a guideline on the craft of the short story for aspiring authors. His creative prose has been translated into several languages, including English, French, German, and Dutch.

He passed away on November 1, 2001.

Further Reading

García Cuevas, Eugenio de J. *Juan Bosch: novela, historia y sociedad*. San Juan, Puerto Rico: Isla Negra, 1995.

Gerónimo, Joaquín. *En el nombre de Bosch*. Santo Domingo, República Dominicana: Editora Alfa Omega, 2001.

—*D. H. Figueredo*

Boukman, Daniel (1936–)

Boukman is an anti-colonialist dramatist from Martinique. His most famous play, *Les Négriers* (1971), is an epic recounting of slavery and the slave trade, contrasting the suffering of the slaves with the oppression experienced by black immigrants in France.

Boukman was born in Fort-de-France with the name of Daniel Blérald, however he opted for the surname of Boukman to render tribute to one of the eighteenth-century leaders of the Haitian revolution. Relocating to France, he studied at the Sorbonne. He was influenced by the writings of **Frantz Fanon** and the Algerians' war of independence from France. Boukman taught French in Algiers from 1966 to 1981.

During the 1968 students' protests in Europe and in the United States, Boukman was inspired to write *Les Négriers*. The play was published in 1971 and performed in Paris the same year. It soon became popular throughout the Caribbean, where it was staged by amateur groups in Martinique and Guadeloupe. During the 1980s, Boukman wrote in Creole several books of poetry celebrating the independence movement. By 1990s, his focus became less Marxist and militant, though he still explored the subject of oppression; for example, in the play *Delivrans* (1996), he writes about a family in which the dictatorial father forces his children to speak French and to favor European culture. His other works include *Chants pour hâter la mort, du temps des Orphée ou Madinina île esclave, poèmes dramatiques* (1967), *Ventres pleins, ventres creux; pièce en deux parties* (1971), and *Et jusqu'à la dernière pulsation de nos veines* (1976).

Further Reading

Jones, Bridget. "Theatre and Resistance? An Introduction to some French Caribbean Plays." In *An Introduction to Caribbean Francophone Writing: Guadeloupe and Martinique*, edited by Sam Haigh, 83–100. New York: Berg, 1999.

—*D. H. Figueredo*

Bourand Family

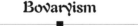

Husband and wife writers from Haiti, Etienne was a poet, playwright, and lawyer, and his wife was a novelist, writing under the pseudonym of Annie Desroys.

Bourand, Etienne (1892–1958). Etienne Bourand was born in Gonaïves, Haiti, on June 10, 1892. He relocated to Port-au-Prince to attend high school and in the 1920s earned a law degree from the l'École du Droit. While attending school, Bourand pursued his passion for drama, writing several plays: *Mènage de poète* (1915), *Le coeur décide* (1915), *L'impréve* (1918), *En retenue* (1921), *Le goût du fard* (1921), and *Feu de paille* (1921). While the plays are melodramatic, presenting such universal issues as love found and lost, they were all staged in Port-au-Prince, proving popular with theatergoers.

In 1928, he published a poetry collection, *L'éternel adolescent*. A successful career in the government, as secretary of the Haitian Legation in Paris and as commissioner of Haiti's Civil Court, demanded much of his time. He was also a law professor at his alma mater.

Desroy, Annie (1893–1943). Desroy was a novelist, playwright, and teacher. Born Anne-Marie Lerebours on May 4, 1893, in Port-au-Prince, Desroy was a teacher and director of the Center for University Studies, a secondary and college-level school for girls. A feminist, Desroy was a member of the Ligue Féminine d'Action.

Desroy wrote comedies for the stage: *El l'amour vient* (1921) and *La centre du passe* (1931). She also wrote the novel *La Joug* (1934), which explored political themes. She devoted much of her time to teaching and to civic activities while also lending support to her husband's career. In the 1990s, feminist scholars began to look at Desroy's work, long neglected by male critics and scholars.

Further Reading

Chancy, Myriam J. A. *Framing Silence: Revolutionary Novels by Haitian Women.* New Brunswick, NJ: Rutgers University Press, 1997.

Herdeck, Donald E. *Caribbean Writers. A Bio-Bibliographical-Critical Encyclopedia.* Washington, DC: Three Continents Press, 1979.

—*D. H. Figueredo*

Bovaryism

This is a term used by Haitian intellectual **Jean Price-Mars** to describe Haitians' attempts to think of Haiti in a way that was not so, that is, portraying an inaccurate view of themselves and their country. The term is an allusion to Emma Bovary's isolation in the world of her own romantic dreams. In his seminal book, *Ainsi parle* *l'Oncle* (1928), Price-Mars asked Haitians to examine their true identity and not think of themselves as colored Frenchmen and -women; he asked them to incorporate ancestral African aspects of their society into their works. *See also* Haitian Literature, History of.

Further Reading

Meehan, Kevin. "A Folio of Writing from La Revue Indigene (1927–28): Translation and Commentary." *Callaloo* 23, no. 4 (Fall 2000): 1377–1380.

Price-Mars, Jean. *So Spoke the Uncle.* Translated by Magdaline W. Shannon. Colorado Springs: Three Continents Press, 1994.

—*Jayne R. Boisvert*

Braithwaite, E. R. (1920–)

Best known for his autobiography, *To Sir, With Love,* made into a successful film in 1966 and starring Sydney Poitier (1927–) as the author, Eustace Edward Ricardo Braithwaite is a writer, teacher, and diplomat. Born in Georgetown, British Guiana—now called Guyana—he attended college in his home country, in the United States, and in England. During World War II, he served with distinction as a pilot in the Royal Air Force.

In the late 1940s, Braithwaite couldn't find employment, despite having a master's degree in physics and an outstanding liberal arts education; in fact, one potential employer simply told him that the white workers in his firm would not work with a black man who was better qualified than they. Frustrated, Braithwaite turned to teaching, finding a position in a London ghetto where the students were unruly and not expected to perform well academically. He taught at the school for five years, and from this experience came his autobiography, *To Sir, With Love,* published in 1959. The book became a bestseller and created a certain type, present in films, if not in books: the superhero black man who is intellectually, academically, and culturally far superior to the white folks around him.

Other works followed: *A Kind of Homecoming* (1962), *Choice of Straws* (1967), *Paid Servant* (1968), *Reluctant Neighbors* (1972), and *"Honorary White": A Visit to South Africa* (1975). *Choice of Straws* is a daring novel. It tells the story from the perspective of an angry white youth who while harassing a black man kills him. A writer who displays self-control and is often self-effacing, Braithwaite's anger erupted in the memoir *Reluctant Neighbors,* damning a racist white society in which a black man must prove himself over and again. In *"Honorary White,"* he describes his experiences as a privileged visitor to apartheid-ridden South Africa, where he was allowed to visit places and stay in hotels where black South Africans were not permitted.

E. R. Braithwaite has traveled extensively, served Guyana as an ambassador, worked for UNESCO, and taught at such prestigious schools as New York University and Howard University. Regarded as a sensitive and honest writer who appeals to a general readership, he is often neglected from serious study of Caribbean literature. *See also* Exile Literature.

Further Reading

Braithwaite, E. R. *To Sir, with Love*. Englewood Cliffs, NJ: Prentice-Hall, 1959.

Wambu, Onyekachi, ed. *Hurricane Hits England: An Anthology of Writing About Black Britain*. New York: Continuum, 2000.

—*D. H. Figueredo*

Brand, Dionne (1953–)

Afro-Caribbean Canadian writer whose novels and poetry attempt to capture the forgotten experiences and voices of the victims of the black diaspora, Dionne Brand is a journalist, filmmaker, gay advocate, and an activist. She belongs to a group of political and socially engaged writers, like the Guyanan **Martin Carter**, who uses literature as a tool for social change.

Dionne Brand was born on January 7, 1953, in Guayguayare, Trinidad. After attending high school in Trinidad, she moved to Canada in 1970, graduating from the University of Toronto in 1975 with a BA in English and philosophy. In 1979, she earned a masters in education from the Ontario Institute for Studies in Education. While in college she became involved in the civil rights and women's movement in Canada and worked for several community-based organizations. In 1983, her Marxist ideology and commitment to the liberation of blacks throughout the world prompted her to travel to Grenada to support the newly established regime of Maurice Bishop (1944–83). She served as information and communication officer of the Agency for Rural Transformation until the murder of Bishop by rival rebels and the island's invasion by a multinational force led by the United States. The invasion of Grenada served as her inspiration for the book of poems *Chronicles of the Hostile Sun* (1984) and the collection of short stories *San Souci and Other Stories* (1989), in which she describes some of the battles she witnessed.

Brand first achieved recognition as poet with the collections *Earth Magic* (1980), *Primitive Offensive* (1982), *Winter Epigrams and Epigrams to Ernest Cardenal in Defense of Claudia* (1983), and *No Language Is Neutral* (1990). In her poems, Brand addresses discrimination against blacks in general and the marginalization of black women in particular. In *No Language Is Neutral* she focuses on sexuality and lesbianism as well. Says scholars Myriam J. A. Chancy in *Searching for Safe Spaces* (1997): "This inclusion of sexuality as part and parcel of Black feminism . . . forces Brand's readers to confront and accept sexuality as a point of difference or of commonality but always as a point of oppression for lesbian women" (119).

As a novelist, Brand has explored the search for African roots and the need to belong to a culture and a tradition in the books *In Another Place, Not Here* (1996), a philosophical exercise on identity, and *At the Full and Change of the Moon* (1999), a **historical novel** about a fictional rebel leader named Marie Ursule. Both works reaffirm Brand's belief that "freedom is not an illusion to be chased, but an experience that is achieved through remembrance, ritual, and renewal," writes critic Salamishah Tillet in the spring 2003 issue of the journal *Callaloo* (916).

Recording the voices and experiences of black women was the objective of Brand's *No Burden to Carry: Narratives of Black Working Women in Ontario* (1991), a series of interviews with transplanted domestic servants from the Caribbean, and the films *Older, Stronger, Wiser* (1989), about five black women in Ontario, and *Sisters in the Struggle* (1991), about black feminists in Canada. *See also* Gay and Lesbian Literature; Literatura Comprometida/Socially Engaged Literature.

Further Reading

Chancy, Myriam J. A. *Searching for Safe Spaces: Afro-Caribbean Women Writers in Exile*. Philadelphia: Temple University Press, 1997.

Garvey, Johanna X. K. "'The She Miss' Exile, Memory, and Resistance in Dionne Brand's Fiction." *Callaloo* 26, no. 2 (Spring 2003): 486–503.

Tillet, Salamishah. "*At the Full and Change of the Moon*: Review." *Callaloo* 26, no. 3 (Summer 2003): 193–912.

—*D. H. Figueredo*

Braschi, Giannina (1953–)

Braschi is a Puerto Rican experimental author who champions the use of **code switching** in literature, the frequent move from one language to another: in this case from English to Spanish and vice versa. Her book *Empire of Dreams* (1994) is her most representative work.

From a well-to-do family, Braschi was born in San Juan, Puerto Rico, on February 5, 1953. She traveled throughout Europe, moving to New York City when she was twenty-two years old. At the age of twenty-seven, she earned a PhD from the State University of New York, and by the time she was thirty, she was gathering scholarly and literary laurels: a grant from Instituto de Cooperación Iberoamericana, in Madrid (1980); the publication of her first book of poetry, *Asalto al tiempo* (1981); a book of criticism, *La poesía de Bécquer* (1982); and an appointment as Minority Faculty at Rutgers University (1983). After two more books—*La comedia profana* (1985) and *Libro de payasos y bufones* (1987)—she published her best-known work, *El imperio de los sueños*, consisting of poems and a short novel, in 1988. It is a book about New York City and the lives of immigrants who live there. Written in three parts, the volume examines the intricacies of the English language, the vitality of street life in Manhattan, and the newcomers' attempts at becoming part of the city and even possessing it. The book, which proved popular in Spain and in Latin America, was translated into English in 1994 as *Empire of Dreams*.

In 1998, Braschi published *Yo-Yo-Boing*. Once again, the novel consisted of three parts: "Close-Up," about a woman evaluating her emotional and intellectual capabilities; "Blow-Up," a Spanish-English conversation about life; "Black-Out," where the author includes herself into the narrative. Comments reviewer Carolyn Kuebler, in *The Review of Contemporary Fiction* (1995): "Braschi writes with a strong poetic tradition behind her, and from her erudite standpoint she forges an odd mixture of poetry, prose, drama, and a little of what could be considered music. She imbues her text with jollity . . . She uses words for their rhythms and image-making, rather than to tell a story or to describe a fixed object or idea" (168).

Further Reading

Kuebler, Carolyn. "Empire of Dreams." *The Review of Contemporary Fiction* 15, no. 1 (Spring, 1995): 168–70.

—D. H. Figueredo

Braschi, Wilfredo (1918–95)

Braschi was a Puerto Rican essayist and short-story writer. His profiles of Puerto Rican actors and writers appeared in numerous journals and popular newspapers such as *El Mundo*.

Born in New York City in 1918 (some sources say 1919), Braschi was raised in Puerto Rico, where he attended the Universidad de Puerto Rico. After working for many years as a teacher and journalist, writing for such newspapers as *La Democracia* and *El Mundo*, he earned a PhD in philosophy and literature from the Universidad de Madrid in 1953. He then taught at the Universidad de Puerto Rico in Río Piedras.

Braschi was interested in theater and wrote extensively on the subject. He also wrote short stories depicting Puerto Rican characters and local settings. His collections of stories include *Cuatro caminos: Crónicas de un viaje* (1963), which won a literary prize from the Instituto de Literatura Puertorriqueña; *Metrópoli* (1968); and *La primera piedra* (1977). His essays on theater were published as *Apuntes sobre el teatro puertorriqueño* (1970).

Through his writings, Braschi treasured Puerto Rican talent while also promoting Puerto Rican culture and traditions. Braschi was also the director of the School of Communication of the Universidad de Puerto Rico.

Further Reading

Enciclopedia puertorriqueña: siglo XXI. Vol 1. Santurce, Puerto Rico: Caribe Grolier, 1998.

—D. H. Figueredo

Brathwaite, Edward Kamau (1930–)

A Barbadian, Brathwaite is one of the Caribbean's most talented and influential writers. An award-winning poet, playwright, and essayist he has spent most of his life as a writer exploring his evolution as a black man as well as reinterpreting Caribbean culture and history. Observes scholar Emily Allen Williams, in *Poetic*

Negotiation of Identity in the Works of Brathwaite, Harris, Senior, and Dabydeen (1999): "To read Brathwaite . . . is to take a historical journey: his journey toward understanding through a culturally, racially, socially, and political complex voyage from the Caribbean . . . to England . . . to Africa . . . and back to the Caribbean" (19).

Lawson Edward Brathwaite was born on May 11, 1930, in Bridgetown, Barbados. Reared during both the summit and decline of colonialism, Brathwaite experienced the racism typical of the colonial era during the 1930s and 1940s and the euphoria of the early independence movements during the 1950s and 1960s. In elementary school in Barbados, he studied the literature that made up the European canon—William Shake-

One of the Carbbean's most important and influential writers, Edward Kamau Brathwaite studies through literature his evolution as a black writer from a regional and international perspective. *Source: Americas Society. Courtesy of Elsa M. Ruiz.*

speare (1564–1616), Victor Hugo (1802–85), etc.—and developed an early interest in writing. He attended Pembroke College, Cambridge, England, graduating in 1953 with a BA in history. A year later, he also earned a diploma in education. In 1968, he received a PhD in philosophy from the University of Sussex.

From 1953 to 1968, Brathwaite led an extremely productive life, both as a writer and as a professional: he published three volumes of poetry—*The Day the First Snow Fell* (1953), *Rights of Passage* (1967), and *Masks* (1968)—a play, *Odale's Choice* (1967), and edited an anthology, *Iouanaloa: Recent Writing from St. Lucia* (1963), while serving in the Ministry of Education of Ghana (1955–62) and teaching literature at the University of West Indies. In 1966, he co-founded in London the **Caribbean Artists Movement**, the first organization to bring together Anglophone Caribbean writers living in Europe and to promote Caribbean writers. During this decade he also met a teacher and librarian, Doris Monica Welcome, with whom he fell deeply in love. Her death of cancer two decades later inspired the book *The Zea Mexican Diary* (1993). Composed of poems, journal entries, and letters, the book details his wife's illness and his suffering after losing her. Comments scholar Sandra Pouchet Paquet in *Caribbean Autobiography: Culture Identity and Self Representation* (2002): "The traumatic events poeticized in this diary . . . are also about the survival of . . . [a]poet . . . whose harrowing experience of death and loss is transformed through poetic elegy into a medium for the understanding of . . . self and community" (233).

In the 1970s, Brathwaite started to use the name Edward Kamau to indicate his African and European cultural identities. In 1973, Brathwaite achieved international recognition with the publication of the trilogy *The Arrivants*, which consisted of the collections *Rights of Passage*, *Masks*, and *Islands*. The poems were of an experimental nature as Brathwaite imitated speech patterns from the Caribbean and Africa while tracing his development as an individual in search of his African heritage. In his second trilogy—*Mother Poem* (1977), *Sun Poem* (1982), and *X/Self* (1987)—he progressed from the personal to the historic as he explored West Indian history. The poems in the two trilogies were a combination of prose and poetry.

Balancing his creative literary process, Brathwaite alternated between the reading and performing of his works with the writing of scholarly essays. He recorded two discs for the Library of Congress, *Kamau Brathwaite Reading his Poems with Comment in the Recording Laboratory* (1970) and *Edward Kamau Brathwaite Reading his Poems* (1982), as well as several recordings for the private label Argo. He also published several scholarly volumes, including *The Folk Culture of Jamaican Slaves* (1969), *The Development of Creole Society in Jamaica,* and *History of the Voice* (1984). In the latter volume, he proposed the concept of the nation language, a blending of European, African, and other languages to produce a lexicon and syntax unique to the Caribbean.

His ever-growing fame is demonstrated by the many awards he has received, including such major recognitions as two **Casa de Las Américas** prizes (1976, 1994), one of Latin America's most prestigious awards. He has also received a Guggenheim Fellowship (1972), the Institute of Jamaica Musgrave Medal (1983), and the Neustadt International Prize for Literature (1994). In 2002, the University of West Indies, in Jamaica, organized a international conference to honor and discuss Brathwaite's oeuvre.

Further Reading

Bobb, June. *Beating a Restless Drum: The Poetics of Kamau Brathwaite and Derek Walcott.* Trenton, NJ: Africa World Press, 1998.

Paquet, Sandra Pouchet. *Caribbean Autobiography: Culture Identity and Self-Representation.* Madison, WI: The University of Wisconsin Press, 2002.

Williams, Emily Allen. *Poetic Negotiation of Identity in the Works of Brathwaite, Harris, Senior, and Dabydeen: Tropical Paradise Lost and Regained.* Queenstown, Ontario: Edwin Mellen Press, 1999.

—*D. H. Figueredo*

Brau Asencio, Salvador (1842–1912)

One of Puerto Rico's most important and prolific writers, Salvador Brau wrote historical dramas, poetry, a classic history of the island's colonization by the Spanish—*La colonización de Puerto Rico (1493–1550)*—and numerous articles and essays addressing colonialism and autonomy. He was an editor, a public servant, and the island's official historian.

Born in Cabo Rojo, Puerto Rico, on January 11, 1842, Brau always wanted to be a writer. His formal education was curtailed due to financial constraints and his need to work after his father's death in 1854. Though he found a job as a clerk at a store, he read voraciously, teaching himself French, and founding a literary and cultural society, Círculo Popular de Enseñaza, so that he could associate himself with like minds and educated people. He also wrote and founded a review, *El Cocuyo,* while writing for other journals, including *El Eco* and *El Buscapié.*

In 1870, he published a text about a local legend, *El fantasma del Puente*. In 1871, his first play, *Héroe y mártir*, set in sixteenth-century Spain, was published and staged. Six years later, his depiction of a rebellion in Sicily against French invaders in 1282, entitled *Los horrores del triunfo*, was staged. These dramas were both romantic and realistic, portraying heroic figures who behaved as if they were regular men and women and also used the popular language of the time, thus bringing the plays closer to the audience. Through his plays, Brau expressed his political philosophy of less colonial influence and more autonomy.

In 1880, Brau moved to San Juan, where he worked in the Treasury Department. He wrote essays on a variety of topics, from labor—*Las clases jornaleras de Puerto Rico* (1882) and *La campesina* (1886), in which he studies the struggles of the Puerto Rican peasant—to dance, *La danza puertorriqueña* (1887), wherein he traces the development of the "danza," a waltzlike dance that emerged on the island in the nineteenth century. In 1889, he purchased the newspaper *El Clamor del País*. He used this paper to present his liberal ideals. His views led to his election as a delegate of the Provincial Assembly of the town of Mayagüez in 1891. He also served as secretary of the Autonomist Party. In 1892, he began his career as a historian with the publication of *Puerto Rico y su historia*, based on a series of lectures he had presented at the **Ateneo Puertorriqueño** and other institutions. In 1893, he published *Lo que dice la historia*.

In the mid-1890s, he conducted research at the Archives of Seville, Spain. From this institution he gathered much of the information that would go into his classic history, *La colonización de Puerto Rico*. From 1895 to 1902, he worked as the deputy collector of Customs in San Juan. But the Spanish-Cuban-American War of 1898 and the separation from Spain disappointed and angered him, for even though he wanted autonomy from Spain he still wished to maintain cultural ties, which he believed that Spain severed after the war, allowing for a greater American influence. As a result, he resigned from all political and public activities.

In 1903, however, he accepted the position of the island's official historian, a post he cherished. In his capacity as a historian he published *De como y cuando nos llego el café* (1906) and *La caña de azucar* (1906), about the coffee and sugar trades respectively, and *La fundación de Ponce* (1909) and *La isla de Vieques* (1912), local histories. As a creative writer, he pursued poetry, *Un poema de Brau* (1905) and *Hojas y caidas* (1909), and wrote a novel, *Lejanias* (1912).

Brau continued to write and to exercise his role of official historian to the very end of his life on November 5, 1912. In San Juan, a bronze statue honors his memory in the heart of a plaza that bears his name. Several Puerto Rican organizations in the United States carry his name. In the 1940s, a merchant ship in the United States was named after Brau.

Further Reading

Córdova Landrón, Arturo. *Salvador Brau; su vida, su obra, su época; ensayo histórico, biográfico, crítico*. San Juan: Editorial Universitaria, Universidad de Puerto Rico, 1949.

Rivera de Álvarez, Josefina. *Diccionario de literatura puertorriqueña*. Vol. 2. San Juan: Instituto de Cultura Puertorriqueña, 1974.

—*D. H. Figueredo*

Breeze, Jinta "Binta" (1957)

■

The first female **dub poet**—poets who perform their works on a stage or platform—Jinta "Binta" Breeze is a Jamaican writer and performer who uses standard English and Jamaican dialect and vernacular in her works. She belongs to a generation of poets who emerged in the 1970s and 1980s and who were interested in exploring the oral aesthetics of poetry rather than its written manifestation.

"Binta" Breeze was born in rural Jamaica in 1957—some accounts say 1956. She grew up in Patty Hill, a small village in Jamaica, before moving to Kingston in 1978, where she attended the Jamaica School of Drama. In 1981, a Rastafarian man saw her writing poetry at the dock on Montego Bay and invited her to perform at a celebration of Haile Sellassie's ninetieth birthday. Breeze accepted it and at a rehearsal met dub poet **Mutabaruka** who liked her poetry and invited her to perform with his band. The performance led to a recording of Breeze reading her poetry. "That's how I became the first female dub poet," Breeze recalled in 2003, in an interview published in the journal *Callaloo* (608).

Her recordings, broadcast over Jamaican airwaves, and her performances in festivals and carnivals made her a celebrity on the island. In 1985, she moved to England. In 1988, she wrote a film script, *Hallelujah Anyhow*. She toured Europe and the United States, and when the American writer Maya Angelou (1928–) turned seventy, she invited Breeze to read her poems at the celebration. Breeze's books of poetry include *Answers* (1982), *Riddym Ravings and Other Poems* (1988), *Spring Cleaning* (1992), *On the Edge of an Island* (1997), and *The Arrival of Brighteye and Other Poems* (2001).

Breeze has been influenced by pioneer poet **Louise Bennett**, the first to write poetry in Jamaican dialect, and like the older poet, Breeze uses the language of the common people, creating a literature of social protest that is nevertheless humorous. Her themes are the African diaspora, exile, and political corruption. In *The Arrival of Brighteye and Other Poems*, Breeze writes about Caribbean women's subjugation, advocating for women to become independent and to cease being defined by men. Criticized for sometimes performing sensuously on stage and writing some erotic poetry, she said in *Callaloo*, "It's critical for Caribbean women poets to explore their sexuality a lot more rather than allowing the men to define [it]" (613). *See also* Dub Poetry; Performance Poetry.

Further Reading

Sharpe, Jenny. "Dub and Difference: A Conversation with Jean 'Binta' Breeze." *Callaloo* 26, no. 3 (Summer 2003): 607–13.

"Jean 'Binta' Breeze." www.contemporarywriters.com (accessed 9/30/05).

—*D. H. Figueredo*

Breville, Pierre. See Hippolyte, Dominique.

Brierre, Jean Fernand (1909–92)

■

A Haitian poet and diplomat, Brierre was one of the leaders of the anti-American movement during Haiti's occupation by American forces. Representative of the **Négritude** movement, which celebrated African heritage and civilization, his poetry is praised for its political message.

Brierre achieved national fame at the age of twenty with his poem "Le Drame de Marchaterre" (1930). The poem, written in the form known as alexandrine—six rhyming lines—was a protest against the killing of thousands of farmers by American forces in November 1929. The poem celebrated the bravery of Haitian farmers, poorly dressed and poorly armed, facing the more superior American soldiers. The impact was immediate. Says Naomi Garret in *The Renaissance of Haitian Poetry* (1963): "The poem fired the ire of the public against the already detested Americans. It was acclaimed by Haitians who saw in the young author . . . the regenerator of circumstantial poetry, speaking out . . . against injustice and in behalf of his . . . compatriots" (149).

Haitian officials recognized Brierre's talents and political abilities, and in 1933, he was dispatched to Paris as secretary of the Haitian Legation. Prior to his departure, he read to his friends poems from a newly written collection, *Chansons secrétes*. The poems in this volume were not political but of a sentimental nature: romantic and melancholic verses. But there were also poems that expressed the poet's sympathy toward the common people and the urban poor. In 1935, he experimented with fiction, writing the novel *Les horizons sans ciel*.

In 1945, the publication *Haïti-Journal* published the poems Brierre had written while in Europe. One of the poems, "Agonie," speaks of his identification with black people the world over. In 1946, he wrote, *Nous garderons le dieu*, his tribute to Haitian novelist **Jacques Roumain**. In 1947, Brierre published his most famous poem "Black Soul," a history of black oppression since the days of slavery.

In the 1950s, Brierre served in Haiti's Foreign Service, where he earned international recognition for his integrity. In the mid-1950s, while serving as Haiti's ambassador to Argentina, Brierre risked his life to protect Argentine dissidents who had sought refuge in his embassy and had then been kidnapped by the military. Brierre tracked down the kidnappers and sought the release of the exiles. In 2004, the Argentine government honored Brierre's courage with a proclamation. *See also* American Occupation of Haiti, Literature of the (1915–34).

Further Reading

Garret, Naomi M. *The Renaissance of Haitian Poetry*. Paris: Présence africaine, 1963.

Pierre-Louis, Ulysse. *L'univers poétique de Jean F. Rrierre* [sic]: *une obsédante quête d'identité*. Port-au-Prince: Editions Christophe, 1997.

—*D. H. Figueredo*

Brodber, Erna (1940–)

Erna Brodber is a Jamaican novelist who uses her professional training as a psychiatrist and anthropologist to explore the fragmentation and sexual, social, and racial oppression experienced by women in the Anglophone Caribbean. She is a psychiatric anthropologist, writer, and cultural activist.

Brodber was born April 20, 1940, in Woodside, St. Mary, Jamaica. She earned a BA from the then University College of West Indies—now the University of the West Indies—and was its first master's graduate. Erna Brodber was awarded a doctoral fellowship to study psychiatric anthropology at the University of Washington. She also read for a PhD in history at the University of the West Indies. She has variously been public servant, teacher, sociology lecturer, and fellow staff member of the Institute for Social and Economic Research in UWI Mona, Jamaica. In 1984, she left UWI to establish Blackspace, a company devoted to facilitating research on the Africans of the diaspora. Brodber has also done numerous assignments as visiting professor and writer in residence at tertiary institutions regionally and abroad. Her stint as a student in the United States stimulated her interest in Black Power and Women's Liberation movements, and these early influences have had an impact on her literary and academic endeavors.

Brodber stated in the journal *Caribbean Writers* that she stumbled into the writing of fiction while grappling with the "boredom with a social science methodology devoted to objectivity and therefore distancing the researcher from the people." In response, she began to write stories based primarily on her speculations concerning the point of her informant's lives. Her fiction, based on her work as a collector of oral histories, includes *Jane and Louisa Will Soon Come Home* (1980) and *Myal* (1988), which was awarded a Commonwealth Regional Prize for Literature in Louisiana.

Brodber terms *Jane and Louisa Will Soon Come Home* a sociological tool with "activist intentions." Based on material written as a case study for her abnormal psychology class, the novel charts the complex interplay of factors that determine the socialization of a middle-strata Jamaican girl as she negotiates the space between the village and the metropolis; between a relatively ungendered girlhood and the demands of sexual maturation; between negation and repossession of familial and ancestral linkages; between avenues of inner-self-development and pathways of valid social commitment. Maneuvering pathways of upward social mobility proves to be mind bending. Nellie, the novel's protagonist, goes through a process of recuperation that reverses the amnesia that has been identified as a key feature of a Caribbean upbringing. She learns to embrace the natives of her person—be they black, white or "sneaking khaki-lipped" (mulatto); moreover, she comes to recognize and refute the historical processes that have made the black woman's womb into the scrap heap of the world.

In *Jane and Louisa*, Brodber set out to craft a narrative that was short, sharp, and topical, possessing space so that people could do their own dreaming. The narrative coheres through a dense network of images that go beyond obvious and public associations. Instead they delve into concentric circles of private meanings, initiated in the magical world of childhood but translated into an adult mode of perception. The title of the novel, after the game song "Jane and Louisa Will Soon Come Home into This Beautiful Garden," signals that the novel is rooted in the child's rich, imaginative world of magic, mystery, and play; of potencies and of vulnerabilities; of extremities of desire, joy, and compelling fear. It announces a recurrent theme of Caribbean literature: journeying, homecomings, explorations of the garden, landscape, and mindscape. These geographical and psychic terrains have become the legacy of the dispossessed and the exiled of the Caribbean. Her subsequent novel *Myal* deals with zombification of a mulatto girl caught between erasure within a black-dominated village and soul theft by her young white husband, who freezes and objectifies her beloved village life as material for a coon show. The novel *Louisiana* traces the interconnectedness for North American and Jamaican blacks and appropriates the anthropologist's tool—a tape recorder for communication with the spirit world.

All three novels explore the interrelatedness of Africans within the diaspora with boldness, intensity, and authority. Brodber explores the souls of black folk as they inhabit a spatial and temporal continuum spanning islands and continents, past, present, and future, the land of the living and the land of the "undead." She unearths and celebrates a diverse range of cultural, social, historical, and personal connections through voyages of discovery that are personal and representative, individual and communal. Brodber's interrelated narratives present powerful arguments—that soul and spirit sickness often lie at the root of physical ailments; that individual sickness often is an externalization of the collective disease of a people; that the trauma of the capture, the middle passage, and enslavement has left scars on the individual and collective psyches; that the hurt runs deep and therefore the healing requires in-depth excavations and radical treatment. Even as Brodber creates increasing acceptance for alternative ways of knowing, the steady scientific orientation of the sociologist-anthropologist-ethnographer-ethnomusicologist crafts the bedrock of the novels, which delves into the abnormal and the paranormal. In the process, she develops and masterfully wields narrative strategies of fragmentation and temporal and spatial dislocation. Psychic wholeness for the protagonist comes from reuniting within the individual psyche all of the opposites that have been fragmented and split off during the individual and collective socialization processes.

Further Reading

Brodber, Erna. "Fiction in the Scientific Procedure." In *Caribbean Women Writers: Essays from the First International Conference*, edited by Selwyn Cudjoe, 164–68. Wellesley, MA: Calaloux Publications, 1990.

Dance, Daryl Cumber. "Go Eena Kumbla: A Coparison of Erna Brodber's Jane Louisa Will Soon Come Home and Toni Cade Bambara." In. *Caribbean Women Writers: Essays from the First International Conference*, edited by Selwyn Cudjoe, 169–86. Wellesley, MA: Calaloux Publications, 1990.

—Paula Morgan

Brouard, Carl (1902–65)

One of the first writers to use Haitian folklore, traditions, and vodouism in his writings, Broaurd was a bohemian poet who was described as a "poéte maudit," a doomed poet who chose a life of alcoholism and sexuality. According to J. Michael Dash, in *The Other America* (1998), Brouard was inspired by nightclubs, prostitutes, and drunks. Brouard helped the Haitianization of his country's literature.

Born into a wealthy family, Carl Brouard, who was educated in Paris, left the comfort of his home to move into Haiti's slums, choosing a bohemian lifestyle and marrying a woman his relatives deemed inferior to his social class. During the 1920s, he became one of the leading writers of the journal *La Revue indigène* and was also one of the best-known members of the literary movement **indigènisme,** which was nationalistic and celebrated Haiti's history and culture. In 1938, he became the editor of the journal *Les Griots*.

Much of his early poetry was published in *La Revue indigène*. His poems describe the life of the poor and use African and Haitian imagery, which include allusions to vodouism, a practice not common at the time. His poetry is sensual, simple, and direct. One of his best-known poems is "J'ai peur de frôler vos doigts si bruns, si longs" (1937):

> J'ai peur de vos yeux de vos regards . . .
> de vos sourires, de votre nom perfumé
> comme un jasmine du Cap

(I'm afraid of your eyes, of your looks / . . . of your smile, your named perfumed / like a jasmine. . . .)

Brouard also explored in his poetry themes of Afro-centricism and political power based along racial lines. In the 1940s, he veered away from liberal ideas and became concerned with mysticism, Catholicism, and French culture. During this period, he grew emotionally unstable. Scholar Naomi M. Garret, in *The Renaissance of Haitian Poetry* (1963), says of the poet: "Abhorring pedantry in any fashion, he has used natural, unadorned language befitting his subjects, to depict the . . . realism of the common people" (129-130). *See also* Haitian Literature, History of.

Further Reading

Dash, J. Michael. *The Other America: Caribbean Literature in a New World Context.* Charlottesville: University Press of Virginia, 1998.

Garret, Naomi M. *The Renaissance of Haitian Poetry.* Paris: Présence africaine, 1963.

—*D. H. Figueredo*

Brown, Lennox (1935–)

Brown is a Trinidadian playwright and musician. He has spent most of his life in Canada.

A native of Port-of-Spain, Trinidad, Brown grew up in a slum. He escaped the poverty and violence that plagued his childhood by spending many hours at the library. He showed a talent for writing as a teenager and wrote for the *Trinidadian Guardian* and *Evening News*, covering gang activities and crime in the slums.

In his early twenties, he worked at the Magistrate's Court. He left for Canada and attended the University of Western Ontario, earning a BA in journalism in 1961. From 1965 to 1968, he was appointed editor of the Canadian Broadcasting Corporation. In 1969, he received an MA in journalism from the University of Toronto. That same year, he published *A Ballet Behind the Bridge*, inspired by his experiences growing up in a slum.

In 1972, his radio drama *Saturday Druid of Man Against Himself* was produced by the Canadian Broadcasting Corporation. That same year, Eugene O'Neill National Playwright Conference premiered his drama *Prodigal Black Stone*. Many of his plays have been read at festivals but have not been published.

As a singer and guitarist, Brown has performed in the Anglophone Caribbean. As a writer and social observer, Brown has been published in Canadian journals, often commenting on what he sees as the absence of a black culture in Canada.

Further Reading

Clarke, George Elliot. "Contesting a model blackness: A meditation on African Canadian African Americanism, or the structures of African Canadianite. *Essays on Canadian Writing*, no. 63 (Spring 1998): 1–55.

—*D. H. Figueredo*

Brown, Wayne (1944–)

A poet from Trinidad, Wayne Brown belongs to the generation of West Indian writers who followed on the footsteps of a group of authors, including Nobel Prize–winner **Derek Walcott**, who first brought international attention to Anglophone Caribbean literature in the 1960s and 1970s. Unlike that previous generation, which was inspired by the independence movements, Brown matured during the era when the former colonies were redefining and reinventing themselves.

Brown was born on July 18, 1944. His mother died while giving birth, and he was raised by an aunt and uncle until he was sent to boarding school. Of a rebellious nature, at the age of sixteen he went to live with his father, a judge. Feeling lonely and nostalgic for his childhood, Brown read extensively, especially the poetry of Derek Walcott, who influenced his writings and anti-colonialist views. When Brown was twenty-one he traveled to Jamaica and enrolled at the Mona campus of the University of West Indies; there, he befriended the would-be poets **Anthony McNeill** and Mervyn Morris.

In 1972, Brown published his first collection of poetry, *On the Coast*. The poems in the volume were lyrical and expressed a combination of the poet's isolation and unhappiness as well as social and political commentary. During this period he researched and wrote a biography of **Edna Manley**, the influential literary editor and mentor and mother of Jamaica's prime minister Michael Manley (1924–97). The book was published in 1976 under the title of *Edna Manley: The Private Years, 1900–1938*. In 1977 Brown returned to Trinidad, where he taught at Fatima College; he was also appointed information officer at the American embassy in Port-of-Spain, Trinidad-Tobago. In 1983, he became a columnist for the *Trinidad Guardian*. In 1989, he published a collection of stories, *The Child of the Sea*, and a book of poems, *Voyages*. In these writings he explored the themes of solidarity with Latin American culture while continuing his fascination with describing the sea and marine life. In the 1990s, he relocated to England.

Critic **Kenneth Ramchand**, writing in *Fifty Caribbean Writers*, describes Brown as a poet who explores literary archetypes—such as the European colonialist and the melancholic fisherman—and who has been influenced by his wide reading of Caribbean and European literature, including such writers as Walcott, **Kamau Brathwaite**, and **Jean Rhys**. But Ramchand concludes that "Brown's voice is distinctive and [his] struggle between form and energy is . . . an epic one" (94).

Further Reading

Ramchand, Kenneth. "Wayne Vincent Brown (1944–)." In *Fifty Caribbean Writers: A Bio-bibliographical Critical Sourcebook*, edited by Daryl Cumber Dance, 83–94. Westport, CT: Greenwood Press, 1986.

—*D. H. Figueredo*

Brown Girl, Brownstones (1959)

Though initially ignored by the media and the general public, this autobiographical novel by **Paule Marshall** was first published in 1959 and then reprinted in 1971. Since then it has become a part of the American literary canon and a favorite of young-adult readers.

The novel tells the story of Selina Boyce and the conflict between her parents. Her father, Deighton Boyce, is a kind but weak man, a musician who longs for a return to Barbados. Her mother, Silla Boyce, works in a factory and manages to buy a brownstone, which she then parcels out into rooms she can rent. The overpowering figure of the mother, represented by the solidly built brownstone, overcomes the romantic father, represented by the hazy memories of his Edenic childhood, who sets out to Barbados to find his own dream but dies, while at sea, a victim of suicide. Selina wants to escape her mother and does so through juvenile rebellion, arguments, forbidden romances, and rejection of her mother's values. However, Selina is as driven as her mother and is quite successful in school; her mother's fighting spirit, which she has inherited, helps her overcome her encounters with racism. By the end of the novel, Selina opts for a return to Barbados.

The novel's appeal rests on the depiction of Selina as she matures from a young girl into a young woman. Her growth contains all the classic elements of a coming-of-age novel: adoration of the parents, rebellion against parental authority, death of a beloved family member, sexual stirrings and first sexual experience, and the cutting of the metaphorical umbilical cord by moving away from home. As appealing, and even more powerful, is the relationship between Selina and her mother, a relationship in which the conflicts are compounded by issues of race and racism. Critic Rosalie Riegle Troester points out in the essay "Turbulence and Tenderness: Mothers, Daughters, and 'Othermorthers' in Paule Marshall's *Brown Girl, Brownstones*" that black mothers sometimes protect their daughters to the point of isolation, creating during the teen years a potential destructive drift between mother and daughter. She adds that the novel through "the turbulent yet occasionally tender connections between Selina and the mother . . . both strengthens our understanding of the Black mother-daughter bond and gives us tolerance toward the inevitable conflicts within such relationships" (164).

The third endearing component in the novel is the father, a romantic figure who nevertheless is representative of sexism. For in his dreams of returning to Barbados, Selina's father imagines owning land and bossing his wife and other women. For Selina's father, success is the ability to assert his masculinity by belittling women's power. As Selina searches for her own persona and her own independence, she knows that ultimately she must rebel against her beloved father. And in doing so and in spite of herself, she grows closer to her mother. Writes Troester:

> Selina finally admits the joining with her mother and this admission frees her to leave. In a final gesture of goodbye to childhood, she throws one of her silver Island bangles to the ghosts of her youth, keeping the other as a sign of bonding with her community. Selina/Silla is a woman. (172)

See also Anglophone Caribbean Literature, History of; Mother-Daughter Relationships.

Further Reading

Marshall, Paule. *Brown Girl, Bronwstones*. New York: Feminist Press and City University of New York, 1981.

Troester, Rosalie Riegle. "Turbulence and Tenderness: Mothers, Daughters, and 'Othermorthers' in Paule Marshall's *Brown Girl, Bronwstones*." In *Double Stitch: Black Women Write About Mothers and Daughters*, edited by Patricia Bell-Scott, et al. New York: Harper Perennial, 1991.

—*D. H. Figueredo*

Buesa, José Ángel (1910–82)

Cuba's most popular twentieth-century love poet, José Ángel Buesa was not taken seriously by literary critics yet had a large readership that has remained loyal decades after his death. He became known for expressing in accessible language the love felt between a man and a woman.

José Ángel Buesa del Regato was born in the province of Las Villas—now Cienfuegos—Cuba, on February 9, 1910. In the late 1920s, he moved to Havana, where he worked in radio, writing scripts, directing, and producing programs. In 1932, he published his first book of poetry, *La fuga de las horas*. By 1963, the year he left Cuba, he had written more than sixteen books of poetry. He traveled to El Salvador, Mexico, and Spain before settling in the Dominican Republic, which he found similar to Cuba and where he felt most welcomed. In the Dominican Republic he worked for a television network, managed the journal *Aula*, and taught at the Universidad Nacional **Pedro Henríquez Ureña**. His Dominican peers, readers, and students appreciated Buesa and his craft to such an extent that the Dominican Academy of the Spanish Language nominated him for the Nobel Prize for Literature in 1974.

Buesa's most famous book of poetry is *Oasis*, published in 1943. The volume contains one of Buesa's most memorable poems, "Poema del renunciamiento," which begins with the line "Pasaras por mi lado sin saber que pasaste," meaning "You will walk past me and not know you did so." This line is memorized and often recited by Buesa's fans, even today. The volume has never been out of print.

Buesa also wrote poems about historical figures and events, such as "Canto a Duarte" (1939), to honor Dominican patriot and writer **Juan Pablo Duarte**, and "Odas por la Victoria" (1943), celebrating Russia's victory over Germany during World War II, and meditative exercises, such as "Los naipes marcados" (1974), wherein he contemplates old age, life after death, and loneliness. His poems are essentially written in rhymed verses and traditional meter. A traditionalist, he advocated versification and believed poems should express genuine emotions rather than experimentation. Many of these ideas were expressed in his book *Método de versificación* (1974), a manual for would-be poets.

Buesa's poems have been translated into English, French, German, Polish, and Portuguese, among others languages. His popularity extends beyond the Caribbean to Latin America, where lines from his love poems are often used in ads for dating services. *See also* Romanticismo/Romanticism.

Further Reading

Buesa, José Ángel. *Año bisiesto: autobiografía informal*. Santo Domingo, República Dominicana: Universidad Nacional Pedro Henríquez Ureña, 1981.

"El Poeta José Ángel Buesa." *Bohemia News* 33, no. 25 (July 2003): 7.

—D. H. Figueredo

Burgos, Julia de (1914–53)

The most renowned woman poet in Puerto Rico, Julia de Burgos wrote about the island's natural beauty, her desire for independence from the United States, and her search for true love. Neglected during her lifetime, Burgos is considered one of the great poets of Latin America. Her passionate poems speak of women's needs to achieve autonomy and equality.

Julia de Burgos was born on February 17, 1914, in Santa Cruz, Puerto Rico, into a poor but literate family. As a child, her father introduced her to such classics as *Don Quixote* and *Robinson Crusoe* and told her about the lives of such great figures as Simón Bolívar (1783–1830) and Napoleon Bonaparte (1768–1821). Her mother nurtured the child's sensibilities and often walked with her on the banks of the Río Grande de Loíza. Years later, in 1938, Burgos wrote

A legendary and tragic figure from Puerto Rico, Julia de Burgos is one of the best poets of the Spanish language. *Source: Centro de Estudios Puertorriqueños.*

¡Río Grande de Loíza! . . . Alárgate en mi espíritu
y deja que mi alma se pierda en tus riachuelos
para buscar la fuente que te robó de niño
y en un ímpetu loco te devolvió al sendero.

(Grande de Loíza river! . . . Stretch out in my spirit / and let my soul get lost in your currents / to find the source that robbed you as a child / and made thrust that returned you to your path.)

Burgos attended primary school in Santa Cruz, often with financial help from her neighbors. In 1928, her family moved to Río Piedras, where Burgos enrolled at the Universidad de Puerto Rico High School and then at the university itself. She earned a teacher's certificate and in 1935 became a teacher at a small rural school. Always interested in education, Burgos used every opportunity she had to take courses at different schools in the cities she lived in throughout her life.

Inspired by the independence movement on the island and by the political actions and rhetoric of the Nationalist Party during the mid-1930s, Burgos wrote the book of political poems, *Poemas exactos a mí misma* (1937), which she printed privately. In 1938, she published *Poema en veinte surcos*, which includes her famous "Río Grande de Loíza." This was followed by *Canción de la verdad sencilla* (1939), love poems that were awarded the poetry prize of the Institute of Puerto Rican Literature.

In 1939, Burgos left her beloved Puerto Rico for New York City, which she found culturally exciting but inhospitable. A year later she went to Cuba, where she stayed until 1942. She felt at home in Cuba, so similar to Puerto Rico, and befriended many illustrious writers, including the Chilean poet Pablo Neruda (1904–73), who was charmed by her looks and talent and promised to write a prologue for the collection she was writing, *El mar y tu*, eventually published in 1954.

Her happy stay in Cuba ended when her lover, a scholar from the Dominican Republic, decided that Burgos needed to return to New York City. Despite that Burgos was a feminist rebelling against the culture of machismo, or the values of a male-driven society, she boarded a plane for Manhattan. In New York City she worked at diverse jobs, ranging from office work to seamstress, though she wrote for the newspaper *Pueblos Hispanos*, where she published many of her poems. She married a musician and lived in Washington, D.C., for a short while.

The several unhappy love affairs that she had experienced—of which she wrote "Here I am / An unruly star, let loose / searching among men for the victim of light / (1939)—the nostalgia for Puerto Rico, the lack of recognition of her genius, and the financial hardships affected her mental and physical health, complicated by her descent into alcoholism. In 1943, she developed cirrhosis of the liver and spent time at various hospitals. One day in July of 1946, while visiting relatives in Brooklyn, she disappeared. She was found unconscious and without personal documents in Harlem and was rushed to a hospital, where she died of pneumonia. Her friends tracked down her remains to the city's morgue and had her transported to Puerto Rico, where she is buried near her beloved Río Grande de Loíza.

Since her death, Burgos's fame has grown throughout Latin America. In the United States, Puerto Ricans from New York City regard her as an early victim of racism and neglect and as a pioneer in the internationalization of Puerto Rican literature. Her poems are regularly anthologized in numerous publications.

Further Reading

Burgos, Julia de. *Obra poética*. San Juan: Instituto de Cultura, 1961.

Rodríguez Pagán, Juan Antonio. *Julia en blanco y negro*. San Juan, Puerto Rico: Sociedad Histórica de Puerto Rico, 2000.

Vázquez, Lourdes. *Hablar sobre Julia: Julia de Burgos: bibliografía 1934–2002*. Austin, TX: SALALM Secretariat, 2002.

—Asela R. Laguna and D. H. Figueredo

Burr-Reynaud, Frédéric (1884–1946)

Burr-Reynaud was a Haitian poet and playwright. He was also a public servant.

Burr-Reynaud was born on July 9, 1884, in Port-au-Prince, Haiti. He attended the Lycée Pétion and was active in cultural and public affairs. In 1930, he was elected to Haiti's Chamber of Deputies. A member of the Society of Letters and

Arts, he promoted Haitian culture. While involved in political activities, he wrote articles and essays for journals and founded the review *La Forge*.

Burr-Reynaud saw an affirmation of a Haitian identity on the island's flora and fauna as well as on its Amerindian heritage. He reflected this view in the book of poetry that became his best-known work: *Poèmes quisqueyens*. In 1911, he wrote the play *Anacaona*, which again celebrated Haiti's original settlers: Anacaona was a Taíno—Amerindian—queen known for her ability to compose music. She opposed the Spanish conquistadores and was executed.

Throughout the 1930s and 1940s, Burr-Reynaud wrote poems that dealt with political issues, *Anathèmes* (1930) and *C'est la guerre* (1943), but did not directly challenge the American forces occupying the nation. In 1940, he also wrote a major study on Haitian's flora: *Visages d'arbres et de fruits haïtiens*.

Overall, though, critic Naomi M. Garret, in *The Renaissance of Haitian Poetry* (1963), believed that Burr-Reynaud was uncomfortable with the American occupation of Haiti and sought escape in the past rather than expressing a political view.

Further Reading

Garret, Naomi M. *The Renaissance of Haitian Poetry.* Paris: Présence africaine, 1963.

Herdeck, Donald, ed. *Caribbean Writers: A Bio-Bibliographical-Critical Encyclopedia.* Washington, DC: Three Continents, Press, 1979.

—*D. H. Figueredo*

Byrne, Bonifacio (1861–1936)

■

Bonifacio Byrne is a nineteenth-century Cuban poet and patriot best remembered for the poem "A mi bandera," written in 1899 and expressing his anger and disappointment at American military presence in Cuba at the end of the Spanish-Cuban-American War of 1898. Described as "the war poet," he was also a prolific journalist and dramatist.

Bonifacio Byrne was born on March 3, 1861 in the province of Matanzas, Cuba. At the age of nineteen he founded two newspapers. In 1893, he wrote the book of poetry *Excéntricas*, which brought him recognition and identified him as a promising young poet. Two years later he wrote a poem describing the execution by the Spanish authorities of a close friend who had conspired against the Spanish Crown. Because of this poem, Byrne was forced to leave Cuba, settling in Tampa, where he promoted Cuba's independence from Spain. He wrote political articles expressing that view in the separatist periodicals *Patria*, *El porvenir* and *El expedicionario*.

In 1899, he returned to Cuba. As the ship entered Havana Bay, Byrne spotted two flags atop the Morro Castle: the Cuban and the American flags. The indignation he felt at seeing the United States attempting to share Cuba's victory in its war against Spain prompted him to write his famous poem "To My Flag." In the poem he describes how the Cuban flag witnessed the many battles against Spanish soldiers where Cuban insurgents fought and died bravely and warns that the presence of the American flag testifies to Americans' desires on the island. Fearing that one day Cuba would lose its independence again, he ends the poem with a stanza that is memorized and often repeated by many Cubans on the island:

> Si desecha en menudos pedazos
> llega a ser mi bandera algún día . . .
> ¡nuestros muertos alzando los brazos
> la sabrán defender todavía! . . .

(If our flag is someday / torn to shreds / Our dead, raising their arms, / Will still know to defend it. . . .)

Inspired by the war of independence, Byrne wrote numerous poems about the conflict, describing battles and celebrating Cubans' courage. He wrote for several newspapers, experimented with drama, and was working on a novel when he died in 1936.

Further Reading

Martínez Carmenate, Urbano. *Bonifacio Byrne*. Habana: Editora Política, 1999.

Moliner, Israel M. *Índice bio-bibliográfico de Bonifacio Byrne*. Matanzas, Cuba: Atenas de Cuba, 1943.

—*D. H. Figueredo*

C

Cabral, Manuel del (1907–1999)

■

Considered one of the greatest poets of Latin America, Cabral was a writer who traveled extensively throughout Latin America and Europe but who nevertheless wrote works that celebrated the beauty and culture of his country, the Dominican Republic. He is one Latin America's most anthologized poets.

Born on March 7, 1907, in Santiago, Dominican Republic, Manuel del Cabral was the descendant of two presidents—José María Cabral (1816–99) and Marcos Cabral (1843–1903). His father expected young Cabral to become an attorney, but the youth was more interested in literature and writing rather than in attending college. Cabral started to write love poetry when he was a teenager, and by his midtwenties he had published two books of poetry, *Pilón, cantos del terruño y otros poemas* (1932) and a privately printed collection, *Color de agua*, written in the 1930s but not issued by a publisher until 1973.

During the thirties, Cabral associated himself with a group of writers that would achieve international recognition: **Juan Bosch, Hector Incháustegui Cabral,** and **Pedro Henríquez Ureña.** These writers, and a few other friends, would meet in a room in Henríquez Ureña's house and would spend hours reading their works and discussing literature; these **tertulias,** informal literary salons, would become known as the group of La Cueva, "the cave," referring to the room where they met.

In 1938, Cabral boarded a steamboat for New York City, where he worked as a window washer. A few months later, he received an unexpected telegram from the Dominican Republic informing him that he had been assigned a minor diplomatic post in Washington, D.C. From that moment on, he became a globetrotter, spending a short time in Washington and then traveling to South America and Europe, befriending along the way such writers as Chilean Pablo Neruda (1904–73). Despite his incessant movement from one country to another, Cabral continued to write, finishing at least six books during the 1940s.

Critic Bruno Rosario Candelier—quoted in *Spanish American Authors* (1992), edited by **Angel Flores**—describes Cabral's productivity as consisting of three themes: black themes, social message, and the metaphysical (147). His poems were essentially rhythmic and rich in metaphors. His most famous poems are "Trópico negro" (1942), "Sangre mayor" (1945), "De este lado del mar" (1948), and "Los huéspedes secretos" (1951). Many of his poems were collected in the volume *Antología poesía* (2002). Cabral also wrote short stories—*Cuentos cortos con pantalones largos* (1981)—novels –*El escupido* (1970) and *El presidente negro* (1973)—and an autobiography, *Historia de mi voz* (1964).

In 1992, he was awarded the Dominican Republic's National Literature Prize. He passed away on May 14, 1999, in Santo Domingo. *See also* Trujillo Era.

Further Reading

Flores, Angel, ed. *Spanish American Authors: The Twentieth Century*. New York: Wilson, 1992.

Prono, Marta, ed. *Manuel del Cabral y su obra: comentarios y crítica*. Santo Domingo, República Dominicana: Comisión Permanente de la Feria del Libro, 2001.

—*D. H. Figueredo*

Cabrera, Francisco Manrique (1908–78)

Cabrera was a poet, essayist, and lecturer from Puerto Rico. He was the author of the first history of Puerto Rican literature, *La historia de la literatura puertorriqueña* (1956).

Born in Bayamón, Puerto Rico, Cabrera graduated as a teacher from the Universidad de Puerto Rica in 1932. He became interested in the depiction of blacks in Spanish literature, and in 1934 he wrote *El negro en la literatura española de ayer*. The work served as his thesis for the completion of his PhD at the Universidad de Madrid in 1934.

Returning to Puerto Rico, he was appointed professor of Hispanic studies at his alma mater. In 1945, he began to write a series of essays on Puerto Rican authors such as **Manuel Alonso, Eugenio María de Hostos,** and **Manuel Zeno Gandía.** These would be collected a decade later in *La historia de la literatura puertorriqueña*. But Cabrera also wrote poetry, *Poemas de mi tierra* (1936), *Antología de literatura infantil* (1943), and *Huella-Sombra y cantar* (1943), which was awarded a prize by the Instituto de Literatura Puertorriqueña.

Poemas de mi tierra is Cabrera's most famous book of poetry. He wrote it while living in Madrid and homesick for Puerto Rico. The verses served as a vehicle of imaginary transportation, and throughout the volume, Cabrera toured his beloved island: the little villages, the huts, the fields, the flora, and the fauna. But rather than producing a sentimental, nostalgic exercise, Cabrera presented a mature work with controlled emotions and linguistic mastery. Scholar José Emilio González, in *Poesía y lengua en la obra de Francisco Manrique Cabrera* (1976), writes: "Cabrera achieved . . . a rarety: a true book of poetry. A book well integrated, coordinated, and in concert. But more importantly . . . one of the best books" expressing a Puerto Rican identity (59).

His second-best-known work, a history of Puerto Rican literature, was both celebrated and condemned when it was first published. Critics commented that the work excluded famous Puerto Rican writers, but Cabrera defended his choice by explaining that fame was relative and a temporary assignation.

Further Reading

González, José Emilio. *Poesía y lengua en la obra de Francisco Manrique Cabrera*. Río Piedras, Puerto Rico: Editorial Cultural, 1976.

—D. H. Figueredo

Cabrera, Lydia (1900–91)

∎

A short-story writer and scholar, Cabrera was one of the first writers in Cuba to explore Afro-Cuban culture and to preserve in print African legends familiar to many Afro-Cubans.

Cabrera was born in Havana, Cuba, on May 20, 1900, the child of a wealthy and long-established Cuban family. Her family traveled extensively, spending time in Europe and in the United States, where they kept an apartment in New York City. Cabrera was sent to private schools in Cuba and also studied at the Sociedad Económica de Amigos del Pais, where her father was the president of the Education Department. She was also tutored at home, which she preferred. As a child, Cabrera spent hours listening to stories told by the black servants in her household. She was fascinated by the African legends they narrated. These tales would serve as the basis of her first book, *Cuentos negros de Cuba* (1936), regarded as classic of Cuban literature.

In 1927, Cabrera went to Paris, where she took art courses, visited museums, attended lectures, and held **tertulias**, literary salons, in her apartment. While in France, she was exposed to Indian mythology and Chinese folklore. She found similarities in all these stories from Asia, Africa, and Cuba and felt encouraged to explore Afro-Cuban traditions, which she did upon her return to Cuba in 1939. In 1940, she wrote *¿Por que? Cuentos negros de Cuba*, which emphasized Afro-Cubans' connections with natural forces as manifestations of African gods. In 1954, she wrote the seminal study *El monte: igbo, finda, ewe orisha, vititi nfinda: notas sobre las religiones, la magia, las supersticiones y el folklore de los negros criollos y del pueblo de Cuba*, an in-depth analysis of the Yoruba religion in Cuba.

Cabrera left Cuba after **Fidel Castro** took over the government in 1959. She settled in Miami, where she supported herself by selling some of the jewels she had been able to take with her from Cuba. The trauma of the Cuban revolution and the experience of exile curtailed her literary productivity, and she was not able to write again until the late 1960s, when she expanded *El monte*. In 1971, she wrote *Ayapá, cuentos de Jicotea*, followed by *Yemayá y Ochún* in 1974.

Cabrera's work is both folkloric and imaginative, making it difficult to assess what pieces are her own short stories, based on Afro-Cuban mythology and her imagination, and which are an actual retelling of a legend. However, the musicality of her prose and her ability to explain complex religious concepts—such as animalism, spirituality, and the like—in an accessible language makes her writing engaging. The many books she wrote helped to popularize Santería, the Afro-Cuban religion. *See also* Santería in Literature.

Cabrera passed away in Miami, Florida, on September 19, 1991.

Further Reading

Gutiérrez, Mariela. *Lydia Cabrera, aproximaciones mítico-simbólicas a su cuentística.* Madrid: 1997.

—*D. H. Figueredo*

Cabrera Infante, Guillermo (1929–2005)

The winner of the 1997 Cervantes Prize, the most prestigious literary award in the Spanish-speaking world, Cabrera Infante was the most outstanding Cuban novelist of his generation and one of the world's great writers. Initially criticized and then ignored for his opposition to the regime of **Fidel Castro,** he was in the late 1990s recognized for his linguistic and comedic genius.

A native of the province of Oriente, Cabrera Infante's parents were members of the Communist Party. When he was twelve years old, his parents moved to Havana, where he studied medicine. He did not complete the degree, deciding to pursue literature and writing instead. In 1951, he cofounded the Cinemáteca Cubana, an organization dedicated to the study and promotion of films. From 1954 to 1960 he was a film critic for the journal *Carteles.* His cinematographic articles were signed G. Cain.

When Fidel Castro overthrew Fulgencio Batista (1901–73) in 1959, Cabrera Infante embraced the revolutionary government. He headed the Cuban film institute and published his first book, *Así en la paz como en la guerra* (1960). In 1961, he confronted the revolutionary regime over the censorship of his brother's film *P.M.,* about Cuba's night life. The confrontation ended with the government closing down the literary

Guillermo Cabrera Infante was a Cuban author often compared to James Joyce for his linguistic novels and clever use of grammar and diction. *Source: Americas Society. Courtesy of Elsa M. Ruiz.*

supplement *Lunes de Revolución*, of which Cabrera Infante had been a cofounder. To protest, Cabrera Infante resigned from the film institute and accepted the post of cultural attaché in Brussels. Three years later, he sought exile, first in Spain and then in England.

In 1967, he published his most famous work, *Tres tristes tigres*, a classic of the literature of the **Latin American Boom,** and one of the great literary works of the second half of the twentieth century. The novel is written in the deepest Cuban vernacular, yet it is accessible to anyone who reads Spanish. The English version, *Three Trapped Tigers* (1971), was more than a translation. Cabrera Infante rewrote it substantially to make all the puns—for which he was notorious—work in English. The novel tells the story of a photographer, an aspiring actor, and a journalist making the rounds of Havana nightclubs, just before the triumph of the revolution. The narrative is filled with places and people typical of the author's beloved city in the 1950s. But *Tres tristes tigres* transcends time and place, rising to the universal.

Though the novel was welcomed as a classic, Cabrera Infante was nevertheless ostracized by intellectuals in Europe. It was a time when writers and academics were in support of Fidel Castro and Cabrera Infante's criticism of the Cuban leader made him persona non grata within literary circles. The isolation he experienced and lack of recognition contributed to a mental breakdown he suffered in the early 1970s. Upon recovering, he plunged into writing once again, publishing over fifteen books. One of the best known from this period is his autobiography, *La Habana para un infante difunto* (1979). Cabrera Infante took the title from a French work by composer Maurice Ravel (1875–1937), *Pavane pour une infante défunte*. Ravel wrote his pavane—a courtly eighteenth-century dance—in memory of a dead, "défunte," child princess, an "infante." Cabrera Infante's book was a eulogy upon a different kind of loss: the death of a self that existed as he grew into adulthood in a pre-Castro era that is forever gone.

In the 1980s, Cabrera Infante wrote several books of essays, including a new edition of *Un oficio del siglo 20: G. Caín 1954–1960* (1981) a collection of his cinema writings, and *Holy Smoke* (1985), a humorous exploration of the cigar industry and cigar smoking written in English. During the 1980s he recorded some of his works for the Library of Congress and lectured to packed audiences in such institutions as the Research Libraries of New York Public Library. In the 1990s, he wrote *Diablesas y diosas: 14 perversas para 15 autores* (1990), *Mea Culpa* (1991), *Delito por bailar el chachachá* (1995), *Ella cantaba boleros* (1996), and *Cine o sardina* (1997).

Cabrera Infante died of a blood infection on February 21, 2005, in London. He was described as Cuba's James Joyce (1882–1941) for mapping a spiritual Havana with linguistic inventiveness, the way Joyce did with Dublin. He was also Cuba's Cervantes (1547–1616): his ironic humor came with a towering compassion for characters lost in mazes of their own making as well as by a society that insisted on trapping its people.

Further Reading

Gil López, Ernesto. *Guillermo Cabrera Infante: La Habana, el lenguaje y la cineomatofía.* Tenerife: ACT, Cabildo Insular de Tenerife, 1991.

Hartman, Carmen Teresa. *Cabrera Infante's Tres tristes tigres: The Trapping Effect of the Signifier Over Subject and Text*. New York: P. Lang, 2003.

—*Roger E. Hernández*

Cade, Robin. See Nicholson, Christopher R.

Cahier d'un retour au pays natal (1939, 1947)

The most discussed literary work in the Francophone Caribbean, this epic poem was the manifesto of the **Négritude** movement—which celebrated African heritage—was a political treatise that forecast the author's own political trajectory as Martinique's longtime mayor, and was considered one of the best-written works in the French language. *Cahier d'un retour au pays natal*, translated in English as *Notebook of a Return to My Native Land* (1995), was written by **Aimé Césaire**.

The surrealist poem uses uncontrolled and free-flowing writing, dismissing poetic forms, such as rhythm and meter, emphasizes sentiments, and employs repetitive patterns. Consisting of seventy pages, the poem begins with a desolate description of the poet's country and the legacy of colonialism. Césaire describes Martinique's capital, Port-au-Prince as "cette ville plate . . . trébuchée de son bon sens, inerte" (a flat town . . . stripped of common sense, inert). This desolation is experienced by the island's inhabitants, the descendants of slaves whose humanity was belittled and silenced by the white colonialist. From this silence, the poet raises a new voice: "Je retrouverais le secret des grandes communications . . . Qui ne me comprendrait pas ne comprendrait . . . le rugissement du tigre" (I would rediscover the secret of great communications . . . He who does not understand me would not understand the roaring of the tiger).

With the new voice, the poet proclaims his African heritage, celebrates Africa's natural condition over a mechanized Europe—seeing in virginal Africa the beginning of the world and in Europe a tired, dying world—and glorifies the color of his skin:

> ma négritude n'est pas une taie d'eau morte sur l'oeil mort de la terre
> ma négritude n'est ni une tour ni une cathédrale
> elle plonge dans la chair rouge du sol

(my negritude is not a spot of dead water over the dead earth / it plunges into the red flesh of the soil).

After inventorying the evils that Europe has visited on Africa and the Caribbean and the attempts at the gradual psychological and physical destruction of blacks by whites, the poet draws a portrait of the raising black man, standing triumphantly on the slave ship, free:

> debout
> et
> libre.

Césaire concludes the poem with an invitation to the world to embrace the black man and for the black man to lead the peoples of the world:

> embrasse, embrasse Nous . . .
> monte . . .
> monte
> monte
> monte
> Je te suis . . . .

(embrace, embrace Us . . . / rise / rise / rise / I follow you).

Césaire wrote the first version of the poem in 1938; it was published in the journal *Volontes* in 1939. Césaire rewrote the poem several times and published in 1947 the version that is known to most readers. Since then, the poem has been reprinted countless times.

Further Reading

Césaire, Aimé. *Cahier d'un retour au pays natal*. Paris: Presence Africaine, 1951.

———. *Notebook of a Return to My Native Land/Cahier d'un retour au pays natal*. Translated by Mireille Rosello with Annie Pritchard. Newcastle upon Tyne, UK: Bloodaxe Books, 1995.

—*D. H. Figueredo*

Cain, G. See Cabrera Infante, Guillermo.

Caliban

■

During the second half of the twentieth century, Caribbean authors saw in Caliban, the monster created by William Shakespeare (1564–1616) in *The Tempest*, a metaphor for Latin America and its treatment of it by the Europeans. Caliban was the Native American, the colonized; Prospero, its master, was Europe, the colonialist. **Roberto Fernández Retamar**, from Cuba, wrote in his famous and controversial essay "Calibán," entitled in English "Caliban: Notes Toward a Discussion of Culture in Our America": "Próspero invadió las islas, mató a nuestros antepasados, esclavizó a Calibán y le enseñó su idioma para poder entenderse con él" (39), meaning "Prospero invaded the islands, killed our ancestors, enslaved Caliban, and taught him his language to make himself understood" (14).

Fernández Retamar was not the first to interpret Caliban in this light. The metaphor surfaced in the 1950s in a book entitled *Prospero and Caliban: The Psychology of Colonization*. The author, the Frenchman O. Manoni, identified Caliban with the colonies. The metaphor was further explored by the Barbadian **George**

Lamming in his autobiography *The Pleasures of Exile* (1960). The theme was picked up again in 1969 by **Aimé Césaire**, from Martinique and one of the founders of **Négritude**, in his play *Une tempête: d'après de "La Tempete" de Sheakespeare: Adaptation pour un théâtre nègre* and, in the same year, by Barbadian poet **Edward Brathwaite** in his collection of poetry *Islands*. This interpretation is commonly accepted by Caribbean writers like **Paule Marshall**, from Barbados, who alludes to it in her fiction, and Cuban American **Virgil Suárez**—Caliban is a character in his book of poetry *Guide to the Blue Tongue* (2002).

Caliban is also representative of "the other," the figure who is neither white nor European and therefore not readily accepted by white Europeans and Americans. *See also* Postcolonialism.

Further Reading

Brathwaite, Edward Kamau. *Islands*. London: Oxford University Press, 1969.

Césaire, Aimé. *Une tempête: d'après "La Tempete" de Shakespeare. Adaptation pour un théâtre nègre*. Paris: Éditions du Seuil, 1969.

Fernández Retamar, Roberto. *Caliban and Other essays*. Minneapolis: University of Minnesota Press, 1989.

———. *Calibán. Contra la Leyenda Negra*. Lérida, España. Ediciones de la Universita de Lleida, 1995.

Lamming, George. *The Pleasures of Exile*. London: M. Joseph, 1960.

—*D. H. Figueredo*

CAM. See Caribbean Artists Movement.

Camille, Roussan (1912–61)

Camille was a politically engaged poet from Haiti. His poetry affirmed the solidarity of the oppressed people of the world.

Camille was born on August 27, 1912—some sources say 1915—in Jacmel, Haiti. Of a comfortable economic background, he attended elementary and secondary schools in his hometown before matriculating at the Institut Tippenhauer and the Lycée Pétion in Port-au-Prince. In his early twenties, Camille was named an official with the Haitian delegation in Paris.

An avid reader, he was initially influenced by French poets, though later on decided to seek solidarity with such writers from Latin America as the Cuban poet **Nicolás Guillén**. He began to write poems at the age of eighteen, publishing them in such journals *La Releve*. But it was in 1940 that the newspaper *Le Temps* initiated Camille's career with the publication of the poem "Nedje." The poem told the story of a young Ethiopian dancer he had seen in Casablanca, Africa, and who is prostituted by capitalists and foreigners, yet manages to survive and to glory in her survival:

> Chacun de tes pas,
> Tes gestes
> Tes regards
> Ta chanson
> Diront au soleil que ta terre t'appartient

(Your steps / Your movements / Your glances / Will show the sun that land that is yours).

Called by scholar Mercer Cook the most moving poem ever written in Haiti, "Nedje" was collected in a volume that excited a generation of students and intellectuals: *Assaut a la nuit* (1940). In the volume, comments Garret, in *The Renaissance of Haitian Poetry*: "Camille sees himself as the embodiment of his race and he suffers from the adversities it experiences" (170).

In 1945, Camille published *Gerbes pour deux amis*, written in collaboration with **Jean Fernand Brierre** and Morisseau Leroy. In 1951, he published *Multiple Presence*. These books revealed his preoccupation with social issues but did not receive the same critical attention as *Assaut a la Nuit*.

Camille, well known in Haiti, where there are schools and streets named after him, has received little attention in Europe and in the United States.

Further Reading

Garret, Naomi M. *The Renaissance of Haitian Poetry*. Paris: Présence africaine, 1963.

"Roussan Camille." www.lehman.cuny.edu/ile.en.ile/paroles/camille.html (accessed 7/24/05).

—*D. H. Figueredo*

Campbell, George (1918–)

Campbell is a poet and playwright from Jamaica. According to scholar Laurence A. Breiner, in *An Introduction to West Indian Poetry* (1998), Campbell was the first Jamaican poet to influence Jamaican writers, who in the past had turned to British authors for their models.

In the 1940s, George Campbell emerged as one of Jamaica's leading poets, attracting readers beyond his island: for example, a young **Derek Walcott** was influenced by Campbell's poetry. In the early 1940s, he befriended **Edna Manley**, the tireless promoter of Jamaican culture and editor of the journal *Focus*. Campbell published much of his early poetry in that journal, and in 1945, he selected some of those for his first collection, aptly titled *First Poems*.

In 1948, he published the drama, *A Play Without Scenery*. The drama and the poetry expressed Campbell's preoccupation with Jamaica's politics and the infighting that occurred as independence approached. In the 1950s, Campbell relocated to the

United States, settling in New York City. He published poems in several journals and anthologies. In 1978, some of his early works appeared in the anthology *Bamboula Dance and Other Poems*, edited by Jose Antonio Jarvis. After his departure from Jamaica, Campbell did not write much. His most famous poem is "Holy" where he writes: "Holy be the white head of a Negro/Sacred be the black flax of a black child" (1987).

Further Reading

Baugh, Edward. "West Indian Poetry 1900–1970." *A Study in Cultural Decolonization.* Kingston, Jamaica: Savacou Publications, 1971.

Breiner, Laurence A. *An Introduction to West Indian Poetry.* Cambridge: Cambridge University Press, 1998.

Donnell, Alison, and Sarah Lawson Welsh, eds. *The Routledge Reader in Caribbean Literature.* London: Routledge, 1996.

—*D. H. Figueredo*

Campbell, Hazel D. (1940–)

A Jamaican short story writer, Campbell is inspired by Jamaica's ongoing search for a political identity. Unlike many writers from the Caribbean who resettle abroad, Campbell has stayed in her country, where she works for the Jamaican government.

Born in Jamaica in 1940, Hazel D. Campbell studied at Mert Grove High School and then went on to the University of West Indies–Mona, where she majored in English and Spanish as well as communications. While in college, she wrote short stories and published her first collection, *The Rag Doll and Other Stories* (1978). The next few years she submitted her stories to several anthologies, including *West Indian Stories* (1981), *Caribanthology* (1981), and *Focus* (1983). In 1985, she published a second collection of stories, *Western Tongue*. In 1993, she wrote *Singerman*. This volume was followed in 1995 by *Tilly Bummie and Other Stories: Life in Jamaican Country and Town*. Campbell's short stories affirm her Caribbeaness and her rejection of American influence on the region. Many of the stories take place in a barrack yard, a Jamaican tenement built around a courtyard, where she explores the culture of poverty and the long-term effects of colonialism. She is praised for prose that is clear and for well-conceived characters. *See also* Barrack Yard Literature.

Further Reading

Lima, Maria Helena. "Beyond Miranda's meanings: Contemporary critical perspectives on Caribbean women's literatures—Out of the Kumbla, edited by Carole Boyce Davies and

Elaine Savory Fido/Caribbean Women Writers edited by Selwyn R. Cudjoe and others."
Feminist Studies 21, no. 2 (Spring 1995): 115–29.

—*D. H. Figueredo*

Canales, Nemesio R. (1878–1923)

Nemesio R. Canales was a Puerto Rican poet, essayist, dramatist, novelist, and journalist who championed women's rights, including their right to popular vote, and fought in favor of workers' benefits. He is praised for his abounding wit, humor, his intellectual brilliance, and above all, his sociopolitical commitment for the betterment of the human condition.

Canales was born in Jayuya, Puerto Rico in 1878. He began his studies in medicine in Zaragoza, Spain, but due to the Spanish-Cuban-American War of 1898 he interrupted his studies and went to the United States, where he received a law degree in 1903 in Baltimore. As a lawyer he worked in Ponce and in San Juan, Puerto Rico, where he joined the law firm of two other important literary figures, the poet **Luis Llorens Torres** and the critic and essayist **Miguel Guerra Mondragón**. In addition to his legal work, he devoted himself to politics and literature.

As a literary figure, Canales achieved prestige mostly as a philosophical and witty journalist. He collaborated on important papers such as *El Día*, *Revista de las Antillas*, and *La Semana* and founded *Juan Bobo* (1915), *Idearium* (1917), and *Cuasimodo* (1919), contributing with about five hundred essays as part of his literary production. In addition to journalistic writings, as evidenced in *Paliques* (1915), a collection of his most important essays, he wrote short novels—*Feliz Pareja, Hacia un lejano sol, Mi voluntad se ha muerto*—and a play, *El héroe galopante*, all published posthumously in 1924.

In all his newspaper writings, Canales voiced his critical viewpoints about topics ranging from local politics and personalities to global concerns about war, hunger, poverty, political corruption, and imperialism. He also expressed his opinions on the *Titanic* disaster, the care and status of children, the future of Spain, Puerto Rican and world writers, grammar, art, love, morality, and feminism. He resorted to irony, satire, and paradox when confronting his readership on controversial topics or when criticizing contemporary customs and conventional ideas. Ideologically he has been considered a revolutionary, an avid reader of Henrik Ibsen (1828–1906), Georges Bataille (1897–1962), John Galsworthy (1867–1933), Gabriele D'Annunzio (1863–1938), Hermann Sudermann (1857–1928), and August Strindberg (1849–1912), but he showed preference for Anatole France (1844–1924) and, above all, George Bernard Shaw (1856–1950), with whom he shared a good part of his socialist credo.

Canales's direct, laconic but richly suggestive and ironic discourse is evident in all his texts, becoming useful in dramatically unveiling social hypocrisy and naive idealism. For example, *Hacia un lejano sol*, written in 1920, is a very short narrative written in the stylistic tradition of Spanish writer Miguel de Unamuno's

(1864–1936) *Nada menos que todo un hombre*. It centers on the disillusionment of the main character, Gloria, when she discovers that her family's fortune, like that of her fiancé, whom she has rejected on moral grounds, originated in shameful exploitative practices. In *El héroe galopante*, a one-act play in prose, Canales ironically demolishes general and conventional Romantic notions of love, honor, patriotism, public opinion, and heroism. Sandoval, the brave proven war hero is seen as a coward because he opted to run rather than confront an assailant in a nonsense street fight, basing his decision on the principle that men should not risk their lives when assaulted by inconsequence and brute actions.

Canales died in 1923 in New York when he was on his way to Washington, D.C., to participate as a legal consultant in a Puerto Rican legislative commission examining American worker-employer relations. *See also* Puerto Rican Literature, History of; Romanticismo/Romanticism.

Further Reading

Babín, María Teresa. *Genio y figura de Nemesio R. Canales*. San Juan, Puerto Rico: Biblioteca de Autores Puertorriqueños, 1978.

Canales, Nemesio R. *Obras completas*. Edited by Servando Montaña Peláez. San Juan, Puerto Rico: Ediciones Puerto, 1992.

—Asela R. Laguna

Capécia, Mayotte (1916–55)

Controversial novelist from Martinique accused of resenting her blackness and wishing to be white, Capécia was the author of two novels, *Je suis Martiniquaise* (1948) and *La Negresse blanche* (1950). The earlier and more celebrated work won the Prix France-Antilles in 1949. Her actual name was Lucette Combette Ceranus.

Mayotte Capécia was born in Carbet, Martinique. An illegitimate child, who never received formal schooling and who spent her youth working in a chocolate factory and later selling merchandise in the capital city of Fort-de-France, Capécia sought better economic opportunities in France toward the end of World War II, relocating to Paris in 1946. Struggling to support her three children, she wrote the autobiographical *Je suis Martiniquaise*. The novel tells the story of a woman attempting to find independence through marriage to a man who is not black. Such an outlook provoked the wrath of fellow Martinican **Frantz Fanon**, who in his book *Peau noire, masques blancs* (1952) saw in Capécia the epitome of the colonized identifying with the colonialist and of a black person accepting European standards of beauty. Recent feminist scholarship, however, concentrates on other aspects of the novel, such as the author's handling of life on the margin and of surviving in a European-male-dominated society. Scholar Joan Dayan observes in "Women, History and the Gods: Reflections on Mayotte Capécia and Marie Chauvet" that Capécia was presenting complex views of race, rejecting the notion that black and white women had to "be clear about . . . alliances, be serious about . . . genealogical inheritance" (70), locating themselves within easily defined categories.

Writing at a time when the people of the French Caribbean were affirming their black identities and when the colonial powers were dwindling, Capécia's novels isolated her. She suffered from cancer and passed away in obscurity in 1955 at the age of thirty-nine.

Further Reading

Dayan, Joan. "Women, History and the Gods: Reflections on Mayotte Capécia and Marie Chauvet." In *Introduction to Caribbean Francophone Writing: Guadeloupe and Martinique.* Oxford: Berg, 1999.

Makward, Christiane. *Mayotte Capecia ou 'Alienation selon Fanon.* Paris: Karthala 1999.

Shelton, Marie-Denise. "Women Writers of the French-Speaking Caribbean: An Overview." In *Caribbean Women Writers: Essays from the First International Conference*, edited by Selwyn R. Cudjoe. Wellesley, MA: Calaloux Publications, 1990.

—*Jayne R. Boisvert and D. H. Figueredo*

Capetillo, Luisa (1879–1922)

Known as the first woman to wear pants in the Hispanic Caribbean, Capetillo was a pioneer feminist and the author of *Mi opinión sobre las libertades, derechos y deberes de la mujer* (1911), the first feminist thesis published in Puerto Rico. She was a labor activist, an advocate of free love, and a journalist.

Capetillo was on October 28, 1879, in Arecibo, the daughter of a French mother and a Spanish father. Her parents were freethinkers and did not believe in marriage—they never married. Capetillo was homeschooled, and as she matured she adopted an anarchist philosophy. In 1900, she worked as a *lector*, a reader at a cigar-making factory, and later a union activist. In 1904, she began to write essays that she published in the periodicals *Unión Obrera*. She also founded her own newspaper, *La Mujer* (1909). Two years later, she published *Mi opinión*.

In 1912, she visited New York City, where she met other cigar workers and labor organizers from Cuba and Puerto Rico. She then traveled to Cuba and became involved in a labor strike. In Cuba, she was briefly arrested for wearing men's pants. Later on, she returned to Puerto Rico. In 1922, she contracted tuberculosis and passed away.

Further Reading

Capetillo, Luisa. *Amor y anarquía: los escritos de Luisa Capetillo.* Edición de Julio Ramos. Río Piedras, Puerto Rico: Ediciones Huracán, 1992.

—*D. H. Figueredo*

Cardoso, Onelio Jorge (1914–86)

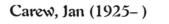

Known as Cuba's national short-story writer, Jorge Cardoso wrote stories depicting the lives of farmers and laborers. He was also a children's writer, a journalist, and a newspaper editor.

Born on May 11, 1914, in the Cuban countryside, in the province of Las Villas, to a farmer who had fought in the 1895 War of Independence, Jorge Cardoso became interested as a child in the way peasants expressed themselves. He attended elementary school in the rural town of Calabazar de Sagua, then went to high school in Santa Clara, the province's capital. Unable to attend college due to financial constraints, Jorge Cardoso taught himself literature, studying European classics, especially the works of the Russian short-story master Anton Chekhov (1860–1904).

Jorge Cardoso wrote his first short stories while still in his teens. He won the first prize for short stories in the journal *Social* in 1936. In 1945, he received the prestigious Hernández Catá National Story Prize for his "Los carboneros," about marginalized charcoal workers. Until 1959, Jorge Cardoso worked as a radio journalist, soap opera, and children's writer. After the triumph of the Cuban Revolution he held several positions in cultural organizations and was editor in chief for such publications as the daily *Granma* and the weekly *Bohemia*.

Over the course of his lifetime, he wrote more than a dozen volumes of short stories, many of which were dramatized and presented by theater companies in Cuba. In 1964, he won the 26th of July literary prize for his writings. Jorge Cardoso also wrote children's stories. His most famous work in this genre, *El caballo de coral* (1960), was choreographed for ballet by Cuba's National Ballet. Some of his writings include *Taita, diga usted cómo* (1945), *El cuentero* (1958), *La techuza ambiciosa* (1960), *El pueblo cuenta* (1961), *El perro* (1964), *Cuentos completos* (1969), *El hilo y la cuerda* (1974), *Cuentos escogidos* (1981), and *Negrita* (1985).

Further Reading

Prada Oropeza, Renato. *Poética y liberación en la narrativa de Onelio Jorge Cardoso: ensayo de interpretación*. Xalapa, Veracruz, México: Centro de Investigaciones Lingüístico-Literarias, Instituto de Investigaciones Humanísticas, Universidad Veracruzana, 1988.

—*Pamela María Smorkaloff*

Carew, Jan (1925–)

A political writer of the generation that came of age during Guyana's struggle for independence from the British, Jan Carew is a prolific novelist, playwright, and poet best known for his studies of the effect of colonialism on the educated individual. He is representative of the writer who lives in exile but writes extensively about the Caribbean.

Jan Rynveld Carew was born on September 24, 1925, in rural British Guiana, now Guyana. As a child he attended Bernice High School, where he studied Latin, French, and literature and was so attracted to science that at one point he contemplated becoming a physician. At Bernice High School he was encouraged to write, and he also demonstrated a talent for painting. After high school graduation, he attended Howard University and Western Reserve University, now Case Western Reserve University, from 1944 to 1948. He also studied at Charles University, in Prague, Czechoslovakia, and the Sorbonne, in Paris. His traveling to these universities was a manifestation of a wanderlust that eventually took him to Africa, the Americas, Asia, and Europe.

As an emerging writer, Carew was personally exposed to several major novelists in his youth: the pioneer Guyanese writer **Edgar Mittelhölzer**, who lived in his neighborhood and wrote historical novels about Guyana; **Sylvia Wynters**, who became his second wife after his first passed away; and **Wilson Harris**, who was his brother-in-law. It was Sylvia Wynter who made Carew appreciate the worth of his own poetry, describing his writing as "genuine West Indian" poetry, as Carew told scholar Daryl Cumber Dance in 1984 in the book *New World Adams* (39). Wilson, on the other hand, was a land surveyor for the British Guiana government and took Carew with him on several expeditions into the rain forest. It was in one of these journeys that Carew met a man who inspired him to write the novel *Black Midas* (1958).

The novel, published in the United States as *The Touch of Midas*, is the story of a Guyanese "pork-knocker"—a diamond miner who is also a frontiersman, an adventurer, and an explorer in the Guyanese jungle—who makes himself a fortune in diamonds, squanders it all, and loses a limb before settling down to a quiet life in a rural village. The narrative frames the protagonist's search for identity and ethnic roots, as he must choose between his European and African Amerindian heritage. Carew's second novel, *The Wild Coast* (1958), is about a well-to-do young man who visits the village of his ancestors; there, while trying to uncover the mystery of his mother's death, he learns about native traditions and such African rituals as the worship of Shango, an African goddess. The novel allows Carew the opportunity to explore the racial and religious tensions between the lower and higher social classes in Guyana.

After the publication of *The Wild Coast*, Carew wrote a novel about an exiled Brazilian artist in Harlem, *The Last Barbarian* (1960), and a critique of racism in the Soviet Union, *Moscow Is Not My Mecca* (1965). He also wrote dozens of children's and young-adult books, several radio and television scripts, and stage plays. Despite his intense and varied productivity, his early novels established his main themes: the cultural and physical annihilations of Africans and Amerindians by the Europeans; the search for identity in a colonial society that held a low image of anyone who was not white; and the conflicts of the racial divide. Carew is often criticized for creating weak characters but the author himself maintains that colonization dwarfed the identity of the people, blinding "us to the truth about ourselves, our history, our humanity," as he expressed in an interview in November 1966 *The Gaither Report* (75).

Carew has received numerous awards and grants, including the Canada Arts Council grant (1969), the Burton International Fellowship (1973), Illinois Art Council award for fiction (1974), **Casa de las Américas** Literature Award (1977), and the National Film Award for the screenplay for *Black Midas* (1985). Princeton University established the Jan Carew Annual Lectureship Award to honor the author in 1975. *See also* Santería in Literature.

Further Reading

Dance, Daryl Cumber. *New World Adams: Conversations with Contemporary West Indian Writers.* Yorkshire, England: Peepal Tree, 1984, 1992.

Gaither, Larvest. *The Gaither Reporter* 3, no. 9 (November 30, 1996); 75–79.

—*D. H. Figueredo*

Caribbean Artists Movement (CAM, 1966–72)

∎

The first transnational association to promote the arts and literature of black artists from the Anglophone Caribbean, the Caribbean Artists Movement was founded in London in 1966 by writers and poets **Kamau Brathwaite, Andrew Salkey, Orlando Patterson, Wilson Harris,** and John La Rose, who was also a publisher. CAM's archivist Anne Walmsley, writing in *The Caribbean Artists Movement, 1966–1972* (1992), listed the founders' objectives as: (1) to discover their own aesthetic; (2) to chart new directions for Caribbean arts and culture; (3) to become acquainted with Caribbean history; (4) to rehabilitate Amerindian inheritance; (5) to reinstate African roots; (6) to reestablish links with the common people through use of popular language and music; and (7) to reassert their own literary tradition in the face of the dominant European and American traditions.

The association started its work in the writers' own apartments in London, then held meetings at the West Indian Students Union Building, with conferences and seminars on the campus of the University of Kent. Topics for discussions were varied and numerous, including "Is There a West Indian Aesthetic?" "Contribution of the West Indies to European Civilization," "Spanish and French West Indian Literature Today." CAM supported the publishing house New Beacon, owned by John La Rose, which specialized in works by African and Caribbean authors and sold those works at CAM's meetings and conferences, published a newsletter and founded the journal *Savacou*. From 1968 to 1972, CAM members attempted to establish the association in the Caribbean but were not successful, probably because of regional and nationalistic differences that were not as strong in London, where all West Indians were seeking solidarity. After 1972, the association as a whole was disbanded. However, CAM members became well-known writers and lecturers and were responsible for holding in the West Indies the first conference on Anglophone Caribbean literature in 1971, called the **Conference of the Association for Commonwealth Literature and Language Studies.** *See also* Anglophone Caribbean Literature, History of; Tertulia/Cénacle/Literary Salon/Soirée.

Further Reading

Walmsley, Anne. *The Caribbean Artists Movement, 1966–1972: A Literary & Cultural History*. London: New Beacon Books, 1992.

—*D. H. Figueredo*

Caribbean Quarterly (1949–)

Published initially to promote the works of Anglophone writers from the Caribbean and to offer its English-speaking readers reliable information on "their own history and culture," as indicated on the back cover of the first issue published in the spring and summer of 1949, this journal evolved into a publication that would eventually cultivate a multilingual and multiregional audience; by 2001, the editorial's were written in three languages: English, French, and Spanish.

The journal publishes creative writings as well as sociological essays, pedagogical treatises, and even information on local governments. The editors have included such important writers as **Sir Philip M. Sherlock** and cultural figures as **Rex Nettleford**. The journal is published and funded by the University of West Indies–Mona, Jamaica.

Further Reading

Caribbean Quarterly (Spring and Summer, 1949). Mona, Jamaica: University of West Indies.

—*D. H. Figueredo*

Caribbean Voices (1943–58)

A British Broadcasting Corporation (BBC) radio program that broadcast from London to the Anglophone Caribbean from 1943 to 1958 and introduced to its listening audience a new generation of Caribbean authors. It was on this program that the prose and poetry of the likes of **George Lamming**, from Barbados, **Samuel Selvon**, from Trinidad, and **Edgar Mittelhölzer,** from Guyana, was first heard beyond their respective countries.

The program was conceived by Jamaican writer **Una Marson,** who was staying in London during the early days of World War II. Concerned over the labor and social unrest that had taken place in the colonies in the late 1930s, the British government had wanted to make sure that the Caribbean region remained loyal to the Crown and had invited Marson, who was well known in Jamaica, to participate in a series of BBC programs meant to rally Jamaicans to the war effort. From these program came forth the genesis for a radio show on the culture and literature of the West Indies. Marson served as the editor of *Caribbean Voices* from 1943 to 1948.

Henry Swanzy followed in her footsteps in 1948, when Marson returned to Jamaica. After 1956, a youthful **V. S. Naipaul** served as editor and contributor.

Initially, *Caribbean Voices* featured writers and literary works from Jamaica, but in the transition from Marson to Henry Swanzy, the program embraced all English-speaking writers from the colonies. Since the emphasis was on performance rather than the written word, *Caribbean Voices*, according to scholar Laurence A. Breiner, was instrumental in developing a "West Indian ear" as well as sound, creating a sort of universal English diction and accent that was true to the Caribbean, rather than London, and that was recognizable by all listeners. The writers would mail their submissions to a BBC representative in Jamaica, who would then dispatch the manuscripts to Swanzy for inclusion in the program. Quite often, though, Barbadian writer **Frank A. Collymore**, editor of the literary journal *Bim* and a friend of Swanzy, would recommend new writers to be featured on the program.

Twenty-nine minutes long, *Caribbean Voices* aired for fifteen years. With the creation of the West Indies Federation in the 1950s, a politically sensitive BBC board felt that the program should no longer originate from London, the capital of a colonial power, and terminated *Caribbean Voices'* tenure on the radio. The program served as the launching pad for over three hundred writers, many of whom went on to greater glory, including Nobel Prize winners **V. S. Naipul**, from Trinidad, and **Derek Walcott**, from St. Lucia. *See also* Literary Journals; Poetry League of Jamaica.

Further Reading

Griffith, Glyne. "Deconstructing Nationalisms: Henry Swanzy, Caribbean Voices and the Development of West Indian Literature." *Small Axe*, no. 10 (September 2001), 1–20.

Jarret-Macauley, Delia. *The Life of Una Marson 1905–65*. Manchester: Manchester University Press, 1998.

—*D. H. Figueredo*

Caridad Doval, Teresa de la. See Dovalpage, Teresa.

Carpentier, Alejo (1904–80)

■

One of most innovative novelists of the twentieth century, Carpentier also wrote literary theories that helped to transform the literary landscape in Latin America and to define the genre that become known as **Magical Realism**. Politically active and a globetrotter, he also helped to internationalize Cuban literature. Like Cuban American and Haitian American writers who chose to write in English, the language of the country where they lived, Carpentier, whose father was French, opted to write in Spanish.

Born in Havana on December 26, 1904, Carpentier was the son of a French architect and a Russian woman. Studying music and architecture, first in France and then in Cuba, Carpentier infused this knowledge into all of his prose, both fiction and nonfiction. In Havana, during the 1920s, he wrote a ballet, worked as a music critic, was one of the founders of the literary journal *Revista de Avance*, and editor of the avant-garde periodical *Carteles*. He was imprisoned in 1927 for opposing the right-wing dictatorship of Gerardo Machado (1871–1939), who was in power from 1924 to 1937. While in prison, Carpentier wrote the first draft of his novel *Ecue Yamba-ó*, a negrista exercise that explored Afro-Cuban themes. The novel was published in Madrid in 1933.

Released from prison, Carpentier returned to Paris, where he participated in the surrealist movement and worked on the documentary *Le Vaudou*. During this time, Latin American mythology was the fashion in literary circles, encouraging the emerging novelist to study Caribbean culture and traditions. In 1936, he went back to Cuba, where he wrote the seminal short story **"Viaje a la semilla."** In this story, the progression goes backward as the aging protagonist grows younger. In 1943, Carpentier traveled to Haiti, a key event in his life: While on the island, he became familiar with Haitian history and the life of Haitian tyrant Henri Christophe (1767–1820), who ruled from 1811 to 1820. His research resulted in his first major novel, *El reino de este mundo* (1949). It is in the introduction to this work where Carpentier proclaimed that the extraordinary and the ordinary and the supernatural and the mundane, coexist harmoniously in Latin America. Calling his notion "lo real maravilloso," the marvelous real, it served as the foundation for **Magical Realism**.

From 1945 to 1959, Carpentier lived in Caracas, working as an executive of a public relations firm. It was while living in Venezuela that he journeyed into the Amazon, another fruitful event in his life. From that experience, he wrote the novel *Los pasos perdidos*, about a musicologist searching for the origins of music in the jungles. The novel was an international sensation, translated into several languages and winning in 1956 the French award for best foreign work, the Prix de Meiller Livre Etranger.

In 1959, Carpentier returned to Cuba to lend his support to **Fidel Castro** and the revolutionary regime. He directed the Imprenta Nacional, the government printing office, organized literary contests that brought to Cuba the best Latin American authors of the period, and served as Cuban consul in France. In 1962, he published *El siglo de las luces*, a **historical novel** about the French Revolution and the invention of the guillotine. During the 1970s, he wrote three novels: *Concierto barroco* (1974), *El recurso del metodo* (1974), and *La consagración de la primavera* (1978), regarded by many critics as homage to Fidel Castro.

Carpentier had a sweeping notion of time, with different ages existing simultaneously. In *Los pasos perdidos*, every step taken into the jungle by the protagonist becomes a step to a primeval past. And in *El siglo de las luces*, all revolutionary ideas, from Robespierre's to the Bolsheviks', are presented as if occurring all at once during the eighteenth century. Carpentier influenced countless authors, including **Jacques Stephen Alexis**, from Haiti, and **Julia Alvarez**, from the Dominican Republic. Carpentier died in Paris on April 24, 1980. *See also* Latin American Boom; Literatura Comprometida/Socially Engaged Literature; Negrista Literature; Novas Calvo, Lino.

Further Reading

González Echevarría, Roberto. *Alejo Carpentier: The Pilgrim at Home*. Ithaca, New York: Cornell University Press, 1977.

Zamora, Louis Parkinson, and Wendy B. Faris, eds. *Magical Realism: Theory, History, Community*. Durham, NC: Duke University Press, 1995.

—Alfonso J. García Osuna and D. H. Figueredo

Carrero, Jaime (1931–)

Puerto Rican novelist, playwright, and poet, Jaime Carrero writes about the Puerto Rican diaspora and the struggles of Puerto Ricans on the island and on the mainland, in the United States. He was the first to coin the term "Neorican" to refer to Puerto Ricans living in New York City.

Jaime Carrero was born in Mayagüez, Puerto Rico, where he was raised. He lived in New York while attending college, earning a graduate degree in fine arts from Pratt Institute. As an innovative and provocative painter he has exhibited his work in the United States, Mexico, and Puerto Rico, and for many years, until his retirement, he directed and taught at the Department of Fine Arts at the Inter-American University in San Germán, Puerto Rico.

Besides being a professional painter, Jaime Carrero is a poet, a dramatist, and a novelist who early in his writing career earned the unique distinction of being the first to use and adopt the term "Neorican" to refer to the experience of Puerto Ricans in the United States; he was one of the pioneers in the use of **Spanglish** for literary purposes and relating to the struggles of the diaspora in New York. During the 1960s, he also collaborated enthusiastically in journals, such as *The Rican, The Revista Chicano-Riqueña*, and in *Revista/Review Interamericana*, the first printed vehicles for the new voices from the diaspora or Puerto Rican living or sharing the United States experience.

Carrero began his literary trajectory as a poet who wrote both in Spanish and English—*Aquí los ángeles/Here the Angels* (1960) and *Tiranosauro Rey amén, amén/Tyrannosaurus Rex, amen, amen* (1963)—and then mixed and experimented in both languages: *Jet neoriqueño. Neo-Rican Jetliner* (1964), where the term "Neorican" was first introduced. In 1970, he published a fourth volume of poetry entitled *Las computadoras del sol*. In addition to his experimenting with **code switching** from Spanish to English, Carrrero's poetry is characterized by its freshness; the freedom to experiment in the form, structure, rhythm, and vocabulary; its use of daring metaphors and comparisons,' the joyfulness between the use of irony and seriousness; and the importance of communicating social commentaries or criticism of the contemporary realities of his time.

In 1965, Carrero began a short and intensive period of writing drama. That year the play *La muñeca de crepé envuelta en celofán* was performed at the

Inter-American University in San Germán. The following year, his second production, *Flag Inside* (1966), received the first place of the Annual Literary Contest sponsored by the **Ateneo Puertorriqueño**. Other plays followed: *Capitán F4C* (1968), *El caballo de Ward* (1971), *Pipo Subway no sabe reír* (1971), *Noo Jork* (1972), *Hit Your Knees for Luck y the FM Safe* (1973), translated as *La caja de caudales FM*, and *Tres chapas tiene mi tía* (1973). Between 1973 and 1983 he published *El Lucky Seven* (1979), and wrote *A Pair of Wings* and *Preciosa y otras tonadas que no fueron al Hit Parade*. Most of his plays were produced either by the Puerto Rican Traveling Theater of New York, founded by Miriam Colón, by the Inter-American University, or by the University of Puerto Rico.

Paradoxical strategies, social and political protest and denunciation, cruelty, irony, humor, the grotesque, experimentation, surprise, and absurd situations are some of the characteristic ingredients that make Carrero's a powerful and compassionate statement of the Puerto Rican human and political condition in Puerto Rico and in the diaspora. Carrero creates a drama that invites meditation or provokes indignation but never entertains frivolously. The political status of the island, Puerto Ricans living in New York, and the Vietnam War serve as the appropriate frame wherein to set the actions of some of his plays and dramatize the tragedy of Puerto Rican families divided by geography, conflicting and opposing ideological positions with regard to the case of the island, and by all sorts of racial and social prejudices.

Carrero has written three novels. The experiences of an optimistic and idealist Neorican who returns to the island as a teacher of English to face cultural rejection is the core of his first novel, *Raquelo tiene un mensaje* (1970). A second novel, *Los nombres* (1972), examines the Puerto Rican experiences in the Korean War; his third novel, *El hombre que no sudaba* (1982), is the story of a university professor of history who suffers from chronic stammering and the inability to perspire. The novels sum up the themes that recur in Carrero's works: the fragmentation of the Puerto Rican family; criticism of the private educational system; the North Americanization of the people and institutions at all levels; cruelty of family relations; the political destiny of the island; the impact of the United States wars in the lives of Puerto Ricans; violence; dehumanization of man; migration; and the experiences of the Puerto Rican diaspora in New York. *See also* Nuyorican Literature.

Further Reading

Mohr, Eugene V. *The Nuyorican Experience: Literature of the Puerto Rican Minority.* Westport, CT: Greenwood Press, 1982.

Rivera de Álvarez, Josefina. *Literatura puertorriqueña: Su proceso en el tiempo.* Madrid: Ed. Partenón, 1983.

Rodríguez-Seda, Asela. "El teatro de Jaime Carrero," *Revista Chicano-Riqueña* 3 (Summer 1977): 26–31.

—*Asela R. Laguna*

Carreta, La (1952)

∎

Possibly Puerto Rico's best-known play, *La Carreta* is a three-act tragedy about a Puerto Rican family looking for a better life who relocate from the countryside to San Juan and then from San Juan to New York City. Written by **René Marqués**, one of Puerto Rico's most famous authors, *The Oxcart* is a retelling of the actual migration of thousands of poor Puerto Ricans beginning in the 1940s.

The principal characters are Luis, a young man who believes in the power of American capitalism to yield wealth and comfort; his sister, Juanita, a small-town girl who is representative of the purity of the land; and his mother, Doña Gabriela, who supportive of her son follows his lead. In act 1, called "estampas," the trio, with a younger brother named, Chaquito, are preparing to leave their farm, which, after the death of Luis's father, they had not been able to maintain. The grandfather appears to bid them farewell and presents his objection to the move. Symbolic of a past that was gentle and pastoral, the grandfather believes that life comes from the land, from the soil. Luis, tired of working as a farmer, rejects his grandfather's notion by saying "the future is not in the land but industry" (25). In act II, the family lives in a slum in San Juan. The promise of a better future does not materialize, and one tragic event after another occurs: the young brother, Chaquito, turns to crime; Luis is unable to find work; his sister is raped and impregnated. Unlike the purity and virginity found in countryside depicted in the first "estampa," the slum is an area of loose morality and easy sexuality, represented by a local store owner whose mistress lives in his household and the owner's wife who has seduced Luis and longs to have an affair with him. After Chaquito is arrested for burglary and Juanita attempts to commit suicide after aborting her fetus, the trio opts to leave San Juan for New York City.

The third "estampa" takes place in a tenement in Manhattan. Luis has a job in a factory, but life has not improved: the tenement is plagued with crime, and they find New York City unwelcoming and rife with bigotry, a city where Puerto Ricans are dehumanized and seen as inferior. The act ends in tragedy when Luis perishes in an accident in the factory. Learning of his fate, his sister and mother decide to return to Puerto Rico to work with a relative who owns a small farm.

In *La Carreta*, the city—both San Juan and New York City—represents inhumanity and the belittlement of men, whereas the countryside represents wholesomeness and spirituality. Says critic **María Teresa Babín Cortes** in the preface to the play: "The return to the soil . . . expresses manhood, human dignity, the personality and the integrity of the individual and the community" (xxix).

Further Reading

Babín, María Teresa. "Prologue." In *La Carreta: drama puertorriqueño* by René Marqués. Río Piedras, Puerto Rico: Editorial Cultural, 1983.

—*D. H. Figueredo*

Carrión, Miguel (1875–1929)

∎

A precursor of feminism in Cuba, Miguel Carrión was a novelist who chose the literary movement known as **naturalismo**, naturalism, to denounce moral hypocrisy and the oppression of women during the early twentieth century. Along with **Carlos Loveira**, he is considered one of the best naturalist writers of Cuban letters.

Miguel de Carrión de Cardenas was born in Havana on April 9, 1875. The son of a physician, Carrión studied medicine, after a brief stint as a teacher, and conducted cancer research. He was the director of the Urologic Institute and professor of anatomy at the Escuela Normal de Maestras—Normal School for Teachers—both in Havana.

Influenced by Émile Zola (1840–1902) and Gustave Flaubert (1821–80), Carrión wrote psychological novels that explored sexual desire in women. He promoted the idea that only through sexual satisfaction could individuals achieve maturity. He criticized Cuban society for curtailing women's sexual growth while encouraging men to philander. His novels, however, also bemoaned political corruption in the recently established republic and lack of economic progress. According to scholar Sintia Molina, writing in *El Naturalismo en la novela cubana*, Carrión represented the frustrations and skepticism expressed by Cuban intellectuals of the era.

His two most famous novels are *Las honradas* (1917) and *Las impuras* (1919). The first novel, written as a diary, tells the story of a woman suffering from frigidity due to her conservative and stifling upbringing coupled with society's expectation that a decent woman doesn't enjoy sexual activities. Only through an affair does she find liberation.

Las impuras is the story of a woman whose affair with a married man signals the beginning of her descent into a world of prostitutes, gigolos, thieves, and corrupt politicians. Ironically though, the character finds her victory when she chooses to become a prostitute: she rejects the middle class's enforced values, the roles assigned to women by men, and affirms her own needs and individuality. Molina points out the irony in the titles: an honest woman is a mere sexual object to her husband, and as such she must be silenced at all times and denied her own individuality; an impure woman, on the other hand, can free herself from society's moral code and choose her own destiny.

Carrión wrote stories and articles for numerous journals as well as political commentaries for popular newspapers; he also wrote an early treatise on the subject of public education for women. A pioneer researcher on the causes and treatment of cancer, Carrión himself succumbed to the disease on July 30, 1929.

Further Reading

Molina, Sintia. *El Naturalismo en la novela cubana*. Lanham, Maryland: University Press of America, 2001.

Toledo Sande, Luis. *Tres narradores agonizantes: tanteos acerca de la obra de Miguel de Carrión, Jesús Castellanos y Carlos Loveira*. Habana, Cuba: Editorial Letras Cubanas, 1980.

—Sintia Molina

Cartagena Portalatín, Aída (1918–94)

One of the most important woman poets from the Dominican Republic, Cartagena Portalatín began her literary career as a member of the group of poets in the literary movement known as **La Poesía Sorprendida,** which flourished in the 1940s. Her poetry is defined by lyricism and a search for language. Her essays are characterized by her identification with the Dominican Republic's African heritage.

Cartagena Portalatín was born in Moca on June 18, 1918. After attending elementary and secondary schools in Santo Domingo, she enrolled at the Universidad de Santo Domingo, where she earned a doctorate in humanities. She then pursued postgraduate work on museum studies and plastic arts at the University of Louvre, in Paris. She directed the publications *Brigadas Dominicanas* and the journal of the School of Humanities at Universidad Autónoma de Santo Domingo. She also edited the publication *Colección Baluarte*, which specialized in publishing works of **literatura comprometida,** socially engaged literature. In 1965, she worked for UNESCO. In 1977, she was a judge in the prestigious **Casa de las Américas** literary contest, held in Havana, Cuba.

Establishing herself as a poet in the Poesía Sorprendida movement—the only woman in a group of men—she traveled throughout Europe, Africa, and Asia. Her travels inspired much of her writings and informed the academic texts she wrote in the field of the history of art. In 1955, she wrote her most famous poem "Una mujer esta sola." The poem explores the themes of loneliness and rebellion while attempting to place women within their rightful place in society; these themes characterize most of her creative productivity.

In 1969, she wrote the novel *Escalera para Electra*, which was a finalist in the Premio Biblioteca Award—competition in Spain. In 1986, she wrote *Las culturas africanas: rebeldes con causa*, a study of black arts and politics. Her other works include *La voz desatada* (1962), *La tierra esta escrita* (1967), *Tablero*—short stories—(1978), *Yania tierra*, (1981), *La tarde en que murió Estefanía* (1983), *En la casa del tiempo* (1984), and *From Desolation to Compromise: A Bilingual Anthology of the Poetry of Aída Cartagena Portalatín* (1988), *Aída Cartagena Portalatín: selección poética* (2000).

She passed away on June 3, 1994, in the Dominican Republic.

Further Reading

Cocco de Filippis, Daisy. *Documents of Dissidence: Selected Writings by Dominican Women*. New York: CUNY Dominican Studies Institute, 2000.

—*Daisy Cocco de Filippis*

Carter, Martin (1927–97)

Described as a political poet, the Guyanan Martin Carter is considered one of the most important writers from the Anglophone Caribbean. His evolution as a poet and his poetic creativity mirrors the ebb and flow of political development in Guyana. His most famous work, *Poems of Resistance from British Guiana* (1955), is representative of the best political and socially engaged literature written in English.

Martin Wylde Carter was born on June 7, 1927, in Georgetown, former British Guiana, now Guyana. He studied at Queen's College in Guyana and joined the British Guiana Civil Service but was soon involved in anti-colonialist political activities as Guyana prepared itself for independence. In 1953, a new constitution was drafted, and Cheddi Jagan, leader of the Progressive People's Party (PPP), was elected to office, but the British, fearing Jagan would create a communist state, suspended the constitution and removed Jagan from power. An activist within the party and supporter of Jagan, Carter was imprisoned. While behind bars, he wrote *Poems of Resistance from British Guiana*, thus belonging to a tradition of great Caribbean writers who wrote behind bars or were inspired by their imprisonment's experience, ranging from the nineteenth-century Cuban poet, **Gabriel de la Concepción Valdés**, to the twentieth-century Jamaican novelist **Roger Mais**.

Praised for its revolutionary aesthetics, identification with the common people, and defiance of the British authorities, as demonstrated in this line "I clinch my fist above my head; I sing my song of FREEDOM," *Poems of Resistance* is often anthologized. Equally popular is his "I Come from the Nigger Yard" (1954) in which he says,

> I come from the nigger yard of yesterday
> leaping from the oppressor's hate
> and the scorn of myself.
> I come to the world with scars upon my soul.

The revolutionary fervor and deep humanism Carter felt during the 1950s lead to a sense of hope in the 1960s as Guyana achieved independence. By the next two decades, however, Carter became somewhat silent and reflective, disappointed by his country's inability to achieve economic equity and the racial and ethnic animosity that evolved between East Indians and blacks. Some writers, however, like Gordon Rohleher, in his essay "West Indian Poetry: Some Problems of Assessment II" (1972–73), believed that Carter had burned himself out as a poet and revolutionary.

In 1980, Carter wrote the collection *Poems of Affinity*, contemplative verses on politics and violence, underlined by a sense of pessimism, the work of a disillusioned poet, as critic Lloyd W. Brown suggests in *Fifty Caribbean Writers* (19). But whether or not the elder Carter might fail to spark fire in his latter poems, his early protest poetry assures him a place in the literary canon. Observes Brown, "The voice itself may have been muted, but the fiery sense of engagement which has made that voice all but unique in the Anglophone Caribbean poetry still burns" (109).

Some of Carter's poetry collections include *The Hill of Fire Glows Red* (1951), *The Hidden Man* (1952), *Poems of Succession* (1977), and *Selected Poems* (1989). As an early performer of his works in the 1950s and 1960s, he anticipated the popularity of performance artists and Dub poets in the Anglophone Caribbean. *See also* Dub poetry; Literatura Comprometida/Socially Engaged Literature; Performance Poetry.

Further Reading

Brown, Lloyd D. "Martin Wylde Carter (1927–)" in *Fifty Caribbean Writers*. Edited by Daryl Cumber Dance. Westport, CT: Greenwood Press, 1986.

Brown, Stewart, ed. *All Are Involved: The Art of Martin Carter*. Leeds, England: Peepal Tree, 2000.

Dance, Daryl Cumber. *New World Adams: Conversations with Contemporary West Indian Writers*. Yorkshire, England: Peepal Tree, 1984, 1992.

Rohlehr, Gordon. "West Indian Poetry: Some Problems of Assessment II." In *The Routledge Reader in Caribbean Literature*, edited by Alison Donnell and Sarah Lawson Welsh, 316–20. London and New York: Routledge, 1996.

—*D. H. Figueredo*

Casa de las Américas

A cultural center in Havana responsible for a prestigious annual literary contest, conferences, the publications of books, and the influential journal of the same name, Casa de las Américas has been responsible for introducing to the world dozens of new and emerging writers, such as Nobel Prize-winner Gabriel García Márquez (1927–) and best-selling novelist Carlos Fuentes (1928–), and for helping to internationalize Latin American culture and literature.

Created by the Cuban government in 1959, the center fostered intellectual dialogue with Latin American nations at a time when the revolutionary government had been shunned by most nations in the Americas, except for Mexico. That year, Casa de las Américas held a literary contest that would become a mainstream of Latin American culture, attracting innovative and experimental writers. The categories were novels, poetry, drama, short stories, and essays written in Spanish. In 1965, however, the center expanded categories to include works concerned with historiography and politics and their relation to literature and culture. It was during this period that Casa de las Américas recognized a new genre, that of testimonial works—**testimonio** in Spanish. During the 1970s, Casa de las Américas began to accept contributions from Latin America authors writing in English, French, and Portuguese. It also included children's literature and essays written in any language as long as they deal with Latin American topics.

Casa de las Américas has been accused of promoting only works that are favorable toward the Cuban Revolution or advocate leftist ideologies, as stated by some of the writers who make up the **Mariel Generation** of the 1980s. But despite this criticism, the center has done much to encourage intellectual discussions in Latin America and to offer such Caribbean authors as Haitian **Paul Laraque** avenues to reach audiences beyond their own countries. See also *Casa de las Américas*, journal; Literary Journals; Literatura Comprometida.

Further Reading

Weiss, Judith. *Casa de las Américas: An Intellectual Review in the Cuban Revolution.* Chapel Hill, NC: Estudios de Hispanófila, 1977.

—*D. H. Figueredo*

Casa de las Américas, Journal (1960–)

Founded and directed by Haydee Santamaría (1922–80), this journal is the official organ of the cultural center of the same name located in Havana. The first issue stated that the journal's philosophical objective was to create a new America and to promote political change. The issue included creative fiction, poetry, essays, and reviews of books. The journal published Cuban writers as well as such international figures as Miguel Angel Asturias (1899–1974) and James Baldwin (1924–87); it also offered space to emerging writers the likes of **Frantz Fanon**. By the second issue, the journal posed an anti-American stance and was careful not to publish works critical of the Cuban Revolution. The objective and format of the journal has remained intact into the twenty-first century. The roster of its editors and contributors—ranging from **Edouard Glissant**, Carlos Fuentes (1928–), and **Roberto Fernández Retamar**—represent the creative and intellectual output of the Caribbean and Latin America during the twentieth and twenty-first centuries.

Further Reading

Weiss, Judith. *Casa de las Américas: An Intellectual Review in the Cuban Revolution.* Chapell Hill, NC: Estudios de Hispanófila, 1977.

—*D. H. Figueredo*

Casal, Julián del (1863–93)

The Cuban poet Julián del Casal was one of the leaders of **Modernismo**—Latin American modernism. His poetry evoked deep pessimism and an intense awareness of death.

Julián del Casal was born in Havana on November 7, 1863. Orphaned at a young age, he had an unhappy childhood. At the age of seven he attended the Real Colegio de Belén in Havana, where he established a handwritten underground newspaper, called *El Estudio*, and began to write poetry. After graduating in 1880, he pursued a degree in law at the Universidad de la Habana but never completed his studies. By 1885, he was a regular contributor to several publications, including *La Habana Elegante*.

In 1888, Casal traveled to Spain, and upon his return he worked as a proof-reader and journalist for *La Discusión*. Around this time, he achieved fame as a man of letters, and many writers frequented his **tertulias,** or literary salons. He befriended the young poet **Juana Borrero** and the Nicaraguan Rubén Darío (1867–1916). His first book of poems, *Hojas del viento*, was published in 1890. His second work, *Nieve* (1892), drew praise from such important figures as the French poet Paul Verlaine (1844–96). His third volume, *Bustos y rimas*, was published after his death in 1893.

Casal's journalistic prose described social life in nineteenth-century Cuba. These pieces were published weekly; they encouraged Cubans to develop culturally and intellectually. His poetry, however, was not concerned with Cuba but with cosmopolitanism and aesthetics. His poetry tended to be philosophical yet simple and direct in its diction. Casal, who suffered from tuberculosis, had a short life, but his contribution to the Modernismo was influential and profound. As a poet, his style is often compared and contrasted to that of his contemporary **José Martí.**

Further Reading

Morán, Francisco. *Casal à Rebours*. Habana: Casa Editora Abril, 1996.

—*Pamela María Smorkaloff*

Casal, Lourdes (1938–81)

Lourdes Casal was an award-winning Cuban poet, short-story writer, and political activist who was initially critical of the Cuban revolution—the reason for which she left the island—but then became a supporter of the revolutionary regime. Terminally ill, Casal returned to Cuba in 1979 and died two years later. Representative of the experience of exile, Casal's poetry reflects an individual caught between two worlds: revolutionary Cuba and exile.

Of European, Chinese, and African descent, Casal was born in Havana on April 5, 1938. She attended the University of Santo Tomás de Villanueva, in Marianao, in the province of Havana. As a student she joined the underground fighting against dictator Fulgencio Batista (1901–73). She remained rebellious and participated in anti-Castro activities after **Fidel Castro** took over the government in 1959. In 1962, she left for the United States, settling in New York City. She earned a masters and a doctorate from the New School of Social Research in 1975. She then taught at several universities, including City University of New York and Rutgers. In the mid-1960s, Casal identified with the civil rights movement in the United States and reevaluated her views and the accomplishments of the Cuban Revolution. She was one of the founders of the journal *Areíto*, which viewed the Cuban experience on the island and the United States from a liberal perspective, organized trips to Cuba, and fostered dialogue between Cubans on and off the island.

Casal wrote scholarly studies on the evolution of the anti-Castro novel and **Cuban American literature.** In 1971, she was the first scholar to document the controversial Padilla case, in which Cuban poet **Heberto Padilla** was jailed for writing poetry deemed critical of the revolution: *El caso Padilla; literatura y revolución en Cuba; documentos.* In 1978, she edited *Contra viento y marea*, a unique account of the experiences of young middle-class Cubans in the United States. Published in Cuba, the volume received a special award from the **Casa de las Américas.** In 1973, she wrote *Los fundadores: Alfonso y otros cuentos*, a collection of autobiographical short stories. In 1981, she wrote the book of poetry *Palabras junta revolución*, which won the literature award from the Casa de las Américas.

A controversial figure in her lifetime—some Cubans in exile perceived her as a traitor—Casal has been adopted by many Cuban American writers, such as **Cristina García,** for her complex view of the Cuban Revolution and her sense of not belonging anywhere, best expressed in one of her poems from *Palabras junta revolución*:

> too habanera to be a Newyorkina
> too newyorkina to be
> —even to become again—
> anything else.

See also Code Switching; Cuban American Literature.

Further Reading

Behar, Ruth. *Bridges to Cuba: Puentes a Cuba.* Ann Arbor, MI: University of Michigan Press, 1995.

Casal, Lourdes. *Itinerario ideológico: antología.* Miami, FL: Instituto de Estudios Cubanos, 1982.

—D. H. Figueredo

Casas, Myrna (1934–)

Erudite dramatist and feminist writer, in her work Casas explores Puerto Rico's cultural identity and women's maltreatment at the hands of men. She is a professor, a theater director, and a producer.

After studying at Vassar College, where she earned a BA, Casas obtained an MA in art from the University of Boston and a PhD in philosophy from New York University. At the age of twenty-one, she taught drama at the Universidad de Puerto Rico and was appointed chair of the Drama Department.

During the 1950s, she began to write for the theater. Her dramas were successfully staged and published. In 1986, she wrote an opera, *El mensajero de plata,* followed by several adaptations of classic children's stories. Her plays, not written for the general public, alternate between traditional presentations and experimental avenues and criticize Puerto Rican society for its consumerism and its male-driven traditions. She usually challenges her audience to bring about social change.

Casas also wrote the anthology *Teatro de vanguardia* (1975). Her published works include: *Cristal roto en el tiempo* (1960), *La trampa (1965), Tres,* (1974), *Este país . . . no existe* (1993). In 2004, the comedy *Tres noches tropicales y una vida de infierno* toured Puerto Rico and Florida. The play told the stories of three women—a New Yorker, a Puerto Rican, and a Cuban American—and their relationships with men. While the comedy promoted independence for women, it also suggested approaches to sexual equality.

Further Reading

Enciclopedia puertorriqueña: siglo XXI. Vol. 2. Santurce, Puerto Rico: Caribe Grolier, 1998.

Rivera, Barbara. "Teatro en Orlando." *La Prensa*, no. 45 (November 25, 2004): 15.

—*D. H. Figueredo*

Casey, Calvert (1924–69)

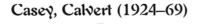

Short-story writer and literary critic who reflects in his writings the loneliness and isolation experienced by homosexual writers in the early days of the Cuban Revolution. The son of a Cuban woman and an American, his short stories explore his cultural duality, sexual insecurities, and the melancholy and solitude he experienced.

Calvert Casey was born in Baltimore, Maryland, but was raised in Havana. In 1934, he returned to the United States, then, in 1958, went back to Cuba. An eager supporter of the revolution, he worked for **Casa de las Américas** and wrote for the prestigious weekly supplement ***Lunes de Revolución*** but fell out of the grace with the revolutionary government, who deemed his homosexuality a social ill. Casey left Cuba in 1965, traveled to Europe, and committed suicide in Rome in 1969.

His best-known work includes the short story "El regreso" (1962) and the volume *Notas de un simulador* (1969), which contained a novella and four short stories. His short stories have a poetic but elusive quality that evoke emotions rather than actual settings and character development.

Further Reading

Casey, Calvert. *Calvert Casey: The Collected Stories*, Translated by John H. R. Polt and edited by Ilan Stavans. Durham, NC: Duke University Press, 1998.

Luis, William. "El lugar de la escritura." *Encuentro de la Cultura Cubana* 15 (1999–2000): 50–60.

—*William Luis*

Castera, Georges (1936–)

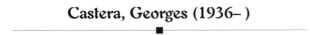

A Haitian poet who writes in Creole or Kreyòl, which he sees as the language of the people, Castera is a politically and socially engaged writer. In his poetry, he advocates an end to oppression, poverty, and racism. As an activist, living in exile New

York City, he organized the Haitian American community into a political presence and founded a theater for Haitian drama.

Of a middle-class background—his father was a physician—Castera was born on December 7, 1936 in Port-au-Prince. He began to write as a teenager, and in his twenties, he befriended such major literary figures as **Jacques Stephen Alexis** and **René Bélance.** He published articles in the local press, often criticizing the dictatorship of **François Duvalier** (1907–71).

In 1956, Castera sought exile in France. While living in Europe, he became familiar with Marxist ideology and **surrealism.** In the 1960s, he went to Spain to study medicine but was attracted by literature and by writing poetry in Kreyòl rather than in French. In 1965, he self-published in Madrid *Klou gagit.* Five years later, he published two more volumes in Kreyòl, again funding the publication with his own money: *Bwa mitan* and *Panzou.* Between 1970 and 2001, he published twelve volumes in Kreyòl of which the collection *Konbèlann* (1976) became the best known. The volume, which includes poems he had written in Haiti, uses experimental typography to represent sounds and expressions in Kreyòl.

Castera, however, also used French, publishing the following books in that language: *Le Retour à l'arbre* (1974), *Ratures d'un miroir* (1992), *Les Cinq letters* (1992), *Quasi parlando* (1993), *Voix de tête* (1996), and *Brûler* (1999). Writing in the two languages has enabled Castera to contemplate the use of language as both a tool of oppression and a tool of liberation. He has also published bilingual editions, in French-Kreyòl, of his poems: *Bòs Jan / Jean le menuisier* and *Pitit papa / Le père et l'enfan* both published in 1999.

During the 1970s and 1980s, Castera lived in New York City, where he wrote numerous plays, including *Lèt ak sitron* (1980) and *Au coeur de la nuit.* (1988), which were staged for the Haitian community. In 1986, he returned to Haiti and founded an association for Haitian writers and taught children how to write poetry. He also edited the journal *Mémoir.* Some of his Kreyòl poems have been set to music by popular Haitian composers. In 1996, he was awarded the prestigious **Casa de las Américas** literature prize. Castera is also a respected artist. *See also* Haitian Literature in Kreyòl (the Haitian Language).

Further Reading

Dominique, Max. *Esquisses critiques.* Port-au-Prince: Editions Mémoire; Montréal: Editions du CIDIHCA, 1999.

Saint-Éloi, Rodney. "Georges Castera." www.lehman.cuny.edu/ile.en.ile/paroles/castera.html (accessed 9/1/05).

—*D. H. Figueredo*

Castillo, Efraím (1940–)

Castillo is a short-story writer and novelist from the Dominican Republic. His works examine urban development in his country.

Castillo was born in Santo Domingo, Dominican Republic, on October 30, 1940. He started to write as a teenager, and by the time he was twenty, he was submitting his writings to local journals. In 1967, his short story "Consígueme la náusea, Matilde" earned a prize in a contest sponsored by the writers group La Máscara. A year later, his short story "Anti Huamán o Eva again" brought him further recognition within the Dominican Republic's literary circles. He received the Casa de Teatro literary prize with the short story "Curriculum Vitae" in 1980. In 2000, he was awarded the National Prize for his novel *El personero*. Much of his writing hints of unfulfilled lives overwhelmed by the simplicity of daily activities and the inability to progress.

Castillo's short stories are often anthologized in the Dominican Republic. He has also written poetry, *Confín del polvo* (1985), and drama, *Viaje de regreso* (1968). His training in the field of public relations informs his use of language as a symbol of power. Some of his other works includes *Los lectores del ático* (1998), *Los ecos tardíos y otros cuentos* (2002), *Guerrilla nuestra de cada día* (2002).

Further Reading

Céspedes, Diógenes. *Antología del cuento dominicano*. Santo Domingo: Editora de Colores, 1996.

—*D. H. Figueredo*

Castro, Fidel (1926–)

Fidel Castro is the dictator of Communist Cuba whose revolution inspired leading literary figures in Latin America, even while his regime censored or imprisoned Cuban poets, novelists, and essayists for writing critically of the regime.

Born on August 13, 1926 in Birán, in the province of Oriente, Castro came to power in January 1959 after a three-year guerrilla war against the dictatorship of Fulgencio Batista (1901–73). The vast majority of the people of his country, as well as many intellectuals throughout the world, initially hailed him as the man who would lead Cuba to a new age of independence, democracy, and social justice. His tall figure, bearded visage, and stirring speeches added an aura of romanticism that persists to this day.

Castro's first few months in power were marked by the summary trials and executions of Batista supporters, yet there were also indications of a Cuban literary renaissance. In 1959, the revolutionary government created **Casas de las Américas**, a cultural institution that fostered intellectual dialogue with Latin American nations, sponsored a literary annual competition, published an influential journal, and established a publishing house that facilitated the international distribution of works by Cuban and Latin American authors, especially those supportive of the revolution. That same year, the novelist **Guillermo Cabrera Infante** became the founding editor of ***Lunes de Revolución***, a literary supplement of the daily newspaper *Revolución* that quickly became perhaps the most influential and widely read literary journal in Latin America. The magazine featured the work not only of Cuba's best-known writers, including **Nicolás Guillén, José Lezama Lima, Heberto Padilla,** and **Virgilio Piñeira,** but also of other internationally renowned authors such as Carlos Fuentes (1928–), Graham Greene (1904–91), Vladimir Nabokov (1899–1977), and Jean-Paul Sartre (1905–80).

But *Lunes* and government censors soon became embroiled in disputes. In June 1961, at a national meeting of writers, Castro gave a speech in which he famously remarked, **"Within the Revolution, everything; outside the Revolution, nothing,"** and in November of the same year he ordered *Lunes* closed. Many of the Cuban writers who had contributed to the magazine went into a period of official ostracism—one exception being Nicolás Guillén, who continued supporting the government and became head of the Cuban Writers Union, **Unión de Escritores y Artistas Cubanos.** In 1966, according to the newspaper *The Guardian,* in article published in 2004, Castro ordered more than hundred Cuban writers to publish an open letter criticizing Pablo Neruda (1904–73) for participating in a conference in New York City, thus socializing with the enemy.

Internationally, though, Castro continued to receive support from leading intellectuals. Then, in 1971, the poet Heberto Padilla was imprisoned on charges of promoting "subversive activities" stemming from the publication of *Fuera del Juego,* or *Out of the Game,* a book of poems critical of the political conformity that Padilla believed Castro had imposed. Padilla was released after a notorious public "confession"—his wife, the poet **Belkis Cuza Malé** says he had been tortured into his mea culpa. As a result, writers and intellectuals who once supported Castro, including Mario Vargas Llosa (1936–), Sartre, Octavio Paz (1914–98), Carlos Fuentes, Simone de Beauvoir (1908–80), Alberto Moravia (1907–90), Juan Goytisolo (1931–) and Susan Sontag (1933–2004), broke with the regime after signing a letter that compared what had happened to Padilla to the worse excesses writers faced in the former Soviet Union under Joseph Stalin (1879–1953). One notable who did not sign was the Colombian Nobel Prize–winning novelist Gabriel García Márquez (1927–), whose personal friendship with Castro continues to be a source of controversy.

Cuban literary life continued to thrive after the Padilla affair, but mostly in exile—Cabrera Infante in London, **Lydia Cabrera** in Miami, for instance—or in the opposition on the island itself. Out of that opposition emerged the generation of writers who had come of age under Castro but chose to flee Cuba in the 1980 Mariel Boatlift. The best-known author of that group is **Reinaldo Arenas.**

A number of dissident writers chose to remain in Cuba through the 1980s and 1990s, however, even though they were unable to publish their work. Some, like the poet **María Elena Cruz Varela,** were imprisoned and harassed by government-sponsored mobs before leaving for exile. The definitive crackdown was ordered by Castro in the spring of 2003, when some eighty intellectuals, were sentenced to lengthy prison terms for "subversive" or "counterrevolutionary" writings.

As a literary figure, Castro has proved an eloquent orator, and many of his speeches are regularly anthologized. Though he himself has not written any texts, his speeches have been published in Cuba as single volumes. Perhaps the most famous are *La historia me absolverá* (1961), his defense speech delivered in 1953 when accused of attacking a fortress in an attempt to remove from power dictator Fulgencio Batista (the act is considered the beginning of the Cuban revolution) and *Porque en Cuba sólo ha habido una revolución* (1975), in which he describes his revolution as the legitimate extension of Cuba's war of independence in the nineteenth century. His rhetoric consists of simplifying complex information, repetitive patterns, and a musicality that rises to the equivalent of a symphonic climax. *See also* Anti-Castro Literature; *Casa de las Américas*, journal; Cuban Literature, History of.

Further Reading

Butts, Ellen, and Joyce R. Schwartz. *Fidel Castro*. Minneapolis: Lerner Publications Co., 2005.

Castro, Fidel. *Palabras a los intelectuales*. Habana: Departamento de Ediciones de Biblioteca Nacional "José Martí," 1991.

Feinstein, Adam. "Cuba: A New History by Richard Gott." *The Guardian*, October 9, 2004.

January, Brendan. *Fidel Castro: Cuban Revolutionary*. New York: Franklin Watts, 2003.

Johnson, Scott. *The Case of the Cuban Poet Heberto Padilla*. New York: Gordon Press, 1977, 1978.

Kurland, Gerald. *Fidel Castro, Communist Dictator of Cuba*. Charlotteville, NY: SamHar Press, 1972.

Press, Petra. *Fidel Castro: An Unauthorized Biography*. Chicago, IL: Heinemann Library, 2000.

—Roger E. Hernández

Cecilia Valdés o La Loma del Ángel; novela de costumbres cubanas (1839, 1882)

———————————————— ■ ————————————————

One of the first Cuban novels, alongside *Sab* (1841) by **Gertrudis Gómez de Avellaneda,** to be accepted in Europe as a serious work of art and to become one of the most popular books read throughout Latin America, *Cecilia Valdés* is an exemplary illustration of the style known as **costumbrismo,** which emphasizes local characters, settings, and traditions. The book is also considered as well as a romance, a **historical novel,** and an abolitionist document. **Cirilo Villaverde** wrote the novel under the guidance of **Domingo del Monte,** Cuba's most important literary promoter of the period. He began it as a short story in 1839 and published a first volume of the novel the same year. For political reasons, Villaverde was forced to leave the island for the United States, and it was there that he completed and published his master work in 1882.

Cecilia Valdés is considered Cuba's national novel. It has been published in just about every Spanish-speaking country in the world and has spawned two operas, several film versions, and television productions. It has influenced a large proportion of Cuban literature. For example, in *Tres tristes tigres* (1965) by **Guillermo Cabrera Infante,** the character Cuba Venegas brings to mind both Villaverde and Cecilia Valdés—they all have the same initials—and **Reinaldo**

Arenas spoofed the masterpiece in his novel *La loma del angel* (1986). The novel helped to popularize the character of the sultry **mulata** as an object of sexual desire as well as the real and symbolic mulatto mixture of the Cuban nation.

The novel, which frames Captain-General Don Francisco Dionisio Vive's corrupt government from 1812 to 1832, is divided into two parts. In the first the wealthy Spaniard slave trader Cándido Gamboa has an affair with a mulata, Charo Alarcón, who becomes mentally ill after her daughter is taken away from her. The grown-up daughter, the beautiful Cecilia Valdés, then falls in love with the handsome and aristocratic Leonardo Gamboa, unaware that he is her half-brother. In the second part, Cecilia has a passionate affair with Leonardo. She believes that he will marry her, but when he doesn't, she asks a mulatto friend, José Dolores Pimienta, who is in love with her, to avenge her. Pimienta waits outside the church where Leonardo is getting married, and as the groom emerges, he knives him and runs away. The grieving bride accuses Cecilia of plotting Leonardo's murder, and Cecilia is sent to an asylum for the insane, the same asylum where her mother is. Before she dies, Charo Alarcón recognizes her daughter, and the two are briefly reunited. In the meantime, Isabel, the widow, retreats to a convent, and Pimienta gets away with his crime.

In *Cecilia Valdés*, Villaverde exposes the evils of slavery, which he associates with the sugar mill, and racism. He even makes references to the well-known Ladder Conspiracy of 1844, which was used to do away with a growing black middle class. Villaverde compares the Gamboa family and their infernal sugar mill—representative of sugar tycoons—with the character Isabel Ilincheta and her interest in the coffee plantation, which promoted a more benevolent form of slavery. Though history heralds the triumph of sugar over coffee, in the novel Villaverde suggests that this ending is not in the best interest of the emerging Cuban culture. *See also* Abolitionist Literature; Cuban Literature, History of.

Further Reading

Schwarts, Kessel. *A New History of Spanish American Fiction. Vol. 1: From Colonial Times to the Mexican Revolution and Beyond.* Coral Gables, FL: University of Miami Press, 1972.

Villaverde, Cirilo. *Cecilia Valdés ó La loma del Ángel; novela de costumbres cubanas.* New York: Impr. de el Espejo, 1882.

———. *Cecilia Valdés,* translated from the Spanish by Helen Lane; edited with an introduction and notes by Sibylle Fischer. New York: Oxford University Press, 2004.

—*William Luis*

Césaire Family, The

■

Aimé and Suzanne are husband and wife writers and philosophers from Martinique. Together, they promoted the **Négritude** movement, black consciousness, and founded the influential journal *Tropiques*. Their daughter, Ina, is a playwright and ethnographer. Of the three, Aimé became the best known and most influential.

Césaire, Aimé (1913–). Called by many Martinicans Papa Césaire and one of the most famous political figures and writers from the Caribbean, Aimé Césaire was one of the founders of the Négritude movement and the author of one of the most discussed literary texts in the Francophone Caribbean, the epic poem *Cahier d'un retour au pays natal*. A cofounder as well of the influential journal *Tropiques*, Césaire is also a successful playwright. He has dominated the politics and culture of Martinique for over a half a century.

Césaire was born to poor parents in Martinique in 1913. His grandmother taught him to read and write in French by the age of four. He attended the Lycée Shoelcher in Fort-de-France, where he demonstrated a talent for writing and excelled at the study of French, English, and Latin. In 1931, he was awarded a scholarship to attend Lycée Louis-le-Grand, a preparatory school in Paris for the École Normale Supérieure. Four years later he earned a teaching degree from the École Normale.

In Paris, Césaire socialized with two men who changed his life: Léopold Sédar Senghor (1906–2001), from Senegal, and **Léon-Gontran Damas**, from French Guiana. These two young intellectuals introduced Césaire to African heritage and culture. Through their friendship and the creation of a short-lived journal, *L'étudiant noir*, Césaire began to affirm his African roots and to develop a black consciousness that led to his rejection of white assimilation. In 1939, he coined the term *Négritude* in his poem *Cahier d'un retour au pays natal*.

Césaire married Suzanne Roussy, and they returned to Martinique in 1939. Both taught at the Lycée Schoelcher and, with a third teacher, **René Ménil**, founded the journal *Tropiques*. Around this time, Césaire became involved in local politics, advocating an anti-colonialist view. In 1945, Césaire, aligned with the Communist Party, was elected mayor of Fort-de-France, a post he maintained for five decades, and was also elected representative to the French National Assembly. In 1946, he supported Martinique's political change into an overseas French department rather than an independent country. He interpreted this move as the way to achieve political equality with France.

After 1946, Césaire published numerous poems in the journal *Tropiques* as well as four books of poetry: *Les armes miraculeuses* (1946), *Soleil cou coupé* (1948), *Corps perdu* (1950), *Ferrements* (1950). In 1950, Césaire wrote a book of essays, *Discours sur le colonialisme*, in which he accuses liberal thinkers of being colonialists. In 1956, he published *Lettre à Maurice Thorez*, explaining his reason for resigning from the French Communist Party, which he saw as using black people to achieve the political objectives of Communist leaders rather than to help black people fight against oppression and achieve equality. He then founded his own political party, the Parti Progressiste Martiniquais (PPM).

From 1960 to 1982, believing that his political and philosophical message could reach a wider audience through drama rather than poetry, he wrote several plays. These works were experimental, highly intellectual, and not easy to stage. *Et les chiens se taisaient: tragédie* (1956) is about a rebel contemplating suicide to protest against the oppression and futility of rebellion. *La tragédie du roi Christophe* (1963) is about Haitian liberator Henri Christophe (1767–1820), who ruled the newly independent nation from 1806 to 1820. The play proved popular and was staged several times. When the drama was presented in Martinique in 1990, it attracted over seventy thousand theatergoers. It was also the first play not written by a French dramatist to be staged by the Comédie Française in Paris in 1991.

In 1960, Césaire told the story of Congo martyr Patrice Lumumba (1925–61) in *Une saison au Congo* (1967). He followed this work with another popular drama, his retelling of Shakespeare's *Tempest, Une tempête; d'après "La tempête" de Shakespeare. Adaptation pour un théâtre nègre* (1969). In it he emphasizes the role of **Caliban** rather than Prospero. The play portrays the conflict between black and white. In the 1970s, Césaire returned to poetry with the publication of *Noria* (1976) and *Moi, laminaire* (1982).

Césaire's poetic style has been discribed as a volcanic explosion in which words rush out onto the page. French philosopher Jean Paul Sartre (1905–80) wrote that Césaire's poetry "bursts and wheels around like a rocket; suns turning and exploding into new suns"—quoted in the 1992 volume *Black Literature Criticism* (359). The surrealist philosopher André Breton (1896–1966) considered Césaire the best twentieth-century writer in the French language.

While Césaire's literary merits are admired, his political choices and philosophy are questioned by many writers, including **Frantz Fanon**, who felt that Césaire had betrayed the independence movement when he'd advocated for unification with France rather than autonomy. Other writers, including **Patrick Chamoiseau** and **Raphaël Confiant**, decried Césaire's support for Négritude as a denial of the ethnic and racial diversity of the Caribbean and criticized his writing in French rather than in Creole. And feminist scholars, the likes of T. Denean Sharpley-Whiting, have suggested that Césaire did not sufficiently acknowledge his wife's contribution to the Négritude movement. Whether admired or criticized, Césaire stands as one of the most influential figures in the Caribbean. His writings have been translated into several languages. His other works include *Toussaint Louverture: la révolution française et le problème colonial* (1960), *Oeuvres complètes* (1976), and *Anthologie poétique* (1996).

Césaire, Ina (1942–). Ina Césaire is a filmmaker, a playwright, and a novelist. Unlike her father, who writes only in French, Césaire uses Creole in her writings. Influenced by the ideology of the Négritude movement and a historical awareness of Martinique and the Caribbean, Ina Césaire has devoted her life to documenting and conserving Martinique's cultural and historical heritage as well as its folklore.

Inspired by oral traditions, Césaire wrote several volumes of stories, anecdotes, and legends: *Contes de mort et de vie aux Antilles* (1976), *Mémoires d'isles: maman N. et maman* (1985), *Contes de nuits et de jours aux Antilles* (1989). All of these works are characterized by her use of Creole.

Believing that the island's oral traditions were best expressed through the theater, Césaire turned to drama, writing *Memoirs d'isle* (1985), about two women recalling their lives in Martinique; *D'infant du passages ou Le Epic du Ti-Jean* (1987), about a teenager and an orphan, *La mansion close* (1991), based on the true story of six women in jail; and *Rosanie Soleil* (1992), about a labor strike.

In 1994, Césaire published her only novel, *Zonzon Square Tete*, the story of a taxi driver.

Césaire, Suzanne (1913–). A brilliant essayist and promoter of Négritude, the Martinican Suzanne Césaire has been long overshadowed by her husband **Aimé Césaire's** literary and political career.

Not much is written about the private life of Suzanne Roussy Césaire. She was born in Trois-Ilets, Martinique, and after completing elementary studies on the island, she traveled to Paris to study philosophy at the École Normale Supérieure There she became active with the Association des étudiants martinquais (Association of Students from Martinique). Through this organization, she met Aimé Césaire and the two fell in love. They were married in 1937.

Returning to Martinique in 1939, in 1941 the Césaires founded, with a few friends and the philosopher René Ménil, the journal *Tropiques*. The journal was meant to be a cultural vehicle that celebrated Martinique's roots. The editors published essays about Caribbean culture, folklore, and even articles about animals and plants from the region. Aimé Césaire published his poetry as well, and Ménil wrote philosophical texts. Suzanne Césaire wrote a series of essays that revolutionized Martinique's cultural life.

The first essays were studies of ethnology and poetry. But in the 1942 issue she wrote a provocative piece entitled "Malaise d'une civilisation," in which she describes Martinique as suffering cultural sterility, the result of French colonialism, racism, and isolation, and encouraging the readers and writers of the island to create a culture of their own, a culture of the tropics: "This land, our land, can only be what we want it to be" (134). In 1945, she wrote the essay entitled "The Great Camouflage," in which she observes that the natural charm and beauty of the island hid centuries of slavery, racism, oppression, and suffering.

This essay was published on the last issue of *Tropiques*. It was also the last piece of writing that Suzanne Césaire did. After 1945, Suzanne Césaire chose silence, devoting her life to raising her family and to supporting her husband, Aimé, who became a major literary and political figure in both Europe and the Caribbean.

Further Reading

Black Literature Criticism. Vol. 1: *Achebe-Ellison*. Edited by James H. Draper. Detroit: Gales Research, 1992.

Miller, Jane Eldridge. *Who's Who in Contemporary Women's Writing*. London: Routledge, 2001.

Rosello, Mireille. "Introduction: Aimé Césaire and the Notebook of a Return to My Native Land in the 1990s." In *Notebook of a Return to My Native Land/Cahier d'un retour au pays natal*, by Aimé Césaire. Translated by Mireille Rosello with Annie Pritchard, 9–68. Newcastle on the Tyne: Bloodaxe, 1995.

Sharple-Whiting, T. Denean. *Negritude Women*. Minneapolis: University of Minnesota Press, 2002.

—*D. H. Figueredo*

Chambertrand, Gilbert de (1890–1984)

Chambertrand was a writer from Guadeloupe whose plays depicted local characters and events and whose decision to write dialogue in Creole rather than French affirmed the author's Caribbeanness.

Chambertrand was born in Pointe-a-Pitre, Guadeloupe, in 1890, descendant of a family that had come to the Caribbean in the 1780s. He started to write at a young age, and his poems were published in the local press when he was fifteen years old. In 1917, he wrote the comedy *L'Honneur des Monviosin*, combining the use of both French and Creole. The successful staging of the comedy in the town of Basse-Terre encouraged him to write two other plays: *Les Méfaits d'Athénaïse* and *Le Prix du Sacrifice*, both written and staged in 1917 and 1918, respectively.

During the 1920s, Chambertrand worked as a librarian, a professor at Lycée Carnot, and a photographer. In 1928, after a hurricane destroyed his home and the library where he worked, Chambertrand moved to France. In the 1940s, he started to write prose and in 1947 published the novel *Titine Grosbonda*. In 1958, he wrote *Coeurs Créoles*, one of his best-known works. Of a restless creative spirit, in the 1960s Chambertrand turned to poetry, writing *L'Album de famille* (1969), *Cantiques pour la déesse, Basse-Terre*, and *Guadeloupe, Jeunes Antilles* (1979).

Further Reading

Jones, Bridget. "Theatre and Resistance? An Introduction to Some French Caribbean Plays." In *An Introduction to Caribbean Francophone Writing: Guadeloupe and Martinique*, edited by Sam Haigh, 83–100. New York: Berg, 1999.

—*D. H. Figueredo*

Chamoiseau, Patrick (1953–)

Considered one of the greatest living writers of the Francophone Caribbean, Chamoiseau has produced a variety of award-winning novels, memoirs, and essays, as well as a volume of folktales. His innovative technique—a blending of French and Creole, oral and written literary styles—has been challenging and dazzling readers since the early 1980s. Complex works, such as his novels *Solibo Magnificent* (1988) and *Texaco* (1992), have prompted critics to compare him to such diverse and outstanding writers as François Rabelais (1483–1553), James Joyce (1882–1941), Gabriel García Márquez (1927–), and Salman Rushdie (1947–).

Born in Fort-de-France, Martinique, Patrick Chamoiseau studied sociology and law in Paris and later became a social worker in metropolitan France. While currently earning a living from writing, he prefers to continue his full-time job as a probation officer in Martinique, helping young offenders who provide inspiration for his literary works. Readers learn more about Chamoiseau's life through his two autobiographies *Antan d'enfance* (1990) and *Chemin d'École* (1994). The former, winner of the Grand Prix Carbet de la Caraïbe, recounts the author's preschool years as one of five children growing up in a working-class family. The tale focuses on Ma Ninotte, the feisty family matriarch whose haggling skills, employed to deal with the local vendors, procures the ingredients for her family's "eternal soup."

Chemin d'Ecole, translated into English in 1997 as *School Days*, sparkles with creativity and humor, while dealing with themes that are serious and dear to the author. Here Chamoiseau explores the absurdity of Martinique's status as an overseas department of France, the denigration of Creole, and the domination of the French mother tongue and culture, which are completely foreign to Martinican children entering the school system for the first time.

In 1986, Chamoiseau published his first novel, the highly acclaimed *Chronique des sept misères*. In this novel, he tells the story of onetime *djobeurs*, workers who perform small jobs to support their families, who found employment by helping vendors cart their loads to market. Pipi Soleil, the protagonist and so-called grand master of the wheelbarrow, cleverly circumvents city traffic in order to get the job done. More than that, however, Pipi embodies the Creole soul—adept at storytelling, gardening under the harsh tropical sun, and communicating with his ancestors. Through Chamoiseau's use of a fresh hybrid language, the great storyteller-author succeeds in creating a narrative that is accessible to Francophone readers while celebrating the Creole language and culture.

Chamoiseau has produced several essays on the subject of language and literature. The best known, *Éloge de la créolité* (1989), or *In Praise of Creoleness* (1993) in English, was written in collaboration with his friends Raphaël Confiant and Jean Bernabé. This brief literary manifesto reacts against the African focus of the **Négritude** movement of the 1930s and seeks to elaborate on ideas first proposed by **Edouard Glissant** in *Le discours antillais* (1981). The authors' main concern is to promote the plurality of the area's peoples in Caribbean writing by restoring the status of the storyteller and breaking down the barrier between written French and spoken Creole.

Winner of France's prestigious Prix Goncourt, the novel *Texaco* is often acknowledged as an illustration of the thesis of **créolité** and Chamoiseau's masterpiece. The complex four-hundred-page epic, which has been translated into over fourteen languages, offers a richly innovative fictional history of Martinique from plantation days and abolition through the eruption of the Soufrière volcano and the effects of the European world wars. Told in a nonlinear fashion, the narrative integrates imaginary personal experience, folk wisdom, and legend within the historical framework. Although there are a multitude of viewpoints, the tale concentrates on the memories of activist Marie-Sophie Laborieux and her father, Esternome. The resulting mosaic—served up in the ebullient, original language typical of Chamoiseau—brings the recent past of Martinique alive.

Some other titles by Patrick Chamoiseau include an early theatrical work, *Manman Dlo contre la fée Carabosse* (1981); the folktales of *Au Temps de l'Antan* (1988); two essays, *Lettres Créoles* (1991) and *Écrire en pays dominé* (1997); a tale set in the time of slavery, *Esclave Vieil Homme et le Molosse* (1997); and his latest novel, *Biblique des derniers gestes* (2002). *See also* Francophone Literature, History of.

Further Reading

Chancé, Dominique. *L'Auteur en souffrance*. Paris: Presses Universitaires de France, 2000.

Dash, Michael. J. "The World and the Word: French Caribbean Writing in the Twentieth Century," *Callaloo* 2, no. 1 (1988): 1, 112–30.

Haigh, Sam, ed. *Introduction to Caribbean Francophone Writing: Guadeloupe and Martinique*. New York: Berg, 1999.

Murdoch, H. Adlai, ed. *Creole Identity in the French Caribbean Novel*. Miami: University of Florida Press, 2001.

Ormerod, Beverley. "The Martinican Concept of Creoleness: A Multiracial Redefinition of Culture." *Mots Pluriel*, 7 (1998). htttp://www.arts.uwa.edu.au/MotsPluriels/MP798bo.html (accessed 5/26/04).

—*Jayne R. Boisvert*

Chanlatte, Juste (1766–1828)

Chanlatte, the count of Rosiers, is an early Haitian poet and dramatist. He was one of the first writers to celebrate Haiti and its people.

Chanlatte was born in Port-au-Prince in 1766. He studied in Paris, at Louis-le-Grand. During the early years of the Haitian revolution in the 1790s, he lived in the United States, but upon his return to Haiti, he became a public official of General Jean-Jacques Dessalines (1758–1806) in 1804. In that capacity, Chanlatte wrote the draft of Haiti's first constitution. After Dessalines's assassination in 1806, Chanlatte served King Henri Christophe (1767–1820) as his personal secretary and the court's poet. He edited the journal *La Gazette du Cap* and the newspaper *Telegraphe*.

His poetry is basically patriotic. The "Cantate a l'Indépendance" (1821) and "La Triple Palme" (1822) are typical of his works: both celebrate Haiti's independence and Haitians' courage on the battlefield. These poems, as all his poems, were published in the newspaper *Telegraphe*. As a playwright, Chanlatte wrote *Nehri* and *La partie de chasse du Roi*. Staged in the court, the plays dramatized Haiti's victory over the French forces that had been sent to crush the revolution in 1803. To date, these works have not been published as books.

Further Reading

Berrou, Raphaël, and Pradel Pompilus. *Histoire de la littérature haitienne*. Tome 1. Port-au-Prince, Haiti: Editions Caraïbes, 1975.

—*D. H. Figueredo*

Charca, La (1894)

The first major novel in Puerto Rican literature, *La charca*—translated into English in 1982 as *The Pond*—is a nearly perfect example of the movement known as **naturalismo/naturalism**, where the characters, usually from lower socioeconomic classes, are doomed and trapped by social circumstances. Written by **Manuel Zeno Gandía**, *La charca* contrasts the fate of two characters: a rich landowner named Juan del Salto and a poor peasant girl, Silvina. Each is representative of a social class, and in between them stands a third group, the merchants: Andújar and Galante.

The narrative, told by an omniscient narrator, focuses on the lives of the poor who are linked to a coffee plantation, though the emphasis is on Silvina's tragic existence. A beautiful girl, Silvina suffers from epilepsy and is sexually abused by her mother's lover, farm owner and rising merchant, Galante. Though she is in love with a young peasant named Ciro, Silvina is forced by her mother to marry an older man named Gaspar, who maltreats her. A dishonest and greedy man, Gaspar, and a criminal named Deblás, plot the murder of local merchant Andujar; they also make an unwilling Silvina an accomplice: while the two men tie Andujar, she is to plunge a knife into his heart. Before the evening of the murder, Marcelo, who is Ciro's brother, discovers the plot and alerts Andujar, who flees town. When Gaspar and Deblás learn that Andujar has left, they agree the deed must be postponed. However, Deblás decides to confirm whether or not Andujar is in town, sneaks into the store and ransacks it. While in the store, Deblás gets drunk and falls asleep. In the meantime, Gaspar and Silvina break into the store. Thinking that Deblás is Andujar, Gaspar murders him. Silvina suffers an epileptic seizure and upon regaining consciousness, runs away.

The following day, the corpse is discovered, and an investigation takes place. Eventually, an old woman, who suspects Gaspar is the assassin, suggests his name to the authorities. When the police is set out to arrest Gaspar, the murderer flees, never to return to the coffee plantation. Freed from her husband, Silvina and Ciro live together. The idyllic romance ends when Ciro's brother, Marcelo, gets drunk and, in a fight, kills his brother. A desolate Silvina mourns her lover, but unable to make a living on her own, she becomes another man's mistress. However, when she is forced to share his bed with another woman, she leaves the man. Desperate, uncertain of what to do with her life, Silvina suffers a seizure and falls off a cliff.

Her tragic existence contrasts with the good fortunes and lifestyle of Juan Del Salto. The rich landowner lives in a mansion, socializes with educated people—he is friends with a priest and a doctor—and is emotionally detached from the plight of the poor people of the mountains. He spends hours thinking of ways to improve the lot of his workers and the people in the mountain but never takes action. Most of his attention is devoted to assuring that his wealth increases so that he can pass it on to his son, who is in Europe. At the end of the novel, as Silvina plunges to her death, Juan Del Salto leaves for Europe to attend his son's college graduation in Spain.

Throughout *La charca*, the characters who possess wealth continue to prosper and those who are poor, like Silvina and Ciro, lead hopeless existences that often end in tragedy. *La charca* is the most famous work of a tetralogy written by Zeno Gandía: *Garduña* (1896), about a crooked lawyer, *El negocio* (1916), about merchants in a city, and *Los redentores* (1925), about Americans in Puerto Rico. Zeno Gandía referred to the tetralogy as "the chronicle of a sick world," which is also the novel's subtitle.

Further Reading

Zeno Gandía, Manuel. *La charca: crónicas de un mundo enfermo*. Ponce, Puerto Rico: Est. Tip. de M. López, 1894.

———. *The Pond*. Translated. By Kal Wagenheim. Princeton: Markus Wiener Publishers, 1999.

—D. H. Figueredo

Charles, Jean-Claude (1949–)

Jean-Claude Charles is a Haitian poet, novelist, and scriptwriter who describes himself as a "nègre errant"—a wandering black man. His poetry and prose are praised for their elusive, telegraphic messages that suggest restlessness and uprootment.

Charles was born in Port-au-Prince, Haiti, on October 20, 1949. After attending elementary and secondary schools in Haiti, he traveled to Mexico to study medicine but soon found himself in the United States—in Chicago—pursuing a literary career. From the United States, he flew to France, where he matriculated at the University of Paris. He earned degrees in journalism and communication and began to work for the influential *Le Monde* during the 1980s. He also became a television producer.

In 1977, he wrote his first novel, *Sainte dérive des cochons*. But critical recognition arrived in the mid-1980s with the publication of the novels *Manhattan Blues* (1985) and *Ferdinand je suis à Paris* (1987). In these two novels, Charles introduced the character of Ferdinand, a writer who travels back and forth between New York City and Paris, describing what he sees and the people he meets. Like Charles, Ferdinand feels that he doesn't belong in any one place in the world.

In 2004, one of his early novels, *Bamboola Bamboche* (1984), was adapted to the stage in France. *Manhattan Blues* and *Ferdinand je suis à Paris* have been translated into Italian and German

Further Reading

Jonassaint, Jean. "Haitian Literature in the United States, 1948–1986." *American Babel: Literatures of the United States from Abnaki to Zuni*, edited by Marc Shell, 43–49. Cambridge: Harvard University Press, 2002.

—D. H. Figueredo

Charlier, Etienne Danton (1904–60)

Charlier was a Haitian historian. He was also an attorney.

Born in Aquin, Haiti, on June 12, 1904, Charlier was sent to Port-au-Prince to attend elementary and secondary schools. When he was in his twenties, he traveled to Paris, earning a law degree from the University of Paris. Returning to Haiti, he established a law office and also taught at the l'École du Droit in Port-au-Prince. His interest in his country's history led to a series of articles that he published in journals such as *La Nation*, *Le Matin*, and *L'Action*.

In 1932, he wrote the law text *De l'aménagement du principe de la liberté individuelle de travail en droit français*, an interpretation of individual rights, labor, and national law. In 1934, he wrote the essay, *Fascime, nazisme ou socialisme scientifique*, an exploration of the rise of fascism. But what brought him national recognition was his historical work, *Aperçu su la formation historique de la nation haïtienne* (1954), a socialist reinterpretation of Haiti's rebellion and the establishment of the Haitian republic.

Further Reading

Herdeck, Donald E. *Caribbean Writers: A Bio-Bibliographical-Critical Encyclopedia.* Washington, DC: Three Continents Press, 1979.

—*D. H. Figueredo*

Chassagne, Raymond (1924–)

∎

Chassagne is a Haitian poet and essayist. Through his writings, Chassagne has sought to introduce Haitian literature to the world.

Born in Jérémie, Haiti, on February 13, 1924, Chassagne attended elementary school in his hometown before going on to high school in Port-au-Prince. While serving in the army during the 1950s, his political activities against dictator **François Duvalier** resulted in his arrest. In 1957, Chassagne went into exile in the United States. During the 1960s, he relocated to Canada, where he matriculated at McGill University. After earning a degree in French literature, he pursued doctoral studies at the University of Montreal. During this period, he wrote essays and conducted conferences on such major Francophone Caribbean writers as **Aimé Césaire** and **Edouard Glissant**.

In 1979, Chassagne returned to Haiti, where he taught literature at l'Université d'État and wrote literary reviews for radio and television programs. During the 1980s, Chassagne and writer Anthony Phelps conducted discussions in a literary salon called the Batafou Club; some of the exchanges and poetry readings were recorded: *Incantatoire, poèmes dits par: Anthony Phelps et Boris Chassagne* (2003).

In the 1990s, Chassagne settled in the town of Port Salut and established a library. Chassagne started publishing books of poetry late in life: *Mots de passé* (1976), *Incantatoire* (1996), and *Carnet de bord.* (2004). In his poetry, Chassagne explores the political situation in Haiti.

Further Reading

Saint-Eloi, Rodney. "Raymond Chassagne." http://www.lehman.cuny.edu/ile.en.ile.paroles/chassagne.html (accessed 8/31/05).

—*D. H. Figueredo*

Chauvet, Marie Vieux (1916–73)

Haitian writer Marie Vieux Chauvet is one of the island's major authors. Her works study the politics of sex and power and the abuses Haitian women have encountered in a male-drive society.

The writing talent of Marie Vieux Chauvet appeared early: she was known in her family as the little scribbler, "la petite écrivassière." She began writing plays and producing them for the family at age ten. Eventually, Marie published four novels, with a fifth appearing posthumously. By the time her fourth novel, *Amour, Colère et Folie*, had appeared in 1968, Marie Vieux had become the first Haitian woman to achieve an international literary reputation, on a par with that of **Jacques Roumain** and **Jacques Stephen Alexis**. Two factors inhibited the further development of her career. First, the Chauvet family bought the rights to the fourth novel and attempted to keep it from being distributed. Secondly, Marie fell seriously ill and died from a brain tumor in New York City.

Because of its prestigious publisher, Gallimard, the fourth novel has received far greater commentary than the other five. In fact, even the first novel, *Fille d'Haïti* (1954), received the prize of the Alliance Française in Haiti. Each novel has its own distinction. *La Danse sur le volcan* (1957)—the only novel to have been translated into English in 1959 under the title *The Dance on the Volcan*—is a long historical novel partially based on the career of the first singer and actress of African origin in Saint-Domingue in the period leading up to the Haitian revolution. The third novel, *Fonds des Nègres* (1960), is the unusual story of a "city girl," raised in Port-au-Prince, who is sent to live with her grandmother in an agricultural village in the mountains of southwestern Haiti. When Marie-Ange, the main character, finds herself trapped in Fonds des Nègres—because of her mother's death abroad—she adapts and chooses to convert to vodou, the traditional religion of Haitian peasants. With the vodou priest, Marie-Ange becomes a leader in the peasant revolt to take back their lands from dishonest politicians and rich entrepreneurs. The three short novels included in *Amour, Colère et Folie* (1968) are all set in the Haiti of **François Duvalier**. Each of them focuses in a different setting on the violence exercised by Duvalier's personal militia, the Tonton Makout, the fearful reaction of Haitian citizens, and the dishonest appropriation of property by the government or its agents. The third part, *Folie*, is centered on the resistance of four young poets to the Duvalier dictatorship and written in a style that has been compared to that of William Faulkner (1897–1962). Joan Dayan states in her essay "Reading Women in the Caribbean: Marrie Chauvet's *Love, Anger, and Madness"* that Chauvet wrote this work "to examine the way women are forced in between two constructs not of their own making: black nationalist and white foreigner". In her later book, *Haiti, History, and the Gods*, Dayan aptly comments that in Chauvet's fiction, "the claims of sex are never far from the mechanics of power and submission" (120). The female protagonist of each novel demonstrates in some manner qualities of self-examination and, in most cases, of rebellion to domination by male wielders of power.

Marie's father, Constant Vieux, was a politician who resigned from his post as Minister of the Interior in 1916; was exiled under the dictatorial regime of President Élie Lescot (1883–1974), which lasted from 1941 to1946 and was a very outspoken journalist. Her mother, Delia Nonez, was from Saint Thomas. After finishing her elementary schooling, Marie began studies at the teacher's college, École Normale, in Port-au-Prince, but interrupted her studies and went to live with her elder brother in Saint-Marc, because of the large family's limited finances. After a divorce from her first husband, Dr. Aymon Charlier, Marie married Pierre Chauvet (1948). Eventually she was married a third time, in New York City, to Ted Proudfort. *See also* Vodou in Literature.

Further Reading

Chauvet, Marrie (Vieux). *Fille d'Haïti*. Paris: Fasquelle, 1954.

———. *Fonds des Nègres*. Port-au-Prince: H. Deschamps, 1960. Excerpt translated by Carrol F. Coates, *Callaloo*, 14, no. 3 (Summer 1991): 564–568.

———. *Amour, Colère et Folie*. Paris: Gallimard, 1968. Excerpt translated by Carrol F. Coates, *Callaloo* 15, no. 2 (Spring 1992): 455–461.

Dayan, Joan. "Reading Women in the Caribbean: Marrie Chauvet's *Love, Anger, and Madness.*" In Joan DeJean & Nancy K. Miller, 228–53. *Displacements: Women, Tradition, Literatures in French*. Baltimore: Johns Hopkins University Press, 1991.

———. *Haiti, History, and the Gods*. Berkeley: University of California, 1995.

—*Carrol F. Coates*

Children's Literature in the English-Speaking Caribbean

∎

The English-speaking Caribbean consists of a number of small countries, mostly islands of varying sizes, that were either former British colonies or are still dependencies. Consequently, for many years there was little incentive for producing indigenous literature, as reading materials were imported from Britain. It was not until the 1960s, when there was a general move toward independence by many of these countries, that a smattering of indigenous books for children started to appear. Now there is a fairly substantial body of literature. Jamaica and Trinidad, two of the larger islands, have produced the majority of the literature from the region, although many of these books still appear under foreign imprints because publishing in the Caribbean is a very costly venture, especially when it comes to children's books. It should also be noted that many of the writers are not necessarily domiciled in the region but live in Britain or North America. Nevertheless; they still write with authenticity about the Caribbean experience at home and abroad.

The available literature covers most of the regular genres, with folktales and realistic fiction dominating the field. Folktales were among the first types of books to emerge, and nearly every country has produced a collection of such tales drawn from the rich oral tradition from Africa and blended with some of the typical features of European folklore. **Anancy,** the West African spiderman and trickster, is the most well-known folk hero with lesser known ones such as Papa Bois and La Diablesse. The best-known writer of such tales over the years is **Philip Sherlock** and more recently, Richardo Keens-Douglas, a talented writer who creates original myths and folktales based on the Caribbean experience. One such book, *Freedom Child of the Sea*, carries a timeless and universal message as the author weaves a powerful myth from strands of his people's harrowing experience during the middle passage from Africa to the West Indies.

Emmanuel and His Parrot (1970), by Karl Craig, was one of the first full-color picture books produced locally, and **John Agard** wrote a number of books, sometimes in verse, that reflected Caribbean realities in Britain as well as locally. Errol Lloyd (1943–), resident of London, is the best-known picture book illustrator from the region, and one of his books, *My Brother Sean* (1973), was runner-up for the prestigious Greenaway Medal in Britain. The combination of art and simple text in Frane Lessac's many picture books suggest a world of childhood innocence, while others portray the realities and unique features of life in the Caribbean. More recently, a steady flow of quality picture book has emerged: for example, **Valerie Bloom's** engaging picture books *Fruits* (1997) and *Ackee, Breadfruit, Callaloo* (1999) which are lavishly and realistically illustrated; Peter Laurie's *Mauby's Big Adventure* (2000); and Barbara Comissiong's *Mind Me Good Now* (1997). As far as poetry is concerned, there is a dearth of single volumes written by an individual. Instead, there are anthologies such as *A Caribbean Dozen* (1996).

Realistic fiction is by far most numerous, especially at the younger age group, with fewer writers at the older level since the eighties. Only a mere handful of historical novels are available from writers like **Vic Reid**—*Young Warriors* (1980)—who builds his stories around key historical events in Jamaica's march toward freedom and political independence, and **Jean Goulbourne's** graphic portrayal of children living under the harshness of slavery. Contemporary stories focus on coming-of-age issues, dealing with racism as immigrants in England or North America (**Rosa Guy,** Errol Lloyd and **Marlene Nourbese Philip**), facing the vicissitudes of life (**Jean D'Costa**) and coping with natural and man made disasters (**Andrew Salkey**). The most prolific writer in this genre to date is C. Everard Palmer, who in vibrant prose has written over a dozen books celebrating all aspects of rural life.

Informational works are few. They are mainly written by foreigners for overseas publishers and focus mostly on the social history of the region. These tend to read like exotic tourist brochures and are sometimes filled with stereotypes. Children's magazines have appeared sporadically and rarely survive for any time due, in part, to high production costs, the scattered nature of the market, the lack of buying power among the readership, and the absence of a recreational reading culture.

Despite the limitations, the future can be viewed with some optimism; since the 1990s, publishers such as Longman, Carlong, and especially MacMillan, have been producing more indigenous children's books for leisure reading. A few more indigenous publishers have also entered the field, such as Morton Publishers in Trinidad, who specializes in picture books with a strong cultural flavor. A few awards for children's books have been introduced, such as the Vic Reid Award for Excellence in Writing for Children & Young Adults in Jamaica, which should serve as an incentive for writers. Finally, the Caribbean Publishers Network (CAPNET) was established in 2000 to promote all aspects of regional publishing, including that of children's books. In light of these developments, an increase in the production of children's literature within the region is anticipated in the years to come. *See also* Anglophone Caribbean Literature; Jamaican Literature, History of.

Further Reading

Breinberg, Petronella. *My Brother Sean*. Illustrated by Errol Lloyd. London: Bodley Head, 1973.

Comissiong, Barbara. *Mind Me Good Now*. Toronto: Annick Press, 1997.

Craig, Karl. *Emmanuel and His Parrot*. London: Oxford University Press, 1970.

D'Costa, Jean. *Escape to Last Man Peak*. Kingston: Longman, 1980.

Goulbourne, Jean. *Freedom Come*. Kingston: Carlong Publishers, 2003.

Gunning, Monica. *Not a Copper Penny in Me House*. Honesdale, PA: Boyds Mills Press, 1993.

Joseph, Lynn. *Coconut Kind of Day. Island Poems*. New York: Lothrop, Lee and Shepard, 1990.

Keens-Douglas, Richardo. *Freedom Child of the Sea*. Illustrated by Julia Gukova. Toronto: Annick Press, 1995.

Laurie, Peter. *Mauby's Big Adventure*. London: MacMillan Caribbean, 2000.

Lessac, Frane. *The Little Island*. New York: HarperCollins, 1984.

Lloyd, Errol. *Many Rivers to Cross*. London: Methuen, 1995.

—Cherrell Shelley-Robinson

Children's Literature in the Hispanic Caribbean
■

Cuba and Puerto Rico dominate the production of children's literature, a production further augmented in the United States in the 1980s and 1990s with children's writers from these two islands recalling their homeland in stories or writing about the immigrant experience in the United States. Overall, it can be stated that the appearance of this genre in the Hispanic Caribbean is a twentieth century phenomenon.

During the nineteenth century, children heard legends and local stories, from relatives and friends, that could be interpreted as fairy tales or children's stories. But the political turmoil in Cuba and Puerto Rico, as these two islands fought for independence from Spain, diverted attention from such activities. There was a pioneer, though, and that was the Cuban patriot and poet **José Martí**. In the 1880s, he edited the first children's magazine in Latin America, *La Edad de Oro* (1889), which consisted of stories, essays, and poems written exclusively for the children. In dealing with children, Martí was unique. During his era, adults treated children as miniature adults. Martí, on the other hand, realized the fragility of childhood and approached children as individuals who were slowly and gradually growing into adulthood. His belief that "los niños son la esperanza del mundo"—children are the hope of the world—prompted him to write stories about heroes and selfless acts, promoting responsible citizenship.

Toward the end of the nineteenth century and beginning of the twentieth, children were exposed to translations of European classics: works by the Grimm brothers—Jacob Ludwig Carl Grimm (1785–1863) and Wilhelm Carl Grimm (1786–1859)—and Hans Christian Anderson (1805–75). In the early 1900s, a Puerto Rican educator and writer, Manuel Fernández Juncos (1846–1928), wrote anthologies for children that were used primarily in schools. In the 1910s, **Cayetano Coll y Toste** collected and wrote popular legends about Amerindians before the arrival of the Spanish, *Tradiciones y leyendas puertorriqueñas* (1914). In 1920s, **Juan B. Huyke** wrote poetry for children and published stories he had meant for his grandchildren, *Rimas infantiles* (1926) and *Un libro para mis nietos* (1928). Though enjoyable, these books revealed didactic characteristics.

In the 1930s, Puerto Rican educators and writers echoed Martí's sentiments toward children and began to write works meant to capture the ways in which children interpreted the world. One of the best volumes published was *Poemas para mis niños* (1938), by **Carmelina Vizcarrondo**. The 1940s were characterized by a series of nursery rhymes based on Puerto Rican legends and depicting Caribbean animals. The series was called *Nanas*—meaning lullabies—and was written by **Ester Feliciano Mendoza**. During this period, Cuba and Puerto Rico also shared a particular story, sometimes written, often presented orally: "La cucarachita Martina," about a little roach who marries a gluttonous mouse. Curiously enough, this folk tale inspired a Puerto Rican librarian working in New York City. **Pura Belpré** was a bilingual storyteller at the New York Public Library who often used puppets to reenact legends and stories from her native Puerto Rico, drawing crowds of children and adults alike. Her first children's book, *Perez and Martina: A Portorican Folk Tale* (1932), was published as a result of its successful reception by library patrons and staff, which impressed the publisher.

In the 1950s, Puerto Rico's Department of Education assumed the role of children's publishers; its principal avenue for exposure was a journal called *Educación*. But the department also published books: the major writer to emerge was once again Carmelina Vizcarrondo. Many of the stories published reflected African, Amerindian, and Spanish traditions and folklore.

In 1959, **Fidel Castro** overthrew Fulgencio Batista (1901–73). The revolutionary government realized that children's literature could serve as an educational tool, and children's stories praising revolutionary accomplishment began to appear in print. In 1966, **Dora Alonso** published *Aventuras de Guille*, a short novel that demonstrated how much the island had progressed under Castro's leadership. Throughout the 1970s, Alonso forsook realistic settings and political messages for more fantastic narratives. In *El cochero azul* (1974), for example, there is house with window shades made of feathers that always take off in flight during the spring.

In 1980s and 1990s, Cuban, Dominican, and Puerto Rican authors living in the United States wrote picture books that dealt with such themes as immigration, families, and recollections from the old country. An example of this category is *When This World Was New* (1999) by D. H. Figueredo. The leading children's writers were **Alma Ada Flor,** whose stories encouraged children to write down their family histories, and **Julia Alvarez**—already an established novelist—whose two children's books, *The Secret Footprints* (2000) and *How Tia Lola Came to Stay* (2001), explored Dominican folklore and family relationships. The appearance of these works signaled a shift: from the Spanish language to English.

The arrival of the twenty-first century suggests the following development: a lull in children's literature in Cuba; more children's stories with realistic settings in Puerto Rico; well-known adult authors writing books for children; and the growing presence of Cuban American, Dominican American, and Puerto Rican American authors in the American market. The predominant themes will be immigration, discrimination, and life in the Caribbean.

Further Reading

Baralt, Blanche Zacharie de. *El Martí que yo conocí*. Habana: Editorial Trópico, 1945.

Figueras, Consuelo. "Puerto Rican Children's Literature." *Bookbird* 38 (2000): 23–28.

Rosell, Joel Franz. "Sense of Place in Cuban Children's Narrative." *Bookbird* 39 (2001): 37–41.

—*D. H. Figueredo*

Ciclón (1955–57, 1959)

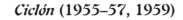

Cuban literary journal founded and edited by José Rodríguez Feo. Educated at Harvard and Princeton universities, Rodríguez Feo (1920–94) had first been involved with the prestigious publication *Orígenes*, edited by poet **José Lezama Lima**. Because of *Orígenes*' Catholic outlook, he parted company in 1954. Using his own financial resources, Rodríguez Feo invited contributions from experimental Cuban writers and established authors from abroad, much as did *Bim* in the Anglophone West Indies. Ciclón published some of the early works of **Severo Sarduy** and **Calvert Casey**. Established authors writing for the journal included **Virgilio Piñera**, Lionel Trilling (1905–75), and W. H. Auden (1907–73). Of limited circulation, Ciclón criticized Cuban culture of the 1950s. *See also* Literary Journals.

Further Reading

Pérez León, Roberto. *Tiempo de Ciclón*. Habana: Ediciones Unión, Unión de Escritores y Artistas de Cuba, 1995.

—Peter T. Johnson

Cinéas, Jean-Baptiste (1895–1958)

A writer who wrote in the genre known as the **peasant novel**—le roman payson—Cinéas promoted Haitian culture and identity, rejecting European influences and models as well as the American presence on the island. He was an attorney.

Cinéas was born in Cap-Haïtien, Haiti, on June 5, 1895, and studied at l'École Notre-Dame du Perpétuel Secours, a Catholic school. He attended the Free Law School of Cap-Haïtien, earning a law degree when he was in his early 20s. He taught at the Collège Notre-Dame, practiced law, and in 1930 was appointed judge to Haiti's Supreme Court.

In 1933, his first novel, *Le drame de la terre*, was published. It was a sympathetic portrayal of Haiti's peasants, emphasizing African influences in their daily lives. That same year, *La vengeance de la terre* was published, again about the struggles of the peasant in the countryside. Both novels initiated literary interest in the dormant genre known as the peasant novel.

Through the 1930s, Cinéas was occupied with his legal responsibilities. In 1945, he published *L'héritage sacré*. In 1948, he published *Le choc en retour*. He also published stories about Haiti's heroes, always emphasizing the nation's connections with the peasants and African roots. *See also* American Occupation of Haiti, Literature of the (1915–34).

Further Reading

Herdeck, Donald E. *Caribbean Writers: A Bio-Bibliographical-Critical Encyclopedia*. Washington, DC: Three Continents Press, 1979.

—D. H. Figueredo

Clarke, Austin (1934–)

Austin Clarke is a Barbadian novelist and short-story writer who examines the themes of colonialism in the Caribbean and the life of the West Indies immigrant in the United Kingdom and Canada. He is the recipient of a prestigious literary prize from **Casa de las Américas**, in Cuba.

Austin Clarke was born in Barbados in 1934. He left the island in 1955 to attend the University of Toronto, taking up residence in that Canadian city, where he has lived more or less continuously ever since. A decade later, in the 1960s, Clarke published his first novels: *Survivors of the Crossing* (1964), *The Meeting Point* (1967), along with a volume of short stories, *Among Thistles and Thorns* (1965). Most of his works explore his experience of Barbados and Canada, while a smaller portion of his writing examines his experience in the United States. Austin Clarke has taught creative writing at a number of American universities and served as cultural attaché to the Barbadian embassy in Washington.

A good introduction to Clarke's Barbados-based works would be a reading of *The Polished Hoe*, his latest novel of 2003, and, alternately, a much earlier memoir in the form of a novel, *Growing Up Stupid Under the Union Jack*, which won the Casa de las Américas Prize in 1980. In this largely autobiographical work, Clarke takes on the topic of colonialism and postcolonial conditions in the British Empire, which he continues to explore in later works. But it is this first coming-of-age in Barbados narrative that allows Clarke to take apart the identity of the island's middle class as he thoroughly deconstructs the British colonial education the narrator receives. The Calibanesque protagonist is, throughout, hard at work positing an alternate identity for himself. An independent-minded hero, he will in all likelihood end up making a life for himself elsewhere.

Clarke's short stories have dealt with the experiences of black people, of West Indian transplants, in Canada. His short-story collections include: *When He Was Free and Young and He Used to Wear Silks* (1971), *When Women Rule* (1985), *Nine Men Who Laughed* (1986), *In This City* (1992), and *There Are No Elders Here* (1993).

Austin Clarke's exploration of identity, colonialism, and resistance among West Indians, both at home and abroad, has taken many forms. *The Polished Hoe* (2003) is set in the 1940s in Bimshire, a fictionalized Barbados, over the course of one single night. Important in its own right is Clarke's culinary memoir, *Pig Tails and Bread Fruit: The Rituals of Slave Food*, which is another inquiry into identity, colonialism, and resistance as it chronicles how food defines home and culture, a topic taken up earlier in *Growing Up Stupid Under the Union Jack*, in which World War II interrupts the arrival of imported foodstuffs from England and people must make do with what they have, rediscovering local cuisine and, in the process, a radical home-grown identity. *See also* Caliban; Postcolonialism.

Further Reading

Algoo-Baksh, Stella. *Austin C. Clarke: A Biography*. Barbados: Press of the University of the West Indies; Toronto: ECW Press, 1994.

—Pamela María Smorkaloff

Cliff, Michelle (1946–)

◼

A Jamaican novelist and poet, Michelle Cliff is preoccupied with history and origins, as well as personal identity and the politics of color. In her writings, she explores feminism and lesbianism as well.

Michelle Cliff was born in Jamaica on November 2, 1946. When she was three her family relocated to New York, yet Cliff would spend her childhood years moving back and forth between Jamaica and the United States. Educated in the United States, Jamaica, and England, Cliff worked in publishing after receiving her masters degree in 1974. In her later thirties, she began to write and has been writing and publishing steadily ever since. As a West Indian immigrant to the United States, a woman of color, and a lesbian, Michelle Cliff engages actively with multiple forms of oppression and resistance in her fiction, prose poems, and essays. At the crossroads of the Americas and Europe, the legacy of slavery and British colonialism, and as a Jamaican who can "pass," Cliff has a rigorous eye and a lot to say on the question of identity and the forging of a Caribbean voice in literature. She makes explicit the very necessary links between the personal and the political, in a global context, in her own development as a Caribbean woman and writer. Her first work was a collection of prose poems dealing with identity and the legacy of colonialism. Along with the best writers of Latin America and the Caribbean, Cliff seeks to explore the unofficial histories of the Caribbean.

Michelle Cliff has been a reporter, a researcher, and an editor. In the academic realm she has held the post of visiting professor at the New School for Social Research, Stanford University, and Trinity College, among others. Her honors include a MacDowell Fellowship at MacDowell Colony, the Eli Kantor Fellowship at Yaddo, National Endowment for the Arts Grant for both fiction and nonfiction, and a Fulbright Scholarship to New Zealand.

Cliff's first book, *Claiming an Identity They Taught Me to Despise* (1980), is a collection of prose poems exploring themes of race, color, class, and gender, followed by *Land of Look Beyond: Prose and Poetry* (1985). Among her works of fiction are *Abeng* (1995), *No Telephone to Heaven* (1987), *Bodies of Water* (1990), *Free Enterprise* (1993), and *Store of a Million Items* (1998).

Further Reading

Agosto, Noraida. *Michelle Cliff's Novels: Piecing the Tapestry of Memory and History.* New York: P. Lang, 1999.

—*Pamela María Smorkaloff*

Cocco de Filippis, Daisy (1949–)

∎

An intellectual and literary investigator from the Dominican Republic, Daisy Cocco de Filippis is an anthologist and essayist who has unveiled the works of little known women writers from her country. An educator and activist, Cocco de Filippis is also known as a literary mentor and the host of **tertulias**, literary salons, where Latina writers and professors from the New York area meet to discuss feminist writers from the Caribbean.

Cocco de Filippis was born on February 25, 1949, in Santo Domingo, the Dominican Republic. In 1962, she moved to New York City and attended public school. In 1975, she graduated from the City University of New York; three years later she earned a masters in Hispanic literature from Queens College; in 1984 she received a PhD in Latin American literature. She taught literature at York College, was a Rockefeller Foundation fellow at the Instítuto de Estudios Dominicanos of the City University of New York, and has been provost and vice president of Academic Affairs at Hostos Community College, the first Dominican in the United States to hold such a high and prestigious position.

Early in her career, Cocco de Filippis realized that half of the literary production in the Dominican Republic, the half written by women, was not well known in that country and was not known at all outside the Dominican Republic. It became her mission to rescue these writers from obscurity. She wrote in the prologue to *This Thing Called Home: Of Diaspora and Books* (2004), "I have endeavored to 'do the right thing' and the 'kind thing' . . . by giving voice . . . to authors who are not heard enough; whose writings are left out from publications by colleagues here and there." With such an objective in mind, she edited numerous anthologies, often translating the selections herself, including *Sin otro profeta que su canto: Antología de poesía escrita por dominicanas* (1998), *Combatidas, combativas y combatientes: Antología de cuentos escritos por mujeres dominicanas* (1992), *Tertuliando/Hanging Out: Compilación bilingüe de escritoras dominicanas en los Estados Unidos* (1997), and *Para que no se olviden: The Lives of Women in Dominican History* (2000). To identify and secure the poems and stories in these anthologies, Cocco de Filippis visited private libraries and searched library holdings of major universities in the New York area and the Dominican Republic.

Cocco de Filippis has written numerous essays and articles about Dominican writers and literature. Though she visits the Dominican Republic quite often, she, like many Caribbean authors, is a person who lives between two worlds and two cultures but chooses to remain in the United States. She writes in *This Thing Called Home* that it is from the United States where she must "write . . . and build . . . [and] be a part of a community of kindred spirits who toil to create a space for those . . . searching answers."

Further Reading

Luis, William. *Dance Between Two Cultures*. Nashville: Vanderbilt University Press, 1997.

Torres-Saillant, Silvio and Ramona Hernandez. *The New Americans: The Dominican Americans*. Westport, CT: Greenwood Press, 1998.

—*D. H. Figueredo*

Code Switching

Code switching is the insertion of a foreign word or phrase into a dialogue or a narrative written in another language. As a literary device it allows the author to create an aura, or ambiance, and to attribute particular traits to a character, such as ethnicity and social background. It also suggests a bond between characters of the same culture or nationality, affirming a cultural heritage.

Code switching also suggests the cultural duality experienced by immigrants or transplanted writers living in the United States. A line from the poem "Bilingual Blues" by Cuban American poet **Gustavo Pérez Firmat** illustrates code switching:

> Soy un ajiaco de contradicciones
> I have mixed feelings about everything.

Code switching is similar to the use of dialect in Francophone and Anglophone Caribbean writings: it stresses the narrator's origin and targets a particular audience, one familiar with the vernacular.

Further Reading

Auer, Peter. *Code-Switching in Conversation: Language, Interaction and Identity*. London: Routledge, 1998.

—*D. H. Figueredo*

Cofiño López, Manuel (1936–87)

Novelist, short-story writer, and author of children's books, Manuel Cofiño López wrote realistic novels that explored the social changes that occurred in Cuba as a result of the revolution in 1959. He wrote for the general public and was unconcerned with literary critics and foreign opinion. Yet his novels were well received in Latin America and were translated into English and Russian.

Cofiño López was born in Havana on February 16, 1936. In the late 1950s, he owned a furniture store that he gave to the new revolutionary regime after **Fidel Castro**'s victory. Cofiño López wrote for all the major journals of the period, including *Casa de las Américas* and *Bohemia*. He also wrote for the foreign publications *Ahora*, published in Chile, and *Tribuna*, from Romania. In 1969, he published his first book, *Tiempo de cambio*, a collection of short stories about revolutionaries combating sabotage and bourgeoisie attitude in Cuba. In 1971, his novel *La útima mujer y el próximo combate* won the **Casa de las Américas** literary award. In 1975, he published *Cuando la sangre se parece al fuego*, which takes place in a "solar," a tenement built like a barrack, and criticizes the practices of **santería**, an African Cuban religion that the author felt undermined the advances made by the revolution.

Cofiño López is identified as a writer of **literatura comprometida**, a literature written to support the Cuban Revolution in particular and political change in general. Compatriot **Edmundo Desnoes**, writing in *Los dispositivos en la flor* (1981), criticized Cofiño López for not commenting negatively on mistakes made by Fidel Castro and his regime. But Cofiño López, like the Jamaican **Vic Reid**, in his novel *A New Day*, preferred to celebrate the revolution's positive accomplishments. *See also* Barrack Yard Literature.

Further Reading

Desnoes, Edmundo. *Los dispositivos en la flor, Cuba: Literatura desde la revolución.* Hanover: Ediciones del Norte, 1981.

García Alzota, Ernesto. *Acerca de Manuel Cofiño.* Habana, Cuba: Editorial Letras Cubanas, 1989.

—D. H. Figueredo

Coicou, Massillon (1867–1908)

■

A patriotic poet, novelist, and playwright, Coicou is probably the first Haitian writer to have been executed by the government. Through his poetry, he expressed, according to scholar Naomi Garret in *The Renaissance of Haitian Poetry* (1963), "a desire for progress for his country . . . guided by patriotic rather than selfish interests" (35–36).

Coicou was born in Port-au-Prince on October 9, 1867. He attended elementary school at the Frères de l'Instruction Chrétienne and high school at the Lycée National. While in school, he demonstrated an early interest in literature and began to write poetry when he was teenager. After high school, he served in the Haitian infantry. In 1895, he became a teacher. During this period, he published his first book of poetry, *Poésies nationals* (1891), and wrote several plays, including *Toussaint au fort de Joux* and *L'Empereur Dessalines* (1896). These works were patriotic and nationalistic.

His creative output brought him to the attention of public officials, and in 1900, President Tirésias Antoine Auguste Simon-Sam (1835–1916), who was friends with the poet's family, appointed Coicou secretary of the Haitian Delegation in Paris. In France, Coicou socialized with writers and intellectuals and was one of the speakers at the celebration of Victor Hugo's centenary. In 1903, he published two books of poetry, *Passions* and *Impressions*. In 1904, he returned to Haiti and he founded the journal *L'Ouvre*. In 1905, he published in the journal *Le Soir* his novel *La noire,* in which he explores colonialism and slavery.

As his literary reputation was growing, Coicou was becoming more involved in political developments, especially in supporting the presidential candidacy of the writer **Anténor Firmin**, who was a good friend of the poet's. His friend's defeat and the unjustified execution of political prisoners by President Nord Alexis (1820–1910) prompted Coicou to join a plot against the government. He was arrested and promptly executed in March 1908.

Further Reading

Berrou, Raphaël, and Pradel Pompilus. *Histoire de la littérature haitienne.* Tome 1. Port-au Prince, Haiti: Editions Caraïbes, 1975.

Garret, Naomi M. *The Renaissance of Haitian Poetry.* Paris: Présence africaine, 1963.

—D. H. Figueredo

Colimon-Hall, Marie-Thérèse (1918–97)

Known by her maiden name *Colimon* as well as by the early pseudonym Marie Bec, this Haitian woman of letters once said that her whole life had been filled with literature. Indeed, from the age of ten she began to be passionate about the written word. Although she did not begin literary production for adult readers until she was in her fifties, Colimon would become one of the most prominent female authors of Haiti.

As devoted to teaching as she was to literature, Colimon began her career as a teacher at the École Smith Duplessis and the Collège Colimon Boisson in Port-au-Prince. She published articles on the Haitian school system and established the École Nationale des Jardinières, a school for the preparation of kindergarten teachers. An activist for the emancipation and defense of women and girls, Colimon served as the president of *La Ligue féminine d'action sociale* (or The Feminine League for Social Action) from 1960 to 1971. She also acted as a member of the jury deciding the Prix littéraire Henri-Deschamps in 1975.

Her bibliography includes a book of poems, three plays, a novel, and an anthology of short stories focused mainly on the topic of women. The six tales from *Le Chant des sirènes* (1980) illustrate such representative themes as poverty, loneliness, dreams, rebellion, and especially exile. In "Bonjour Maman! Bonne Fête Maman!" a fourteen-year-old girl balks at a class assignment of writing a Mother's Day letter because her parents have been living apart from her in exile since she was an infant. Seemingly exiled herself as a boarding school student in the capital city, Dolcina Désilius envies the family life of her classmates as well as the comfortable existence that she imagines her parents and younger siblings enjoy in the United States.

Colimon's only novel, *Fils de misère,* won her a major literary prize, the Prix France-Haïti, in 1973. Inspired by an unknown woman and baby passing by her on a Haitian street, Colimon created the strong and memorable character of Lamercie Mercidieu. The proud Cicie, as she is called, lives in the poverty-stricken, oppressed Cour Ravette section of Port-au-Prince, where she struggles at a variety of low-paying jobs to survive. Because her hopes and dreams are centered on her only child, a son nicknamed Ti-Tonton, Cicie proves that she is determined to do whatever is necessary to provide him with food and an education and to protect him against the cruel and powerful members of the political regime.

Titles of some of Colimon's other writings include her plays *La Fille de l'esclave* (1949) and *Marie-Claire Heureuse* (1955).

Further Reading

Author unknown. "Mémoire de femmes: Marie-Thérèse Colimon-Hall." http://www.haitiwebs.com/femmes/html/37.htm (accessed 5/28/04).

Condé, Maryse. *La Parole des Femmes: essai sur des romancières des Antilles de langue française.* Paris: L'Harmattan, 1979.

Serrano, Lucienne J. " 'Elle porte l'enfant comme on porte un bouquet' *Fils de misère* de Marie Thérèse Colimon." *Elle écrivent des Antilles: Haïti, Guadeloupe, Martinique,* edited by Suzanne Rinne, and Joëlle Vitiello, 71–75. Paris: L'Harmattan, 1997.

Shelton, Marie-Denise. "Haitian Women's Fiction." *Callaloo* 15, no. 3 (Summer 1992): p. 770–77.

Wainwright, Edith. "La Présence africaine dans les æuvres féminines haïtienne: Marrie Chauvet, Marie-Thérèse Colimon, Paulette Poujol Oriol." *Journal of Haitian Studies* 3, no. 4 (1997–98): p. 96–102.

—Jayne R. Boisvert

Coll, Edna (1906–)

Coll is a Puerto Rican artist, essayist, and educator. Her extensive traveling reinforced a universal vision of the arts and literature which, in turn, encouraged her to promote not only the literature of Puerto Rico but of Latin America as well.

A native of San Juan, Coll traveled throughout Europe and the United States before matriculating at the Universidad de Puerto Rico in 1938. Four years later, she received a BA in education. In 1945, she earned an MA in Hispanic studies. In 1949, she founded a school that bore her name, Academia de Bellas Artes Edna Coll. In 1954, she began to teach at her alma mater but at the Mayagüez campus.

While teaching, she was writing articles that were published in the popular and academic press, including *Diario de Puerto Rico*, *Revista Hispánica Moderna*, and *Atenea*. She wrote literary essays, publishing in 1947 *Chile y los chilenos en las novelas de Joaquín Edwards Bello*, and in 1964 *Injerto de temas en las novelistas mexicanas contemporáneos*. In the mid-1970s, she worked on a massive reference source, *Índice informativo de la novela hispanoamericana*.

Coll also wrote short stories, *Simplemente cuentos* (1986), and the memoirs *Vida y literatura* (1972) and *Instantes en el tiempo: mis memorias* (1986,1988). An artist, Coll received the 1981 Andres Bello Medal of Honor from the Venezuelan government and in 1983 a literary award from the Academia de Artes y Ciencias de Puerto Rico.

Further Reading

Toro-Sugrañes, José A. *Nueva enciclopedia de Puerto Rico de la geografía, historia, y cultura*. Tomo 4. Hato Rey, Puerto Rico: Editorial Lector, 1994.

—D. H. Figueredo

Collado Martel, Alfredo (1900–30)

Considered one of Puerto Rico's best writers of short stories within the **Modernismo** movement—which advocated an intense awareness of aesthetics, preferred metaphorical language, and controlled expression of emotions—Collado wrote stories that addressed universal themes within a Puerto Rican setting. He was a journalist and wrote poetry as well.

Born in the Dominican Republic of Puerto Rican parents, Collado and his family returned to Puerto Rico when he was eight years old, settling in Mayagüez. Economic hardship interrupted his education, and from a young age he had to find employment. He worked at a sugar mill until he relocated to San Juan, where he began to publish his short stories in local publications. In 1929, he befriended writers **Antonio S. Pedreira**, Vicente Geigel Polanco, and **Samuel R. Quiñones**, and they founded the journal *Índice*, which published the works of young writers of the era.

Critic **Concha Meléndez**, in *El arte del cuento en Puerto Rico* (1961), considered that his best and most representative work is the story "La última aventura del patito feo," a tragic retelling of Hans Christian Anderson's *The Ugly Duckling*.

Collado died very young. In 1931, his short stories were published under the title *Cuentos absurdos*.

Further Reading

Meléndez, Concha. *El arte del cuento en Puerto Rico*. New York: Las Américas Publishing, 1961.

Vázquez, Margarita, and Daisy Caraballo. "Cuento: El cuento en Puerto Rico." In *La gran enciclopedia de Puerto Rico*, edited by Vicente Báez, 83–87. San Juan: Puerto Rico en la Mano y La Gran Enciclopedia de Puerto Rico, 1981.

—*D. H. Figueredo*

Collective Bovaryism. See Bovaryism.

Collins, Merle (1950–)

■

Poet, short-story writer, and novelist from Grenada, Merle Collins has written extensively about the Grenadian revolution of the 1980s and about her self-exile in England. Like the Guyanese **Martin Carter**, with whom she is often compared, Collins is a political writer committed to the use of literature as a vehicle for social change.

Born in Aruba of Grenadian parents on September 29, 1950, Merle Collins was raised in Grenada, where she attended elementary and secondary schools before enrolling at the University of West Indies–Mona. Graduating in 1972, she returned to Grenada to work as a teacher. She then went to graduate school at Georgetown University, specializing in Latin American studies; she graduated in 1981.

Though she wasn't a Marxist, the ideology attracted her. She wrote in the essay "Writing Fiction, Writing Reality," published in *Caribbean Women Writers* (1999): "What Marxism-Leninism meant for me was . . . equality of classes, better living conditions for everybody, education available to all" (23). Because of her views, in 1982 she became a supporter of the revolutionary regime in Grenada, the People's Revolutionary Government led by Maurice Bishop (1944–83), and worked for the Ministry of Foreign Affairs. The social changes occurring on the island inspired her poetry, which she performed at public gatherings and official events. Through her poetry, she praised, and sometimes criticized, the revolutionary government. She also contemplated the ill effects of colonialism. In one of her most famous poems, "The Lesson" (1984), she describes how her grandmother was quite familiar with British history but knew little of the Caribbean or of her African heritage.

In 1983, Maurice Bishop was assassinated by rival rebels, the revolutionary government was toppled, and American armed forces landed on the island. The events devastated Collins, but her compatriots' reaction baffled her even more, for most Grenadians favored the invasion and those who didn't remained silent. To sort out her emotions, Collins moved to Britain, where she attended the School of Economics and Political Science at the University of London, earning a PhD in government studies.

In 1987, Collins wrote *Angel*, her first novel. The Grenadian revolution, its failures, and the invasion of Grenada by the United States serve as the background for the novel. Three years later, she published a collection of short stories entitled *Rain Darling*. The seven stories in the volume explore West Indian culture, language, and the role of women in the Caribbean. In 1992, she wrote about her experiences in Grenada and in England in the collection of poems *Rotten Pomerach*. In 1995, she wrote the *Colour of Forgetting*, an epic novel about slavery, emancipation, and colonialism. The focus is on the need for the people of the Caribbean to affirm their cultures and remember their histories and to reject European versions of the conquest and colonization of the West Indies.

Aside from the political themes, Collins uses her poetry and prose to give a voice to the silent women of the Caribbean, praising their ability to survive slavery, family separation due to immigration and exile, and the values imposed on women by a male-driven society. Her other writings include *Because the Dawn Breaks! Poems Dedicated to the Grenadian People* (1985) and *Lady in a Boat: Poems* (1999). She is the editor—with Rhonda Cobham—of *Watchers and Seekers: Creative Writing by Black Women in Britain* (1987) and *Jump-Up-and-Kiss Me: Two Stories of Grenadian Childhood* (1990). *See also* Literatura Comprometida/Socially Engaged Literature; Postcolonialism.

Further Reading

Collins, Merle. "Writing Fiction, Writing Reality." In *Caribbean Women Writers: Fiction in English*, edited by Mary Conde and Thorunn Lonsdale, 23–31. New York: St. Martin's Press, 1999.

—*D. H. Figueredo*

Collymore, Frank A. (1893–1980)

Called the "enabler of West Indies literature," Barbadian Frank Collymore is fondly remembered as the enthusiastic editor of the literary journal *Bim*, the first such publication in the region, and a promoter of West Indian literature. He was also a poet and a short-story writer.

In 1942, friends asked Collymore to edit the floundering *YMPC Journal*, the newsletter and organ of the Young Men's Progressive Club; from this seed came forth *Bim*, a literary magazine that would in time feature the works of such major writers as **George Lamming** and **Edgar Mittelhölzer**. While favoring authors from Barbados, Jamaica, and Trinidad, Collymore, always eager for new talent and new ideas, also published creative works by Haitian writers, thus bringing to the West Indies an exciting literature unknown to most Anglophone readers. During the 1940s and 1950s, Collymore introduced new writers to the BBC producers of the influential radio show **Caribbean Voices**, which originated in London and was broadcast in the Caribbean. Often, a piece that was read or discussed in *Caribbean Voices* would make its way onto the pages of *Bim*.

As a writer, Collymore wrote macabre short stories reminiscent of works by Edgar Allan Poe (1809–49), whom Collymore treasured, and Ambrose Bierce (1842–1914?). Two of his most famous stories are "Shadows" and "Some People Are Meant to Live Alone." In the first, the eerie mood of the mansion where a couple lives propels the husband to murder his wife; he remarries only to discover the deceased has possessed the second wife. In the second story, the narrator learns that his eccentric relative has a tendency to do away with anyone who talks too much and disturbs the silence of his home . . . and much to his surprise, the narrator discovers that he shares the sentiment!

As a poet, Collymore wrote pastoral poems, "Seaplunge" for example, that depict the natural beauty of the Caribbean; he penned antiwar poems, such as "V. C. Invictus," which honors the memory of a friend killed in combat; and satirical verses, such as "Roman Holiday," in which he compares a funeral to a coronation. His verses are light and playful, which is a reflection of how the very modest Collymore saw himself: a good enough poet but not a genius. Collymore also penned the seminal *Notes for a Glossary of Words and Phrases of Barbadian Dialect* (1955), considered the first attempt at presenting the richness of West Indian language in a scholarly manner and to approach West Indian dialect as a subject worthy of linguistic exploration.

Frank A. Collymore was a teacher, an artist, an actor—called by George Lamming one of the best actors in West Indies—and a member of the committee that selected Barbados's national anthem in 1996. As a literary figure, scholars have yet to study his works. As a literary mentor, historians agree that it was Collymore who inspired dozens of writers to write and to get their output onto the world's arena. *See also* Literary Journals; Tertulias/Literary Salons/Soirées.

Further Reading

Baugh, Edward, "Frank Collymore." In *Fifty Caribbean Writers*, edited by Daryl Cumber Dance, 122–33. Westport, CT: Greenwood Press, 1986.

Collymore, Frank A. *Collected Poems*. Bridgetown, Barbados: Advocate Co., 1959.

———. *The Man Who Loved Attending Funerals and Other Stories*. Oxford: Heinemann International Literature and Textbooks, 1993.

—*D. H. Figueredo*

Coll y Toste, Cayetano (1850–1930)

Cayetano Coll y Toste was one of the most important literary figures of the second half of the nineteenth and first decades of the twentieth centuries for his many intellectual contributions to the history of Puerto Rican culture. His *Tradiciones y leyendas puertorriqueñas* (1924–25) serves not only to popularize most of the well-known legends and stories about the early process of conquest and colonization of Puerto Rico but also became a foundational narrative that depicts the process of acculturation, miscegenation, cultural clash, and the founding of the first settlements on the island.

Cayetano Coll y Toste was born in Arecibo, Puerto Rico, on November 30, 1850. He studied medicine at the Universidad de Barcelona, earning his MD in 1874. Back in Puerto Rico, he served as director of hospitals, as member of several political parties in different times—Liberal Party, Puerto Rican Republican Party, Union Party—and was appointed to important positions such as Regional Governor of the North (1897), Assistant Secretary of Agriculture, Industry and Commerce (1898), Civil Secretary of Puerto Rico (1899), and Interior Commissioner (1900). In 1913 he received the distinction of becoming the Official Historian of Puerto Rico.

A foundational researcher of Puerto Rican historiography, Coll y Toste gathered as many important documents relevant to the history of the island as he could in the Archives of the Indies in Seville, collecting, editing, and publishing an amazing number of texts that became required readings to anyone interested in the Puerto Rican historical memory. Among his numerous publications are *Crónicas de Arecibo* (1891), *Colón en Puerto Rico-Disquisiciones histórico-filológicas* (1893), *Reseña del estado social, económico e industrial de la Isla de Puerto Rico al tomar posesión de ella los Estados Unidos* (1899), *Prehistoria de Puerto Rico* (1907), and *Historia de la instrucción pública en Puerto Rico hasta 1898* (1910). Perhaps his most important historical contribution is a compendium of fourteen volumes published between 1914 and 1927 with the title of *Boletín histórico de Puerto Rico*.

Coll y Toste was also a fiction writer, mostly remembered for his famous historical and romantic legends compiled under the title of *Tradiciones y leyendas puertorriqueñas* (1924–25). Among the most famous legends and myths in the volume are "Guanina," "Becerrillo," "La hija del verdugo," "El pirata Cofresí," "Carabalí," "La campana del ingenio," "Los negros brujos," and "El prodigio de Hormigueros."

These short legends capture, in a romantic fashion, historical and fictional stories that in the decades of the twenties, when Puerto Rican intellectuals were engaged in the examination of their cultural roots, represented an affirmation and celebration of the indigenous past. "Guanina," probably one of his most anthologized legends, retells the story of the tragic love between the beautiful Taíno Indian Guanina and the young Spanish conquistador and settler Don Cristóbal de Sotomayor. Guanina, aware that Sotomayor is in danger because her brother, Chief Guaybaná, is plotting to rebel against the Spaniards, warns him, but Sotomayor refuses to change his plans to go to the capital. The following day, he leaves with some of his men. They are attacked by the Taínos and Sotomayor is killed. When informed of what has happened, Guanina tries to revive him with her passionate kisses and does not let anyone come close or touch her lover's body. The Taíno Indians decide to sacrifice Guanina the next day in order for her to accompany Sotomayor in the other life, but when they reach the site of the tragedy, they find Guanina dead, resting on the chest of her lover. They are buried at the base of the giant native tree called "ceiba," in a tomb crowded with wild red poppies and white lilies.

This beautifully narrated legend is typical of those dealing with incidents and figures of the colonization of the island. In these stories, Coll y Toste captures the struggles, conflicts, and collision of two different worldviews, but also the emotions and experiences that different people share, such as love, loyalty, respect, and commitment. History and fiction mix. Spanish expressions incorporate Taíno words that refer to anything from names of the people, religious and class divisions—Guanina, Guaybaná; zemi, nitayno, naiboa—to words about war, places and nature. It is a strategy that not only authenticates the stories and the epoch, but establishes the continuity of the impact and legacy of a culture which formed the Puerto Rican people. He died November 19, 1930, in New York. *See also* Historical Novel; Indianist Literature; Puerto Rican Literary, History of; Romanticismo/Romanticism.

Further Reading

Coll, Edna. *Cayetano Coll y Toste; síntesis de estímulos humanos*. San Juan: Editorial Universitaria, Universidad de Puerto Rico, 1970.

Coll y Toste, Cayetano. *Folk Legends of Puerto Rico*. Translated by Coll Y Toste, José L. Vivas and Ulises Cadilla. [s.i.]: Trans Caribbean Airways, [n.d.].

—*Asela R. Laguna*

Colón, Jesús (1901–74)

∎

Noted Puerto Rican journalist and political activist, Jesús Colón was born into a working-class Afro–Puerto Rican family in Cayey, Puerto Rico. Colón's writings are considered landmarks in the development of Puerto Rican literature in the continental United States: he was one of the first writers to become well known through his use of English and because of his identification with the working class and his ideas on race. He was the forerunner of the Nuyorican writers who began to appear in the 1960s and 1970s.

Colón started writing in Spanish for Latino periodicals in New York in the 1920s. Having arrived in the city at age sixteen as a stowaway, Colón worked in a series of jobs that exposed him to the exploitation and abuse of immigrants, lower-class, and unskilled workers. He became involved in literary and journalistic endeavors while working as a laborer, trying to establish a newspaper, and writing translations of English-language poetry. As he strived to develop his literary and journalistic career, he encountered racial prejudice, mainly because of his dark skin color. Despite discrimination, Colón became active in community and progressive politics.

In the late 1940s, Colón switched to English for his writing and became a columnist for the *Daily Worker*, the official organ of the Communist Party. He also founded and operated a publishing house, Hispanic Publishers, or Editorial Hispánica, which issued history and literary books, as well as political information in Spanish. In 1952 and 1969, Colón ran unsuccessfully for public office on the Communist Party ticket.

A columnist and observer of Latino life in the United States during the early 20th century, Jesús Colón was probably the first to create the Nuyorican persona: a Puerto Rican from New York. *Centro de Estudios Puertorriqueños.*

Colón published a selection of his newspaper columns and essays in 1961 in book form under the title of *A Puerto Rican in New York and Other Sketches*. Two other collections have been published posthumously, *The Way It Was and Other Sketches* (1993) and *Lo que el pueblo me dice* (2001). In these essays, or sketches, as Colón preferred to call them, his major themes are (1) the creation and development of a political consciousness; (2) the development of Puerto Rican nationalism; (3) advocacy for the working-class poor; and (4) the injustices of capitalist society in which racial and class discrimination are all too frequent, and individual worth does not seem to exist. The collections are richly expressive of a socially conscious and humanistic point of view. *See also* Immigrant Literature; Nuyorican Literature.

Further Reading

Acosta-Belén, Edna, and Sánchez-Korrok. "The World of Jesús Colón," introduction to *The Way It Was and Other Sketches* by Jesús Colón. Houston, Texas: Arte Público Press, 1993.

—*Nicolás Kanellos*

Commonwealth Literature. See Anglophone Caribbean Literature, History of.

Compère Général Soleil (1955)

———————◼———————

Written by **Jacques Stephen Alexis**, this is a novel about a Haitian couple who are symbolic of the honest, diligent, and the disenfranchised lower classes, and the massacre of Haitian workers in the Dominican Republic in 1937. Hilarion, the hero, is a worker of peasant origin who, forced by the lack of employment, has been involved in petty crimes until he meets Claire-Heureuse, a young Haitian woman with whom he falls in love, and Jean-Michel, a young physician who cures him of epilepsy and introduces him to communism as well as a to humanitarian way of contemplating life and his compatriots.

Hilarion and Claire-Heureuse, who becomes pregnant, set up a small grocery store in downtown Port-au-Prince. Following the store's destruction by a disastrous fire, Hilarion and Claire-Heureuse, leave Haiti for the northwestern Dominican Republic, where he works as a cane cutter. Caught in the massacre of Haitians ordered by President Rafael Leónidas Trujillo (1891–1961) in late September 1937, the couple flees with their baby, who dies from malnutrition. As they cross the Massacre River back into Haiti, a Dominican soldier wounds Hilarion. He dies urging his companion to find another man and bear more children to carry on the fight for the survival and dignity of the people.

Alexis conceived the novel around 1949 and sent the manuscript to the French publisher Gallimard in 1954, when Alexis was thirty-two years old. The novel was praised in France and was seen as part of the French literary corpus but also as an expression of Haitian literature. It was translated into English as *General Sun, My Brother* by Carrol F. Coates in 1999.

In 1998, Haitian writer **Edwidge Danticat** wrote a complement novel to *Compère Général Soleil*, entitled ***The Farming of Bones*** and dedicated to Jacques Stephen Alexis. *See also* Trujillo Era; Haitian Literature, History of.

Further Reading

Alexis, Jacques Stephen. *Compère Général Soleil*. Paris: Éditions Gallimard, 1955.

———. *General Sun, My Brother*. Translated by Carrol F. Coates. Charlottesville: University Press of Virginia, 1999.

—Carrol F. Coates

Condé, Maryse (1934–)

———————◼———————

A major international writer from Guadeloupe, Condé is a novelist, playwright, and essayist who, according to scholar Leyla Ezdinli, in *Conde: Land of Many Colors and Nanna-ya*, employs "a powerful voice in addressing issues of the black diaspora and of women's experiences within that diaspora" (vii). Her most famous works are the historical novels *Ségou: Les Murailles de Terre* (1984) and *Ségou II,* a chronicle of an African family before and during colonialism in the eighteenth and nineteenth centuries.

Condé was born as Maryse Boucolon on February 11, 1937, in Pointe-a-Pitre, Guadeloupe. Her father was a banker and her mother a schoolteacher. She became interested in writing through her love of reading. In the essay "What about those who don't have grandmothers," Condé recalled:

> My father had a superb library, quantities of books, bound and unbound, carefully arranged in alphabetical order. The library resembled a forbidden city. No children were allowed to enter there or touch the books, not even me . . . I transgressed that rule . . . I began paying secret visits to the library. . . .(308)

At the age of sixteen, her parents sent her to Paris to study. She attended the Lycée Fénelon and the University of Paris. In 1958, she married an actor, Mamadou Condé; later on they were divorced. She traveled throughout Africa and taught at different schools on the Ivory Coast, Guinea, Ghana, and Senegal. In 1968, she moved to London where she worked at the BBC as a producer. Two years later, she returned to Paris and worked as an editor at the journal *Présence Africaine*. She also enrolled at the Sorbonne, earning a PhD in 1975. While in graduate schools she wrote two dramas, which were staged in Paris—*Dieus nous l'a donné* and *Mourt d'Oluwemi d'Ajumako*—and her first novel *Hérémakhonon*, an autobiographical narrative about an educated black woman who marries a black actor and has an affair with a white professor. Initially, this novel was not well received by the critics.

During the late 1970s, she taught literature at the University of Paris and in the 1980s, Condé was course director at the Sorbonne. She met her academic responsibilities with the publications of several texts of literary criticism, including *La civilisation du bossale: réflexions sur la littérature orale de la Guadeloupe et de la Martinique* (1978) and *Le profil d'une oeuvre: Cahier d'un retourn au pais natal*. In 1984 and 1985 she published the two *Ségous* novels, which became bestsellers in France.

Recognition as a scholar and writer afforded her teaching opportunities in the United States, where she taught at such prestigious universities as the University of California in Santa Barbara, Columbia, and Princeton University. In 1986, she received the Grand Prix Littéraire de la Femme, in France, for the novel *Moi, Tutuba sorciére*. Translated into English that same year as *I, Tituba, Black Witch of Salem*, the novel brought her fame in the United States.

Spending half the year in her native Guadeloupe since 1986, Condé wrote *La vie scélérate* (1987), about class

An international figure, Maryse Condé gained recognition for incisive novels that explored the African Diaspora and women's role within the Diaspora. *Courtesy of Maryse Condé. Photo by John Foley.*

conflict, and *Traversée de la Mangrove* (1989), about the awkwardness of her own return to Guadeloupe after decades of living abroad. In 1995, Condé offered *La migration des coeurs*, a reinterpretation and retelling of the classic British novel *Wuthering Heights* (1847), by Emily Brontë (1818–48), this time set in the Caribbean.

Condé has written in an array of different genres—romance, historical, and autobiographical—and styles, from traditional narratives to experimental studies; however, she has essentially addressed the same themes throughout her prolific career. Critic Ezdinli lists the themes as "the search for identity in the context of the African diaspora; the political significance of history; class struggles; the effects of colonialist ideology in the Caribbean; fraught relations between the sexes." In 2003, Conde retired from teaching.

Further Reading

Condé, Maryse. "What About Those Who Don't Have Grandmothers?" In *Contemporary Women Writing in the Other Americas: Contemporary Women Writing in the Caribbean*, vol. 2, edited by Georgiana M. M. Colville, 307–11. Lewiston, NY: Edwin Mellen Press, 1990.

Ezdinli, Leyla. "Introduction." In *Maryse Condé: Land of Many Colors and Nanna-ya*. Translated by Nicole Ball, vii–xviii. Lincoln, NE: University of Nebraska Press, 1999.

Scarboro, Ann Armstrong. "(Re)writing History: Strategies of Telling in Maryse Condé's Une Saison à Rihata." In *Contemporary Women Writing in the Other Americas*, edited by Georgiana M. M. Colville, 292–305. Lewiston, NY: Edwin Mellen Press, 1990.

—D. H. Figueredo

Conference of the Association for Commonwealth Literature and Language Studies (1971)

∎

This was the first formal academic gathering where writers from the Anglophone Caribbean met to discuss the aesthetics and literature of the English-speaking islands. The setting was Kingston, Jamaica, rather than the usual locale for literary conferences, which was London. Presenters included **Edward "Kamau" Brathwaite**, from Barbados, and **V. S. Naipul**, from Trinidad. The conference demonstrated that there was an audience for West Indian literature, an idea often disputed by British scholars and even by some writers from the West Indies, called for the writers from the region to form communities, rather than work in forced geographic isolation, and promoted the serious study of West Indies literature. In essence, the conference claimed that there was a West Indian literary canon. According to Laurence A. Breiner, the conference meant that "the center was no longer in London but at home, that the language was West Indian and not British." *See also* Anglophone Caribbean, Literature of; Caribbean Artists Movement.

Further Reading

Breiner, Laurence A. *An Introduction to West Indian Poetry*. Cambridge: Cambridge University Press, 1998.

—*D. H. Figueredo*

Contreras, Hilma (1913–)

Alongside **Delia Weber, Virginia Elena Ortea,** and **Aída Cartagena Portalatín,** Contreras is one of the first woman short-story writers from the Dominican Republic. Her stories reveal the author's struggle to find a voice and to witness the existential silence imposed on women by a male-driven society. Contreras is an essayist, a diplomat, and an educator as well.

Born in San Francisco de Macorís, Dominican Republic, in 1913, she attended elementary school in her hometown before moving to Paris, where her father was serving as a diplomat while also studying medicine. When she returned to the Dominican Republic, she studied philosophy and literature at the Universidad de Santo Domingo. In the 1920s, she went back to France, where she studied French at the Víctor Duruy school in Versailles. While at the school, she befriended the daughter of the popular French author Colette (1873–1954).

In 1937, she mailed her short stories to author and political figure **Juan Bosch,** who encouraged her to continue writing. Through the 1940s, her stories were published in local newspapers and journals. In 1953, she published her first collection of short stories, *Cuatros cuentos*. This volume was followed by *El ojo de Dios: cuentos de la clandestinidad* (1962), *Entre dos silencios* (1987), and *Facetas de la vida* (1993). During this period, she traveled extensively throughout Europe, sometimes serving as a diplomat, sometimes on her own. In 1986, she published the novel *La tierra está bramando*. Her book-length essay *Doña Endrina de Calatayud* (1955) reflects on the definitions of the code honor in the Hispanic culture and the weight of sexual harassment and abuses inflicted on women throughout Latin America.

In 2002, Hilma Contreras received the Dominican Republic's National Literature Award.

Further Reading

Cocco de Filippis, Daisy. *Documents of Dissidence: Selected Writings by Dominican Women*. New York: CUNY Dominican Studies Institute, 2000.

—*Daisy Cocco de Filippis*

Cooper, Afua (1957–)

∎

Feminist poet from Jamaica, Afua Cooper uses her poetry to fight racism and the values imposed on women by a male-driven society. She belongs to a generation of Caribbean woman writers who have migrated to Canada.

Cooper was born in Westmorland, Jamaica, and moved to Kingston in 1963. She began to write poetry while in high school but did not publish her works until she relocated to Canada in 1980. Her first book of poems, *Breakin Chains*, came out in 1983. This was followed by *The Red Caterpillar on College Street* (1989), a children's book, and *Memories Have Tongue* (1992). The latter, possibly her best-known work, is a collection of poetry that was the first runner-up in the 1992 **Casa de las Américas** literary prize. In the volume, Cooper pays tribute to her grandmother, presenting her as a prototype of a connection to the past and an extension to the future:

> Seh her memory bad
> but she memba
> 1938
> Frome
> di riot
> Manley
> Busta
> but what she memba most of all
> is dat a pregnant woman was shot
> and killed
> by di soldiers

Cooper's poetry is influenced by Jamaican vernacular and reggae music. Observes poet and scholar **Kwame Dawes,** in his book *Talk Yuh Talk* (2001): "Cooper's work is constantly trying to reconcile two seemingly disparate spheres of experience: political action and activism . . . bringing those two into . . . meaningful dialogue" (215).

Cooper reads her poetry at universities, schools, and libraries. Her doctoral dissertation is on Canadian abolitionist Henry Bidd. Her poetry has been recorded in *Woman Talk* (1985) and *Poetry Is Not a Luxury* (1987). *See also* Grandparents in Caribbean Literature.

Further Reading

Cooper, Afu. "Finding My Voice." In *Caribbean Women Writers: Essays from the First International Conference*, edited by Selwyn R. Cudjoe, 301–05. Wellesley, MA: Calaloux Publications, University of Massachusetts Press, 1990.

Dawes, Kwame, ed. *Talk Yuh Talk: Interviews with Anglophone Caribbean Poets*. Charlottesville: University Press of Virginia, 2001.

—*D. H. Figueredo*

Corchado y Juarbe, Manuel (1840–84)

A nineteenth-century Puerto Rican essayist and dramatist, Corchado y Juarbe was a prominent orator who espoused liberal ideals, such as opposing the death penalty, and supported the abolitionist movement. He was an attorney who devoted as much time to law and political causes as to literature.

Manuel María Corchado y Juarbe was born in Isabela, Puerto Rico. After attending elementary school in his hometown, Corchado y Juarbe went to high school in Spain. He graduated with a law degree from the Universidad de Barcelona in 1864. While in school, he wrote essays and poems that were published in San Juan and Barcelona.

Back in San Juan, he set up a law office and wrote essays advocating progressive political reforms on the island. In 1868, he cowrote, with José Feliu, *Abraham Lincoln*, a biography, and in 1870, the essays *Las barricadas* and *Dios*. In 1872, he wrote the collection of short stories, *Historias de ultratumba*, eerie tales that demonstrated his belief in the afterlife. That same year, he represented Puerto Rico before the Cortes, Spanish Parliament, advocating the abolition of slavery.

He returned to the island in 1879. He was elected president of the **Ateneo Puertorriqueño** and wrote the historical drama, *María Antonieta* (1880), which was a polite criticism of Spanish colonialism, the comedy *Desde la comedia al drama* (1885), and the adventure story *El capitán Correa* (1885). In 1884, he was a candidate for Spanish Parliament once again but lost the elections due to fraud. He traveled to Spain to dispute his defeat, but died suddenly.

Further Reading

Morfi, Angelina. *Historia crítica de un siglo de teatro puertorriqueño*. San Juan, Puerto Rico: Instituto de Cultura Puertorriqueña, 1980.

—*D. H. Figueredo*

Corretjer, Juan Antonio (1908–85)

A Puerto Rican poet who dedicated his life to his country's independence and to the writing of poetry, Correjter wrote poetry that celebrated the island's Amerindian and African heritage. Though he spent many years in prison in the United States accused of plotting political violence against the American government, he managed to write over a dozen books.

Corretjer was born on March 3, 1908, in Ciales, Puerto Rico, the descendant of patriots who had participated in an insurrection against Spain in 1898. He started to write poetry at the age of twelve and published his first poem, "De otoño," when he was sixteen years old. During his teen years he was inspired by

Puerto Rico's landscape, but from 1927 on, when he moved to San Juan, he espoused Marxist ideology in his writings.

In 1928, Corretjer relocated to New York City, where he supported revolutionary movements in Nicaragua and protested against the American military presence in Haiti. Two years later, he returned to Puerto Rico, where he met the nationalist Pedro Albizu Campos (1893–1965). Joining the Partido Nacionalista—of which Albizu Campos was the leader—he participated in numerous anti-American and pro-independence activities—he even traveled to Cuba to seek support for the Puerto Rican cause. Yet, during the early 1930s, he managed to publish several books of poetry, including *Agueybaná* (1932), *Ulises: Versos al mar de un hombre de tierra adentro* (1933), *Amor de Puerto Rico* (1937), and *Cántico de guerra* (1937). The themes he addressed in these volumes were love of country, celebration of the life and struggle of the Puerto Rican peasant, and solidarity with the poor.

In 1936, Corretjer was accused of conspiring to overthrow the American government. He, Albizu Campos, and a group of writers, including **Clemente Soto Vélez**, were sent to prison in Atlanta, Georgia. Released in 1942, he was not allowed to return to Puerto Rico. Settling in New York City, he founded the newspaper *Pueblos Hispanos* and published the patriotic poem, *El Leñero: poema de la revolución de Lares* (1944), a celebration of the insurrection of the Grito de Lares, which took place in Puerto Rico against Spanish rule in 1868. The publication received the Poetry Prize from the Instituto de Literatura Puertorriqueña. He also wrote several essays on patriotic and nationalistic themes, including *La lucha por la independencia de Puerto Rico* (1949). He continued his political labor inspired by Consuelo Lee Tapia, a Marxist intellectual with whom he fell in love and with whom he spent the rest of his life.

Back in Puerto Rico, Corretjer was accused in 1950 of inciting a political revolt known as the Revuelta Nacionalista when members of the Partido Nacionalista led an uprising against the American government in several towns. Again he was imprisoned, and during this time, he wrote *Los Primeros años* (1950) and *Tierra nativa* (1951), patriotic poems. In 1959, he visited Cuba where he befriended revolutionary leader Ernesto "Che" Guevara (1928–67) and then toured several Latin American nations, including Mexico and Venezuela, seeking support for the independence of Puerto Rico. In 1962, he returned to Puerto Rico to organize the Liga Socialista and to oppose the draft. Again he managed to write several books of poetry, of which his *Albizu Campos, hombre histórico* (1963), his tribute to his friend and independence leader, is one of the best known.

In 1970, there was an assassination attempt on Corretjer and Consuelo Lee. A year later, accused of plotting the violent overthrow of the United States, Corretjer and Lee were briefly incarcerated. During the 1970s, Corretjer delivered a series of talks on radio programs and at Puerto Rican universities and libraries. He also edited the journal *El Correo de la Quincena* and continued publishing books of poetry, including *Mujer boricua* (1997), which he cowrote and copublished with his beloved Consuelo. In 1978, the Instituto de Cultura Puertorriqueña collected his works in the volume *Obras completas*.

Corretjer died on January 19, 1985. To the end of his life, he remained involved in the political struggle for Puerto Rican independence, supported revolutionary causes in Latin America, including the Cuban Revolution, and wrote poetry. A few months before his death, he recorded poems about his hometown, *Vivo: Ciales en dos tiempos*, expressing his undying love for his island.

Further Reading

Meléndes, Joserramón. *Juan Antonio Corretjer, o, La poesía inevitable*. Río Piedras, Puerto Rico: qeAse, 1996.

—D. H. Figueredo

Corsen, Joseph Sickman (1855–1911)

A pioneer in the literature of the Dutch Caribbean, Corsen was the first poet to publish in Papiamentu, the language of the people of Curaçao. A musician, Corsen was also a promoter of a native Curaçao culture and identity.

Born in Curaçao on December 13, 1855, Corsen was self-educated. He taught music, played the piano for a musical society, called Harmonie, and was a church organist, all to make a living. With a Hispanist named Ernesto Romer, Corsen founded and directed the journal **Notas y Letras, semanario de literatura y bellas artes.**

Lasting from 1886 to 1888 and totaling seventy-two numbers, the journal was published in Spanish and in English. This was a period when Curaçao witnessed many publications published in Spanish even though Dutch was the official language; this publishing activity was the result of the many Spanish-speaking Jews and other immigrants from Venezuela, Colombia, and the Dominican Republic. *Notas y Letras* was the first literary journal in Curaçao. It published translations of works by European writers—with Corsen translating many of the pieces—submissions by Spanish-speaking writers, and news and articles published in journals in neighboring islands. Corsen published many of his poems in the journal.

But it was in another journal, the weekly *La Cruz*, where Corsen made history. *La Cruz* was published by the Catholic Church. At the end of the nineteenth century, the Church had intensified its campaign to reach the poor communities of Curaçao where Dutch was not the primary language and where there were high levels of illiteracy. Hymns for the mass were sung in Papiamentu, composed by the Dutch friar P. J. Poiesz and the writers Willem M. (Shon Wein) Hoyer and Corsen. These three collaborated in *La Cruz*.

In 1905, Corsen published the poem "Atardi" in the weekly. It was the first published poem in Papiamentu. In writing in this language, Corsen was demonstrating the creative potential of Papiamentu for the expression of the finer and more artistic sentiments of the human experience. "Atardi" was also affirming a Dutch Caribbean identity while offering Papiamentu as a way of breaking cultural and linguistic links with Europe.

The editorial note that accompanied "Atardi" underlined the aesthetic character of the poem:"This poem was not destined for publication, which makes it the more beautiful and natural. We have been told that Papiamentu can not express tender sentiments. Read this poem and be assured you will change your opinion. Here, it is the depth of sentiment and the simplicity of expression that unites what is beautiful and gentle. In addition, the reader will be able to judge the sweetness of the language of Curaçao." The poem, written in traditional rhyme and meter, observed the relation that exists between dusk or the death of the day, and the sadness or melancholy dwelling in the poet's soul. The poem also compared the passing of the day with the passing of life.

Many critics have commented on the poem. The writer **Henry Habibe**, in the journal *Amigoe* (1995), observed that the poem brings the reader closer to the Spanish romantic poet Gustavo Adolfo Becquer (1836–70), and Aart G. Broek, in an essay in the volume *Swirling Columns of Imagination*, detected influences of the German Heinrich Heine (1797–1856). Both affirmed how influential the poem was in introducing literature in Papiamentu.

Corsen's pioneering writing encouraged others to follow in his footsteps in the twentieth century. His own direct influence is present in his grandchildren, Oda Blinder—her real name was Yolanda Corsen—and Charles Corsen, who in the 1940s became known as writers whose works appeared in the journal *De Stoep*. *See also* Literary Journals; Romanticismo/Romanticism.

Further Reading

Broek, Aart G. *Pa saka kara, tomo I: Historia di literature papiamentu*. Willemstad: Fundashon Pierree Lauffer, 1998.

———. "Literary Writing in the Dutch Caribbean." In *Swirling Column of Imagination*. Curaçao: Maduro and Curiel's Bank N.V., 1997.

Habibe, Henry. "De avondschemering van J. S. Corsen (1853–1911): De bakermat van de Papiamentu-poëzie." *Amigoe* 26, no. 8 (1995).

Lauffer, Pierre. "Joseph Sickman Corsen." *Antillano* 1, no. 7 (1954): 7–11.

Terligen, J. *Las Antillas Neerdandesas en su vecindad: lengua y literatura Española en las Antillas Neerlandesas*. Curaçao: Ministerio de Asuntos Culturales de las Antillas Neerlandesas, 1961.

—Emilio Jorge Rodríguez

Costumbrismo

A style or genre that may be described as "local color," *costumbrismo* emerged in Spain during the sixteenth century, and its popularity continued well into the modern era. In Latin America, and specifically in the Spanish-speaking Caribbean, *costumbrismo* flourished in the nineteenth century, evolving out of the Romantic Movement but also bearing touches of nationalism, realism, and the **historical** novel. The genre helped to affirm nationhood, that is, it differentiated what was Caribbean from what was Iberian.

Costumbrismo depicted "cuadros de costumbres," meaning a sketch or snapshot of a local subject. The elements of the *cuadros* were emphasis on local types, such as the town's drunk, and language; preference for the picturesque; social satire; commentaries on local politics; attempts at accurately depicting physical settings. *Costumbrista* writers favored pastoral settings. Poet **Nicolas Ureña de Mendoza** serves as a good illustration with his idyllic description of the Dominican Republic countryside in his poem "Un guajiro predilecto":

> No muy lejos descollar
> se ve un grupo de colinas
> y entre lindas clavellinas
> matizadas de colores,
> cual salido de entre flores
> se ve el pueblo de Los Minas

> (Not too far stands
> A cluster of hills
> And amidst the pretty carnations,
> Blooming in the colors
> That the flowers bring,
> The town of Las Minas can be seen).

The desire was to conjure up a view of paradise in the tropics. That is what **Manuel A. Alonso**, from Puerto Rico, did with his *El gíbaro*, a volume consisting of verse and prose, the first literary effort to celebrate the Puerto Rican countryside and the ways of the farmers. Likewise, the Cubans **José Victoriano Betancourt** and his son **Luis Victoriano Betancourt** depicted rural and town scenes in articles and poems they published in popular newspapers. One of the most famous novels of the genre is *Cecilia Valdés, o La Loma del Angel: novela de costumbres cubanas*, meaning "Cecilia Valdes or Angel Hill: a Novel of Cuban Customs," written by **Cirilo Villaverde**. The novel is rich, almost voluptuously so, in the description of local characters—how they spoke, dressed, and the carriages they rode—and settings, including detailed descriptions of churches, government buildings, and theaters.

If in the nineteenth century *costumbrismo* was a path taken by writers in search of a national identity, in the twentieth century the genre served as a window to a nostalgic past. In Puerto Rico, after the Spanish-Cuban-American War of 1898, when the island's dream of independence from Spain was shattered by the American occupation, *costumbrismo* painted Edenic scenes of the island before the arrival of Americans. During the second half of the twentieth century, Cuban writers living in the United States recounted local episodes from a pre-Castro Cuba; typical is the book by the popular writer **Eladio Secades** who in 1969 published *Las mejores estampas de Secades: la Cuba de antes y la Cuba comunista,* with its nostalgic allusion to the Cuba of yesteryear.

Costumbrismo was popular throughout Latin America and not just in the Spanish-speaking nations. In Haiti, the poet **Oswald Durand** and the novelist **Jacques Roumain** used *costumbristas* techniques to describe Haitian cities and the countryside, rendering tribute to the physical beauty and hard work of the urban residents and the peasants. *See also* Romanticismo/Romanticism.

Further Reading

Rosa-Nieves, Cesáreo, ed. *El Costumbrismo literario en la prosa de Puerto Rico.* San Juan, Puerto Rico: Editorial Cordillera, 1971.

Ruiz del Vizo, Hortensia. *Antología del costumbrismo en Cuba: prosa y verso.* Miami, FL.: Ediciones Universal, 1975.

Secades, Eladio. *Las mejores estampas de Secades.* México: Medinas Hermanos, 1969.

—*D. H. Figueredo*

Courtois, Félix (1892–1984)

■

Courtois was a Haitian novelist and government official. His novels depict his youth and the political figures he met during his long life in government.

Courtois was born in Port-au-Prince, Haiti, on February 4, 1892. He came late to writing, pursuing a political and public service career that saw him as chief of the Division of Foreign Affairs of the Haitian government and as secretary of the Haitian Legation to Paris. A cautious man, he survived several political changes and Haitian presidents.

That sense of caution is present in his first novel, *Duex pauvres petites* (1922), written when he was thirty years old. The work is an autobiographical account of his life in Haiti, filled with nostalgia for his childhood. Throughout the 1960s, he wrote stories that were published in journals. In 1975, he published his second novel, *Scènes de la vie port-au-princienne*, and in 1977, his third, *Durin Belmour.* These works were peopled with politicians and government officials realistically and humorously portrayed. However, the novels did not criticize Haitian politics. Courtois's prose—discreet, rich, and opulent—was influenced by his love for the works of French writers Gustave Flaubert (1821–80) and Guy De Maupassant (1850–93).

When he passed away on November 16, 1984, obituaries in national newspapers celebrated his contribution to Haitian politics and culture. He was admired for his sense of decorum and his loyalty to the nation.

Further Reading

Herdeck, Donald E. *Caribbean Writers. A Bio-Bibliographical-Critical Encyclopedia.* Washington, DC: Three Continents Press, 1979.

Hoffmann, Léon-François. *Bibliographie des études littéraires haïtienes 1804–1984.* Vanves: EDICEF/AUPELF, 1992.

—*D. H. Figueredo*

Covarrubias, Francisco (1775?–1850?)

Considered the first Cuban dramatist to adapt Spanish one-act plays—known as "entremeses"—into Cuban dramas, substituting Spanish characters with Cuban characters, Covarrubias was also a physician and an actor. He is credited with founding the Teatro Nacional in Havana and is often described as the father of Cuban theater.

He was trained as a physician and worked as such at sugar mill plantations. However, theater attracted him, and he soon became an actor, traveling throughout the island. While performing, he also Cubanized numerous Spanish plays, writing a few one-acts of his own to which he usually added music. Not much is known of his private life, and his plays were not published, though scholars and critics, the likes of **Max Henríquez Ureña,** have studied programs of the performances and articles in contemporary publications.

Further Reading

Henríquez Ureña, Pedro. *Panorama histórico de la literatura cubana.* Tomo II. Habana: Editorial Arte y Literatura, 1979.

—*D. H. Figueredo*

Craig, Christine (1943–)

A Jamaican short-story writer and poet, Craig combines the use of standard English with the Jamaican vernacular to create a Caribbean voice. She is also a journalist and an editor.

Christine Angela Craig was born on June 24, 1943, in St. Andrew, Jamaica. As a child, she spent time in the countryside; years later, the island's natural beauty, the farmers, and the undervalued daily struggle of Jamaican women on the farms would inspire her writings. When she was twenty-one years old she traveled to London where she was a trainee journalist for the *Guardian* and was one of the co-founders of the **Caribbean Artists Movement (CAM),** the first transnational association to promote the arts and literature of black artists from the Anglophone Caribbean. Upon her return to Jamaica, she worked for the Women's Bureau.

Interested in children's literature, in 1970 she published the picture book *Emmanuel and His Parrot.* She followed it up with a sequel, *Emmanuel Goes to Market,* a year later; her husband, artist Karl Craig (1936–) illustrated both volumes. The next ten years, Craig was involved in diverse activities, earning a BA from the University of West Indies in 1980, working for a multimedia company, and participating in training program for Peace Corps Jamaica. In 1984, she published the book of poems, *Quadrille for Tigers.*

During the 1980s, she directed a children's television series in Jamaica, and in 1989 she received a fellowship to attend the International Writers Program at the

University of Iowa. In 1993, she published the collection of short stories *Mint Tea and Other Stories*. One of her best-known poems, "Elsa's Version" (1987), criticizes how Jamaican men see women as representations of their country while belittling their humanity:

> You rass man
> stop put we down
> in duty song or
> high up editorial.

Further Reading

Donnell, Alison and Welsh, Sarah Lawson. *The Routledge Reader in Caribbean Literature*. London and New York: Routledge, 1996.

Fister, Barbara. *Third World Women's Literature: A Dictionary and Guide to Materials in English*. Westport, CT: Greenwood Press, 1995.

—*D. H. Figueredo*

Creole. See Créolité; Haitian Literature in Kreyòl.

Créolité

This is a literary movement from the Francophone Caribbean that emphasizes and celebrates the diversity of the Caribbean people. Créolité emerged as a response to the **Négritude** movement, which was founded in the 1930s by the Martinican **Aimé Césaire**, Léopold Senghor, from Senegal, and **Léon-Gontran Damas**, from French Guiana, and which focused exclusively on the African roots of the Caribbean. The founders of Créolité were the writers Jean Bernabé, **Edouard Glissant**, **Patrick Chamoiseau**, and Raphaël Confiant. The movement's manifesto is the text *Eloge de la créolité* (1989) written by Bernabé, Chamoiseau, and Confiant. This text claims that Négritude replaced Europe with Africa. *Eloge de la créolité*, on the other hand, advocates for a new Caribbean persona: a Creole composed all of the races and people in the region; it also proposes the use of Creole, which derived from a combination of French and several African languages, as the true language of the Francophone Caribbean. Explains scholar Lise Morel, in her essay "In Praise of Creoleness?" that Creole is "a language at least capable of including all of the various influences that the peoples of the Caribbean bear within themselves" (153). *See also* Haitian Language in Literature.

Further Reading

Bernabé, Jean, Patrick Chamoiseau, and Raphaël Confiant. *Eloge de la créolité*. Paris: Gallimard, Presses universitaires créoles, 1989.

Morel, Lise. "In Praise of Creoleness?" In *An Introduction to Caribbean Francophone Writing: Guadeloupe and Martinique*, edited by Sam Haigh, 149–58. Oxford: Berg, 1999.

—D. H. Figueredo

Crime Fiction. See Detective Fiction.

Cruz, Nilo (1960–)

The first Latino in the United States to win the Pulitzer Prize for Drama, Nilo Cruz is a playwright who writes predominantly about Cubans in Cuba and Cuban Americans in the United States.

Nilo Domingo Cruz was born on October 10, 1960, in Matanzas, Cuba. He came to the United States ten years later, settling in Miami, where his father, a former political prisoner, opened up a shoe store. After attending Miami-Dade Community College's Wolfson Campus, he went on to earn a masters from Brown University. Initially interested in acting, his drama coach encouraged him to write drama instead. Unlike his compatriot dramatists, like **Matías Montes Huidobro,** who studied Spanish drama and wrote in Spanish, Cruz preferred American playwrights and chose to write in English.

Nilo Cruz is a Cuban-American playwright who was the first Latino to win a Pulitzer Prize for drama. *Courtesy of Peregrine Whittlesey.*

In the early 1990s, several awards, grants, and residencies at such theaters as the prestigious McCarter Theater in Princeton, New Jersey, afforded him the opportunity to write a series of plays in which he perfected his craft. In 1999, he wrote *Two Sisters and a Piano*, inspired by the arrest in Cuba of the poet and dissident **María Elena Cruz Varela,** followed by a dramatic adaptation of the Gabriel García Márquez (1927–) short story "A Very Old Man with Enormous Wings." In 2002, he wrote *Ana in the Tropics*. This was the first play ever to win a Pulitzer Prize before being staged in New York City; the judges indicated that the play won solely on strength of its prose and characterizations.

In *Two Sisters and a Piano*, the playwright depicts the conflict between the yearning for freedom, in the person of the poet under arrest, and the need of totalitarian regimes, personified by the officer guarding the poet, to silence those who are different. In *Ana in the Tropics*, a lector—a professional reader hired by cigar-tobacco workers to read to them as they worked—changes the lives of Cuban cigar workers in Tampa with his dramatic reading of the novel *Anna Karenina*. Both plays illustrate the liberating effects of art and literature in every day life. Cruz's dialogue is poetic and his characters display a determination and fragility reminiscent of Tennessee Williams's heroes and heroines.

Though inspired by Cuban themes, Cruz is equally interested in writing about the Latino experience in the United States. His *Night Train to Bolina* (1994) is about children from Central America and *Lorca in a Green Dress* (2003) is about Spanish poet Federico García Lorca (1898-1936). *See also* Anti-Castro Literature; Cuban American Literature.

Further Reading

Anders, Gigi. "Work and All Play." *Hispanic* (June 2003): 34–35.

—*D. H. Figueredo*

Cruz, Victor Hernández (1949–)

At the age of seventeen, Cruz published and distributed five hundred copies of his first book of poetry, *Papo Got his Gun* (1966); one copy was purchased by the editor of *Evergreen Review*, a New York City literary journal, and some of the poems were published in the review. A year later, Cruz was the editor of the journal *Umbra* and had become friends with such important literary figures as Amiri Baraka (1934–) and Nikki Giovanni (1943–). In less than a decade, Cruz became a major poet, a representative of the **Nuyorican** literary movement, a literary style that combines English with some Spanish and that addresses the social concerns of the Puerto Rican community in New York. However, Cruz, like Cuban American **Virgil Suárez**, is representative of the Latino author who writes in English and who alphabetizes his surname in the English style, that is, the very last surname takes priority over the first surname, the opposite of the practice in Spanish where he would identify himself as Hernández Cruz.

Born in Aguas Buenas, Puerto Rico, on February 6, 1949, Cruz moved with his family to New York City when he was about five years old. His parents were soon divorced and he was raised by his mother. He started to read voraciously, and words formed in his head. When he was fourteen years old, he found himself writing as much as he was reading, capturing in poetry what he saw as the tragedy and vitality of the ghetto.

After his early start as a writer with *Papo Got His Gun*, Cruz was one the founders of the East Harlem Gut Theater, where some of his plays were performed. Sometime in 1968, Cruz left for California; the next twenty years he traveled back and forth between the East and West Coasts. In 1969, Random House published one of his manuscripts: *Snaps*. The poems in this collection depicted the gritty side of Manhattan, all written in a style that was energetic and musical. Though not all the critics liked the book, *Snaps* was widely reviewed in the major press. In 1973, Cruz published another collection with Random House: *Mainland*. In this volume, Cruz wrote about his experiences across the United States. In 1976, he wrote *Tropicalization*, a celebration of the Hispanic experience in the United States. That same year, some of Cruz's poems were printed on city buses in New York City.

As his recognition increased during the 1970s, Cruz taught writing in prisons, senior centers, and in city festivals, won two grants from the Creative Artists Program Service of New York City, worked as contributor of the *Revista Chicaño-Riquena*, and gave poetry readings in Holland, Germany, and France. In the 1980s, he experimented with short fiction, recalling his parents' and relatives' experiences in Puerto Rico. Curiosity and longing for the island encouraged him to return to Puerto Rico. His return served as the inspiration for *Red Beans* (1991) and for the memoir *Panoramas* (1997), a work reminiscent of Telluric literature or the **peasant novel** of Haiti.

Cruz is one of the most anthologized Latino writers in the United States, appearing in at least twelve anthologies. He has been featured in films and interviews in television, including a 1995 PBS production with journalist Bill Moyers (1934–).

Further Reading

Hernández, Carmen Dolores. *Puerto Rican Voices in English*. Westport, CT: Praeger, 1997.

—*D. H. Figueredo*

Cruz Varela, María Elena (1953–)

Sometimes called the "angel of freedom" by Cuban exiles, Cruz Varela is an award-winning poet and political activist who was arrested in 1991 for challenging **Fidel Castro**'s regime. Her confrontation with the revolutionary government was the basis for the play *Two Sisters and a Piano* (2002) by playwright **Nilo Cruz**.

Cruz Varela was born in Matanzas and moved to Havana at the age of twenty. At the Universidad de la Habana she studied art but was soon attracted to literature and started to write poetry. In 1987, she published the collections *Afuera esta lloviendo* and *Mientras la espera el agua,* poems that celebrate freedom and the human spirit. Two years later, she received the prestigious award Premio Poesía **Julian del Casal**. Disillusioned with the Cuban government, she met other dissidents, and in 1990 Cruz Varela chaired an organization that promoted peaceful political change in Cuba. She also signed a manifesto critical of Fidel Castro. Charged with defamation of state institutions, she was placed under house arrest, was regularly harassed by a mob of Castro supporters and was once forced to eat her own writings.

In 1992, she published *El angel agotado*, her best-known book. That same year she was nominated for the Nobel Peace Prize. A year later, PEN honored her poetry and political commitment with the Poetry International Prize. In 1994, Cruz Varela was able to go into exile in Spain. In 1995, she wrote *Ballad of Blood/Ballada de la sangre*. In 2001 she wrote the testimonial novel *Dios en las cárceles de Cuba*, about her imprisonment. Two years later she penned *Juana de Arco, el corazón del verdugo*, in which she recounts the Joan of Arc legend through the eyes of the martyr's executioner.

A feminist, Cruz Varela uses her poetry to encourage women's liberation and the rejection of stereotypical images of women conceived by men. She advocates the use of the arts as a tool for peaceful social change. *See also* Anti-Castro Literature; Feminism in Caribbean Literature; Literatura Comprometida/Socially Engaged literature; Testimonial Novel.

Further Reading

Cámara, Madeline. *Vocación de Casandra: poesía femenina cubana subversiva en María Elena Cruz Varela*. New York: Lang, 2001.

—*D. H. Figueredo*

Cuban American Literature

Cuban American literature refers to that body of work written in the United States by Cubans who were either born in the United States or arrived there at an early age. Writing in English, and for an English-speaking audience, these authors came into prominence in the late 1970s and 1980s. Their works essay on the duality of the exile experience: living in the United States while also longing for the old country.

Cuban American literature explores several themes: (1) Cuban diaspora after 1959, the onset of the Cuban revolution; (2) conscious examination of what it means to be a Cuban living outside the island; (3) an attempt at understanding the historical dimensions of the Cuban revolution; (4) a longing for roots; and (5) critical evaluation of the United States and its role in Latin America. Typical examples of this literature are the novels *Dreaming in Cuban* by **Cristina García** (1992), and *Havana Thursdays* by **Virgil Suárez** (1995), the memoir *Next Year in Cuba*, by **Gustavo Pérez Firmat**, (1995) the book of poems *Floating Island* by **Pablo Medina** (1999), and the play *Ella/She* by **Dolores Prida** (1991).

Not all scholars accept the notion that Cuban American literature started after 1959. Noted critic **Pamela María Smorkaloff** maintains that Cuban writers have penned literary works in the United States long before the Cuban Revolution. As such, she points out that **José Martí** did most of his writing in the United States and that the classic novel *Cecilia Valdés*, by **Cirilo Villaverde**, was completed and published in New York in the late nineteenth century.

Within the larger scope of Caribbean literature, Cuban American writing represents the conscious choice not to write in the author's home language or the language of the parents. Many of works, such as the novel *Our House in the Last World* by **Oscar Hijuelos**, serve almost as sociological and anthropological texts that explain Cuban culture, history, and tradition to an outsider.

Cuban scholars and writers, both on the island and in exile, have debated whether Cuban American literature is part of the American literary experience, something akin to the ethnic literature produced by Italian American and Jewish American writers, or part of the Cuban literary canon. Novelist **Reinaldo Arenas**, for example, maintained that works written in English, even though they were about Cubans and Cuban matters, belonged within the American literary tradition. In the 1990s, however, a change occurred as Cuban critics on the island and in the United States, anticipating the eventual reunion of Cuban exiles with their compatriots on the island, professed the view that although Cuban American literature was written in English, it was still an expression of national letters. *See also* Anti-Castro Literature; Exile Literature; Immigrant Literature.

Further Reading

Behar, Ruth, ed. *Bridges to Cuba—Puentes a Cuba*. Ann Arbor: University of Michigan Press, 1995.

Figueredo, Danilo H. "Ser Cubano (To Be Cuban): The Evolution of Cuban-American Literature" in *Multicultural Review* 6 (March 1997): 18–27.

Smorkaloff, Pamela María. *Cuban Writers on and off the Island*. New York: Twayne Publishers, 1999.

—*Rolando Pérez and D. H. Figueredo*

Cuban Literature, History of

Cuban literature begins with the poem "Espejo de paciencia." Written in 1608 by **Silvestre de Balboa Troya y Quesada**, the poem told of the kidnapping of a bishop by a pirate, his rescue, and of the killing of the pirate by an African slave, the first instance in Latin American literature in which a black character is presented in a favorable light. Though no major writers emerged after "Espejo de paciencia," it was a time when a national cultural and identity began to develop, manifested in the poem "A la piña," where its author, **Manuel de Zequeira y Arango**, celebrates the beauty of the Cuban pineapple, and in so doing, takes pride on the island's flora, which in turn is suggestive of taking pride in a national identity separate from Spain. Also during this period, schools were founded, cultural centers were established, a printing press was introduced, and a newspaper was published (*Papel periódico de la Habana*).

The first major Cuban poet was the romantic **José María Heredia**, who was forced into exile by the Spanish authorities in the nineteenth century. While visiting Niagara Falls in 1824, he wrote one of the most popular poems of the period,

"Oda al Niágara." The poem was representative of **Romanticismo**, the Romantic Movement taking hold of the continent: it celebrated the vastness, the beauty, and the majesty of the Americas. Heredia was also an early prototype of the Caribbean writer who is condemned, either by choice or by force, to live away from his or her country but devotes his or her life to writing about the homeland. Drama was the province of José Jacinto Milanés, though he was a poet as well. His two plays, *El conde Alarcos* (1838) and *Un poeta en la corte* (1840), hinted of the evolving conflict between Cuba and Spain over sovereignty and of a desire for a national consciousness. During this century, prose was characterized by analytical essays on economics, nationhood, and slavery; the two major essayist and philosophers were educator Father **Félix Varela y Morales** and economist **José Antonio Saco**. Their analysis of colonialism, their promotion of self-rule, and their anti-slavery stance would influence pro-independence writers and patriots a generation later.

In the 1840s, the first Cuban writer of Spanish and African origins achieved recognition; his name was **Gabriel de la Concepción Valdés** but was known as "Plácido." A versifier and popular performer of his works in **tertulias**, literary salons, he was falsely accused of conspiring against the Spanish authorities, was arrested, and executed. During the same decade **Gertrudis Gómez de Avellaneda** wrote an anti-slavery novel, *Sab* (1841), scores of poems, and over ten plays, which were performed in Spain. A pioneer feminist, Gómez de Avellaneda was the first great woman writer in Cuba.

In 1868, war against Spain broke out in Cuba. The conflict was known as the Ten Years' War, for it ended in 1878. Many of the Cuban writers who rejected Spanish rule looked toward France for literary models; one such writer was the Romantic poet **Juan Clemente Zenea,** whose writings attempted to define the nature of the soul and whose style had a liquid, dreamy quality about it. He lived in exile most of his life; returning to Cuba to meet the Cuban leaders of the war, he was captured and executed by Spanish forces. Another writer who spent much of his life in exile was Cuba's most beloved poet and writer, the patriot **José Martí**. A practitioner of **Modernismo**, the first literary movement to originate in Latin America, Martí wrote poetry, essays, drama, children stories, and novels. His essays, collected in the volume *Nuestra América* (1891), warned of American imperialism in Latin America; his children's magazine *La Edad de Oro* (1889) was the first of its kind in Latin American literature; the collection of poems *Versos sencillos* (1891) contained the popular poem "**La rosa blanca,**" memorized by virtually all Cubans. The supreme idealist, Martí advocated independence for Cuba, the equality of all races, and tolerance of all ideas and dissenting viewpoints. In 1895, when Cuba and Spain were at war once again, Martí, who from the United States had orchestrated the independence movement, returned to the island. He was killed in a skirmish between insurgent and Spanish troops.

A contemporary of Martí and a modernist as well was **Julián del Casal**; his poetry was philosophical and melancholic with a hint of self-destructiveness. Like Martí, he died young, of tuberculosis, in 1893. Toward the end of the nineteenth century two novelists were at the forefront of Cuban letters: **Cirilo Villaverde**, whose *Cecilia Valdés* (1879, 1882) is considered Cuba's national novel, and **Nicolás Heredia**, author of *Leonora*, a realistic novel about a tragic love affair in the countryside.

The Spanish-Cuban-American War ended in 1898, and Cuba became a republic in 1902. Literary criticism flourished under the authorship of **Enrique Piñeyro** during the early 1900s. The genre known as **naturalismo,** naturalism, which emphasized the seedier side of life, expressed the sentiment of many Cubans who were disappointed that independence had not brought about social equality and democratic governments. The best-known exponents of naturalism were **Carlos Loveira,** a union leader, and **Miguel Carrión,** a physician. The poet **Agustín Acosta** wrote poetry of social protest, specifically the poem "La zafra" (1926), which condemned American interventionism in the sugar industry. The short story prospered in the hands of **Lydia Cabrera** and **Lino Novás Calvo**; both wrote about Afro-Cuban legends and traditions, incorporating magical elements into their realistic narratives.

Afro-Cuban motifs were the inspiration for the one writer who dominated the 1930s, the poet **Nicolás Guillén.** He incorporated Cuban vernacular and Afro-Cuban parlance with classic rhyming and meter; his poetry celebrated racial diversity. Innovation was the objective of **Enrique Labrador Ruiz,** who in 1936 wrote a novel, *El laberinto de sí mismo,* with no clear beginning and no clear ending, forecasting the experimental techniques that Latin American writers would use in the 1960s. Equally experimental was **Alejo Carpentier,** whose baroque prose was ornate and whose plots were often more of a philosophical exercise than a matter of storytelling; his *El reino de este mundo* (1949) tells the early history of Haiti through the eyes of a former slave and rebel.

The 1940s were defined by the founding of the journal *Orígenes* (1944–56), which emphasized abstract poetics, lyricism, and modern art. The founder of the journal was the poet and novelist **José Lezama Lima,** regarded as the icon of the Cuban baroque, **barroco,** movement. Lezama Lima achieved fame with his poem "Muerte de Narciso" (1937). His complex concept of art and aesthetics was summarized in his masterpiece, the novel *Paradiso* (1966). In between these two works, Lezama Lima wrote challenging poems and stories that claimed literature—poetry in particular—as the true force of the universe. Lezama Lima befriended and mentored countless Cuban writers, including the playwright **Virgilio Piñera.**

Piñera's experimental work brought about a renaissance in Cuban drama, drawing audiences to the theater to watch productions of his plays, *Electra Garrigo* (1941), *Jesús* (1943), and *Falsa alarma* (1957). His plays, novels, and short stories, charged with sexual energy, influenced such younger talents as the playwright **Matías Montes Huidobros** and novelist **Reinaldo Arenas,** who crafted works that universalized Cuban themes while also questioning Cuban values and mores.

The Cuban Revolution of 1959 was probably the most significant development in Cuban literature, nurturing the writers who supported it, forcing into exile those who didn't follow the party line, and bringing unprecedented international attention to Cuban letters. Many established writers, such as Enrique Labrador Ruiz, Agustín Acosta, and Montes Huidobros, to name but a handful, went into exile. Others, like Nicolás Guillén and Alejo Carpentier, embraced the revolution, prospering as their books were published and distributed throughout the world and as they were allowed to travel to international conferences. Somewhere in the middle were writers who initially supported the revolutionary agenda but soon found their lifestyles and beliefs in opposition to the regime. Authors such as José Lezama Lima, Virgilo Piñera, and Reinaldo Arenas, who were gay and free-thinkers, were either imprisoned or ostracized. The most famous case of censorship was that of the poet

Heberto Padilla, who in 1971 was arrested for writing anti-revolutionary poetry. Despite, or because of the conflicts and controversies, dozens of Cuban writers produced an extraordinary output during the 1970s, both on the island and in exile. In Cuba, such authors as **Roberto Fernández Retamar, Nancy Morejón,** and **Miguel Barnett** wrote poetry, essays, and novels that were experimental, anti-American, and committed to the Cuban Revolution, serving as examples of the literature of social engagement or **literatura comprometida.** In exile, the likes of **Guillermo Cabrera Infante, Calvert Cassey,** and **Severo Sarduy** produced a body of work that sought experimentation but that also exposed to the world human rights violations in Cuba. The political division continued into the 1980s as the members of the **Mariel Generation** went into exile—through a massive boatlift that originated in the port of Mariel in the summer of 1980. Led by Reinaldo Arenas, these writers cultivated an innovative literature that engaged in art for art's sake but that was also highly critical of **Fidel Castro.**

In the United States, a new body of literature emerged from Cuban American writers who wrote about life away from the island and the impact of the revolution and who preferred to write in English, as **Oscar Hijuelos** did with *Our House in the Last World* (1983) and **Cristina García** with *Dreaming in Cuban* (1992). On the island, authors had to negotiate censorship by venturing into genres that were not commonly practiced before the revolution: the detective novel—its most famous writer is **Leonardo Padura**—and historical narratives. The economic hardships after the collapse of the Soviet Union in the mid-1980s resulted in escapism through excessive sex; typical erotic novels were *La vida cotidiana* (1995) by **Zoé Valdés** and *Trilogía sucia de La Habana* (1998) and *Rey de la Habana* (2000) by **Pedro Juan Gutiérrez.** Short stories and anthologies proliferated, showcasing in particular feminist stories by a generation of Cuban women who came of age in the 1990s. Writers like **Anna Lidia Vega Serova, Aida Bahr,** and **Marylin Bobes** cultivated erotic stories from a lesbian perspective.

Toward the end of the twentieth century, Cuban authors who had left the island at a young age or who were born in cities like Miami or New York, expressed an interest in bypassing politics and reaching out to writers in Cuba, as shown in the anthology *Bridges to Cuba: Puentes a Cuba,* edited by Ruth Behar (1995). While there were still writers, such as the pro-revolution **Roberto Fernández Retamar** and anti-Castro **Carlos Alberto Montaner,** battling each other in print, there were some Cuban American critics, such as **Emilio Bejel** and **Pamela María Smorkaloff,** who were studying the works of Cuban writers on the island and abroad—regardless of whether they wrote in English or Spanish—as a manifestation of one culture and one literature. In essence, these critics were defining Cuban literature as an expression bound neither by geography nor history but by their Cubanness. To this end, no other literary and cultural critic has done more to articulate a theory of "lo cubano," or Cuban (self)-identity than **Gustavo Pérez Firmat** in his many incisive books: sometimes with a look toward the past, and at others looking at the present and beyond it, when "Cuban" literature and culture may mean something else.

Further Reading

González, Mirta. "Cuba." In *Encyclopedia of Latin America Theater*, edited by Eladio Cortés and Mirta Barrea-Marlys, 188–200. Westport, CT: Greenwood Press, 2003.

Henríquez Ureña, Max. *Panorama histórico de la literature cubana*. 2 vols. Habana: Editorial Arte y Literatura, 1979.

Martínez, Julio A., ed. *Dictionary of Twentieth Century Cuban Literature*. Westport, CT: Greenwood Press, 1990.

Montes Huidobro, Matías. "Cuba." *Handbook of Latin American Literature*, edited by David William Foster. New York: Garland Publishing, Inc. 1992.

Romeu, Raquel. *Voces de mujeres en las letras cubanas*. Madrid: Editorial Verbum, 2000.

Smorkaloff, Pamela María. *Cuban Writers on and off the Island*. New York: Twayne Publishers, 1999.

—Rolando Pérez and D. H. Figueredo

Cuevas, Clara (1933–)

∎

Sometimes known as Ysa Di'Rivel, Cuevas is a love poet from Puerto Rico. She is also a journalist and a playwright.

Born in Río Piedras, Puerto Rico, on October 30, 1933, Clara Cuevas studied at the Universidad de Puerto Rico where she earned a BA in humanities. She also majored in journalism and wrote for the school newspapers. Using the pen name of Ysa D'Rivel, she began to publish her poems in such important newspapers as *El Mundo*.

In 1972, Cuevas was appointed assistant editor of Librería International; that same year she took a similar position for the literary review *Inter-American University of Puerto Rico*. While working as journalist for *Revista Bohemia* and a translator for the journal *Pro Tempo*, she wrote several books of poetry, including *Canto al amor profundo* (1956), *Tríptico del amor, del dolor y de la muerte* (1969), and *Amor ultraterreste* (1976). The themes that she explored in her poetry were love, complex relationships between men and women, and immortality. Her poetry is accessible, characterized by clarity of emotion. Cuevas also cultivated the short-story genre, publishing the collections *La carcel del tiempo* (1970) and *Maremagnum* (1976). She also wrote plays, *El rompecabezas* (1970) and *Los buitres del alma— The vultures of the soul* (1976), and a memoir, *La extraña paradoja de mi vida* (1975).

In 2001, in concert with the Puerto Rican government Cuevas set up a workshop for young writers. She is a member of the Society of Puerto Rican Women Authors.

Further Reading

Enciclopedia puertorriqueña. Siglo XXI. Vol. 2. Santurce: Caribe Grolier, 1998.

"Clara Cuevas." *Contemporary Authors on Line*. http://www.galenet.galegroup.com (accessed 11, 2001).

—D. H. Figueredo

Cuevas Regis, Carmen Leila (1910–)

Cuevas Regis was a journalist and a biographer from Puerto Rico. She was one the earliest woman journalists on the island in the twentieth century.

A native of Ponce, Puerto Rico, Cuevas Regis was attracted to journalism during an era when many women did not pursue such a profession. She also had a great interest in chronicling life on the island as seen through her experiences. She wrote for the newspapers *El Mundo* and *Puerto Rico Ilustrado*. Many of her articles were anecdotes that belonged within the genre known as **costumbrismo**, stories of local characters and traditions. She gathered many of these stories in the volume *Desde mi palomar* (1966).

Through the 1960s, she researched the life and works of the Puerto Rican poet and patriot **Lola Rodríguez de Tió**. In 1969, Cuevas Regis published the poet's biography, *Lola de America*. The volume received the literature prize from the Instituto de Literatura Puertorriqueña. Throughout her writings, Cuevas Regis emphasized the development of a Puerto Rican identity and celebrated the island's cultural traditions.

Further Reading

Enciclopedia puertorriqueña. Siglo XXI. Vol. 2. Santurce: Caribe Grolier, 1998.

—*D. H. Figueredo*

Cuza Malé, Belkis (1942–)

Belkis Cuza Malé is a Cuban poet and writer who was imprisoned, along with her husband **Heberto Padilla**, by the Cuban government in 1971 for writing antirevolutionary poems. Though both were released shortly after, her works were censored and her activities monitored until she went into exile in 1979.

Born on June 15, 1942, in Guantanamo, she and her parents moved to Santiago de Cuba in 1954. She attended the Universidad de Oriente, earning a masters in Spanish American and Cuban literature in 1964. In 1962, the Department of Culture of the same university published her first book of poetry, *El viento en la pared*. In this volume, Cuza Malé examined her growth as a poet, revealing a fascination with words and the creative process; the poems were light and celebratory. In 1964, Cuza Malé relocated to Havana, where she continued literature studies at the University of Havana while also writing for the cultural section of the newspaper *Hoy*. When the paper ceased publication, she was transferred to *Granma*, the official organ of Cuba's Communist Party; she was fired two years later for expressing critical views of the revolution. In 1967, she was hired by the **Unión de Escritores y Artistas de Cuba**, editing the journal *La Gaceta de Cuba*. In 1967, she married poet Heberto Padilla.

During this period she wrote three books of poems, *Tiempo de sol* (1963), *Cartas a Ana Frank* (1966), and *Juego de damas* (1970). *Tiempo de sol* is a somber volume in which the poet contemplates a world filled with anxiety and destruction. *Cartas a Ana Frank* was written as a diary; the poems are sad and lament man's inhumanity to man. Both volumes received honorary citations in the **Casa de las Américas** literary contests. The third volume, *Juego de damas*, was deemed subversive and was shredded by Cuban authorities.

After her and Padilla's release from prison, Cuza Malé lived in virtual silence and isolation in Cuba. In 1979, she migrated to the United States. In 1980, her husband joined her in exile, and they moved to Princeton, New Jersey, where they edited the literary journal *Linden Lane*. In 1984, she authored *El clavel y la rosa*, a fictionalized biography of the Cuban poet **Juana Borrero**, who died in 1898 while still a teenager. In 1994, she wrote *Elvis: la tumba sin sosiego*, and in 1996, *En busca de Selena*, explorations of the cultural impact of the two legendary performers and their tragic deaths. In 1997, she relocated to Fort Worth, Texas, where she found La Casa Azul: Centro Cultural Cubano, a cultural institution and art gallery. After her husband's death in 2000, Cuza Malé added his name to the society: Centro Cultural Cubano Heberto Padilla.

Cuza Malé writes for several periodicals in Argentina, France, Mexico, and Spain. Through the Casa Azul, she is involved in charity work and assistance to the Latino community in Texas. In 2002, she published her censored book, *Juego de damas*.

Further Reading

Cuza Malé, Belkes. Interview with author. November 2003.

Niurka, Norma "El más allá de Belkis Cuza Malé." *El Nuevo Herald,* December 17, 2000.

Weiser, Nora. *Open to the Sun: A Bilingual Anthology of Latin American Women Poets.* California: Perival Press, 1980,

—*D. H. Figueredo*

D

Dabydeen, Cyril (1945–)

A poet and writer from Guyana, Dabydeen has lived most of his life in Canada, where he has worked as a professor and government official while writing dozens of books. He was the Poet Laureate of Ottawa from 1984 to 1987.

Dabydeen was born on October 15, 1945, in Berbice, British Guiana, now Guyana. He grew up in a poor rural family but was able to use the British Council Library, where he read the works of T. S. Eliot (1888–1965) and W. H. Auden (1907–73). He also read the works of such emerging Caribbean writers as **Derek Walcott** and **V. S. Naipul**. He was influenced by the Guyanese **Martin Carter** and his very first book of poetry, *Poems in Recession*, written when he was a teenager but published in 1972, was his response to Carter's classic work *Poems of Resistance* (1955).

At the age of twenty-five, Dabydeen migrated to Canada. He graduated from Lakehead University and earned a masters in art and a masters in business from Queens University. White teaching at Algonquin College, in Ottawa, Ontario, he wrote poetry, which he published in two volumes in 1977: *Distances* and *Goatsong*. His poetic productivity continued into the next two decades, during which he published over ten volumes. His poetry was shaped by his Marxist ideals and his realization of the universality of oppression felt by those on the margin of society, regardless of location.

Dabydeen has achieved recognition as a poet. But he is also a short-story writer and a novelist. *Still Close to the Island* (1980), one of his best-known collections, explores the presence of poverty in the developed world. The novel *Dark Swirl* (1989) is a mystical study of Guyana's hinterlands. Like his poetry, his prose addresses political themes, though Dabydeen doesn't describe himself as a political writer.

Dabydeen has won numerous awards, including **A. J. Seymour** Lyric Poetry Prize (1967), the Ontario Arts Council Award (1977–80), and the Canadian Council Award (1983). Despite his recognition in Canada and the Caribbean, Dadydeen's works have yet to attract wide scholarship. His cousin is the writer **David Dabydeen**. *See also* Literatura Comprometida/Politically and Socially Engaged Literature.

Further Reading

Dawes, Kwame. *Talk Yuh Talk: Interviews with Anglophone Caribbean Poets.* Charlottesville: University Press of Virginia, 2001.

—D. H. Figueredo

Dabydeen, David (1955–)

∎

East Indian and Guyanese writer who explores the double oppression experienced by East Indians who feel discriminated by the black population in Guyana and by whites in England, Dabydeen is a poet, novelist, and scholar. Poet and literary critic **Kwame Dawes**, in *Talk Yuh Talk* (2001), calls him one of the leading talents of a new wave of immigrant writers who live in Britain.

David Dabydeen was born in an old sugar plantation in British Guiana, now Guyana, in 1955. As a child, walking about the plantation and the sugarcane fields, he could envision the ghosts of black slaves toiling in the field. The ambiance and the sense of history would inspire his poetry and inform his scholarly work decades later.

At the age of twelve, his family moved to England in search of better economic opportunities. Dabydeen earned a BA from Cambridge University in 1978. Three years later, he received his PhD from the University of London. He conducted postdoctoral work at Oxford University from 1983 to 1987. His writing is influenced by the works of the Guyanan **Wilson Harris** and the Barbadian **Kamau Brathwaite**, often using in his novels and poetry characters and situations created by those writers. He told poet Kwame Dawes in *Talk Yuh Talk* that he writes to "Harris and to Naipul, write back, quarrel with, borrow from, love, praise, worship them" (205).

Dabydeen's first book of poetry was *Slave Song* (1984), a daily account of life on a colonial plantation. In re-creating the lives of the exploitation of the slaves, Dabydeen uses Creole: "Tell me how me haniamal / African orang-utan / Tell me how me cannibal / Fit fo slata fit to hang." The book of poetry received the 1984 Commonwealth Poetry Prize. He then alternated between creative writing and scholarly work, and a year after the publication of *Slave Song*, he published *The Black Presence in English Literature*. This volume was followed by several critical studies, including *Hogarth's Blacks: Images of Blacks in Eighteenth Century English Art* (1985) and *Black Writers in Britain, 1760–1890* (1991), both well received by critics. Dabydeen also wrote several novels: *The Intended* (1991), *Disappearance* (1993), *The Counting House* (1996), and *Harlot's Progress* (1999).

In his poetry and novels, Dabydeen explores his dual African and East Indian heritage, the nuances of language as used by people in the Caribbean and in England, and the impact of colonialism on the indentured East Indian servants who migrated to Guyana in the nineteenth century. There is often the affirmation of the past as in the poetry collection *Coolie Odyssey* (1988), where the narrator chooses the Creole language used by his grandmother over the educated language he has employed to assimilate into British society. Dawes observes that Dabydeen "offers fresh approaches to the themes of exile and cultural schizophrenia that are distinguished by [the] capacity to examine . . . the construction for race and difference in British literature and art."

Dabydeen directs the Caribbean Studies Department at the University of Warwick. He has served for many years as Guyanese ambassador to the United Kingdom. His cousin is the writer **Cyril Dabydeen**.

Further Reading

Dawes, Kwame. *Talk Yuh Talk: Interviews with Anglophone Caribbean Poets*. Charlottesville: University Press of Virginia, 2001.

Williams, Emily Allen. *Poetic Negotiation of Identity in the Works of Brathwaite, Harris, Senior, and Dabydeen: Tropical Paradise Lost and Regained*. Lewiston, NY: Edwin Mellen Press, 1999.

—*D. H. Figueredo*

D'Aguiar, Fred (1960–)

D'Aguiar is a British-Guyanese poet and novelist who first achieved fame with the publication of his first book of poetry *Mama Dot* (1985). His poems, long and musical, and his prose, innovative and with shifting viewpoints, explore the themes of the African diaspora in the Caribbean and the racist legacy of the colonial era.

D'Aguiar was born in London on February 2, 1960. His Guyanese parents had emigrated to Great Britain to look for employment, but when they found it difficult to raise D'Aguiar due to their work schedule, they sent him to his grandparents in Guyana. He lived in the interior of the country with his paternal grandparents but also spent time in the capital, Georgetown, with his maternal grandparents. At the age of twelve he returned to London. But the years in Guyana provided him with materials needed for his fiction and poetry: memorable grandparents, a diversity of the ethnic experience, since his Guyanese relatives were of African, Amerindian, British, and East Indian descent, and the musicality of the Creole language, which is a combination of standard English and Guyanese vernacular.

In London, D'Aguiar studied literature at the University of Kent, graduating in 1985. That same year, he published his first book of poetry, *Mama Dot*. The volume, consisting of a series of long poems, was the author's recollections and celebrations of his Guyanese grandmothers. The collection was a critical success; comments poet and critic **Kwame Dawes** in his book *Talk Yuh Talk* (2001): "The poems' control, formal dexterity, and carefully rendered sentiment, along with their fresh articulation of the Guyanese experience in a language that was clearly shaped by British life, combined to assure . . . a positive critical response" (226). The volume earned D'Aguiar the 1985 Guyana Prize for poetry and brought him recognition; he was featured in cultural discussions—on television and radio—with such important literary figures as Nobel Prize winner **Derek Walcott** and poet **Linton Kwesi Johnson**.

Three years later, D'Aguiar published *Airy Hall*, an exploration of his years in Guyana and of the effects of colonialism on that nation. Again, the controlled but musical diction of his poetry made the volume popular with English readers. Other successes followed: *A Jamaican Airman Foresees His Death* (1991), a play about discrimination in Great Britain; and the novels *The Longest Memory* (1994), about slavery; *Dear Future* (1996), about his stay in Guyana and return to London; and *Feeding the Ghosts* (1999), about the forced journey of enslaved Africans to the New World. Though these books were not written as poems, the author's poetic style and distinct voice renders the works a sense of intimacy. The novels were of experimental nature with a multiplicity of characters and shifting narratives.

D'Aguiar also ventured into radio drama, writing in 1992 a play about Christopher Columbus. Entitled *1492*, it was produced by the British Broadcast Corporation (BBC). He has written for television and has edited an anthology, *The New British Poetry* (1988). In the late 1990s, D'Aguiar left Great Britain for the United States, where he teaches at the University of Miami, in Florida. It was his first encounter with the American South that prompted D'Aguiar to explore the subject of his slavery in two of his books. *See also* Postcolonialism.

Further Reading

Dawes, Kwame, ed. *Talk Yuh Talk: Interviews with Anglophone Caribbean Poets.* Charlottesville: University Press of Virginia, 2001.

—*D. H. Figueredo*

Damas, Léon-Gontran (1912–78)

∎

Alongside the Martinican **Aimé Césaire** and Léopold Senghor (1906–2001) from Senegal, Damas was one of the founders of **Négritude**, the black consciousness movement of the Francophone Caribbean. Of these three men, he was the first to publish a book, *Pigments* (1937), representative of Négritude. A native of French Guiana, Damas was a pioneer poet in portraying the colonized personality, a psychological condition that a generation later **Frantz Fanon** would write about as a psychiatrist.

Damas was born in Cayenne, the capital of French Guiana, on March 28, 1912, the son of a well-to-do mulatto family. His mother died in his childhood, and he was raised by an aunt. After attending elementary school in Cayenne, he was sent to the high school Lycée Schoelcher in Martinique, where he befriended the would-be poet and political figure Aimé Césaire. From Martinique, Damas traveled to Paris to study at the University of Paris in the early 1930s. He collaborated on three journals, *La revue du monde noir, Légitime défense*, and *L'étudiant noir*; though short-lived, these journals served as the seed for the influential publication **Tropiques**, which Césaire would publish in Martinique a few years later.

In 1937, Damas published his first book of poetry, *Pigments*, which lashed out at racism and French colonialism while celebrating blackness and the Caribbean's African roots. In the volume, Damas chose the word "négre" over "noir." The latter was the traditional expression used by the French. The first was a pejorative term, similar to "nigger" in English. In choosing "négre," Damas was affirming in print, for the first time, his African heritage and his rejection of European values.

The book was a sensation. Scholar Ellen Conroy Kennedy, in *The Negritude Poets*, describes why: "In a blunt, dry, vivid style, marked by fresh images, unashamedly plain language, staccato rhythms, and acridly witty puns, Damas' short poems lay bare the author's often violent rejection of European 'ci-vi-li-za-tion'" (42). A typical and exemplary poem is "Sell Out," translated by Kennedy: "I feel ridiculous / in their shoes / their dinner jackets" (50).

Damas's next book was *Retour de Guyane* (1938). This narrative about his return to Guyana was also a denunciation of French colonialism and a rejection of assimilation into the white culture. *Retour de Guyane* and *Pigments* were both censured by the French colonial government. In 1943, he published *Veillées noires*, a collection of tales from Guyana.

After World War II, Damas was elected to represent his country before the French Assembly, a post he held from 1945 to 1951. In 1948, he published *Poemès nègres dur des airs Africains*, his adaptations of African folklore and poems.

During the 1950s, he traveled throughout Africa and worked for UNESCO. He published two works of poetry during this decade: *Graffiti* (1952) and *Black-Label* (1956). Though not as famous as his friend Aimé Césaire, Damas was often invited to read his poetry on American campuses, which he did throughout the 1960s. In 1970, he settled in the United States, teaching literature at Howard University. In 1972, he published a collection of short stories, *Veillès noires*.

Damas passed away at the age of sixty-five while still working as a professor at Howard University. His knowledge of the English language and the friends he made in the United States, including Langston Hughes (1902–67), enabled him to internationalize the Négritude movement. *See also* Postcolonialism.

Further Reading

Kennedy, Ellen Conroy, ed. *The Negritude Poets: an Anthology of Translations from the French*. New York: Viking Press, 1975.

Ojo-Ade, Femi. *Léon-Gontran Damas: The Spirit of Resistance*. London, England: Karnak House, 1993.

—*D. H. Figueredo*

Danticat, Edwidge (1969–)

∎

Edwidge Danticat is a Haitian-American novelist who writes about the immigration experience of Haitians in the United States and the political oppression experienced by Haitians in their homeland. Like many writers from the Caribbean, Danticat chose to write in English rather than in her mother tongue.

Edwidge Danticat was born on January 19, 1969, in Port-au-Prince, Haiti, and emigrated to the United States in 1981. She began writing as a teenager; the publication of her historical novel *The Farming of Bones* catapulted her to prominence as one of the most important American artists under the age of thirty.

The novel takes place in 1937 and depicts an event known as the "kout kouto," translated from Creole or Kreyòl (Haitian's vernacular based on French) as "stabbing," the popular term for the massacre by Dominican soldiers and paramilitaries of up to fifteen thousand Haitian guest workers. *The Farming of Bones* tells this story in the voice of a young Haitian woman, Amabelle Desir, who since childhood has worked as a servant in the home of a wealthy Dominican family. She is planning to marry a Haitian cane worker from a nearby plantation, Sebastian Onius, when the Dominican Republic's newly installed military dictator, Rafael Leónidas Trujillo (1891–1961), orders the expulsion of all the Haitian workers. Along with thousands of other Haitians, Sebastian dies in the massacre that follows, and despite the promise of Amabelle's employers that they will protect her, she must flee. After a harrowing journey in which being black and non-Spanish-speaking leads to death, she crosses the aptly named Massacre River (named for an early nineteenth-century massacre of Dominican soldiers by Haitian forces) to a life of safety but crushing poverty and loneliness in Haiti. The novel depicts Haiti's tortured history and its conflicts with the Dominican Republic, neighbors on the island of Hispaniola divided by race, language, experiences of colonialism, and its legacy in the global economic system.

The publication of *The Farming of Bones* followed two other significant works of fiction that brought notice to Danticat. Her first novel, *Breath, Eyes, Memory* (1994), is a coming-of-age story drawn from her own experience of emigrating from Haiti to Brooklyn, New York, at the age of twelve. That novel, which she began writing in adolescence, portrays the relationships among teenager Sophie Caco, struggling to adjust to a life in a new country, her aunt who raises her in Haiti and demands strict conformity to traditional mores, and her mother in Brooklyn, who is still haunted by a brutal rape in Haiti years before. In 1995, Danticat's short story collection, *Krik? Krak!* appeared. The title comes from the Haitian storytelling tradition, which employs a call and response between teller and audience. The stories portray life in Haiti under the cruel, corrupt Jean-Claude Duvalier (1951–) dictatorship, the travails of Haitian refuges fleeing to the United States, often on rickety boats; and the intergenerational conflicts within immigrant families.

With her own experience as an immigrant teenager still fresh, Danticat has remained active within her Brooklyn community, conducting workshops for high school students and helping them enter competitive colleges. She credits her undergraduate years at Columbia University and graduate years at Brown with giving her the skills, contacts, and confidence to succeed in her chosen field. In 2002 she published her first novel for young readers, *Behind the Mountains*, which portrays a mother and daughter forced by political violence to leave Haiti and join the father in Brooklyn; Danticat concludes the novel with a brief essay detailing her own immigration experience. Danticat has also edited the anthology *The Butterfly's Way*, published in 2001, in which thirty-three contributors—writers, college students, and professors—discuss their journeys from Haiti to the United States. *See also* Alexis, Jacques Stephen; Haitian Literature in Kreyòl; Mother-Daughter Relationships.

Further Reading

Contemporary Authors, Volume 129. Detroit, MI: Gale, 2002.

Johnson, Kelli Lyon. "Both sides of the Massacre: collective memory and narrative on Hispaniola." *Winnipeg* 36, no. 2 (2003): 75–81.

—*Lyn Miller-Lachman*

Das, Mahadai (1954–2003)

∎

A passionate and politically committed poet from Guyana, Mahadai Das wrote a poetry that attempted to capture her cultural heritage and to protest the discrimination Indo-Caribbean people experienced in the Caribbean and in the United States. She was one of the first Indo-Caribbean women poets to be published.

Mahadai Das was born in Eccles, Guyana, the oldest of ten children. Talented and beautiful, she was elected beauty queen of her town in 1971. That same year, her mother passed away and Das became responsible for the upbringing of her siblings. Despite her responsibilities, she continued to study, attending Bishops High School, in Georgetown, and graduating from the University of Guyana.

In 1972, she joined a group of young Guyanese writers called "**The Messenger Group**," where she was exposed to nationalistic and leftist ideals. To continue her studies, Das then relocated to the United States, earning BA in philosophy from Columbia University and an MA in philosophy from New York University. While pursuing doctoral studies at the University of Chicago, she had to undergo open-heart surgery.

In 1977, she published the collection of poems *I Want to Be a Poetess of My People*, a history of East Indians in the Caribbean. In 1982, her second collection was published, *My Finer Steel Will Grow*, an examination of **postcolonialism** in Guyana and her expression of disappointment over the conflicts between Afro-Guyanese and Indo-Guyanese in her native country. In *Bones* (1998), Das changed her focus from the Caribbean to the United States, where she had experienced discrimination.

Shortly after the publication of *Bones*, Das's health deteriorated, and at a time when critics and scholars were becoming more interested in her works, she had to stop writing. Before her death on April 3, 2003, Das discussed with the editors of

Peepal Tree Press the publication of her last work, *A Leaf in Her Ears: Selected Poems*, which included poems published in previous collections and some of her earlier works. The volume was published in 2005. *See also* Literatura Comprometida/Politically and Socially Engaged Literature.

Further Reading

Miller, Jane Eldridge. *Who's Who in Contemporary Women's Writing*. London: Routledge, 2001.

"Mahadai Das: *A Leaf in His Ear: Selected Poems*." http://www.peepaltreepress.com (accessed 8/31/05).

—*D. H. Figueredo*

Dathorne, O. R. (1934–)

Guyanese novelist and scholar Oscar Ronald Dathorne has written about the immigrant experience in London and the need for the people of the Caribbean to search for their African roots. His academic work, which explores how Europe used and abused Africa and the Caribbean, has been compared to the works of the Trinidadian historian and political figure **Eric Williams**.

Dathorne was born on November 19, 1934, in Georgetown, in the former British Guiana, now Guyana. While attending elementary school in Georgetown, he was awarded at the age of twelve a scholarship to Queen's College, the prestigious government high school in Guyana. His plans were to become a rural teacher, but when his father lost his job, he and his parents moved to England. To help his family, Dathorne worked for two years before enrolling at the University of Sheffield. Graduating in 1957, he then earned a masters in education from the University of London.

The years as an undergraduate and graduate student, and the many immigrants he met in London, provided him the inspiration for his novel *Dumplings in the Soup*. Published in 1963, the novel tells the story of several West Indians rooming together in London. It is a humorous look at the immigrant experience and the alienation experienced by outsiders. Underneath the humor, though, there is a veneer of cynicism and criticism of the British, who often see themselves as liberated and unbiased while being perceived by others as quite prejudiced.

In the early 1960s, Dathorne accepted teaching positions in Nigeria and was also a UNESCO adviser in Sierra Leone. Africa served as the setting for his second novel, *The Scholar Man* (1964), about a man's search for his African roots. The novel was not only an philosophical exploration of race and identity but also a satire on the African educational system, for at the time an educated African knew more about Europe than about Africa.

In the mid-1960s, Dathorne received his PhD from the University of Sheffield. He was invited to teach at several American universities, including Yale, Howard, and Ohio State, before settling at the University of Miami, in Florida, where he was first appointed director of American studies and then director of Caribbean, African, and Afro-American studies. In 1969, he founded the *Journal of Caribbean Studies*. His academic activities encouraged him to pursue scholarly writings, which he did for two decades, publishing *The Black Mind: A History of African Literature* (1976), *Dark Ancestor: The Literature of the Black Man in the Caribbean* (1981), *In Europe's Image: The Need for American Multiculturalism* (1994), and *Worlds Apart: Race in the Modern Period* (2000), among others. In 1986, Dathorne returned to fiction with *Dele's Child*. But whereas his first two novels used humor, this latest work is a more serious, though poetic, examination of African culture. Dathorne also wrote a book of poems, *Kelly Poems* (1977).

Dathorne's creative work has been widely reviewed in such international publications as **Bim, Caribbean Quarterly**, and *Times Literary Supplement*. His academic work has received praise and commendations from his peers and students. For example, in 1972 the International Biographical Center of Cambridge, England, honored him with "The Men and Women of Distinction" award, and in 1980 and 1982, the United Black Students Organization of the University of Miami rendered him tribute for "Outstanding Services and Contributions to Black Culture." *See also* Immigrant Literature.

Further Reading

Lawrence, Leota S. "O. R. Dathorne (1934–)." In *Fifty Caribbean Writers: A Bio-Bibliographical Critical Sourcebook*, edited by Daryl Cumber Dance. Westport, CT: Greenwood Press, 1986.

—*D. H. Figueredo*

Daubón, José Antonio (1840–1922)

A writer who cultivated the genre of **costumbrismo**, writings of local color, Daubón was an essayist and promoter of Puerto Rican culture.

Daubón was born, raised, and died in San Juan. He received his elementary education in that city and conducted secondary studies at the Seminario Conciliar, also in San Juan. From very early on, he felt the desire to describe Puerto Rican traditions and customs as a way of affirming a Puerto Rican identity separate from an Iberian identity. This was the objective of his most famous work, *Cosas de Puerto Rico* (1893), a costumbrista volume that sketched local activities, festivals, and cultural expressions that were purely Puerto Rican.

Daubón also experimented with theater, writing in 1899 the drama *El próceso*. In 1900, he published a volume of his poetry, *Poesías*. He was a prolific writer of articles and essays, which were published in journals such as *Plumas amigas, El boletin mercantil, Diario de Puerto Rico,* and *El Clamor del País*.

Further Reading

Enciclopedia puertorriqueña. Siglo XXI. Santurce, Puerto Rico: Caribe Grolier, 2000.

—*D. H. Figueredo*

Davertige (1940–2004)

Though Davertige published only one book of poetry during his lifetime—*Idem* (1962)—his politically charged poems have assured him international recognition. He was also an artist, using his actual name—Villard Denis—to indicate that activity while adopting the name *Davertige* to identify himself as a poet.

Born on December 2, 1940, in Port-au-Prince as Villard Denis, his parents raised him in a loving environment of comfort and books. A frail child, Davertige spent his childhood indoors, reading French literature and drawing. Noticing his gift for art, his parents sent him at the age of twelve to Centre de Céramique de l'Éducation Nationale to study ceramics. In his early twenties, he enrolled at Foyer des Arts school. Around this period, he started to become aware of social inequities in Haiti and to espouse communism. He was also writing poetry. Becoming part of a literary group called Samba, he decided at this time to adopt his pen name.

Between 1960 and 1961, he wrote the poems that make up the collection *Idem*. A year later, Davertige financed the publication of the volume. In the next three years or so, word of mouth, the poet's own readings of his work at conferences and salons, and the support of friends helped to promote the book in Haiti and Paris; it was then reprinted in Paris in 1965. That same year, he arrived in Paris after living in New York City for a year.

In 1968, Davertige joined a group of Haitian exiles who were interested in overthrowing the dictatorship of **François Duvalier**. They traveled to China in the hope of obtaining financial backing, but the effort failed. Davertige grew discouraged with Communist ideology and with Paris. He gave up poetry, began the draft of an autobiographical novel, which he didn't finish, and moved to Montreal in 1976. Ten years later, he returned to Haiti, where he exhibited his paintings to great acclaim. He re-edited *Idem*, which was published in Montreal under the title of *Davertige, secret anthologie*, in 2003. This version consisted of old and new poems and drawings.

Davertige passed away in Montreal on July 25, 2004.

Further Reading

Crosley, Bernadette Carré. "La modernité créole chez Davertige." *Journal of Haitian Studies*, no. 3–4 (1997–1998): 110–23.

—*D. H. Figueredo*

Dávila Family

■

The Dávilas were father and son poets from Puerto Rico. The father, Virgilio, was a local politician and popular teacher; the son was a physician. Both wrote poetry that was popular with the general reading public.

Dávila, José Antonio (1898–1941). Dávila achieved popularity with a romantic and nationalistic poetry that attempted to create a Puerto Rican persona. He often identified the characters in his poems with natural elements, as expressed in "Pulpa" (1940): "Mi sangre tiene el rojo del crepúscolo / mi cuerpo, húmedo y fresco de rocío / dorado con el sol . . . (My blood has the red of the dusk / my body the freshness of the dew / made golden by the sun).

José Antonio Dávila was born in Bayamón, Puerto Rico, on October 7, 1898. A physician, he set up his practice in his hometown. His medical knowledge and his sickly constitution made him intensely aware of life's frailty, a theme he also addressed in his poetry.

Encouraged and inspired by his father, Dávila contributed poetry to local publications, beginning in 1917 and ending in 1939. Many of these poems were collected after his death and published in 1940 under the title of *Venimia*. The poems depicted local scenes and celebrated Puerto Rican culture and traditions. Comments critic **Margot Arce de Vázquez**, in *Lecturas puertorriqueñas*, (1968): "The island's natural beauty appears as decorative element or personification of the land, expressing its colors and types with a great deal of strength. [The poems] incorporate the local vernacular . . . making them accessible to the average person." Davila also wrote children's poetry, collected in the volume *Almancén de baratijas* (1941). Fluent in English, he often translated into Spanish the poems of William Shakespeare (1564–1616) and John Milton (1608–74); he even translated from Spanish to English the poetry written by his father.

Dávila, Virgilio (1869–1943). Dávila was a Puerto Rican poet representative of the island's **costumbrismo**, literature of local color. According to critic **Margot Arce de Vázquez**, in *Lecturas puertorriqueñas* (1968), at a historic time when Spanish influences were receding from Puerto Rico and the American presence was growing as a result of the Spanish-Cuban-American War of 1898, Dávila was affirming Puerto Rican traditions and values.

Dávila was born on January 28, 1869, in Toa Baja, Puerto Rico. He graduated from secondary school in 1895 and was elected mayor of Bayamón in 1905, serving for six years. Dávila was also a teacher and a farmer. He founded a seminary in 1909.

Influenced by Victor Hugo (1802–85), Dávila wrote poetry that was romantic in its identification with nature and the countryside. Sensing changes in urban and rural settings, he longed for the past and the old towns of his childhood and attempted to preserve them in his poetry. He also celebrated the beauty of the Puerto Rican women, which he interpreted as a symbol of the country. Many of his poems have been set to music.

His most popular books are *Patria* (1903), *Viviendo y amando* (1912), *Aromas del terruño* (1916), *Pueblito de antes* (1917), and *Un libro para mis nietos* (1928). *See also* Romanticismo/Romanticism.

Further Reading

Arce de Vázquez, Margot et al. *Lecturas puertorriqueñas: poesía*. Sharon, CT: Troutman Press, 1968.

Ramos Mimoso, Adriana. *Vida y poesía en José Antonio Dávila*. 2nd ed. rev. Río Piedras, Puerto Rico: Editorial de la Universidad de Puerto Rico, 1986.

—D. H. Figueredo

Dawes Family

Neville and Kwame are father and son writers born in Africa but raised in Jamaica. Together, they have promoted Caribbean culture and Pan-Africanism over six decades through numerous writings and cultural and scholarly activities.

Dawes, Kwame (1962–). Born in Ghana, raised in Jamaica, educated there and in Canada, and a United States resident, Kwame Dawes embodies Pan-Africanism: the presence of Africa in the world at large. A renaissance man, Dawes is a poet, writer, scholar, musician, and an actor.

Kwame Senu Neville Dawes was born in Ghana on July 28, 1962, but he and his family relocated to Jamaica. He graduated from the University of West Indies–Mona in 1983. Ten years later, he earned a PhD from the University of New Brunswick, Canada. In the 1980s and 1990s, he wrote over a dozen plays, including *Warmth of the Cold* (1982), *And the Gods Fell* (1983), *The Martyr*

Poet, playwright, and critic Kwame Dawes writes about colonialism and racism, while also promoting the works of other Caribbean writers. *Courtesy of Kwame Dawes.*

(1985), *Friends and Almost Lovers* (1986), *Coming in From the Cold* (1988), *Charades* (1990), *Stump of the Terebith* (1994), and *A Celebration of Struggle* (1995), all produced in Jamaica and in Canada. His appreciation of Jamaican writer **Roger Mais** and his interest in the common people led Dawes to his stage adaptation of Mais's classic novel *Brother Man* (1954), about Rastafarianism in Jamaica. Titled *One Love*, the drama was successfully staged at Old Vic and the Lyric Theater in London.

Attracted to and inspired by reggae music, Dawes's poetry is musical and rhythmic while exploring such subjects as colonialism, diversity, and pride in

African heritage. His many volumes of poetry include *Progeny of Air* (1994), *Resisting the Anomie* (1995), *Prophets* (1995), *Requiem* (1996), *Jacko Jacobus* (1996), *Mapmaker* (2000), and *New and Selected Poems, 1994–2002* (2002). Like many other Jamaican writers, the bulk of his work was published in England. However, the volume *Midland* (2001) was published in the United States, a logical choice, since the poems in the collection celebrate Dawes's new home: South Carolina.

As a scholar, he essayed on the religiosity of Reggae in *Natural Mysticism: Towards a New Reggae Aesthetics in Caribbean Writing* (1997), and he interviewed Caribbean writers in *Talk Yuh Talk: Interviews with Anglophone Caribbean Poets* (2000), a seminal work that introduces several newcomers and established authors to American readers. He has received numerous honors, including the Honorary Fellow of the University of Iowa's writing program (1987), Associate Fellow of the University of Warwick (1997), the Pushcart Prize for Poetry (2001), and Individual Artist Fellowship from the South Carolina Arts Commission (2001).

Dawes, Neville (1926–84). Known for satirical novels that questioned the political process on the island while advocating revolutionary change, Neville Dawes was a scholar and a teacher. He belonged to a generation of intellectuals, like **Andrew Salkey** and **John Hearne**, who felt the need to relocate abroad but, unlike his compatriots, returned home.

Neville Dawes was born in Nigeria on June 16, 1926, the son of Baptist missionaries from Jamaica. In 1929, the family returned to Jamaica, and nearly ten years later, young Dawes was awarded a scholarship to attend Jamaica College in Kingston. From 1948 to 1951, he studied at Oriel College, Oxford. Upon graduation, he returned to Jamaica, where he taught literature at Calabar High School and at the University College of the West Indies. In 1955, he went back to Africa, where he taught in Ghana and where his son Kwame Neville was born.

Welcomed as if he were a native son, Neville Dawes was soon involved in political activities and cultural work in his new home, editing the literary journal of the Ghana Society of Writers. In the mid-1960s, he traveled to Guyana, and in 1970, he settled once again in Jamaica, where he was the director of the Institute of Jamaica, the first director of the African-Caribbean Institute of Jamaica, and was involved in the administration of libraries, museums, and cultural center. He passed away in 1984 as a result of a fall.

In his novel *The Last Enchantment* (1969), Dawes chronicled the development of modern Jamaica in the rise to political power of two friends, one who becomes a leftist leader, probably modeled on labor leader Alexander Bustamente (1884–1977), while the other, based on Norman Manley (1893–1969), espouses a conservative ideology. Rich in characterization, Dawes's humorous perspective renders a cartoonlike ambiance of a political gathering where the crowd mistakes one politician for another and a government official has difficulty speaking because of the false teeth he is wearing. In his second novel, *Interim* (1978), Dawes proposed a more radical change for Jamaica through a socialist revolution that promised social equality. However, before political reforms could be implemented, anti-revolutionaries plotted with the United States government to remove from power the revolutionary leaders. Scholar Edward Baugh, writing in *Fifty Caribbean Writers*, points out that in *Interim* Neville Dawes had the vision to imagine how the establishment of a socialist regime in Caribbean, especially after the Cuban revolution of 1959, would lead to military intervention by the Americans, as it occurred in Grenada a decade later.

Dawes also wrote *In Sepia* (1958), a book of poems, and *Prolegomena to Caribbean Literature* (1978). He wrote for the influential daily *The Gleaner*, several literary journals, and for the BBC.

Further Reading

Baugh, Edward. "Neville Dawes (1926–1984)." In *Fifty Caribbean Writers: A Bio-Bibliographical Critical Sourcebook*, edited by Daryl Cumber Dance. Westport, CT: Greenwood Press, 1986.

Dathorne, O. R. *Caribbean Narrative: An Anthology of West Indian Writing*. London, Heinemann, 1966. Reprinted 1979.

Newson-Horst, Adele. "*Kwame Dawes. New and Selected Poems, 1994–2002* (Book Review)." *World Literature Today* 77, no. 3–4 (October–December 2003): 81.

—*D. H. Figueredo*

D'Costa, Jean (1937–)

■

D'Costa is a popular young-adult writer from Jamaica, where her novels are included in the literary canon. She is also a scholar and anthologist who has mentored younger writers and who eagerly promotes Jamaican literature.

Jean Constance D'Costa was born in St. Andrew, Jamaica, on January 13, 1937. Her parents were school teachers who taught in rural Jamaica. The countryside and the people from the villages charmed and inspired the would-be writer. Years later, she would be praised by her readers for her accurate depiction of the Jamaican landscape.

D'Costa attended the Half-Way-Tree Elementary School with another student who would also achieve fame as a poet, **Mervyn Morris**; after attending high school in the town of St. Ann, D'Costa won a scholarship to attend the University College of the West Indies. She was an honor student, and upon graduation, she received a scholarship to study at Oxford University. In 1952, D'Costa returned to Jamaica, where she taught English literature at the University of West Indies. She also worked for the Ministry of Education. In the 1960s, she relocated to the United States to teach at Hamilton College, New York.

In the mid-1960s, she wrote her first novel, *Sprat Morrison*, a story about a young boy getting ready to take a high school entrance examination in Jamaica. The book was published by Ministry of Education Publications Department in 1968. The novel was well received and it soon became mandatory reading in public schools. A few years later, she published *Escape to Last Man Peak* (1976), an adventure and thriller about a group of young orphans seeking refuge in a mountain after an epidemic strikes their orphanage and the surrounding villages. This novel earned her the Children's Writers Award from the Jamaican Reading Association. In 1978, she published *Voice in the Wind*, a historical novel about the impact of World War II on Jamaica. In 1980, she coedited with **Velma Pollard** a collection of short stories, *Over Our Way*. Her desire to promote Jamaican literature outside the island inspired her to write, with **Barbara Lalla**, *Voices in exile: Jamaican texts of the 18th and 19th centuries* (1989). Her interest in the Jamaican vernacular, which she uses in her novels, led her to coauthor, again with Barbara Lalla, the book *Language in Exile: Three Hundred Years of Jamaican Creole* (1990).

Further Reading

Johnson, Joyce. "Jean D'Costa (1937–)". In *Fifty Caribbean Writers: A Bio-Bibliographical Critical Sourcebook*, edited by Daryl Cumber Dance. Westport, CT: Greenwood Press, 1986.

—*D. H. Figueredo*

Deana, La (1790–1852)

∎

Pseudonym of Dominican writer Manuela Aybar o Rodríguez, a pioneer feminist and author of a seminal essay, entitled "Story of a Woman" (1849), on the condition of women in nineteenth-century Dominican society. The essay, daring for its time, sketches a life free of expectations for women from Latin America, in general, and from the Dominican Republic in particular.

There is little information on the life and works of La Deana. The unmarried godchild of Dean José Gabriel de Aybar, with whom she lived, her involvement in politics and community affairs exceeded the norm. As a spinster, La Deana was expected to play a supportive role in society, volunteering her services to the Church. Instead, she occupied herself as a contractor of masons working on the reconstructions of historic buildings. Convention required her to be genteel and less willing to speak about her own illegitimacy and modest financial circumstances. She chose, however, to wear these traits as badges of honor.

La Deana kept a hand-cranked press at home that she used to reproduce her verses, mostly political and in favor of President Pedro Santana (1801–64), who defeated the Haitian invasion of 1849 and annexed the Dominican Republic to Spain. La Deana distributed her verses to anyone requesting a copy, especially to members of the working class, including the stone masons who worked with her. The poems were of poor quality, but the author, as La Deana indicates in "Story of a Woman," did not have much of an opportunity to study. The poems are significant, however, because they present a portrait of nineteenth-century politics; also at a time when women were expected to remain silent, the poems depict La Deana's sentiments and her own fascination with the political process. The essay

"Story of a Woman" is constructed with irony and subterfuge. In the essay, La Deana goes to great pains to explain that as a woman she has no political aspirations, as mandated by the male-driven society of the era. However, she uses her writings to promote her views and her criticism of those who apposed president Santana.

La Deana is an example of a woman of independent spirit. She was not only a spinster but one who was happy to have found a role beyond that of a wife. *See also* Dominican Republic, Literature, History of

Further Reading

Cocco de Filippis, Daisy. *Documents of Dissidence: Selected Writings by Dominican Women*. New York: CUNY Dominican Studies Institute, 2000.

—Daisy Cocco de Filippis

De Boissière, Ralph (1907–)

Political novelist from Trinidad, De Boissière has lived most of his life in Australia. He is known for his sympathetic portrayals of workers and common people.

The descendant of French settlers who migrated to Trinidad during the 1700s, Ralph Anthony Charles De Boissière was born in 1907. Orphaned at an early age, he was brought up by his stepmother and was influenced by an uncle who often wrote and talked about the ways society shaped an individual's personality. Rebellious by nature, De Boissière refused to attend church, and he let his hair grow long, a behavior not acceptable in the 1920s. Graduating from Queen's Royal College, he became a traveling salesman, visiting towns and villages in Trinidad. During the 1920s, he befriended the writers who were known as the Beacon Group—**Alfred Mendes, Albert Gomes**, and **CLR James**—the publishers of the influential journal *The Beacon*.

During the 1930s, he contributed stories to *The Beacon* and became involved in local politics, campaigning for Albert Gomes, who won a seat in Port of Spain City Council. In 1947, De Boissière left Trinidad, moving first to the United States and then to Australia, where he worked in a factory. With a group of friends he founded the Australian Book Society, which served as the publisher for his first book, *Crown Jewel* (1952). Though the novel was sold initially at gatherings of the Australian Book Society and trade union meetings it eventually became one of the major novels written about the Anglophone Caribbean. It told the story of a labor leader in Trinidad before World War II, detailing the abuses Trinidadian workers experienced at the hands of colonial authorities and ruthless capitalists.

In 1956, De Boissière published *Rum and Coca Cola*, which narrated the struggles of urban dwellers in Trinidad as they demanded equal rights and better living and working conditions. This novel was followed by *No Saddles for Kangaroos* (1964), based in Australia; the kangaroos in the title are industrial workers attempting to organize a union. These three novels became popular in the former Soviet Union, where they were translated into Russian. During the 1960s, the novels were reprinted and distributed throughout the United Kingdom. De Boissière's novels depict realistic characters and situations. Critic Frank Birbalsingh, writing in *Passion and Exile* (1988), describes De Boissière as a "passionate" and "genuine" novelist, a man of the people.

Further Reading

Birbalsingh, Frank. *Passion and Exile: Essays in Caribbean Literature*. London: Hansib Publishing, 1988.

—*D. H. Figueredo*

Debrot, Cola (1902–81)

A novelist, dramatist, and poet from Curaçao, Debrot advocated creolization, the mixing of several races and ethnic origins and traditions, for the establishment of literature in the Dutch Caribbean. He was a governor of the Dutch Caribbean region and a tireless promoter of a Caribbean identity and culture.

Nicolaas Cola Debrot was born in Bonaire on May 4, 1902, into an elite white protestant family, though his mother was Catholic and from Venezuela. From the age of fourteen, he lived in Europe, earning a law degree and a medical degree in Utrecht and Amsterdam. He spoke Spanish, Papiamentu, and English.

Among his first texts is the short novel *Mijn zuster de negerin*, written in Dutch and published initially in the literary journal *Form* in 1934. A year later, it was published as a book. In 1958, the novel was translated into English as *My Sister the Negro*, translated by Estelle Debrot-Reed and published in the periodical *Antilliaanse Cahiers*. The novel tells of the incestuous relationship between a white man and a mulatto woman who happens to be the illegitimate daughter of the man's father. Since the novel parted from the traditional literature of the time, of a didactic nature and influenced by Catholicism, *Mijn zuster de negerin* was considered polemical when it first appeared in Curaçao.

This novel placed Debrot in a pioneering position, initiating Dutch literature in the Dutch Caribbean. The development of this literature was further augmented by the creation of the journal *De Stoep*, which appeared in 1940. From 1940 to 1942, Debrot was editor of the literary review *Criterium*, published in Holland, which also influenced the production of a literature written in Dutch in the Caribbean.

During World War II, Debrot practiced medicine in Holland and then in Curaçao. He was a member of the board of Sticusa, a Dutch foundation for cultural cooperation with the Caribbean, established in 1948. That same year, he was assigned to promote the foundation's activities in the Dutch Caribbean; to do so, he settled in Curaçao. He was the first president of Cultureel Centrum Curaçao, founded in 1949, and directed—with Henk Dennert and Jules de Palm—the journal *Antilliaanse Cahier*, from 1955 to 1962, and then in 1976. This journal was an initiative of the Cultureel Centrum Curaçao and was financed by the foundation Sticusa.

Debrot wrote dramas and didactic dialogues: "De automaten," "Camind' I Cruz, un dialog na Corsow" (published in Papiamentu in *La Cruz*, under the pseudonym of Chandi Lagun), and "Bokaal aan de lippen." He also wrote accounts of literary history and development in the Dutch Caribbean, which contributed to and influenced the organized study of literature of the region. Those works included "Literatuur in de Nederlandse Antilles," published in *Antilliaanse Cahiers* (1955), and "Verworvenheden en leemten van de Antilliaanse literatuur" (1977).

Debrot advocated for creolization as a viable concept for the creation of a social and cultural identity endemic to the Dutch Caribbean and its literary production, based on the assimilation of African, European, and Latin American traditions and emphasizing ethnic contributions and successive migrations. He highlighted the similarity of this process with similar cultural development throughout the Caribbean. However, his concept of creolization was criticized in the 1970s by writers who were intent on revitalizing the African presence in the Caribbean and the exclusive use of Papiamentu.

Debrot served in various public-service positions: Plenipotentiary Minister of the Dutch Caribbean in the Hague and governor of the region (1962–70). In 1968, the island's government created the Cola Debrot Award to recognize artistic and scientific accomplishments. In 1970, Debrot relocated to Holland. He spent the last years of his life in Rosa Spierhuis, a retirement home for authors, artists, and scientists. He passed away on December 2, 1981, in Laren. *See also* Créolité.

Further Reading

Broek, Aart G. "Ideological Controversies in Curaçaoan Publishing Strategies." In *History of Literature in the Caribbean. Vol. 2: English- and Dutch-Speaking Regions*. Edited by A. James Arnold, 375–85. Philadelphia: John Benjamins Publishing Co., 2001.

Martinus Arion, Frank. "Het tragische sentiment bij Cola Debrot." In *De eenheid van het kristal*. Edited by Alex Reinders, 157–73. Curaçao: Kolibri, 1988.

Oversteegen, J. J. In *Het schuim van grauwen wolken. Het leven van Cola Debrot tot 1948. Biography I and II*. Amsterdam: Meulenhoff, 1994.

—*Emilio Jorge Rodríguez*

Degetau González, Federico (1862–1914)

Degetau was a Puerto Rican novelist, essayist, short-story writer, and poet. A patriot, he favored autonomy from Spain during the nineteenth century, but in the early years of the twentieth century considered American statehood as beneficial to the island.

Degetau was born in Ponce on December 5, 1862. He studied in Spain, graduating with a law degree from the Universidad Central de Madrid in 1888. The year before he founded in Madrid the journal *La Isla de Puerto Rico*, which promoted his autonomist ideals and criticized the colonial government on the island.

Degetau was a prolific writer. During the 1880s and 1890s, he wrote numerous short stories, which where published in Spain, France, and Puerto Rico. Many of the stories, as those collected later on in the volume *Cuentos literarios y pedagógicos* (1925), were written within the **naturalismo** genre, which depicted scenes of violence and sexual innuendos and evoked a social system where the poor were controlled by the rich. Other stories, as those included in *Cuento para un viaje* (1894), forecast the experimental literature of the twenteith century. The stories in this volume were presented as newspaper clippings and articles that an unknown reader glued together for a future reader.

After the Spanish-Cuban-American War ended in 1898, Degetau González returned to Puerto Rico. From 1901 to 1905 he served as Resident Commissioner of Puerto Rico in Washington, D.C. He passed away in San Juan on January 20, 1914. Some of his novels include *El secreto de la domadora* (1886), *El fondo del aljibe* (1886), and *Juventud* (1895).

Further Reading

Mergal, Angel. *Federico Degetau, un orientador de su pueblo*. NY: New York: Hispanic Institute, 1944.

Vázquez, Margarita, and Daisy Caraballo. "El Cuento en Puerto Rico." In *La gran enciclopedia de Puerto Rico*, edited by Vicente Báez, 36–37. San Juan: Puerto Rico en la Mano and La Gran Enciclopedia de Puerto Rico, 1981.

—*D. H. Figueredo*

De Haarte, Norma (1933–)

Canadian-Guyanese author, Norma De Haarte writes about her experiences in her native country. Her works reflect a preoccupation with the nature of exile and the need for a return to the homeland.

De Haarte was born in Georgetown, Guyana, on July 28, 1933. Interested in teaching, she attended Guyana's Teachers College, graduating in 1966. She relocated to Canada, where she matriculated at Brandon University, Manitoba, earning a second teaching degree in 1977. She returned to Guyana to work for the Ministry of Education. In 1982, she moved to Canada.

In 1991, she wrote her best-known work, the *Guyana Betrayal*, an exploration about her ethnic heritage and the legacy of colonialism. In 1992, she published *Little Abu, The Boy Who Knew Too Much*, a children's story. In 1997, she wrote the scholarly volume *Mr. Jimmy and the Blackpudding Man: A Short History of*

Immigrants. Throughout her writings, there is a nostalgic coloring of events in Guyana as well as the awareness that the arrival of independence did not solve all of the nation's problems and, furthermore, brought political corruption and demagogy. *See also* Exile Literature; Postcolonalism.

Further Reading

"Guyana Betrayal." http://www.landofsixpeople.com (accessed 9/1/05).
"Norma De Haarte." http://www.writersunion.ca/d/dehaarte.htm (accessed 7/16/05).

—D. H. Figueredo

Deive, Carlos Esteban (1935–)

Though born in Spain, dramatist, novelist, and essayist Deive has lived most of his life in the Dominican Republic. His works reflect his love and fascination of his adopted country.

Deive was born on December 26, 1935, in Sarria, Spain, but emigrated to the Dominican Republic in the 1950s. In 1957, he entered and won a drama contest with the play *Los señores impertinentes*. In 1963, he published the major study *Tendencias de la novela contemporánea*, on the development of the novel in Europe and the Americas, and in the Dominican Republic in particular. This was the first scholarly work to rank Dominican Republic's literary history with that of such nations as France, Germany, and the like. For his effort, Deive received the National Prize for Essays. A year later, he published his first novel, *Magdalena*.

Equally intrigued by anthropology and history, during the 1970s and 1990s he wrote over twenty volumes on such subjects as slavery in the Dominican Republic, the Haitian revolution, and African influences in Caribbean cookery. But what earned wider recognition was his 1979 novel, *Las devastaciones*, set in the Dominican Republic during the seventeenth century. The novel earned him the literary prize Premio Siboney de Literatura.

Deive has taught literature at Universidad Nacional **Pedro Henríquez Ureña**. In 2001, he was awarded the National Prize for Literature. In 2004, he was appointed president of the Dominican Republic's International Book Fair.

Further Reading

Escritores dominicanos. http://www.escritoresdominicanos.com/deive.html (accessed 6/1/05).

Veloz Maggiolo, Marcio. *Cultura, teatro y relatos in Santo Domingo.* Santiago de los Caballeros, Republica Dominicana: Universidad Católica Madre y Maestra, 1972.

—D. H. Figueredo

Delgado, Emilio (1904–67)

■

A Puerto Rican journalist and poet, Delgado was associated in his youth with experimental literary movements on the island. He was an editor and a correspondent for several publications from Spain.

A native of Corozal, Puerto Rico, Delgado was a self-taught writer. As a poet, he participated within the experimental movements known as **Diepalismo**, which created poetry based on onomatopoetic combinations, and **Noismo**, which rejected foolish and effeminate literature and artworks with utilitarian purposes. As such his poetry played with the sound of words and used obscure, though humorous, imagery.

Delgado, is best known as a journalist. He wrote for the newspapers *El Imparcial*, *El Mundo*, and was the editorial director of *La Correspondencia de Puerto Rico*. In 1942, the Instituto de Literatura Puertorriqueña awarded him a prize, El Premio del Periodismo, for his labor as a journalist. In 1958, he published the book of poems, *Tiempos del amor breve*.

Further Reading

Delgado, Emilio. *Antología, en recuerdo de su vida y su obra* San Juan, Pureto Rico: Instituto de Cultura Puertorriqueña, 1976.

Enciclopedia puertorriqueña. Siglo XXI. Vol. 2. Santurce: Caribe Grolier, 1998.

—*D. H. Figueredo*

Delgado Pantaleón, Mélida (1885–1967)

■

Delgado Pantaleón is a playwright, poet, and short-story writer from the Dominican Republic. Writing at a time when Dominican society did not expect women to pursue intellectual activities, she wrote in silence, devoting much of her visible energy to her family and the community.

Delgado Panteleón was born in, Salcedo, Dominican Republic, on November 11, 1885. The daughter of a Puerto Rican father, who was a physician and a Dominican mother, Mélida Pantaleón concluded her formal studies to marry at the age of fifteen. Widowed a year later, she then married her cousin Manuel de Jesús Rojas Delgado. The mother of eleven children, her interest in assuring her children a solid education led to community work and the promotion of public education. She founded the Escuela de la Comunidad de Conuco as well as several cultural and social organizations.

Quietly, she pursued her literary vocation, devoting a few hours daily to the writing of poetry and drama. Around the turn of the nineteenth century, she submitted her poems to local papers. Her drama, *La criolla*, a celebration of local customs and traditions, was published in the collection *Diccionario de criollismo* by

Rafael Brito in 1930. In 1967, she trusted a friend, Monsignor Hugo Eduardo Polanco Brito with her unpublished poems, short stories, and plays. In 1989, Polanco Brito, edited the papers into a volume titled *La cítara campestre cibaeña*. *See also* Costumbrismo.

Further Reading

Amoro, Lesbia E. *Perfil de la mujer dominicana: ayer y hoy*. Santo Domingo, República Dominicana: Universidad Autónoma de Santo Domingo, ADOMUVI, 1992.

—*D. H. Figueredo*

Deligne Brothers

Playwrights and poets from the Dominican Republic, Gastón Fernando and Rafael Alfredo explored national themes in their works. Both were tragic figures who suffered poverty as children, limited economic opportunities as adults, and illness. The two brothers suffered from leprosy, and both committed suicide

Deligne, Gastón Fernando (1861–1913). Called the "Father of National Poetry," Gastón Deligne was the first poet in the country to explore psychological themes as well as writing political poetry. He has been described as both a modernist and a postmodernist. He led a tragic life, wherein economic conditions and illness served as barriers to his talent. Nevertheless he managed to become what another major poet, **Manuel del Cabral**, in *10 poetas dominicanos* (1980), considered as the nation's "most cultured and accomplished poet" (9).

Gastón Deligne was born on October 23, 1861, in Santo Domingo, Dominican Republic. Orphaned and raised in poverty, a local philanthropist paid for his education at the Colegio San Luis Gonzaga. Graduating from high school when he was sixteen years old, he found an office job at a general store located in the colonial section of the capital. When he was thirty years old, he attempted to set up a few businesses of his own but was not successful and spent the rest of his life working at a German bank. An avid reader and of a studious nature, he learned several languages, including English, French, German, and Italian. He wrote for several newspapers and translated into Spanish the poetry of Paul Verlaine (1844–96), Victor Hugo (1802–85), and Henry W. Longfellow (1807–82).

His passion, however, was poetry. In his mid-twenties he self-published his first book, *Soledad* (1887). Financial conditions did not allow him to publish his next book until two decades later, *Galaripsos* (1908), his most important work. In this volume were gathered the poems that made him a national figure and revealed the depth of his talent: "Angustia," about a mother's love for her son; "De Luto," a description of an unknown individual who is mourning; "Ololoi," a rally against political oppression. Deligne also wrote lyrics for the opera *María de Cuellor* and the musical comedy *Soleda, pulpera y comendador*.

On January 18, 1913, suffering from leprosy, Deligne committed suicide.

Deligne, Rafael Alfredo (1863–1902). Rafael Alfredo was a playwright, poet, and drama critic. He contributed to numerous newspapers and spent much time in the theater. Leprosy plagued him, robbing him of physical strength and curtailing his talent. Toward the end of his life, he lost use of his hands and had to dictate his poetry to his physician.

He wrote for the newspaper *El Cable* and directed and edited the journal *Prosa y Verso*. In 1894, he wrote the play *La justicia y el azar*. During that decade, he experimented with poetry and short stories and published the book of poems, *A Dios* (1901). A year before his death, he wrote the play *Vidas tristes* (1901). Both of his plays were staged and were popular productions. *See also* Modernismo/Modernism.

Further Reading

Alcántar Almánzar, José. *Dos siglos de literatura dominicana (XIX-XX)*. Santo Domingo, República Dominicana: Colección Sesquicentenario de La Independencia Nacional, 1996.

Cabral, Manuel Del. *10 poetas dominicanos: tres poetas con vida y siete desenterrados*. Santo Domingo: Publicaciones América, 1980.

—*D. H. Figueredo*

De Lisser, Herbert George (1878–1944)

An early-twentieth-century Jamaican novelist known for creating realistic and sympathetic portrayals of black heroines, de Lisser was nonetheless controversial for his racist and imperialist views. He was a journalist and the editor of the influential newspaper *The Daily Gleaner*.

De Lisser was born in Falmouth, Jamaica. Of African, Portuguese, and Jewish descent, his light complexion and European surname allowed him entry into Jamaica's elite white society. As a young man he was influenced by the writings of James Anthony Froude (1818–94), an Englishman who believed Jamaican society had been culturally debased by slavery, which had also made blacks culturally inferior. Furthermore, Froude saw Jamaican culture as derivative and imitative of British culture. De Lisser adapted this perspective in his novels, especially in the depiction of black male characters.

De Lisser's first novel, and the one best remembered, was *Jane's Career* (1914), a story with a plot reminiscent of *Pamela*, by Samuel Richardson (1689–1761). *Jane's Career* narrates the life of an attractive young black woman who leaves her village to move to Kingston, where she finds employment as a servant to a lower-middle-class mulatto woman. After suffering psychological abuses at the hand of her employer, Jane moves in with a friend who secures her a job at a factory but who eventually, jealous of Jane's good looks, turns against her. Alone and fending off sexual advances by her boss at the factory, Jane meets a black foreman who falls in love with her. The novel ends with their marriage and the promise of a comfortable middle-class life for Jane.

Jane's determination to succeed echoes de Lisser's own struggles. Left penniless by the death of his father, de Lisser found employment at the age of fifteen as a library assistant at the Institute of Jamaica. Five years later he became a proofreader for *The Gleaner*. Within a short time, he was one of the newspaper's brightest journalists, and by the age of twenty-six, he was appointed editor, a position he held for four decades. A respected member of Jamaican society, de Lisser served on the board of directors of the Institute of Jamaica, was secretary of the Imperial Society, and befriended such celebrities as George Bernard Shaw (1856–1950). De Lisser was presented with the Musgrave Silver Medal for Literary Work and the British Empire Journalistic and Literary Achievement Award.

Jane's Career proved a popular novel, and in 1942, de Lisser wrote a sequel. Entitled *Myrtle and the Money*, it tells the story of Jane's youngest daughter, but, more importantly, the novel serves as a study of the new black middle class that was emerging on the island. In between these works, de Lisser wrote seven other novels, some of which were political satires and others historical romances. Trained as a journalist, de Lisser wrote an accessible and flowing prose, duplicated realistic dialogues—using Jamaican dialect as needed—and contrived enough suspense to propel the narrative.

Popular during the early decades of the twentieth century, by the late 1930s de Lisser fell out of favor. Scholar Delia Jarret-Macauley, in her book *The Life of Una Marson*, recalls that at a gathering of young Jamaican nationalists the audience booed de Lisser, who was "humiliated and rebuffed." In his imperialist views, de Lisser was similar to conservative thinkers from the nineteenth-century Spanish Caribbean. His racial attitude echoed sentiments expressed by other writers from the 1800s, including the Haitian **Oswald Durand**. But unlike white intellectuals, such as the Cuban **Fernando Ortiz**, who matured from Negrophobia to a true appreciation of Afro-Caribbean culture and traditions, de Lisser was not able to alter his beliefs. Some of his other works include *Triumphant Squalitone* (1917), *Revenge* (1919), *The White Witch of Rosehall* (1929), *Under the Sun* (1937), *Psyche* (1952). *See also* Jamaican Literature, History of.

Further Reading

De Lisser, Herbert George. *Jane's Career; A Story of Jamaica*. New York: Africana Pub. Corp., 1971.

Jarret-Macauley, Delia. *The Life of Una Marson: 1905–65*. Manchester: Manchester University Press, 1998.

Ramchand, Kenneth. *An Introduction to the Study of West Indian Literature*. Jamaica: Thomas Nelson and Sons Ltd., 1976.

—*D. H. Figueredo*

Del Monte, Domingo (1804–51)

■

Literary mentor and promoter of Cuban culture and writers, it was Del Monte who prompted Cuban authors to write antislavery texts, thus helping to launch **Abolitionist literature** on the island. A writer and bibliophile, Domingo del Monte hosted in his home **tertulias**, informal gatherings or symposiums on culture, literature, and politics, which attracted Havana's emerging writers and intellectuals, including economist **José Antonio Saco**, novelist **Cirilo Villaverde**, and the poet-slave **Juan Francisco Manzano**.

Del Monte was born August 4, 1804, in Maracaibo, Venezuela, but moved to Cuba in 1810. He attended the Seminario de San Carlos and Universidad de la Habana, befriending along the way educator and writer **Félix Varela** and legendary poet **José María Heredia**. Becoming a lawyer in 1827, he traveled to Europe and the United States. Back in Cuba in 1829, he was elected president of the Sociedad Económica de Amigos del País, a national organization which promoted culture and education. In 1835, he found in the province of Matanzas the first public library outside of Havana. He also wrote for and founded numerous influential journals, including *Revista bimestre cubana* and *La moda.*

In 1834, Del Monte began to host tertulias, where he coordinated and led discussions on European literature, politics, and slavery. The members of the tertulia also read aloud poems and stories they had written, then the group would comment on the works. The tertulias were so popular that the Spanish authorities suspected the gatherings were an occasion to conspire against the Crown. Thus, in 1843, del Monte had to flee Cuba to avoid arrest. This was not the case with one of the participants in the tertulia: Juan Francisco Manzano, who was imprisoned for a year. While living in Paris, del Monte was accused of participating in the Conspiracy of the Ladder, a supposedly abolitionist plot against the colonial government. He proved his innocence and was able to relocate to Madrid.

In Spain, del Monte lobbied for colonial reforms that would improve relations between Cuba and Spain and suggested the replacement of slavery with the paid labor of white workers. He passed away in Spain in 1851, and his body was sent to Cuba for burial in 1852.

Del Monte wrote hundreds of letters, which were collected in seven volumes—entitled *Centón epistolario de Domingo del Monte*, the volumes were published between 1926 and 1957—and a bibliography of Cuban works, *La isla de Cuba tal cual esta* (1836). His true contribution, however, was the friendships he made with the likes of Manzano and Villaverde, encouraging them to write. He edited Manzano's autobiographical manuscript and passed it on to a British abolitionist who published the book in England under the title of *Poems by a Slave in the Island of Cuba* (1840); del Monte also collected funds to purchase Manzano's freedom. Del Monte suggested to two other Cuban authors, **Anselmo Suárez y Romero** and **Antonio Zambrano**, the theme of slavery, documenting in particular the true story of a slave named Francisco who was not allowed to have relations with the slave woman he loved. Suárez y Romero wrote the story as *Francisco*, the first antislavery novel in Cuba, while Zambrano titled his version *El negro Francisco*. Both stories promoted the stereotype of the passive slave who suffers in silence. *See also Cecilia Valdés o la Loma del Ángel;* Cuban Literature, History of.

Further Reading

Andioc, Sophie. *Centón epistolario / Domingo del Monte; ensayo introductorio.* Habana: Imagen Contemporánea, 2002.

Bueno, Salvador. *Domingo del Monte.* Habana: Unión de Escritores y Artistas de Cuba, 1986.

Martínez Carménate, Urbano. *Domingo del Monte y su tiempo.* Maracaibo, Venezuela: Dirección de Cultura de la Universidad del Zulia, 1996.

—*D. H. Figueredo*

Delorme, Demesvar (1831–1901)

A theoretician and novelist, Delorme was an influential Haitian thinker and politician. Despite an active life in politics, where he survived several governmental changes and the animosity of at least two presidents, he was able to write several books, of which *Les théoricens au pouvoir* (1870) is the best known and most controversial. He traveled widely and befriended such major literary figures as Victor Hugo (1802–85).

Born on February 10, 1831, in Cap-Haïtien, Delorme lost his father at an early age. When his mother remarried, she trusted the young boy's education to his older brother, a public notary. While his brother taught him to write, Delorme developed a love for reading, which he did voraciously. When he was eleven years old, an earthquake destroyed his home, and Delorme and his family went to live near an uncle in La Grande Rivière du Nord. The young boy loved the countryside and spent hours roaming the region.

A brilliant student, in 1844, Delorme attended the newly established secondary school Philippe-Guerrier, where he studied ancient Greek classics and French literature. Upon graduation, he worked as a teacher at the school Adélina; there, one of his students was the would-be poet **Oswald Durand**. In the late 1850s, Delorme visited the United States, and upon his return to Haiti in 1859 he founded the journal *L'Avenir*. Critical of the government of President Fabre Geffrard (1806–79), the journal was shut down by the authorities. In 1862, Delorme was elected deputy, and in the Haitian congress he continued to express his opposition to President Geffrard. Four years later, he supported a rebellion led by a general. When the revolt was crushed, Delorme went into exile in Brussels, where he wrote the volume *L'Indépedance belge* (1866). When President Geffrard was overthrown a year later, Delorme returned to Haiti and served in the Ministry of Foreign Relations.

Political intrigue and governmental change found Delorme once again in Europe, first in England, and then in France. While living for nearly a decade in Paris, he published his most important works: *Les théoricens au pouvoir* (1870), the novel *Francesca* (1873), *Réflexions diverses sur Haïti* (1873), *Les Paisibles* (1874), and *Le Damné* (1877), his second work of fiction. In *Les théoricens au pouvoir*, probably his most controversial, he promoted the notion that governmental power should be only in the hands of the educated elite.

Returning to Haiti, he was again elected deputy in 1878 and wrote for the publication *Ralliement*. When Lysius-Félicité Salomon (1815–88) assumed the presidency, Delorme was sent to prison and was saved from being sentenced to death by the president's niece, the educator Argentine Bellegard Foureau (1842–1901). Delorme became the director of the journal *Moniteur* in 1884. From 1891 to 1901, he traveled throughout Europe either as a representative of the new president, Florvil Hippolyte (1827–96), or as a tourist. He did not return to his country and passed away in Paris on December 26, 1901.

Further Reading

Berrou, Raphaël, and Pradel Pompilus. *Histoire de la littérature haitienne*. Tome 1. Port-au-Prince, Haiti: Editions Caraïbes, 1975.

—*D. H. Figueredo*

Denis, Lorimer (1904–57)

■

One of the founders of **Les Griots** movement in Haiti, Denis was a promoter of Haitian and African culture. He was an essayist and a public servant who befriended would-be dictator **François Duvalier** during the early 1930s.

Denis was born in Cap-Haitien on October 20, 1904, into a poor family. He went to primary school in his hometown before winning a scholarship to the prestigious secondary school the Lycée Pétion in Port-au-Prince. Around 1926, he earned a law degree from the Faculty of Law but chose instead to teach high school. His opposition to the **American occupation of Haiti**, which lasted from 1915 to 1934, coupled with his desire to cultivate a Haitian national identity, led him in 1932 to write articles about African culture and to use the term *Griot* to indicate a storyteller from Africa. From this term came the concept for the creation of a cultural movement and a journal. Along with Denis, the other founders of the **Les Griots** movement were François Duvalier, **Carl Brouard**, and **Clement Magloire St-Aude**.

His friendship with Duvalier resulted in several literary collaborations, though journalists Bernard Diederich and Al Burt in *Papa Doc* (1969) assert that Denis was the actual talent in the collaboration: *Les tendances d'une génération* (1934), *Evolution stadiale du vodou* (1944), and *Le problème des classes à travers l'histoire d'Haiti* (1948). The latter volume was a popularization of the **Négritude** ideals expressed by **Jean Price-Mars** in *Ainsi parla l'oncle* (1928), which years later Duvalier converted into a sort of black fascism to justify his dictatorship.

In 1942, Denis was appointed assistant director of the Bureau of Ethnology—Jean Price-Mars was the director—which attempted to preserve Haitian folklore and traditions, including voudism. In 1947, he was Haiti's representative at the Centennial of the Republic of Liberia.

Denis influenced much of Duvalier's earlier political ideals and introduced him to political figures. Denis, however, passed away on August 17, 1957, a month before his protégé was elected president.

Further Reading

Diederich, Bernard, and Al Burt. *Papa Doc: The Truth About Haiti Today*. New York: McGraw Hill, 1969.

—*D. H. Figueredo*

Denis, Villard. See Davertige.

Depestre, René (1926–)

A poet who in the 1940s, according to Léon-François Hoffmann, in *Essays on Haitian Literature*, laid the foundation for modern Haitian poetry—by his selection of political themes and celebration of Haiti's blackness—Depestre is also a novelist. A political activist, he has spent most of his life away from his country, where conservative governments have not welcomed his Marxist ideals.

Depestre was born in Jacmel, Haiti, on 1926. An orphan, he was raised by his grandmother. The poverty he experienced as a child shaped his concerns for the common people of his country and of the world. He attended high school in Port-au-Prince. In that city, he befriended would-be novelist **Jacques Stephen Alexis** and was influenced by the writings and the ideology of **Jacques Roumain**, one of Haiti's greatest writers. Writing poetry as a teenager, Depestre achieved early fame at the age of nineteen with his book of poems, *Étincelles* (1945). The poems in the collection advocated for revolutionary change, a perspective willingly accepted by college students and Haitian intellectuals. A year later, Depestre came out with a second collection of poems, *Gerbes de sang*. In between the publication of these two books, Depestre edited a militant journal, *La Ruche*, and partook, with Alexis, of the students' revolution that overthrew the dictatorial regime of President Elie Lescot in 1946. The new government then awarded Depestre a scholarship to study in Paris.

While living in France during the 1950s, he became a Communist. He visited Berlin and Moscow as well as traveling throughout Latin America, where he befriended such international authors as **Nicolás Guillén**, from Cuba, and Pablo Neruda (1904–73), from Chile. Influenced by Marxism, most of his writings celebrated this political philosophy. However, in 1956, he published a collection, *Mineral noir*, which also contained love poems.

In 1957, Depestre returned to Haiti, but his opposition to the dictatorship of **François Duvalier** led to his exile in Cuba. Welcomed in Havana by Castro's government in 1959, Depestre worked as a librarian and wrote scripts for a radio program broadcast from Cuba to Haiti. He participated in cultural events and wrote a volume which expressed his anti-American sentiment, *Un arc en ciel pour l'occident Chretien* (1967). Though his *Poete a Cuba* (1976), celebrated the Cuban Revolution, Depestre began to grow uneasy with censorship on the island, especially when a novel he wrote in 1973, *Alleluia pour une femme jardin*, was considered too erotic and not political enough by Cuban Communist intellectuals.

The novel indicated a change in the poet, and from the mid-1970s onward, he has cultivated fiction: *Le mat de cocagne* (1979), critical of Duvalier and celebratory of Vodou and sexual freedom, *Hadriana dans tous mes reves* (1988), an experimental work, and *Eros dans un train chinois* (1990). The trajectory from poetry to prose revealed more universal concerns, wherein Depestre became less of a Marxist and more of a humane writer preoccupied with such universal themes as love and mortality.

In the mid-1970s, Depestre returned to Paris. In 1988, he was awarded the Prix Renaudout for *Hadriana dans tous mes reves*. *See also* Vodou in Literature.

Further Reading

Crosley, Bernadette Carré. *René Depestre et la défense et l'illustration de la créolité/haïtianité dans Bonjour et adieu à la négritude (1980) et Hadriana dans tous mes rêves (1988)*. Port-au-Prince, Haiti: Impr. H. Deschamps, 1993.

Hoffmann, Léon-François. *Essays on Haitian Literature*. Washington, DC: Three Continents Press, 1984.

—*D. H. Figueredo*

Desnoes, Edmundo (1930–)

The author of *Memorias del subdesarrollo* (1965), a celebrated novel about the Cuban Revolution made into an equally celebrated film in the 1960s, Desnoes is a journalist and short story writer. In 1981 he edited, along with Cuban American scholar **William Luis**, the anthology *Los dispositivos en la flor: Cuba, literatura desde la revolución*, the first book to include in one volume selections from writers in Cuba and from Cuban writers in exile.

Edmundo Pérez Desnoes was born in Cuba on October 2, 1930, the son of a Cuban father and Jamaican mother. Graduating from high school in Havana, in 1953 he went to New York City, where he attended New York University and Columbia University, majoring in journalism. After the triumph of the Cuban Revolution, he returned to Havana. He collaborated in the periodical *Revolución* and its literary supplement **Lunes de Revolución** and was one of the founders of the influential literary journal *Casa de las Américas*. Desnoes held various government positions, working for the Ministry of Education, the Editorial Nacional de Cuba, and El Instituto del Libro. In the 1960s he served as a cultural agent for the Cuban government, attending international conferences to identify writers from the Caribbean who could then be invited to Cuba, thus fostering cultural solidarity between Cuba and other Caribbean islands.

In 1961, Desnoes wrote his first novel, *No hay problemas*, which takes places in Cuba in the 1950s, during the dictatorship of Fulgencio Batista (1901–73). In 1965, he wrote *Cataclismo* and *Memorias del subdesarrollo*; the latter becoming an immediate success and quickly translated into half a dozen languages. The English version appeared under the title of *Inconsolable Memories* (1967).

Written in the first person, *Memorias del subdesarrollo* is an autobiographical exercise: the story of Sergio, a well-to-do Cuban who can neither support the revolutionary government nor turn against it. Spending his days wandering around Havana, noticing all that is negative about the Revolution while claiming that he could never go into exile, Sergio is unable to make a political choice. Like the characters in the novels of **Garth St. Omer**, from St. Lucia, Desnoes's protagonist remains undefined, something of a dangling man. The novel, with a script written by Desnoes, was made into a film in 1968. It played to packed art houses in the United States and Europe and was incorporated into the canon of Latin American cinema.

In 1979, Desnoes surprised his friends in Cuba: he defected while attending a conference in Venice. He relocated to the United States, where he taught at Dartmouth College, in New Hampshire. The publication in 1981 of the anthology *Los dispositivos en la flor* proved quite controversial. In Cuba, intellectuals criticized Desnoes for including such antirevolutionary authors as **Guillermo Cabrera Infante**. In the United States, novelist **Reinaldo Arenas**, who had been imprisoned in Cuba, resented being included in a book that contained speeches by **Fidel Castro** and Ernesto Che Guevara (1928–67), whom he did not consider writers. Comfortable with controversies, Desnoes surprised his friends in Cuba and in the United States once again when in 2002 he returned to the island to serve as a juror of a literary competition sponsored by the cultural center **Casa de las Américas**. Like his alter ego in his famous novel, Desnoes defies easy classification as either a pro- or an anti-Castro intellectual. *See also* Anti-Castro Literature; Cuban Literature, History of; Literatura Comprometida/Socially Engaged Literature.

Further Reading

Desnoes, Edmundo and William Luis, eds. *Los Dispositivos en la flor: Cuba, literatura desde la Revolución*. Hanover, N.H: Ediciones del Norte, 1981.

Memories of underdevelopment: Tomás Gutiérrez Alea, director. Inconsolable memories: Edmundo Desnoes, author. Introduction by Michael Chanan. New Brunswick: Rutgers University Press, 1990.

—*D. H. Figueredo*

Desperate Generation.   See Generación del 45.

Desroys, Anne.   See Bourand Family.

"Dessalinienne, La," The National Anthem of Haiti

■

In 1903, Justin Lhérisson, a journalist and lawyer who had been a member of the "Société du Centenaire"—the society of the Centenary—since 1893, submitted this poem, of five stanzas of four-syllable lines, to a national jury for the selection of a national anthem. The members of the jury were novelist **Fernand Hibbert**, poet Arsène Chevry, and journalists Sténio Vincent and Solon Ménos. Lhérisson's "La Dessalinienne," set to music by Nicolas Geffrard, was selected. It was first performed at the "Autel de la Patrie"—Altar of the Fatherland—in Saint-Marc on October 17, 1903, when a bust of Haitian liberator Jean-Jacques Dessalines (1758–1806) was unveiled. Official recognition did not come until the State Council voted the law of August 5, 1919, declaring "La Dessalinienne" the "Chant National Haïtien" (Corvington 112 n.). It is likely that the execution of the Caco hero, Charlemagne Péralte (1886–1919), who had opposed the American invasion of 1915, following his betrayal by Jean Conzé, was in the minds of the Council members when they voted: "Pour le Pyas, / Pou les Ancêtres, / Marchons unis (bis) / Dans nos rangs point de traîtres. . . . (For the nation, / For the Ancestors, / Let us march united / With no traitors in our ranks . . .).

Pour le Pays, pour les Ancêtres
Marchons unis, marchons unis
Dans nos rangs point de traîtres
Du sol soyons seuls maîtres
Marchons unis, marchons unis
Pour le Pays, pour les Ancêtres
Marchons, marchons, marchons unis
Pour le Pays, pour les Ancêtres

Pour les Aïeux, pour la Patrie
Béchons joyeux, béchons joyeux

Quand le champ fructifie
L'âme se fortifie
Béchons joyeux, béchons joyeux
Pour les Aïeux, pour la Patrie
Béchons, béchons, béchons joyeux
Pour les Aïeux, pour la Patrie
Pour le Pays et pour nos Pères

Formons des Fils, formons des Fils
Libres, forts et prospères
Toujours nous serons frères
Formons des Fils, formons des Fils
Pour le Pays et pour nos Pères
Formons, formons, formons des Fils
Pour le Pays et pour nos Pères

Pour les Aïeux, pour la Patrie
O Dieu des Preux, O Dieu des Preux
Sous ta garde infinie
Prends nos droits, notre vie
O Dieu des Preux, O Dieu des Preux
Pour les Aïeux, pour la Patrie
O Dieu, O Dieu, O Dieu des Preux
Pour les Aïeux, pour la Patrie

Pour le Drapeau, pour la Patrie
Mourir est beau, mourir est beau
Notre passé nous crie:
Ayez l'âme aguerrie
Mourir est beau, mourir est beau
Pour le Drapeau, pour la Patrie
Mourir, mourir, mourir est beau
Pour le Drapeau, pour la Patrie

March on! For ancestors and country,
United march, United march;
Loyal subjects all remain,
And lords of our domain
United march, March on!
United march for ancestors and country,
March on, united march, march on!
Unite for ancestors and country!

For sacred soil,
For sires of old
We gladly toil.
When teem field and would
The soul is strong and bold.

We gladly toil, we gladly toil
For sacred soil,
For sires of old.

For land we love
And sires of old
We give our sons.
Free, happy, and bold,
One brotherhood we'll hold.
We give our sons, we give our sons
For land we love
And sires of old.

For those who gave
For country all,
God of the brave,
To thee, O God, we call;
Without thee we must fall,
God of the brave, God of the brave.
For those who gave
For country all.

For flag on high
For Native land
'Tis fine to die.
Our traditions demand
Be ready, heart and hand,
'Tis fine to die, 'tis find to die
For flag on high,
For Native land.

See also American Occupation of Haiti, Literature of the (1915–34).

Further Reading

Corvington, Georges. *Port-au-Prince au cours des ans*. Vol. 4: *Lemétropole haïtienne du XIXe siècle, 1888-1915*. Port-au-Prince: Deschamps, 1994.

Desquiron, Jean . *Haïti à la une. Une anthologie de la presse haïtienne de 1724 à 1934*.Vol. 2, *1870-1908*; Vol. 4, 1915-1921. Port-au-Prince: L'Imprimeur II, 1994; 1996.

Laroche, Maximilien. "La littérature en haïtien." Pp. 119-217 in *L'avènement de la literature haïtienne*. Sainte-Foy: Université Laval (GRELCA), 1987.

Supplice, Daniel. *Dictionnaire biographique des personnalités politiques de la République d'Haïti, 1804-2001*. Tielt, Belgium: Lanoo Imprimerie, 2001.

—*Carrol F. Coates*

Detective Fiction

■

Caribbean writers started to cultivate the genre of detective fiction relatively late in the twentieth century. The genre was created by Edgar Allan Poe (1809–49) in 1841 with the short story "Murders in the Rue Morgue," where he introduced the amateur sleuth C. Auguste Dupin, who employed deduction to solve a crime. Detective fiction was further popularized by Sir Arthur Conan Doyle (1859–1930), with his detective Sherlock Holmes, and by Agatha Christie (1891–1976), who created the character of Hercule Poirot. Holmes and Poirot were cerebral investigators who were representative of the middle and upper classes in Europe. A tougher approach was used by American writers Dashiell Hammett (1894–1961) and Raymond Chandler (1888–1959) during the 1920s and 1930s with the invention of the physically aggressive detectives Sam Spade and Phillip Marlowe, respectively, who used fists and brains as tools of investigation.

It was the rough-and-tough American detectives that served as models for the Caribbean detective story. The writers from the Caribbean rejected the British model because it was based on the assumption that governments and societies ran smoothly and that the criminal was an aberration; once the crime was solved, the world returned to its Victorian order and primness. The American version, on the other hand, depicted a dark world of corrupt politicians and capitalists. The concept of a society that was slightly chaotic appealed to writers who had grown up in countries where the political system did not always work and where strong corrupt rulers proliferated.

The first detective story written in the Caribbean was *The Mind Reader* (1929), by the Jamaican **Walter Adolphe Randolph**. During the 1930s and 1940s, the Cuban **Lino Novas Calvo** wrote crime and detective short stories, presented as articles, that were published in the weekly *Bohemia*. A radio program introduced to Cuban listeners a Chinese detective named Chan Li Po. But it was not until after the triumph of the Cuban Revolution that the genre flourished on the island.

Two types of detective narrative emerged. The first, which evolved in the late 1960s and throughout the 1970s, were secret-agent stories in which the protagonist worked with a group of investigators, consisting of policemen, spies, members of the Committee for the Defense of the Revolution, a neighborhood watchdog organization, to solve a crime or deter one from occurring. The nemesis was usually a CIA agent or a Cuban counterrevolutionary. The Cuban hero was portrayed as all good; the villains were evil, cowards, and effeminate. The most representative novel of this period is *Y si muero mañana* (1978) by Luis Rogelio Nogueras (1945–86). In the 1990s, the second type of Cuban detective novel evolved embodied in the person of sleuth Mario Conde, an alcoholic would-be writer who sees the failings of the Cuban Revolution; this detective was created by writer **Leonardo Padura Fuentes**. By this decade, the villains were not people outside of the revolution but often officials within the revolutionary government. The work most representative of this type of detective fiction is *Máscaras* (1997) by Padura Fuentes.

In Puerto Rico, **Luis López Nieves** wrote *Seva: historias de la primera invasión norteamericana de la isla de Puerto Rico ocurrida en mayo de 1898*, a historical mystery in which a professor investigates a secret American invasion of the island prior to the Spanish-Cuban-American War of 1898. Presented as if it were a true story in the journal *Claridad* in 1983, the novel convinced many readers of the event.

In the United States, during the 1980s and 1990s, writers from the Hispanic Caribbean entered the genre. The Puerto Rican judge **Edwin Torres** wrote *Q & A* (1977), about racism and corruption within the New York City police force. The Cuban Americans **Alex Abella** and **Carolina Aguilera-García** created a series of novels with Cuban-American sleuths. Abella developed Charlie Morell—probably modeled on Sam Spade—and Aguilera-García created Lupe Solano, a feminist detective whose territory is the Miami of the wealthy Cubans. From the Anglophone Caribbean, Trinidadian **Rosa Guy** created a savvy young-adult detective, named Imamu Jones, in the novels *The Dis-Appearance* (1979) and *New Guys Around the Block* (1983), both set in Harlem.

Further Reading

Braham, Persephone. *Crimes Against the State, Crimes Against Persons: Detective Fiction in Cuba and Mexico*. Minneapolis: University of Minnesota Press, 2004.

—*D. H. Figueredo*

Dévieux, Liliane (1942–)

∎

This short-story writer from Haiti, also known as Dévieux-Dehoux, is one of the leaders of Haitian women's literature. She belongs to a generation of Caribbean women writers who in the 1970s left their countries to seek academic and publishing opportunities in Canada, Great Britain, and the United States. In her writings, Dévieux contemplates the possibility that women living away from the Caribbean might not be able to return home after decades of self-exile. This is a view expressed by such other writers as **Cristina Garcia**, from Cuba.

Dévieux was born and raised in Port-au-Prince, Haiti, but as a young woman moved first to France and then Canada, settling in Montreal. As a short-story writer, her works have been published in numerous journals but have not been the subject of many critical studies. Her short story "Piano Bar," which first appeared in the review *Conjonction* in 1988, has been translated into English by Lizabeth Paravisini-Gebert. In 1976, she published *L'Amour, oui: La Mort, non*, a novel concerning the effects of the Vietnam War on a family.

Dévieux's narratives examine such themes as political and economic migrations. As critics Carmen C. Esteves and Lizabeth Paravisini-Gebert observe in *Green Cane and Juicy Flotsam:* "Dévieux . . . explores the ways in which women have found the experience of migration the means to break away from the patriarchal aspects of Caribbean cultures which hampered their full development while remaining true to the nurturing values of their native culture" (xxv). *See also* Exile Literature.

Further Reading

Esteves, Carmen C., and Lizabeth Paravisini-Gebert. *Green Cane and Juicy Flotsam: Short Stories by Caribbean Women*. New Brunswick, NJ: Rutgers University Press, 1991.

Jonassaint, Jean. "Liliane Dévieux." *Le Pouvoir des mots, les maux du pouvoir; des romanciers haïtiens de l'exile*. Montréal: Les Presses de l'Universite de Montréal, 1986.

—*Jayne R. Boisvert*

Dévieux-Dehoux. See Dévieux, Liliane.

Díaz, Jesús (1941–2002)

∎

Jesús Díaz was a Cuban author and filmmaker who documented the revolutionary struggle against the dictatorship of Fulgencio Batista (1901–73) during the 1950s and the implementation of a revolutionary regime after **Fidel Castro**'s victory in 1959. He was a philosophy professor and a journalist as well.

Jesús Díaz was born on July 10, 1941. As a teenager he participated in the insurrection against Batista. After the triumph of the revolution, he studied international politics at the Universidad de la Habana. During this time, he founded the journal *El caimán barbudo*. In 1966, he was awarded the prestigious **Casa de las Américas** literary prize for his collection of short stories *Los años duros*, which told of the struggle against Batista. In 1978, he filmed the documentary *55 Hermanos*, about young Cubans who had left the island in the early 1960s and had returned for a visit. In 1979, he published *De la patria y el exilio*, a companion piece to the film: it consisted of interviews he had conducted with the young Cubans.

After a long absence from publishing due to political pressures, when he was perceived by some militants as being antirevolutionary, Díaz published in 1987 the novel *Los iniciales de la tierra*, which depicted a Cuban intellectual caught between political dogma and social inertia. In 1991, he wrote *Las palabras perdidas*, a novel that questioned the revolutionary process on the island. Shortly after the publication, Díaz went into exile in Spain.

In 1996, Díaz founded in Madrid the journal *Encuentro de la Cultura Cubana*, which published writings by Cubans on the island and in exile. He also wrote several books: *La piel y la máscara* (1996), *Dime algo sobre Cuba* (1998), and *Siberiana* (2000). He directed over dozen documentaries and feature films; his two most famous are *Polvo rojo* (1981), about a young revolutionary managing a nickel plant in Cuba during the 1960s, and *Lejanía* (1985), about the reunion between a mother and son separated by the Cuban revolution. In 2002, Díaz passed away in Spain.

Further Reading

Collmann, Lilliam Oliva. *Jesús Díaz: el ejercicio de los límites de la expresión revolucionaria en Cuba.* New York: Lang, 1999.

—Wilfredo Cancio Isla

Díaz, Junot (1968–)

Though Dominican American Junot Díaz has only published one book, his reputation is well established within literary circles in the United States and has been praised by such popular publications as *Newsweek* and the *New York Times*. The fame rests on his collection of short stories called *Drown* (1996). After **Julia Alvarez**, Junot Diaz is the second Dominican to publish works of fiction originally written in English.

Junot Díaz was born in the Dominican Republic but was raised in Parlin, New Jersey. Living in a neighborhood where most people went either to work or into the armed forces, Díaz didn't think he would go to college. But after working at a factory and as a delivery man and dishwasher, he decided to enroll at Rutgers University. While working, Díaz wrote stories when he was off the job. He continued to write upon entering college and eventually submitted the stories to such journals as *Story* and *The New Yorker*.

In 1995, the stories were collected in the volume *Drown*, which was published to general acclaim. The stories are about drug dealers, dysfunctional families, and immigrants. Though there is a naturalist element to the tales, there is also a sense of hope and beauty. A writer in a November 2000 issue of *Hispanic* described Diaz's style as "a narrative voice and dialogue that straddles two cultures, mixing street-smart New Yorkese with Spanish to lyrically re-create an authentically immigrant language" (p 32).

A writing professor at Syracuse University, Díaz often returns to Rutgers University to mentor minority students. Despite the fame, he remembers and celebrates his heritage: "It's real nice that *The New Yorker* wants to publish me, but *The New Yorker* didn't raise me," he told *Hispanic* magazine. *See also* Dominican-American Literature; Naturalism/Naturalismo.

Further Reading

Kanellos, Nicolás. *Hispanic Literature of the United States.* Westport, CT: Greenwood Press, 2003.

Radelat, Ana. "Junot Díaz." *Hispanic* (November 2000): 32.

—D. H. Figueredo

Díaz Alfaro, Abelardo (1920–99)

Like **Juan Bosch**, from the Dominican Republic, Díaz Alfaro is one of the Caribbean's best short-story writers. Inspired by the struggles of Puerto Rican farmers and the beauty of the countryside, his stories, often depicting animals with human qualities, celebrated Puerto Ricans' abilities to maintain their Hispanic traditions despite American influence on the island. He is much revered by his compatriots.

Díaz Alfaro was born on July 24, 1920—some sources say either 1918 or 1919—in Caguas. In the early 1940s, he earned a BA in art from the Universidad Interamericana and found work as a social worker in the countryside. While working, he also took courses on social work at the Universidad de Puerto Rico.

The years of work with the poor peasants of the island inspired him and served as the basis for the short stories that appeared in the volume *Terrazo* (1947). Critics immediately noticed the literary quality of the work. Readers in general appreciated the linear storyline and clear narrative. One of the best-known stories in the collection is "El Josco," about a bull that after years of service as a stud and protector of the herd is replaced by a younger bull from the United States. Rather than live humiliated, El Josco jumps off a cliff.

The story was a parable for the political and economical conditions in Puerto Rico and the establishment of American businesses on the island. The story also evoked some of the writer's favorite themes: the humility, sincerity, and fatalism of Puerto Ricans. The collection received a literary award from the Instituto de Literatura Puertorriqueña.

In 1956, Díaz Alfaro published a second collection, *Los perros*. The best-known piece in the volume, "Los perros," is about an old horse fighting off wild dogs trying to eat it. Again, in this short story, Díaz Alfaro studied the political situation on the island but without ever saying so. Again, the collection was well received by critics and the public, establishing the author as one of the leading short-story writers in Latin America.

Díaz Abelardo read many of his stories on the radio and produced radio programs, such as *Retablo en el solar*, which examined current events on the island. He also wrote for numerous newspapers and literary journals, including *El Mundo*, *La Nueva Democracia*, and the influential **Asomante**. In 1967, he published his radio scripts, *Mi isla sonada*. His short stories have been translated into several languages, including English, French, and Czechoslovakian. Upon his death in San Juan, on July 22, 1999, the victim of multiple strokes, the *New York Times* described Díaz Abelardo as an author "whose short stories gave voice to Puerto Ricans' quest for identity" (9).

Further Reading

Honan, William H. "Abelardo Díaz Alfaro; 81. Author of Puerto Rican Stories." *New York Times*, July 26, 1999.

Vázquez, Margarita, and Daisy Caraballo. "Cuento: El Cuento en Puerto Rico." In *La gran enciclopedia de Puerto Rico*. Tomo. 4. Edited By Vicente Báez, 111–14. San Juan: Puerto Rico en la Mano and La gran enciclopedia de Puerto Rico, 1980.

—*D. H. Figueredo*

Díaz Quiñones, Arcadio (1940–)

Essayist and cultural and literary critic, Arcadio Díaz Quiñones is regarded as one of the preeminent scholars of the intellectual and literary history of the Hispanic Caribbean.

Born in Mayagüez, Puerto Rico, in 1968 he obtained a PhD from the Universidad Central de Madrid. He taught at the Universidad de Puerto Rico, Río Piedras, from 1970 to 1982 before joining Princeton University in 1983. He directed the Program in Latin American Studies between 1988 and 1994, and currently holds the Emory L. Ford Chair at the Department of Spanish and Portuguese Languages and Cultures.

His publications include *El almuerzo en la hierba* (1982), an edition of *El prejuicio racial en Puerto Rico*, by **Tomás Blanco** (1985), a study on the Cuban poet *Cintio Vitier: La memoria integradora* (1987), a book of essays on Puerto Rican culture entitled *La memoria rota: ensayos de cultura y política* (1993), and most recently, the book of essays *El arte de bregar* (2000). His many articles have often been devoted to major intellectual and literary figures of the Hispanic Caribbean and Latin America such as **José Martí, Salvador Brau, Pedro Henríquez Ureña, René Marqués, Luis Palés Matos, Antonio S. Pedreira, Fernando Ortiz**, and Juan José Saer. He has edited *El Caribe entre imperios* (1997), the Cátedra edition of *La guaracha del Macho Camacho* by **Luis Rafael Sánchez** (2000), and works by Tomás Blanco, Nobel laureate Juan Ramón Jiménez (1881–58), and **Luis Lloréns Torres**. He also wrote an introduction to *Cuentos completos* by **José Luis González** (1997), and has published interviews with José Luis González, the Argentine Ricardo Piglia (1941–), and **Cintio Vitier**.

Díaz Quiñones's writings explore the intersection of politics, literature, and culture in an extended vision of the Caribbean that includes the metropolis and the broader American continent. Some of the unifying themes in his work are the construction of collective memories and, relatedly, the spatial fluctuations of intellectuals and Caribbean populations in general.

Díaz Quiñones has taught as visiting professor at the Universidad de Puerto Rico in Río Piedras and Cayey, the University of Pennsylvania, Rutgers University, the University of Washington–Seattle, the Universidad de Buenos Aires, the Universidad de Cartagena in Colombia, and Swarthmore College.

Further Reading

Duany, Jorge. "Imagining the Puerto Rican nation: Recent works on cultural identity." *Latin American Research Review* 31 no. 3 (1996): 28–268.

—*Fernando Acosta-Rodríguez*

Díaz Valcárcel, Emilio (1929–)

The youngest of the writers who composed the **Generación del 45** in Puerto Rico, Díaz Valcárcel—alongside **José Luis González, René Marqués,** and **Pedro Juan Soto**—led the thematic change in the national literature from rural to urban settings. He also incorporated into Puerto Rican literature the innovative techniques that were being used at the time in Latin America as part of the **Latin American Boom.**

Díaz Valcárcel was born in Trujillo Alto, Puerto Rico, on October 16 1929. He attended secondary and elementary schools in his hometown. In 1951, he was drafted into the U. S. Army, serving two years in Korea during the war. Upon his return, he took courses at the School of Social Sciences of the University of Puerto Rico while working in the Editorial Section of the Division of Community Education of the Department of Education from 1955 to 1969. At the Department of Education, he conducted research on Puerto Rican history and wrote educational texts and scripts for documentaries. During this period, he wrote the drama *Una sola puerta hacia la muerte*, which was produced on Puerto Rican television on the station WIPR-TV.

At the age of nineteen, Díaz Valcárcel published his first short story, "Idilio criollo," in the journal *Puerto Rico Ilustrado*, and continued his literary career in the 1950s writing for such journals as *Alma Latina* and *Asomante*. While in the armed forces, he was a journalist for the magazine *Presente*. In 1956, his story "La última sombra" was awarded the prize from the **Ateneo Puertorriqueño** and again, in 1959, he won for the short story "Sol negro." In the early 1960s, he received a Guggenheim scholarship to study Puerto Rican immigration to New York.

From 1969 to 1975, he resided in Madrid, where he worked as a translator. When he returned to Puerto Rico in 1976, he founded a writing workshop for the Instituto de Cultura Puertorriqueña. In 1971, his novel *Figuraciones en el mes de marzo* was a finalist in the competition Premio Biblioteca Breve sponsored by the publisher Seix-Barral, in Spain. This novel, characterized by humor, a variety of narrative techniques, and linguistic experimentation, is considered by critics as Puerto Rico's entry into the Latin American literary boom of the 1960s.

Díaz Valcárcel essays on several themes. The Korean War is the background for his second collection of short stories, *Proceso en diciembre* (1963), and the volumes *Napalm* (1971) and *Mi mamá me ama* (1986). The theme of immigration is present in the short story 'La muerte obligatoria," from the collection *El asedio y otros cuentos* (1958), where the enfant terrible of a family returns to the island when he is told his mother is gravely ill, forcing himself into her presence at all costs, since he had gone home only to attend her funeral. In this story appears a tendency to project the Puerto Rican returning home as alien to the island's reality and to familial tradition. The same motif recurs in the story "La mente en blanco," where an encounter between an immigrant who has become a hoodlum and an unemployed head of a family end with the hoodlum getting away with a crime and the unemployed father being arrested for a criminal offense he did not commit. The images presented in the stories are stereotypical of the Puerto Rican immigrant as either a criminal or unemployed. Díaz Valcárcel evolved from these images with the novel *Harlem todos los días* (1978), a complex rendering of New York City as modern Babel. In this novel he deepens his understanding of the psychology of the immigrant and his children; the relationships between diverse groups of immigrants; the many aspects of life in the metropolis, from unemployment to political struggles, while depicting coexistence at different levels of survival. The novel also balances social documentation with the imagined, humor with social criticism, and fantasy as a metaphor for reality.

Díaz Valcárcel taught at the University of Puerto Rico until 1994 when he retired with the rank of associate professor.

Further Reading

Casanova-Sánchez, Olga. *La novela puertorriqueña contemporanea*. San Juan: Instituto de Cultura Puertorriqueña, 1986.

Joset, Jacques. "Figuraciones del novelista sofocado." *Revista de Estudios Hispánicos* 25, no. 1–2, 1998.

Moran, Carlos Roberto. "Figuraciones en el mes de marzo de Emilio Diaz Valcarcel." *Sin Nombre* 3, no. 3 (Enero-Marzo 1973): 75–81.

—*Emilio Jorge Rodríguez*

Diego, Eliseo (1920–94)

Considered one of Cuba's greatest contemporary poets, Diego was the winner of the island's first National Prize for Literature, issued in 1986 by the Ministry of Culture, and the 1993 Juan Rulfo International Award for Literature, in Mexico. He was also a translator and English teacher, as well as the director of the children's department of the **José Martí** National Library, in Havana. Writing to Puerto Rican critic **Angel Flores** for inclusion in the volume *Spanish-American Authors: The Twentieth Century* (1992), Diego defined poetry as "the act of paying attention in its utmost purity."

Eliseo Julio de Diego Fernández-Cuervo was born July 2, 1920, in Havana. As a child, he spent time in Europe with his parents but returned to Cuba to attend secondary school. Upon graduating from high school, he enrolled at the Universidad de la Habana to study law but withdrew two years later. In 1942, he became editor of the journal *Clavileño*. In 1944, he founded, with poet **José Lezama Lima** and other friends, the literary journal *Orígenes* in which he published many of his early poems. During the 1940s and 1950s, he worked as an English teacher and as inspector for the Ministry of Education. After the triumph of the Cuban Revolution, he worked at the national library and represented the government at numerous conferences throughout Europe. In the 1989s, he traveled to Niagara to place on the Canadian side of the falls a plaque honoring the memory of the Cuban romantic poet **José María Heredia**, who in the 19th century penned "Oda al Niágara" (1824), one of most famous poems of the period.

Despite his full schedule, Diego translated into Spanish the works of Hans Christian Andersen (1805–75) and the Grimm Brothers—Jacob (1785–1863) and Wilhelm (1786–1859). He also continued writing poems and stories, including *En la Calzada de Jesús del Monte* (1949), his most famous work, *Por los extraños pueblos* (1958), *El oscuro esplendor* (1966), *Noticias de la quimera* (1975), *Los días de tu vida* (1977), and *Libro de quizás y de quién sabe* (1989). In his poetry, he attempted to recreate with words the essence of colors and sounds and the relationship between space and the passing of time.

Eliseo Diego died in Mexico City in 1994.

Further Reading

Fuentes, Ivette. *Nombrar las cosas: sobre la poética de Eliseo Diego*. Habana: Ediciones Extramuros, 1993.

—*D. H. Figueredo*

Diego, José de (1866–1918)

∎

Called the defender of Hispanic culture—El Caballero de la Raza—and the knight of the mother country—El Caballero de la Patria—José de Diego was a Puerto Rican poet, patriot, and public servant. A gifted orator, in his speeches he rallied Puerto Ricans to fight for the preservation of the Spanish language on the island, versus the imposition of English as the official language or language of cultural influence, and to uphold Puerto Rican culture and Hispanic traditions. To the end of his life, he advocated for the island's independence.

Born in Aguadilla, Puerto Rico, on April 16, 1866, José de Diego y Martínez received his primary education in Mayagüez and attended a private high school in Logroño, Spain, where he remained after graduation. It was during his stay in Spain that he began to publish poetry. One poem was considered anti-Catholic, however, and the authorities sentenced him to prison for a few months.

His return to Puerto Rico in 1886 was bittersweet. He fell in love with a young woman, but her parents opposed the relationship. The heartbreak inspired the love poem "A Laura" (1888), which became and still is one of his most popular works. At the age of twenty-two, he began his law studies, first in Spain, and then in Cuba, graduating in 1892. He founded the journal *La República* and was appointed judge in 1897. During this period, he was active in local politics, being one of the founders of the Partido Liberal Fusionista, which advocated political reforms for the island, served as a judge, and was elected to the Chamber of Representatives. He also wrote numerous texts on administration, published in local and government publications.

In 1904, he published the book of poetry, *Pomarrossas*. In the early 1900s, he toured Cuba and the Dominican Republic and was praised in both countries for his oratory skills. A favorite theme was independence for Puerto Rico from the United States, which he passionately invoked. A similar theme was present in his book of poetry, *Cantos de rebeldía* (1916). His advocacy for Hispanic culture in Puerto Rico, which American officials were attempting to Anglicize, earned him the appellation of "El Caballero to de la Raza," meaning the Knight of Hispanic Culture.

José de Diego was president of the **Ateneo Puertorriqueño** and member of several prestigious international associations: the Real Academia Hispano-Americana de Cádiz, Unión Ibero Americana de Madrid, and the Academia Internacional de la Historia de Paris. He died on April 16, 1918, in New York City, where had gone for surgery. In 1949, *Cantos de Pitirre* one of his now most famous book of poems, was published. His poetry was anticlerical and patriotic, advocating for Puerto Rico's independence, which he claimed he would do even after death. *See also* Puerto Rican Literature, History of.

Further Reading

Arrigoitía, Delma S. *José de Diego, el legislador: su visión de Puerto Rico en la historia (1903–1918)*. San Juan, Puerto Rico: Instituto de Cultura Puertorriqueña, 1991

Rodríguez Escudero, Néstor A. *José de Diego: el caballero de la patria*. Quebradillas, Puerto Rico: Imprenta San Rafael, 1992.

—*D. H. Figueredo*

Diego Padró, José I. de (1899–1974)

∎

Puerto Rican novelist who wrote extensively about what it meant to be Puerto Rican, Jose I. de Diego Padró was also a poet who attempted to find new modes of expressing poetry. He was a cofounder of the literary movement known as **diepalismo**.

José I. de Diego Padró began his literary career as a Modernist poet deeply influenced by Nicaraguan poet Rubén Darío (1867–1916) and Uruguayan Julio Herrera Reissig (1875–1910), as evidenced in his first poetry book, *La última lámpara de los dioses* (1921). However, he soon distanced himself from the Greek themes and myths used in **Modernismo** to join other contemporary poets, the likes of **José P. Hernández, Luis Palés Matos, Emilio R. Delgado,** to produce an innovative poetry, influenced by avant-garde writers such as the Italian Filippo Tommaso Marineti (1876–1944). With Luis Palés Matos he created the diepalismo movement. The term—a neologism created by combining their last names—referred to the writing of a poetry mostly based on onomatopoetic combinations that intended to replace logic by phonetics to apprehend reality. Their first joint poem, "Orquestación diepálica," appeared in the newspaper *El Imparcial* on November 7, 1921. By 1924, Diego Padró was contributing as a cofounder with Antonio Coll Vidal, Luis Palés Matos, Bolívar Pagán, José E. Gelpí, and Juan José Llovet, to the monthly publication *Los Seis*. The aims of the publication were, on the one hand, to promulgate less traditional forms of writings and to seek more iconoclastic positions toward the establishment and its institutions, and, on the other hand, to contribute to the affirmation of the Puerto Rican identity. In 1952, Diego Padró published a text that is representative of his maturity as a poet—*Ocho epístolas mostrencas*. With irony and pessimism, he philosophically deals with subjects such as freedom, death and time. Another book of poetry followed, *Escaparate iluminado: autobiografía poética* (1959).

Diego Padró also published criticism and particularly a series of important novels characterized not only by their length but by enormous emphasis on erudition and by the centrality of life in all its complexities. *En Babia, manuscrito de un braquicéfalo* (1940), *El tiempo jugó conmigo* (1960), and *El minotauro se devora a sí mismo* (1965) all attempt to capture, with innuendoes and details, the universe of a single, sensible, and imaginative, but at times almost schizophrenic, character-narrator, Jerónimo Ruiz, who possesses a scientific and encyclopedic education. While *En Babia* centers mostly in Ruiz's relationship with an extravagant and eccentric rich Cuban, named Sebastian Guenard, in New York, *El tiempo jugó conmigo* describes Ruiz's return to Puerto Rico, focusing on his difficulties in adapting to Puerto Rican society. This text is rich in sociohistorical comparisons between the Puerto Rico under the golden era of coffee versus the sugar plantations, and between the native landowners and North American investors, intertwined with the love affair between Ruiz and his cousin Arabela.

In this novel, Jerónimo Ruiz is a character who embodies the ideological stand represented by **Zeno Gandía**'s character Juan del Salto in the seminal novel *La charca* (1892) and Antonio S. Pedriera's characterization of the Puerto Rican based on the country's geographical isolation. Jerónimo is the very thoughtful, conscious man able neither to adapt to his milieu nor become an active agent of change. His deterministic vision of the Puerto Rican falls within the textual tradition of Zeno Gandía and Antonio S. Pedreira when he states that "we are positively a country of slaves, of malnourished, of weak and disoriented people. We are devoured by a chronic inferiority complex, of smallness that obeys . . . to the smallness of the soul of our people" (30). Ironically, Jerónimo shares some of the traits he harshly criticizes in others.

In *El minotauro se devora a sí mismo*, Jerónimo is an old, retired, and boring man who evokes and remembers things that are not told in the two previous novels. It is a slow novel in which the character details his daily mundane life while philosophically arguing about the existential and cultural significance of living. Diego Padró's novel *Un cencerro de dos badajos* (1969) centers around the Nationalist Movement and its political activities in the island, whereas his last novel, *El hombrecito que veía en grande* (1973), is a brutal but funny parody of a Caribbean dictator. *See also* Puerto Rican Literature, History of.

Further Reading

Diego Padró, J. I. *Luis Palés Matos y su trasmundo poético; estudio biográfico-crítico*. Río Piedras: Ediciones Puerto, 1973.

Diego Padró, J. I. *Relatos*. San Juan, Puerto Rico: Instituto de Cultura Puertorriqueña, 1997.

Soto, Pedro Juan, Alicia de Diego, and Carmen Lugo Filippi. *En busca de J. I. Diego Padró*. Río Piedras: Ediciones de la Universidad de Puerto Rico, 1990.

—Asela R. Laguna

Diepalismo

This was a short-lived literary movement created by Puerto Rican poets **José I. de Diego Padró** and **Luis Palés Matos** in 1921. The term—a neologism created by combining their last names, Diego and Palés—referred to the writing of a poetry mostly based on onomatopoetic combinations, or the imitation of sounds, that intended to replace logic by phonetics to apprehend reality. The first and only poem written in collaboration was "Orquestación diepálica" which was published in the newspaper *El Imparcial* on November 7, 1921:

> Guau! Au-auhummmmm . . .
> La noche. La luna. El campo . . . hummmmm
> Zi,zi, -zi, -zi, co-quí, co-quí, co-quí . . .
> Hierve la abstrusa zoología en la sombra
> Silencio!Hummmmm.

(Guau! Au-au . . . hummmmm . . . / The night. The field . . . hummmmm / Zi,zi, -zi, -zi, co-qui, co-qui, co-qui . . . / The abstruse zoology boils in the shadow / Silence! Hummmnn . . . .) This movement had no literary influences.

Further Reading

Soto, Pedro Juan, Alicia de Diego, and Carmen Lugo Filippi. *En busca de J. I. Diego Padró*. Río Piedras: Ediciones de la Universidad de Puerto Rico, 1990.

—Asela R. Laguna

Domacassé, Pacheco (1941–)

A dramatist, theater director, and musician from Bonaire, Domacassé has used the theater as a vehicle of protest against colonialism. He is a promoter of the preservation of Caribbean culture and traditions.

Born on April 1, 1941, in Bonaire, Venancio Benjamin Domacassé attended high school and college in Curaçao. He was a member of the Troubadors and the Teenage Shadows, pop musical trios. This experience sparked in him an interest in theater, and in 1966, he made his debut as an actor. Two years later, he toured the Caribbean, the United States, and Europe with a traveling company.

In 1970, after riots that occurred in Curaçao to protest the Dutch colonial administration, Domacassé premiered his first drama, *Opus I*. The work reflected the social events of the period and its staging at the Pro-Art Center in Willemstad was a catalyst for political confrontations between the Dutch and the people of Curaçao over a vision of a Caribbean identity. In 1971, he wrote the historical drama *Tula*, inspired by the leader of the 1795 slave rebellion that took place in Curaçao. The production was staged by the theatrical group Nos Causa. The same group adapted Domacassé's next drama, *Tochi*. Both plays, *Tula* and *Tochi*, were immensely popular with theatergoers on the island. During the same period, Domacassé was active in a writer's workshop, "Tayer Antiyano pa Arte Dramatiko," conducted by Dutch writer Tone Brulin (1926–). Simultaneously, Domacassé organized theatrical groups, called Pro-Identidad Propia, which performed throughout Curaçao.

In 1973, he was invited by the organization Sentro Kultural di Boneiru to write the play *Konsenshi di un pueblo*, about governmental corruption and a riot similar to the disturbances that had occurred in May 1969. In 1974, Domacassé directed the children's play *Buchi van pia fini*, written by **Diana Lebacs** (1947–). In 1980, his musical *E pida baranka 'ki ta di mi e ta*, interpreted the **Anancy stories** present in Curaçao's folklore. Five years later, he wrote the film script *Boka Sanantonio*, which explored superstitions endemic to the Caribbean and their effects on the people.

Domacassé's work as a playwright, director, and cultural promoter was based on a generational commitment of creators who brought about social consciousness through the exposition of political ideals and confrontations with the Dutch administration of the time. In 1977, he refused an award from the Dutch Foundation for Cultural Cooperation on the basis that the foundation represented colonialism. Years later, with more political autonomy, Domacassé accepted the post of head of the Kultura Insular de Curaçao where he supported the maintenance of folklore and popular culture.

Further Reading

Broek, Aart G. *Pa saka kara, tomo I: Historia di literature papiamentu*. Willemstad: Fundashon Pierre Lauffer, 1998.

Casimiri, Nel. "Pacheco Domacassé: Het trekken van het schip is mij te zwaar geworden." *Amigoe-Ñapa* (Aug.15, 1992).

Rutgers, Win. "Di nos e ta! Outside and Inside Aruba Literature." In *A History of Literature in the Caribbean. Vol. 2: English and Dutch Speaking Regions*. Edited by James Arnold, 451–61. Amsterdam: John Benjamins Publishing Co., 2001.

—Emilio Jorge Rodríguez

Domínguez, José de Jesús (1843–98)

A romantic poet from Puerto Rico, Domínguez was an essayist and journalist.

A native of Anasco, Puerto Rico, Domínguez traveled to France to study medicine at the Sorbonne. In Paris, he was influenced by the works of such French writers as Victor Hugo (1802–85) and Theophile Gautier (1811–72) as well as the American Edgar Allan Poe (1809–49), who was in vogue in France at the time. While in Paris, Domínguez started to write a poetry that was of a romantic vein in message and with a traditional rhyming structure. Two of the poems from this period are "Seducciones" and "La Suicida," both written in 1870 and reflective of the elusiveness of life. That year, Dominguez joined the French army to fight against the Prussians during the Franco-Prussian War.

After the war, Domínguez returned to Puerto Rico, settling in Mayagüez. Though he established a medical office, he continued to write, submitting his poems to several reviews, including *La Revista Blanca* and *La Revista Puertorriqueña*. Interested in medical research, in 1876 he published *Estudios científicos*. Preoccupied with the island's struggle for autonomy, he wrote in 1886 *La autonomia administrativa en las Antillas*. That same year, he wrote his most famous volume, the long poem *Las huríes blancas*. The poem is exploration of death and the need for the poet to create, to prolong life through the arts:

> La fuerza misteriosa y escondida
> que, en fecunda corriente, allí circula
> provoca la creación, vierte la vida . . .

(The powerful and hidden mystery / that propogates in currents/provokes creation, gives life . . . .) Domínguez was also the mayor of Mayagüez.

Further Reading

González, José Emilio. "La poesía en Puerto Rico." In *La gran enciclopedia de Puerto Rico*. Tomo 3. Edited by Vicente Báez, 55–57. San Juan: Puerto Rico en la Mano and La Gran Enciclopedia de Puerto Rico, 1981.

—*D. H. Figueredo*

Dominican American Literature

Dominican literature written in the United States is not a recent phenomenon, contrary to what is commonly believed by many. It was not born with the arrival of the so-called diaspora during the decades of the sixties and seventies. There is an early Dominican presence in literary circles and in publications that includes works by the Modernist poet **Fabio Fiallo** and the earliest creations by a young **Pedro Henríquez Ureña,** who was living in Washington, D.C., and, under the pseudonym of E. P. Garduño, submitted a number of chronicles on life in the

United States during the first decades of the twentieth century to the Cuban news-paper *El Heraldo*. From this period, we also find the poetic portraits of life in New York written by the young **Jesusa Alfau de Solalinde** in *Las Novedades*, a weekly edited by Caribbean intellectuals in the second and third decades of the last cen-tury. Her literary portraits contributed to the enrichment of a Latino literary tradi-tion in New York that includes among its highest representatives the writings by **José Martí, Pachín Marín,** and **Bernardo Vega**. Also significant are the *Seis novelas cortas* by **Virginia de Peña de Bordas**, written in English while she studied art in Boston, and intended to be submitted for publication to North American women's journals. The translation was published posthumously in Santo Domingo in 1951.

By the middle of the twentieth century, Dominican writers, among them **Camila Henríquez Ureña** and her better-known sibling, Pedro Henríquez Ureña, were contributing to the incipient creation of programs of Latin American studies in North American universities. Pedro Henríquez Ureña's *Las corrientes literarias en América Hispánica* have been, for many decades now, part of any serious course on the development of Latin American literary history. Camila Henríquez Ureña's three seminal essays on the condition of women in society, *Feminismo, La mujer y la cultura,* and *La carta como forma de expresión literaria femenina,* have yet to be equaled and serve as the base for the study of gender and the role of women in Latin American society. During this period, there is also the emergence of a body of anti-Trujillo literature written by Dominicans in the United States. Among the most notable in this category are the volumes *Yo también acuso* by Carmita Landestoy and *Cementerio sin cruces* by Andrés Francisco Requenqa, a publication that cost the latter his life, in New York, at the hands of the regime's henchmen.

The literature of young poets and short-fiction writers during the so-called great diasporic wave of the seventies and eighties has been collected by Franklyn Gutiérrez (1950–) in a series of anthologies, among them *Espiga del siglo* (1984) and *Voces del exilio* (1986). Later on, **Daisy Cocco de Filippis** edited *Poemas del exilio y de otras inquietudes,* with Emma Jane Robinett, (1988), *Historias de Washington Heights y de otros rincones del mundo,* with F. Gutiérrez, (1994), *Tert-uliando/Hanging Out, Dominicanas and Friends* (1997). These writings, at first of rather nostalgic tone and themes, and then as translators of "otherness," gather ele-ments that mark a defining moment in Dominican literature: authors who are for the most part working class, and a good number of them female. In a very signifi-cant way, the Dominican diaspora offers the democratization of Dominican literary circles. Never before had such a consistent and numerous occurrence of publica-tions representative of groups been given entry in Dominican letters, such as the ex-emplary works of Diógenes Abreu, Josefina Báez, José Carvajal, José Cornielle, José de la Rosa, Franklyn Gutiérrez, Francisco Gutiérrez, Marianela Medrano, Héctor Rivera, Tomás Rivera Martínez, Yrene Santos, and **Miriam Ventura**. More recently, Dinorah Coronado and Virginia Moore, among others.

With the publication of *How the García Girls Lost Their Accents* in 1990, **Julia Alvarez** enters the imagination and the literature read by English mainstream America. The work of Julia Alvarez is to be singled out because of its recovery of Dominican historical feminine figures and for her sensitive and often painful inhab-iting of two cultures.

At the beginning of the new millennium, the contribution of emerging writers who publish in English is being read. These recent literary works portray in many instances generational conflicts, poverty in urban areas, and the changes brought about in family structures as a result of the education and emancipation of children and, in particular, women. Male adolescence, its challenges, clashes, and human value find a voice in the stories of **Junot Díaz**, published in *The New Yorker* in the nineties and in the collection titled *Drown* (1996). Transnationalism finds its most jarring and painful expressions in the novels of emerging Dominican American women authors, particularly in such works as *Geographies of Home* (1999) by Loyda Maritza Pérez, *Soledad* (2000) by Angie Cruz and *The Song of the Water Saints* (2001) by Nelly Rosario. *See also* Dominican Republic Literature, History of; Trujillo Era.

Further Reading

Augenbraum, Harold, and Margarite Fernández Olmos. *The Latino Reader*. New York: Houghton Mifflin, 1997.

Cocco de Filippis, Daisy. *Combatidas, combativas y combatientes, antología de cuentos escritos por dominicanas*. Santo Domingo: Taller, 1992.

———. *Documents of Dissidence, Selected Writings by Dominican Women*. New York: CUNY Dominican Studies Institute, 2000.

———. *Sin otro profeta que su canto, antología de poesía escrita por Dominicanas*. Santo Domingo: Taller, 1988.

———. *The Women of Hispaniola, Moving Towards Tomorrow*. New York: York College, Executive Report No. 1, 1993.

Evora, José Antonio. "Tres autores en siete días." *El nuevo herald*, May 21, 2004.

Fernández, Roberta. *In Other Words, Literature by Latinas in the U.S.* Houston, Texas: Arte Público Press, 1994.

Gutiérrez, Franklin, ed. *Antología histórica de la poesía dominicana*. New York: Alcance, 1997, and Puerto Rico: Editorial de la Universidad de Puerto Rico, 1999.

Gutiérrez, Franklin, ed. *Niveles del imán*. New York: Alcance, 1983.

Hernández, Ramona, et al. *Dominican New Yorkers: A Socioeconomic Profile*. New York: CUNY Dominican Studies Institute, Dominican Research Monograph Series, 1995.

Rodríguez de León, Francisco. *El furioso merengue del norte, una historia de la comunidad dominicana en los Estados Unidos*. New York: n.p., 1998.

Sención, Viriato. *Los que falsificaron la firma de Dios*. Santo Domingo: Taller, 1991.

—Daisy Cocco de Filippis

Dominican Republic Literature, History of

Though the Dominican Republic is known for its poetry, the genre that has dominated the nation's literature, drama and prose have flourished as well. In the late 1580s, **Cristobal de Llerena** was the first dramatist in the Caribbean. A cleric, Llerena wrote for the Catholic Church plays that were initially staged within the religious edifice but were later performed outside on a public square. In the same century, Leonor de Ovando, a nun, wrote poetry, making her one of the first poets in the region.

True literary production, however, began in the nineteenth century with the works of two women writers: **La Deana** and **Josefina Antonia Perdomo**. La Deana was a pioneer feminist who wrote a seminal essay entitled "Story of a Woman" (1849) on the condition of women in nineteenth-century Dominican society. The essay, daring for its time, sketches a life free of expectations for women from Latin America, in general, and from the Dominican Republic in particular. Perdomo was one of the first woman poets to be published in the nation.

The major poet to emerge during this period was **Salome Ureña de Henríquez** who wrote nationalist verses advocating for a Dominican identity and criticizing the repressive governments that took power after the Dominicans had driven Haitian forces out of the national territory in 1844 (the Haitians had occupied the Dominican Republic for two decades). The daughter of **Nicolás Ureña**, who was a costumbrista, a writer of local customs, **Ureña de Henríquez** was also the founder of the first school for women in the Dominican Republic in 1881. **Ureña de Henríquez** was part of a group of writers called Los Dioses Mayores—the Major Gods. Two other members of the group included **Gastón Deligne**, the first poet in the country to explore psychological themes as well as writing political poetry, and **José Joaquin Pérez**, who celebrated the Amerindian roots of the Dominican Republic.

Glorification of the Amerindians was one of the objectives of the novel *Enriquillo* (1882) a work widely known throughout Latin America and written by **Manuel de Jesús Galván**. Together Pérez and Galván defined the Dominican identity as originating from Spain and the Caribbean, ignoring African heritage; their stance also meant a rejection of Haitian influences. Other novelists in the early twentieth century followed their leads, including Federico García Godoy and Tulio Manuel Cestero.

The twentieth century saw the development of several important and unique literary movements in the Dominican Republic and the rise to power of dictator Rafael Leónidas Trujillo (1891–61); in fact, some of the movements that emerged in the later twentieth century were direct responses to Trujillo's dictatorship. The first movement was **Vedrismo**. Founded in 1917, the movement promoted a poetry that was experimental and free from traditional forms and rhymes, while rejecting nationalistic poetry. The movement's founder was the poet **Otilio Vigil Díaz**. **Postumismo**, meaning beyond **Modernismo**, was founded by **Domingo Moreno Jimenes** in 1921 and joined by Rafael Augusto Zorrilla and Andres Molino. These poets favored nationalistic themes over European subjects and in so doing affirmed a Dominican consciousness.

In 1940, the poets **Tomás Hérnández Franco, Héctor Inchaustegui Cabral, Manuel del Cabral**, and **Pedro Mir** formed the group known as the **Poetas Independientes del 1940**. This group of writers was loosely connected, rejected a literary agenda, and preferred free verse as a poetic expression. All of these poets became major cultural figures. Hernández Franco wrote the epic poem *Yelidá* (1942), which, unlike the works of Pérez and Galván, acknowledged the African presence in the Dominican Republic: Yelidá, is the beautiful daughter of a European and a black woman. However, by making Yelidá a mulata, Hernández Franco was asserting that the beauty of the Dominican woman emerged from being not black but light-skinned. Pedro Mir was the only member of the group to achieve international fame. His book of poems *Hay un país en el mundo* (1949), which contrasted the economic and political imbalance between the rich and the poor, is a seminal text in the Caribbean and a classic example of **literatura comprometida**, politically and socially engaged literature.

In 1943, the movement **La Poesía Sorpredida** was established. Its members were **Aída Cartagena Portalatín, Franklin Mieses Burgos, Freddy Gatón Arce**, and **Manuel Rueda**. These poets tempered their criticism of Trujillo by writing in an elusive style. When addressing social issues in their country, they pursued a universal approached that masked their true comments. Of these poets, there were two who earned recognition in other genres later on. Manuel Rueda was a successful playwright who in 1957 received the National Prize for Literature for the play *La trinitaria blanca*, and Cartagena Portalatín wrote an experimental novel, *Escalera para Electre* (1969), which received honorable mention in a prestigious international competition held in Spain.

Cartagena Portalatín had received early attention in her career in the 1930s when **Juan Bosch** had read one of her short stories and had written her a letter praising her talent. It was not an empty praise, since Bosch was already by that time an important personage in the Dominican Republic. A politician, who was for a few months president of the nation in the 1960s, Bosch is the best-known short-story writer from the Dominican Republic. He wrote masterful short stories—*Cuentos escritos en el exilio* (1976)—and was an insightful student of the political process: *Crisis de la democracia de América en la República Dominicana* (1966), *El próximo paso: Dictadura con respaldo popular* (1967), and *El pentagonismo, substituto del imperialismo* (1968).

Bosch influenced many of the young writers who in 1965 made up the generation known as **Joven Poesía Dominicana** or Poesía de Postguerra. These writers came of age after the death of Trujillo in 1961 and the civil war of 1965, which was the result of the overthrowing of Bosch from office. They wrote stories and poems celebrating and reaffirming nationalism and proclaiming a commitment to social change. Some of the writers in this group include the essayist and poet Norberto James Rawlings and **Enriquillo Sánchez**, a poet and short-story writer whose writings explored, often with humor, issues of national and cultural identities.

By the 1970s, a major change was taking place: mass migration to the United States, where a generation of young writers would mature away from their homeland. The literature of these young poets and short-fiction writers formed the "great diasporic wave" of the seventies and eighties. Much of their works have been collected by Franklyn Gutiérrez (1950–) in a series of anthologies, among them *Espiga del siglo* (1984) and *Voces del exilio* (1986). Later on, **Daisy Cocco de Filippis** edited *Poemas del exilio y de otras inquietudes*, with Emma Jane Robinett, (1988), *Historias de Washington Heights y de otros rincones del mundo*, with F. Gutiérrez, (1994), *Tertuliando/Hanging Out, Dominicanas and Friends* (1997). These writings, at first of rather nostalgic tone and themes, and then as translators of "otherness," gathered elements that marked a defining moment in Dominican literature: authors who were for the most part working class, and a good number of them female. In a very significant way, the Dominican diaspora offered the democratization of Dominican literary circles.

With the publication of *How the García Girls Lost Their Accents* in 1990, **Julia Alvarez** entered the imagination and the literature read by English mainstream America. The work of Julia Alvarez is to be singled out because of its recovery of Dominican historical feminine figures—in novels such as *In The Name of Salomé* (2000), about Salome Ureña de Henríquez and her daughter **Camila Henríquez Ureña,** a literary critic—and for her sensitive and often painful inhabiting of two cultures.

At the beginning of the new millennium, the contribution of emerging writers who publish in English is being read. These recent literary works portray in many instances generational conflicts, poverty in urban areas, and the changes brought about in family structures as a result of the education and emancipation of children and, in particular, women. Male adolescence, its challenges, clashes, and human value, find a voice in the stories of **Junot Díaz,** published in *The New Yorker* in the nineties and in the collection titled *Drown* (1996). Transnationalism finds its most jarring and painful expressions in the novels of emerging Dominican American women authors, particularly in such works as *Geographies of Home* (1999) by Loyda Maritza Pérez, *Soledad* (2000) by Angie Cruz, and *The Song of the Water Saints* (2001) by Nelly Rosario. *See also* Dominican American Literature; Trujillo Era.

Further Reading

Balaguer, Joaquín. *Historia de la literatura dominicana.* Ciudad Trujillo, Dominican Republic: Librería Dominica, 1956.

Chow, Rey. *Writing Diaspora, Tactics of Intervention in Contemporary Cultural Studies.* Bloomington: Indiana University Press, 1993.

Cocco de Filippis, Daisy. *Documents of Dissidence, Selected Writings by Dominican Women.* New York: CUNY Dominican Studies Institute, 2000.

Fernández, Roberta. *In Other Words, Literature by Latinas in the U.S.* Houston, Texas: Arte Público Press, 1994.

Sommer, Doris and Esteban Torres. "Dominican Republic." In *Handbook of Latin American Literature*, edited by David William Foster, 271–86. New York: Garland Publishing, 1992.

—*Daisy Cocco de Filippis and D. H. Figueredo*

Dominique, Jan J. (1953–)

Dominique is a Haitian journalist and novelist. Her childhood experiences in Haiti and her adult years in Canada informed her writings.

Born into a middle-class family in Port-au-Prince on January 25, 1953, Dominique attended schools in Haiti and then emigrated to Montreal, Canada, to pursue a college education. After a long period abroad, Dominique returned to her homeland, where she worked as a radio journalist for Radio Haïti Inter. Her radio program Entre nous—with the writer **Yanick Lahens,**—focused on the difficulties encountered by Haitians living in exile.

In 1984, Dominique's published first novel, *Mémoire d'une amnésique*, won the Prix Henri Deschamps. This autobiographical work explores racial and social relations in Haiti as seen through the eyes of a middle-class mulatto adolescent. In 2000, Dominique published her second novel, *Inventer . . . La Célestine*. It was a genealogical history of a family as well as a history of Haiti. Containing elements of **magical realism**—realismo mágico—both works question the nature of reality and combine history, memory, and spirituality to evoke an image of Haiti rather a realistic portrayal.

Dominique is also the author of *Évasion* (1996), a collection of articles, essays, and short stories exploring the difficulties exiled Haitians encounter when they return to their native country.

Further Reading

"Jan J. Dominique." *http://www.lehman.cuny.edu/ile.en.ile/paroles/dominique.html* (accessed 6/1/05).

Serrano, Lucienne J. "Les Maux por écrire." *Elles écrivent des Antilles: Haïti, Guadeloupe, Martinique.* Edited, by Susanne Rinne and Joëlle Vitiello, 79–84. Paris: L'Harmattan, 1997.

—*Jayne R. Boisvert and D. H. Figueredo*

Don Rafa. See Ramírez de Arellano, Rafael W.

Dorcely, Roland (1931–)

■

Haitian poet and artist, Dorcely celebrated the poor people of Haiti in his writings and paintings. His poetry is praised for its simplicity and lack of pretense.

A native of Port-au-Prince, Dorcely's father was a butcher. Dorcely attended high school in his hometown and at the age of nineteen received a scholarship from the Institut Francais d'Haiti to study art in Paris. Upon his return to Haiti, he wrote poems that appeared in local publications.

A modest man, his poetry, which often depicts everyday sights and the experiences of the average citizen, is available only through journals and anthologies. Some of his most famous poems are "La Genèvese" (1949), a commentary on poverty, "La Brume est un clown gris" (1949), and "Instants' (1949). Observes critic Naomi M. Garret, in *The Renaissance of Haitian Poetry* (1963), "Dorcely shows no class consciousness and very little concern over the problems growing out of economic or social conditions. Yet, Dorcely is not indifferent to the suffering about him . . . [and is] interested in the seconds of happiness that life allows . . . those fleeting moments of joy" (198).

Today, Dorcely is better known as an artist. His paintings hang at the Museum of Modern Art in Paris and the Museum of Modern Art in New York City.

Further Reading

Garret, Naomi M. *The Renaissance of Haitian Poetry*. Paris: Presence Africaine, 1963.

—D. H. Figueredo

Dorsainvil, Justin Chrysostome (1880–1942)

Like **Jean Price-Mars,** Dorsainvil was a respected Haitian essayist and educator. He was also a physician.

J. C. Dorsainvil was born in Port-au-Prince on December 20, 1880. After attending elementary school in his hometown, he graduated from the Lycée Pétion, a prestigious high school in Port-au-Prince. He studied medicine at the Faculty of Medicine, from where he graduated in 1905. His concern over hygienic conditions in his country led to the study *Militarisme et hygiène social* (1905). Realizing the need for a better education for all Haitians, he wrote *Le problème de l'enseignment primaire en Haiti* (1922).

His commitment to public education, as well as his writings, brought him national recognition. He taught at the Lycée Pétion and also served as Head of the Education Division at the Department of Public Education during the 1920s. He continued writing, though, publishing a major work on vodouism, *Una explication philologique de vodou* (1924), and a psychological study of this religion's influence on Haitians, *Vodou et néurose* (1931).

A renaissance man, Dorsainvil, lectured on the history of his nation and wrote several texts, including *Manuel d'histoire d'Haiti* (1924). Dorsainvil advocated for a political process in Haiti that was more ethically responsible and less driven by individualistic desires. He was widely admired for his years of public service and his intellect. He passed away on September 8, 1942. *See also* Vodou in Literature.

Further Reading

Herdeck, Donald E. *Caribbean Writers. A Bio-Bibliographical-Critical Encyclopedia.* Washington, DC: Three Continents Press, 1979.

—D. H. Figueredo

Dorsinville Family

Roger and Max Dorsinville are uncle and nephew novelists and literary critics from Haiti. Together they wrote nearly fifty books on Haitian themes and the Haitian Diaspora.

Dorsinville, Max (1938–). Max Dorsinville is a literary critic, scholar, and novelist who writes in English and French.

Born in Port-au-Prince, Max Dorsinville studied abroad as he accompanied his family to various posts in Haiti's diplomatic service. In his twenties, he studied literature at McGill University. Afterward he relocated to New York City, earning a PhD in comparative literature from City University of New York.

In 1974, he published the literary study *Caliban Without Prospero: Essay on Quebec and Black Literature.* This analysis of postcolonialism and the Haitian diaspora proved one of his most popular works. In 1976, he published *Exile and Tradition: Studies in African and Caribbean Literature.* As he established his reputation as a literary critic, in the 1990s he turned to fiction, writing two novels *James Wait et les lunettes noires* (1995) and *Erzulis Loves Shango* (1998).

With the arrival of the twenty-first century, he began to translate stories and criticism written by his uncle Roger, including: *Post colonial stories by Roger Dorsinville: In the shadow of Conrad's Marlow* (2001) and *A critical edition of writer Roger Dorsinville's Haitian memoirs of Africa* (2003).

Dorsinville, Roger (1911–92). A novelist who was the first Haitian to write a novel about Africa, *Kimby,* (1973), Dorsinville was a prolific writer whose career might be described as consisting of two phases: the writer of Haitian novels and poetry and the novelist who wrote about Africa. Like many Caribbean authors, such as **Juan Bosch**, from the Dominican Republic, Dorsinville spent many years of his life in exile. He was also a dramatist and essayist.

Dorsinville was born in Port-au-Prince on March 11, 1911, the son of a journalist. His father, Hénec Dorsinville, introduced him to literature and to writing. From very early on, he expressed a concern with the political corruption and the social injustices plaguing Haiti. In 1945, he wrote the drama *Barrières,* about racism within Haitian society, and in 1955, he wrote the poem "Pour célébrer la terre," in which he renders tribute to Haitian peasants. As his fame grew in Haiti, Dorsinville worked as a teacher and pursued a career in the Foreign Service. In the 1950s, he was appointed ambassador to several South American countries.

In 1957, his opposition to the dictatorship of **François Duvalier** resulted in his exile, first in the United States and then Canada before settling in Africa. In 1962, he wrote the epic poem "Le Grand devoir," lamenting the tragedy of slavery and portraying Haiti as a paradise destroyed by such corrupt rulers as Duvalier. Three years later, Dorsinville published *Toussaint Louverture; ou, La vocation de la liberté,* a biographical study that served as a vehicle to analyze the trajectory of Haitian politics since independence in 1806. In the 1970s, Dorsinville stopped writing about Haiti and turned to Africa for inspiration. It was during this period when he began to cultivate long fiction, eventually publishing five novels about Africa of which *Kimby, ou, La loi de Niang* (1973), and *L'Afrique des rois* (1975) are probably the best known. These novels examined African politics and corruption with a critical eye, not that of a white European assuming a superior and racist attitude, but that of a son of African expressing his love for the mother country. In 1980, Dorsinville returned to the topic of Haiti, publishing *Mourir pour Haïti, ou, Les croisés d'Esther.* Combined, the novels about Africa and Haiti allowed the author to advocate for black unity, regardless of national boundaries.

In 1986, with the Duvalier dictatorship at an end, Dorsinville went back to Haiti. Three years later he published the novel, *Les vèvès du Créateur*. Using the literary device known as **magical realism**—realismo mágico—he again explored Haitian politics and reality.

Dorsinville also wrote numerous essays on topics ranging from politics to literature. His nephew Max Dorsinville, writing *Research in African Literatures*, observed Dorsinville's works as "a defining act of the African-Caribbean imagination" (171). He passed away on January 12, 1992.

Further Reading

Dorsinville, Max. "Remembering Roger Dorsinville." *Research in African Literatures* 25, no. 3 (Fall 1994): 171.

Dumas, Pierre-Raymond. *Panorama de la litératture haïtienne*. Tome I. Port-au-Prince: Promobank, 1996.

—*D. H. Figueredo*

Doval, Teresa de la. See Dovalpage, Teresa.

Dovalpage, Teresa (1966–)

A Cuban novelist whose writings reflect the moral and economic collapse of post-Soviet Cuba, Dovalpage began to write first in Spanish and then, like many other Hispanic or Francophone Caribbean writers who live in the United States, switched to English. She also writes under the name of Teresa de la Caridad Doval.

Dovalpage was born in Havana, Cuba, on October 1, 1966. As an only child, she developed an early interest in literature and has often described her childhood as that of a bookworm with an unquenchable curiosity for things spiritual. In 1990, Dovalpage graduated from the School of Foreign Languages at the University of Havana with a BA in English literature and an MA, in Spanish literature. How she came to the United States is an interesting story in itself. From 1990 to 1996, she attended Silent Quaker meetings in Havana, where she got the opportunity to meet diverse groups interested in exploring alternative pathways of spirituality. It was at one of the Silent Quaker meetings that she met her husband to be, Hugh Page, an American psychologist and former U.S. Air Force chaplain, for whom she initially acted as translator when he visited the Quaker group. They married in 1994, and two years later they came to live in the United States, first settling in San Diego, California, where Dovalpage taught Spanish in several community colleges. In 2002, Dovalpage and her husband moved to Albuquerque, where she is presently a doctoral candidate in the Spanish and Portuguese Department of the University of New Mexico.

The year 2004 saw the publication of *Posesas de La Habana* and *A Girl Like Che Guevara*. *Posesas de La Habana* is cross-generational novel, involving four women, La Abuelonga, Barbarita, Elsa, and Beiya. The novel takes place during a power outage in Havana: giving each of the women the opportunity to narrate the story of her life and the parallel history of Cuba. Whenever the eleven-year-old Beiya speaks, for instance, the language is graphic and rough, as it reflects the degraded world of a contemporary Cuban teenager. The fact that the story takes place during a power outage already signals a world without light or any possible means of escape. The family unit that may have offered some comfort and sense of security in the past fails to function as a nucleus of support. If anything, it is only the world of women that seems to provide some modicum of cultural cohesiveness in corrupt, contemporary Cuban society.

Penned under the name of Teresa de la Caridad Doval, *A Girl Like Che Guevara* was directly written in English. Set in 1982, *A Girl Like Che Guevara* tells the story of sixteen-year-old Lourdes Torres, child of a mixed-race marriage who comes of age in a School-in-the-Fields work-camp program, where schoolchildren known as "pioneros"—or pioneers—are sent to contribute to the Revolution for a period of forty-five days to three months every year until they graduate from high school. Little by little, the idealist Lourdes, admirer of Ernesto "Che" Guevara (1928–67), comes to see through the lies and hypocrisy of Castro's Communist society. The tobacco fields in Pinar del Rio, where she is sent to work along with other teenagers, become an unexpected source of social, racial, and sexual education for Lourdes. Her white father, a professor of Marxism at the university, and her black mother, lead a less than ideal, racially harmonious life. And when Lourdes's parents visit her in the fields with food, it becomes obvious that they are much better off than others, giving us a glimpse into one of Cuba's most contentious contradictions. *Publishers Weekly* called *A Girl Like Che Guevara* "an intimate portrait of life inside Communist Cuba" with "sensitive characterizations."

Dovalpage is currently working on an English-language novel on the theme of **Santeria**, an Afro-Cuban religion. *See also* Anti-Castro Literature; Castro, Fidel; Cuban American Literature.

Further Reading

Anonymous. Review of *A Girl Like Che Guevara*. *Publishers Weekly Forecasts*, March 1, 2004.

Crone, Thomas. "Cuban Teen Tests Limits of Farm Growing Tobacco and Communists." Review of *A Girl Like Che Guevara*. *St. Louis-Post Dispatch*, May 23, 2004.

Evora, José Antonio. "Tres autores en siete días." *El nuevo herald*, May 21, 2004.

Mabe, Chauncey. "Promising Author Captures the Essence of Cuban Life." *South Florida Sun-Sentinel*, June 4, 2004.

—*Rolando Pérez*

D'Rivel, Ysa. See Cuevas, Clara.

Duarte Siblings

∎

Brother and sister from the Dominican Republic who were patriots and writers. **Juan Pablo Duarte** is considered the father of the Dominican Republic. **Rosa Protomártir Duarte y Diez** was a historian responsible for recording the patriotic events that took place in their country during the nineteenth century.

Duarte, Juan Pablo (1813–76). Called both the Father of the Country—El Padre de la Patria—and the Christ of Freedom, Duarte was a Dominican patriot who led a successful rebellion against Haiti, which had invaded the country in 1822. He was a poet, though his patriotic activities did not allow him sufficient time to write or even publish what he did manage to write. Much of what is known about his life comes from what his sister Rosa Duarte y Diez saved and wrote in the volume *Apuntes para la historia de la historia de la isla de Santo Domingo y para la biografía del general dominicano, Juan Pablo Duarte,* written during the 1880s.

Duarte was born in Santo Domingo on January 26, 1813; his father was Spanish and his mother was a native of the Dominican Republic, but with Spanish ancestry. During his youth, he traveled throughout the United States and Europe, where he was influenced by liberal philosophy and where he was attracted to the **Romantic Movement**. Returning to the Dominican Republic, he founded at the age of twenty-five a revolutionary movement called La Trinitaria, consisting of secret cells spread throughout the nation.

Duarte organized an armed rebellion that forced the Haitian governor to capitulate. But Haitian forces returned, arresting anyone connected with the revolt. Duarte fled to Venezuela to reorganize the insurrection. While he was away, a friend and conspirator, Ramón Mella, staged an uprising on February 27, 1844. The Haitian troops opted not to fight, and the following day, negotiations resulted in a peaceful agreement that granted the Dominican Republic its independence.

The poetry Duarte wrote was romantic and patriotic. He seldom had the opportunity to revise, thus the poems reveal a potential not fully realized. A typical poem is "Tristezas de la Noche," written during his youth, where using a repetitive pattern the poet describes how different people—a vagabond, a sailor, a wealthy man—contemplate life. Researchers at the Dominican Republic's National Library recently found what might be the last poem written by Duarte while living in exile. It is a tribute to a dead friend and it reveals a more mature approach to his questions about mortality. The trajectory between the poems of his youth and the poems in exile suggest an artistic growth that the poet was never able to fulfill. Nevertheless, his memory and his poetry are revered in the Dominican Republic.

Duarte y Diez, Rosa Protomártir (1820–88). Historian from the Dominican Republic, Rosa Duarte dedicated her life to the support of the lofty ideas behind the Dominican independence movement and the creation of a new nation. Chronicler of the history of her nation, she preserved for posterity the biography of her brother and the importance of the historical moment she lived.

Duarte was born in Santo Domingo, Dominican Republic, on June 26, 1820. In her twenties she participated in revolutionary plots to expel Haitian invading forces from the Dominican Republic. Forced to go into exile in Venezuela with her family in 1845, she realized the importance of documenting the revolutionary struggle as well as her brother's life and ideas. Such a realization inspired her to write *Apuntes para la historia de la historia de la isla de Santo Domingo y para la biografía del general dominicano, Juan Pablo Duarte* during the 1880s. In 1970, the volume was published in the Dominican Republic by the Instituto Duartiano de Santo Domingo as *Apuntes de Rosa Duarte*.

The volume was one of the first histories written by a woman in the Dominican Republic. It attested to Duarte's keen sense of the importance of recording history and her role as a participant, thinking person, chronicler, and preserver of historical truth. She died in Venezuela in 1888. Her burial site remains unknown.

Further Reading

Cocco de Filippis, Daisy. *Documents of Dissidence: Selected Writings by Dominican Women*. New York: CUNY Dominican Studies Institute, 2000.

Duarte, Rosa. *Apuntes de Rosa Duarte. Archivo y versos de Juan Pablo Duarte*. Santo Domingo: Editora del Caribe, 1970.

"Juan Pablo Duarte." http://www.bnrd.gov.do/poesia1/1900-1974.htm (accessed 9/1/05).

—Daisy Cocco de Filippis and D. H. Figueredo

Dub Poetry

Dub Poetry is a term arguably coined by **Linton Kwesi Johnson,** one of the principle architects of the art form. Dub poetry may be seen as a form of **performance poetry** in that the artist often sees him- or herself as a part of the poem itself. "The poet," according to poet **Mutabaruka,** "is bringing to life the poem. You (the poet) actually become the poem." In this respect, it draws on African oral traditions and the rhythm is frequently held by djembe or kettle drums, which add to the African quality of the performance. It is typically recited in Caribbean vernacular, which gives it a certain "chant" sound and clipped quality to the poetic meter. The following lines from Johnson's famous poem, "Sonny's Lettah (anti-sus poem)" are typical:

> Dem tump 'im in 'im belly
> an' it turn to jelly
> Dem lick 'im pon 'im back
> an 'im rib get pop
> Dem lick 'im pon 'im head
> but it tuff like lead.

The theme of this poem is police brutality related to the anti-suspect laws passed in England in the late 1970s and early 1980s which many social and political activists saw as racist. It is also related to the themes of dub poetry promulgated by artists in Jamaica, Canada, South Africa, Trinidad, and elsewhere. Ahdri Zhina

Mandiela, Lillian Allen, Clifford Joseph, Mutabaruka, **Mikey Smith**, Oku Onuora, and Osbourne Ruddock (King Tubby) did much to promote the dub-poetic style. Like Johnson, these *poets*—a term many like Mutabaruka and Johnson himself insist on despite their rise to prominence through popular reggae music of the 1970s and 1980s—address issues of social inequality, political oppression, and racial injustice, often critiqued in the poems on a global scale with sharp criticisms of institutions like the International Monetary Fund. Dub poetry cannot be seen outside of its raison d'être: a voice of protest for and by Caribbean nationals both at home in the Caribbean and in regions of the British Commonwealth to which they have historically migrated.

Further Reading

Batson-Savage, Tanya. "Dub Poetry on Page." *The Jamaica Gleaner*.com, January 1, 2004. http://www.jamaica-gleaner.com/gleaner/20040101/ent/ent1.html (accessed 11/20/04).

Habekost, Christian. *Verbal Riddim: The Politics and Aesthetics of African-Caribbean Dub Poetry.* Rodopi Press. Amsterdam, 1993.

Johnson, Kwesi Linton. 1997. Interview with Billy Bob Hargus. *Furious.com*, January. http://www.furious.com/perfect/lkj.html (accessed 11/19/04).

Mutabaruka. Telephone Interview.

—*Ian H. Marshall*

Dupré, Antoine (?–1816)

Called the bard of Haiti, Dupré was a patriot whose poetry praised the accomplishments of the emerging Haitian nation and the bravery of its leaders. His most famous poem, "Hymne à la liberté" (1812), recounts how Haiti fought for and won its liberty. Dupré was also an actor.

Dupré was born in Cap-Haïtien, Haiti, though there is no record of his exact birth. It is believed that he studied in France and spent some time in Great Britain. During the civil wars that followed the Haitian revolution, Dupré distinguished himself by writing and reciting verses that encouraged Henri Christophe (1767–1820) to continue fighting the rebellious forces on the south of Haiti. During this period, around 1810 or 1811, Dupré wrote a play about this conflict: *La morte de Lamarre.*

Dupré was killed in a duel in 1816. His writings capture the excitement and confusion of the early Haitian Republic, offering valuable historical insight.

Further Reading

Berrou, Raphaël, and Pradel Pompilus. *Histoire de la littérature haïtienne.* Tome 1. Port-au Prince: Editions Caraëbes.

—*D. H. Figueredo*

Durand, Oswald (1840–1906)

∎

Haiti's most beloved poet, Oswald Durand is the author of nationalist and romantic poems. His best known piece, "Choucoune," was written in Creole or **Kreyòl** in 1880 and set to music in 1883 by New Orleans pianist Michel Mauleart Monton (1855–98). A variation of the song emerged in the 1950s as "Yellow Bird," performed by the singer Harry Belafonte (1927–). Durand was inspired by Haiti's landscape and by Haitian culture, using his country's flora and fauna, a practice not common at the time when Haitian writers used France's flora—oaks and apple trees, for example—to describe Haiti. A ladies' man, the physical beauty of Haitian women was also one of Durand's favorite themes.

Durand was born in Cap-Haïtien, Haiti, on September 17, 1840. When his parents were killed in an earthquake in 1842, his grandmother, a relative of general Alexandre Dumas, the father of the famous author of the same name, raised him. Self-educated, he became a teacher in 1860. Two years later he married poet **Virginie Sampeur,** but due to his philandering, she divorced him in 1871.

In 1866, Durand was appointed director of a secondary school in the town of Gonaïves. Then, in the 1880s, he was sent to prison for criticizing the government, though the reason is still not clear. After his release in 1885, he was elected to the legislature. He managed and published the legislature's official organ, *Le Moniteur,* and the review *Les Bigailles.* In 1888, he was elected president of the Haitian Parliament.

Encouraged by **Demesvar Delorme,** one of the most famous Haitian men of letters of the day, Durand began writing and submitting poems to local newspapers as a youth. In time, he became a prolific writer, but most of his work, published in little known newspapers and in his own notebooks, has yet to be uncovered. Durand did not publish his first book, *Rires et pleurs,* until 1896. In 1900, he published the collection *Quatre nouveaus poemes.* His poetry was and is highly popular, presenting themes that are still relevant to the average Haitian. For instance, in the poem "Le Fils du noir" (1896), he writes about racial discrimination while "Chant national" (1896) is a tribute to Haiti's patriots. But it is his love poetry that receives popular attention: In "Idalina" (1896), he compares a woman's figure to Haitian fruits, and in "Sonnets de femmes," he glorifies all Haitian women.

Durand did not make much money from his writings. In 1905, the Haitian government, at the urging of novelist **Frédéric Marcelin,** who was at the time Minister of Finance, awarded the poet a pension. He died suddenly on April 22, 1906.

Further Reading

Berrou, Raphaël, and Pradel Pompilus. *Histoire de la littérature haitienne.* Tome 1. Port-au Prince, Haiti: Editions Caraïbes, 1975.

Garret, Naomi M. *The Renaissance of Haitian Poetry.* Paris: Présence africaine, 1963.

—*Léon-François Hoffmann and D. H. Figueredo*

Duvalier, François (1907–71)

∎

Though known as a ruthless dictator who controlled the destiny of Haiti for nearly twenty years, "Papa Doc" Duvalier was one of the founders of the **Les Griots**, a literary group, a literary revue, and a weekly newspaper that emphasized and celebrated the island's connections with Africa. Duvalier wrote over a dozen books, ranging from cultural studies, political pamphlets, articles on medicine, and his own memoirs.

Born in Port-au-Prince, Haiti, on April 14, 1907, he was the son of a teacher and a baker. He attended the Lycée Pétion and graduated as a physician from medical school in 1934. During this period he seemed concerned with literary activities and medical work. He cowrote ethnographical articles with **Lorimer Denis**—though biographers Bernard Diederich and Al Burt maintain in *Papa Doc* (1969) that Denis was the actual thinker and writer—and was involved in the journal *Les Griots*. In 1934, he and Denis cowrote *Les tendances d'une génération*, which promoted nationalism in the face of the American military presence and encouraged Haitian writers to create a national literature. During this period, he was participating in the medical campaign to wipe out yaws, a disease which afflicts the skin and bones, making it difficult for the afflicted to walk, and which brought him national attention. In 1945, he published *Contribution à l'étude du pian en Haiti*, and in 1948, *La valeur de la pénicilline dans le traitement du pain en Haiti*, both medical studies. In 1948, he also wrote, with Denis, who again masterminded the writing, *Le problème des classes à travers l'histoire d'Haiti*, which advocated a form of black fascism.

Since he appeared to have no political ambitions, he was encouraged to aspire to the presidency, which he did, winning the election in 1957. His hunger for power was insatiable, and thus he declared himself President for Life. He purged the armed forces of those who were disloyal and established a secret police that suppressed dissent. He ordered the execution of writer **Jacques Stephen Alexis**, who had participated in a plot against Duvalier, sent to prison newspapers editors and writers, and forced out of the country such major authors and intellectuals as **René Depestre**.

Toward the end of his life, Duvalier saw himself as political prophet and considered his political pamphlet *Breviaire d'une révolution; extraits des "OEuvres essentielles" du Docteur François* (1967) similar to Mao Zedong's (1893–1976) *Little Red Book* (1966). He also published, in 1968, his memoirs, written under a pseudonym, Abderrahman, which he had used in the 1930s, *Souvenirs d'autrefois (bric-à-brac), 1926–1948*. It could be said that Duvalier himself was something of a literary parody: he often talked about himself in the third person, claimed supernatural powers, and greeted spirits while in the presence of foreign officials.

After amending the constitution so that his son could take over the government, Duvalier died on April 21, 1971. His other works include *Pour affronter les temps durs* (1960), *Face au people et à l'histoire* (1961), and *Hommage au Marron inconnu* (1969).

Further Reading

Diederich, Bernard, and Al Burt. *Papa Doc: The Truth About Haiti Today.* New York: McGraw Hill, 1969.

Dorsinville, Roger. *The rule of Francois ("Papa Doc") Duvalier in two novels by Roger Dorsinville: realism and magic realism in Haiti/edited and translated by Max Dorsinville* Lewiston, NY: E. Mellen Press, 2000.

—D. H. Figueredo

E

Edgell, Zee (1940–)

The most famous writer from Belize, Edgell was one of the first novelists to write about her country and her compatriots. Her novels address a multiplicity of themes, ranging from colonialism and racism to women's oppression and sexual relationships.

Edgell was born as Zelma Inez Tucker in Belize City, Belize, on October 21, 1940. She attended Catholic school in Belize and spent hours at home reading and listening to radio dramas. In the 1960s, she traveled to Great Britain and, in 1965, graduated from the Polytechnic of Central London with a degree in journalism. After working as a reporter for the *Daily Gleaner* in Kingston, Jamaica, in 1966, she was appointed editor of a monthly newspaper called *The Reporter*.

During the 1970s, she visited Africa, the Middle East, and Great Britain with her husband Al Edgell. Returning to Belize, she became director of the Women's Bureau in 1981. Aware that her country was changing, she wrote in 1982 her first novel, *Beka Lamb*, about Belize's struggle for independence from Britain. The book was well received, winning the British Fawcett Society Book Prize. In 1991, she wrote *In Times Like These*, about a woman returning to Belize as the country was achieving autonomy. Her third novel is *The Festival of San Joaquin* (1997), a story about a woman who murders her husband. Edgell writes in a realistic, direct style. Her books are read throughout the Caribbean and are included in the curriculum in Great Britain and many schools in the United States

Edgell has explained that her novels are as much about women as about Belize. "Belize is always a major character. It's not just a backdrop, it's an integral part of the narrative," she told scholar Irma McClaurin in the journal *Americas* in 1994.

Further Reading

About Zee Edgellenglishscholar.com/ZeeSite/about.htm (accessed 4/17/05).

McClaurin, Irma. "A writer's life: A country's transition." *Americas* 46, no. 4 (July 1994): 38–44.

—D. H. Figueredo

Elzaburu y Vizcarrondo, Manuel (1851–92)

An attorney, writer, translator, and promoter of Puerto Rican culture, Elzaburu was one of the founders of the **Ateneo Puertorriqueño**, the influential cultural center where writers met to discuss literature and read their own works.

Of Basque descent, Elzaburu was born in San Juan, Puerto Rico, on January 2, 1851. He attended Catholic elementary and secondary schools in Puerto Rico and earned his law degree from the University of Madrid, Spain. He set up an office in San Juan, and during his spare time wrote poetry under the name of Fabian Montes. Fluent in French, he also translated the works of Charles Baudelaire (1821–67), among others, which he read to friends who gathered in his home for literary soirées. These gatherings, or **tertulias,** resulted in the introduction of contemporary French literature to young Puerto Rican writers and in the eventual creation of the Ateneo Puertorriqueño.

The Ateneo was founded in 1876. To promote its ideals, Elzaburu created with poet **José Gautier Benítez** the scholarly and literary journal *Revista Puertorriqueña de Literatura y Ciencia*, which was distributed to Ateneo's members. In 1888, he published his ideas on the promotion of education in Puerto Rico, *La institución de la enseñanza superior de Puerto Rico.*

Elzaburu passed away suddenly at the age of forty-one. His portrait hangs at the entrance to the Ateneo.

Further Reading

Ribes Tovar, Federico. *100 Outstanding Puerto Ricans.* New York: Plus Ultra, 1976.

—D. H. Figueredo

Encarnación Rivera, Ángel (1952–)

Encarnación Rivera is a Puerto Rican poet and short-story writer.

Encarnación Rivera was born in Santurce, Puerto Rico, on January 24, 1952. He attended primary and secondary schools in Carolina and, in 1969, matriculated at the Universidad de Puerto Rico. As a student, he founded the journal *La Gotera* and submitted his poems to such influential literary reviews as *Zona Carga y Descarga.*

In 1973, he earned a BA in art. The year of his graduation, he published *Poemas de la servilleta* and *El vuelo del buitre vestido de paloma.* That same year, his novel *Noches ciegas* won the literary contest sponsored by the **Ateneo Puertorriqueño**. The novel was published three years later to positive reviews.

In the 1970s and 1980s, he cultivated the genre of short stories, publishing stories in numerous journals. In 1979, he collected some of the stories into the volume *Cuadernos de juglaria;* the stories, some experimental in format, revealed a sarcastic interpretation of life and a preoccupation with the erotic. His work awaits further study.

Further Reading

Cuentos modernos: Antología. Río Piedras, Puerto Rico: Editorial Edil, 1975.

Vega, José Luis. *Reunión de espejo.* Río Piedras, Puerto Rico: Editorial Cultural, 1983.

—*D. H. Figueredo*

Endicott, Stephen. See Roberts, Walter Adolphe.

Equiano, Olaudah, *also called* Gustavus Vassa, the African (1745–97)

■

The first to write a slave narrative entirely on his own, Equiano was an extraordinary individual who bought his own freedom; sailed in a scientific expedition; wrote, published, and sold an account of his life, which became an eighteenth-century best-seller. Upon his death he was able to leave his children an inheritance of about $150,000, by today's standard. His autobiography, *The Interesting Narrative of the Life of Olaudah Equiano, or Gustavus Vassa, the African* (1789), narrated his life from enslavement to freedom and contained several chapters on the horrors of slavery in the Caribbean, thus assuring his position in the canon of Anglophone Caribbean literature.

Equiano was born in 1745 in modern-day Nigeria. When he was about eleven years old, he and his sister were captured by slave traders. The two were separated, and when Equiano was twelve, he arrived at England. From there he was shipped to Barbados, where he witnessed the selling of slaves as if they were animals and the purposeful separation by the white colonialists of friends and families: "Why are parents to lose their children, brothers their sisters, husbands their wives? Sure this is a new refinement in cruelty," he wrote (88).

Equiano was taken to Virginia, where he was sold to a Royal Navy officer who named him Gustavus Vassa, a common strategy used to take the slave's identity away by denying use of his or her original name. As personal servant to the officer, Equiano took part in the Seven Years' War, carrying ammunition from cannon to cannon aboard a ship. When in England, the officer allowed Equiano to attend schools, where he learned to read and write. To Equiano's surprise, the officer sold him to another sea captain, who took him to Montserrat and, in turn, sold him to a Quaker merchant. In Montserrat, Equiano described the tortures visited by the masters upon the slaves: "I have seen a negro beaten til some of his bones were brokin, for . . . [the crime of] letting a pot boil over"(213). Sailing throughout the islands in the Caribbean, Equiano began to purchase and sell merchandise—glassware, predominantly—and saved forty pounds, the money needed buy his freedom. He returned to England as a freed man and worked as a hairdresser before signing himself on a ship as a sailor. He sailed the Mediterranean, went on an expedition to the Arctic in 1772, and spent some time with Mesquite Indians on the Caribbean coast of Central America. In 1733, he befriended the abolitionist Granville Sharp. In 1787, he was Appointed Commissary for Stores in charge of acquiring provisions for an expedition to resettle freed slaves in Sierra Leone. Equiano realized the enterprise would not work due to poor planning and because many of the white organizers were stealing funds from the project. When he made his observations public, Equiano was reprimanded and removed from his post. The expedition was a failure and Equiano vindicated.

A most extraordinary man who participated in scientific expeditions and fought in the Seven Years' War, Olaudah Equiano was an ex-slave who wrote the first major denunciation of slavery and the slave trade; his slave narrative became the model for the genre. *Source: Schomburg Center for Research in Black Culture, The New York Public Library, Astor, Lenox, and Tilden Foundations. Courtesy of Lisa Finder.*

Around this time, Equiano began to write his memoir with the intention of stirring "a sense of compassion for the miseries which the Slave-Trade has entailed on my unfortunate countrymen"(iii). To print the volume, he sought funds from numerous abolitionists, who persuaded by the well-spoken and well-read Equiano contributed toward the publications; the contributors included the Prince of Wales and the Duke of York. Upon publishing his memoir, Equiano promoted it through lectures and discussion in England, Wales, Scotland, and Ireland. The narrative was a best seller: it was reprinted eight times in Great Britain and it was published in the United States.

In 1792, Equiano married a white English woman and had two daughters. During the 1790s, he devoted his energy to campaigning against slavery, using his book and his own life as an abolitionist document. He died in 1797, having planted a seed toward the eventual abolition of slavery.

There are two controversies regarding Equiano and his autobiography. At a conference at Kingston University, Surrey, United Kingdom, in 2003, it was suggested by scholar Vincent Carreta, based upon his study of birth records and slave inventories in North Carolina for a new edition of Equiano's work, that Equiano was born in the American colonies and that the account of his youth in Africa was collected from different stories he had heard. Not all scholars agree with this conclusion, but whether or not it's true, the narrative remains a realistic portrayal of eighteenth-century Africa and a powerful indictment of the cruelties of the slave trade. It has also been suggested that Equiano was assisted in the writing of his autobiography, but most scholars believe that if this was the case, the aid consisted in checking spelling errors and sentence structure. As evidence of Equiano's authorship, scholars point to a manuscript letter in the Liverpool City Library written by Equiano and demonstrating his excellent command of the English language.

As literature, the narrative effectively denounces the inhumanity of all those involved in slavery, draws ethnographic scenes of life in Africa during the eighteenth century, and renders one of the first travelogues of the Caribbean. His account of his conversion to Christianity is an excellent example of religious literature. What keeps the text together, though, and makes it engaging, is Equiano's persona: likable, imaginative, and modest. He finishes his autobiography thus: "What makes any event important, unless by its observation we become better and wiser"(255). *The Interesting Narrative of The Life of Olaudah Equiano, or Gustavus Vassa, the African* predates Frederick Douglass's autobiography and **Juan Manzano**'s seminal *Autobiografía de un esclavo*, also published in England, by at least fifty years.

Further Reading

Equiano, Olaudah. *The interesting narrative and other writings*. Edited with an introduction and notes by Vincent Carretta. New York: Penguin Books, 2003.

———. *The Life of Olaudah Equiano or Gustavus Vassa, the African*, 1789. In two volumes with a new introduction by Paul Edwards. London: Dawsons of Pall Mall, 1969.

Walvin, James. *An African's Life: The Life and Times of Olaudah Equiano, 1745–1797*. London: Cassell, 1998.

—*D. H. Figueredo*

Escalona, Rafael E. (19th century)

Escalona was a pioneer in the development of Puerto Rican theater and drama toward the end of the nineteenth century.

He is a mysterious figure from that era. Very little is known of his life except that he was involved in Puerto Rican theater during the 1880s and wrote several popular comedies. Information about him comes from programs and contemporary commentaries about theatrical productions, actors, and performances of Escalona's plays. Influenced by "teatro bufo," similar to vaudeville but often with a social message, Escalona wrote in 1883 the comedies *Flor de una noche* and *Amor a la Pompadour*. In 1888, he wrote *Cada loco con su tema*. His works depict love stories where the protagonists are separated and overcome opposition to their union.

Escalona discarded European conventions of presenting characters that reflected middle-class values and spoke in a manner acceptable by society. Instead, he used black characters and duplicated the vernacular of the era and the Afro-Spanish–Puerto Rican parlance, thus, according to Angelina Morfi in *La Gran enciclopedia de Puerto Rico* (1981), "saved for posterity the richness of expressions of the blacks and Puerto Rican peasants"of the nineteenth century.

Further Reading

Morfi, Angelina. "El Teatro en Puerto Rico."In *La gran enciclopedia de Puerto Rico*. Vol. 6. Edited by Vicente Baéz, 59–61. San Juan: Puerto Rico en la Mano and La Gran Enciclopedia de Puerto Rico, 1981.

—*D. H. Figueredo*

Espaillat, Rhina Polonia (1932–)

Dominican American poet who writes both in English and Spanish, Espaillat is known for writing poetry that captures the beauty of the mundane and the routine. Often compared to poet Anthony Hecht (1923–), she is considered a member of the New Formalist school, that is, a poet who writes within certain poetic forms, be it sonnet or couplets.

Espaillat was born in La Vega, Dominican Republic, on January twentieth, 1932, the daughter of a diplomat. Influenced by her grandmother, who wrote poetry and who introduced the young girl to verses and music, Espaillat began to write in Spanish by the age of five. When she was seven years old, her parents moved to New York City, where Espaillat quickly mastered English. Ten years later, her teachers in high school were reading and praising her poetry. When she was fifteen years old, *Ladies Home Journal* published some of her poems. A year later, she was accepted into the Poetry Society of America.

In 1953, Espaillat graduated from Hunter College and became a teacher. During the 1960s, she attended graduate school at Queens College. Her family responsibilities—she has three children—and her studies curtailed her writing. But in 1980 she returned to poetry. Her poems appeared in numerous literary journals, and in 1992 she published her first collection, *Lapsing to Grace: Poems and Drawings*. She followed the collection with four other volumes: *Where Horizons Go* (1998), *Mundo y Palabra/The World and the Word* (2001), *Rhina P. Espaillat: Greatest Hits* (2002), and *Rehearsing Absence* (2002).

While her poetry, usually consisting of rhythmic sonnets, describes family life and domestic settings, which she has called "snapshots,"she also addresses such issues as ancestry, assimilation, and immigration. Her poem "You Call Me by Old Names"(2000) serves as an example:

> And suddenly I think of people
> dead many centuries ago
> my ancestor, who never knew . . . snow.

Observes poet and critic Robert B. Shaw of Espailla's poetry in the journal *Poetry* (2002): "She notices what we typically overlook, and she delineates it with lucid intelligence, tolerance, and good humor. Hers is a voice of experience, but it is neither jaded nor pedantic. She speaks not from some cramped corner but from somewhere close to the center of life."

Further Reading

Espaillat, Rhina Polonia. "You Call Me By Old Names."*Callaloo* 23, no. 3. (Summer 2000): 1052–56.

Shaw, Robert. B. "Straws in the Wind."*Poetry* 180, no. 6 (September 2002): 345–56.

—D. H. Figueredo

Espinet, Ramabai (1948–)

A Trinidadian writer who belongs to a generation of Caribbean women who migrated to Canada in the late 1960s and early 1970s, Espinet is one of a handful of Indo Caribbean writers—like **Samuel Selvon**—to achieve international recognition. She is a poet, a children's writer, and a novelist. She is also an actor.

Espinet was born in Princes Town but grew up in San Francisco in Trinidad-Tobago. She was raised in a Christian Indian community and was exposed to American and British writers—Alfred Lord Tennyson(1809–92), Henry Wadsworth Longfellow (1807–82)—along with Caribbean authors, the likes of **V. S. Naipul** and **Derek Walcott**, in her teen years. After studying at Naparima College, in Trinidad, she migrated to Canada around 1970. She supported herself by driving a taxi while attending York University. Eventually, she earned a PhD in postcolonial literature at the University of West Indies in St. Augustine, Trinidad.

Traveling back and forth between Canada and Trinidad, Espinet has described herself as an Indo-Caribbean Canadian woman. Her creative writings explore the need to give voice to the silent Indian women of the Caribbean, silenced by their own patriarchal communities and by years of colonialism, and the understanding of the complexities of creolization, the mixing of European and Caribbean cultures. Her desire to make American readers aware of the literary expression of women in the Caribbean led her to compile the anthology *Creation Fire* (1990), one of the few volumes to include the work of women authors who write in English, Dutch, French, and Spanish.

Espinet's reputation as a writer emerges from her poetry, her children's stories, and her novel. In 1991, she published the book of poems *Nuclear Seasons*, in which a dominant theme is the quest for a type self-identity that challenges society's assumption of racial and gender identities. Her first children's book, *Princess of Spadina* (1992), is a fantasy about a tall princess with dreadlocks helping three girls—one Italian, one Chinese, and one Trinidadian—to subdue a thief; her second, *Ninja's Carnival* (1993), tells of a child homesick for Trinidad. In 2003, her novel *The Swinging Bridge*, about the multiplicity of the Indian diaspora—from India to the Caribbean and to Canada—was well received by the mainstream media in Canada and in the United States.

Espinet is also a performer, acting out her poem "Shay's Robber Talk"(1998) at several festivals throughout Toronto. She teaches literature at York University and Seneca College, both in Toronto.

Further Reading

Esteves, Carmen C., and Lizabeth Paravisini-Gebert. *Green Cane and Juicy Flotsam: Short Stories by Caribbean Women.* New Brunswick, NJ: Rutgers University Press, 1991.

—*D. H. Figueredo*

Espinosa, Victoria (1922–)

Espinosa is drama critic who has written extensively about Puerto Rican theatre. She is a producer, director, and drama professor at the Universidad de Puerto Rico.

A native of San Juan, she attended elementary and secondary schools in that city. In 1949, she earned a BA in theater from the Universidad de Puerto Rico. Twenty years later, she received a PhD in theater from the Universidad Nacional Autónoma de México.

Espinosa promoted Puerto Rican theater, and with that objective she often staged the works of dramatists that represented the best of the genre, such as **René Marqués** and **Myrna Casas**. Espinosa managed the university's theater and its traveling company. She also directed children's theater.

In 1969, she published *El teatro de René Marqués y la escenificación de su obra, Los soles truncos,* a major review of Puerto Rican drama during the twentieth century and of dramatist René Marqués.

Further Reading

Enciclopedia de Puerto Rico. siglo XXI. Vol. 3. Santurce, Puerto Rico: Caribe Grolier, 1998.

—*D. H. Figueredo*

Esteves, José de Jesús (1881–1918)

Esteves was a Puerto Rican poet who wrote about the island's natural beauty and who was inspired by nostalgia for his youth and the island's past.

Esteves was born in Aguadilla, Puerto Rico, on October 15, 1881 (some sources say 1882). He studied law through correspondence school and served as municipal judge of the town of Manatí, where he shared an office with the attorney and writer, **Luis Llorens Torres**. When he was not working as an attorney, he devoted time to the writing of poetry, which he contributed to local publications.

Influenced by the literary movement known as **Modernismo**, which advocated for an intense awareness of aesthetics, the controlled expression of emotions, and a cultivated longing for the past, Esteves wrote poems that celebrated the island's Hispanic heritage, *Crisálidas* (1909), and love poems, *Rosal de amor* (1917).

However, it was the poetry describing and taking joy in the beauty of the Puerto Rican countryside and Puerto Rican women that made him popular on the island. Typical of his work is the poem *Mi musa* (1909), in which he sings that his inspiration comes from a

> trigueña,
> hija del sol borincano,
> que refleja en su figura
> los tropicales encantos

(a dark woman / daughter of the Puerto Rican sun / in whose anatomy is reflected / the enchantment of the tropics).

Further Reading

Arce de Vázquez, Margot et al. *Lecturas puertorriqueñas: Poesía*. Sharon, CT: Troutman Press, 1968.

—*D. H. Figueredo*

Estévez, Abilio (1954–)

Poet, dramatist, novelist, and short-story writer, Abilio Estévez is a Cuban writer known for depicting allegorical images of a decaying Havana during the 1990s, a period of economic hardship dubbed the "Special Period." Estévez belongs to a generation of writers who grew up under the revolutionary regime but who nevertheless question the accomplishments of the regime.

Abilio Estévez was born on January 7, 1954, in Havana. He graduated from the Universidad de la Habana, earning a BA in literature in 1977. He has conducted writing workshops in Cuba and has been visiting professor at several universities in the United States and Latin America. As a youth, he was mentored by playwright **Virgilio Piñera**, who introduced him to other Cuban dramatists and helped him with his writing as well.

In 1987, Estevez's drama *La verdadera culpa de Juan Clemente Zenea* received the Cuban National Theater Award. The drama was staged in Miami, Florida, in 1991. His subsequent plays, *Perla marina* (1993), *Santa Cecilia* (1994), and *El enano en la botella* (1994), were performed in Berlin, Germany, and Caracas, Venezuela. The drama *La noche* (1996) was awarded the Tirso de Molina literary prize in Spain.

His book of poems *Manual de las tentaciones* (1989) won the Luis Cernada Award in Madrid. His novel *Tuyo es el reino* (1997) brought him further international recognition. It is a story about a decaying mansion filled with phantasmagorical images. In 1992, he wrote *Los palacios distantes* (2002), about a gay man and a prostitute who, kicked out of their homes, find refuge in a crumbling old theater in Havana. He has also written two collections of short stories, *Juego con Gloria*

(1987) and *El horizonte y otros regresos* (1998). His fiction has been translated into English, French, German, Greek, and Finnish.

Further Reading

Carreo Mendía, Raquel. "La verdadera respuesta: apuntes para una lectura del tercer personaje."*Conjuntos* 71 (January–March 1987): 65–80.

—*Wilfredo Cancio Isla*

Étienne, Franck (1936–)

■

Haitian educator, writer, actor, and artist, who writes under the pen name of Frankétienne and was the first to publish a novel in the Haitian language, **Kreyòl**. Étienne can claim the most prolific production of any Haitian writer of the twentieth century. He has published some forty volumes of poetry, fiction, and theater (the clear generic distinction is difficult, since he subtitles many works as a "spirale," spiral), without speaking of his ongoing production in the graphic arts: paintings, graphics, ceramics, and so on. His novel *Dézafi* (1975) was the first literary work published in Haitian Kreyòl; a revised version was published in France in 2002, completely recast with the standard orthography of Kreyòl, which was not fully developed and recognized in 1975. His plays are also written and produced in Kreyòl, a language comprehensible to popular audiences whether literate or not.

Born in Saint-Marc on April 12, 1936, Frankétienne says he was the son of an American industrialist who raped his thirteen-year-old mother. She left Saint-Marc and settled with her son in Bel-Air, a northside neighborhood of Port-au-Prince. He finished his secondary studies at the Lycée Alexandre Pétion in 1953 and, for two years, worked as a mechanic for the Haitian electric company. He opened his own school, "L'École Franck Étienne," in 1959, continuing as teacher and principal until 1992.

In an interview in *Haïti en Marche* in October 2003, Frankétienne said: "My writing is of a schizophrenic nature. It is inscribed in *la spirale* ('**spiralism**')"(11). To the author, *la spirale* means a rebellion against oppression, an affirmation of insanity against censorship. He refers to spiralist discourse as "semantics without substance" that participates in the "subversion of current hierarchies." Spiralism interprets the creative process as an upward circling movement that includes elements of past experience or knowledge without ever returning to a precise point of the past.

In *Dézafi/Les affres d'un défi*, Frankétienne gives voice to a group of zombies who are forced to work for a pitiless *bòkò*—sorcerer—under threat of punishment, torture, and execution. What appears at first glance to be a cacophonic series of non-sequential utterances by unidentified voices, typographically shown by different typefaces—Roman, bold, italic—clearly becomes the increasingly rebellious discourse of zombies, with occasional dialogue between the sorcerers Sentil/Saintil, his daughter Siltàna/Sultana, and Zofè/Zofer, the assistant who oversees the zombie-slaves. Asked how he was able to publish such a subversive novel under the regime of Jean-Claude Duvalier (1951–), Franketienne responded that presidential advisers recognized the nature of the work but were unconcerned because Franck was not politically active, and few Haitians could read the book.

Franketienne has achieved international recognition. His Kreyòl-language plays have been produced in Haiti and France, and at least *Kaselezo*, in a French version by the author, was produced in Montréal in 1987. His latest novel *H'éros-chimères* was awarded the Prix Carbet de la Caraïbe in 2002. Franketienne's insistence on producing his own texts in order to avoid the dictates and restrictions of the commercial book industry has inhibited to some extent the recognition and publicity that could come from commercial publication, but he has achieved wide recognition among readers of Haitian and francophone literature. A significant number of theses have been written at both the masters and doctorate levels.

Franketienne's works have yet to appear in English in book format, but several translations have been published in journals, including *Kaselezo* (Childbirth-a play), in *Callaloo* (1992), translation and presentation by Asselin Charles; "*Les affres d'un défa*," an excerpt in *Callaloo* (1996), translation and presentation by Carrol F. Coates.

Further Reading

"Franketienne." An interview by Charles H. Rowell; trans. by Mohamed B. Taleb-Khyar. *Callaloo* 15, no. 2 (Spring 1992): 385–92.

"Franketienne: entre l'exil et le tragique." *Haïti en Marche* 17, no. 36 (October 8, 2003): 11.

—*Carrol F. Coates*

Étienne, Gérard (1936–)

A Haitian writer who has written about political abuses in Haiti, Étienne is a novelist, poet, and essayist. His writings document the brutal dictatorship of **François Duvalier**.

Born in Cap-Haïtien, Haiti, on May 28, 1936, Étienne felt compelled to leave his home at the age of fifteen: he could not stand his father's physical abuse of his mother. His sense of injustice prompted him to join an insurrection against the dictatorial regime of Paul Magloire (1907–2001) during the 1950s. He was arrested and tortured; the experience would influence his writings later on. From 1955 to 1957, he was a cadet in the air force. In the 1960s, he joined a second conspiracy, this time against dictator François Duvalier.

Despite his political involvement, Étienne managed to write poetry, which he read over local radio stations. In 1960, he published two books of poetry, *Au milieu des larmes* and *Plus large qu'un rêve*. He followed this success with two books of criticisms and essays: *Essai sur la négritude* (1962) and *Le Nationalisme dans la littérature haïtienne* (1964). He was also writing articles and literary criticism for local publications.

In 1964, Étienne sought exile in Canada. While working in a factory and also as a nurse, he attended the University of Montreal, earning a BA in literature in 1968; and later earning a PhD in linguistics from the University of Strasbourg. In 1965, he published the book of poems *Lettres à Montréal*. He also wrote for the journals *La Voix canadienne* and *Le Matin*.

In 1974, he published one of his best-known novels, *Le Nègre crucifié, récit*, an anti-Duvalier narrative characterized by violence and the author's descriptions of tortured bodies. In 1979, he wrote *Un ambassadeur macoute à Montréal*, about a Duvalier agent tracking down Haitian exiles in Canada. Recovering from brain surgery in the mid-1980s, Étienne wrote several novels, books of essays, and poetry collections, including: *La Reine Soleil Levée* (1987), *La Charte des crépuscules, Oeuvres poétiques—1960–1980* (1993), *La Question raciale et raciste dans le roman québécois—essai d'anthroposémiologie et sémiotique appliqué* (1995), *La femme noire dans le discours littéraire haïtien*, (1998), and *L'Injustice, la désinformation, le mépris de la loi.* (1998). In exile, his literary and political preoccupation is informed by his memories of Haiti and contemporary developments in that nation.

Étienne has been awarded numerous honors, including the Prix du meilleur éditorialiste, in 1988, the 1991 Médaille de l'Association des écrivains de la Guadeloupe, the 1994 Prix de la meilleure émission de radio communautaire, and the 1996 Certificat d'honneur Maurice Cagnon du Conseil International d'Études Francophones (CIEF), and the 1997 Médaille d'or de La Renaissance française (Montréal).

Further Reading

Walker, Keith L. *Countermodernism and Francophone Literary Culture: The Game of Slipknot*. Durham: Duke University Press, 1999.

—*D. H. Figueredo*

Eulate Sanjurjo, Carmela (1871–1961)

Puerto Rican novelist and short-story writer who lived most of her life in Spain, Eulate Sanjurjo was a pioneer feminist and translator. A world traveler, she was also an accomplished opera singer and concert pianist.

A native of San Juan, Eulate Sanjurjo studied literature and music in Cuba before relocating to Spain, where she studied and mastered several languages, including Catalan, English, French, German, and Italian. She wrote short stories and translated poems that were published in such journals as *La Ilustración Puertorriqueña, La Mujer,* and *El Correo de Ultramar,* published in Cuba, Puerto Rico, and Spain.

In 1895, she published her first novel, *La muñeca*, which included a prologue by her compatriot **Manuel Zeno Gandía**. She followed this work with the novels *La familia Robredo* (1907) and *Marqués y Marquesa* (1911). In 1915, she published two volumes on the lives of celebrated and famous women from Europe and the Americas: *La mujer en la historia* and *La mujer en el arte*. Throughout the first decade of the twentieth century, she traveled to Africa and Holland, where she studied Russian and Arabic. In 1920, she published *Cantigas de amor*, translations into Spanish of Arabic poems. She also published *Antología de poetas orientales*, which she cotranslated with a Russian friend, Nikolai Goncheff; the anthology, one of the first of its type in Spanish, included works by Persian, Chinese, Japanese, and Afghan writers.

Her *La mujer moderna* (1924) was an early feminist document that promoted education for all women. Her biography *Los amores de Chopin* (1926), proved very popular. She followed this successful attempt with several other biographies, including *María Antonieta* (1929), *Santa Teresa* (1933), and *Wolfgan Amadeus Mozart* (1936). She then wrote four novels—*Desilusión* (1926), *Teresa y María* (1927), *Las veleidades de Consuelo* (1930), and *El asombroso doctor Jover* (1930). These novels were of a sentimental nature, with characters, settings, and dialogues realistically drawn.

In 1933, she published the anthology, *Antología de poetas occidentales* (1933), her translations of poems written in English, French, German, and Russian. When she passed away in Barcelona, she left boxes of unpublished novels and biographies. Critic Rivera de Álvarez, in *La gran enciclopedia de Puerto Rico* (1981), describes Eulate Sanjurjo's talent as "responding to her extensive intellectual foundation, founded on fine aesthetics sensibilities, which were enriched by musical training, knowledge of foreign languages, and her wide readings"(80).

Further Reading

Rivera de Álvarez, Josefina. "La novela puertorriqueña desde sus orígenes." In *La gran enciclopedia de Puerto Rico*. Vol. 5. Edited By Vicente Báez, 8, 80. San Juan: Puerto Rico en la Mano and La Gran Enciclopedia de Puerto Rico, 1981.

—*D. H. Figueredo*

Exile Literature

———————————————■———————————————

This is a body of creative work written by writers who have been exiled or have left their respective native countries due to political reasons. A difference between emigration and exile is that in general the first process might allow for departure preparations, including taking some funds from one country to another, whereas exile might occur suddenly or the would-be exiled might not be allowed by the government to take either money or personal documents out of the country. Once safely abroad, however, writers have used literature to expose to the world the abuses committed either by dictators or political regimes at home. While addressing topics of assimilation and some of the themes dominant in **immigrant literature**—such as the tribulations of immigration, exploitation, and discrimination—writers in exile see their responsibility as combating through literature the despot leaders at home—and sometimes through participation in aggressive plots, such as was done by novelist **Jacques Stephen Alexis**, who in the 1960s participated in an invasion to overthrow Haitian dictator **François Duvalier**.

The first example of exile literature in the United States was the volume *El Laúd del Desterrado* (1858), an anthology of poems written by Cuban poets who were critical of Spanish rule on the island. During the nineteenth century, the best-known exiled writer was the Cuban poet **José Martí**, who dedicated his life to Cuba's independence and whose poems criticized colonialism. In the twentieth century, the Puerto Rican **José Luis González** served as example of the writer in exile. Opposing American presence in Puerto Rico and the creation of the Commonwealth State on the island, advocated by governor and writer **Luis Muñoz Marín**, González lived in exile in Mexico. The majority of his short stories and essays condemned the United States for taking over Puerto Rico after the Spanish-Cuban-American War of 1898. The Dominican poet and politician, **Juan Bosch,** fought against the dictatorship of Rafael Leónidas Trujillo (1891–1961) while in exile in Cuba during the 1940s and 1950s.

Haitian writers throughout the nineteenth and twentieth centuries have sought exile in Europe and in Latin America. One of the first histories of that nation, *Etudes sur l'histoire d'Haïti*, was written in Paris in 1847 by **Beaubrun Ardouin**, whose brother had been executed by President Faustin Éli Soulouque (1782–1867). Similarly, in 1848 his compatriot **Emeric Bergeaud** wrote the first Haitian novel, *Stella,* while in exile in St. Thomas. During the 1950s and 1960s, several Haitian poets who opposed Duvalier achieved international recognition while living abroad: **René Depestre**, who settled in Cuba after the triumph of **Fidel Castro**'s revolution in 1959, and **Paul Laraque** are probably two of the best known writers of that generation. Laraque penned a poem entitled "Exile is Stale Bread" (2004), in which he says:

> exile is bitter coffee
> curdled milk
> a rotten avocado
> a mango full of worms.

Writing in Canada in the 1980s, novelist **Dany Laferrière** published *Le goût des jeunes filles* (1992), his depiction of the Duvalier dictatorship. In the United States, the most famous Haitian writer is **Edwidge Danticat**, whose novels have explored the corruptive and persuasive power of dictatorial regimes.

Exile from the Anglophone Caribbean was often not the result of governmental action but rather a matter of choice for those individuals who elected self-exile to protest colonialism and racism in the English-speaking islands. **Una Marson** was the first writer from Jamaica to spend years in Great Britain, during the 1930s and 1940s, where she criticized lack of culture in Jamaica and colonialism while also attempting to make Caribbean writers famous in Europe through her participation in conferences and radio programs. The decade of the 1950s witnessed a wave of talented writers heading for England: **Roger Mais**, who was once arrested for criticizing

British policies in Jamaica, Barbadian **Kamau Brathwaite**, and Trinidadian **Samuel Selvon**, to list a handful. The late 1960s and 1970s experienced a shift from Great Britain to Canada and the United States as well as the rising presence of women writers seeking escape from societies they deemed as male-driven and anti-feminists: **Donna Brand** and **Merle Collins** became two of the best-known writers of this generation. One of the best explorations of self-exile of Anglophone Caribbean writer is **George Lamming's** autobiography, *The Pleasures of Exile* (1960), a seminal study of the African diaspora, exile, and colonialism.

Regardless of language and origin of country, exile literature contains these characteristics: (1) exposure of human rights abuses (2) criticism of the ruling powers, (3) lashing out against individual political figures such as **Fidel Castro** and François Duvalier; and (4) promoting political and social changes. Often, exile literature may lack literary quality, since political message takes precedence over artistic intent; however, numerous works have met with critical success and wide readership beyond the writer's compatriots. Some well-known examples of exile literature are *Le nègre crucifie* (1974) by **Gérard Étienne** (critical of the Duvalier regime); *Angel* (1987) by Merle Collins (about the American invasion of Grenada); *Antes que anochesca* (1990) by **Reinaldo Arenas** (an anti-Castro memoir); and *In The Time of the Butterflies* (1994) by **Julia Alvarez** (an anti-Trujillo novel). *See also* Anti-Castro Literature; Trujillo Era.

Further Reading

Bevan, David, ed. *Literature and Exile*. Amsterdam, Atlanta: Rodopi, 1990.

Glad, John. *Literature in Exile*. Durham, NC: Duke University Press, 1990.

Hernández-Miyares, Julio E., ed. *Narrativa y Libertad: Cuentos cubanos de la Diáspora*. 2 Vols. Miami, Florida: Ediciones Universal, 1996.

—D. H. Figueredo

F

Fanon, Frantz (1925–61)

The best-known intellectual from Martinique and regarded as the voice of the third world, Fanon was a political essayist and philosopher who, after leaving his homeland, became an Algerian citizen and joined that country's war of independence from France during the 1950s. Though in his first book, *Peau noire, masques blancs* (1952), he explained that his theories on race, psychology, and racism applied only to the Caribbean, his observations have been generally accepted, and also criticized, the world over. Fanon was a practicing psychiatrist.

The son of a prosperous family, Fanon was born in Fort-de-France, Martinique, on July 20, 1925. He was as equally inclined to sports, soccer specifically, as to spending hours reading at the school library. He studied at the Lycée Schoelcher under **Aimé Césaire**, one of the founders of the **Négritude**, the black consciousness movement. It was Césaire who first made Fanon realize that it was good to be black. Fanon's awareness of his blackness increased during World War II, when he served with the Free French Army and experienced discrimination. At the end of the war, Fanon returned to Martinique and campaigned for Césaire in the mayoral race of Fort-de-France.

In 1946, Fanon traveled to France to study medicine at the University of Lyon. Choosing psychiatry, he noticed while interning that French psychiatrists treated Arab patients with disdain, belittling their humanity and dismissing their illnesses. The result was the article "Le Syndrom nord africain," which he published in the journal *Esprit* in 1952. That same year, his most influential book, *Peau noire, masques blancs*, came out. The fundamental premise was that whites dehumanized blacks and deemed them inferior and that blacks accepted this notion, concluding that to be successful a person had to be white. In the volume, Fanon attacked the novelist **Mayotte Capécia** for writing a novel, *Je suis Martiniquaise* (1948), in which the black protagonist sees social and racial advance only through a marriage to a white man, an act that not only denies her blackness but presents it as inferior to the white race. Though the argument appealed to his initial readers, years later, feminist scholars took issues with Fanon, especially when in the same book he criticized a black author who marries a white woman but excuses his action by saying that the black author was suffering from mental problems.

In 1953, Fanon accepted the post of psychiatrist at a hospital in Algeria. In 1954, the Algerian war broke out, and Fanon sided with the Front de Liberation Nationale. In 1957, the French authorities expelled him from Algeria, and he traveled to Tunisia, participating in clandestine operations against the French and surviving several attempts on his life. In 1959, he published his account of the Algerian conflict, *L'an v de la révolution algérienne*, and wrote a series of essays and articles that were published posthumously as *Pour la révolution africaine; écrits politiques* (1964). Some of the articles detailed how the French colonialist pitted one minority group against another and referred to the Algerian war as a riot in an attempt at discrediting the insurgents before world opinion.

In 1960, Fanon was appointed representative of the provisional Algeria government in Ghana and spoke at several conferences in Africa, seeking support for the Algeria cause. Fanon began to feel ill and fatigued: he was diagnosed with leukemia. He was treated first in the former Soviet Union and then in the United States. Fanon dictated to his wife his last book, *Les damnés de la terre*, probably his most famous work. In this book, he theorized on the nature of colonialism, saying the colonialist must possess everything and the colonized nothing and advocating the need for the colonized to use violence to bring about freedom and equality. Explains scholar Emmanuel Hansen in, *Frantz Fanon: Social and Political Thought* (1977): "Fanon argues that it is only by violence that the colonized can achieve their freedom. Violence first liberates consciousness, and second, it destroys the social and political institutions of the colonial society. It is necessary to destroy these institutions because they were set up . . . as instruments of oppression" (115–116). This was a view applauded by revolutionaries like **Fidel Castro** but criticized by such writers as Fanon's former teacher, Aimé Césaire.

Fanon died on December 6, 1961, shortly after completing *Les damnés de la terre*. Jean-Paul Sartre wrote the preface to the volume. *Les damnés de la terre* became popular throughout Latin America and Africa, regarded as the Bible of the underprivileged. Fanon's language was nonclinical, accessible, and at times poetic-as demonstrated in *Black Skin, White Masks* (1967): "the alienated, the neurotic, was my brother, my sister, my father" (225)—made him popular on American campuses. While his message of revolutionary violence might not be as acceptable today, his studies of the colonized self and the alienation created by racism still foster discussions.

Further Reading

Hansen, Emmanuel. *Frantz Fanon: Social and Political Thought*. Columbus: Ohio State University Press, 1977.

Johnston, Guillemette. "Frantz Fanon: 1925–1961." *Dictionary of Literary Biography*. *Literature Resource Center:* http://www.galenet.galegroup.com (accessed 8/31/05).

Macey, David. *Frantz Fanon: A Biography*. London: Granta Books, 2000.

—*D. H. Figueredo*

The Farming of Bones (1998)

The novel that catapulted Haitian-American author **Edwidge Danticat** to prominence as one of the most important American artists under the age of thirty, *The Farming of Bones* takes place in 1937 and depicts an event known as the "kout kouto," translated from Kreyòl (Haitian's vernacular based on French) as "stabbing," the popular term for the massacre by Dominican soldiers and paramilitaries of up to fifteen thousand Haitian guest workers. The novel tells this story in the voice of a young Haitian woman, Amabelle Desir, who since childhood has worked as a servant in the home of a wealthy Dominican family. She is planning to marry a Haitian cane worker from a nearby plantation, Sebastian Onius, when the Dominican Republic's newly installed military dictator, Rafael Leónidas Trujillo (1891–1961), orders the expulsion of all the Haitian workers. Along with thousands of other Haitians, Sebastian dies in the massacre that follows, and despite the promise of Amabelle's employers that they will protect her, she must flee. After a harrowing journey in which being black and non-Spanish-speaking leads to death, she crosses the aptly named Massacre River (named for a early-nineteenth-century massacre of Dominican soldiers by Haitian forces) to a life of safety but crushing poverty and loneliness in Haiti. The novel depicts Haiti's tortured history and its conflicts with the Dominican Republic, neighbors on the island of Hispaniola divided by race, language, experiences of colonialism, and its legacy in the global economic system.

The novel complemented a fictional account of the same incident written by Haitian novelist **Jacques Stephen Alexis** and titled *Compère Général Soleil* (1955). *The Farming of Bones* is dedicated to Alexis. *See also* Haitian Literature, History of.

Further Reading

Danticat, Edwidge. *The Farming of Bones*. New York: Soho Press, 1998.

—Lyn Miller-Lachman

Faubert, Ida (1882–1969)

A member of the group of Haitian writers associated with the influential journal *La Ronde*, Faubert, a pioneer feminist, was the first woman author in Haiti not to use a pseudonym in the pursuit of a literary career.

Born in Port-au-Prince on February 14, 1882, Ida Solomon was the only daughter of Haitian president Lysius Solomon (1815–1888). When she was six years old, her father was ousted from power by a military rebellion; the family sought exile in Paris, where the young girl attended secondary school. In 1903, she returned to Haiti, where she married Andre Faubert.

In Port-au-Prince, Ida Faubert befriended the writers and intellectuals, the likes of **Leon Laleau**, who lived in the capital and frequented literary salons. Attractive and gifted, she was soon a favorite in literary circles. She became the only woman associated with the **Géneration de la Ronde**, a group of writers who were interested in achieving artistic perfection in poetry and who published their works in the journal *La Ronde*. In 1912, she began to publish her poetry, but while her work was praised, many Haitian men could neither accept her intellect nor feel comfortable in the presence of an articulate woman. Thus, seeking personal and artistic freedom, Ida Faubert returned to Paris in 1914.

In Europe, Faubert and her husband were divorced. In her apartment she held literary salons that were frequented by Haitian writers living in Paris, including **Jean Price-Mars**, and she continued writing poetry. In 1920, editor Louis Morpeau included some of her poems in the volume *Anthologie haïtienne des poètes contemporains*; many of her poems also appeared in literary reviews in France and Italy. Her first collection, published in 1939 under the title of *Coeur des iles*, won the Prix Jacques Norman de la Societé des gens de letters. The volume consisted of melancholic poems written to honor the memory of her deceased daughter, Jacqueline; of gently erotic poems; and of poems evocative of Haiti. In 1959, Faubert published a collection of nostalgic stories about life in Haiti entitled *Sous le ciel caraibe*.

Faubert did not return to Haiti. She died in Paris in 1969. *See also* Feminism Literature in the Caribbean.

Further Reading

Charles, Christophe. *La poésie féminine haitienne: histoire et anthologie de Virginie Sampeur á nous jours*. Port-au-Prince: Editions Choucoune, 1980.

http://idafaubert.ifrance.com (accessed 9/15/05).

—Jayne R. Boisvert and D. H. Figueredo

Faubert, Pierre (1806–68)

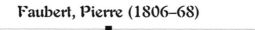

Faubert was an early Haitian poet and dramatist who wrote about the social customs and manners of his era while also essaying on patriotic themes. His works captured the hopes and conflicts of the newly independent Haiti.

Faubert was born in Cayes, Haiti, in 1806. A general in the army of the emerging republic of Haiti, he served President Jean-Pierre Boyer (1776–1850) as his personal secretary. From 1837 to 1842, he earned recognition as the director of the school the National Lyceum. Attracted to literature, he wrote a play entitled *Ogé ou le préjugé de couleur*, which was performed in 1841 and published in 1858. He also wrote a book of poetry, *Les poésies fugitives* (1856). In the 1860s, he traveled to France where he socialized with politicians and intellectuals, even finding favor with Napoleon III.

Ogé ou le préjugé de couleur was a patriotic drama with characters voicing ideals representative of colonialism and autonomy. *Les poésies fugitives* consisted of poems that explored a variety of subjects, from patriotism to lost loves. The strength of the book is apparent is such poems as "Aux Haïtiens," in which the poet expresses in lyrical language his love of Haiti.

Further Reading

Berrou, Raphaël, and Pradel Pompilus. *Histoire de la littérature haïtienne*. Tome 1. Port-au-Prince: Editions Caraëbes, 1975.

—D. H. Figueredo

Felices, Jorge (1911–)

Felices is a journalist from Puerto Rico. His only novel, *Enrique Abril, héroe* (1947) can be read as a political parable of those who trade in ideology for capitalist gains.

A native of San Juan, Felices had planned to study medicine but decided to become a journalist instead. He founded the magazines *Zig-Zag* (1933) and *Páginas* (1936). He published articles, short stories, and poems in several newspapers and reviews, including *El Mundo*, *Puerto Rico Ilustrado* and *Revista del Ateneo Puertorriqueño*.

Enrique Abril, héroe traces the progression of a university student from a youth of idealism to a middle age of comfort and political compromise. In 1989, he collected his poems into the volume *Una isla para ese grito: poemas, 1970–1987*.

Further Reading

Rivera de Álvarez, Josefina. "La novela puertorriqueña desde sus orígenes hasta el presente." In *La Gran enciclopedia de Puerto Rico*. Vol. 5. Edited by Vicente Báez, 44. San Juan: Puerto Rico en la Mano and La Gran Enciclopedia de Puerto Rico, 1981.

—D. H. Figueredo

Feliciano Mendoza, Ester (1917–87)

Feliciano Mendoza is a children's author from Puerto Rico who wrote about the island's folklore and natural beauty. She was an educator and a short story writer as well.

A native of Aguadilla, she earned a teaching degree from the Universidad de Puerto Rico in 1938. During the 1940s, she began to write children's stories and poems while raising a family. In 1945, she published her first children's book, *Nanas*, a celebration of motherhood. In 1951, she published *Arco iris*, and in 1957, *Coquí*, both tributes to the island's fauna and flora. She also published the volume *Voz de la tierra mía*, reflective essays, with a touch of sadness, about her love for her island. Matriculating at her alma mater, Feliciano Mendoza earned an MA in arts in 1959.

Throughout the 1960s, she taught at the Universidad de Puerto Rico, lectured on children's literature, and wrote poetry, winning a poetry prize from the Unión de Mujeres Americanas in 1962. She also pursued doctoral studies, earning a PhD in philosophy in 1970 from the Universidad de Puerto Rico. That same year, she published *Sinfonía de Puerto Rico*, a collection of Amerindian and Puerto Rican legends and myths. In 1979, she was invited to the Library of Congress, where she recorded some of her poetry and children's stories. In the 1980s, she began to cultivate the genre of the short story, writing realistic portrayals of Puerto Rican characters and addressing such concerns as racism and social inequality. These stories appeared in journals and textbooks.

In 1983, Feliciano Mendoza was elected Woman of the Year by the Unión de Mujeres Americanas. A middle school in Aguadilla is named in her honor. Her other works include *Nanas de Navidad* (1959), *Nanas de la adolescencia* (1963), *Cajita de música* (1968), *Ala y trineo* (1980), and *Ilán-ilán* (1985). *See also* Children's Literature in the Hispanic Caribbean.

Further Reading

Figueras, Consuelo. "Puerto Rican children's literature." *Bookbird* 38, no. 2 (2000): 23–28.

Lastra, Sarai. "Juan Bobo: A Folkloric Information System." *Urbana* 47, no. 3 (Winter 1999): 529–58.

—*D. H. Figueredo*

Feminism in Caribbean Literature

While feminism in general focuses on women's rights and women's equality to men in all arenas of life, in literature, feminist approaches concentrate on female fictional characters and female writers, and thus these works have been very important to the study of the literature of the Caribbean. Because Caribbean literature often expresses vividly the struggles of various oppressed peoples, it connects naturally to feminism, which looks at women through an historical lens and sees the extent to which women and their contributions have been marginalized. Many works of literature from the Caribbean are written by women, and many more focus on female characters. These works help to shift the focus from women as a side story in men's literature to a focus on women's own story.

A good example of Caribbean feminist literature would be **Jean Rhys's** novel *Wide Sargasso Sea* (1966), which inverts Charlotte Brontë's (1816–55) novel *Jane Eyre* (1847) to demonstrate the unique ways in which West Indian women have been bought and sold out by English men. In that work, Rhys focuses on the fictional character Bertha Rochester, the protagonist's first "crazy" Caribbean wife to explain how English values and patriarchal traditions led to Bertha's spiritual annihilation and ultimate imprisonment. More recently, Caribbean authors such as **Edwidge Danticat, Esmeralda Santiago,** and **Jamaica Kincaid** have highlighted the particular challenges of women in the Caribbean, subjugated both by geography and gender. Danticat and

Kincaid, in different ways, deal with the burdens of traditional female life as passed on from mothers to unwilling daughters. These matters are further complicated when the younger generation of women are immigrants to North America and have to try to square the American practices with traditional ones. Works by Esmeralda Santiago, **Paule Marshall**, and **Audre Lorde** address this kind of cultural and generational conflict as it applies especially to taboos and controls on women's sexuality. The stories told by these writers often involve a mother trying hard to hold onto a traditional way of life, including restrictions on women's sexual behavior, while the daughters face increasing pressure from the new environment to acculturate to the new nation, which usually means more sexual freedom. Overlaid upon these personal struggles are the political and social struggles of the women to maintain their unique Caribbean identity while understanding how they fit into the new culture. The relationships, thus, are complex. Why would women whose lives were often impoverished by European-style hierarchical notions of gender and geography impose those same visions on their daughters? The answers result in a rich literature that accounts for the true-life experiences of many women, before and during the changes brought on by the Women's Movement, in the wider context of the imperialist impositions upon the life of island people.

Other feminist writers include **Luisa Capetillo** and **Olga Nolla**, both from Puerto Rico; **Zoe Valdés** and **Aida Bahr**, from Cuba; **Julia Alvarez** and **Daisy Cocco de Filippis**, from the Dominican Republic; **Una Marson** and **Jinta "Binta" Breeze**, from Jamaica; **Maryse Condé**, Guadeloupe; **Suzanne Césaire**, Martinique; **Claire Harris**, Canada and Trinidad; **Ida Faubert** and **Yanick Lahens**, Haiti; **Zee Edgell**, from Belize. *See also* Mother-Daughter Relationships.

Further Reading

Cocco de Filippis, Daisy. *Documents of dissidence: selected writings of Dominican women.* New York: CUNY Dominican Studies Institute, 2000.

Mohammed, Patricia. *Gendered Realities: Essays in Caribbean Feminist Thought.* Barbados: University of the West Indies Press and Mona, Jamaica: Centre for Gender and Development Studies, 2002.

Showalter, Elaine, ed. *The New Feminist Criticism: Essays on Women, Literature, and Theory.* New York: Pantheon Books, 1985.

—Angela Conrad

Fernandes, Carlos M. See Lauffer, Pierre A.

Fernández, Roberto G. (1951–)

■

Roberto G. Fernández is a Cuban American writer who first began writing in Spanish and then, like the poet **Gustavo Pérez Firmat** and many other Hispanic Caribbean writers, opted to write in English. His novels detail the experiences of Cuban Americans in the Miami area, exploring such themes as assimilation, homesickness, and racism.

Born in Havana, Cuba, on September 24, 1951, Roberto G. Fernández and his parents left for the United States in 1961. Living near Miami, Fernández grew up surrounded by Cubans who longed to return to the island while building a new life in the United States. Fernández witnessed the Cubanization of Miami as the exiles opened up businesses in the city's southwest, established cultural centers that bore the names of Cuban towns and provinces, and became involved in anti-Castro activities. But Fernández also noticed how his compatriots maintained a sense of humor and viewed their prospects in the United States with a sense of optimism. When he was in his mid-twenties and in graduate school, Fernández began to write short stories about his compatriots and their lives in the Miami area.

Fernández earned a BA and a master's in Spanish from Florida Atlantic University. In 1977, he received a PhD in Spanish from Florida State University. In 1975, he published the collection of short stories *Cuentos sin rumbos*; this was followed by *El jardín de la luna* in 1976. In 1981, he wrote the novel *La vida es un especial*; four years later he wrote *La montaña rusa*. These short stories and novels used the Cuban vernacular, poked fun at the extreme anti-Castro views held by some of the exiles, and explored Cubans' and Americans' misconceptions of each other.

The books received favorable reviews in the Spanish press, but eager to reach a wider audience, Fernández decided to write in English and to find a publisher that could distribute his books in the American market. In 1988, he published his first novel in English, *Raining Backwards*. This was followed in 1995 by *Holy Radishes*. These two novels essayed the same themes as in his previous works. What was missing, however, was the linguistic playfulness he had used when writing in Spanish. Yet, he still created credible characters that were as eccentric and lovable as the Cubans he had met in Miami: the former tycoon turned day-laborer who remembers the wealth he left behind in Cuba; the guerrilla organizer conducting military drills in the Everglades; and the cook who became a millionaire baking guava pastries.

Fernández has been influenced by the writers of the **Latin American Boom**, who in the 1960s attempted to devise new ways of writing novels, like his compatriot **Guillermo Cabrera Infante**, who told stories without discernable plots and toyed with the Spanish language. Fernandez's novels use diverse view points to tell a story, employ multiple characters, and offer no clearly chronology of events. The novels, however, do render tribute to the struggles and successes of the Cuban community in Florida. *See also* Cuban American Literature.

Further Reading

Rivero Marín, Rosanna. *Janus Identities and Forked Tongues: Two Caribbean Writers in the United States*. New York: P. Lang, 2004.

—*D. H. Figueredo*

Fernández de Juan, Adelaida (1961–)

A Cuban short-story writer, Adelaida Fernández de Juan belongs to a generation of Cuban women writers who matured during the period of economic hardships known as the "Special Period," faced by Cuba in the 1990s. As a writer she explores the role of women within Cuba's revolutionary society.

Fernández de Juan was born in Havana in 1961. She attended medical school at the Universidad de la Habana and upon graduation volunteered for medical service in Africa. She worked in Zambia from 1988 to 1990. Returning to Cuba, she wrote a collection of short stories that dealt with her experiences in Africa. Entitled *Dolly y otros cuentos africanos*, the volume was published in 1994 and was quickly translated into English and published in Canada. In 1996, she won the **Cecilia Valdés** literary award for her second collection of stories *Clemencia bajo el sol*. Two years later, she was awarded a literary prize by the **Unión de Escritores y Artistas de Cuba** for her third book, *Oh Vida*.

Fernández de Juan writes stories that address Cuban issues confronted by Cuban women: sexual equality on the island, the double roles of Cuban women as revolutionaries and as mothers, and the daily difficulties encountered on the island as a result of economic hardship. Her narrative, usually written in the first person, is contemplative and filled with subtleties that hint at tabooed subjects: the sexual tensions between mother and son, brother and sister. A major preoccupation is the sense of the missing Cubans, those who left for the United States. She exposes, according to critic Olga Marta Pérez in *Mujeres como islas* (2002), the "deep . . . drama: the forsakenness, the absence" of family separation as a result of the Cuban Revolution (11). Fernández de Juan's stories have been translated into French, German, Hebrew, and Italian. In 2005, she received the **Alejo Carpentier** Short Story award for her writings. *See also* Feminism in Caribbean Literature.

Further Reading

Berg, Mary G. *Open Your Eyes and Soar: Cuban Women Writing Now*. Buffalo, New York: White Pine Press, 2003.

—*D. H. Figueredo*

Fernández Méndez, Eugenio (1924–94)

A major contributor to the study of the appreciation of Puerto Rican culture and history, Fernández Méndez was a writer, a historian, and an anthropologist. He often wrote for the popular media.

Born in Cayey, Puerto Rico, on July 11, 1924, Fernández Méndez obtained his PhD in anthropology from Columbia University while in his mid-twenties and soon afterward began to teach at the Universidad de Puerto Rico. Ten years later, he was appointed coordinator of the Department of Social Sciences as well as editorial director of the university press, Editorial Universitaria. A patriotic and social concern served as the backbone of his academic work: a preoccupation with a Puerto Rican identity and the national development of a culture. Such are the themes of many of the volumes he wrote in the 1950s, some of which include *Filiación y sentido de una isla* (1951), *Unidad y esencia del ethos puertorriqueño* (1954), and *La identidad de la cultura* (1959).

In the 1960s, Fernández Méndez also wrote texts in English, exploring both the history and anthropology of the island, *Puerto Rico: Sources on Puerto Rican Cultural History, a Critical Appraisal* (1967), and *Art and Mythology of the Taíno Indians of the Greater West Indies* (1972). He often wrote for such major newspapers as *El Mundo*, inviting his compatriots to create a Puerto Rican civilization.

A lecturer, he presented numerous conferences on the island. In his writings and speeches, there was always a sense of urgency, and excitement, at appreciating Puerto Rican culture. He was an expert on Haitian art and wrote on Puerto Rican literature as well, *Salvador Brau y su tiempo* (1958). His two collections of his own poetry, *Tras siglo* (1958) and *Poesía viva: nuevo cuaderno (1939–1991)*, were published two years before his death in 1994.

Further Reading

Duany, Jorge. "Imagining the Puerto Rican nation: Recent works on cultural identity." *Latin American Research Review* 31, no. 3 (1996): 248–68.

Toro-Sugrañes, José A. "Geografía, historia y cultura." In *Nueva enciclopedia de Puerto Rico*. Tomo 4. Hato Rey, Puerto Rico: Editorial Lector, 1994.

—*D. H. Figueredo*

Fernández Retamar, Roberto (1930–)

A Cuban poet and intellectual who is best known for his essays on the legacy of colonialism and his criticism of the United States' policies toward Cuba and Latin America. In 1950, Fernández Retamar published his first book of poetry; entitled *Elegía como un himno*, the poems examined the nature of the creative process and the loneliness experienced and cultivated by poets. In the 1960s, his poems shifted away from the personal to the political, focusing particularly on the accomplishments of the Cuban Revolution. A notable work from this period is *Revolución nuestra, amor nuestro*, published in 1976.

In 1971, Fernández Retamar wrote the essay "Calibán," published in the journal *Casa de las Américas*, where in a scholarly tone, and with a bit of sarcasm, he deplored how colonial powers, such as Spain and England in the seventeenth and eighteenth centuries, stifled Latin America's cultures, glorifying anything that was European and caucasian and dismissing that which was colored and not from Europe. The direct tone used by Fernández Retamar, who accused certain Latin

American writers of being imperialists and puppets of the American government, prompted authors, such as **Reynaldo Arenas** and **Guillermo Cabrera Infante,** to accuse the Cuban intellectual of serving as **Fidel Castro's** mouthpiece.

Aside from writing, Fernández Retamar has taught at Yale University and the University of Havana and has served as editor of the prestigious literary journal *Casa de las Américas.* His works have been translated into numerous languages, including English and Russian. For many liberals, Fernández Retamar is a shining example of a practitioner of politically committed literature, **la literatura comprometida.** *See also* Casa de las Américas; Castro, Fidel.

Further Reading

Fernández Retamar, Roberto. *Caliban and Other Essays.* Translated by Edward Baker. Minneapolis: University of Minnesota Press, 1989.

Sklodowska, Elzbieta, and Ben A. Heller. *Roberto Fernández Retamar y los estudios latinoamericanos.* Pittsburgh: Instituto Internacional de Literatura Iberoamericana, Universidad de Pittsburgh, 2000.

— *D. H. Figueredo*

Fernández Spencer, Antonio (1922–95)

∎

A poet, essayist, diplomat, and library administrator from the Dominican Republic, Fernández Spencer was a member of the **Poesía Sorprendida** movement, created in 1943, which challenged **costumbrismo**—regional writing or writing of local color— and traditional and realistic poetry, emphasizing universal themes. His poetry revealed a preoccupation with the brevity of life, expressed elegantly and filled with allusions to universal literature.

He was born in Santo Domingo on June 22, 1922. While studying philosophy at the Universidad de Santo Domingo, he befriended the members of the Poesía Sorpredida movement, which included poets **Freddy Gatón Arce** and **Franklin Mieses Burgos,** and published his first book of poetry, *Vendaval interior* (1944). In 1945, he earned a PhD in philosophy from the University of Salamanca, Spain. He remained in Spain for six years and he founded Tertulia Hispanoamericana, a cultural organization where literary salons were held to discuss Latin American literature. In Madrid, he wrote *Bajo la luz del día* (1952). A year later, he published *Nueva poesía dominicana,* an anthology of works by Dominican writers.

He spent the 1950s and early 1960s pursuing a career in education and in the diplomatic corps. He was vice secretary of the Ministry of Education, a professor at Universidad Nacional **Pedro Henríquez Ureña,** and ambassador in several Latin American nations, including Uruguay. In the 1960s, he founded a publishing house, Colección Arquero, and published several books of criticism, including *A orillas del filosofar* (1960), *Ensayos literarios* (1960), and *Caminando por la literatura hispánica* (1964). These studies explored the Hispanic roots of Latin American literature.

Throughout the 1970s, he was active in cultural activities with the Academia Dominicana de la Lengua and was a representative of Real Academia Española. The 1980s saw his return to poetry: *El regreso de Ulises* (1985), *Obras poéticas* (1986), and *Poemas sin misterio* (1988). In 1988, he was appointed director of the National Library of the Dominican Republic, a post he held until his retirement in 1991. *See also* Tertulia/Cénacle/Literary Salon/Soirée.

Further Reading

Brown, Isabel Zakrzewski. *Culture and Customs of the Dominican Republic.* Westport, CT: Greenwood Press, 1999.

"Galería de directores BNPHU." http://www.bnrd.gov.do/gdirectores.htm (accessed 8/31/05).

—*D. H. Figueredo*

Ferré, Rosario (1938–)

Feminist and controversial Puerto Rican writer whose novels and short stories, written and published in both English and in Spanish, are widely read in Latin America and in the United States, Rosario Ferré has used her position within the island's aristocracy to criticize the treatment of Puerto Rican women of all economic levels and to question the island's politics from both a leftist and a conservative perspective. Her father, Luis A. Ferré (1904–2003), was Puerto Rico's governor from 1968 to 1972, her aunt Sor Isolina Ferré (1914–2000), a Catholic nun, was a prominent social worker and activist for the poor, and her cousin Maurice Ferré (1935), was elected mayor of Miami, Florida, during the 1980s.

Feminist Puerto Rican author Rosario Ferré has achieved international recognition with novels that condemn the male-driven culture of Latin America. *Source: Americas Society. Courtesy of Elsa M. Ruiz.*

Rosario Ferré was born on September 28, 1938, in Ponce, Puerto Rico. Her introduction to the pleasures of reading and writing came through her nanny, who was only ten years older than the young Rosario and who loved to read. Together they would find a secluded spot where they would read out loud to each other; the fairy tales and adventure stories that Ferré heard prompted her to create her own stories. Her second thrust into writing came after her divorce in the 1970s from her well-to-do husband and the realization that she needed to affirm her own independence. She believed she could accomplish this through writing.

In 1976, she wrote a short story based on a true incident in which a beautiful cousin of hers was used as an artifact by a husband who abused her and cloistered her away so that he could pursue a life of drink and women. The short story was entitled "La muñeca menor" and it was an instant success. Translated into English as "The youngest doll" (1986), the piece explored Ferré's dominant theme: that of women as objects of pleasure who are good enough for bedroom antics but deemed inferior for full participation in society. In 1980, Ferré published a collection of essays, *Sitio a Eros*, on women writers, focusing primarily on the literary silence assigned to them by male critics, a theme that later on became popular with Caribbean feminist scholars, such as **Daisy Cocco de Filippis**.

In 1995, Ferré opted to write a novel in English, *The House on the Lagoon*, an epic about a wealthy family whose storyline parallels the island's history. The novel, which was published in Spanish the following year, contrasted the telling of the narrative from a woman's and a man's perspective through the changes each individual makes on a dairy chronicling the family's history. Highly successful and reviewed in the major media in the United States and the Spanish-speaking world, the novel established Ferré as a writer of international recognition. She followed this work with two other novels, *Eccentric Neighborhoods* (1998) and *Flight of the Swan* (2001), both written in English and equally well received; for example, *Eccentric Neighborhoods* was a National Book Award finalist.

Ferré's literary career has been by followed by controversies. Her criticism of women's treatment at the hands of Puerto Rican men, regardless of social and economic background, was seen as disrespectful by the aristocracy. Her initial support of independence from the United States disappointed her father and his friends, all of whom supported statehood. Then, her switch to a pro-statehood stance in the 1990s upset the island's intellectuals and liberals, who viewed her as a traitor. Even her decision to write in English prompted accusations that she was selling out to American publishers because they paid more than their Spanish counterparts. Her answer to these criticisms affirms her independence: "When people begin to me tell what to do, I always do the opposite," she told a reporter from *El Diario La Prensa* in June 2002.

Her other works include *Papeles de Pandora* (1976), *Los cuentos de Juan Bobo* (1981), *El árbol y sus sombras* (1989), *El coloquio de las perras* (1990), *La batalla de las vírgenes* (1993), *A la sombra de tu nombre* (2001), and *Language duel— Duelo de lenguaje* (2002). *See also* Feminism in Caribbean Literature; Hispanic Caribbean Literature, History of; Puerto Rican Literature, History of.

Further Reading

Henao, Eda B. *The Colonial Subject's Search for Nation, Culture, and Identity in The Works of Julia Alvarez, Rosario Ferré, and Ana Lydia Vega*. Lewiston, NY: E. Mellen Press, 2003.

Hintz, Suzanne S. *Rosario Ferré: A Search for Identity*. New York: Lang, 1995.

Sachis, Eva. "Rosario Ferré: El duelo de una puertorriqueña dual." *El Diario La Prensa*, June 9, 2002.

—*D. H. Figueredo*

Ferrer Canales, José (1913–)

Ferrer is a Puerto Rican essayist and educator. Using a Pan-Caribbean perspective, he devoted his life to the study of Caribbean culture and language. He also wrote numerous articles on such important Puerto Rican figures as **Eugenio María Hostos** and Pedro Albizu Campos (1893–1965).

A native of San Juan, Ferrer Canales earned both a BA and an MA in literature from the Universidad de Puerto Rico when he was in his mid-twenties. He matriculated at the Universidad Nacional Autónoma de México where he was awarded a PhD in philosophy and literature. When he was twenty-six years old, he published his first collection of essays, *Marginalia*. Two years later, his study of language, culture, and politics was published as *Por nuestra lengua y nuestra soberanía*.

Through the 1940s and 1950s, Ferrer Canales taught at numerous universities, including Dillard, Howard University, and City University of New York. In the 1960s, he promoted Caribbean culture and identity in the volumes, *Hora de Puerto Rico* (1961), *Imagen de Varona* (1962), and *Regionalism and Universitality* (1965). In works such as *Acentos cívicos, Martí, Puerto Rico y otros temas* (1972), *Martí y Hostos* (1990), and *Hostos y Giner* (1997), he explored the political philosophies of the Puerto Rican Hostos and Cuban poet **José Martí**.

Further Reading

Enciclopedia puertorriqueña. siglo XXI. Vol. 3. Santurce, Puerto Rico: Caribe Grolier, 1998.

—*D. H. Figueredo*

Fiallo, Fabio (1866–1942)

Erotic and love poet, Fiallo, who was something of a Casanova, is one of the Dominican Republic's most popular poets. He was a diplomat and served in numerous governmental posts.

Fiallo was born on February 3, 1866, in Santo Domingo, Dominican Republic. He attended elementary and secondary schools in Santo Domingo and then matriculated at the Instituto Profesional with the objective of becoming an attorney. His political work and dedication to literature took much of his time, and so he did not complete his legal studies. He worked as a journalist, founding several newspaper and magazines, including *El Hogar* (1894), *La Bandera Libre* (1899), *La Campana* (1905), and *Las Noticias* (1920). He was a contributor to the influential periodicals *Listín Diario* and *El Lápiz*.

Fiallo befriended the Nicaragua poet Rubén Darío (1867–1916) but preferred the poetry of the Spaniard Gustavo Adolfo Bequer (1836–70), whose love poems influenced Fiallo's writing. In 1902, Fiallo published his first book of poetry, *Primavera sentimental*, and in 1908, he published a collection of short stories,

Cuentos frágiles. Of the two volumes, the first became more popular: readers were attracted to his descriptive poems about beautiful women and to his polite eroticism.

In between the publication of these two volumes, Fiallo served as consul in Havana in 1905. He was then appointed consul to New York City in 1905 and to Hamburg in 1910. Three years later, he served as the governor of Santo Domingo. During this period, he wrote the book of poetry, *Canciones de la tarde* (1910).

When American forces occupied the Dominican Republic in 1916, Fiallo opposed the intervention and was sent to prison in 1920. He wrote a series of patriotic poems that were published in 1924 under the title of *Canto a la bandera.* Though he wrote a treatise on political consciousness in the Dominican Republic, *Mensaje a las asociaciones independientes de jovenes de la República Dominicana* (1922), and a second collection of short stories, *La manzana de Mefisto* (1934), his preference was for love poetry. His poems were so popular that it was common for young men to memorize verses when courting their sweethearts.

Fiallo passed away in Cuba on August 28, 1942. He was buried on that island, but in 1977 his body was exhumed and returned to the Dominican Republic.

Further Reading

Cabral, Manuel del. *10 poetas dominicanos: tres poetas con vida y siete desenterrados.* República Dominicana: Publicaciones América, S.A., 1980.

"Fiabo Fiallo." http://www.escritoresdominicanos.com (accessed 8/31/05).

—*D. H. Figueredo*

Fignolé, Jean-Claude (1941–)

Haitian writer and intellectual, Fignolé is the founder, with writers and compatriots Frankétienne and **Rene Philoctète,** of the experimental **Spiralist Movement,** which maintained that artistic patterns emerge from apparently random forms and that literature extends beyond social realism and nationalistic expressions. Fignolé is a novelist, an art critic, and a businessman.

Fignolé was born on May 24, 1941, in Jérémie, Haiti. A lawyer and agronomist, he worked as an art critic in the 1970s and was a journalist for the publication *Petit samedi soir.* During this decade, he published a series of literary criticism that brought him national attention: *Etzer Vilaire, ce méconnu* (1970), *Pour une poesie de l'authentique et du solidaire* (1971), *Sur Gouverneurs de la rosée: hypothèses de travail dans une perspective spiraliste* (1974), and *Voeu de voyage et intention romanesque* (1978).

Influenced by Marxism and the works of the Colombian author Gabriel García Márquez (1927–), Fignolé, with Rene Philoctète and Frankétienne, beginning in the 1950s and through the 1970s, developed the concept of "Spiralisme," or Spiralist Movement, which they defined as a dialectical process of the spirit that carries the thinker beyond rigid political, artistic or social structures, a semantic without substance that participates in the subversion of current hierarchies. His *Les*

Possédés de la pleine lune (1987) and *Aube tranquille* (1990) were written in the Spiralist mode.

While writing novels, articles, lecturing on literature in Haiti and throughout the Caribbean, Fignolé worked in the town of Les Abricots dans la Grande Anse, helping its residents to build roads and introducing new agricultural methods. During the 1990s, he promoted the Gulf of Gonâve as a tourist area and established a small boating company that serviced foreign hotels and resorts. He also founded and directed the school College **Jean Price-Mars**. His other works include *Hofuku* (1993), *La dernière goutte d'homme* (1999), and *Moi, Toussaint Louverture . . . avec la plume complice de l'auteur* (2004). His writings have been translated into Italian and Spanish.

Further Reading

Large, Josaphat-Robert. "Jean Claude Fignolé." http://www.lehman.cuny.edu/ile.en.ile/paroles/fignole.html (accessed 4/18/05).

—*D. H. Figueredo*

Figueroa, John Joseph Maria (1920–99)

∎

A Jamaican poet who celebrated the diverse ethnic heritage and traditions that formed Caribbean society, John Figueroa was an educator, a promoter of Caribbean literature, and a scholar. He was the editor of the first major multivolume anthology of Anglophone Caribbean poetry, *Caribbean Voices* published between 1996 and 1971.

John Figueroa was born on August 4, 1920, in Kingston, Jamaica. His ancestors came from Panama, when it was part of Colombia, and from Cuba. As a child, he was exposed to the Spanish language and read widely in English, from Thackeray to Tennyson to Eliot. After graduating from high school in Jamaica, Figueroa attended Holy Cross College in Massachusetts. In 1946, he studied at the University of London, earning a graduate degree in education. While in London, he worked for the BBC as a reader for the legendary radio program **Caribbean Voices**. In 1960, he conducted postgraduate work at the University of Indiana–Bloomington.

Figueroa traveled extensively throughout Africa, Europe and the Caribbean. He taught at numerous universities—in Great Britain, Jamaica, Nigeria, and Puerto Rico—and lamented that his need to work for a living limited his output as a poet. Nevertheless, Figueroa published five books of poetry—*Blue Mountain Peak* (1944), *Love Leaps Here* (1962), *Ignoring Hurts: Poems* (1976), *The Chase 1941–1989* (1991), and *The Project* (1996)—and edited and coedited several anthologies and references sources, including *Caribbean Writers: A Bio-Bibliographical Critical Encyclopedia* (1979), and wrote numerous pedagogical studies. Like many writers in the Caribbean, Figueroa self-published his first two book of poetry. By the late 1960s, however, his poetry readings and contacts in academia introduced him to major publishing houses, such as Three Continents Press, that paid for and promoted his work.

Figueroa was influenced by European literature—he read Federico García Lorca (1898–1936), from Spain, and the Frenchman Paul Valery (1871–1945), to name but two. He wrote sonnets and verses in standard English, for example "At Home the Green Remains" (1948):

> New England's hills are flattened as crimson-lake
> And purple columns, all that now remain
> Of trees, stand forward as hillocks do rain,
> And up the hillside ruined temples make.

But like his contemporary **Louise Bennet,** he also used Jamaican dialect: "Mek I advise yu boy / If yu trouble white people toy. . . ." He was inspired by religious themes—he was a devout Catholic—the Caribbean landscapes, especially the Blue Mountains of Jamaica, and classical literature.

John Figueroa was of the generation of Jamaican poets who achieved maturity after independence. His radio performances, the anthologies he edited, and his travels throughout the world made him a promoter of the emerging Anglophone Caribbean literature. Of dual citizenship, Jamaican and British, he was living in England at the time of his death on March 5, 1999; he was buried in England.

Further Reading

Mordecai, Pamela. "John Joseph Maria Figueroa." In *Fifty Caribbean Writers: A Bio-Bibliographical Critical Sourcebook*, edited by Daryl Cumber Dance, 178–86. Westport, CT: Greenwood Press, 1986.

—*D. H. Figueredo*

Figueroa Berríos, Edwin (1925–)

Figueroa Berrios is an award-winning Puerto Rican short-story writer. He is known for capturing in his stories the nuances of the Puerto Rican vernacular and expressions.

A native of Guayama, Figueroa Berrios's mother, who was a teacher, introduced him to reading and literature when he was a young child. Closely bonded with his maternal grandmother, he often listened to her anecdotes and the stories her friends shared with her. Expressing an interest in theater and acting, he attended the Universidad de Puerto Rico during the 1940s, earning a BA and an MA in art from the same school. While studying, he performed on radio dramas and was also a radio announcer. After working as a researcher for the Council on Education, he began to teach at his alma mater in 1955.

His short stories were published in local newspapers and received numerous awards through the 1950s from such institutions as the **Ateneo Puertorriqueño.**

Some of these stories he gathered for the volume *Sobre este suelo* (1962). These stories reflect his interested in linguistics and Puerto Rican folklore. In 1978, he published *Seis veces la muerte*, where in stories such as "La vida comienza a los doce años" he examines the fragile bridge between childhood and adolescence. Critic **Luis de Arrigoitia**, in the preface to the second edition of *Sobre este suelo*, described Figueroa as a writer who "knows the succinct details of the short story genre and takes advantage of the least connotation of a word . . . [also] his stories carry the lyricism of the popular vernacular . . . [expressing a] love for the regional." In 1999, he published *Cuentos de todos los tiempos y una crónica de guerra*, stories exploring the conflict between the lifestyle and traditions of farmers in Puerto Rico against growing urbanization on the island.

Further Reading

Arrigoitia, Luis de. Preface. *Sobre este suelo*, by Edwin Figueroa. Río Piedras, Puerto Rico: Editorial Cultural, 1973.

—*D. H. Figueredo*

Filoktèt, Rene. See Philoctète, René.

Firmin, Anténor (1850–1911)

One of Haiti's most influential thinkers, Firmin was probably the first black anthropologist and a pioneer in challenging the concept of race as scientific. He was also one of the earliest proponents of Pan-Caribbeanism.

Firmin was born on October 18, 1850, in Cap-Haïtien. After attending elementary school in his hometown, he was then tutored by a retired French professor who had taught at École Normale Supérieure de Paris. Firmin taught school for nearly five years before accepting a post at the customs house and then at a private business, Stapehorst et Cie. While working, he studied at a small private college called Nelson Desroches; there, he mastered his knowledge of French, Latin, and Greek.

Highly intellectual and attracted to writing, in 1873 he found the journal *Le Messager de Nord*, contributing essays that expressed his liberal ideas. In 1883, President Lysius Salomon (1815–88) appointed him the country's representative at the celebrations of Simón Bolívar's (1783–1830) centennial in Caracas, Venezuela. From Caracas, Firmin traveled to St. Thomas and later on to Paris. In France, he joined the Anthropological Society.

Participation in that society proved a turning point in Firmin's life. For he learned how readily Europeans accepted the scientific theories expressed by Count Arthur de Gobineau (1816–82) who in his book *Essai sur l'ingaliti des races humaines* (1853–55) asserted that blacks were inferior and primitive while whites were members of a superior race. Firmin countered the racist argument with a brilliant 650-page treatise entitled *De l'egalite des races humaines* (1885), in which he denounced racial superiority as unscientific and reflective of a colonialist mentality. His scholarly approach in this volume contributed to the birth of modern anthropology.

Firmin returned to Haiti in 1889, and the new president, Florvil Hippolyte (1827–96), welcomed him with the post of Minister of Foreign Affairs. Firmin successfully opposed the establishment of an American naval base in Haiti, but sensing that the president's desire to industrialize the nation and to please the United States would result in an increasing American presence, Firmin resigned his post and went back to Paris in 1891. In France, he wrote three books: *Haïti et la France* (1891), *Haïti au point de vue administrative, politique et économique* (1891), and *Une défense* (1892).

During the next two decades, Firmin sailed back and forth between Haiti and France. He was often involved in political activities and in 1902 presented himself as presidential candidate but lost the bid. Concerned over potential political chaos, he wrote, in 1908, *M. Roosevelt, président des Etats-Unis et la République d'Haïti* where he foresaw America's military intervention—it actually occurred seven years later. In 1910, he wrote *Lettres de Saint-Thomas*, wherein, according to scholar J. Michael Nash in "Nineteenth-Century Haiti and the Archipelago of the Americas: Antenor Firmin's Letters from St. Thomas," Firmin proposed new ways of looking at nationhood and the racial and political nature of the Caribbean, advocating for Pan-Caribbeanism.

It was on the island of St. Thomas where Firmin passed away. His early work as an anthropologist has yet to be fully recognized, and most of his writings have not been translated into English. *See also* Haitian Literature, History of.

Further Reading

Berrou, Raphaël, and Pradel Pompilus. *Histoire de la littérature haitienne*. Tome 1. Port-au Prince, Haiti: Editions Caraïbes, 1975.

Dash, J. Michael. "Nineteenth-Century Haiti and the Archipelago of the Americas: Antenor Firmin's Letters from St. Thomas" *Research in African Literatures* 35, no. 2 (Summer 2004): 44–54.

—*D. H. Figueredo*

Flanagan, Brenda (1946–)

Flanagan is a novelist and short-story writer from Trinidad. Her dialogue captures the musicality and energy of Caribbean diction and lexicon.

Brenda Flanagan was born on December 6, 1946, in Trinidad into a large family. As a child, she loved to listen to the voices of the women around her. When she was ten years old, she started to write poetry. By the age of thirteen, she was writing and singing her own calypsos. She worked at a factory to help her family and then became a trainee reporter for the newspaper *The Nation* from 1965 to 1967.

In 1967, she left Trinidad for the United States, where initially she worked as a servant and then at a variety of jobs, from sales consultant for a furniture company to a clerk with Pepsi Cola. She was twice married to husbands who appreciated her energy and enthusiasm but who nevertheless attempted to silence her creative energy. She had three children, whom she raised as a single mother while attending the University of Michigan. She graduated with distinctions in 1977. A year later, she earned an MA in education technology and journalism, and, in 1986, she obtained a PhD, both from the University of Michigan.

Flanagan taught at several schools, from preparatory schools to community colleges until settling in the 1990s at Davidson College, where she teaches Creative Writing and African and Caribbean Literature. In 1994, she was a visiting professor at the University of Hawaii.

The first African American-Caribbean writer and cultural ambassador to Kazakhstan and Turkmenistan, Brenda Flanagan celebrates Caribbean culture and the zest for life in her writings and teachings. *Courtesy of Brenda Flanagan.*

During the 1980s, she published short stories in numerous journals, including *Calalloo, Journal of Caribbean Studies*, and the *Indian Review*. In 1990, she published her novel *You Alone Are Dancing*. The narrative, about citizens of a Caribbean island combating corrupt government officials and American businesses, was well reviewed in the general press, including in the *New York Times*. In 1991, she published the play *When the Jumbie Bird Calls* in the anthology *In Roots and Blossoms: African American Plays for Today*. In 2004, she published a collection of short stories, *In Praise of Older Women and Other Crimes*.

In 2003, Flanagan was asked by the United States government to serve as its first African American Caribbean writer and cultural ambassador to Kazakhstan and Turkmenistan. In advance of her arrival at those nations, the State Department shipped hundreds of copies of her novel.

Flanagan has received numerous honors, including a National Endowment for the Humanities grant (1978), a Mellon Foundation Award (1981), and the James Michener Fellowship for Creative Writing (1992). She is currently working on a new collection of short stories.

Further Reading

"Brenda A. Flanagan." *Contemporary Authors Online.* The Gale Group, 2001. http://web2.infotrac.galenet.com (accessed 9/19/05).

Flanagan, Brenda. *Curriculum Vitae.* February 2005.
Figueredo, D. H. *"Interview with Brenda Flanagan."* February 2005.

—D. H. Figueredo

Flax, Hjalmar (1942–)

Flax is an award-winning Puerto Rican poet and film critic. He was born and raised in San Juan, where he studied literature at the Universidad de Puerto Rico in the early 1960s. In 1969, he earned a PhD in Spanish literature from the University of Pennsylvania. While in school, he wrote poetry, publishing his first collection, *44 poemas*, the same year he finished his doctoral studies. *44 poemas* was part of a collaborative project: another poet, Arturo Trías (1947–), included 100 poems; the book was actually titled *144 poemas en dos libros.*

In 1978, Flax published *Los pequeños laberintos*, which he reissued in 2003. In the interim, he published several collections, including *Tiempo adverso* (2002), *Confines peligrosos* (1987), *Cuestión de oficio* (1998), and *Abrazos partidos y otros poemas* (2003). During this time, he was a film critic, a shipping merchant, and an airplane pilot.

In 2004, Flax was awarded Puerto Rico's national literary award. His poems range from verses with the brevity and evasiveness of haiku to love poems describing an intimate moment. Throughout his poetry, there is an awareness of the creative process and the natural simplicity of art:

> Quiero pensar
> . . . que pudiera
> abrir la ostra hermética
> donde mi alma duerme
> . . . Comérmela
> y sacar una perla de mi boca (1969)

(I want to think / that I could / open the hermetic clam / where my soul sleeps / . . . eat it / and take out from my mouth a pearl). Some of his poems recall the simplicity and ease of **José Martí's** verses.

Flax's poetry is published in Mexico, Spain, and in the United States. Since the 1990s, he has been promoting Puerto Rican literature, ever aware of the unique limitations being a commonwealth imposes on a writer: "The Puerto Rican author writes in Spanish but his metropolis is Washington, where they speak in English. His ancient ex-metropolis is Madrid, where no one likes Latin American literature," he wrote in July 2004 on the Internet site *Portal.*

Further Reading

Flax, Hjalmar. "La fama y otras desgracias." *Portal.* http://www.hflaxg.web.prw.net/page11 (accessed 8/31/05).

Serrano, Pío E. "Prólogo." In *Abrazos partidos y otros poemas*, by Hjalmar Flax. San Juan, Puerto Rico: Editorial Plaza Mayor, 2003.

—*D. H. Figueredo*

Flores, Ángel (1900–92)

■

Near the end of his long life, critic and translator Ángel Flores had a mission: to finish one last major reference source on Latin American literature. The volume was entitled *Spanish-American Authors: The Twentieth Century*, and it was published shortly after Flores passed away. It was symbolic of a life dedicated to the cultivation and promotion of literature.

Born on October 2, 1900, in Puerto Rico, Flores moved to New York City as a teenager, graduating from New York University in 1923 and attending graduate school at Lafayette College and Cornell University. A polyglot, Flores was fascinated by the writings of Franz Kafka (1883–1924) and in 1926 traveled to Germany to meet Kafka's literary executor and friends, thus becoming one of the first scholars to introduce Kafka to a North American audience. In 1928, he translated *The Waste Land* into Spanish, introducing T. S. Eliot (1888–1965) to Latin American readers. Two years later, Flores reversed the process and translated into English the poetry of Pablo Neruda (1904–73), introducing the poet to North American readers. During World War II, Flores remained in Washington, D.C., where he edited the first *Handbook of Latin American Studies* (1935), an annual publication used the world over by students and scholars. It is also during this period that he noticed a change in Latin American literature: the combined use of surrealist techniques with fantastical and magical elements. In 1954, he dubbed this literary trend **Magical Realism**.

Highly intelligent and charming, Flores was the toast of many literary circles throughout the world. He traveled extensively through the Americas and Europe, befriending and encouraging hundreds of writers, the likes of the Cubans **Alejo Carpentier** and **Nicolás Guillén**, **José Luis González** and **René Marqués**, from Puerto Rico, and **Juan Bosch** and **Pedro Mir**, from the Dominican Republic, among others. He wrote, edited, and translated nearly a hundred titles in English and Spanish, covering a wide range of topics and national literatures, including *Spanish Literature in English Translation* (1926), *Lope de Vega: Monster of Nature* (1930), *Cervantes across the Centuries* (1947), *Masterpieces of the Spanish Golden Age* (1957), *The Medieval Age* (1963), *The Literature of Spanish America*, five volumes (1966–69), *The Kafka Debate: New Perspectives for Our Times*, (1977), *The Defiant Muse: Hispanic Feminist Poems from the Middle Ages to the Present*—written with his wife, Kate—(1986), *Great Spanish Plays in English Translation* (1991). His textbook *First Spanish Reader*, published in 1964 and reissued in 1988, is still being used today.

Flores edited the journals *Alhambra* and *Literary World*. He taught at numerous prestigious institutions, including Cornell University, Rutgers University, and the University of Wisconsin. Like the **Hernández Ureña** siblings from the Dominican Republic, Flores shaped the twentieth-century Latin American canon and influenced thousands of students and readers. Always a traveler, he passed away in Guadalajara, Mexico.

Further Reading

"About Angel Flores." In *Spanish American Authors: The Twentieth Century*, edited by Angel Flores. New York: Wilson, 1992.

Flores, Angel. "Magical Realism in Spanish American Fiction." In *Magical Realism: Theory, History, Community*, Edited by Lois Parkinson Zamora and Wendy B. Faris. Durham, NC: Duke University Press, 1995.

—*D. H. Figueredo*

Florit, Eugenio (1903–99)

A poet and scholar who despite the fact that he was born in Spain, spoke with a Castilian accent, lived half his life in the United States, and became a naturalized American citizen, considered himself a Cuban above everything else. Toward the latter years of his long life, he exclaimed that the correspondence he received from readers and writers in Cuba made him feel closer to the island.

Florit manifested his love of Cuba in the book of poems *Trópico*, written in 1930. Writing in rhythmic verse, in ten-line stanzas, he approaches scenes familiar to anyone who has visited Cuba and the Caribbean: the royal palm tree, the sugarcane mills, the coffee plantations, and the "cocuyo"—a firefly endemic to the region. Yet his descriptions are elusive, far from the stereotypical; for example, he doesn't name the "cocuyos" but describes them as "flying lights, atomic diamonds" (Brillan luces voladoras / . . . son átomos de diamante); likewise, he doesn't use the words *palm tree*; instead he says an "arrow in green ectasy" (flecha en un extasis verde). In *Trópico*, Florit avoids the sentimental and the obvious, as often practiced by poets writing about nature, raising the Cuban countryside from the local to the universal.

The universal is present in what might be his most famous poem "Martirio de San Sebastián," a meditation on martyrdom. In this religious poem, allusions to peace and serenity abound, so much so that from then on critics always commented that Florit gave his readers a great sense of serenity. Both *Trópico* and "San Sebastián" made of Florit a favorite among the luminaries of his time, from the Cuban intellectual **Jorge Mañach** to the Nobel Prize–winner Juan Ramon Jiménez (1881–1958), from Spain.

Though Florit described himself as a slow writer, he was quite prolific, writing hundreds of poems, articles, and essays, including the books, *Conversación a mi padre* (1949), *Hábito de esperanza; poemas, 1936–1964* (1965), *Versos pequeños 1938–1975* (1979), *A pesar de todo* (1987), and *Antología personal* (1992). His textbook *Literatura hispanoamericana; antología e introducción histórica* (1960), cowritten with Enrique Anderson Imbert (1910–2000), served for decades as the standard college introduction to Latin American literature.

Florit was born in Madrid of a Spanish father and a Cuban mother and moved to Cuba when he was fourteen years old. After studying law at the Universidad de la Habana, he served in the Cuban consulate in New York City from 1927 to 1940. In 1942, he accepted a teaching position at Columbia University where he taught until his retirement in 1968. He passed away in 1999 in Miami, Florida. *See also* Romantism/Romanticism.

Further Reading

Núñez, Ana Rosa, et al., eds. *Homenaje a Eugenio Florit*. Miami: Ediciones Universal, 2000.

Vitier, Cinto. *Lo cubano en la poesía*. 2nd edición. Habana: Instituto del Libro, 1970.

—*D. H. Figueredo*

Focus (1943–60)

∎

Jamaica's first literary magazine was founded by writers **Philip M. Sherlock, Vic Reid**, and **Roger Mais**; it was edited and managed by **Edna Manley**, who was a sculptor, writer, promoter of Jamaican culture, wife of Norman Manley (1893–1969), a politician and labor leader, and mother of Michael Manley (1924–97), the would-be prime minister. The journal emerged out of the weekly *Public Opinion*, the organ of the People's National Party, which featured a literary supplement. As *Public Opinion* began to fail due to administrative problems, the members of its board, which included Manley and the poet **Una Marson**, decided to publish a literary journal. In the first issue, editor Manley observed that Jamaica was changing and that the journal would address those changes by expressing an interest in developing a nationalist approach to culture as well as criticizing social conditions on the island. A major preoccupation was that of a national identity and the poems, short stories, and essays published addressed that concern from both a European and an African perspective. Many of the writers featured in the journal, and referred to as the Focus Group, went on to international acclaim, including **George Campbell** and **John Hearne**. *See also* Jamaican Literature, History of; Literary Journals.

Further Reading

Breiner, Laurence A. *An Introduction to West Indian Poetry*. Cambridge: Cambridge University Press, 1998.

—*D. H. Figueredo*

Focus Group. See *Focus*.

Fouchard, Jean (1912–)

Fouchard was a Haitian journalist and historian. He was a diplomat and public servant.

Born in Port-au-Prince, Haiti, on March 2, 1912, Fouchard studied at the Séminaire Collège Saint-Martial before earning a law degree from the Faculty of Law when he was in his twenties. Attracted to journalism, he began to write for local publications while he was in college, publishing essays and articles in such journals as *Petit Impartial* and *Haïti-Journal*. He was also the managing editor of the review *La Relève*. During the 1930s, President Sténio Vincent (1874–1959) appointed him chief of his cabinet. Fouchard also served as minister of Haiti in Cuba during the same period.

Fouchard began to publish books when he was in his forties. He wrote on theater history and on theatrical depictions of Haiti: *Le théâtre à Saint-Domingue* (1955) and *Artistes et réportoire des scènes de Saint-Domingue* (1955). In the 1960s and 1970s, he cultivated the literary essay, publishing *Cahies de Guinée* (1966) and *Langue et littérature des aborigènes d'Ayti* (1972). His history of the Haitian revolution, *Les marrons de la liberté* (1972), which explored the development of Maroons societies and their role during the conflict, became of one his best-known works. His history of the evolution of the dance known as "meringue," *La méringue* (1973), is often cited by musicologists from the Caribbean.

A well-known orator, Fouchard published a collection of his speeches in 1962, *Trois discours*. His other works include *Toussaint Louverture* (1983), *Regards sur l'histoire* (1988), and *Les marrons du syllabaire* (1988).

Further Reading

Herdeck, Donald E. *Caribbean Writers. A Bio-Bibliographical Critical Encyclopedia.* Washington, DC: Three Continents Press, 1979.

James, CLR. "Preface." In *The Haitian Maroons: Liberty or death*, by Jean Fouchard. New York: Blyden Press, 1981.

—*D. H. Figueredo*

Fouché, Frank (1915–78)

Fouché was one of the pioneer Haitian writers to publish in **Kreyòl** rather than in French. His writings were inspired by Spanish and Greek as well as Haitian folklore.

Fouché was born in Saint-Marc, Haiti, on November 27, 1915. Growing up during the **American occupation of Haiti,** he affirmed Haitian nationalism by studying his country's folklore and by writing in Kreyòl. In 1946, he published his first book of poetry, *Massage*. In the 1950s, he turned to the theater, adapting into Kreyòl the Spanish drama *Yerma*, by Federico García Lorca (1898–1936) and the

Greek classic *Oedipus Rex*. These plays were staged in 1955 and 1956. During this period, he wrote essays and poems that were published in several journals, including *Optique* and *Le National*.

Attracted to communism, he visited in Cuba in 1960 and befriended the poet **Nicolás Guillén,** to whom he gave a copy of his book of poetry *Les lambis de la Sierra* (1960); later on, Guillén translated the volume into Spanish. From Cuba, Fouché traveled to the former Soviet Union and then China. In 1976, he wrote a seminal study of theater in Haiti titled *Vodou et théâter*.

Fouché was killed in a car accident in Canada in early January 1978. *See also* Haitian Literature in Kreyòl (the Haitian Language).

Further Reading

Dumas, Pierre-Raymond. *Panorama de la litterature haïtienne de la diaspora*. Tome. II. Port-au-Prince, Haiti: Promobank, 1996.

—*D. H. Figueredo*

Francisco, Ramón (1929–)

Ramón Francisco is an experimental poet from the Dominican Republic who combines the dual role often performed by writers in the Caribbean: a working professional who is also a published poet.

Francisco was born in Puerto Plata, 1929. He was raised in Santiago, where he attended public school. In the late 1950s, he enrolled at the Universidad de Santo Domingo, earning a degree in accounting. During this decade, he started to read the poetry produced by the movement known as **La Poesía Sorprendida**—the surprised or bewildered poetry—and was influenced by its use of symbolism and experimentalism.

Francisco taught at the Universidad Pública and was founder and editor of the accounting journal *Revista del contador*. He also served as vice minister of finance after the fall of Rafael Leónidas Trujillo's (1891–1961) dictatorship in 1961.

While pursuing a career as an accountant and public servant, he also wrote poetry and promoted literature through participation in conferences and literary contests. In 1960, Francisco wrote *Las superficies sólidas*, experimental poems that were critical of Trujillo's dictatorship. In 1969, he wrote the volume *Literatura dominicana 60*, where he lamented the absence in the Dominican Republic of literary criticism. In 1987, he cowrote, with **Manuel Rueda,** *De tierra morena vengo*, experimental and traditional poems about the Dominican Republic. He followed this work with two other texts, *Critic-A-demas* (1987) and *La patria montonera* (2001).

Further Reading

Pina Contreras, Guillermo. *Doce en la literatura dominicana*. Santiago, República Dominicana: Universidad Católica Madre y Maestra, 1982.

—*D. H. Figueredo*

Franco Oppenheimer, Félix (1912–)

Franco Oppenheimer was a Puerto Rican poet and scholar. His poetry explores metaphysical concepts as well as celebrates the natural beauty of the island. A scholar and educator, his *Antología general del cuento puertorriqueño* (1959) was a popular college textbook for many years.

Franco Oppenheimer was born in Ponce on July 10, 1912. His family lacked the economic means to send him to school. Instead, after the sixth grade, he had to work as a typist and proofreader. While working at a printing press in San Juan, he attended night school. Upon graduation, he matriculated at the Universidad de Puerto Rico. In 1947 he earned his BA. Four years later, he received his MA in arts from his alma mater. While studying, he befriended Puerto Rican writers and poets and was involved in several poetic groups. In 1950, he published the book of poems *El hombre y su angustia*.

During the early 1950s, Franco Oppenheimer taught at different schools. In 1953, he was appointed professor at the Universidad de Puerto Rico. In 1956, he published his second volume of poetry, *Del tiempo y su figura*. He then traveled to Mexico, where he received a PhD in philosophy and literature from the Universidad Nacional Autónoma de México in 1964.

Through the 1960s, he wrote poetry, essays, and short stories. In 1964, he published the scholarly study *Imagen y vision edénica de Puerto Rico*. He also published four volumes of stories within the **costumbrismo** genre, stories of local color: *Imagenes* (1957, 1962, 1966, and 1972). In 1976, the Instituto de Cultura Puertorriqueña published an anthology of his works, *Antología poetica*.

Further Reading

González Torres, Rafael A. *La obra poética de Félix Franco Oppenheimer*. Río Piedras: Editorial Universitaria de Puerto Rico, 1981.

Rosa-Nieves, Cesáreo. *Del contorno hacia el dintorno; notas sobre el LiBRO de ensayos: Contornos de Félix Franco Oppenheimer*. San Juan, Editorial Yaurel, 1961.

—*D. H. Figueredo*

Francophone Caribbean Literature, History of

French, Creole, or Kreyòl, is spoken in French Guiana, Guadeloupe, Haiti, and Martinique, territories and countries initially settled by the Spanish but taken over by the French through either force or negotiations in the seventeenth and eighteenth centuries. During that era, the literature of the Francophone Caribbean consisted of folk stories and legends. Comments Mickaëlla L. Pèrina in *African Caribbeans: A Reference Guide* (2003): "At first, this oral literature referred exclusively to Africa, but its contact with European literary norms transformed not only its themes but its language—into Creole" (133). There were travelogues and accounts written by European visitors who viewed themselves superior to the people in the Caribbean. The theater was particularly active, and artists of color began to appear onstage.

The revolutionary change in the literature occurred with the onset of the Haitian revolution. **Antoine Dupré** is credited as the first poet in Haiti and therefore in the French Caribbean. In 1817, the first major journal appeared, *L'Abeille Haytienne*, founded by **Jules S. Milscent**. These Haitian developments characterized the nineteenth century, and much of the writing from this period occurred in Haiti, where the first black republic in the world had been established in 1804—and the second republic in the Americas, after the United States—and where there was no slavery and blacks were allowed to read (that was not so throughout the rest of the Caribbean).

The first Francophone Caribbean novel was *Stella*, written by **Emeric Bergeaud**, and published in 1859. **Oswald Durand** was the first French-speaking Caribbean poet to achieve recognition in Haiti and in France. Dozens of poets appeared, though much of the literature was influenced by French romanticism. Some of these writers were the **Nau Brothers**—Émile and Ignace—the **Ardouin Brothers**—Beaubrun, Céligni, and Coriolan—who were writers and politicians, and **Massillon Coicou**.

A true explosion of literary activity occurred in the twentieth century. Again, Haiti was in the lead but Martinique was not far behind. In 1915, American forces occupied Haiti and remained in the country until 1934. In reaction to the American military presence, Haitian intellectuals set out in anger to demonstrate the racist nature of the occupiers but also to understand the reasons that had placed Haiti in such a political conundrum. Dr. **Jean Price-Mars** criticized educated Haitians for their "**bovaryism**"—an allusion to fictional character Emma Bovary, who sought refuge in romantic world of her own creation—and for isolating themselves from the world and shying away from Haiti's African roots. His book *Ainsi parla l'oncle* (1928) revolutionized Haiti's intelligentsia. Poets and novelists **Carl Brouard, Émile Roumer**, and **Phillipe Thoby-Marcelin** condemned the Americans and began to celebrate Haiti's folklore and tradition, including the vodou religion. The most famous writer to emerge from this cluster and to write one of the best novels written in French was **Jacques Roumain**. His novel *Gouverneurs de la rosée* (1944) depicted the lot of the poor peasants of Haiti; the novel is the best example of a genre popular in Haiti, the **peasant novel**.

While Haiti was discovering and redefining its national culture, Martinique was experiencing a similar growth and making a dramatic entrance onto the stage of world literature. In 1938, a teacher and would-be politician named **Aimé Césaire** penned a poem considered a masterpiece of the French language: *Cahier d'un retour au pays natal*. In this poem, Césaire proclaimed his African heritage, celebrated Africa's natural condition over a mechanized Europe, and glorified the color of his skin. The poem became the manifesto of the **Négritude** movement and would influence countless writers and activists the likes of **Frantz Fanon**, also from Martinique, and Stokley Carmichael (1941–98), from the United States. A prolific author and controversial political figure—he favored the departmentization of Martinique, making it a state of France rather an independent nation—Césaire quickly outshone his own wife, **Suzanne Roussy Césaire**, a philosopher and one of the editors the influential journal *Tropiques*. Along with her husband, the other editor was **René Ménil**, also a philosopher. These three authors and intellectuals were censored by the authorities who at the time represented the fascist regime of Vechy—Germany had already invaded France.

In France, during World War II, several writers from Guadeloupe suffered a unique fate: they were but a handful from the Caribbean to directly experience the Nazi regime. These writers had arrived in Paris during the 1930s to either study or work. **Saint-John Perse** was serving in the diplomatic corps when Paris surrendered to the German forces. A poet—who would become the first writer from the Caribbean to win the Nobel Prize for literature in 1961—Perse's manuscripts were burned by the Nazis when he sought exile in 1940. **Paul Niger** eluded the invaders and joined the underground in Paris. After the war, he would achieve fame for writing works that promoted Négritude and an anticolonialist stance. **Guy Tirolien** was captured and sent to a camp, where he met Léopold S. Senghor (1906–2001), who introduced him to Négritude. In his poetry, Tirolien would fight racism and rally all black men to seek freedom. **Jean-Louis Baghio'o** set up a clandestine radio station. This experience served as the basis for his first work, *Fugue mineure*.

In Martinique after World War II, **Mayotte Capécia** wrote the romance *Je suis Martiniquaise* (1948), a controversial love story wherein the heroine sees salvation for her and her children only through marriage to a white person. In 1950, what would become a popular international novel was published: *La rue cases nègres*. Written by **Joseph Zobel**, the novel depicted the lot of the poor and abused sugarcane workers who lived on a plantation in Martinique. During this decade, one of the best-known writers from the Caribbean, and the most famous from Martinique, would make his appearance with a theoretical volume on the psychology of racism and oppression. The book was *Peau noire, masques blancs* (1952) and the author was Frantz Fanon. Fanon's writings, especially *Les damnés de la terre* (1961), justified the use of violence against repressive regimes; this philosophy would inspire liberation movements throughout Africa and Latin America. During this decade, Haiti experienced the beginning of the dictatorship of **François Duvalier**, who in his youth had cultivated literature and had promoted a fascist version of Négritude in *Le problème des classes à travers l'histoire d'Haiti* (1948).

The repressive regimes of François Duvalier, from 1957 to 1971, and his son, Jean-Claude, from 1971 to 1986, brought about a massive emigration of Haitian intellectuals, giving rise to an important body of diasporic Haitian literature. One of the first to seek exile was **Jacques Stephen Alexis** who was also one of the casualties of the regime: returning to Haiti in a plot to overthrow of Duvalier, he was captured and murdered by the dictator's secret service. Other writers who went into exile were **René Depestre**, **Jean Métellus**, and **Lilas Desquiron**, who settled in France; **Roger Dorsinville** and **Félix Morisseau-Leroy**, in Africa; **Émile Ollivier**, **Gérard Étienne**, Roland Morisseau, Joël Des Rosiers, Robert Berrouët-Oriol, and **Dany Laferrière**, who went to Canada; and **Paul Laraque**, the United States.

Duvalier's black fascism and the rise of liberation movements in the Third World prompted concerns over Négritude in the Caribbean, explorations of the **postcolonialism**, and exposition of racism and sexual inequality at home. In 1960, **Michèle Lacrosil** published *Sapotille et le serin d'argile*, followed a year later by *Cajou*; each of these novels tells the story of a mulatto woman who faces discrimination in Guadeloupe because of the color of her skin. In 1967, **Simone Schwarz-Bart**, published *Un plat de porc aux bananes vertes* (1967), coauthored with husband

André Schwarz-Bart, a novel that addressed multiple themes in the complicated construction of identity for a Martinican woman experiencing alienation from French society and searching for her Caribbean roots.

In the 1970s, writers challenged racial relations in Martinique and the government's structure. **Jacqueline Manicom** suggested in her novel *Mon examen de blanc* (1972) that to be in the ruling class you had to be male and more importantly light-skinned, and **Vincent Placoly**, a novelist and a playwright, used novels such as *L'Eau-de-Mort-Guildive* (1973) and dramas such as *Dessalines, ou, La passion de l'indépendance* (1983) to criticize the island's semicolonial status. In the 1980s, **Créolité** became a dominant ideology. This movement emphasized and celebrated the diversity of the Caribbean people.

Créolité emerged as a response to Négritude. The founders of Créolité were the writers Jean Bernabé, Raphaël Confiant, **Edouard Glissant**, and **Patrick Chamoiseau**, both from Martinique. The movement's manifesto was the text *Eloge de la créolité* (1989), written by Bernabé, Chamoiseau, and Confiant. This text claimed that Négritude replaced Europe with Africa. *Eloge de la créolité* advocated for a new Caribbean persona: a Creole composed of all the races and people in the region; it also proposed the use of Creole, which derived from the French and several African languages, as the true language of the Francophone Caribbean.

One of the first writers to espouse Creole was Césaire's own daughter **Ina Césaire**, who became a well-known playwright with works such as *Contes de mort et de vie aux Antilles* (1976), *Mémoires d'isles: maman N. et maman* (1985), and *Contes de nuits et de jours aux Antilles* (1989). Implicit in her stance was the need for women writers to voice their own concerns in their own voices. Other women writers who emerged were the Haitian **Yanick Lahens**, whose collection of short stories *Tante Résia et les dieux* (1994) chronicled everyday life in Haiti, and **Maryse Condé**—from Guadeloupe—and Haitian American **Edwidge Danticat**, who earned international recognition for their novels.

Condé and Danticat represented one half of a trend: women writers who live away from their home countries but write about their countries. But the other half included a new twist: women writers who relocate abroad and then return to the land of their birth. Probably the most representative of this development is **Jan J. Dominique**, who after living abroad returned to Haiti to write novels and become a radio personality.

The traveling back and forth to their islands as well as the increasing presence of women authors might forecast the literature of the twenty-first century: exploration of two worlds and two cultures—the islands and Europe and the United States. It might be a restaging of the traveling narratives so popular during colonial times, but with a difference—the travelers now are writing about their own homes.

Further Reading

Condé, Maryse. *La Parole des Femmes: essai sur des romancières des Antilles de langue française.* Paris: L'Harmattan, 1979.

Hoffmann, Léon-François. *Essays on Haitian Literature.* Washington, DC: Three Continents Press, 1984.

Ormerod, Beverly. *Center of Remembrance: Memory and Caribbean Women's Literature.* London: Mango Publishing, 2002.

———. *An Introduction to Caribbean and Francophone Writing: Guadeloupe and Martinique.* New York: Berg, 1999.

Pèrina, Mickaëlla. "Martinique." In *African Caribbeans: A Reference Guide,* edited by Alan West-Duran. Westport, CT: Greenwood Press, 2003.

—*D. H. Figueredo*

Frankétienne. *See* Étienne, Franck.

G

Galib, Hamid (1947–)

A Puerto Rican poet, Galib is a physicist and humanitarian admired for his fight during the 1990s for the relinquishment of the island of Vieques from the U.S. Navy. Galib describes himself as a poet who happens to practice medicine.

Of Lebanese descent, Galib was born in San Germán, Puerto Rico, on March 26, 1947. Raised in a well-to-do family, he felt the call for two vocations in his youth: literature and medicine. He began to write poetry at the age of nine and continued to do so through his undergraduate studies at Georgetown University, Washington, D.C. Graduating in 1968, he returned to Puerto Rico, where he attended medical school at the Universidad de Puerto Rico. After establishing his practice in Santurce, he published his first book of poem in 1976, *Aleluya para un clavel*. The poems revealed his deep love for humanity and his advocacy for peaceful social change.

Through the 1980s, he taught in medical school and was also active in political causes, such as the removal of an American naval base on the island of Vieques, a few miles east of Puerto Rico. In 1985, he published *Solemnidades*, echoing once again his call for a compassionate society. In the 1990s, he published several volumes, including *Borrón y patria nueva* (1990), *Los presagios* (1991), and *Contravida* (1992). He was also featured on a television program where he recommended the reading and writing of poetry as beneficial to good health.

A friend of President Bill Clinton (1946–), Galib lobbied the leader to relinquish Vieques to Puerto Rico. In 2000, he went on a hunger strike to protest the navy's presence on the island—the Navy did leave in May 2003. For his work as a humanitarian and a writer, Galib was awarded the Doctor **Agustín Stahl** medal by the Puerto Rican government.

Further Reading

Lluch Mora, Francisco. *Tres estancias esenciales en la lírica de Hamid Galib: Solemnidades, Revoque, Los presagios, 1985–1991*. San Juan: Ediciones Mairena, 1991.

—*D. H. Figueredo*

Galván, Manuel de Jesús (1834–1910)

■

During the nineteenth century, when most Dominican Republic writers favored poetry, Galván chose the genre of the novel for his entry into the national literature.
His novel, *Enriquillo* (1879, 1882) is considered one of Latin America's best examples of the **historical novel** and of **costumbrismo**, stories of local color. Galván was
a public servant and skillful politician.

Manuel de Jesús Galván was born on January 13, 1834, in Santo Domingo.
Not much is written about his childhood and youth except that he demonstrated an
interest in literature and in the study of law. He cultivated both through his life and
became a lawyer at the age of forty-five.

In 1854, Galván founded the newspaper *Oasis*. The articles he wrote expressed
his conservative views, his fear of a Haitian invasion—the black republic had occupied its neighbor from 1822 to 1844—and his admiration for Spanish culture. During this period, he became friendly with government officials and politicians and
served in several government posts from secretary of the Senate, to editor of the government publication *La Gazeta*, to master general of the post office.

In 1861, when President Santana (1801–64) annexed the Dominican Republic
to Spain, as an act of protection from Haiti, Galván founded the journal *La Razón*,
where he celebrated the annexation. President Santana named Galván his personal
secretary and Galván also served as the minister of Public Works. In 1865, he traveled to Puerto Rico, where he published his articles in the journals *El buscapié*, *La
democracia*, and *Boletín mercantil*. Ten years later, he was elected deputy to the
Dominican Republic's national convention and served in a number of prestigious
posts: minister of Foreign Relations, president of the Supreme Court, and interim
director of the Department of Interior.

In the 1870s, he began to work on the novel. *Enriquillo* told the story of the
Amerindian Anacaona who rebelled against the Spanish conquistadores during the
colonization of Hispaniola in the sixteenth century. The protagonist wins the uprising and is able to persuade the Spanish to treat the Amerindians with dignity and
free them from forced labor. The novel depicted historic events as the work of individuals and not heroic figures, thus granting the narrative a sense of intimacy. The
first version was published in 1879. Galván then edited and improved a second and
final version, published in 1882. According to critic Raimundo Lazo, in *Historia de
la literatura hispanoamericana* (1967), the novel became well known throughout
Latin America because of its "plain diction, the author's engaging expression . . . and
his conciliatory interpretation of history" (287).

From 1896 to 1902, Galván taught law at the Derecho de Instituto Profesional, in
Santo Domingo. In 1904, he studied and wrote a study of the Dominican Republic's
foreign debt. He was in Puerto Rico when he passed away on December 13, 1910. His
remains were transferred to the Dominican Republic in 1917. *See also* Dominican
Republic Literature, History of; Hispanic Caribbean Literature, History of.

Further Reading

Alcántara Almánzar, José. *Dos siglos de literatura dominicana (XIX–XX)*. Santo Domingo:
Colección Sesquicentenario de la Independencia Nacional, 1996.

Gutiérrez, Franklin. *Enriquillo: radiografía de un héroe galvaniano* Santo Domingo: Editora Búho, 1999.

Lazo, Raimundo. *Historia de la literatura hispanoamericana.* México: Editorial Porrua, 1967.

—D. H. Figueredo

García, Cristina (1958–)

The author of one of the most popular novels written about Cuban Americans and the Cuban Revolution—*Dreaming in Cuban* (1992)—Cristina García is a journalist, novelist, and short-story writer. She is representative of the Caribbean writer, along with **Julia Alvarez, Edwidge Danticat,** and **Virgil Suárez,** who was not born in the United States and whose native tongue is not English yet chooses to write in that language.

García was born in Cuba but left for the United States with her family at the age of four. Raised in New York City, she was surrounded by avid anti-Castro Cubans. Wanting to know more about the revolutionary process, García, who was by then a journalist for the *New York Times*, visited Cuba in 1984. It was an experience that inspired her to write *Dreaming in Cuban*. The novel narrates the life of Pilar, a child of the 1960s who attempts to reconcile her mother's pro-American and anti-Castro sentiments with the pro-Castro sentiments of her grandmother, who lives in Cuba. Pilar's trip to the island allows her to uncover her family past, represented by letters her grandmother Celia wrote to her Spanish lover, Gustavo. The novel expands Cuban history from the 1930s to 1980, when thousands of Cubans fled through the Mariel Boatlift. García's second novel, *The Agüero Sisters* (1997), continues to examine Cuban and American cultures through the eyes of Reina, who lives in Cuba, and Constancia, who lives in the United States; both sisters represent the separation of Cuban families as a result of the Cuban Revolution. The novel traces the family past to the end of the nineteenth century, from the period of insurrection to the mid-twentieth century, when Constancia's father, Ignacio, attempts to preserve Cuba's dying past and kills Blanca, Constancia and Reina's mother. The murder is symbolic of Cuba: Ignacio was born on October 4, the day of Orula, the orisha of divination, who in Santería is Saint Francis of Assisi, and kills his wife, Blanca, on September 8, the day of Oshún, Our Lady of Mercy, Cuba's patron saint. With his actions, Ignacio foretells the violent and chaotic future of his country. Her third novel, *Monkey Hunting* (2003), is the story of a Cuban Chinese family from the nineteenth century to the Vietnam War. In Garcia's novels, history, culture, and Afro-Cuban religions serve as the background to the action. The stories, however, are about the coming to terms with the loss of the homeland and separation from loved ones. *See also* Anti-Castro Literature; Cuban American Literature; Mariel Generation; Santería in Literature.

Further Reading

Alvarez Borland, Isabel. *Cuban-American Literature of Exile: From Person to Persona.* Charlottesville: University Press of Virginia, 1998.

Luis, William. *Dance Between Two Cultures: Latino Caribbean Literature Written in the United States*. Nashville, TN: Vanderbilt University Press, 1997.

Méndez Rodena, Adriana. "En búsqueda del paraíso perdido: La historia natural como imaginación diaspórica en Cristina García," *MLN* 116, no. 2 (2001): 392–481.

Pérez Firmat, Gustavo. "Cuba sí, Cuba no. Querencias de la literatura cubana/americana." *Encuentro de la cultura cubana* 14 (Fall 1999): 131–37.

—William Luis

García-Aguilera, Carolina (1949–)

Carolina García-Aguilera is a popular Cuban American mystery writer whose protagonist ads a unique addition to the genre: a Cuban American woman detective. In less than a decade since the publication of her first novel, *Bloody Water* (1996), García-Aguilera has achieved notoriety as a writer, and her works have been translated into several languages.

García-Aguilera was born in Havana, Cuba, on July 13, 1949, into a middle-class family. After the triumph of the Cuban Revolution in 1959, her family went into exile in the United States, settling in New York City. She attended Rollins College, earning a BA in history. She received a master's in finance from the University of South Florida in 1983. In 1986, she set up her own detective agency, working as a private investigator for nearly a decade. Her experience as a detective, affording her realistic descriptions of bureaucratic procedures, and her intimate knowledge of Cuban political refugees, provided her with credible characters and storylines for her mystery novels.

The first novel she wrote was *Bloody Water* (1996), about an illegal adoption ring in Miami. The protagonist is Lupe Solano, a Cuban detective representative of integrated Cuban Americans: as independent as an American but as respectful of family traditions as a Cuban. Solano was a success with readers. Critic and fellow mystery writer Rolando Hinojosa (1919–) describes her, in a *Multicultural Review* article, as "wise, hip, takes no claptrap from anyone." Soon Solano surfaced in several mystery novels: *Bloody Shame* (1997), *Bloody Secrets* (1998), *Havana Heat* (2000), *Bitter Sugar* (2001), *One Hot Summer* (2002), and *Luck of the Draw* (2003). The novels are fast-paced, using occasional Spanish words for ambiance. But throughout the narrative there are comparisons of life in the United States versus life in Cuba, as illustrated in this passage from *Bloody Secrets*: "Honor in Miami was almost exclusively discussed by older people who recalled where they came from. My contemporaries—second generation Cubans—rarely mentioned it. They were too busy with the present and the future to contemplate the past" (93).

Further Reading

Figueredo, Danilo H. "The Stuff Dreams Are Made Of: The Latino Detective Novel." *Multicultural Review* 8, no. 3 (September 1999): 22–29.

"Writers Reveal Secret at Keynote Luncheon." *ACRL Footnotes*. Chicago: Association of College and Research Libraries. Saturday, April 9, 2005.

—*D. H. Figueredo*

García Marruz, Fina (1923–)

A Cuban poet known for her religious verses, poems about motherhood as the origin of all things, and political poetry, Fina García Marruz was the only woman in the group of influential writers who edited the journal *Orígines* during the 1940s and 50s. Working under the shadows of such colleagues as **José Lezama Lima**, the co-founder of *Orígines*, and married to one of Cuba's leading intellectuals and poets, **Cintio Vitier**, García Marruz was often neglected until the development of feminist studies on the island in the 1980s.

García Marruz was born on April 28, 1923, in Havana. When she was thirteen years old, she met the poet Juan Ramón Jiménez (1881–1958) who sparked her interest in poetry and in writing. At the age of nineteen, she published her first book of poems, *Poemas*; a year later she was on the editorial board of the literary journal *Clavileño*. In 1944, she started writing for *Orígines*, a publication that maintained political changes in Cuba could only come about through cultural developments, and befriended the editors and contributors: José Lezama Lima, José Rodríguez Feo, Cintio Vitier, and **Eliseo Diego**. In 1951, she published *Las miradas perdidas*, dedicated to her parents. The collection, described by critic Catherine Davies as "exceptionally beautiful" in her book *A Place in the Sun?* (91) contains poems that are delicate and evocative of faith, love, sweetness, and tenderness:

> Una dulce nevada está cayendo
> detrás de cada cosa, cada amante
> una dulce nevada comprendiendo
> lo que la vida tiene distante

(A sweet snow is falling / behind each object, a lover / a sweet snow understanding / what life holds at a distance).

Las miradas perdidas received some recognition on the island but García Marruz was still far from achieving literary fame. In 1961, she earned a doctorate in social science from the Universidad de la Habana and was appointed researcher at Cuba's national library. In 1967, she wrote one of her best-known poems "On the death of Ernesto Che Guevara," included later on in the collection *Visitaciones* (1970). In 1969, she coauthored with her husband the literary study *Temas martianos*, about Cuban nineteenth-century poet and patriot **José Martí**—one of many treatises she would write with her husband. In 1971, she published a critical analysis of the Spanish poet Gustavo Adolfo Bécquer (1836–70), *Bécquer o la leve bruma*. In 1984, the book that finally brought her recognition, *Poesías escogidas*, was published.

García Marruz's themes are often summarized as consisting of Catholic mysticism, a Cuban identity, and motherhood. It is the latter that is attracting critical feminist attention. For motherhood is also symbolic of woman's voice, the silence to which women have been subjected, and the objectification of women. In 1990, García Marruz received Cuba's National Literary Award. Some of her other books include *Hablar de la poesía* (1986), *Créditos de Charlot* (1994), *Textos antiimperialistas de José Martí* (1996), *Habana del centro* (1997), *Antología poética* (2002).

Further Reading

Davies, Catherine. *A Place in the Sun? Women Writers in Twentieth-Century Cuba*. London: Zed Books Limited, 1997.

Méndez, Roberto. *La dama y el escorpión*. Santiago de Cuba: Editorial Oriente, 2000.

—*D. H. Figueredo*

García Ramis, Magaly (1948–)

■

Along side **Rosario Ferré**, García Ramis is one of Puerto Rico's women writers to achieve recognition beyond the island, winning honors and awards from such important cultural institutions as Cuba's **Casa de las Américas** (1974). García Ramis is an educator, an artist, and newspaper columnist.

Born in San Juan, Puerto Rico, on September 20, 1948—some sources say 1946—she grew up in a comfortable middle-class environment—her father was a government official—where she was introduced to the arts at an early age. She attended private elementary and secondary schools, and, in 1964, she enrolled at the Universidad de Puerto Rico. While a college student, she worked as an editor for the newspaper *El Mundo* and upon graduation received a merit scholarship to conduct graduate studies at Columbia University. In 1969, she returned to Puerto Rico, where she worked in the publicity department of the Universidad de Puerto Rico. A year later, she went back to New York to find a position as a journalist. While she was not successful, the experience proved advantageous: working as a waitress, she gathered ideas for her first short story and materials for her novels.

In the early 1970s, she worked for several newspapers and became editor of the journal *Avance*. In 1976, she traveled to Mexico to pursue doctoral studies at the Universidad Nacional Autónoma de México. It was while she was in Mexico that her first collection of short stories was published, *La familia de todos nosotros*. The volume brought her instant recognition in Puerto Rico. In 1986, she published the novel *Felices días, Tío Sergio*, which received the Pen Club Puertorriqueño literary award. The novel was quickly translated into English and German. The novel and the short stories explore two themes: the inner workings of middle-class families contrasted with political and social events occurring in Puerto Rico.

As her reputation grew through the 1980s, García Ramis taught literature at the Universidad de Puerto Rico, was a visiting professor at Yale University, and set up and managed with her brother an art studio where she worked in ceramics. In

1988, she received a Guggenheim Fellowship. In 1993, she published a collection of the essays and articles she had written for several newspapers, *La ciudad que me habita*, about her passion for the city of San Juan. In 1995, she published *Las noches del riel de oro*, a collection of short stories and essays. Her compatriot **José Luis Vega**, a critic and poet, describes García Ramis as a "perceptive observer of the world about her, a friendly chronicler of reality."

García Ramis wrote a script for television production in Puerto Rico—*A flor de piel* (1994). She teaches literature and communication at the Universidad de Puerto Rico and is a columnist for the daily *El Nuevo Día*.

Further Reading

Torres, Víctor Federico. *Narradores Puertorriqueños del 70. Guía biobliográfica*. San Juan: Plaza Mayor, 2001.

Vega, José Luis. *Reunión* de Espejos. Río Piedras, Puerto Rico: Editorial Cultural, 1983.

—*D. H. Figueredo*

Garduño, E. P. See Henríquez Ureña, Pedro.

Garrastegui, Anagilda (1932–)

A feminist, Garrastegui is a Puerto Rican poet whose writings define femininity and feminism through a female perspective freed from man's control. Critics praise Garrastegui for writing a poetry that is both playful and serious.

Born in San Sebastián, Puerto Rico, on October 8, 1932, she attended the Universidad de Puerto Rico in the mid-1950s, befriending such writers as **Hugo Margenat** and **Jaime Carrero,** among others. In her poetic development, she was influenced by poet Juan Ramón Jiménez (1881–1958), with whom she corresponded, and studied under Puerto Rican poet **Francisco Matos Paoli.**

In 1956, she published *Desnudez*, a book of feminist poems where she presented the female body as a woman, and not a man, saw it. In the 1960s, she taught literature at her alma mater and published the books of poetry, *Niña íntima* (1961), and *Abril en mi sangre* (1969). These poems reflected woman in her many roles: lover, mother, and creator. In the 1970s, a militant voice was evident in her books *Shizaad* (1972) and *De mis soledades vengo* (1979), which critic José Torres, in a 1994 article in *El Diario La Prensa*, saw as "a revolutionary call" to erotic writing.

Garrastegui also cultivated the novel, writing in 1998 *Semillas de fuego*, wherein she used experimental techniques, such as excerpts from diaries, letters, and poems to again explore feminist themes. Scholar Yasmín Cruz Rivera describes Garrastegui as "incarnating the feminine culture and projecting expressions of women who are diverse, unique, and contradictory. Her poetic production develops from a definition of what is feminism to a magnificent profile of what women are and want to be."

Further Reading

Cruz Rivera, Yasmín. "Voces de mujer: poesía de Anagilda Garrastegui y la nueva poesía" *Primer Congreso Virtual Humanístico del Caribe 2002*. Universidad de Puerto Rico en Humacao. http://cuhwww.upr.clu.edu (accessed 9/5/05).

Torres, José. "La poesía erótica de Sandra García." *El Diario La Prensa*, May 2, 1994.

—*D. H. Figueredo*

Garvey, Marcus (1887–1940)

The founder of the Universal Negro Improvement Association, an organization dedicated to black consciousness and economic gains for blacks, and the leader of the "Back to Africa" movement, Garvey, also known as "the Black Moses," was a Jamaican political activist, social thinker, journalist, and writer. He published several newspapers and mentored numerous young black writers.

Born as Marcus Moziah Garvey Jr. on August 17, 1887, in St. Anne's Bay, Jamaica, Garvey was the son of a stonemason who was believed to be descendant of Maroons, the slaves who had fled to the Jamaican hills during the seventeeth century and had established their own independent communities, and a devout Christian woman. Garvey's father was a voracious reader, which allowed young Garvey to educate himself; he also admired the rhetoric and oratory skills of the Protestant preachers of the area.

Garvey worked as an apprentice with his godfather, who was a printer, and at the age of sixteen he moved to Kingston, where he became a leader of the Printers Union. After publishing his own newspapers, *Garvey's Watchman*, Garvey went to Costa Rica and then to Great Britain. While traveling throughout Europe,

Jamaican social activist, writer, and poet, Marcus Garvey founded the Universal Negro Improvement Association and advocated for a return to Africa. *Source: Schomburg Center for Research in Black Culture, The New York Public Library, Astor, Lenox, and Tilden Foundations. Courtesy of Lisa Finder.*

Garvey studied public speaking. He read Booker T. Washington's *Up from Slavery* (1901), which inspired Garvey to promote black unity.

He returned to Jamaica in 1914 and founded the Universal Negro Improvement Association (UNIA). In 1916, he traveled to the United States, establishing the UNIA's headquarters in Harlem. In 1917, he began publishing the weekly *Negro World*, in which he wrote about black unity and the need for a return to Africa. The journal also published the early works of major would-be American and Caribbean writers like Zora Neale Hurston (1891–1960) and **Eric Walrond**. In 1919, Garvey created a shipping line, the Black Star Line, meant to transport blacks to Africa, which he viewed as the homeland, and to establish commerce between blacks in the United States and nations in Africa and the Caribbean. The experiment failed as a result of Garvey's poor managerial skills and dishonest business partners.

By now his advocacy for a homeland for all blacks, known as the "Back to Africa" movement, was internationally known. Flamboyant, supportive of racial purity and separatism, Garvey had numerous critics and enemies, both black and white. Accused of mail fraud, he was sent to prison for five years in 1925. While incarcerated, his wife, Amy Jacques Garvey (1885–1973), who had published in 1923 *Philosophy and Opinions of Marcus Garvey*, released a second volume in 1925; she funded both publications, and to recover the expense, she toured the United States, lecturing on her famous husband. *Philosophy and Opinions of Marcus Garvey* consisted of articles and speeches. As such, the pieces were short and conversational, clearly expounding on Garvey's political and racial ideas. The volume also contained a number of sayings meant to work in the manner of proverbs, for example: "Men who are in earnest are not afraid of consequences" (9).

Responding to a plea for the release of Garvey, whom his supporters felt had been unjustly accused, President Calvin Coolidge commuted Garvey's sentence in 1927 and deported him to Jamaica. That same year, Garvey wrote a book of poetry, *The Tragedy of the White Injustice*, his condemnation of the whites:

> Lying and stealing is the whiteman's game;
> For rights of God nor man he has no shame.

From Jamaica, Garvey traveled to England, where he founded the magazine *Black Man* and a school, the School of African Philosophy. Suffering from asthma, pneumonia, and two debilitating strokes, Garvey died in London on June 10, 1940. His influence continued to grow, though: his advocacy for the return to Africa helped to launch the Rastafarian movement in Jamaica, his face appeared on a Jamaican stamp, numerous cultural centers were named in his honor in the United States, and, in 1971, the Jamaican government honored him with the Order of the National Hero. In 1983, many of his poems were published under the title of *The Poetical Works of Marcus Garvey* and his speeches and article were published in 2004 as *Selected Writings and Speeches of Marcus Garvey*.

Further Reading

Donovan, Sandra. *Marcus Garvey*. Chicago: Raintree, 2003.

Martin, Tony. *Marcus Garvey, Hero: A First Biography*. Dover, MA: 1983.

Taylor, Ula Y. *The Veiled Garvey: the Life & Times of Amy Jacques Garvey*. Chapel Hill: University of North Carolina Press, 2002.

—*D. H. Figueredo*

Gatón Arce, Freddy (1920–94)

■

A poet from the Dominican Republic, Gatón Arce belonged to the movement known as the **Poesía Sorprendida**, which sought universal themes and shied away from nationalistic poetry. He was a journalist and an educator.

Gatón Arce was born in San Pedro de Macorís, Dominican Republic, on March 27, 1920. By the time he graduated with a law degree from the Universidad Autónoma de Santo Domingo in 1946, Gatón Arce had already published a book of experimental poetry entitled *Vlía* (1944). The volume was one long prose poem, part philosophical, part surrealist, and with Biblical allusions. *Vlía* brought him literary recognition in the Dominican Republic.

From 1944 to 1947, Gatón Arce managed the journal *Poesía Sorprendida*, published by the group of writers who made up the movement of the same name. In 1949, he worked as a journalist for the daily *El Caribe*. During the 1950s, he continued his journalist career while also teaching law at his alma mater. In 1962, he reorganized the school of communication at the Universidad Autónoma and was appointed its director. In 1967, he was his country's representative before the transnational writers group called Comunidad Latinoamericana de Escritores— known as CLE.

Retiring from journalism in 1974 to accept the position of vice president of the newspaper *El Nacional de Ahora*, Gatón Arce focused on writing poetry. The 1980s, therefore, were for him a fruitful period with the publication of several volumes, including *Son guerras y amores* (1980), *Y con ayer el tanto tiempo* (1981), *Cantos comunes* (1983), *Los ríos hacen voca. Tengo sed* (1986), and *Discursos de los alborotos* (1988). He also wrote short stories, which he called biobrevis, short narrative pieces with a moral.

Gatón Arce's writing is complex and playful, filled with contradictory sentiments. In one volume of poetry, he can be celebratory of love; in the next, he can depict love as a barrier to a happiness. Gatón Arce passed away on July 22, 1994.

Further Reading

Diccionario de autores dominicanos, 1492–1994. 2nd ed. Santo Domingo: Editora Colorscan, 1994.

Veloz Maggiolo, Marcio. *Cultura, teatro y relatos in Santo Domingo*. Santiago de los Caballeros, Republica Dominicana: Universidad Católica Madre y Maestra, 1972.

—*D. H. Figueredo*

Gautier Benítez, José. See Benítez Family.

Gay and Lesbian Literature

∎

This is a body of work depicting manifestations of love, sex, and relationships between couples of the same sex. Until recently, such literary output was either silenced or ignored. When the subject was approached, the tendency was to create stereotypical characters or present them in a negative light, such as suffering some form of emotional unbalance or simply portrayed as perverts. In such instances, redemption came in the act of suicide, as demonstrated in the novel *El ángel de Sodoma* (1928) by Alfonso Hernández Catá (1885–1940) and *Hombres sin mujer* (1938) by Carlos Montenegro (1900–81).

Another complexity related to this issue is the fact that the category of "homosexual" is a slippery one because it often depends on the identity of the person in question. It is not only a matter of the denial of homosexuality by people who practice some form of same-sex activity, but of the often arbitrary classification of the historical term *homosexual*. In Latin America, as in some other parts of the world, not every same-sex practice classifies the person as a homosexual. For example, in his autobiography, *Antes que anochezca*, **Reinaldo Arenas** commented how many men in the Caribbean did not consider themselves gay if they perceived themselves as the penetrators in the sexual relation.

Neither governments nor society treated gay and lesbian writers well. Probably the most extreme illustration of discrimination of homosexuals in modern times happened in Cuba after the revolution of 1959. During the 1960s, various social forces that had been present for many years converged. Radical nationalism's homophobia, as well as that of international Stalinism, united in Cuba with all sorts of positions inherited from religion and positivism, gave rise to the persecution of gays and lesbians. Thus, in 1961, gay writer **Virgilio Piñera** was arrested, and although he was freed a few hours later, his detention concerned many Cuban writers. And from 1966 to 1968, gay men were incarcerated in labor camps for being "antisocials." By the middle of the 1970s, homosexual persecution in Cuba diminished, but the old attitudes surfaced in 1980 during the Mariel Boatlift when gay people seeking permission to leave the island were verbally and physically abused and described as "the scum of the earth." The 1990s, however, saw a softening of the homophobic attitude in Cuba. In 1993, the film *Strawberry and Chocolate*, based on the short story "El lobo, el bosque y el hombre nuevo" by **Senel Paz**, dealt explicitly with the discrimination against gays in Cuba. Since the release of the film, many of the writers began to explore their sexuality, be it heterosexual or homosexual, in a frank and direct manner, among them, **Aida Bahr**, Pedro de Jesús López Acosta, and many others.

Whether institutionalized or through the practice of individuals, gay and lesbian writers from elsewhere in the Caribbean encountered discrimination. **Manuel Ramos Otero**, from Puerto Rico, had to move to New York City to express his sexuality. Likewise, the Jamaican American short story writer **Thomas Glave** published articles in *The Gleaner*, protesting against discrimination in Jamaica. In the United States, the eloquent and forceful poetry of **Audre Lorde**, from St. Croix, demanded the removal of the cultural and political barriers that had silenced and ostracized gay and lesbian people and writers for generations. Similar sentiments were expressed by the poet **Dionne Brand** in Canada during the 1980s.

Towards the end of the twentieth century, the emergence of such important writers and scholars as Lourdes Argüelles, Daniel Balderston, **Emilio Bejel**, Emilie Bergmann, Arnaldo Cruz-Malavé, David William Foster, Víctor Fowler, Donna Guy, Jesús Jambrina, Marvin Leiner Ian Lumsden, E. M. Martínez, Oscar Montero, **Shami Mooto, Achy Obejas**, José Quiroga, Ruby Rich, Paul Julian Smith, and **Alfredo Villanueva Collado**, among many others, have improved the acceptance of Caribbean gay and lesbian studies in academia and in literature.

Further Reading

Bejel, Emilio. *Gay Cuban Nation*. Chicago: University of Chicago Press, 2001.

Bergmann, E., and P. J. Smith, eds. *Entiendes? Queer Readings, Hispanic Writings*. Durham, NC: Duke University Press, 1995.

Foster, David William. *Gay and Lesbian Themes in Latin American Writing*. Austin, TX: University of Texas Press, 1991.

Martínez, E. M. *Lesbian Voices from Latin America*. New York: Garland, 1996.

—Emilio Bejel and D. H. Figueredo

Generación del 48

■

This was a group of writers from the Dominican Republic who wanted to present through poetry a nationalist and political image of their nation; they explored biblical themes while also attempting to convey the universality of the arts. Their aim was to engage poets in social issues, though they refrained from any overt criticism of the dictatorship of Rafael Leónidas Trujillo (1891–1961). The members of this group were **Máximo Avilés Blonda**, Rafael Lara Cintrón, Ramón Cifre Navarro, Víctor Villegas, **Lupo Hernández Rueda, Rafael Valera Benites**, Alberto Pena Lebro, and Luis Alfredo Torres. Based in the southern region of the Dominican Republic, these poets began to publish their works in the cultural section— "Colaboración escolar"—of the newspaper *El Caribe* in 1948, thus the term *Generación del 48*. Poet and critic **Marcio Veloz Maggiolo**, in *Cultura, teatro y relatos en Santo Domingo*, considered this generation an extension of the more famous movement known as **Poesía Sorprendida**. *See also* Trujillo Era.

Further Reading

Sommer, Doris, and Esteban Torres. "Dominican Republic." In *Handbook of Latin American Literature*, edited by David William Foster, 271–86. New York: Garland, 1992.

Veloz Maggiolo, Marcio. *Cultura, teatro y relatos in San to Domingo*. Santiago de los Caballeros, República Dominicana: Universidad Católica Madre y Maestra, 1972.

—D. H. Figueredo

Generación del 45, or The Desperate Generation

This term refers to a literary movement in Puerto Rico that broke away from **costumbrismo**, literature of local color, and criollismo, a literature that emphasized the national and the native, to focus on urban issues, be it on the island or in the Puerto Rican communities living in the United States. The movement appeared at the end of World War II and received its first recognition in 1948 with the publication of the book of short stories *El hombre en la calle* by **José Luis González**. Though some poetry was produced by the members of this generation, it consisted mainly of novelists and short-story writers.

The most famous members of this generation were: González, who wrote about Puerto Ricans in New York City; **César Andreu Iglesias**, who penned novels about the struggle between colonialism and separatism; **René Marqués**, playwright, short-story writer, and novelist who studied the effects of colonialism on individuals; and **Emilio Díaz Valcarcel**, an experimental writer who focused on the Puerto Rican intellectual who lived abroad, detached from the island's political problems. Artistically, these writers were influenced by the likes of Ernest Hemingway (1899–1961), William Faulkner (1897–1962), and Alberto Moravia (1907–90). Politically, they favored nationhood for Puerto Rico and expressed feelings of desperation upon seeing nationalism yield to Americanism and the creation of a commonwealth state, thus the appellation the Desperate Generation. Ranging in styles from **realism** to **surrealism**, all of these writers shaped Puerto Rican letters during the twentieth century, and some, like González and Marqués, went on to achieve international recognition.

Further Reading

"La Novela." In *La Gran enciclopedia de Puerto Rico*. Vol. 5.

—*D. H. Figueredo*

Generación del Mariel. See Mariel Generation.

Generación del 60

Influenced by the Cuban Revolution of 1959 and by opposition to the dictatorship of Rafael Leónidas Trujillo (1891–1961), this generation, which flourished from 1960 to 1965, consisted of a group of writers and artists from the Dominican Republic who were intent on writing poetry of nationalism and social protest, promoting their belief that literature should serve as a vehicle for social change. The members of this generation, which included **Miguel Alfonseca, René del Risco y Bermúdez,** Antonio Lockward Artiles, Juan José Ayuso, **Jeannette Miller,** Grey Coiscou Guzmán, Pedro Caro, Anez Bergex, Jacques Viaux Renaud, and Héctor Dotel, rejected regionalism and the concept of art for art's sake, preferring social realism and the clarity of political language. In 1965, when the United States intervened in the civil war raging in Dominican Republic, these writers participated in the struggle against the American forces. The Generación del 60, like Cuba's **Mariel Generation** of 1980, was more of historical development than a literary movement.

Further Reading

Sommer, Doris and Torres, Esteban. "Dominican Republic." In *Handbook of Latin American Literature*, edited by David William Foster, 271–86. New York: Garland, 1992.

—*D. H. Figueredo*

Generación del 30

A Puerto Rican literary movement that was inspired by the island's countryside, the agrarian worker or peasant, and local costumes and traditions and opposed America's culture and political influence on the island. Though the members of this generation continued publishing beyond the decade of the thirties, it was during this period that they achieved maturity as writers. As a group, they were responsible for abolishing the obligatory teaching of English in Puerto Rican schools, thus maintaining the Hispanic culture of the island.

The work most representative of this movement is the novel *La llamarada* (1935) by **Enrique A. Laguerre,** which deals with the exploitation of sugarcane workers. The other creative writers who made up this generation were **Manuel Meńdez Ballester,** whose historical romance *Isla cerrera* (1937) was an exploration of the island's colonial past, and **Tomás Blanco,** short-story writer and novelist whose *Los vates: Embeleco fantástico para niños mayores de edad* (1949) was a philosophical exercise about the conflicts between idealism and materialism. Essayists and literary critics included **Margot Arce de Vázquez, Concha Meléndez,** and **Antonio S. Pedreira.** The poet and dramatist **Emilio S. Belaval** was the best-known member of this generation.

Further Reading

González, Anibal. "Puerto Rico." In *Handbook of Latin American Literature*, edited by David William Foster. New York: Garland, 1992.

—*D. H. Figueredo*

Generación de la Ronde, La

∎

Associated with the journal *La Ronde*, published from 1898 to 1902 and founded by members of the literary club "Les Emulateurs," the writers of this generation shared an ambition to expand the horizons of Haitian literature and to take their place among francophone writers; they demonstrated an interest in literary forms—such as meter and rhyme—and in improving their verses to achieve a state of near perfect poetry.

The foremost poet in the group was **Etzer Vilaire**, a lawyer and judge. Etzer's poetry focused on broader themes of love, moral values, and reflections on life and death, largely leaving behind both political and historical themes. Another writer was **Georges Sylvain**, who produced a volume of fables—*Cric? Crac!* (1901), inspired by La Fontaine (1621–95)—that was the most important early example of a literary work completely written in Haitian or **Kreyòl**. Members of this group included critics, jurists, teachers and two would-be presidents: Louis Borno (1865–1942) and Sténio Vincent (1874–1959).

The generation lasted from 1896 to 1915. Considered imitators of European literary models, the **American occupation of 1915** switched Haitian writers' interest from Europe to the broader national stage and from the external to the internal. *See also* Haitian Literature, History of.

Further Reading

Antoine, Jacques C. "Literature: From Toussaint Louverture to Jacques Roumain." In *An Introduction to Haiti*, edited by Mercer Cook, 93–120. Washington, DC: Pan American Union, Department of Cultural Affairs, 1951.

Laroche, Maximilien. "Haiti." In *Handbook of Latin American Literature*, edited by David William Foster, 333–45. New York: Garland Publishing, 1992.

—Carrol F. Coates and D. H. Figueredo

Gilroy, Beryl (1924–2001)

∎

A teacher and a psychologist, Beryl Gilroy was the first author from the Anglophone Caribbean to write about elderly people, and their treatment in modern society, and to document her experiences as a black Caribbean woman living in England during the 1950s. She was an acclaimed educator and psychologist whose autobiography, *Black Teacher* (1976), like the better-known *To Sir, With Love* (1959), by **E. R. Braithwaite**, described the racism she faced as a teacher in London's slums.

Beryl Gilroy was born on August 30, 1924, in Berbice, British Guiana, now Guyana. After graduating from the Government Technical Institute in 1945, she moved to London and enrolled at London University, earning a bachelors degree in psychology and English in 1954. She earned a master's in English as a second language at Sussex University in 1965 and a PhD in counseling psychology at Century University in 1980. During the late 1940s, she worked for UNICEF. In London, she was the first black woman appointed headmistress of a school. She was also one of the first psychologists to open a counseling clinic for black women.

Gilroy's writing was inspired and informed by her professional background and clinical experiences. In the essay "I Write Because . . ." in the anthology *Caribbean Women Writers* (1990), she recalls that she began to write for children and young adults to fight off cultural imperialism, which "breeds bigots, who in turn breed sturdier and more determined bigots" (198). From that effort came a series of pedagogical exercises and stories entitled "Nippers and Little Nippers Readers" and included *Bubu's Street, My Dad,* and *In Bed,* all published in 1972 and all detailing actual experiences of students in her classes. As a psychologist, she understood the alienation experienced by elderly black women in England and in the Caribbean, where often younger members of the family left their parents behind to seek opportunities abroad. In 1986, she wrote *Frangipani House,* about the "marginalizations that are enforced through ageism," observed scholar Myriam J. A. Chancy in her 1997 volume *Searching for Safe Spaces* (67). It is the story of an elderly woman abandoned by her daughter in a Guyana nursing home. In 1990, Gilroy wrote *Boy-Sandwich,* about a young boy trying to determinate his ethnicity: is he British or is he Guyanese? Gilroy examined colonialism in two historical novels, both published in 1996, *Gather the Faces* and *Inkle and Yarico.* That same year she also wrote *In Praise of Love and Children,* an autobiographical novel about her experiences in London.

Gilroy died of heart failure on April 4, 2001.

Further Reading

Chancy, Myriam J. *Searching for Safe Spaces: Afro-Caribbean Women Writers in Exile.* Philadelphia: Temple University Press, 1997.

Gilroy, Beryl. "I Write Because . . ." in *Caribbean Women Writers: Essays from the First International Conference,* edited by Selwyn R. Cudjoe, 195–201. Wellesley, MA.: Calaloux Publications, 1990.

—*D. H. Figueredo*

Glave, Thomas (1964–)

∎

The second black gay writer to win an O. Henry Award for short fiction, Glave is a Jamaican American short-story writer and educator.

Born in the Bronx, New York, of Jamaican parents, he spent his early years in Kingston, Jamaica, where he was exposed to a culture of storytelling and the expressiveness and musicality of the Jamaican vernacular. Fascinated by the stories he heard, he began to write at the age of five.

When his parents returned to New York City, they enrolled him in Catholic schools. In 1989, he matriculated at Bowden College, majoring in Latin American studies. In 1998, he earned a master of fine arts from Brown University. He traveled to

Jamaica as a Fulbright scholar to study Caribbean intellectual history. He also founded the Jamaican Forum of Lesbians, All-Sexuals, and Gays (J-Flag). In the late 1990s, his short stories began to appear in prestigious literary journals, including the *Kenyon Review* and *Callaloo*. In 1997, he won the O. Henry short-story award, the second black gay author to win such an honor—James Baldwin (1924–87) was the first.

In 2000, he was appointed literature professor at the State University of New York–Binghamton. That same year, he published the collection of short stories called *Whose Song?* The stories depict acts of violence against gay men as well as gentle love stories. The volume was published to great acclaim by numerous publications, such as the *Village Voice* and *Library Journal*.

Glave maintains dual citizenship: American and Jamaican. In Jamaica, he has published articles critical of gay men's oppression on that island. Glave has received numerous awards, including the James Michener Scholar (1993), a National Endowment Arts Travel Grant (1995), and a fiction fellowship from the New York Foundation for the Arts.

Further Reading

Glave, Thomas. "Whose Song." In *Black Like Us: A Century of Lesbian, Gay and Bisexual African American Fiction*, edited by Devon W. Carbado, Dwight A. McBride, and Donald Weise, 456–70. San Francisco: Cleis Press, 2002.

"Thomas Glave." *Contemporary Authors Online*, 2004. http://www.galenet.galegroup (accessed 5/9/05).

—*D. H. Figueredo*

Glissant, Edouard (1928–)

Glissant is a major Caribbean writer, philosopher, poet, and cultural activist from Martinique. He switched from exploring **Négritude,** or black consciousness, as the affirmation of the Caribbean identity to a complex vision of a region that includes multiple ethnicities and cultural heritages. As a writer, his main preoccupation has been to define what it means first to be a Martinican, and second, to be an individual from the Caribbean.

Glissant was born on September 21, 1928, on the hills of Martinique in the town of Sainte-Marie. In 1938, he left his hometown to attend the Lycée des Jeunes Filles, in Fort-de-France, where he studied under **Aimé Césaire,** one of the founders of the Négritude movement. He became involved in the political activities that led in 1945 to Cesaire's election as mayor of Fort-de-France.

When he was eighteen years old, Glissant left for France on a scholarship. He studied at the Sorbonne and the Musee de l'Homme, but because of his political work with several anticolonialist Caribbean organizations, including the Front Antillo-Guyanais, and his participation in the First Congress of Negro Writers and Artists in 1956, he was closely watched by the French government and was not allowed to leave France. During this period, Glissant wrote a play, *Monsieur Toussaint* (1961), about the Haitian revolution, several books of poetry, including

Un champ d'iles (1953), and *Les Endes: Poemes de l'une et l'autre terre* (1955), and his first novel, *La Lezarde* (1958). The poems, which are metaphysical and challenging, illustrate his preoccupation with a Caribbean identity; most of the poems were translated into English in 1998 under the title *Black Salt*. The novel, on the other, proved more popular and was translated into English a year after its original publication as *The Ripening*. Through the story line of a plot to assassinate a Martinican official and the hero's development as an adult, the novel muses on the politics of the Caribbean and the legacy of colonialism.

In 1965, Glissant returned to Martinique to teach philosophy at his former school, the Lycée des Jeunes Filles. In 1971, he founded the journal *Acoma*, which attempted to look at the Caribbean as a single entity rather than a

A major writer from Martinique, Edouard Glissant views the Caribbean identity as composed of several ethnic groups and a diversity of cultural tradition. *Source: Americas Society. Courtesy of Elsa M. Ruiz.*

collection of islands, and, in 1974, he created the school Institut Martiniquais d'Études, devoted to the study of Caribbean history. In 1977, he earned a doctorate from the Sorbonne and three years later was appointed to an editorial post within UNESCO. During the 1980s he taught at Louisiana State University and City University of New York before settling in Manhattan, where he now resides.

His cultural and academic activities have not interfered with his writings. During the 1970s and 1980s he wrote several novels and books of essays and poetry. The novels feature reappearing characters, a nonlinear timeline, and extensive philosophical and political musings; aside from *La Lezarde*, his best-known novels are *Malemort* (1975), *La case du commandeur* (1981), and *Mahagony* (1987). His book of essays *Le discourse antillais* (1981), was translated into English as *Caribbean Discourse* (1989). Scholar and translator **J. Michael Dash** describes the volume as "an exploration of a poetics of the Martinican unconscious" (xxi) and a presentation of the region as "a forest of becoming in the untamed landscape . . . [a] human forest [becoming] Caribbean space" (xli).

Glissant has received numerous awards, including the Ordre des Francophones D'Amerique (1958), the Prix Charles Veillon (1965), and the Roger Callois International Prize (1991). Alongside the Cuban **Alejo Carpentier** and the Guyanan **Wilson Harris**, Glissant is considered one of the most intellectual and philosophical writers of the contemporary Caribbean.

Further Reading

Britton, Celia. "Collective Narrative Voice in Three Novels by Edouard Glissant." In *An Introduction to Caribbean Francophone Writing: Guadeloupe and Martinique*, edited by Sam Haigh, 135–47. New York: Berg, 1999.

Dash, J. Michael. "Introduction." In *Caribbean Discourse: Selected Essays*, by Edouard Glissant; translated by J. Michael Dash. Charlottesville: Caraf Books; University of Virginia Press, 1989.

—*D. H. Figueredo*

Golden, Max. See Marryshow, Theophilus Albert.

Gomes, Albert (1911–78)

∎

A poet, editor, journalist, and politician, Gomes was the founder of the *Beacon*. He was a well-known cultural and political figure in Trinidad from the 1930s to the 1950s. He championed the right of steel bands to play music and was one of the first public officials to call calypso a genuine art form.

Born on March 25, 1911, into a middle-class family of Portuguese and Moorish descent, Albert Maria Gomes was sent to the United States to study journalism at City College of New York. Before his departure from Trinidad, he had expressed an interest in literature, thus while he was away, a friend mailed him a collection of Trinidadian poetry gathered together by would-be author **Alfred M. Mendes.** Excited by the poems he had read, Gomez returned to Trinidad in 1930 and soon befriended Mendes. The two men, and other young writers, met to discuss literature. From these meetings, in 1931 emerged the journal *The Beacon*, funded by Gomes with money his mother gave him. Soon enough, *The Beacon* proved an influential vehicle for the promotion and creation of Trinidadian literature. The journal also challenged British rule.

Gomes published some of his poems in the journal as well as an influential article, "A West Indian Literature" (1933), calling for the development of a national literature. He also became involved in politics, siding with the common workers, espousing a leftist ideology, and advocating for independence. He won a seat in the Trinidadian House and held it for nearly three decades. In 1937, he edited the volume *From Trinidad: Poems and Short Stories.*

In the 1950s, Gomes campaigned for the establishment of the West Indian Federation, meant to bring together all the Anglophone islands of the Caribbean. When the federation was dissolved in 1962 and when he lost his seat in the House, Gomes left the island and settled in England, where he wrote his autobiography, *Through a Maze of Colour* (1974). The volume is an account of his life on the island, political development in Trinidad, and a portrayal of such great writers and friends as A. M. Mendes and **CLR James.** The autobiography is also an astute study of racial relations in Trinidad and Great Britain and of the whimsical nature of racism. In the autobiography, Gomes recalled how in Trinidad he was considered white while in England he was considered "coloured."

Gomes passed away on January 13, 1978, having completed the autobiographical novel *All Papa's Children*. Trinidadian journalist Jeremy Taylor sums up Gomes thus: "Gomes was a man who enjoyed controversy. He relished a fight. He loved a good cause, and adopted plenty of them during thirty years of public life in Trinidad." Much of Gomes's poetry and many of his articles have yet to be published in book format.

Further Reading

Gomes, Albert. "Through a Maze of Colour" (an excerpt). In *The Routledge Reader in Caribbean Literature*, edited by Alison Donnell and Sarah Lawson Welsh, 166–71. London: Routledge, 1996.

Taylor, Jeremy. "Missing Action." *Caribbean Beat*, September/October 2005. http://www.meppublishers.com (accessed 9/5/05).

—*D. H. Figueredo*

Gómez de Avellaneda, Gertrudis (1814–73)

Alongside poet **José María Heredia**, Gómez de Avellaneda is considered one of the most important literary figures produced by Cuban **Romanticismo**. She was an early feminist and an abolitionist.

Gómez de Avellaneda was born on March 23, 1814, in Camagüey, Cuba, to a Spanish father and a Cuban mother. She went to live in Spain at the age of twenty-two, after rejecting the offer of a "good" marriage in Cuba—an unheard of decision at a time when society ladies were expected to marry well and to accept such offers. In 1845, she bore a daughter out of wedlock to Spanish poet Gabriel García Tassara (1817–75), but the infant died a few months later. In 1846, Gómez de Avellaneda married Pedro Sabater, a politician, who died three months later. After a conventional period of mourning, Gómez de Avellaneda returned to Madrid.

In 1841, Gómez de Avellaneda wrote the abolitionist novel *Sab*, the first work in Spanish to condemn slavery. Between 1846 and 1858, she entered a

Gertrudis Gómez de Avellaneda was a feminist who wrote the first novel in Spanish to attack slavery and promote emancipation. *Source: Otto G. Richter Library of the University of Miami, Cuban Heritage Collection. Courtesy of Lesbia Varona.*

period of intense creative and intellectual activity, writing over a dozen plays, all of which were staged in Madrid to great acclaim. In 1853, she tried to become a member of the Academia Española but was denied entry because she was a woman. Later on, she married Colonel Domingo Verduo, who was assigned a military post in Havana; she returned to Cuba with her husband in 1859.

In Havana, she presided over the journal *Album Cubano de lo Bueno y lo Bello,* in which she published works by **Juan Clemente Zenea** and **Gabriel de la Concepción Valdés**. When her husband passed away in 1863, she traveled with her brother to the United States, Great Britain, and France before returning to Spain. She wrote for numerous journals and translated poetry from French to Spanish. She used the pseudonym "La peregrina." Gómez de Avellaneda died of diabetes in 1873. *See also* Abolitionist Literature; Cuban Literature, History of.

Further Reading

Albin, María C. *Género, poesía y esfera pública: Gertrudis Gómez de Avellaneda y la tradición romántica* Madrid: Editorial Trotta, 2002.

Alzaga, Florinda. *La Avellaneda: intensidad y vanguardia.* Miami, FL: Ediciones Universal, 1997.

—*Pamela María Smorkaloff*

Gonzalez, Anson (1936–)

Gonzalez is a poet, publisher, radio broadcaster, and promoter of Caribbean literature from Trinidad and Tobago.

Gonzalez started to write at an early age to escape monotony and to understand his own growth as an individual. In 1967, he wrote *Quinquennial,* which was included in the publication *Writing: Anniversary 5.* The poem brought him recognition, and he continued to publish his writings in numerous journals and anthologies. In the 1970s, he became interested in promoting poetry and cultural life in the Caribbean, and, in 1973, he founded the journal *The New Voices.* Through this journal, Gonzalez published the reference volume *Bibliography of Creative Writing in Trinidad and Tobago* (1962).

In 1979, he established Poetry Day in Trinidad-Tobago and produced two radio programs, *Self-Discovery Through Literature* and *Trinidad and Tobago Literature,* and featured the works of neglected women writers from the Caribbean. During this decade, he also wrote several children's books, including *Daaga, the Warrior* (1975) and *Towards Lagos* (1978). In 1981, he founded *The New Voices Newsletter,* which provided information on emerging writers.

His work as literary promoter and his own poetry resulted in an invitation by the **Casa de las Américas** to serve as judge in a literary contest. In 1988 and 1990, Gonzalez was awarded the Writers' Union of Trinidad and Tobago Writer of the Year Award, and in 1996 the James Michener Fellowship, from the University of

Miami. His works include: *Collected Poems, 1964–1979* (1979), *Merry-Go-Round: and Other Poems* (1992), *Crossroads of Dream* (2005).

Further Reading

"A brief biography of Anson Gonzalez." http://www.users.rcn.com/alana.interport/anson-bio.html (accessed 9/5/05).

Donnell, Alison, and Sarah Lawson Welsh. *The Routledge Reader in Caribbean Literature.* London: Routledge, 1996.

—*D. H. Figueredo*

González, José Luis (1926–96)

■

One of Latin America's great writers, González preferred to see himself as a true son of all the Caribbean, with all its ethnic manifestations. He wrote to critic **Ángel Flores,** for the volume *Spanish-American Authors: The Twentieth Century*, "To sum it all up: José Luis González, a Puerto Rican, Caribbean, and Latin American writer." Nevertheless, the island of Puerto Rico and the lives of Puerto Ricans served as the inspiration for his writings.

González was born in the Dominican Republic on March 8, 1926, some sources say 1929, the son of a Puerto Rican father and a Dominican mother. When he was four years old, his family moved to Puerto Rico. He attended elementary and secondary schools in San Juan and was tutored by short-story writer **Juan Bosch**, from the Dominican Republic. Bosch introduced him to literature and taught him writing techniques. At the age of seventeen, González published his first book of short stories, *En la sombra* (1943). Two years later, González's second collection of stories, *Cinco años de sangre* (1945), received the literary prize from the Institute of Puerto Rican Literature. By now, critics were claiming that González's experimental style was changing the writing of short stories on the island, which tended to imitate nineteenth-century models of realistic fiction.

Upon graduation from the Universidad de Puerto Rico, he earned a graduate degree in literature from the New School of Social Research in 1948. During his stay in Manhattan, he finished *El hombre en la calle* (1948), a collection of stories with an urban setting, and gathered the material for a book about Puerto Ricans in New York City, *En Nueva York y otras desgracias*, which he would publish in 1973.

Rejecting Puerto Rico's commonwealth status—which he interpreted as a form of colonialism—González moved to Mexico, becoming a Mexican citizen in 1955. In Mexico, he was appointed professor of literature at the Universidad Nacional Autónoma de México, in Coyoacán, and at the Universidad de Guanajuato. After publishing two more collections, *Paisa* (1950) and *En este lado* (1953), González did not publish another book for two decades. When questioned why, he always explained that he was working on his memoirs—*La luna no era de queso: memorias de infancia*, published in 1988.

In 1972, he published a short novel, *Mambrú se fue a la guerra*, in which his anti-American sentiment and socialist philosophy made the book a best seller in the former Soviet Bloc countries, where the novel was quickly translated into Rumanian and Polish. In 1978, he was awarded the Xavier Villaurutia Prize for literature for his novel *Balada de otro tiempo*. Scholarly work attracted his attention as well, and during the 1970s he wrote several books of literary theory and criticism, including *Literatura y sociedad en Puerto Rico* (1976) and *Plebeyismo y arte en el Puerto Rico de hoy* (1979).

In the decade of the 1980s, González continued to write short stories while also crafting political and social essays: *El país de cuatro pisos y otros ensayos* (1980), which he updated and revised in 1985 and 1989. In this controversial volume, González combines memoirs, essays, and short fiction to comment on the political situation in Puerto Rico, affirming the need to acknowledge the island's African heritage, a notion denied by earlier scholars, who were more interested in emphasizing Puerto Rico's ties to Spain. He also revised some of his short-story collections, including a new edition of *Balada de otro tiempo*. The revised and reissue of an older work supported his notion of writing as an ongoing process in which a writer has the ability to improve his work with age and experience. Throughout his productive life as a writer, he remained a professor. Expressing his solidarity with workers, he wrote in *Spanish American Authors*: "I earn my own living, without exploiting anybody" (380).

He passed away on December 8, 1996.

Further Reading

Díaz Quiñones, Arcadio. *Conversación con José Luis González* Santa Rita, Río Piedras, Puerto Rico: Ediciones Huracán, 1977.

Falcón, Rafael. *La emigración puertorriqueña a Nueva York en los cuentos de José Luis González, Pedro Juan Soto y José Luis Vivas Maldonado*. New York: Senda Nueva de Ediciones, 1984.

González, José Luis. "Jose Luis Gonzalez." In *Spanish American Authors: The Twentieth Century*, edited by Angel Flores, 378–81. New York: H. W. Wilson Company, 1992.

—D. H. Figueredo

González Echevarría, Roberto (1943–)

González Echevarría is, without a doubt, the most important Hispanist of our time. He stands tall next to luminary figures of any literary field, including those of the likes of critics and theorists Harold Bloom (1930–), Paul de Man (1919–83), and Stanley Fish (1938–). He is the leading scholar in Peninsular and Latin American literatures and feels at home in both areas of research. As the Sterling Professor of Hispanic and Comparative Literature, Yale University has bestowed upon him the highest honor possible. González Echevarría has also been recognized by other universities, having received honorary degrees from Columbia University, University of South Florida, and Colgate University. Other tributes include a symposium sponsored by the University of Puerto Rico, Arecibo (2002), and a special issue of *Encuentro de la Cultura Cubana* (2004) devoted to his work.

Born November 28, 1943, in Sagua la Grande, in the province of Santa Clara, Cuba, González Echevarría's family, like many other Cubans, sought exile in Miami after **Fidel Castro**'s rebels overthrew the Batista (1901–73) dictatorship in 1958. As a recent exile, he held odd jobs, including a stint as a semi-pro baseball player, as he completed his high school diploma. He received a BA from the University of South Florida (1964), an MA from Indiana University (1966), and a MPh (1968) and PhD (1970) from Yale University. He began his career at Yale (1970–71), continued it at Cornell University (1971–77), and, since his return to Yale in 1977, will most likely retire there. In the meantime, he continues to influence students and colleagues alike.

Considered the leading Hispanist of our times, Roberto González Echevarría has influenced generations of literary critics. *Courtesy of Roberto González Echevarría.*

González Echevarría is a prolific writer whose scholarship knows no boundaries. He has published extensively in both Peninsular and Latin American literatures, from the earliest to the most recent periods. He is well read not only in the field of literature but also in anthropology, history, politics, and philosophy, among others. His works will have an immeasurable impact for many decades to come.

González Echevarría published his first article, as a graduate student, on the Spanish writer Azorín (1873–1967), in the prestigious *Revista de Occidente* in 1969, and his first books on *Calderón ante la crítica: Historia y antología*, 2 vols. (with Manuel Durán) and *Relecturas: estudios de literatura cubana* in 1976. But it was his *Alejo Carpentier: The Pilgrim at Home* (1977) that established him as a major figure in literary criticism. In this exemplary book, González Echevarría studies **Alejo Carpentier**'s life and works, from his early poems and short stories to his novels, in a perceptive and analytical manner that went beyond anything previously written on that author or any other author, for that matter.

Like his Carpentier book, *La ruta de Severo Sarduy* (1987) considers the writings of another Cuban, albeit younger, writer. Here González Echevarría combines close readings of **Severo Sarduy**'s production, from the novels *Gestos* (1963) and *De donde son los cantantes* (1967) to *Colibrí* (1984), with other canonical Cuban texts and political events before and after the Cuban Revolution. In search of nostalgia, origin, and absence, this book underscores the brilliance of Sarduy, but also of González Echevarría.

The Voice of the Masters: Writing and Authority in Modern Latin American Literature (1988) confirmed González Echevarría's preeminence in the field. To the works of Cuban writers like **Guillermo Cabrera Infante, Fernando Ortiz, Miguel Barnet**, and Carpentier, he studies those of José Enrique Rodó (1872–1917), Julio Cortázar (1911–1984), Carlos Fuentes (1928–), Mario Vargas Llosa (1936–), and Gabriel García Márquez (1927–). With his deft analysis of contemporary master writers, González Echevarría adds his own voice as a master among the writers.

Myth and Archive: A Theory of Latin American Narrative—winner of the 1992 Latin American Studies Association's Bryce Wood Award for Outstanding Book on Latin America—studies the origin and development of the Latin American novel. *Celestina's Brood: Continuities of the Baroque in Spanish and Latin American Literature* (1993) is a collection of ten essays that shows the interconnection of the **baroque** in Peninsular and Spanish American literatures. Beginning with Fernando de Rojas's (1473 or 1476–1541) *Celestina*, González Echevarría addresses the baroque as an excess and exorbitant producer of multiple meanings in the *Lazarillo*, and works by Cervantes (1547–1616), Lope de Vega (1562–1635), and Calderon de la Barca (1600–1681); and in the New World by **Silvestre de Balboa**, Juan de Espinosa Medrano (1632–1688), Carpentier, **Nicolás Guillén** and Sarduy.

The Pride of Havana (1999) addresses the author's personal interest with scholarship and combines autobiography with research. The book is about baseball, Cuba's pastime. And through recollections, extensive research, and interviews, González Echevarría traces the history of Cuban baseball and reads it as a metaphor of Cuban culture, from its origin in the 1860s to Fidel Castro's coming to power. This book was named a Notable Book of 1999 by the *New York Times Book Review* (1999) and was the winner of the first Dave Moore Award for Most Important Book on Baseball from *Elysian Fields Quarterly* for 2000.

Crítica práctica/Práctica Crítica (2002) proposes a new approach to Spanish American literature, one that brings together teaching, research, and journalism. As with his book on baseball, González Echevarría allows his personal voice to surface. *Crítica práctica/Práctica Crítica* relates the old and the new, the chronicles with contemporary narrative, Cervantes with Jorge Luis Borges (1899–1986) and Carpentier, Luis de Góngora y Argote (1561–1627) with **José Lezama Lima**, literature with dance and baseball. It is a hybrid text, featuring personal comments and scholarly analysis, as well as essays, articles, notes, a review, a letter, a telegram, and pictures of the author with writers.

Last but not least, with Enrique Pupo Walker, González Echevarría coedited three volumes of *The Cambridge History of Latin American Literature* (1996), which is the definitive source on the subject of Latin American literature.

Further Reading

Contemporary Authors Online. The Gale Group, 2001. http://www.Galenet.galegroup.com (accessed 5/9/05).

Sánchez, Miguel Angel. "Universidad de Columbia otorga doctorado 'honoris causa' profesor cubano: Roberto González Echevarría y su carrera ejemplar." *El Diario La Prensa*, June 3, 2002.

—*William Luis*

González García, Matías (1866–1938)

The author of the first naturalistic novel in Puerto Rico, *Cosas* (1893), González García was a prolific short-story writer and novelist. He was also a journalist and a newspaper editor.

Born in Gurabo, Puerto Rico, on December 9, 1866, he attended private elementary school in his hometown and a Jesuit high school in Spain, where he was sent to prepare for a medical career. He matriculated in medical school at the Universidad de Santiago de Compostela, but after two years of study, he opted to return to Puerto Rico. Back on the island, he passed a pedagogical examination and obtained a teaching certificate, enabling him to practice a vocation he cherished and providing him with the time he needed to write.

Though González García wrote some poetry and a few plays, he essentially cultivated prose, writing over four hundred short stories and several novels. His stories are representative of **costumbrismo**, sketches of local color, and express his love for the countryside and the Puerto Rican peasant. However, González García was also influenced by **naturalismo**, which depicted the tragic lives of characters from the lower socioeconomic spheres, and some of his novels were written in that vein.

González García wrote *Cosas*, about poor farmers, in 1893. He then wrote *Ernesto* (1895), *Carmela* (1903), and *Gestación* (1905). The latter novel, which tells of the struggle of peasants to organize into a cooperative, had been serialized in newspapers a decade earlier and is considered his best novel. During this period, he founded the newspapers *El Correo del Este* and *Rocinate*.

Also active in politics, he was elected to the Puerto Rican Congress in 1904 and served as municipal secretary in Gurabo. In 1924, he was elected mayor of Gurabo. In 1922, he published his only book of poetry, *Cosas de antaños y cosas de ogaño*, a nostalgic view of the nineteenth century. Many of his short stories were gathered into one volume in 1922 under the title of *Cuentos*. In 2000, a forgotten novel, *Guerra*, about the American occupation of Puerto Rico in 1898, was published.

Further Reading

Rivera de Álvarez, Josefina. "La novela puertorriqueña desde sus orígenes hasta el presente." In *La Gran enciclopedia de Puerto Rico*, vol. 5, edited by Vicente Báez, 88. San Juan: Puerto Rico en la Mano and La Gran Enciclopedia de Puerto Rico, 1981.

—*D. H. Figueredo*

González Torres, Rafael A. (1922–)

A novelist from Puerto Rico, González Torres is a literary critic and academician. His best-known work is the existentialist novel *Un hombre se ha puesto de pie* (1970), in which he toys with the relationship between the novelist and the reader, playfully suggesting literature's inability to duplicate reality.

Torres was born in Utuado, Puerto Rico, on December 17, 1922. A passion for literature and traveling took him to the University of Munich, Germany, and Universidad de Madrid, Spain, before returning home to the Universidad de Puerto Rico, where he earned a PhD in philosophy and literature. From 1967 to 1972, he chaired the Spanish Department at the Colegio Universitario del Cayay and edited the journal *Revista de Estudios Generales.*

During this period he wrote his most famous work, *Un hombre se ha puesto de pie.* Though written in short chapters in language that is sparse and direct, evocative of the style used by Albert Camus (1913–60) in *L'Etranger* (1942), the novel was both an existentialist statement and a psychological game between writer and characters, readers and the novel, creating the uncertainty as to whether the volume was the author's memoir or a narrative about a character who wants to be as real as the author. *Un hombre se ha puesto de pie* was an instant success, both in Puerto Rico and abroad.

In 1976, González Torres wrote a second novel, *El retrato de oro,* which received the literary prize from the Instituto de Literatura Puertorriqueña. A year later, his literary study *Los cuentos de Emilia Pardo Bazán* was published; the work was well received by the critics who praised the author's accessible language. In 1978, he published *La busqueda de lo absoluto o la poesía de Francisco Matos Paoli,* an idelogical analysis of the Puerto Rican poet, and, in 1981, *La obra poética de Félix Franco Oppenheimer.* In these literary studies, while searching for the universal in these writers' works, Gonzalez Torres affirmed their Puerto Rican identities and nationalism. In 1996, he published a nostalgic memoir, *Mi niñez y juventud en Utuado: retratos de una época y de una familia puertorriqueña*

Further Reading

Ciarlo, Héctor Oscar. *El escritor y su obra: al encuentro de Concha Meléndez y otros ensayos.* Río Piedras, Puerto Rico: Editorial de la Universidad de Puerto Rico, 1982.

Fernández de Encinas, Serapio. Prologo. *Un hombre se ha puesto de pie,* by Rafael González Torres. Río Piedras, Puerto Rico: Editorial Universitaria, 1981.

—*D. H. Figueredo*

Goodison, Lorna (1947–)

An internationally acclaimed poet, Lorna Goodison employs traditional form, metaphor, and **code switching** to create a poetry that celebrates language and the senses as well as meditates on history. Goodison's poetry is testimonial and at times ecstatic. Her portraits of ancestors and local personalities not only evoke her native Jamaica but speak to larger social issues. Among the themes she explores are the legacy of slavery, the family as a source of solace, and the mystery and splendor of nature.

Goodison, who is of African and European heritage, was born on August 1, 1947, in Kingston, Jamaica. She recounted in a BBC interview in 2002 her early experience of reading Wordsworth's poem about daffodils and wanting to write about flowers she knew in her own country. She also felt the impulse to "make things true." She started writing in the 1960s and was influenced by William Wordsworth (1770–1850) and other icons of European literature, such as William Butler Yeats (1865–1939) and Anna Akhmatova (1889–1966), as well as by the Persian poet Rumi (1207–1273), and by popular cultural icons such as Bob Marley (1945–1981). The politics of the time—it was the period when Jamaica gained its independence—also influenced her worldview.

Goodison attended the Jamaican School of Art, in Kingston (1967–68) and the Art Students League, in New York (1968–69). She was a fellow at the University of Iowa International Writing Program (1983) and a Bunting fellow at Radcliffe College (1986–87). She presently lives and works in Toronto.

She is the author of eight books of poems, from *Tamarind Season* (1980) to *Travelling Mercies* (2001). In addition to her poetry, she has published a work of fiction, *Baby Mother and the King of Swords* (1990). Her work has appeared in *The Vintage Book of Contemporary World Poetry* and *The Norton Anthology of World Masterpieces*. She has received the Commonwealth Writers Prize (1976) and the Musgrave Gold Medal (1999). Goodison has also distinguished herself as a painter; many of her images appear on the covers of her books.

Lorna Goodison combines traditional form, a bold narrative style, and resonant, metaphorical imagery to produce a highly personal and lyrical poetry. At times, she "switches" between standard English and Creole, creating a textural language that conveys the immediacy of the spoken word, as illustrated in "Crossover Griot"(2001):

> Still they ask her
> why you chant so
> And why she turn poet
> not even she know.

Her poems celebrate language as well as the natural world. "About the Tamarind" (2001), for example, sensually relates the history and symbolic properties of that versatile fruit, which is "still here, still bearing after five hundred years." "To Us, All Flowers Are Roses," in her *Selected Poems* (1992) as well as the title poem of one of her more recent books (1995), evokes a sense of place through an accumulation of images drawn from picturesque names of towns such as "Heart-ease," "Amity," and "Friendship," names that Goodison has called "aspirational."

Portraits of family members, especially "For My Mother (May I Inherit Half Her Strength)"—in *Selected Poems*—and "Leanna" (2001) explore the poignancy of attachment and loss. "Elephant," "The Lace Seller," and "The Woman Speaks to the Man Who Has Hired Her Son," all published in 1995, portray unnamed local characters that the poet dignifies by telling their stories. These portraits also provide social commentary on class, race, and exploitation. In the last poem, a desperate mother wonders

> what kind of father
> would give a son hot and exploding
> death when he asks for bread.

Other poems throughout her collections are dedicated to icons such as **Marcus Garvey**, Rosa Parks (1913–2005), and Nelson Mandela (1918–). The poet also addresses the legacy of Africa—the brutal history of slavery as well as ancestral traditions. In "Inna Calabash" (1995), a slave girl learns how to outwit "Massa" by feigning pregnancy with an empty gourd. In "Birthstone" (1995), an elder passes on folk wisdom to a woman about to have her first child. These pieces help record and honor the poet's heritage through language and memory. Her anthem-like "Mother, the Great Stones Got to Move" (1992) decries past and present oppression but culminates with an image of "anise and star water, bright fragrant for our children's future," thus revealing the poet's larger vision of hope.

Finally, Goodison is an ecstatic poet, as demonstrated in poems that evoke a spiritual dimension, whether through religion, the invisible world, or art. "Mysteries" and "Was It Legba She Met Outside the Coronation Market?" (1995) both exemplify this vein—the former through the enigmatic image of "peridots," the latter through a colorful anecdote about the Yoruba god. The last line of the transcendent "Deep Sea Diving" (2001) invites the speaker to learn "the infinite possibilities of flying," an apt metaphor for the poet's oeuvre as a whole.

Lorna Goodison's love of language, far-ranging imagination, and rich subject matter animate her poems, instilling them with great emotional and historical resonance.

Further Reading

Chamberlin, J. Edward. *Come Back to Me My Language: Poetry and the West Indies.* Chicago: University of Illinois Press, 1993.

Chang, Victor L. *Three Caribbean Poets on Their Work: E. Kamau Brathwaite, Mervyn Morris, Lorna Goodison.* Mona, Jamaica: Institute of Caribbean Studies, 1993.

—*Daniel Shapiro*

Gouraige, Ghislain (1925–78)

Gouraige was an educator and historian from Haiti. During the first phase of his life as a writer and professor, he wrote about Haitian literature. The second half of his life, living in exile, he wrote about the African diaspora.

Gouraige was born in Port-au-Prince, Haiti, where he conducted his primary and secondary studies. He wanted to attend college in Paris, but due to World War II, he traveled to Canada instead, where he earned a BA from the University Laval, in Quebec. When the war was over, he matriculated at the Sorbonne, earning a PhD in literature in 1954. Upon his return to Haiti, he taught at the Lycée Pétion and the Institute of International Studies.

In 1955, he published his first book, a history of the island titled *L'Indépendance d'Haïti et la France*. Combining his love of history and literature, he wrote his second volume, *Histoire de la littérature haïtienne* (1960). In 1963, he published an anthology, *Les meilleurs poètes et romanciers haïtiens*.

The political and economic situation on the island forced him to leave in 1966. He settled in New York, where he taught literature at the State University of Albany. His experiences in exile inspired him to write the play *Mon exil et toi*, which was performed in New York City. He also published the books of essays, *La Diaspora d'Haïtie et l'Afrique* (1974), which was awarded the Prix des Caraïbes prize. His other works include *Amour: révolution de la feme* (1976), and *Continuité Noire*.

Further Reading

Dumas, Pierre-Raymond. *Panorama de la littérature haïtienne de la diaspora. Tome I.* Port-au-Prince: Promobank, 1996.

Herdeck, Donald E. *Caribbean Writers: A Bio-Bibliographical-Critical Encyclopedia.* Washington, DC: Three Continents Press, 1979.

—D. H. Figueredo

Gouverneurs de la rosée (1944)

■

One of the Francophone Caribbean's most popular works and Haiti's best-known novel, *Gouverneurs de la rosée*, written by Jacques Roumain and translated into English as *Masters of the Dew* (1947), is a **peasant novel**, a literary work that expresses solidarity with and celebrates poor rural workers; it's the story of an individual's sacrifice to bring unity and economic salvation to a poor village.

The protagonist is Manuel Jan-Josef, a Haitian who returns home after spending years away in Cuba, working as a sugarcane cutter. In Cuba, he learns about solidarity with other workers and participates in a strike. The experience teaches him that a group of people can bring about changes that one person alone cannot realize. Such mentality helps him address his village's blight: years of drought have destroyed the fields, crops are not growing, and everyone is malnourished. Manuel concludes that the solution to the drought is to irrigate the land, canaling the waters from a stream on a nearby mountain. This plan can only work if Manuel is able to confront the second problem plaguing the village: a bitter land dispute that has divided the families in the village, with the residents siding either with Manuel's relatives or with the novel's villain, a vengeful man named Gervilen.

Manuel first persuades his family and relatives to make peace with Gervilen's people. Then, he meets with the village's elder and convinces him to ask Gervilen's relatives to befriend Manuel's relatives. After addressing Gervilen's relatives and inviting them to work together to build a canal, Manuel is certain that the dispute would be set aside for the betterment of the whole village. But as he returns home, Gervilen, who is jealous of Manuel who has captured the heart of a woman Gervilen desires, knives him. Manuel crawls to his home, and as he lay dying, he begs his mother not to reveal the name of his assailant; furthermore, he asks her to tell the people of the village that his blood should serve as the sacrifice to bring about reconciliation. His mother obeys his wishes, and after his burial, everyone in the village unites to bring water to their fields.

The novel was published posthumously. Considered the best example of the peasant novel, it was soon translated into twenty language with the English version rendered by American poet Langston Hughes (1902–67). *Gouverneurs de la rosée* has been adapted to the stage and was released as a feature film in 1975.

Further Reading

Roumain, Jacques. *Gouverneurs de la rosée*. Port-au-Prince, Imprimerie de l'état, 1944.

———. *Masters of the Dew*. Translated by Langston Hughes and Mercer Cook. Oxford: Heinemann International, 1978.

—*D. H. Figueredo*

Grandparents in Caribbean Literature

Much of the writing of Caribbean authors highlights the relationships between the members of younger generations family or in a community and the older generations as embodied by grandparents, or characters assuming the role of grandparents. Common themes include the grandparents adopting the role of parents, the grandparents' efforts to assure the grandchildren a better life, the struggle of a younger generation to break away from traditions held sacred by the grandparents, and grandparents as a link to the past and Caribbean history. Often by learning the history of their grandparents, characters come to understand the challenges and rewards of their grandparents' lives and the choices they made.

Perhaps one of the best known depictions of a grandparent doubling as a parent while assuring the child has better life and future is the novel *La rue cases nègres* (1950), by **Joseph Zobel**. The grandmother, M'man Tine, is a richly developed character that is caring but dictatorial, gentle but demanding. Her objective in life is to assure that her grandson doesn't become a sugarcane cutter by helping him get an education and move out of the plantation into a city, or even another country.

In the novel *New Day* (1949), by **Vic Reid**, the younger member of the family humors his grandfather—actually, an uncle who has assumed the role—and belittles his knowledge of Jamaican history, breaking away from concepts of nationalism in favor of a more British and aristocratic lifestyle. In *Brand New Memory* (1988), by **Elías Miguel Muñoz**, a husband and wife, successful members of the middle class and representative of American consumerism, view the grandmother as a relic with little relevance in a fast-paced modern society. It is their daughter who can appreciate the spirituality that the grandmother brings to the household. For the young girl, the grandmother is a bridge to a Cuban past and to the girl's roots.

Examples of the grandparents' link to nostalgic and biblical paradise can be found in the poetry of **Roberto Valero** when he writes: Abuela esta dormida en mi cartera / Se que flota una sonrisa de recuerdo / La ausencia de un cuerpo conocido (Grandmother sleeps in my ballet / I know she floats a smile of remembrance / The absence of a known person . . .) In David Dabydeen's poetry volume *Coolie Odyssey* (1988), the grandmother's funeral affirms his responsibility as a writer to revisit the past and to honor the memory of his ancestors. In essence, his grand-mother becomes the tale he has to tell. *See also* Mother-Daughter Relationships.

Further Reading

Figueredo, Danilo H. "Ser Cubano (To Be Cuban): The Evolution of Cuban-American Liter-ature" in *Multicultural Review 1*, no. 6 (March 1997): 25.

Williams, Emily Allen. *Poetic Negotiation of Identity in the Works of Brathwaite, Harris, Se-nior, and Dabydeen: Tropical Paradise Lost and Regained*. Queenston, Ontario: Edwin Mellen Press, 1999.

—Angela Conrad and D. H. Figueredo

Gratiant, Gilbert (1895–1985)

∎

Described as "the 'mulatto' poet of New World metissage (race mixing)" by critic Lucien Taylor—in "Creolite Bites: A Conversation with Patrick Chamoiseau, Raphael Confiant, and Jean Bernabe" (1997), the Martinican Gratiant was one of the first to promote the use of Creole in Caribbean literature. Though proud of his African heritage, he also acknowledged the diverse ethnic roots present in the Caribbean experience.

A native of Fort-de-France, Gratiant grew up in a household where his parents affirmed their African heritage, an uncommon practice at the time. After gradua-tion from the Lycée Schoelcher, he traveled to France, where he studied English. Upon his return to Martinique, he founded in 1927 the journal *Lucioles*, which ex-plored Martinique's African roots and promoted the use of Creole as the language for artistic and literary expression. A year later, Gratiant returned to France to ac-cept a teaching post at the Lycée de Toulouse and the Lycée Molière.

A Communist, Gratiant espoused social causes, yet his love of French culture and his racial mixing often created conflicts with the founders and the members of the **Négritude** movement, including philosopher **René Ménil**, who viewed Gratiant as something of an elitist. During this period, Gratiant was also praising the racial diversity of the Caribbean and promoting the use of Creole.

In 1950, he published, in French, his most important work, *Credo des sang-mêê*. That same year, he published a volume in Creole, *An Moué*. In 1958, he pub-lished another book of poetry in Creole, *Fab' compè Zicaque*. Initially, these books were not welcomed by such compatriots as **Aimé Césaire**, who preferred to write in French and who believed in the need for all Anglophone Caribbeans to embrace their blackness. However, a generation later, writers like **Patrick Chamoiseau** and

Raphaël Confiant, believers of **Créolité**, which embraced the ethnic and racial diversity in the Caribbean, celebrated Gratiant's writings. By the 1990s, Césaire himself was appreciative of Gratiant's efforts, writing the prologue to the monograph *Fable créoles et autres récits* (1995).

Further Reading

Foster, David William. *A Dictionary of Latin American Authors*. Tempe: Arizona State University, 1975.

Taylor, Lucien. "Creolite bites: A conversation with Patrick Chamoiseau, Raphael Confiant, and Jean Bernabe." *Transition*, no. 74 (Summer 1997): 124–62.

—*D. H. Figueredo*

Grimard, Luc (1866–1954)

Grimard was a Haitian poet and a journalist. He served in the diplomatic corps and was also an educator.

Born in Cap-Haïtien, Haiti, on January 30, 1866, Grimard studied in his hometown and became a teacher at Lycée Philippe Guerrier during the period of the **American Occupation** of his country. As a teacher, Grimard advocated pride in Haitian culture and identity, challenging his students to reject American influence. In 1927, he wrote one of his best-known poems, "The Legend of the First Flag," where he narrated how revolutionary hero and leader Jean-Jacques Dessalines (1758–1806), tore the midsection of the French flag to create Haiti's flag in 1803. That same year, he published two books of poetry, *Ritournelles poémes* and *Sur ma flûte de bambous*.

His nationalist activism resulted in his appointment as inspector of the Normal School system in Haiti. Prior to World War II, he served as Haitian Consul in France. Upon his return to Haiti in 1941, he published a collection of short stories, *Du sable entre les doigts*. In 1943, he collaborated with writer **Frédéric Burr-Reynaud** and **Dominique Hippolyte**, in the volume of poems, *La corbeille*. In 1953, he was invited by the Library of Congress to record some of his poetry at that institution. His poetry was accessible, gentle, and celebratory of Haiti.

Grimard passed away on October 24, 1954, while visiting New York City in his capacity as the first president of the University of Haiti.

Further Reading

Herdeck, Donald E. *Caribbean Writers. A Bio-Bibliographical-Critical Encyclopedia*. Washington, DC: Three Continents Press, 1979.

Trouillot, Ernst. *Hommage à Luc Grimard*. Port-au-Prince, Haiti: Impr. de l'État, 1955.

—*D. H. Figueredo*

Griots, Les

———————————————————●———————————————————

This was a Haitian literary group, a literary revue, and a weekly newspaper. In the late twenties, three young men—"les trois D"—Louis Diaquoi, **Lorimer Denis**, and **François Duvalier**, met regularly to discuss their nationalist views. While the idea of black consciousness or noirism—"le noirisme"—can be traced back to the beginnings of the Republic of Haiti, the idea of the genius of Africans and those of African descent had been advanced seriously by Louis Étienne Lysius Félicité Salomon jeune—the younger—who was president of Haiti from 1879 to 1888.

Diaquoi announced the formation of the "Griots" group in 1932. Following his death that year, Duvalier and Denis continued to stress the importance of African civilization and, following the French ideologue, Joseph Arthur Gobineau, to accept the doctrine of the inequality of races, disagreeing of course as to the superiority of Europeans. **Jean Price-Mars's** research into Haitian archeology and, in particular, into vodou, with its African roots, was also influential for the Griot group. In 1938, the group brought out the first issue of the literary and cultural revue, *Les Griots*, with the poet **Carl Brouard** as editor. Four additional volumes appeared, the last numbered 5–6, October 1939–March 1940. One of the early contributors to *Les Griots* was the poet **Magloire-Saint-Aude**. After World War II, a weekly newspaper appeared under the same title from 1948 to 1950.

After World War II, **René Piquion** joined Duvalier and Denis in praising vodou and the importance of African traditions. Piquion attacked the role of Christianity in Haiti, maintaining that the Christians taught a doctrine of despair and weakness rather than the vital traditions brought from Africa. As postwar politics became more unsettled, Duvalier and Denis further attacked the liberal "mulattoes"—who were traditionally the elite in power—and promoted the need for a rising black middle class to ally itself with the masses of Haitians. *See also* Négritude.

Further Reading

Dash, J. Michael. *Literature and Ideology in Haiti, 1915–1961*. London: Macmillan, 1981.

Nicholls, David. *From Dessalines to Duvalier: Race, Colour and National Independence in Haiti*. Rev. ed. New Brunswick, NJ: Rutgers University Press, 1996.

—*Carrol F. Coates*

Grupo La Cueva. See Cabral, Manuel del.

Guanina

———————————————————●———————————————————

A popular Puerto Rican legend retold by writer **Cayetano Coll y Toste** in his book *Tradiciones y leyendas puertorriqueñas* (1924–25), Guanina is the story of the tragic love between the beautiful Taíno Indian Guanina and the young Spanish conquistador and settler Don Cristóbal de Sotomayor. Guanina, aware that Sotomayor is in danger because her brother, Chief Guaybaná, is plotting to rebel against the Spaniards, warns him, but Sotomayor refuses to change his plans to go to the capital. The following day, he leaves with his some of his men. They are attacked by the Taínos, and Sotomayor is killed. When informed of what has happened, Guanina tries to revive him with her passionate kisses and does not let anyone come close or touch her lover's body. The Taíno Indians decide to sacrifice Guanina the next day in order for her to accompany Sotomayor into the other life, but when they reach the site of the tragedy, they find Guanina dead, resting on the chest of her lover. The lovers are buried at the base of the giant native tree called "ceiba," in a tomb crowded with red wild poppies and white lilies.

This beautifully narrated legend is typical of those dealing with incidents and figures of the colonization of the island. In this story Coll y Toste captures the struggles, conflicts, and collision of two different world visions, but also the emotions and experiences that different people share, such as love, loyalty, respect, and commitment. History and fiction mixes, Spanish expressions accommodate Taíno words that refer to names of the people, religious and class divisions— Guanina, Guaybaná; zemi, nitayno, naiboa—to words about war, places and nature—guasábara, bohique; it is a strategy that not only authenticates the stories and the epoch, but establishes the continuity of the impact and legacy of a culture that formed the Puerto Rican people.

Coll y Toste's retelling of the legend has been included in numerous anthologies and is read and studied in schools in Puerto Rico.

Further Reading

Coll y Toste, Cayetano. *Folk Legends of Puerto Rico*. Translated by Coll Y Toste, José L. Vivas, Ulises Cadilla. Trans Caribbean Airways, [n.d.].

—Asela R. Laguna

Guerra Mondragón, Miguel (1880–1947)

Guerra Mondragón was a Puerto Rican politician and public official who wrote essays on the political and cultural formation of the island. He was a translator and a journalist.

Miguel Guerra Mondragón y Mártinez de Andino was born in San Juan on September 29, 1880. After graduating from the high school Instituto de Segunda Enseñanza de Puerto Rico, he began his law studies in Spain while he was still a teenager. However, the beginning of the Spanish-Cuban-American War of 1898 forced him to return to Puerto Rico. A year later, he went to Pennsylvania, and from there to Washington, D.C., where he studied at Washington National University. He became a lawyer in 1903 and returned to Puerto Rico, setting up a law office with writers **Nemesio Canales** and **Luis Llorens Torres**.

He devoted his life to politics, serving in the Puerto Rican Congress and organizing several political parties, including the Unión de Puerto Rico and the Liberal Puertorriqueño. He also taught at the Universidad de Puerto Rico. Guerra Mondragón wrote for several newspapers and reviews, including *La Democracia, Puerto Rico Ilustrado,* and *Juan Bobo.* He founded and wrote for *Revista de las Antillas.* In his writings, he proposed and elaborated on a form of government for the island that would later on serve as the model for the commonwealth status. But, he also wrote essays on the emerging Puerto Rican literature, revealing a preoccupation with establishing a Puerto Rican cultural identity.

Guerra Mondragón translated into Spanish many classics of British literature, including the play *Salome* by Oscar Wilde (1854–1900). His articles and essays have yet to be collected in book format.

Further Reading

Figueroa, Javier. "Diccionario: Diccionario Histórico-Biográfico." In *La gran enciclopedia de Puerto Rico,* edited by Vicente Báez, 157–58. San Juan: Puerto Rico en la Mano and La Gran Enciclopedia de Puerto Rico, 1980.

"Miguel Correa Mondragón." *Historia del Capitolio.* http://www.linktopr.com/capitolio.html (accessed 9/5/05).

—*D. H. Figueredo*

Guilbaud, Tertulien (1856–1937)

∎

Patriotic poet and admired civil servant, Guilbaud's two books of poetry were inspired by his love of Haiti. His optimistic and nationalistic poetry led the way for other nationalist writers, including the poet **Massillon Coicou.**

Guilbaud was born on May 22, 1856, in Port-de-Paix. He attended elementary school in his hometown and went to the town of Cap-Haïtien for his secondary education. After graduation from high school, he matriculated at Lycée Pétion, where he studied literature and rhetoric. In 1875, he became a high school teacher and was also involved in cultural and political activities.

In 1884, President Lysius Félicité Salomon Jeune (1815–88) appointed him inspector of schools, a post that Guilbaud held for a year. In 1885, Guilbaud traveled to Paris, where he published the book of poems *Patrie.* In 1888, he published *Feuilles au vent.* These books expressed the author's desire to be a guiding light for his country and for his countrymen to unite under the Haitian banner. The poems emphasized the value of education and the need for industry in order for Haiti to advance as a nation.

Guilbaud returned to Haiti in 1889. In 1895, he founded in Cap-Haïtien a school, known as the Free School of Rights, which he directed. A year later, he became actively involved in politics, serving in President Tiresias Simon Sam's (1835–1916) cabinet from 1896 to 1900, secretary of the Ministry of State and Education from 1911 to 1913, and secretary of the Ministry of Justice and Culture in

1915. After the assassination of President Vilbrun Guillaume Sam (?–1915) and the occupation of Haiti by American marines in 1915, Haiti's National Assembly nominated Guilbaud president of the republic, but he declined.

His career as an educator and his involvement in politics did not allow Guilbaud sufficient time for writing. However, his limited output demonstrated his faith in his countrymen and the future of his nation. In one of his best-known poems, "Hymne de foi" (1885), he asks Haitians not to be discouraged because of political uncertainties but to continue nourishing the tree of liberty: "L'arbre de liberté, ne cesse de verdir." *See also* American Occupation of Haiti, Literature of the (1915–34).

Further Reading

Berrou, Raphaël and Pompilus, Pradel. *Histoire de la littérature haïtienne*. Tome 1. Port-au-Prince: Editions Caraëbes.

—*D. H. Figueredo*

Guillén, Nicolás (1902–89)
∎

One of the best poets of the Spanish language, Nicolás Guillén was born on July 10, 1902, in the Cuban city of Camagüey. His father was a senator in the provincial legislature, and during his childhood his family enjoyed a middle-class economic and social position. But in 1917, his father was murdered, and the family was left without economic support. At age fifteen, Guillén began working as a typesetter in the printing office of the Camagüey newspaper *El Nacional*; in the evening he took classes at a private academy. In 1902, Guillén obtained a secondary education degree from Camagüey's Instituto de Segunda Enseñanza and went to Havana to study law at the Universidad de la Habana. But since he did not have the financial means to stay in the capital, he had to return to Camagüey. In 1923, he published a literary journal, *Iris*, while earning a living at the newspaper *El Camagüeyano*. He stayed in Camagüey until 1926, when he was offered a job as a typist in Havana, where he settled permanently.

Guillén began writing poetry during his adolescence, and by the time he had moved to Havana, he had a collection of unpublished poems entitled *Cerebro y corazón*. He started his literary career in Havana when he was asked to contribute to "Ideales de una Raza," a supplement addressed to Afro-Cubans in the prestigious Havana newspaper *El Diario de la Marina*. It was in "Ideales de una Raza" in 1930 that he published his first Negrista poems, a collection he titled *Motivos de Son*. Poems inspired in the life, customs, and speech patterns of the Afro-Cuban masses had been written before, but Guillén was the first Afro-Cuban to do so. The following year he published another collection of Negrista poems, entitled *Songoro Cosongo*, and he included some poems in this style in the collection *West Indies Ltd.*, published in 1934. But in *West Indies Ltd.*, Guillén went beyond the folkloristic to write about the socioeconomic conditions of the Afro-Cuban masses and of the economic and political dependence of Cuba under what he called American imperialism. In 1937 he joined the Cuban Communist Party, and with the collection *Cantos para soldados y sones para turistas*, published in Mexico City, he started his career as a revolutionary poet.

Guillén saw Cuban society as a mixture of Spanish and African cultures, a theme explored in one of his most famous poems, "Balada de los dos abuelos," about a child with white and black grandparents, included in the book *West Indies Ltd*. In 1937, he showed his affection for Spain in the collection *España*, his homage to the Second Spanish Republic. Guillén wrote his last Negrista poems in 1947, in the collection *El son entero*, but he never ceased writing revolutionary poems. Political and social themes are present in all the collections of poetry that he wrote after 1937: *La paloma de vuelo popular* (1958), *Tengo* (1964), *El gran zoo* (1968), *El diario que a diario* (1968), *La rueda dentada* (1972), and *Por el Mar de las Antillas anda un barco de papel* (1977). In 1959, he supported the revolutionary government of Fidel Castro, seeing in its laws which favor the working classes and advocate racial equality—the beginning of a new era in Cuba, when the sociopolitical ideals of the Cuban national hero **José Martí** would become reality. **Fidel Castro** decorated him with the José Martí Order Medal and named him Cuba's National Poet. Nicolás Guillén kept his faith in the Cuban revolutionary government until his death in Cuba in 1989.

The Negrista poems that Nicolás Guillén wrote are among the best in the genre, but he was a gifted poet in all styles and formats, as well as an accomplished prose writer who contributed articles to Cuban periodicals as diverse as *El Diario de la Marina* and the Cuban Communist Party newspaper *Hoy*. *See also* Ballagas, Emilio; Literature Comprometida/Socially Engaged Literature; Negrista Literature; Négritude.

Further Reading

Augier, Angel I. *Vida y obra de Nicolás Guillén*. Habana: Editorial Pueblo y Educación, 2002.

Guillén, Nicolás. *Obra poética, 2. v.* Habana: Unión de Escritores y Artistas de Cuba, 1982.

Márquez, Roberto. "Racism, Culture and Revolution: Ideology and Politics in the Prose of Nicolás Guillén." *Latin American Research Review* 17, no. 1 (1982): 43–68.

Morejón, Nancy. *Nación y mestizaje en Nicolás Guillén*. Habana: Unión de Escritores y Artistas de Cuba, 1982.

—*Rafael E. Tarrago*

Gutiérrez, Pedro Juan (1950–)

The author of scatological stories that paint a picture of the desolation, misery, and despair of an otherworldly city in ruins called Havana and the disturbing exploits of its dehumanized inhabitants during the so-called Special Period, a time of economic shortage in Cuba during the 1990s, Gutiérrez is representative of the Cuban authors who questioned the advances of the Cuban Revolution toward the end of the twentieth century. He is a novelist and a short-story writer.

Pedro Juan Gutiérrez was born on January 27, 1950, in Matanzas, Cuba. His parents had recently moved to that city from the western province of Pinar del Río, having failed at a bar-restaurant business they had established there. In their new city, his parents tried their hand, more successfully, at the ice cream business.

Matanzas has been called the "Cradle of Cuban culture," a city that has traditionally given Cuba more than its share of poets, novelists, musicians, industrialists, artists, and historians, including **José María Heredia** and **Cintio Vitier**. Growing up in that milieu, young Pedro Juan matured in an environment that imbued him with an appreciation for the arts. Because Matanzas is a major port city, Gutiérrez was able to meet and interact not only with the prostitutes that abounded in its La Marina neighborhood, but also with the countless sailors that came ashore. These characters occasionally bought some of the ice-cream cones that he peddled in that district and around the world-famous Sloppy Joe's Bar, or traded him perfume, cigarettes, or clothing for the beautiful seashells he'd pick up by the seashore. This dynamic combination—the arts and the underclass world of pimps, prostitutes, and sailors—would be a key contributing factor in the election of style and content for his work. Also implicated in his intellectual growth, Matanzas's first-rate public library was a refuge where young Pedro Juan would spend limitless hours reading comics and a great variety of books, both Cuban and foreign.

In 1961, Gutiérrez's parents' business and bank accounts were confiscated by the new revolutionary government; here begins a period of penury and destitution for the family. In 1966, Gutiérrez was drafted and served four years in the military, from which he was discharged honorably but with an attached secret file that stated he was undisciplined, conflictive and self-sufficient, incapable of occupying supervisory positions. In order to keep body and soul together, he worked as a farmer, draftsman, union executive, construction worker, radio show host, news reporter, and radio actor. He obtained a degree in journalism in 1978 from the Universidad de la Habana, having enrolled in a special course for workers that met only on Wednesdays. Once he graduated, he worked as a journalist on television and radio, and for the well-known magazine *Bohemia*.

During the 1980s he completed several broadcasts based on his research on, among other things, the penal system, the Brazilian ghettos, the United States—Mexico border, and southern Spain; these won him several national awards for excellence in journalism. In 1987, he finished a book on astronautics that bears the title *Vivir en el espacio*; it was published in 1989 in Havana by Editorial Científico Técnica for its "Vulcano" collection. During the 1980's he also began to write *Melancolía de los leones*, a collection of short stories in which poetry, the absurd, and the strange coalesce in a captivating homage to his two spiritual mentors, Franz Kafka (1883–1924) and Julio Cortázar (1914–84). This work took him thirteen years to complete and was published in 2000 in Havana by Editorial Unión.

Gutiérrez has always been interested in painting, and he attempted to register at the Escuela de Artes Plásticas in Matanzas, but his father disallowed it. At eighteen he received a scholarship to study at the Escuela Nacional de Arte, but military service impeded his entry into that prestigious school. This hasn't prevented him from taking up painting. Some of his works of art hang in private collections in some fifteen countries, in addition to which his experiments with "visual poetry" have gained him much praise.

International acclaim for his writing began in 1998 with the publication by Editorial Anagrama, in Barcelona, of his *Trilogía sucia de La Habana*. An immediate upshot of this was his sudden and unexplained dismissal from his post at the magazine *Bohemia* on January 11, 1999. This dismissal allowed him the time to become a full-time writer. Between 1998 and 2003 he wrote the five books that constitute his "Ciclo de Centro Habana." The first of these is the already mentioned *Trilogía sucia de La Habana*. This novel is in reality a series of vignettes brought together by the main character, an alter ego of the writer named Pedro Juan. This work earned Gutiérrez the soubriquet "the Cuban Bukowski," in view of the similarities critics have found in the works of Gutiérrez and the American author Charles Bukowski (1920–94). The second novel in this cycle is *El Rey de La Habana*, published in 1998 in Barcelona by Anagrama. It takes up where *Trilogía* left off, narrating the tale of a young man who journeys through the streets and barrios of Havana in his quest to survive. Hungry and futureless, Rey, the protagonist, manages to eat just enough to engage in a never-ending spree of sexual encounters of every kind. The next novel in the series is *Animal Tropical*, also published in Barcelona by Anagrama, in 2000. The protagonist is the same from *Trilogía*, but this time he's fifty years old and attempting to write a novel. His sexual exploits continue, although here he curtails his gargantuan appetite, sleeping with only two women. Anagrama published the fourth novel in the series in 2002; its title is *El insaciable hombre araña*, and it follows in the same neo-picaresque mode as the previous three novels. The series is capped by *Carne de perro*, published by Anagrama in 2003, a work wherein the main character—again the author's alter ego—attempts a spiritual-psychological withdrawal—unsuccessful—from his miserable, gloomy environment. During this period Gutiérrez also published three books of poetry and a detective novel.

Pedro Juan Gutiérrez presently lives in Havana, where writing and painting are his principal pursuits.

Further Reading

Obejas, Achy. "From Havana with Love and Squalor." *The Village Voice*, Feb. 13, 2001.

—*Alfonso J. García Osuna*

Guy, Rosa (1925 or 1928–)

Born in Trinidad, Rosa Guy is a young-adult novelist who writes about urban decay and its impact on American black youth. She is praised for her realistic descriptions of Harlem and Brooklyn. Many of her novels are part of the curriculum for schools in the United States and Great Britain.

Rosa Cutbert Guy was born in Trinidad in September of either 1925 or 1928. When she was a young child, her parents left her in Trinidad with a relative while they went to New York City to look for employment. In 1932, Rosa joined her parents in Harlem, but it was a short-lived reunion: within a year her mother became ill and died, her father remarried and divorced, and then, since it was the height of the Depression, he lost his job and was unable to find employment. The sudden and rapid changes in her family life, as well as the process of Americanization, which included exposing the young Rosa to racism, laid the foundation for the books she would write. Her experiences as an orphan, as a young black girl in the United States, and as a minority—a West Indian—within a larger minority—African Americans—enabled her to sympathize with those on the margin of society and to create psychologically and culturally rich characters.

At age sixteen, Rosa married Warner Guy, a soldier. To divert herself from her work at a factory and her responsibilities as a young wife, she joined the American Negro Theater, where she met such would-be legends as Sidney Poitier (1927–), Ruby Dee (1924–), and Harry Belafonte (1927–). However, her primary interest was in writing, thus, in 1951, she and a group of fellow writers formed the Harlem Writers Guild; other members included **Paule Marshall** and Maya Angelou (1928–).

While learning the craft of writing at the guild—where the members would critique each other's works—Rosa Guy noticed Harlem's decay, which had commenced at the end of the 1920s. Her first novel, *Bird at My Window*, published in 1966, documented this decay while telling the story of the relationship between a black mother and her children and the tragic life of a self-destructive young black man. The assassinations of Dr. Martin Luther King (1929–68) and Malcom X (1925–65) and the summer riots that took place in 1968 inspired Guy to compile and edit *Children of Longing* (1970), a collection of interviews with black youth from across the United States. The real young men and women she met became characters in her subsequent novels.

In the early 1970s, she began to work on the trilogy that made her famous: *The Friends* (1973), *Ruby* (1976), and *Edith Jackson* (1978), young-adult novels about three girls, their friendships, and their growth into adulthood. The novels depict the cultural conflict between African Americans and West Indians, family disputes as a result of young West Indian girls rebelling against their parent's cultural upbringing, and the pangs of adolescence, loneliness, and forbidden love—the novel *Ruby* tells of the affair between two of the girls. In 1979, Guy switched from writing about girls to writing about a young boy, in the novel *The Disappearance*. The protagonist is a streetwise teenager who is sent to a foster home in Brooklyn; when the youngest girl in the household disappears, the family accuses the protagonist of abducting her. The protagonist, named Imamu Jones and modeled after African American playwright and poet Amiri Baraka (1934–)—whose birth name was Leroy Jones and whom Rosa Guy had met in the 1960s—was so well crafted that it prompted Guy to write two more mystery novels with Jones as the hero: *New Guys Around the Block* (1983) and *And I Heard a Bird Sing* (1987). Rosa Guy has also written novels for adults, *A Measure of Time* (1983), based on her stepmother's life, and *The Sun, the Sea Touch of the Wind*, about an artist living in Haiti. Guy's success emerges from her realistic characters and engaging narrative.

Observes her biographer Jerrie Norris, in the preface to *Presenting Rosa Guy*, "Rosa Guy is a true storyteller. Twice blessed by the African oral tradition through her Trinidadian roots and Harlem upbringing, she writes novels that both entertain and convey the history of a people" (preface). *See also* Detective Fiction; Realismo/Realism.

Further Reading

Norris, Jerrie. *Presenting Rosa Guy*. Boston: Twayne Publishers, 1988.

—D. H. Figueredo

Guyanese Literature, History of

Many of the great contemporary writers of the English language come from Guyana: **Wilson Harris, Martin Carter,** and the popular **E. R. Braithwaite,** to name a few. Their presence in world literature is indicative of the development of Guyanese culture during the twenteith century. However, as is the case with many other Caribbean countries and territories, cultural activities and literature existed in Guyana before the 1900s.

Although Guyana is located in South America, geography makes its citizens regard themselves as members of the Caribbean. This is because on one side of Guyana lies the Atlantic Coast and on the other, an impenetrable forest stretches for four hundred miles. Thus, Guyana is not connected to the rest of South America, and any communication and contact with the world occurs out of and through the coastline. It is on the thin stretch of land between the coast and the jungle that nearly eight million people live.

In 1581, the Dutch attempted to colonize Guyana. The French soon followed. But in 1814, Great Britain gained control, creating the colony of British Guiana in 1831. Those who attended school during this period, and learned to read and write, were exposed to British literature. Thus, early writings were imitative of literary works from England.

The first major Guyanese writer to emerge was **Leo G. Martin,** who in 1883 published a book of poetry, *Leo's Poetical Works*, which he dedicated to the governor of British Guiana. In 1887, Martin achieved notoriety in England with his addition of two stanzas to "God Save the Queen," written in 1887. His poems, romantic in vein, celebrated and glorified the natural beauty of Guyana.

Through the end of the nineteenth century and the beginning of the twentieth, many poets wrote minor works that were published in local newspapers; some of the names that appeared were Henry Dalton, Harold Moore, and S. E. Wills. True literary flowering occurred in the late 1930s with the poetry of **A. J. Seymour.** This poet became a seminal figure in Guyanese culture when in 1945 he started publishing the review *Kyk-Over-Al*—known as *Kyk*. *Kyk*'s objective was to create a national literature by giving voice to Guyanese writers. Seymour's effort paid off, and the pages of the magazine served as a home to the writers who would dominate Guyanese literature for the next three decades, including the revolutionary Martin Carter and the novelist and innovator Wilson Harris. The journal made Seymour the chief mover of Guyanese literature.

Equally influential was **Edgar Austin Mittelhölzer**, a prolific writer who is often described as the father of the novel not only in Guyana but also in the Anglophone Caribbean. A tragic figure who committed suicide by setting himself on fire in 1965, Mittelhölzer published his first major novel in 1941: *Corentyne Thunder*, about a wealthy mulatto in love with a Hindu peasant girl. One of the few Caribbean writers who actually made a living from writing during the second half of the twentieth century, Mittelhölzer wrote the Kaywana trilogy—*The Children of Kaywana* (1952), *The Harrowing of Hubertus* (1954), and *Kayana Blood* (1958)—perceived as Guyana's national novels.

The 1950s were a turbulent period for the emerging nation. The decade before, the British and the Guyanese people had paved the path for self-government, and in 1953, a new constitution was adopted and Cheddi B. Jagan (1918–97) was elected governor. However, fearing that the new governor was a Communist, the British suspended the constitution, removed Jagan from office, and dispatched British marines to Georgetown, the capital. One of the poets arrested for supporting Jagan was Martin Carter. While behind bars, he wrote *Poems of Resistance from British Guiana* (1955), one of the most eloquent examples in English of socially engaged literature.

During this period, a promising poet switched from writing poetry to fiction. His name was Wilson Harris, and his first novel, **The Palace of the Peacock**, published in 1960, revealed a highly philosophical, cerebral, and oblique mind that has continued to challenge readers in the last four decades. *The Palace of the Peacock* was followed by *The Far Journey of Oudin* (1961), *The Whole Armour* (1962), and *The Secret Ladder* (1963), making up what is now known as "Guyana Quartet."

In 1958, Harris left Guyana for Great Britain. Other writers had preceded him. Many others followed. Like Wilson, these writers were looking for better economic and publishing opportunities. A key factor was the need to work with publishers who could distribute and disseminate books beyond a single country. Some of the writers who left Guyana were **Jan Carew, John Agard, Cyril Dabydeen, Grace Nichols**, and **Fred D'Aguiar**.

Carew was Harris's brother-in-law, and Harris had often taken him on expeditions into the rain forest. It was in one of these journeys that Carew met a man who inspired him to write the novel that made him famous—*Black Midas* (1958). This novel is the story of a Guyanese "pork knocker"—a diamond miner who is also a frontiersman, adventurer, and explorer in the Guyanese jungle—who makes himself a fortune in diamonds, squanders it all, and loses a limb before settling down to a quiet life in a rural village.

Agard became a prolific writer of children's books. A poet and short-story writer, his writings were inspired by Guyana and his love of Afro-Caribbean traditions. In 1982, he wrote *Man to Pan*, about the steel drums used to play calypso. For this work, the prestigious **Casa de las Américas**, in Cuba, awarded him a literary prize. At the age of twenty-five, poet Cyril Dabydeen migrated to Canada. His poetry—*Distances* and *Goatsong* (1977)—was shaped by his Marxist ideals and his realization of the universality of oppression felt by those on the margin of society, regardless of location.

Grace Nichols moved to Great Britain in 1977. Her separation from her homeland inspired her to write. In 1983, she published *I Is a Long Memoried Woman*, haunting poems about the atrocities committed on black people by racists, illustrated by the role of the master during slavery. But the poems also affirmed the need to remember and to rectify the errors of the past: in the poem "I'm coming back," the narrator tells the master that she will bend before him, as expected by the master, but only "to rise and strike." Fred D'Aguiar achieved fame with the publication of his first book of poetry, *Mama Dot* (1985). His poems, long and musical, and his prose, innovative and with shifting viewpoints, explored the effects in the Caribbean of the racist legacy of the colonial era.

Through the 1960s and 1980s, new voices were heard in and outside Guyana. Critic Laurence A. Breiner, in *Introduction to West Indian Poetry*, described these voices as "something unique in the Anglophone Caribbean . . . an almost independent tradition . . . that draws exclusively on the East Indian cultural heritage" (81).

Peter Lauchmonen Kempadoo wrote *Guyana Boy* (1960), one of the first novels to depict the lives of East Indians working on a sugar plantation. **Rajkumari Singh** was one of the first published Indo-Caribbean women. A poet, her most famous piece of writing is the poetic essay, "I am a Coolie" (1973), in which she reshaped the pejorative term *coolie* into an expression of Indian pride. In 1972, she founded the **Messenger Group**, a cultural association that influenced the careers of such emerging writers as **Mahadia Das**.

Mahadia Das was a passionate and politically committed poet; she wrote poems that attempted to capture her cultural heritage and to protest the discrimination Indo-Caribbean people experienced in the Caribbean and in the United States. *My Finer Steel Will Grow* (1982) is one of her best-known collections of poems. Her compatriot **Rooplall Motilal Monar** documented the traditions and customs of East Indians in the Caribbean and depicted the daily struggles of the Indian peasant community in Guyana in such volumes as *Backdam People* (1985).

The arrival of the twenty-first century was marked by a Guyanese literature that is reflective of the diaspora and that it is at home both in Guyana and abroad. Representative of this development is **David Dabydeen**. In his writings—*The Intended* (1991), *Disappearance* (1993), *The Counting House* (1996), and *Harlot's Progress* (1999)—he explored the schizophrenic relationship between the cultural pull from home and the cultural mandates of exile and the host society.

Exile will probably be the dominant experience of the Guyanese writers of the early twenty-first century. But with exile, there will also be a longing for the native country. As such, then, much of the country's literature will be geographically borderless and culturally universal. Fred D'Aguiar phrases it thus in *Talk Yuh Talk*: "I have two landscapes in mind and heart when I think of home" (234). *See also* Anglophone Caribbean Literature, History of; Literatura Comprometida/Socially Engaged Literature.

Further Reading

Breiner, Laurence A. *An Introduction to West Indian Poetry*. Cambridge: Cambridge University Press, 1998.

Dawes, Kwame. ed. *Talk Yuh Talk: Interviews with Anglophone Caribbean Writers*. Charlottesville: University Press of Virginia, 2001.

McDowell, Robert E. *Bibliography of Literature from Guyana*. Arlington, TX: Sable Pub. Corp., 1975.

Temple, Bob. *Guyana*. Philadelphia: Mason Crest Publishers, 2004.

—D. H. Figueredo

H

Habibe, Henry (1940–)

Habibe is a literary editor, critic, and poet from Aruba. He was born on May 6, 1940, in Aruba, of Arabic descent. After attending primary and secondary schools in Aruba, he relocated to Holland at the age of twenty-six. There, he earned a BA in Spanish language and literature from the University of Nijmegen in 1971. While at the university, he, with other students from the Dutch Caribbean, founded the journal *Watapana*, named after the dividivi tree, which is endemic to the islands.

The journal's philosophy, as Habibe saw it, was that the Papiamentu language was the authentic language of the Dutch Caribbean, and, as such, literature from the region needed to be written in that language. In time, this preoccupation widened to examine the essential elements that make up a national literature and culture. The journal was subsidized by the foundation Sticusa, a Dutch organization that promoted cultural cooperation. In 1976, the foundation presented Habibe with an award for his writings and literary labor as editor of *Watapana*.

Habibe's work as a writer consists of two activities: poetic production and literary studies. Critics have noted the social contexts of Habibe's poetry, as well as the intense rhythmic design and use of metaphors. His best-known collections are *Keresentechi* (1980) and *Yiu di tera* (1985). His most famous poem is *Papiamentu na kaminda* (1988), a linguistic saga about the evolution, the past, and the future of Papiamentu. As far as his critical studies, Habibe has written for numerous publications, including *Kaliña, Kristòf, Skol y komunidad, Independiente, Amigoe di Curaçao*, and *Beurs-en Nieuwsberichten*. His literary essays have examined the works of such major Caribbean figures as **Pierre A. Lauffer, J. S. Corsen,** and **Elis Juliana,** among others. He has also compared and contrasted works in Papiamentu with literature produced in Spanish elsewhere in the Caribbean: *El compromiso en la poesía afroantillana de Cuba y Puerto Rico* (1985).

Habibe has a PhD from the University of Leiden and is a Spanish language and literature professor at Arubano College. *See also* Literatura Comprometida/Socially Engaged Literature; Literary Journals.

Further Reading

Broek, Aart G. *Pa saka kara, tomo I: Historia di literature papiamentu*. Willemstad: Fundashon Pierre Lauffer, 1998.

Rutgers, Wim. *Beneden en bowen de wind: Literatuur van de Nederlandse Antillen en Aruba*. Amsterdam: De Bezige Bij, 1996.

———. "Di nos e ta! Outside and Inside Aruba Literature." In *A History of Literature in the Caribbean*, vol. 2: *English and Dutch Speaking Regions*, edited by James Arnold, 451–61. Philadelphia: John Benjamins Publishing Co., 2001.

—*Emilio Jorge Rodríguez*

Haitian Language. See Haitian Literature in Kreyòl.

Haitian Literature, History of

It was illegal to teach slaves to read in prerevolutionary Saint-Domingue, although some, like the would-be liberator Toussaint Louverture (1743?–1803), learned, anyway. The theater was particularly active, however, and artists of color began to appear onstage. Original musical comedies presented scenes of colonial life. **Marie Chauvet's** novel, *Dance on the Volcano* (1959) gives an extensive view of life from the standpoint of slaves and liberated people of color.

Literature by Haitians began to appear in print soon after independence—January 1, 1804. **Boisrond-Tonnerre** (1776–1806), educated in France, wrote the Haitian Act of Independence for General Jean-Jacques Dessalines (1758–1806). **Antoine Dupré** is credited as the first poet of Haitian literature. **Jules Milscent** founded one of the first journals, *L'Abeille Hayitienne* (1817). After Charles X, king of France (1824–30), recognized Haitian independence in 1825, many Haitians were able to study or work in France, gaining exposure to French romanticism.

The poetry of **Coriolan Ardouin**, who died in 1835, was an important source of inspiration for a group of friends called the Cenacle of 1836. Major figures in this group were **Émile Nau**, who would produce a *Histoire des caciques d'Haïti* (a history of the caciques of Haiti; 1855), and his brother **Ignace**; Céligny and **Beaubrun Ardouin**; Beauvais and Dumay Lespinasse, and others. Ignace Nau founded the newspapers *Le Républicain* (1836) and *L'Union* (1837), both publishing poetry and prose by this group.

The first Haitian novel, **Emeric Bergeaud's** *Stella*, was published in the year Emperor Faustin the First died, 1859. In 1860, the Haitian government signed a Concordat with the Vatican, allowing the Catholic Church to establish schools in Haiti. This began a period (to about 1896) of ideological and political contestation between the Liberal and National Parties, reflecting the instability of the government. Liberals tended to be pro-mulatto, anti-military, Catholic, and French-oriented. The

Nationalists were apt to be anti-clerical, pro-military, and attracted by African traditions.

Recognized in Paris as well as in Haiti, **Oswald Durand** is one of the best poets of the period, although his first collected volume of poetry appeared late, *Rires et pleurs* (1896). Durand was a master of genres used by nineteenth-century French poets. **Massillon Coicou** worked briefly in the Ministry of War and taught at the secondary level. "L'alarme," a warning against civil war, is among the most famous poems in his *Poésies nationales* (1892). He was also successful with patriotic dramas such as, *L'Empereur Dessalines* (1906) and satirical plays such as *Fifi Candidat* and *Fifi Ministre,* about the Haitian political scene. President Nord Alexis (1820–1910) had Massillon Coicou arrested for suspicion of subversive activities, and he was summarily executed in 1908.

Among other writers of the period are poets Alcibiade Fleury-Battier (1841–83), Emmanuel Édouard (1858–95), and **Tertulien Guilbaud** (1856–1937). Although she never published an entire volume, **Virginie Sampeur,** the ex-wife of Oswald Durand, should be mentioned as the first woman to publish poetry. Henry Chauvet (1863–1928) and **Isnardin Vieux** were productive dramatists. The themes of drama range broadly from patriotic historical dramas to the evocation of satirical scenes, while philosophical reflection, colorful evocations of the Haitian landscape, and melancholic reminiscences of love past or lost are themes favored by poets.

The early twentieth century brought the emergence of a new Haitian literature and a gradual departure from the thematics of French romanticism. The writers of the **Generation of La Ronde** (1898–1902) share an ambition to expand the horizons of Haitian literature and to take their place among francophone writers. The foremost poet to begin publishing in *La Ronde* was **Etzer Vilaire,** a lawyer and judge. His first volumes of poetry were *Pages d'amour* and *Dix hommes noirs* (both published in 1901). Etzer's poetry focused on broader themes of love, moral values, and reflections on life and death, largely leaving behind both the political and historical thematics of the preceding generations. **Georges Sylvain** produced a volume of fables, inspired by La Fontaine, that was the most important early example of a literary work completely written in Haitian or **Kreyòl.** Sylvain, who had served as Haitian ambassador to France (1909–11), became a leader in the intellectual protest against the United States occupation of Haiti of 1915. Also active were novelists **Frédéric Marcelin, Ferdinand Hibbert, Justin Lherisson,** the author of "La Dessalinienne," Haiti's national anthem, and playwrights **Frédéric Burr-Reynaud, Dominique Hippolyte,** and **Charles Moravia.**

The occupation of Haiti by the U.S. Marines, from 1915 to 1934, brought a form of externally imposed stability back into Haitian affairs. Only the capture and summary execution of Charlemagne Péralte, in October 1919, ended the Caco rebellion in the north. In reaction to the American military presence and Washington's domination, Haitian intellectuals set out in anger to demonstrate the falseness of racist views of the Black Republic. Dr. **Jean Price-Mars,** who had worked in the Haitian embassy in Washington, returned to Haiti and began his efforts to rally discouraged Haitian intellectuals. His major work, *Ainsi parla l'oncle* (1928), focused on African cultural traditions along with the development of popular culture and folklore in Haiti. Price-Mars gave the lie to prejudices about a lack of culture in Haiti. He studied vodou as a religion with its own belief in divinity and moral values, arguing against the idea that religious ecstasy or possession is a form of "racial psycho-neurosis" (Jean-Chrysostome Dorsainville; Berrou & Pompilus, III, 724). He criticized educated Haitians for their "**bovaryism,**" an allusion to Emma Bovary's isolation in the world of her own romantic dreams. The Indigenist movement soon formed around *La Revue Indigène* (1927), edited by **Normil Sylvain**. Among associated writers were **Carl Brouard, Émile Roumer, Jacques Roumain, Philippe Thoby-Marcelin,** and Milo Rigaud. Roumain and Rigaud both continued research and writing on Vodou. Novelists Philippe Thoby-Marcelin, Jacques Roumain, and Milo Rigaud, and Charles-Fernand Pressoir all worked to highlight elements of folklore and popular culture and to bring to public attention the heritage of the Caribbean Indians.

In the wake of the Indigenists, a new revue, *Les Griots*, was founded by Carl Brouard (1938). Principal writers included Kléber Georges Jacob, Léon Diaquoi, **François Duvalier, Lorimer Denis,** and **Magloire-Saint-Aude** (Clément Magloire fils). Jean Price-Mars and Jacques Roumain associated with the revue, but took a distance when Duvalier and Denis began developing their "noiriste" doctrines—a Haitian version of black power.

The repressive regimes of François Duvalier, from 1957 to 1971, and his son, Jean-Claude, from 1971 to 1986, brought about a massive emigration of Haitian intellectuals, giving rise to an important body of diasporic Haitian literature. In Montréal, the members of the group "Haïti Littéraire" founded a journal, *La Nouvelle Optique*, and an associated publishing enterprise. Haitians settled in France—**René Depestre** and **Jacques Stephen Alexis**, followed by **Jean Métellus** and **Lilas Desquiron**; in Africa—**Roger Dorsinville** and **Félix Morisseau-Leroy**; in Canada—**Émile Ollivier, Gérard Étienne, Roland Morisseau,** followed by younger writers Joël des Rosiers, **Robert Berrouët-Oriol,** and **Dany Laferrière**; and the United States—**Paul Laraque** and, much later, **Edwidge Danticat**. Among writers who stayed in Haiti are **Franketienne, Georges Castera,** and **Yanick Lahens**. In spite of financial problems, literary journals continue to appear in Haiti—*Conjonction* and *Chemins critiques*, among others—and a number of authors publish literary and historical works, sometimes in coeditions with French or Canadian publishers. *See also* American Occupation of Haiti, Literature of; Literary Journals.

Further Reading

Berrou, F. Raphaël, and Pradel Pompilus. *Histoire de la littérature haïtienne illustrée par les textes.* 3 vols. Port-au-Prince: Éditions Caraïbes, 1975–77.

Chauvet, Marie. *Dance on the Volcano.* Translated by Salvator Attanasio. New York: William Sloane, 1959.

Gouraige, Ghislain. *Histoire de la littérature haïtienne. De l'indépendance à nos jours* (1960). Geneva: Slatkine Reprints, 2003.

Herdeck, Donald E., ed. *Caribbean Writers. A Bio-Bibliographical-Critical Encyclopedia.* Washington, DC: Three Continents Press, 1979.

Nicholls, David. *From Dessalines to Duvalier: Race, Colour and National Independence in Haiti,* 1979. Rev. ed. New Brunswick, NJ: Rutgers University Press, 1996.

Price-Mars, Jean. *So Spoke the Uncle.* Translated by Magdalin W. Shannon. Washington, DC: Three Continents Press, 1983.

—Carrol F. Coates

Haitian Literature in Kreyòl (the Haitian Language)

∎

In Haiti, Kreyòl, the Haitian spelling of "Creole," is evolving as the language of the people, of commerce, and as an increasingly important vehicle of literary expression. Kreyòl has been the primary language since before independence in 1804 and has, like all living languages, undergone a complex evolution of which the history has yet to be written. The Constitution of 1987 states that "Sèl lang ki simante tout Ayisyen ansanm, se lang kreyòl. Kreyòl ak franse, se lang ofisyèl Repiblik d Ayiti" (all Haitians are united by a common Language: Creole or kreyòl. Kreyòl and French are the official languages of the Republic of Haiti).

Oswald Durand, the best-known Haitian poet of the nineteenth century, wrote in Kreyòl one poem, "Choucoune," which virtually every Haitian knows by heart. At the turn of the century, **Georges Sylvain** published a volume of fables written in Kreyòl, *Cric? Crac! Fables de La Fontaine racontées par un montagnard haïtien* (1901). The subjects are taken from La Fontaine, but the tone, language, and poetic form are completely inscribed in the folk traditions of Haiti.

The first modern writers to begin working in Kreyòl were born toward the beginning of or during the **American occupation of Haiti** (1915–34) and grew up during that period with **Jean Price-Mars** leading the movement to emphasize Haiti's cultural heritage—folklore, the Kreyòl language, vodou, and soon. Among those intellectuals were **Feliks Moriso-Lewa** (Félix Morisseau-Leroy) and **Frank Fouche** (Franck Fouché). Moriso-Lewa published a first volume of poetry, *Dyakout*, in 1951. Both he and Fouche wrote and produced plays deriving their inspiration both from Greek tragedy—Moriso-Lewa, *Antigòn*; Fouche, *OEdipe Roi*—and Haitian folk characters—Fouche, *Bouki nan paradis*. **Paul Laraque** is one of the best poets publishing mostly in Kreyòl from the sixties onward.

Frankétienne is the first Haitian to publish an entire novel in Kreyòl: *Dezafi* (1975). Like Fouche and Moriso-Lewa, he has also recognized and exploited the communicative possibilities of theater in Kreyòl. Several of his plays have been published, but a number of others have been produced without publication. Also born in 1936, **Georges Castera** has published many volumes of poetry in Kreyòl. Now many younger writers—born in the 1940s and later—give expression to wide segments of concerns and feelings of the Haitian people. Among the better-known *sanba* poets, in the broad sense, are Syto Cave, Jozafa Wobè Laj (Josaphat Large), Jan Mapou, Patrick Sylvain, Denize Lotu, and many others.

Apart from the fact that Kreyòl song, storytelling, and theater are deeply ingrained in Haitian culture and comprehensible to everyone, regardless of their facility in reading, a major problem in the dissemination of print literature in Kreyòl has been the lack of a standard orthography. The early writers of Kreyòl used a more or less gallicized and personal orthography. This was true of many major writers—**René Depestre** and **Jacques Stephen Alexis**, for example—when they included proverbs, songs, or samples of conversation within the French discourse of their fiction. With the efforts of Yv Dejan (Yves Déjean) and other Haitian linguists, a standard orthography with relatively few ambiguities has been made official. Franketienne, among others, has recognized this, and his *Dezafi* was republished in France in 2002 in standard Kreyòl orthography. Younger writers have been using the standard orthography for more than ten years now. *See also* Code Switching; Créolité.

Further Reading

Lang, George. *Entwisted Tongues: Comparative Creole Literatures*. Amsterdam: Rodopi, 2000.

Laraque, Paul. *Fistibal/Slingshot*. Translated by Jack Hirshman. San Francisco/Port-au-Prince: Seaworthy Press/Éditions Samba, 1989.

Laraque, Paul and Jack Hirschman, eds. *Open Gate. An Anthology of Haitian Creole Poetry*. Translations by Jack Hirschman and Boadiba. Willimantic, CT: Curbstone Press, 2001.

Morisseau-Leroy, Félix. *Haitiad & Oddities*. Translated by Jeffrey Knapp, et al. Miami: Pantaléon Guilbaud, 1991.

—*Carrol F. Coates*

Harris, Claire (1937–)

∎

A Canadian Trinidadian writer, Harris is a feminist poet who writes on the theme of racial identity in the twentieth century. She uses her poetry to combat stereotypical images of blacks held by Canadian readers. Poet and scholar **Kwame Dawes**, in *Talk Yuh Talk* (2001), observes that Harris has "managed to locate herself as a writer devoted to exploring the landscape and culture of a Canada that is transcultural" while remaining a writer who is "rooted in the Caribbean landscape" (61).

Claire Kathleen Patricia Harris was born on June 13, 1937, in Port of Spain, Trinidad. In her youth, she traveled widely and attended numerous schools in different countries: University College, Dublin, in 1961, earning a BA in English literature; University of West Indies for a diploma in education in 1963; University of Lagos for a diploma in communications. Her international experience, coupled with a longing for the Caribbean, shapes her poetic work.

Harris began to write in her late thirties while she was on sabbatical from her position as a high school teacher in Canada. In 1984, she published her first collection of poems, *Fables from the Women's Quarters*; some of the pieces in this volume were inspired by the works and life of Rigoberta Manchu (1959–), a Guatemalan revolutionary and the 1992 Nobel Peace Prize recipient. Two years later, Harris published *Travelling to Find a Remedy*. The poems in this volume, some in haiku style and others in long, uneven meditative stanzas, were more of a personal nature than those in her first book.

In 1989, her *Conception of Winter* was published. This collection was followed by *Drawing Down a Daughter* in 1992, a collection of poems and stories written to an unborn daughter awaiting delivery. Aside from writing poetry, Harris was also the editor of two literary journals, *Dandelion* (1981–89) and *Blue Buffalo* (1984–87), of which she was cofounder.

During the 1990s, Harris began to travel throughout the world, reading her poems and conducting writing workshops. She is an active member of Amnesty International.

Further Reading

Dawes, Kwame. *Talk Yuh Talk: Interviews with Anglophone Caribbean Poets.* Charlottesville: University Press of Virginia, 2001.

Williams, Emily Allen. *Poetic Negotiation of Identity in the Works of Brathwaite, Harris, Senior, and Dabydeen: Tropical Paradise Lost and Regained.* Lewiston, NY: Edwin Mellen Press, 1999.

—*D. H. Figueredo*

Harris, Wilson (1921–)

One of the Caribbean's greatest writers, Guyanan Wilson Harris writes complex and challenging novels that express the universality of man while introducing new approaches to storytelling and the use of words; his writings evoke the diversity of the Caribbean, expanding from the national to the global. Harris's best-known works are the tetrology the "Guyana Quartet," set in the Guyanese jungles, and the "Da Silva" trilogy, based in London.

Theodore Wilson Harris was born on March 24, 1921, in New Amsterdam, in the former British Guiana, now Guyana. Of mixed ancestry—European, African, and Amerindian—he attended Queen's College in Georgetown, becoming a land surveyor. He worked for the British

Originally from Guyana, Wilson Harris is one of the Caribbean's most intellectual and gifted novelists. *Source: Americas Society. Courtesy of Elsa M. Ruiz.*

Guiana government from 1942 to 1958, surveying the country's interior, where he studied in depth the topology of the region, met Amerindian tribes on the brink of extinction, and dealt with government agents, land developers, and explorers. The experience provided him with the canvas for his writings. Like the nineteenth-century Romantics who were awed by the vastness of the New World, the enormity of the Guyanese jungle made Harris aware of how insignificant the local political struggle was and how minuscule nations were when compared to nature and the universe.

In 1959, Harris retired and moved to London to write full-time. In 1968, he was appointed delegate to UNESCO and visited Cuba and Australia. He was also a visiting scholar at numerous universities in the United States and the Caribbean. In 1986, he relocated from London to Chelmsford, England.

Harris began his writing career as a poet. Using the pen name Kona Waruk, he wrote four books of poetry, *Fetish* (1951), *Eternity to Season* (1952), *The Well and The Land* (1952), and *Eternity to Seasons: Poems of Separation and Reunion* (1954). His first novel, **The Palace of the Peacock**, was published in 1960. This work was followed by *The Far Journey of Oudin* (1961), *The Whole Armour* (1962), and *The Secret Ladder* (1963). These novels, which make up the "Guyana Quartet," take place in the Guyanese jungle and explore the conflicts that evolve between a surveyor, or government agent, the workers who report to him, and the Amerindians who live in the jungle. The descriptions of the power of nature are realistic and palpable, as evidenced in this passage from *The Secret Ladder:* "The sun stood directly overhead, the sun of equatorial Guiana, of the inchoara Amazon basin. . . . All shadow had ceased save within veined grassroots, and along lines of . . . a couple of leaves clinging to an arm and branch, belonging to a solitary plant in the clearing" (142–43).

Ultimately, the Guyana novels are not about the jungle and its inhabitants but about the human condition in general, as scholar Kenneth Ramchand points out in the volume *West Indian Literature*. The human condition and timelessness is also one of the themes of the Da Silva trilogy. Consisting of *Da Silva da Silva's Cultivated Wilderness* (1977), *The Tree of the Sun* (1978), and *The Angel at the Gate* (1982), the trilogy also examines the multiple levels of the human experience: "Da Silva moved to the studio door of carven wood in which the sap of lost gardens stood like a milestone tree that shone with invisible lakes and rivers along which explorers had stumbled into" (75).

In 1996, Harris wrote about the Jonestown massacre, when, in 1978, a demented cult leader, Jim Jones, forced hundreds of his followers to commit mass suicide. In the novel *Jonestown*, Harris essays on his preoccupation with one Caribbean ethnic group rising over another group and controlling it, the dangers of nationalism, and the potential for charismatic leaders to turn against the very people they aimed to help.

Alongside the Cuban **Alejo Carpentier**, Wilson Harris is often regarded as one of the most intellectual, abstruse, and challenging writers from the Caribbean. His novels cite philosophical concepts from across the centuries—from classical Greek to the German philosophers—and allude to mythological figures from diverse cultures; his use of symbolism requires the reader to be familiar with multiple texts as well as with Harris's previous works. Scholar Michael Gilkes sums up Harris's novels as "complementary explorations of impressive depths into the 'divine' comedy of modern existence"(158).

Some of Harris's works include *Heartland* (1964), *Tamatumari* (1970), *Companions of the Day and Night* (1975), and *The Dark Jester* (2001). His works of nonfiction include *Tradition and the West Indian Novel* (1965), *History, Fable and Myth in the Caribbean and Guianas* (1970), *The Womb of Space: The Cross-Cultural Imagination* (1983), and *Selected Essays of Wilson Harris* (1999). *See also* Romanticism/Romanticismo.

Further Reading

Durrant, Sam. *Postcolonial Narrative and the Work of Mourning: J. M. Coetzee, Wilson Harris, and Toni Morrison.* Albany: State University of New York Press, 2004.

Gilkes, Michael. *The West Indian Novel.* Boston: Twayne Publishers, 1981.

Jonas, Joyce. *Anancy in the Great House: Ways of Reading West Indian Fiction.* Westport, CT: Greenwood Press, 1990.

Ramchand, Kenneth. *An Introduction to the Study of West Indian Literature.* Jamaica: Nelson Caribbean, 1976.

Wilson-Tagoe, Nana. *Historical Thought and Literary Representation in West Indian Literature.* Gainesville: University of Florida Press, 1998.

—*D. H. Figueredo*

Hearne, John (1926–95)

■

John Hearne was a major Jamaican novelist who wrote about the island's middle class during the early days of independence. He coined the fictional name of "Cayuna" for Jamaica. A literary critic as well, Hearne was one of the first to recognize the talent of St. Lucian writer **Derek Walcott**, a Nobel Prize winner, and the first to study the works of Guyanese novelist **Wilson Harris**.

John Edgar Caulwell Hearne was born on February 4, 1926, in Montreal, Canada. In 1928, his family returned to Jamaica, where he attended several private schools, as well as having his own tutor, until matriculating at Jamaica College in 1937. At the beginning of World War II, he left for England, volunteering for service as an air gunner. After the war, he enrolled at Edinburgh University, earning a degree in art. In 1950, he received a teaching diploma from the University of London. Hearne traveled back and forth between Jamaica and England, holding several teaching positions.

His novels might be characterized as expressing two distinct sentiments: the early works express optimism in the political process transforming the Caribbean as a result of Jamaica's independence, the rise to power of prime minister Michael Manley, and the triumph of Cuban revolution; his last novel betrays the author's weariness with Caribbean politics and the inability of the region to become economically independent. Underlying these novels is an awareness of the racial divide.

The early novels were *Voices Under the Window* (1955), written when Hearne was in his twenties; *Stranger at the Gate* (1956); *The Faces of Love* (1957), published a year later in the United States under the title of *The Eye of the Storm*; *The Autumn Equinox* (1959); and *Land of the Living* (1961). *Voices Under the Window* might be the most representative of the group: it is story of an attorney who is mistakenly slain by a rioter with whom the attorney sympathizes; as the attorney dies, flashbacks reveal his involvement with Jamaican politics and social issues and his own awareness of his African and European heritage. Though the protagonist perishes, there is a sense of hope and redemption in the novel. For his death can be interpreted as a sacrifice toward the creation of a better Jamaican society.

Between 1961 and 1981, Hearne wrote short stories and articles but didn't write a novel. Instead, he became active in Jamaican politics and in higher education, serving as an information officer, special assistant to Michael Manley, chairman of the Council of the Institute of Jamaica, and secretary of the Creative Arts Center of the University of West Indies–Mona.

In 1982, he wrote *The Sure Salvation*, a historical novel, reminiscent of the sea stories of Joseph Conrad (1857–1924) that Hearne had read as a child, about a ship with an illegal cargo of slaves. The ship served as a metaphor for Jamaica. Observes **Barbara Lalla** in *Defining Jamaican Fiction* (1996): "Hearne looks out at the world and back at the past from a Jamaican present to reconstruct points of view other than those of traditional history but also other than those that are politically correct in the Caribbean" (152). Hearne's conclusion was that despite independence and progress in racial relationships, skin pigmentation still defined the individual, separating one person from another. Critic **Kenneth Ramchand**, in *West Indian Narratives*, commented that all of Hearne's novels take place in a society where "automatic responses to colour tend to overshadow the behaviour of the individual and to work against the possibilities of personal relationship" (158).

Further Reading

Dance, Daryl Cumber. "Conversation with John Hearne." In *New World Adams*, edited by Daryl Cumber Dance, 97–107. Yorkshire, England: Peepal Tree, 1992.

Lalla, Barbara. *Defining Jamaican Fiction: Marronage and the Discourse of Survival.* Tuscaloosa: University of Alabama Press, 1996.

Ramchand, Kenneth. *West Indian Narratives: An Introductory Anthology.* Nelson: London, 1966.

Samad, Daizal R. "In Quest of the Dialogue of Self: Racial Duality in John Hearne's *Voices Under the Window.*" *Journal of Commonwealth Literature* 25, no. 1 (1990): 10.

—*D. H. Figueredo*

Heath, Roy A. K. (1926–)

Heath is one of Guyana's major novelists. Moving to Great Britain at a time when many other writers from the Caribbean, like **Kamau Brathwaite**, were living there, Heath chose not to write about life in exile, preferring Guyana for his subject. In his novels, the saga of Guyanese families parallels the development of that country from colony to independence.

Roy Aubrey Kelvin Heath was born in Georgetown, Guyana, in 1926. As a child, he listened intently to the folktales family members and friends told each other; he was also fascinated by the geography and history of Guyana. After graduating from Queen's College High school, in 1950 he left for Great Britain, where he attended the University of London. In the 1950s, he became a high school teacher. Though he studied law and was admitted to the English bar in 1964 and the Guyanese bar ten years later, he remained a teacher. The position afforded him the time needed for writing.

In 1966, Guyana's independence prodded him to write the novel that would later on form the basis for the Armstrong trilogy: *From the Heat of the Day* (1979), *One Generation* (1981), and *Genetha* (1981). The work was too long, and since Heath was unknown, he could not find a publisher. Rather than feeling discouraged, he decided to write a shorter novel, which he titled *A Man Come Home*. Published in 1974, it is set in a **barrack yard**, a tenement area where residents live in small rooms clustered about an open courtyard, and it tells the story of a man who becomes rich through the magic intervention of a spirit. The portrayal of poverty, corruption, and easy sexuality is meant to be a parable of the social and racial chaos in Guyana the 1970s. The novel was well received by critics in Great Britain and in the Caribbean.

In 1978, Heath published *The Murderer*, about a man who murders his unfaithful wife. As in the works of **Wilson Harris**, the characters in this novel are as affected by each other as by Guyana's geography. The novel received the prestigious Guardian Prize for Literature. In 1994, the Armstrong trilogy was published as a single volume, as the author had originally planned. The story of one of family, from the 1930s to the 1950s is also the story of Guyana from the beginning of the independence movement to the actual struggle with England. Critics from Europe have commented on Heath's ability to conjure up an exotic, sensuous world while their counterparts in the Caribbean praise Heath's realistic portrayal of cities and towns and his rendition of corrupted politicians and merchants. His other works include *Kwaku: Or the Man Would Could Not Keep His Mouth Shut* (1982), *Orealla* (19), and *The Shadow Bride* (1988). *See also* Barrack Yard Literature.

Further Reading

Saakana, Arnon Saba. *Colonization and the Destruction of the Mind: Psychosocial Issues of Race, Class, Religion and Sexuality in the Novels of Roy Heath*. London: Karnak House, 1996.

—*D. H. Figueredo*

Hendriks, Arthur Lemiére (1922–92)

Hendriks was a popular Jamaican poet. He was a television executive who worked in Jamaica and in Great Britain. Hendriks came to writing late in his life after a successful career in television.

Hendriks was born on April 17, 1922, the son of a financial adviser and investor. He attended primary and secondary schools in Kingston, Jamaica, and then enrolled at the Open University of the West Indies while managing his own business, the Arthur Hendriks Co., a furniture company. In 1950, he switched careers and became the manager of the Jamaica Broadcasting Corporation. In the early 1960s, he left Jamaica to manage Thomas Television in the Bermudas. By the mid-1960s, he moved to England.

During the 1960s, he began to write poetry and short stories. In 1962, he edited the *Independence Anthology of Jamaican Literature*, which included some of his own works. In 1965, he published *On This Mountain and Other Poems*. His poems, celebratory of the Caribbean's beauty, were of an optimistic nature and did not address political concerns.

Through the 1970s, he published several volumes, *These Green Islands* (1971), *Muet—Poems* (1972), and *Madonna of the Unknown Nation* (1974). These poems proved highly popular in Jamaica, and a few were set to music. In the 1980s, he published *The Islanders and Other Poems* (1983) and *To Speak Simply: Selected Poems* (1988).

Hendriks was modest about his writing and preferred not to talk about it. He was active in cultural activities in Jamaica and in England. Louis James, in *Encyclopedia of Latin America and Caribbean Literature*, describes his style as "elegant, precise and objective . . . [reflecting] an inner peace uncharacteristic of most contemporary Jamaican verse" (257).

Further Reading

"Arthur Lemiere Hendriks." *Contemporary Authors Online*, Gale, 2002. http://www.galenet.galegroup.com (accessed 8/31/05).

James, Louis. "Hendrinks, Arthur Lemiere." *Encyclopedia of Latin America and Caribbean Literature 1900–2003*, edited by Daniel Balderston and Mike González, 257. London: Routledge, 2004.

—*D. H. Figueredo*

Henfrey, June (1939–92)

∎

A Barbadian short-story writer, Henfrey was a community activist. She spent most of her life in England.

A native of June Gollop, Barbados, Henfrey was raised in St. David's Village, sugarcane country. She found beauty in the fields of sugarcane surrounding her and admired how poor Barbadians toiled in those fields as sugarcane cutters. Highly intelligent but poor, in 1957 Henfrey won a merit scholarship to attend Oxford University.

At Oxford, she studied French and was attracted to the writings of the great Martinican poet and politician **Aimé Césaire**, one of the founders of the **Négritude** movement. After visiting the United States and touring Brazil, she settled in Liverpool, where she raised her family. In the mid-1970s, she was a community activist, involved in projects that helped women and black families gain economic advantages. She also taught at the University of Liverpool.

Throughout her life, she wanted to write, but family and social commitments limited her output. However, when at the age of fifty one she learned she had cancer, Henfrey dealt with her plight by writing stories about her childhood and Barbados. She passed away in 1992. Two years later, a collection of her stories were published under the title *Coming Home and Other Stories*. In Liverpool, a library was named in her honor.

Further Reading

"June Henfrey." Peepal Tree Press, April 2005. http://www.peepaltreepress.com (accessed 4/2/05).

"June Henfrey: Coming Home and Other Stories." *New Statesman and Society* 7, no. 329 (November 18, 1994): 54.

—*D. H. Figueredo*

Henríquez Ureña, Camila. See Henríquez Ureña Family.

Henríquez Ureña Family

Distinguished family of writers and scholars from the Dominican Republic whose combined literary output surpasses hundreds of books and thousands of articles, shaping the canon of Latin American literature and helping to promote the literary cultures of Argentina, Cuba, Dominican Republic, Mexico, and Puerto Rico, among others. There were three siblings: Camila, Max, and Pedro—a fourth brother, Francisco, also called Fran, did not follow in his siblings' footsteps. Their grandfather was **Nicolás Ureña**, a costumbrista, a writer of local customs, and one of the Dominican Republic's first major poets. Their father was Francisco Henríquez y Carvajal (1859–1935), who served as a president of the republic during 1916, and their mother was **Salomé Ureña de Henríquez**, the country's national poet. After Salomé's death, Francisco remarried and had a second family, but those children led quiet lives.

Henríquez Ureña, Camila (1894–1973). Essayist, literary critic, and one of the finest Latina Caribbean intellectuals of the twentieth century, Camila Henríquez Ureña was the fourth child and only daughter of Salomé and Francisco. Born in the Dominican Republic on April 9, 1894, three years before the death of her mother, Camila Henríquez Ureña's figure has often been shadowed by the presence of her two better-known siblings, Pedro and Max.

Camila Henríquez Ureña spent a good deal of her life in Cuba, where she moved with her father and his second wife and family in 1904. Her mother had died in 1897. Henríquez Ureña received her doctorate in philosophy, letters, and pedagogy from the Universidad de la Habana in 1917. Her thesis was on the

"Pedagogical Ideas of **Eugenio María de Hostos**," honoring the memory of the illustrious Puerto Rican educator and her mother's mentor and supporter of her founding the first Normal School for Girls in the Dominican Republic. From 1918 to 1921 Henríquez Ureña lived in Minnesota, where she studied and taught classes at the University of Minnesota. Returning to Cuba in the early 1920s, Camila Henríquez Ureña became a Cuban citizen in 1926. She lived in Paris and studied at the Sorbonne from 1932 to 1934. While living in Cuba in the 1930s, she was an active organizer of feminists as well as cultural institutions and events. Most notable among her activities are her role as cofounder and president of the Lyceum, a feminist cultural organization, and the Hispanic-Cuban Institute. In 1942, she moved back to the United States and taught at Vassar College until 1959, in the Department of Hispanic Studies, where she served twice in the capacity of chairperson and was a tenured professor. During a number of summers in her 1942 to 1959 residence in the United States, Camila Henríquez Ureña was also on the faculty of the prestigious language and literature summer program at Middlebury College. Her contribution is notable, for she represents one of the earliest instances of a Latina Caribbean academic earning tenure and chairpersonship at a prestigious academic institution in the United States. Camila Henríquez Ureña, however, gave up her pension as Professor Emerita at Vassar College to return to Cuba and participate in the restructuring of the Universidad de la Habana, where she taught in the Department of Latin American Literature until her retirement in 1970. At the time of her death, while visiting her native Dominican Republic, Camila Henríquez Ureña held the titles of Professor Emerita from the University of Havana as well as Vassar College, a rare if not unique accomplishment, worthy of note.

The breadth of knowledge to be found in Camila Henríquez Ureña's writings gives evidence of her erudition and life-long commitment to learning. Camila was a woman of many and varied interests. Pedro Henríquez Ureña's letters collected in the family's *Epistolario* (1995) record his own amazement for his sister's capacity for learning and her curious intellect. In several "testimonios," provided by Mirta Yáñez in her "Camila y Camila," one finds out how truly diverse Camila's interests were: her knowledge of, and participation in and even singing of operas in various languages; her ability with music and her fine, distinguished but very Caribbean way of dancing; her work as an educator and in women's movements; her ability to learn foreign languages, ostensibly so that she might read works in the original by some of her favorite authors: Dante, Ibsen, Racine, Shakespeare, and others. Furthermore, a selection of her essays, collected posthumously and edited by Mirta Aguirre, one of her most distinguished students and later colleague at the Universidad, gives evidence of a sound liberal education and a serious intellect. In brief, her intellectual capacity is evident in the subject matters she chose: her doctoral dissertation on Hostos; her introduction to a Spanish version of Dante's *Inferno* published in Cuba in 1935; her collaboration with the Spanish poet laureate Juan Ramón Jiménez (1881–1958) in the now classic *La poesía en Cuba* in 1936; her studies of the pastoral genre in Spain and on the theater of Lope de Vega (1562–1635), to name just some of her known works.

Camila Henríquez Ureña's most significant contributions to the genre of the essay, however, is her now classic collection of essays on the condition of women, her formidable trilogy: "Feminismo" (1939), "La mujer y la cultura" (1949), and "La carta como forma de expresión literaria femenina" (1951). Literary critics **Mirta**

Yáñez, Daisy Cocco de Filippis and **Chiqui Vicioso**, among others, have pointed out the importance of these essays to the history of the feminist essay in the Spanish Caribbean. In "Feminismo," Camila Henríquez Ureña traces the history of the role women have played in societies from prehistoric time to her day. In this essay, Henríquez Ureña takes to task the male creation of "exceptional women" to justify denying women's rights. In "La mujer y la cultura," an essay she first wrote in 1939 but did not publish until 1949, Camila explains that true change comes about as a result of collective efforts (translation by Daisy Cocco de Filippis):

> Las mujeres de excepción de los pasados siglos representaron aisladamente un progreso en sentido vertical. Fueron precursoras, a veces, sembraron ejemplo fructífero. Pero un movimiento cultural importante es siempre de conjunto, y necesita propagarse en sentido horizontal. La mujer necesita desarrollar su carácter, en el aspecto colectivo, para llevar a término una lucha que está ahora en sus comienzos. Necesita hacer labor de propagación de la cultura que ha podido alcanzar para seguir progresando
>
> (Exceptional women in past centuries represented isolated cases of progress in the vertical sense. They were precursors, at times they planted fruitful examples. But an important cultural movement is always a group effort, and it needs to be propagated in a horizontal sense. Women need to develop character, in a collective sense, to bring to fruition a struggle that it is now in its inception. She needs to work on propagating the culture that she has acquired in order to be able to continue to make progress).

In a certain sense, in reading "La mujer y la cultura," one finds understanding of why Camila Henríquez Ureña would return years later to Cuba to help out, as she would say, putting in practice the theories expounded in her essay. Indeed, this fine intellectual and teacher approached many of her studies and writings as a woman. In her essay "La carta como forma de expresión literaria femenina," Camila chooses four authors whose correspondence serves as a barometer, an expression, and an answer to the historical moment they lived. Among them we find two writers whose names ought to head any history of the essay written in Spanish: Santa Teresa de Jesús (1515–82) and Sor Juana Inés de la Cruz (1648–95). Camila's essay is a tour de force in the art of reading and the importance of the reader's response to giving meaning to the literature written by women. Tellingly, today, having gone through various stages of readings as women and as feminists, many feminist thinkers find themselves back where Camila Henríquez Ureña was fifty years ago: understanding more than ever the importance of reader's response, "de leer con la sensibilidad de las mujeres las obras de las mujeres" (to read with a woman's sensibility other women's writings), to the creation of a feminine and feminist aesthetic.

Camila Henríquez Ureña earns a place in the history of Latinas in the United States as a pioneer who was able to transcend borders and whose work continues to have resonance in the development of new generations of readers, as evidenced by the publication in the year 2000 of Julia Alvarez's *In the Name of Salomé*, a fictionalized retelling of Camila's and Salome's lives.

Henríquez Ureña, Maximiliano "Max" (1885–1968). Diplomat, professor, poet, and orator whose histories of Cuban and Dominican literature helped to disseminate knowledge of those Caribbean nations to readers throughout Latin

America; his volume on the history of **modernismo,** *Breve historia del Modernismo* (1954), is one of the classic texts on the subject. He was born on November 16, 1885, in Santo Domingo, where he studied under professor and poet **Emilio Prud'Homme.** He began writing in his teens, and by the time he was fifteen years of age, Max was a drama and literary critic for a major newspaper, *La Lucha.*

He relocated to Cuba with his father in his twenties and earned a doctorate in philosophy and letters from Universidad de la Habana in 1913. Interested in promoting drama and theater in Cuba, he was one of the founders of the Sociedad de Fomento del Teatro, which facilitated the staging of works written by young dramatists. He was also cofounder of the Sociedad de Conferencias, which hosted public conferences on literature and history.

A much-sought-after speaker, Max lectured at major universities in Argentina, Brazil, Mexico, Puerto Rico, and the United States. While serving for numerous cultural institutions in Cuba, he was also a diplomat for the Dominican Republic, appointed to that country's embassies in London and Washington. Returning to the Dominican Republic in the 1960s, he taught at the National University and Autonomous University of Santo Domingo until his death on January 23, 1969.

A renaissance man, who could write with equal ease about music and contemporary political matters, his initial scholarly interests lay in the belles lettres from Spain. As he matured as a scholar, Max focused on Latin America letters, penning essays that were not only literary studies but also sketches of major Latin American writers, many of whom he knew personally. His scholarly texts include *Tablas cronológicas de la literatura cubana* (1929), *El retorno de los galeones* (1930), *Les influences Francaises sur la poésie Hispano-Americaine* (1938), *Panorama histórico de la literatura dominicana* (1945), *De Rimbaud a Pasternak y Quasimodo: ensayos sobre las literaturas contemporáneas* (1960) *Panorama histórico de la literatura cubana* (1963). As a poet, he wrote three books of poetry: *Anforas* (1914), *Fosforescencias* (1930), and *Garra de la luz* (1958). His novels *La conspiración de los Alcarrizos* (1941) and *El arzobispo Valera* (1944) recounted historical events from the Dominican Republic. Max Henríquez Ureña was a lively and accessible writer; his prose and poetry was controlled, elegant, and erudite. His literary contribution, according to Cuban critic José Fernández Pequeño, writing in *Espíritu de las islas* (2003), was the consecration of all that was intellectual in the Caribbean with the objective of enriching Caribbean society.

Henríquez Ureña, Pedro (1844–1946). Pedro was born in Santo Domingo on June 29, 1884. A precocious child, he published his first book of poetry, *Aquí abajo* (1898), at the age of fourteen. Graduating from Columbia University, he first went to Cuba and then moved in 1906 to Mexico, where he earned a law degree. Eight years later, he returned to the United States, where under the pseudonym of E. P. Garduño he wrote articles about life in the United States that were published in Cuba in *El Heraldo.* In 1921, he went back to Mexico to teach for two years before moving to Argentina, which became his permanent home. In Argentina, he led a fruitful life, teaching at several prestigious institutions, supervising the work of doctoral students; leading **tertulias,** or literary salons; writing and editing articles; and working on his series *Cien obras maestras de la literatura y del pensamiento universal.* In the mid-1930s, he left his home in Argentina to serve for two years in his native Dominican Republic as supervisor of national education, a position from which he resigned in protest against Dominican dictator Rafael Leónidas Trujillo

(1891–1961), who was in power from 1930 to 1961. From 1940 to 1941 he occupied the Charles Eliot Norton chair at Harvard University, delivering eight lectures that were collected in the book *Literary Currents in Hispanic America* (1945). During his last years in Argentina, he felt persecuted by the military junta ruling the country. He died in Buenos Aires on May 11, 1946 on his way to teaching a class.

Pedro Henríquez Ureña knew such literary and historical giants as Eugenio María Hostos, Alfonso Reyes (1889–1959), and Jorge Luis Borges (1899–1986). He was well versed in the works of William Shakespeare (1564–1616) and George Elliot (1819-80), admired French literature, and could confer comfortably about Italian and Russian authors. Borges said of his friend, writing in the prologue to *Henríquez Ureña's Obras Completas* (1960), "His memory was an exact literary museum" (viii). Pedro Henríquez Ureña devoted many years of research to developing a definition of Spanish verse, studying rhyme and meter and the uses of language. Though he wrote extensively on linguistics, literature, and literary history, his analyses were never presented in a vacuum but rather within the context of society at large. He was an idealist but did not separate ideas from action, aesthetics from the practical; he believed in a just world and advocated for economic equality. He viewed literature as a living entity, with the power to change individuals and political systems. "Nationalism," he wrote in *La Utopía de América*, "is born out of the qualities of a people when transformed into art." The Dominican Republic's national university bears his name.

His many books include *Horas de estudio* (1910), *Tablas cronológicas de la literatura española* (1913), *La Utopía de América* (1925), *Seis ensayos en busca de nuestra expresión* (1928), *La versificación irregular en la poesía castellana* (1933)—a seminal work on the study of Spanish poetry—*La cultura y las letras coloniales en Santo Domingo* (1936), *Gramática castellana* (1940)—which is still being used in schools throughout Latin America—and *Historia de la cultura en la América Hispánica* (1947). *See also* Costumbrismo; Dominican Republic Literature, History of; Exile Literature; Trujillo Era, The.

Further Reading

Alvarez, Julia. *In the Name of Salomé: A Novel*. Chapel Hill, NC: Algonquin Books of Chapel Hill, 2000.

Andrade Coello, Alejandro. *Tres poetas de la música, la obra del dominicano Max Henríquez Ureña*. Segunda ed. Quito, Ecuador: Talleres gráficos de Educación, 1942.

Castillo Vega, Marcia. *Catálogo de los documentos manuscritos de Camila Henríquez Ureña*. Santo Domingo: Publicaciones ONAP, 1994.

Cocco de Filippis, Daisy. *Documents of Dissidence, Selected Writings by Dominican Women*. New York: A Publication of the CUNY Dominican Studies Institute, 2000.

———. *Madres, maestras y militantes dominicanas*. Santo Domingo: Búho, 2001.

Familia Henríquez Ureña. *Epistolario*. Santo Domingo: Publicación de la Secretaría de Educación, Bellas Artes y Cultos, 1995.

Henríquez Ureña, Camila. *Estudios y conferencias*. Habana: Instituto Cubano del Libro, 1971.

Yáñez, Mirta. *Camila y Camila*, Premio Nacional de Ensayo, Cuba, 2000.

—Daisy Cocco de Filippis and D. H. Figueredo

Henríquez Ureña, Max. See Henríquez Ureña Family.

Henríquez Ureña, Pedro. See Henríquez Ureña Family.

Henríquez y Carvajal, Federico (1848–1952)

A patriotic poet and beloved teacher from the Dominican Republic, Henríquez y Carvajal was a member of an illustrious and literary family: his brother Francisco was president of the republic, his sister-in-law was **Salomé Ureña de Henríquez**, the country's national poet, and his nephews and niece, the **Henríquez Ureña** siblings, achieved international fame as writers and literary critics. Henríquez y Carvajal himself had a long literary career that spanned nearly six decades.

Henríquez y Carvajal devoted his life to teaching. He taught at numerous schools, including the Colegio San Luis Gonzaga, the Instituto de Señoritas, and the Colegio Central. He wrote for several newspapers and journals and was director of the publications *Ateneo* and *Clio*. In his teachings and journalistic writings, he promoted public education for women. He started to publish books of poetry when he was in his thirties, beginning with *La hija del hebreo* (1883), and he published his last volume, *El poema de la historia* (1948), when he was one hundred years old. In between, his output exceeded over twenty-five volumes.

Henríquez y Carvajal practiced two poetic styles: a traditional verse of four lines with every other line rhyming, and longer verses, which consisted of two or three words per line with an increasing number of stanzas, going from six to ten:

> Con la aurora
> se colora
> del Peravia la cimera
> Canta un gallo
> mi caballo . . .

(With the arrival of the dawn / my helmet changes color . . . a rooster sings to my horse).

Henríquez y Carvajal's early poems were descriptive of the countryside. His matured production was marked by **Romanticism**. Both types of poems, though, as illustrated in *Romances históricos* (1937) were characterized by patriotic sentiments. When Henríquez y Carvajal passed away at the age of 104 he was still writing and editing a newspaper.

Further Reading

"Federico Henríquez y Carvajal." http://www.bnrd.gov.do/poesia/1848-1952.htm (accessed 9/5/05).

Veloz Maggiolo, Marcio. *Cultura, teatro y relates en Santo Domingo*. Santiago de los Caballeros, República Dominicana: Universidad Católica Madre y Maestra, 1972.

—D. H. Figueredo

Heredia, Nicolás (1855–1901)

Nicolás Heredia was a Dominican Cuban journalist and writer who chronicled in the newspaper *El Figaro* the early battles of Cuba's war of independence in 1895 and wrote realistic stories and novels. His most famous work is the novel *Leonela* (1893).

Nicolás Heredia was born in Baní, Santo Domingo, Dominican Republic, in 1855. Relocating with his parents to the province of Matanzas, in Cuba, around the 1880s, he founded and became director of the daily *Diario de Matanzas*. He also wrote for several newspapers, including *El Figaro*, where he reported on the war of independence. When the newspaper was closed by the Spanish authorities, Heredia moved to New York City, where he joined the Cuban revolutionaries in exile and plotted against the Spanish government. At the end of the war, Heredia returned to Cuba. He was appointed national director of public education and taught at the Universidad de la Habana.

In 1893, Heredia wrote *Leonela*, a realistic account of an attempt by a Cuban American businessman to establish an industrial site in the countryside. The protagonist, a Cuban who lived in the United States, is representative of the industrialist who believes machines can create new societies, however the town he builds—modeled on American factory towns—is soon wiped out by a deluge. The novel also tells of the protagonist's tragic love affair with Leonela. Heredia describes in realistic details the landscape, the houses, and the characters in the novel, photographing, as it were, a moment in their lives. *Leonela* proved a popular Cuban novel during the early decades of the twentieth century. Its depiction of an American company town in a Latin American setting was a motif that appeared in many twentieth-century novels, including *Cien años de soledad* (1967) by the Colombian Gabriel García Márquez (1927–).

Heredia also wrote the novel *Un hombre de negocios* (1882) and several works of nonfiction, including *Puntos de vista* (1892), *La sensibilidad en la poesía castellana* (1898), and *El utopista y la utopía* (1899). His *El lector cubano* was a popular school text reprinted several times during the second decade of the twentieth century. *See also* Cuban Literature, History of.

Further Reading

Martínez Carménate, Urbano. *Nicolás Heredia*. La Haban: Editora Política, 1999.

—*D. H. Figueredo*

Heredia y Heredia, José María (1803–39)

The prototype of the writer in exile who waxes sentimental for his country—a common occurrence throughout all of the Caribbean across the centuries—José María Heredia was a romantic poet whose ode to Niagara Falls was one of the most popular poems in nineteenth-century Cuba. He was also a playwright, a literary critic, orator, and patriot.

Heredia was born in Santiago de Cuba on December 31, 1803. His parents were Dominicans who, fearing that the Haitian revolution would expand to the Dominican Republic, had come to Cuba. A precocious child, Heredia was introduced to the classics by his father, started to write poetry when he was ten years old, and by the age of sixteen had penned a drama, *Eduardo IV o el usurpador*, which was staged in Havana in 1819. In 1820, he traveled to Mexico, where he wrote the ode "En el Teocalli de Cholula," a celebration of Mexico's pre-Columbian cultures. Returning to Cuba after his father's death, he earned a law degree and joined the conspiracy called Soles y Rayos de Bolívar—Bolívar's suns and rays, after the legendary South American liberator—which advocated separation from Spain. In 1823, he went into exile in the United States, visiting Niagara Falls the following year. The overwhelming beauty and majesty of the cataracts inspired him to write his famous ode. But the ode is not only a celebration of the falls, it's also a song of exile: before the spectacle of the cascading waters, the homesick poet sees Cuban palm trees.

In 1825, he published his first book of poetry, *Poesías*, and moved to Mexico. In that country, he married a Mexican woman, worked as a critic for the newspapers *El Iris* and *La Miscelanea*, taught history and literature, while also achieving acclaim as a public orator, usually discoursing on political themes. In 1836 he returned to Cuba after writing a letter to the Spanish authorities, wherein he recanted his separatist activities. Reproached by his friends for his change of heart, especially literary mentor and cultural promoter **Domingo del Monte**, with whom he had been friends for decades, Heredia had to leave his beloved Cuba once again. He died in Mexico on May 7, 1839.

As famous as his Niagara ode is his 1825 poem "El himno del desterrado," a dramatic lament about exile and his longing for Cuba:

> Cuba, Cuba, que vida me diste
> dulce tierra de luz y hermosura,
> ¡cuánto sueño de gloria y ventura
> tengo unido a tu suelo feliz!

(Cuba, you gave me life Sweet land of light and beauty / How many glorious and happy dreams I link to your happy soil.)

Heredia was a passionate poet who not only depicted dramatic images of nature with the use of colors and classical allusions but also chose words that conveyed sounds and speed: in his ode to Niagara, the reader can hear the water rushing down a precipice. His love poetry, on the other hand, was gentle, almost as if he were whispering into his beloved's ear.

Heredia was one of the initiators of Cuban poetry and one of the earliest writers from the Spanish-speaking Caribbean to be translated into English, first in 1844, *Selections from the poems of Don José Maria Heredia*, and then, in 1852, *Modern poets and poetry of Spain*, both translated by James Kennedy. On a wall at Niagara Falls a plaque, reprinting his poem in English, renders tribute to the poet. *See also* Exile Literature; Romanticismo/Romanticism; Tertulia/Cénacle/Literary salon/Soirée.

Further Reading

Aparicio Laurencio, Ángel. *¿Es Heredia el primer escritor romántico en lengua española?* Miami, FL: Ediciones Universal, 1988.

Padura, Leonardo. *José María Heredia: la patria y la vida.* Habana: Ediciones Unión, 2003.

—D. H. Figueredo

Hernández, Ángela (1954–)

Ángela Hernández is one of the most respected intellectuals in the Dominican Republic. A community organizer, activist, poet, and fiction writer, she is a tireless worker on behalf of human rights. Hernández has coauthored a series of handbooks designed to explain women's legal and moral rights.

Ángela Hernández was born in Jarabacoa, Dominican Republic, on July 16, 1954. She attended elementary and secondary schools in her native town and then enrolled at the Universidad Autónoma de Santo Domingo, where she earned a degree in Chemical Engineering. While a student, she was active in political activities and during the 1980s, she joined the feminist movement. She wrote for numerous national newspapers and journals. Her short stories have appeared in several anthologies, including *Out of the Mirrored Garden*, edited by Delia Poey; *Antología del cuento dominicano*, edited by Diógenes Céspedes; *Dos siglos de literatura dominicana*, compiled by José Alcántara Almánzar; and *Combatidas, combativas y combatientes*, compiled by **Daisy Cocco de Filippis**. Hernández's short stories, according to critic Catharina Vallejo, writing in *Mujeres como islas* (2002), depict realistic occurrences of the daily life of women struggling for equality. Her stories are characterized by humor, irony, and elusive dialogue. On her literary studies, such as the volume *De críticos y creadores* (1987), Hernández elucidates on male writers and critics who through the centuries have silenced, by either not publishing or acknowledging, the creative output of women in the Dominican Republic in particular and Latin America in general.

In 1998, Hernández won the Dominican Republic's National Award for Short Stories for the collection *Piedra de Sacrificio*. Her other works include the short-story collections *Las mariposas no le temen a los cactus* (1985), and *Alótropos* (1989); the poetry volumes, *Desafío* (1985), *Tizne y crystal* (1987), and *Arca despejada* (1994); the novel *Mudanza de los sentidos* (2001); and the books of essays *Machismo y aborto* (1985) and *Las mujeres en la coyuntura actual: algunas reflexiones* (1991).

Further Reading

Cocco de Filippis, Daisy. *Documents of Dissidence: Selected Writings by Dominican Women.* New York: CUNY Dominican Studies Institute, 2000.

Vallejo, Catharina. "Innovación, calidad y riqueza en la cuentística dominicana femenina contemporánea." In *Mujeres como islas.* Habana: Ediciones Unión; Santo Domingo: Ediciones FERILIBRO, 2002.

—Daisy Cocco de Filippis

Hernández, José P. H. "Peache" (1892–1922)

One of Puerto Rico's most beloved writers, Hernández was a tragic poet whose literary promise was cut short by an early death. His poem "Madrigal"—also known as "Ojos astrals"—published posthumously, is a memorable farewell to those he loved.

"Peache" Hernández, as he was called—sounding out in Spanish the initials "P" and "H"—was born in Hatillo, Puerto Rico. When he was fifteen years old, he moved to San Juan, where he studied music and attended high school. He wrote poetry for a young woman, Carmen Sánchez, with whom he fell in love and later married.

Peache Hernández mastered several languages, including English, Greek, and Latin, and frequented the **tertulias**, or literary salons, of the poets **Luis Llorens Torres** and **Evaristo Ribera Chevremont**, to whom he read his poetry. In 1912, he became a pharmacist and set up a pharmacy in Hatillo, where he was also the director of the municipal band.

Tragedy struck in 1919 when he lost one of his children. Hernández grew despondent and developed tuberculosis. The collections of poetry *Coplas de la vereda* (1919) and *El último combate* (1921) expressed the sadness he experienced. At the age of twenty-nine, Peache Hernández lost his battle with tuberculosis. Though his poetic work was interrupted by illness and death, over the years his popularity in Puerto Rico has grown. Comments **Margo Arce de Vázquez**, Laura Gallego, and **Luis de Arrigoitia** in *Lecturas puertorriqueñas*: "The intimate lyricism of his verses and the . . . the sickly figure marked by death have created a . . . legendary creature" (143).

Further Reading

Arce de Vázquez, Margot, et al. *Lecturas puertorriqueñas: poesía*. Sharon, CT: Troutman Press, 1968.

—D. H. Figueredo

Hernández Aquino, Luis (1907–88)

The first Puerto Rican to examine through fiction the American presence on the island as the result of the Spanish-Cuban-American War of 1898, Hernández Aquino was a poet, novelist, and literature professor. He was one of the founders of the literary movements known as **Atalayismo** and Integralismo.

Hernández Aquino was born in Lares, Puerto Rico, and died in San Juan in 1988. He was educated in Puerto Rico, attended the Universidad de Puerto Rico, and obtained a doctoral degree in philosophy and letters from the Universidad de Madrid.

Before becoming a full-time professor and scholar—he taught at the Universidad de Puerto Rico from 1953 to 1972—he earned many distinctions as a journalist and poet. He collaborated in the daily *El Mundo* and in 1941 founded his first literary journal, *El Día Estético*, which later became *Insula* and in 1950 changed its name to *Bayoán*. He also became the director of the *Revista Colegial*, the official publication of the Universidad de Puerto Rico in Mayagüez. In 1949 the Instituto de Cultura Puertorriqueña recognized his work as a first-rate journalist with an award.

As a poet he was prolific, and was a key founding figure of several avant-garde poetic movements, such as Atalayismo, tendencies that took him and other poets who were writing in the 1930s to experiment both with the poetic forms and subject treated. If the Atalayismo stressed novelty, daring images, and experimentation with punctuation or not to deal with metaphysical and love themes, "Integralismo," promoted by Hernández Aquino after 1941, would instead focus on Puerto Rico, its history and existence from a more existential perspective as evidenced, for example, in *Isla para la angustia* (1943). Among his most representative books of poetry are *Niebla lírica* (1931), *Agua de remanso* (1939), *Poemas de vida breve* (1940), *Voz en el tiempo* (1952), *Memoria de Castilla* (1956), *Del tiempo cotidiano* (1961), and *Entre la alegría y el réquiem* (1968). In addition, he published several important anthologies: with Ángel Valbuena Briones, *Nueva poesía de Puerto Rico* (1952), and then *Poetas de Lares* (1966), *Cantos a Puerto Rico* (1967), and *El modernismo en Puerto Rico: poesía y prosa* (1977).

His love for and interest in the history of Puerto Rico is manifested not only as a poet but as a scholar and novelist as well. Hernández Aquino was a researcher who left a very important poetry study, *Nuestra aventura literaria: los ismos en la poesía puertorriqueña, 1913–1948* (1964), and a reference study on the Taíno language and its legacy in Puerto Rico, *Diccionario de voces indígenas de Puerto Rico*, published in 1969. This volume received an award from the Instituto de Cultura Puertorriqueña.

In the novelistic tradition of the island, Hernández Aquino was the first writer who wrote a text fully devoted to examining the subject of the American arrival, or invasion, of Puerto Rico in 1898 in his only novel, *La muerte anduvo por el Guasio* (1959)–the other novels are *La llegada: crónica con ficción* (1980) by **José Luis González** and *Seva: historia de la primera invasión norteamericana de Puerto Rico ocurrida en mayo de 1898* (1982) by **Luis López Nieves**. The conflict in Hernández Aquino's novel is not formulated from the perspectives of key historical figures or by those in power, but throughout the actions and loyalties of the particular stories of many characters who are living at the margin or have been forgotten by official versions of the history. Among the many characters, there are two who played leading roles because they synthesized and became symbols of two opposing political stands: Panchito Machirán and Tomás Cáceres. Machirán is the leader of those who defend Spain while Cáceres is like a "rebel Nazareth" who fights for the absolute autonomy for the island. His separatist ideals are summed up in his statement that he does not want to see a new "master" substituting a vanquished one.

Further Reading

Martínez, Edgardo. "A dos años de la muerte de *El Mundo*." *El Diario La Prensa*, Dec. 23, 1992.

—Asela R. Laguna

Hernández Espinosa, Eugenio (1936–)

A Cuban dramatist, Hernández Espinosa is known for his artistic explorations of Cuba's African roots and the idiosyncrasies of Cuban blacks. He is the founder and directon of a theatrical group, El Teatro Caribeño.

Hernández Espinosa was born in Havana and as a child attended a Seventh-day Adventist School. In 1960, he participated in the Seminario de Dramaturgia, a drama workshop organized by the Teatro Nacional de Cuba. Seven years later, he staged his drama *María Antonia*, about a Cuban **mulata** who falls in love with a boxer who uses her for his own pleasure and advancement. The work fleshes out racial stereotypes to offer a new theatrical vision of the Afro-Cuban universe.

In 1967, Hernández Espinosa received the **Casas de las Américas** drama prize for the play *La Simona*. In 1984, his play *Patakín*, which uses **Santería** motifs and incarnate African gods to tell a story of love and betrayal, was adapted to the screen. In 1991, *María Antonia* was also adapted for the screen.

Hernandez Espinosa's plays are performed throughout Latin America and Europe. His other works include *Calixta Comité* (1980), *Odebí, el cazador* (1982), *Oba y Shangó* (1983), *Mi socio Manolo* (1988), and *Emelina Cundiamor* (1989). In 2005, he received Cuba's National Theater Award.

Further Reading

Martiatu, Inés María. "Una Carmen Caribeña." In *Teatro cubano contemporáneo: Antología*, edited by Carlos Espinosa Domínguez. Madrid: Fondo de Cultura Económica, 1992.

—Wilfredo Cancio Isla

Hernández Franco, Tomás (1904–52)

A diplomat during the **Trujillo era**, this poet from the Dominican Republic achieved fame with his epic *Yelidá* (1942), which conceived of the Caribbean as the offspring of the marriage between Europe and Africa. Hernández Franco was also a short-story writer and an essayist.

Hernández Franco was born in Santiago, Dominican Republic, on April 29, 1904. As a child, he studied under the tutelage of a Venezuelan professor before enrolling at Santiago de los Caballeros secondary school. As a teenager he wrote for the publications *El progreso* and *La Información de Santiago*, published his first book of poetry, *Rezos bohemios* (1921), and a collection of short stories, *Capitulario* (1921). When he was seventeen years old, he traveled to Paris, where he lived for six years. He studied law at the Sorbonne and socialized with French writers and intellectuals.

In 1930, he became supporter of dictator Rafael Leónidas Trujillo (1891–1961), and in 1932 he wrote a book favorable of Trujillo's government, *Los dos años del gobierno del presidente Trujillo*; he updated the volume two years later. His support of the regime earned him several government posts as well as service in the diplomatic corps. In that capacity, he served as consul in El Salvador and in Belgium. Whether working for the government or on his own, Hernández Franco toured dozens of cities in Europe and in Latin America. When he was home in the Dominican Republic, he spent time with the important writers of the era, including **Hector Incháustegui Cabral**.

While in El Salvador in 1936, he published his most important work, *Yelidá*. In this epic poem, a Norwegian named Erick tracks down the sounds of drums in the Caribbean jungle and meets a beautiful Haitian woman named Suqui. From their union, comes the mulata Yelidá:

> Y así vino al mundo Yelidá en un vagido de gato tierno
> mientras se soltaba la leche blanca de los senos negros de Suquí

(Thus to the world arrived Yelidá in wailing of a gentle cat / while white milk licks out from Suquí's black breast).

In *Yelidá*, Hernández Franco melded together his knowledge of European culture and mythologies with voudism and Afro-Caribbean traditions. After this epic poem, Hernández Franco did not publish any more books of poetry, though it is believed he wrote at least two other volumes which are now lost. In 1942, he wrote a study of black poetry, poesía negrista, titled *Apuntes sobre poesía popular y poesía negra en Las Antillas*. In 1951, he published a collection of short stories, *Cibao: Narraciones cortas*. He passed away a year later. *See also* Negrista Literature.

Further Reading

Cabral, Manuel del. *10 poetas dominicanos: tres poetas con vida y siete desenterrados*. Santo Domingo, Republica Dominicana: Publicaciones América, S.A., 1980.

"Tomas Hernández Franco." http://www.escritoresdominicanos.com (accessed 9/7/05).

—*D. H. Figueredo*

Hernández Rueda, Lupo (1930–)

Dominican poet Hernández Rueda is representative of the Caribbean writer who works as a professional and leads an active civic life while still involved in the creative arts. He has won several national awards from the Dominican Republic.

Born in Santo Domingo on July 29, 1930, Hernández Rueda went to elementary and secondary schools in the nation's capital. At the age of twenty four, he earned a law degree from the Universidad de Santo Domingo. That same year, he published his first book of poetry, *Como naciendo aun*. Three years later, he published his second collection, *Trío*. These two volumes were well received within literary circles, and in 1960 he was awarded the National Prize for Poetry. In 1965, he wrote one of his best-known poetry collections, *Crónica del sur*, in which he depicted the sufferings and daily toil of the peasants from the countryside.

Hernández Rueda coupled his writing career with his work as an attorney and public servant. He directed the Labor School at the Universidad Nacional **Pedro Henríquez Ureña** and the National Labor and Social Welfare Association of the Dominican Republic. His interest in labor relations brought him recognition throughout Latin America. In 1974, he wrote a law manual, *Manual del Derecho Dominicano*.

In the 1970s, he wrote four books of poetry, of which *Del tamaño del tiempo* is the best known. He also edited the anthology *Antología panorámica de la poesía dominicana contemporánea*. In 1980, he published the book-length essay *La generación del 48 en la literatura dominicana*, for which he was awarded the National Essay Prize. In 1983, he traveled to Europe to study labor relations in Italy, Spain, and Switzerland. His literary productivity continued through the 1990s with the collections *Por el mar tus ojos* (1993) and an expanded edition of his first collection, *Como naciendo aun*. In 1994, he wrote a second law text, *Derecho del proceso del trabajo* based on his studies in Europe.

Hernández Rueda has served in numerous cultural and civic organizations. He is a member of the prestigious Academia Dominicana de la Lengua.

Further Reading

Gutiérrez, Franklin. "Lupo Hernández Rueda." In *Antología histórica de la poesía dominicana del siglo XX*. San Juan, Puerto Rico: Editorial de la Universidad de Puerto Rico, 1998.

Veloz Maggiolo, Marcio. *Cultura, teatro y relatos en Santo Domingo*. Santiago de los Caballeros, República Dominicana: Universidad Católica Madre y Maestra, 1972.

—*D. H. Figueredo*

Hibbert, Fernand (1873–1928)

A novelist and dramatist who exposed the ills of Haitian society, Hibbert denounced the financial corruption and the political and economic instability brought about by Haiti's dependence on foreign powers. As a businessman, the constant disputes between the liberals and the nationalists bankrupted him.

Hibbert was born on October 3, 1873, in Miragoäne, a town on the northern coast of Haiti. In 1883, after followers of the rebel leader Boyer Bazelais (1836–83), who was opposing dictator Pierre Boyer (1776–1850), landed in the region, took over, and destroyed Miragoäne, the young Hibbert and his mother sought refuge in Port-au-Prince, where they stayed permanently. In Port-au-Prince, he attended secondary school at the École de Saint-Martial for five years. He then went to France, where he studied at the Law School of Paris, the College of Political Science, and the College of France. In 1894, he returned to Haiti and found work as an accountant in the Department of Finance. Two years later he married Marie de Pescaye. One of his daughters, Nicel, would become novelist **Jacque Roumain**'s wife. In 1904, Hibbert started to teach history and French literature at the Lyceum Pétion, in Port-au-Prince. In 1912, he was named chief of the Ministry of Foreign Relations. From 1915 to 1921 he was Haiti's ambassador in Cuba. From 1921 to 1922, under the government of Sudre Dartiguenave, he was appointed Minister of Public Education.

Hibbert began his career as a writer in 1901 with a series of articles he wrote — "Une mulâtresse fille de Louis XIV," "Le néronisme de Rochambeau," and "Un nègre à la cour de Louis XIV, le Prince Zaga"—for the journal *La Ronde*. The following year he published in the same journal a short story entitled "La Bacchnate," which takes place in the Rome of Emperor Claudius (10 BCE–AD 54). His subsequent literary production is characterized by the sentiments and aesthetics of the contributors to *La Ronde*: descriptions of Haitian scenes, both from a physical and moral perspective, and a search for a national identity. The title of his first and most popular novel, *Sena* (1905), which was an instant success, alludes to the nickname given to senator Jean Baptiste Renelus Rorrottee, a terse and aggressive man who achieved a position of power in Haiti as a result of family connections and stolen funds, which he kept in European banks. In the novel, Sena, like all the rich Haitians of the period, travels to Paris, where his mistress betrays him. Heartbroken, he seeks solace from a compatriot who encourages him to visit universities, such as the Sorbone and the College of France, and to attend performances of the Comédie Française and the opera. The exposure to culture and liberal philosophy transforms Sena, who returns to Haiti to advocate liberal and social reforms. Sena is arrested and imprisoned; one morning he is found dead in his cell. The novel, lyrical and using popular vernacular, offers a pessimistic view of a society defined by disloyalty, hypocrisy, vanity, intrigue, and political frustration.

In his next novel, *Romulus*, a historical romance, Hibbert re-creates the political events of 1883. Romulus tells the story of Etienne Trévier and how Bazelais destroyed the town where Trévier lived. This work was followed by a collection of short stories, *Masques et visages* (1910). Both works were well received by the public, who praised Hibbert's humorous depictions of the upper classes, which he knew quite well, since he himself belonged to such a class. Other works that followed include *Une affaire d'honneur* (1916), *La réclamation Hopton* (1916), *Le manuscript de mon ami* (1923), and *Les simulacres; l'aventure de M. Hellénus Caton* (1923).

Hibbert has been praised for his abilities as an engaging narrator, his social criticism, and his usage of Creole or Kreyòl expressions and descriptions. But he has also been criticized for portraying characters that are not fully developed. In 1920, a suitcase containing his manuscripts caught fire when Hibbert arrived at the French port of Habre; the manuscripts were never reproduced, and the works were lost. Hibbert passed away on December 19, 1928, in Port-au-Prince, Haiti.

Further Reading

Dominique, Jean L. "Le manuscrit de mon ami, de Fernand Hibbert." *Conjonction* 133 (March–April 1977): 101–3.

Gindine, Yvette. "Satire and the Birth of Haitian Fiction (1901–1905)." *Caribbean Quarterly* 21, no. 3 (September 1975): 30–40.

Lahens, Yannick J.P. "Le paraître féminin, sa estructure, sa stratégie dans le roman de Fernand Hibbert Les Thazar." *Conjonction* 136–137 (February 1978): 45–55.

Thadal, Roland. "Fernand Hibbert fait tomber les masques." *Le Nouveau Mond* March 28–29, 1981.

—*Emilio Jorge Rodríguez*

Hijuelos, Oscar (1951–)

One of the most widely read Latino authors in the United States, Oscar Hijuelos was the first Latino novelist to receive the Pulitzer Prize in 1990 for his novel *The Mambo Kings Play Songs of Love*. His detailed and poetic descriptions of New York City, the setting for most of his books, have been compared with Charles Dickens's (1812–70) descriptions of Victorian London.

Hijuelos was born August 24, 1951, in New York City, of Cuban parents who had left their homeland in search of employment. He attended the City University of New York, graduating in 1975; a year later, he earned an MA in creative writing. He worked in advertising for a few years before publishing his first novel, *Our House in the Last World* (1983), which tells the story of an immigrant family in New York City and the dictatorial and mercurial patriarch who rules over it. His second novel, *The Mambo Kings Play Songs of Love*, is the story of two brother musicians who achieve a certain level of fame when they make a guest appearance on the television show *I Love Lucy*. The novel was praised for its realistic portrayal of Latino cabarets during the 1950s and 1960s. Some critics, however, were disturbed by the numerous sex scenes, which are graphically described in the narrative.

In 1993, Hijuelos wrote *The Fourteen Sisters of Emilio Montez O'Brien*, a family saga spanning nearly a hundred years and a nostalgic re-creation of turn-of-the century America. This novel was followed by *Mr. Ives' Christmas* (1995), a heart-wrenching story of a man who must accept the death of his son, and *The Empress of the Splendid Season* (1999), about a Cuban woman who works as a maid during the 1950s and the impact she has on those who hire her, in particular on a wealthy New Yorker who, taken by her beauty, becomes her son's protégé. In 2002, Hijuelos wrote *A Simple Havana Melody (When the World Was Good)*, a fictional biography of Cuban composer Moses Simons (1888–1945), the creator of the world-renowned song *El manisero—The Peanut Vendor*.

Cuban American critic and poet **Gustavo Pérez Firmat** describes Hijuelos' as an explicator of Cuban culture, but the depth of Hijuelos's characterizations and the complexities of his narrative have made him an insightful chronicler of the human condition in general: his heroes and heroines might be Cuban, but their triumphs and defeats are universal. Hijuelos has also been criticized for portraying women as mere sex objects and for glorifying men who are womanizers; as an answer to this criticism, the author wrote *The Fourteen Sisters of Emilio Montez O'Brien* and *The Empress of the Splendid Season*, both of which depict strong, multidimensional heroines.

Hijuelos has won several prestigious scholarships, including the American Academy Fellowship, a Cintas award—administered by UNESCO—and a Guggenheim Fellowship. *See also* Cuban American Literature; Immigrant Literature.

Further Reading

Pérez Firmat, Gustavo. *Life on the Hyphen: The Cuban-American Way*. Austin, TX: University of Texas Press, 1994.

—*Daniel Shapiro and D. H. Figueredo*

Hill, Errol Gaston (1921–2003)

Errol Gaston Hill, Trinidadian-born actor, director, playwright, poet, professor, theater historian, and scholar, was a champion of West Indian drama and indigenous performance traditions, particularly of the Anglophone Caribbean. His book, *The Trinidad Carnival: A Mandate for National Theatre*, published by University of Texas Press in 1972 and republished by New Beacon Books in 1997, is a classic, seminal work on the history of Carnival and the Carnival arts. Hill proposes in this scholarly book, as well as in his doctoral thesis at Yale University, that the theatrical talent of people involved in Carnival should form the foundation of an authentic national theatre in Trinidad.

Born in Port-of-Spain, Trinidad, on August 5, 1921, Errol Hill was the author of 11 published plays, writer or editor of more than 15 books and periodicals and of over 25 articles on drama and theater history. He directed and produced more than 120 plays and pageants in the Caribbean, England, Nigeria, and the United States with amateur, semiprofessional, and professional companies. Hill's deep knowledge of theater and versatility is demonstrated in the selection of these plays, which ranged from classical Greek dramas to Shakespeare and contemporary African, American, Caribbean, and European plays. An actor and announcer for the BBC radio, Hill performed in over thirty major roles in amateur and professional productions in the Caribbean, England, Wales, Nigeria, and the United States. He also wrote poetry that was published, mainly during the 1940s, in a variety of Caribbean periodicals. Hill's poetry, like his plays, reflected his origins and addressed themes such as the Caribbean landscape, death, despair and love.

Errol Hill's plays celebrated the survival of indigenous arts and performances in Trinidad, despite colonial oppression. *Source: Dartmouth College. Courtesy of Lisa Finder.*

After receiving a British Council scholarship to study at the Royal Academy of Dramatic Arts in 1951, Hill won a Rockefeller Foundation Fellowship to study at Yale University, where he received a BA and an MFA, as well as a DFA from the Yale School of Drama in 1966. Hill spent two years teaching drama and directing plays at the University of Ibadan, Nigeria, as a Rockefeller Foundation Fellow. He returned to the United States, where he taught for one year at Richmond College in New York, before being appointed to the faculty of the Drama Department at Dartmouth College in 1968. The first tenured faculty member of African descent at Dartmouth College, Hill taught a portfolio of thirteen courses on acting, directing, playwriting, and theater history. He directed thirty-three full-length plays in his thirty-five years at Dartmouth—twenty-one years on the faculty—chaired the Drama Department, and served for two years as the college's first official Affirmative Action Officer. Hill retired from Dartmouth College in 1989 as the John D. Willard Professor of Drama and Oratory, Emeritus.

Man Better Man, Hill's best-known play, was first performed at the Yale School of Drama in 1964. The plot revolves around stick fighting and an obeahman—sorcerer—with characters from Trinidadian village life, and is set to calypso verse and music. The play, which was written entirely in verse, was a celebration of the region's indigenous performance tradition, which endured despite suppression during the colonial era. *Man Better Man* was so well received that it was chosen to represent Trinidad and Tobago at the 1965 Commonwealth Arts Festival in Britain. Members of the cast were recruited in Trinidad and performed in London, Croydon, and Glasgow. Later, the play was performed by the Negro Ensemble Company in New York in 1969, at Dartmouth in 1975, and by theater groups throughout the Caribbean, United States, and Canada.

An earlier play, *The Ping Pong* (1958), was revolutionary in that it attracted a large urban working-class audience when initially performed. Thought to be the first play written about the Trinidad steel band, it is a window to the complex feelings of jealousy among steel band members and their loyalties on the night before a major competitive festival. *The Ping Pong* is written in Creole dialect, but the successful reception of the play was due to the fact that it speaks to all socio economic levels of society. The play celebrates popular culture, while highlighting the steel band and heralding it as Trinidad and Tobago's national music.

As with his other plays, such as *Wey Wey* (1958), his two open-air plays, Dimanche Gras Carnival extravaganzas (1963 and 1964), *Dance Bongo* (1965) *Oily Portraits* (1966), and *Strictly Matrimony* (1966), Hill sought to place Caribbean peoples as central characters within plots set within a Caribbean context and often involving political satire. He chose to recognize the folk expression of the Caribbean, utilizing the vernacular in speech without demeaning the indigenous forms of expression. *Wey Wey* had as its theme the Chinese numbers game in Trinidad, while *Dance Bongo* centered on a ritual dance for the dead. *Strictly Matrimony*, a comedy set in Jamaica, was based on an unsuccessful attempt by colonial powers in Jamaica to reduce the number of common-law couples and convince them to get legally married.

In Port of Spain, Trinidad, Hill was founder with **Errol John** of the Whitehall Players in 1946. This groundbreaking theatre group was thought to be the first Trinidadian theater company of persons of color. The Whitehall Players, which merged with the New Company to form the Company of Players, served as a training ground for Caribbean actors, directors, and future playwrights such as Osbourne Ashby and Errol John. In 1951, Hill directed **Derek Walcott's** *Henri Christophe* for the BBC radio in London and, a year later, on the stage to critical acclaim. As drama tutor at the Extramural Department of the University of the West Indies (UWI) in 1953, Hill traveled throughout the Caribbean, lecturing and organizing theater workshops and coordinating productions of plays. He spent a total of eight years at UWI and pioneered the collection, editing the publication the "Caribbean Play Series," which continues to this day.

Hill's numerous scholarly contributions to theater research include the *Theatre of Black Americans: A Collection of Critical Essays* (1980), *Shakespeare in Sable: A History of Black Shakespearean Actors* (1984), *Black Heroes: Seven Plays* (1989) and *The Jamaican Stage 1655–1900: Profile of a Colonial Theatre* (1992). A prolific scholar right up to his death, Hill completed the award-winning *History of African American Theatre* (2003) with coauthor James Hatch. His chapter on "The Caribbean Connection" in this book chronicled the development of Caribbean theater and the impact of theater personages of Caribbean origin on the development of African American theater in the United States and abroad.

Hill married Grace Hope in 1956, and they had four children. His personal papers and library were acquired by Dartmouth College in 2003 and serve as a complement to his administrative papers, which were a gift to the college in 1994. He passed away in Hanover, New Hampshire, on September 15, 2003. *See also* Anglophone Caribbean Literature, History of; Obeah Practices in Literature.

Further Reading

Banham, Martin, Errol Hill, and George Woodyard, eds. *The Cambridge Guide to African and Caribbean Theatre.* Cambridge: Cambridge University Press, 1994.

Gullick, Todd. "Celebrating Errol Hill: At the Centre of Creation." *Trinidad & Tobago Review* (October 6, 2003): 27–30.

Hill, Errol, and James Hatch. *A History of African American Theatre.* Cambridge: Cambridge University Press, 2003.

———. "The Papers of Errol G. Hill in the Dartmouth College Library." Dartmouth College, Rauner Special Collections Library, Hanover, NH, Sept. 1994, ML-77. http://diglib.dartmouth.edu/library/ead/html/ml77.html (accessed 8/31/05).

Stone, Judy S. J. *Curtain Rise: The Pioneers of West Indian Theatre 1900–1950: Errol Hill in Theatre.* London: Macmillan Press, 1994.

—*Claudia Hill*

The Hills Were Joyful Together (1953)

A classic of **barrack yard literature**, *The Hills Were Joyful Together*, by Jamaican **Roger Mais**, was the first novel in Jamaica to depict life in a slum. The setting is a barrack yard, an enclosed slum with a yard in the center where the tenants cook and conduct other household chores that can't be performed in their small apartments or rooms. The yard serves as a gathering place where a great deal of social interaction takes place.

The novel doesn't have a protagonist; rather, it narrates the incidents in the life of many of the yard residents. At the very beginning of the narrative, Roger Mais lists the names of the residents, followed by a brief description, for example: "Zephyr. A prostitute. She is continually being embarrassed by the bigness of her heart." Divided into three parts, part one—called Book One—introduces the residents and potential conflicts. The major issues that emerge are poverty, incest, poor health, and delinquency. But the residents do not let their circumstances depress them: one evening, there is a cookout and they enjoy each other's company, sharing anecdotes and singing. By the end of Book One, though, some of the conflicts erupt: a resident named Bedosa is run over by a locomotive, and a tenant named Surjue, who was planning to rob a store, is betrayed by a friend named Flitters and is arrested.

In Book Two, tensions build: Shag, one of the yard dwellers, discovers that his woman, Euphemia, is unfaithful; Surjue's wife, Rema, loses her sanity; Surjue is beaten up in prison; Flitters, planning to leave Jamaica for Cuba, is tracked down by a couple of Surjue's friends, who murder him. In this part of the novel, much of the action takes place in prison, where the author details the abuses committed by the guards and the wardens. In Book Three, Rema burns herself to death, Shag chops up Euphemia with a machete, and Surjue is shot to death while attempting to escape from prison. The only hope for a better life is expressed by a young tenant named Lenny, who is boarding a ship for America.

The different plots are presented by an omniscient narrator in a straightforward and realistic narrative. The exceptions are the rambling thoughts of Shag as he contemplates the murder of his woman and the marijuana-induced rumination of a Rasfatarian dweller named Ras. Throughout the text, Mais comments on the ills of poverty and the ruling class' indifference to the plight of the poor:

> The smell of wet tar-roads scarred and sun-blistered and night-sweating rose up to his nostrils, mingled with the odours of rancid vegetable oil stale. . . . The wind blew across the carelessly swept-up heaps of untended roadside garbage where dogs, scuffling, snarling, fighting, had been before. . . . There were nice people who thought, ain't old slums awfully quaint-looking and romantic, and in their own way beautiful? (228)

Further Reading

Mais, Roger. *The Three Novels of Roger Mais*. London: Jonathan Cape, 1966, 1970.

—*D. H. Figueredo*

Hippolyte, Dominique (1889–1967)

Hippolyte devoted his life to two activities: his career as an attorney and his work as a dramatist. He also served the Haitian government in several posts, including president of his country's Commission on Intellectual Cooperation.

Born on August 4, 1889, in Port-au-Prince, Hippolyte was raised in that city and attended school there, graduating from the prestigious Lycée Pétion in 1904. He earned a law degree from the Faculty of Law around 1908, and after teaching in high school for a short time, he was appointed commissioner of the Civil Court at Port-au-Prince.

Beginning in the second decade of the twentieth century, Hippolyte cultivated theater, writing and staging several theatrical pieces over the next two decades: *Quand elle aime* (1917), *La baiser de l'aieul* (1924), *Le Força* (1933), and *Le Torrent* (1940). The latter work, a retelling of the birth of Haiti as a republic in 1804, was cowritten with historian Placide David and is Hippolyte's most famous work.

Hippolyte viewed the creative process not only as an individualist exercise but also a work of partnership. In that spirit, he cowrote with **Luc Grimard** *Jour de gloires* in 1941 and with **Frédéric Burr-Reynaud** the historic drama *Anacaona* in 1911. Though Hippolyte earned his living as an attorney, he also wrote poetry under the pen name of Pierre Breville; he published his poems in such literary journals as ***La Revue Indigène***, *La Relève*, and *Les Griots*. In 1953, he visited the Library of Congress in Washington, D.C., where he recorded some of his poetry. *See also* Les Griots.

Further Reading

Dayan, Joan. *Haiti, History, and the Gods*. Berkeley: University of California Press, 1995.

Herdeck, Donald E. *Caribbean Writers. A Bio-Bibliographical-Critical Encyclopedia*. Washington, DC: Three Continents Press, 1979.

—*D. H. Figueredo*

Hispanic Caribbean Literature, History of

The Hispanic Caribbean consists of Cuba, the Dominican Republic, and Puerto Rico. These three claim Fray **Bartolome de las Casas** as one of their earliest writers and heroes. Las Casas was the first priest ordained in the Americas and one of the first to protest against the abuses inflected on the Amerindians by Spanish colonists; his best-known work, *Brevísima relación de la destrucción de las Indias* (1552), was one of the earliest books that attempted to bring about social changes in the Caribbean.

The first dramatist was **Cristóbal de Llerena** who in the Dominican Republic in 1580s wrote plays for the Catholic Church. In 1582, **Juan Ponce de Leon II**, grandson of explorer Juan Ponce de Leon (1460–1521), wrote the *Memoria de Melgarejo*, a chronicle of the conquest and colonization of Puerto Rico. In 1608, the first black Caribbean character presented in a likable vein appeared in the poem "Espejo de Paciencia," written by **Silvestre de Balboa Troya y Quesada**. The poem told of the kidnapping of a bishop in Cuba by a pirate and of the bishop's rescue by a slave, who also killed the kidnapper. In 1691, a Puerto Rican priest, Francisco de

Ayerra Santa María, living in Mexico gained recognition for writing sonnets that described historical events.

Most scholars agree that true literary activities in the Hispanic Caribbean began in the nineteenth century. Some general characteristics evolved: poetry began to emerge as the dominant genre in the Dominican Republic, questions of a national cultural identity informed the Puerto Rican discourse, and the writing of abolitionist and pro-independence novels and essays were favored by Cuban writers. The poetry from the Dominican Republic was unique and revolutionary: its major exponent was a woman. At a time when men in the Dominican Republic, as well as throughout Latin America, expected women to manage the household and to do so in silence, **Salomé Ureña de Henríquez** wrote nationalist verses criticizing the repressive governments ruling the nation. She was also the founder of the first school for women in that country. Other Dominican women who rebelled against the silence imposed on them were **La Deana, Josefa Antonia Perdomo**, and **Virginia Elena Ortea**.

Puerto Rico also featured a woman pioneer in the creation of a national literature. **María Bibiana Benítez**, whose poem "La ninfa de Puerto Rico" (1832) celebrated the natural beauty of the island, contributed poems to an anthology credited with inaugurating Puerto Rican literature, *Aguinaldo puertorriqueño* (1843). Another contributor to this anthology was the poet **Manuel Alonso**, who, in 1849, attempted to define the characteristics of Puerto Rican identity with his book *El gíbaro*, containing poems that duplicated the lexicon and diction of Puerto Rican farmers and stories that described local events. A book that further explored Puerto Rico's heritage and cultural traits was the volume *Biblioteca histórica de Puerto Rico* (1854), written by **Alejandro Tapia y Rivera,** based on extensive research conducted in Spain. Tapia y Rivera is considered the great man of Puerto Rican literature, writing in all genres—essays, dramas, fiction, and poetry. Also described as the father of Puerto Rican theater, Tapia y Rivera expressed his abolitionist sentiments in the play *La cuarterona* (1867).

An antislavery agenda inspired the writing of many nineteenth-century Cuban writers. **Gertrudis Gómez de Avellaneda** wrote *Sab* (1841), her criticism of the slave trade and plantation life. Educator **Félix Varela** and economist **José Antonio Saco** produced analytical and philosophical essays that condemned slavery and promoted self-rule; their anticolonialist stance would influence the Cuban patriots who went to war against Spain during the 1870s and 1890s. Probably the best-known work outside of Cuba written during this period was *Celia Valdés o La Loma del Ángel*. **Cirilo Villaverde** began to write this novel, about a doomed interracial love affair, in 1832 and finished it fifty years later.

The end of the nineteenth century saw the appearance of three figures who would achieve fame throughout the Americas: **Manuel de Jesús Galván, José Martí,** and **Eugenio María de Hostos**. Galván, from the Dominican Republic, authored the internationally reknowned novel *Enriquillo* (1882), which proclaimed that Dominican heritage was rooted in Iberia and in the pre-Columbian Caribbean. The Cuban poet José Martí was a romantic figure who devoted his life to freeing the island from Spanish rule. One of the initiators of **Modernismo** movement, Martí was killed in action in Cuba. The philosopher Eugenio María Hostos advocated autonomy for his beloved Puerto Rico and toured Latin America, creating schools and promoting free public education in such countries as Chile, the Dominican Republic, and Peru.

He believed in the creation of a Caribbean federation consisting of Cuba, the Dominican Republic, and Puerto Rico.

Hostos's dream was denied: in 1898, when the United States declared war on Spain. The conflict, called the Spanish-Cuban-American War, lasted a few months and ended with Spain's defeat, the acquisition of Puerto Rico by the United States, and the eventual birth of the Cuban Republic. A pessimist mood characterized the Caribbean's response to the growing American influence after the war. In Puerto Rico, intellectuals saw their Hispanic heritage and Spanish language threatened. Writers like **José de Diego, Luis Llorens Torres,** and **Nemesio Canales** espoused the modernist notion of culture as an artificial entity and sought to shape and develop a Puerto Rican national culture. As in the nineteenth century, the Puerto Rican farmer and peasant emerged once more, in *La canción de las Antillas y otros poemas* (1929) by Llorens Torres, as the embodiment of the island's culture and spirit. In Cuba, novelists **Carlos Loveira,** a union leader, and **Miguel Carrión,** a physician, chose **Naturalismo,** which emphasized the seedier side of life. The poet **Agustín Acosta** wrote poetry of social protest, specifically the poem "La zafra" (1926), which condemned American interventionism in the sugar industry.

In the Dominican Republic two literary movements contradicted each other: **Vedrismo,** founded in 1917 by **Otilio Vigil Díaz,** rejected nationalist poetry and favored experimental literature and **Postumismo,** created in 1921 by **Domingo Moreno Jimenes,** criticized European influences and affirmed a Dominican consciousness. Other movements emerged: the **Poeta Independientes del 1940** and **La Poesía Sorprendida. Poeta Independientes** were a cluster of loosely connected writers who rejected a literary agenda or program—out of this group emerged **Pedro Mir,** who achieved distinction for his socially engaged literature. **La Poesía Sorprendida,** grouped around the journal of the same name (1943), promoted the works of the poet **Manuel Rueda,** who later on became a successful playwright, and **Aída Cartagena Portalatín,** who switched from poetry to experimental fiction. The latter movement, to a certain extent fearsome of the political repressive characteristic of the **Trujillo era**—which lasted from 1930 to 1961- produced a type of poetry that was elusive and explored universal themes rather than national issues. In the early 1960s, the **Joven Poesía Dominicana** emerged. Its most representative poet was Norberto James Rawlings, who advocated for nationalism, social change, and flirted with leftist ideology.

As important as these poetic groupings were, they did not attract to their ranks two men who were probably the most famous cultural figures from the Dominican Republic: **Juan Bosch,** a master of the short story, and **Joaquín Balaguer,** a literary historian and critic. These two writers were the complete opposite of each other. Bosch was a liberal and was the first elected president after the assassination of dictator Rafael Leónidas Trujillo in 1961. Balaguer was Trujillo's associate—some say puppet—was a conservative, and was elected president on numerous occasions. Bosch and Balaguer were lifelong rivals.

Persecuted by Trujillo, Juan Bosch had sought refuge in Puerto Rico and in Cuba during a period when these islands were experiencing exciting political and cultural developments. In Puerto Rico, through the 1930s, 1940s, and 1950s, the concept of the commonwealth status, something akin to a colony, was being fermented and then implemented, vigorously promoted by poet and politician **Luis**

Muñoz Marín. Many writers opposed the commonwealth, favoring either statehood or independence. The debate—a passionate one at that—in turn fostered literary generations that introduced to Latin American memorable essayists, short-story writers, and dramatists. The **Generación del 30** opposed America's culture and political influence and was inspired by the island's countryside, local customs and traditions. **Antonio S. Pedreira** wrote the volume *Insuralismo* (1934), which defined Puerto Ricans as white and of Iberian origins, denying the African presence. **Luis Palés Matos** maintained the opposite view, writing poetry that portrayed Puerto Rico as the offspring of blacks, whites, Africans and Spanish. Matos became one of the creators of **negrista literature**, which celebrated and acknowledged the African roots of the Caribbean.

The **Generación del 45, or the Desperate Generation,** consisted mainly of writers who expressed a sense of desperation at seeing the island plunge into economic chaos and being overwhelmed by American capitalism, culture, and traditions. **René Marqués** wrote the tragedy *La carreta* (1952), probably the best-known play outside Puerto Rico. **José Luis González** crafted realistic and political short stories that established him as one of Latin America's great short-story writers. Other important writers were **Julia de Burgos** and **Jesús Colón.** Both of these writers went to New York City. But for de Burgos, Manhattan translated into unanonymity and death: in 1943, the poet was found unconscious in Harlem, and it took a few days for her friends to find her body at the morgue. Colón fared better, becoming an activist and a noted journalist. Highly identified with the Puerto Rican working class and staking out a piece of Manhattan as part of a Puerto Rican identity, Colón can be seen as an inaugurator of a New York–Puerto Rican persona, a Nuyorican.

From the 1930s to the 1950s, Cuba witnessed the fall of dictator Gerardo Machado (1871–1939), the emergence of strongman Fulgencio Batista (1901–73), and the seeding of the Cuban revolution. The volatile political scene coupled with social changes and racial awareness energized **Nicolás Guillén,** whose Afro-Cuban poetry acknowledged Cuba's African roots and celebrated racial diversity. **Alejo Carpentier** also explored African themes in his novels, but his interpretation of baroque, **barroco,** and his literary theories would lay the foundation for the genre known as **magical realism.**

In the 1940s, another baroque writer, **José Lezama Lima,** founded the journal *Orígines* (1944–1956) which emphasized abstract poetics, lyricism, and modern art. A contributor to the journal was **Virgilio Piñera,** whose experimental dramas revitalized Cuban theater. His plays *Electra Garrigo* (1941) and *Falsa alarma* (1957) were charged with sexual energy and attracted audiences to the theater to watch dramatizations of his works. These authors, critical of Batista's dictatorship, eagerly welcomed the triumph of the Cuban Revolution in 1959.

The revolution was probably the most significant development in Cuban literature, nurturing the writers who supported it—**Miguel Barnet, Roberto Fernández Retamar, Nancy Morejón,** for example—imprisoning those who were seen as a threat—the likes of **Reinaldo Arenas** and **Heberto Padilla**—and bringing unprecedented attention to Cuban and Caribbean letters. The revolutionary government established such publishing and cultural houses as **Casa de las Américas** to promote Latin American literature, especially a literature that was friendly towards the government's goals and critical of capitalism. In Cuba, the Puerto Rican José Luis González and the Dominican Pedro Mir found a receptive audience, but many Cuban writers and intellectual like **Jorge Mañach** and **Lino Novas Calvo** sought exile in the United States. Their children, **Himilce Novas**, for example, followed in their literary footsteps but with a difference: they were writing outside their country and in a foreign language.

Novas's experience was not a unique enterprise. For the decades before the end of the twentieth century were characterized by the production of an exciting and innovative literature that challenged easy definition of a national canon: Cuban, Dominican, and Puerto Rican authors writing about life in the United States. Initially Cuban Americans penned works of anti-Castro sentiment, anti-Castro literature, especially in the 1960s and early 1970s, but by the 1980s a new generation had taken center stage, lead by **Oscar Hijuelos**, the first Latino writer to win a Pulitzer Prize, whose novels *Our House in the Last World* (1983) and *The Mambo Kings Play Songs of Love* (1987) were about the immigrant experience in New York City and not about the old country.

Nuyorican literature, a body of work produced by Puerto Rican authors born or raised in New York, flourished in the 1960s and 1970s. Some of its best exponents were **Miguel Algarín**, **Tato Laviera**, **Nicholasa Mohr**, and **Piri Thomas**. Their works captured the vitality of street life and the heroism of the average Puerto Rican surviving poverty and discrimination in the United States. Similarly, a decade later, writers from the Dominican Republic who had grown up in the United States began to write about immigrants and the working poor. In 1996, **Junot Díaz** published a collection of short stories, *Drown*, that best exemplified this trend.

The trend, however, contained a new element: the voice of women writers. It is possible to perceive of Hispanic Caribbean literature in the United States as dominated by feminist critics, narrators, and scholars. These women were not only gifted but also moneymakers, creating best sellers, almost one after another: *How the García Girls Lost Their Accents* by **Julia Alvarez** (1990), *Dreaming in Cuba* by **Cristina García** (1992), and *When I Was Puerto Rican* (1994), by **Esmeralda Santiago**. Scholars and critics, such as the Cuban **Pamela María Smorkaloff, Daisy Cocco de Filippis**, from the Dominican Republic, and the Puerto Rican **Asela Rodríguez de Laguna**, unearthed feminist and revolutionary texts, drew attention to the bicultural experience of the Caribbean writer, and emphasized the Pan-Caribbeanness experience. Collectively, the creative writers and the critics were helping to redefine the Caribbean canon and suggesting new evaluations of Caribbean literature, including the acceptance of gay and lesbian literature and themes explored by such poets and scholars as **Luz María Umpierre**, Puerto Rican American, and **Emilio Bejel**, Cuban American.

Transnationalism might be the norm in the twenty-first century with Dominican writers traveling back and forth to their country, Cuban exile reaching out to the island, and Nuyorican writers being accepted in Puerto Rico as creators of a Puerto Rican experience, regardless of the language. The evidence at hand is the volume *Mujeres como islas* (2002), written by feminist writers from the Hispanic Caribbean, published simultaneously in Cuba, the Dominican Republic, and Puerto Rico and presenting stories set in the Caribbean and in the United States. It might appear that at least in literary output, the federation that Eugenio María Hostos had dreamed of is a reality.

Further Reading

Cabrera, Francisco Manrique. *Historia de la literatura puertorriqueña*. Río Piedras, Puerto Rico: Ediciones Cultural, 1979.

Chow, Rey. *Writing Diaspora, Tactics of Intervention in Contemporary Cultural Studies*. Bloomington: Indiana University Press, 1993.

Cocco de Filippis, Daisy. *Documents of Dissidence, Selected Writings by Dominican Women*. New York: CUNY Dominican Studies Institute, 2000.

Fernández, Roberta. *In Other Words, Literature by Latinas in the U.S.* Houston, TX: Arte Público Press, 1994.

López Baralt, Mercedes, ed. *Literatura puertorriqueña del siglo XX: antología*. San Juan, Puerto Rico: Editorial de la Universidad de Puerto Rico, 2004.

Martínez Fernández, Luis, et al., eds. *Encyclopedia of Cuba*. Westport, CT: Greenwood, 2003.

Rodríguez de Laguna, Asela. *Images and Identities: The Puerto Rican in Two World Contexts*. New Brunswick, NJ: Transaction Books, c. 1987.

Smorkaloff, Pamela María. *Cuban Writers on and off the Island*. New York: Twayne, 1999.

—*D. H. Figueredo*

Historical Novel

∎

This is a genre in which the author inserts fictional characters into events that actually occurred years before the novel was written; the fictional characters also interact with actual historical personages. For example, in the Jamaican historical novel *New Day* (1949), by **Vic Reid**, the fictional protagonist and narrator socializes with real-life people such as rebel Deacon Paul Bogle (1822?–65) and the aristocrat George William Gordon (1820?–65), both leaders of the 1865 insurrection known as the Morant Bay Rebellion.

The first historical novel by a Hispanic Caribbean author was *Jicoténcal* (1826), written by the Cuban **Félix Varela**; the second was *Enriquillo* (1882) by the Dominican **Manuel de Jesús Galván**. Both of these works retold historical events but used the retelling as an opportunity to criticize colonialism and Spain's maltreatment of the natives. In Haiti, **Emeric Bergeaud** wrote *Stella* (1859), that nation's first novel, which captured the era of the Haitian revolution; the author used the main character as a representation of Haiti.

Through the nineteenth and twentieth centuries, critics debated over the importance and aesthetic value of the historical novels. Many saw the genre as lacking literary importance, thus discouraging serious writers from producing historical fiction. The change occurred in the 1940s when **Alejo Carpentier** wrote works that depicted historical events peopled with complex and multidimensional characters while employing an inventive narrative and experimental techniques—*El reino de este mundo* (1949), *El arpa y la sombra* (1979), and *El siglo de las luces* (1962). In the 1960s, **Reinaldo Arenas** revisited the genre with his *El mundo alucinante* (1969), a fictional and fantastical biography of the real-life Fray Servando Teresa de Mier (1765–1827); the novel allowed Arenas the means to criticize **Fidel Castro**'s dictatorship. In Puerto Rico, novelist **Olga Nolla** brought a feminist perspective to her retelling of the colonization of the island and the life of conquistador Juan Ponce de Leon (1460–1521) in *El castillo de la memoria* (1996). **Maryse Condé**, with her fictional biography of *Moi, Tutuba sorciére* (1986) retold the tragic story of the Caribbean slave transplanted to Massachusetts and accused of starting the Salem witch hysteria of the seventeenth century.

In the United States, **Orlando Patterson** depicted the eighteenth-century world of the plantations in *Die the Long Day* (1972). A popular novel was *Silent Wings* (1998) by **José Raul Bernardo**, a re-creation of nineteenth century Guatemala and retelling of the supposed love affair between Cuban poet and patriot **José Martí** and a young aristocratic woman. *See also* Cuban Literature, History of; Dominican Republic Literature, History of; Puerto Rican Literature, History of.

Further Reading

Menton, Seymour. *Latin America's New Historical Novel*. Austin: University of Texas Press, 1993.

Wilson-Tagoe, Nana. *Historical Thought and Literary Representation in West Indian Literature*. Gainesville, Tallahassee: University of Florida Press, 1998.

–*D. H. Figueredo*

Hodge, Merle (1944–)

∎

Novelist, short-story writer, and educator Merle Hodge is known for her fictional creation of unforgettable, powerful, and larger-than-life matriarchs who fiercely treasure their autonomy and who love and scold their broods, by blood or informal adoption, with equally excessive generosity and passion. As an educator, she is widely admired for teaching young students to value their Caribbeanness, including its hybrid "nation language," an English-based Creole that emerged out of the confluence of indigenous Indian, African, East Indian, and European cultures, while encouraging them to communicate and master standard English.

Merle Hodge was born in Calcutta Settlement, Carapichaima, Trinidad, on January 15, 1944. Winner of a scholarship based on her secondary school performance at the Bishop Anstey High School, Port of Spain, in 1961, Hodge graduated from the University of London in 1967, having acquired a BA (Hons.) in French and a masters in French for research on French African and French Caribbean Literature. Since 1970, she has taught in secondary schools and universities throughout the West Indies, including the University of the West Indies–Mona, the University of the Virgin Islands–St. Croix; the Grenada Teacher College, where she served as curriculum consultant and lecturer in language arts for the National In-Service Teacher Education Programme during Maurice Bishop's Socialist Revolutionary Government in 1979. She wrote about this experience in *"Is Freedom We Making": the New Democracy in Grenada* (1982). Hodge returned to Trinidad two years later when Bishop was assassinated in an internal coup and the United States government invaded the island.

Hodge has been passionate in her campaigns to realize a decolonized Caribbean educational system and culture, and by extension a decolonized Caribbean mind. She remains fascinated with socialization, education, and particularly the school environment, which she sees as a microcosm and the seedbed of the wider social order. This is the major focus of her two novels *Crick Crack, Monkey* (1970) translated into French and Dutch, and *For the Life of Laetitia* (1993), also translated into French, Italian, and German. Published two decades apart, both novels deal with young girls as they transition from childhood to adulthood at pivotal points of Caribbean sociocultural development.

Merle Hodge's published short fiction includes "Millicent" in *Shell Book of Trinidad Stories* (1973), "Inez" in *Pepperpo* (1975)—and reprinted in *The Faber Book of Contemporary Caribbean Short Stories* (1990)—"Jeffie Lemmington and Me" in *Over Our Way* (1980), and "Gran-Gran" in *Venture* (1996). Her key essays include "In the Shadow the Whip: Male-Female Relations in the Caribbean" in *Is Massa Day Dead?* (1974), "Towards a Discussion on: The Emergence of a Caribbean Aesthetic" in *El Caribe* (1980), and "Towards People's Participation in Caribbean Development" in *A Caribbean Reader on Development* (1986). She is the author of the instructional text *The Knots in English: A Manual for Caribbean Users* (1977).

Hodges identifies her impulse to write as rooted protest against the arrogant colonialist's assumption "that I and my world were nothing and to rescue our selves from nothingness, we had best seek admission to the world of their storybook." She rallies against the Europeans' and Americans' tendencies of negating the Caribbean and offering Europe and the United States as the world's salvation. *See also* Caliban; Postcolonialism; Feminism in Caribbean Literature; Mother-Daughter Relationships.

Further Reading

Rafis, Iris Fawzia. *You of age to see about yourself now! So pull up you socks!: Themes of "bildung" in select novels by West Indian women writers.* Ann Arbor, MI: University Microfilms International, 1996.

—Paula Morgan

Hostos, Eugenio María (1839–1903)

∎

Alongside the Cuban **José Martí**, Eugenio Maria Hostos is one of Latin America's most beloved patriots and cultural figures. A philosopher, educator, and writer, Hostos had a dream: To form one federation out Cuba, the Dominican Republic, and Puerto Rico. The dream was shattered in 1899 when at the end of the Spanish-Cuban-American War the United States occupied Puerto Rico. That same year Hostos asked President William McKinley (1897–1901) to grant freedom to his beloved island, a request that was denied. Disillusioned, Hostos retired to the Dominican Republic.

Eugenio María de Hostos y Bonilla was born on January 11, 1839, near Mayagüez, Puerto Rico. He was taught at home by tutors and then attended the Lyceum in San Juan, from where he traveled to Spain to attend secondary school. After graduation, he matriculated in law school but didn't complete his studies. While in Spain, he wrote the novel *La peregrinación de Bayoán*, an anticolonialist work.

In 1869, he traveled to New York City. Conceiving of Cuba's and Puerto Rico's independence movements as similar struggles, he joined the Cuban Revolutionary Junta and became editor of the journal *La Revolución*. From 1870 to 1874 he toured Latin America, seeking support for Cuba's and Puerto Rico's causes. While in Peru, he witnessed how Chinese railroad workers were abused by the employers and cam-

Bust of Eugenio María Hostos in San Juan, Puerto Rico. Hostos is a beloved philosopher, essayist, and educator who promoted Pan-Caribbeanism during the 19th century. *Source: D. H. Figueredo.*

paigned successfully for better working conditions for these laborers. From 1875 to 1888, he reformed the educational system of the Dominican Republic and Chile—advocating for the establishment of public education for women, a novel notion at the time—and taught philosophy at the Universidad de Buenos Aires. During these years he also founded and edited several newspapers, including *La Patria*, in Peru, and *Ferrocarril* and *Sud América*, in Chile. In 1888, he published his best-known work, the philosophical *Moral social,* in which where he maintains that personal behavior that is ethical and honest benefits both the individual and society.

After 1898, Hostos spent the remaining years of his life in the Dominican Republic, where he was a revered teacher. He passed away in Santo Domingo on August 11, 1903. Throughout Latin America he is called "The Citizen of the Americas." Numerous schools in the Caribbean and in the United States are named in his honor. *See also* Hispanic Caribbean Literature, History of; Puerto Rican Literature, History of.

Further Reading

Arpini, Adriana. *Eugenio María de Hostos, un hacedor de la libertad*. Mendoza, Argentina: Editorial de la Universidad Nacional de Cuyo, 2002.

Ferrer Canales, José. *Martí y Hostos*. Río Piedras: Instituto de Estudios Hostosianos, Universidad de Puerto Rico, San Juan: Centro de Estudios Avanzados de Puerto Rico y el Caribe, 1990.

—*D. H. Figueredo*

House for Mr. Biswas, A (1961)

■

The novel *A House for Mr. Biswas*, by **V. S. Naipaul**, has been termed, by Robert Hamner in *V. S. Naipul* (1973), "easily one of the finest to be written by a West Indian author and is considered by many to be among the best in English Literature." It explores the acculturation of Indian immigrants within the burgeoning, chaotic Trinidadian society during the period 1931 to 1948.

Based loosely on the life story of V. S Naipaul's father, **Seepersad Naipaul,** and the writer's own formative years in Trinidad, the novel traces the life path of his hero from birth into disadvantageous circumstances, through adulthood. But this is certainly a Bildungsroman, Trinidad style. The anomie and social disorder allow for no clear predictable pathway to success; the diversity and spiritual paucity allow for no smooth spiritual integration.

The central concerns of the novel include the Hindu culture under assault in the new world; the process of creolization; the individual caught between the decaying closed Asiatic culture and the anomie of the emerging West Indian culture; the nature of the intimate family relationships that surface within such a framework; the rebellion of diminished man within a sociocultural framework that threaten to nullify him. Naipaul portrays the East Indian community as a world within a world, driven by fierce competition and loyalties, a strong sense of cultural superiority, bitter gender conflicts: all of these against a background of a disparate Creole society characterized by anomie and crawling shakily toward self-government.

Naipaul's skill in characterization is magnificently displayed on the novel's broad six-hundred page canvas. His observation of human character is precise. His focus on human foibles is single-minded. His biting sarcasm and irony is constantly at work, but not without the tempering compassion that surfaces often at the most unexpected moments.

Biswas is the quintessential unaccommodated man. Small and unassuming in stature, he is beset with disadvantages. Through the workings of fate, from birth Biswas is dogged by a prophecy that casts him in the role of outsider—born the wrong way, with an unlucky sneeze and six fingers, a liar, spendthrift and a lecher. He is denied the tragic stature of an Oedipus, whose prophetic downfall is crafted in terms of a grand design.

Biswas's diminutive stature is overshadowed only by the ridiculousness of the situations in which he finds himself. Without a home and even adequate shelter and nourishment, beset by physical discomfort, Biswas cannot assume a heroic posture. He is flabby, clownish, inclined to be overlooked. The smallness of his stature and status is emphasized by numerous descriptions of his clothes and mannerisms. But he possesses a streak of recklessness and determination, which surfaces when he is down—an irrational defiance that causes him to fight in the face of impossible circumstances. It is at these moments that his endearing personality surfaces and he lays claim to what he perceives as his rights, airs his grievances, and takes his revenge. Biswas is also extremely naive. As a result of his innocence and idealism, he repeatedly takes the world on trust and is repeatedly hoodwinked. He often becomes incensed by cruelty and reacts with futile rage.

Yet Naipaul never constructs Biswas as a fool. Indeed his triumph by the end of the novel takes on the largest possible dimensions. Reader and character alike are "amazed" at his audacious feat; the acquisition of a house, jerry-built, heavily mortgaged, and in disrepair is the acquisition of his very own portion of the earth, the successful, though qualified fulfillment of mankind's ultimate quest to evade the human predicament of being unnecessary and unaccommodated.

Further Reading

Hamner, Robert D. *V. S. Naipaul*. New York: Twayne, 1973.

Naipaul, V. S. *A House for Mr. Biswas*. New York: McGraw-Hill, 1961.

———. *Reading & Writing: A Personal Account*. New York: New York Review of Books, 2000.

—Paula Morgan

Huyke, Juan B. (1880–1961)

■

Huyke is representative of the Caribbean politician who cultivates literature, like **Eric Williams** in Trinidad-Tobago, and **Juan Bosch** from the Dominican Republic. He was a Puerto Rican novelist and short-story writer who also served as governor of the island.

Born on June 11, 1880 in Arroyo, Puerto Rico, Huyke studied at the Instituto Provincial in San Juan, where he earned a teaching certificate and a law degree. At the turn of the century, he taught in elementary school and was promoted to administrator. His pedagogical interests coupled with the need to create educational materials prompted him to write several school texts: *Libro de lectura* (1913), *Niños y escuelas* (1919), and *Lecturas* (1923), among others. His reputation as an educator led to his appointment as Commissioner of Public Education in Puerto Rico from 1921 to 1930. He was also a skilled politician, serving in the Puerto Rican Congress and as interim governor of the island in 1922.

The 1920s was a fecund period for the politician-educator. He wrote several comedies for the theater—*El batey* (1926), *La sentimental* (1926), *Días de reyes* (1929), and *Abuelo y nieto* (1929)—and several novels—*Vida escolar* (1925), *Pepe el abogado* (1926), and *El joven ingeniero* (1927). He also published short stories, two collections of autobiographical articles, *Combatiendo* (1922) and *Triunfadores* (1926–27), and children's books *Rimas infantiles* (1926) and *Un libro para mis nietos* (1928).

When Huyke was fifty years old, he focused his energies on the management of two important Puerto Rican newspapers, *El País* and *The Puerto Rican School Review*.

Further Reading

Toro-Sugrañes, José A. Nueva. *Enciclopedia de PuertoRico*. Vol 4, Biografías. Hato, Rey, Puerto Rico: Editorial Lector, 1994.

—D. H. Figueredo

I

Immigrant Literature

This is a body of creative work that documents the immigrants' experience in the host country, that offers a connection with the homeland, and that facilitates the immigrant's transition from the original country to the adopted country. Observes scholar **Nicolás Kanellos** in *Hispanic Literature of the United States* (2003): "The predominant themes in the literature of immigration are the description of the Metropolis . . . [the] trials and tribulations of immigrants . . . exploitation . . . and discrimination [of] foreigners and racial others"(25).

The immigrant literature that is written in the immigrants' language and that helps the reader understand the host country's customs, laws, and traditions often appears in small newspapers or publications published by small presses. Newspapers were the main source of Hispanic Caribbean immigrant literature in the United States during the nineteenth century. A frequent contributor to the press was the Cuban poet **José Martí** whose articles and essays detailed life in the United States.

In the twentieth century, the Puerto Rican **Bernardo Vega** edited a journal, *El Gráfico*, which in Spanish and in English published articles and essays about American culture as well as editorials on racism and discrimination. During the same decade, **Jesús Colón**, from Puerto Rico, also wrote about discrimination. His pieces, though, were written in English.

Since the 1950s, writing immigrant literature in English is the practice of Francophone or Hispanic Caribbean writers who were either born or raised in the United States. Novels such as *Our House in the Last World*, by Cuban American **Oscar Hijuelos,** and the novels of Haitian writer **Edwidge Danticat,** are written for immigrants who read English and also for a general audience. With that perspective in mind, many of these works, such as *Our House in the Last World*, serve as ethnographic studies that explain to the novice the traditions and customs from the homeland.

Anglophone Caribbean writers did not have to address the issue of language, since they were already writing in English. The novels and poems these writer published did emphasize the new surroundings and process of assimilation as well evoking images from the homeland. Caribbean immigrant literature in English flourished during the second half of the twentieth century as authors migrated to Great Britain, Canada, and the United States. One of the best novels to document this experience was the *Lonely Londoners* (1956) by Samuel Selvon. A popular work, as far as the non–Caribbean reading public is concerned, was the autobiography *To Sir With Love* (1960), in which teacher **E. R. Braithwaite** narrated his experiences in a London ghetto in the late 1950s. **Rosa Guy** and **Paule Marshall** vividly described New York City and the life of islanders during the same period. In her bestselling novel, ***Brown Girl, Brownstones*** (1959), Marshall also addressed a salient theme: the longing for a return to the homeland, a return that never occurs. For these writers, though, the link with the old country is crucial for their work. **Jamaica Kincaid**, for example, is a longtime U.S. resident who maintains her Antigua passport as a reminder of her native country.

In the francophone Caribbean, the appearance of immigrant literature occurred after the late 1950s as Haitian writers migrated to France and Canada. Like their Anglophone counterparts, the writers from the French Caribbean did not have to write in a new language for they were reaching a French reading audience—the exception was Danticat in the United States. **J. C. Charles** wrote two novels *Manhattan Blues* (1985) and *Ferdinand je suis à Paris* (1987), where the protagonist travels back and forth between New York City and Paris, describing what he sees and the people he meets. Other excellent examples of immigrant literature include *Strange Fruit* (1981), a play by **Caryl Phillips**, *Lucy's Letter and Loving* (1982), poems by **James Berry**, *How The Garcia Girls Lost Their Accents* (1991), a novel by **Julia Alvarez**, and *When I Was Puerto Rican* (1994), a memoir by **Esmeralda Santiago**.

Further Reading

Kanellos, Nicolás. *Hispanic Literature of the United States*. Westport, CT: Greenwood Press, 2003.

Luis, William. *Dance Between Two Cultures: Latino Caribbean Literature Written in the United States*. Nashville: Vanderbilt University Press, 1997.

Mendoza, Louis, and S. Shankar. *Crossing Into America: The New Literature of Immigration*. New York: The New Press, 2003.

—*D. H. Figueredo*

Incháustegui Cabral, Héctor (1912–79)

Popular poet from the Dominican Republic who was one of the few able to criticize through his poetry the dictatorship of Rafael Leónidas Trujillo (1891–1961), Incháustegui Cabral was also a critic, a novelist, and a journalist. He was a member of the literary groups **La Poesía Sorprendida** and the **Independentistas del 40**.

Born in Bani, as a child he grew up in a home frequented by writers and surrounded with books. His father was a journalist and his grandaunt read to him Spanish poetry and children's stories at bedtime. He spent numerous hours reading, and as an adult he always spoke fondly of the books he had read while growing up: *The Arabian Nights*, adventure yarns by Emilio Salgari (1862–1911), and Shakespeare's plays, among others. The reading and the contact with writers such as **Domingo Moreno Jimenes** and **Vigil Díaz** led him to writing short stories when he was still a young boy.

In 1939 he published a collection of poems, *Poemas de una sola angustia*, that brought him national attention. The poems were openly critical of social conditions and poverty in the Dominican Republic:

> Mientras el hombre tenga que arrastrar
> enfermad y hambre,
> . . . no deberá haber sosiego
> ni deberá haber paz

(As long as man must drag / diseases and hunger . . . / there should no be rest / no peace).

Though Incháustesgui Cabral risked censorship and even imprisonment for his criticism of Trujillo's regime, he did not seek exile like other writers, such as **Juan Bosch** and **Pedro Mir**. He told journalist Guillermo Piña Contreras, in *Doce en la literatura dominicana* (1982), that dictator Trujillo, who was his friend, did not arrest him because he realized that the poet had no political aspirations and was only expressing universal conditions in his poetry (118).

In 1942, Incháustegui Cabral published *Rumbo a la otra vigila* and *En soledad de amor herido*. The poems in these collections continued to reveal his preoccupation with social conditions, expressed in a style that consisted of long phrases, philosophical musings, biblical allusions, and a certain musicality; these volumes solidified his popularity in the Dominican Republic. In 1951, he published in Mexico a novel, written in verse, *Muerte en el Eden*, which became a best seller. In 1965, the civil war in the Dominican Republic and the arrival of American troops inspired him to write *Diario de la guerra* and *Los dioses ametrallados*, reflections on the shame and pain experienced by his compatriots due to the political situation. With the objective of encouraging critical study of the literature of the Dominican Republic, he wrote two volumes of literary history and criticisms: *De literatura dominicana Siglo XX* (1969) and *Escritores y arstistas dominicanos* (1979).

While writing, Incháustegui Cabral supported his family through numerous positions as a newspaper editor and radio producer. He also worked for the government as vice secretary of the ministry of education, arts and culture, and vice secretary of foreign relations. He was appointed ambassador to Brazil, El Salvador, Mexico, and Venezuela. *See also* Dominican Republic Literature, History of; Trujillo Era.

Further Reading

Enciclopedia ilustrada de la Republica Dominicana. Vol. 6. Santo Domingo: Eduprogreso, S.A., 2003.

Incháustegui Cabral, Héctor. *El pozo muerto*. Ciudad Trujillo, República Dominicana: Impr. Librería Dominicana, 1960.

—*D. H. Figueredo*

Independentistas del 40

This was a group of writers from the Dominican Republic who opposed the dictatorship of Rafael Leónidas Trujillo (1891–1961) during the 1940s and who often preferred exile rather than stay in their country. Once in exile, these writers used a poetry that was direct and passionate and that criticized Trujillo's dictatorship. Their poems also denounced world capitalism and advocated for political reform beyond the dictatorship. The most renowned members of this group were **Manuel del Cabral, Tomás Hernández Franco, Héctor Inchaústegui Cabral,** and **Pedro Mir.** The most famous poem to emerge from this group is the volume *Hay un país en el mundo* (1949), written by Pedro Mir. The poem, an excellent example of politically and socially engaged literature, criticized capitalism and rallied the working poor to fight against American imperialism. *See also* Literatura Comprometida/Socially and Engaged Literature; Trujillo Era.

Further Reading

Brown, Isabel Zakrzewski. *Culture and Customs of the Dominican Republic.* Westport, CT: Greenwood, 1999.

—*D. H. Figueredo*

Indianism or Indianismo. See Indianist Literature.

Indianist Literature

In the nineteenth century, Indianist literature idealized and romanticized the Native Americans—the Caribs, Siboneys, and Taínos—from the Caribbean and portrayed the Europeans, in particular the Spaniards, as all evil. Indianist novels and poetry usually depicted the Caribbean as an earthly paradise shattered by the arrival of the Spanish conquistadores. One of the best examples of the genre is the novel *Enriquillo* (1879, 1882), by **Manuel de Jesús Galván,** from the Dominican Republic. Enriquillo is a Taíno chief who is at first sympathetic towards the colonizers but upon encountering their greed, ruthlessness, and treacherous ways rebels against them; the novel is a retelling of what occurred in the island of Hispaniola, known as Quisqueya to the aborigines, when the Taínos first welcomed Christopher Columbus only to have his men rape Taíno women and murder Taíno men. Other representative works include the collection of poems *Fantasías indígenas* (1877), written by **José Joaquín Pérez,** and the epic poem "Anacaona" (1880) by **Salomé Ureña Henríquez,** both from the Dominican Republic; and *Cantos del Siboney* (1855) by José Fornaris as well as some of the poetry of **Joaquín Lorenzo Luaces,** both from Cuba.

During the nineteenth century, according to G. R. Coulthard, in Cuba and Puerto Rico, Indianist literature, or Indianism, fostered nationalism and protested against the Spanish colonial presence while in the Dominican Republic, it strengthened the Dominicans' resolve against the Haitians who had invaded the country in the early 1800s and still had their eyes on that side of the island. In Haiti, Indianism appeared as **indigènisme,** which was a rejection of European culture and a reaction against the American invasion of 1915; indigènisme affirmed Haitian nationalism and its African roots.

In the Caribbean, Indianism is essentially a literary movement. In the countries in Latin American where there is large Native American population—Bolivia, Guatemala, Mexico, among others—Indianism, known as Indigenismo, refers to a political agenda for the integration of Native Americans into the political process. In Cuba, this genre is also known as "siboyenismo." *See also* Créolité; Négritude.

Further Reading

Berger, Thomas. *A Long and Terrible Shadow: White Values, Native Rights in the Americas, 1492–1992.* Vancouver: Douglas & McIntyre; Seattle: University of Washington Press, 1992.

Coulthard, G. R. *Race and Colour in Caribbean Literature.* London: Oxford University Press, 1962.

Galván, Manuel de Jesús. *Enriquillo: leyenda histórica dominicana, 1503–1533.* Santo Domingo: Ediciones de la Fundación Corripio, 1990.

—*D. H. Figueredo*

Indigenism. See Indianist Literature. See also Indigènisme.

Indigènisme

This was a Haitian literary movement that rejected European traditions and criticized Haitian elites for denying their African heritage and favoring French literature, culture, and manners. The movement was also a reaction to the **American occupation of Haiti** in 1915 and was influenced by the writings of Haitian intellectual **Jean Price-Mars.** The movement's literary organ was *La revue indigène,* published from 1927 to 1928. Indigènisme promoted voudism as the nation's true religion, rather than Catholicism, and also the writing of a literature that celebrated Haiti's common people, such as the rural, or **peasant novel.**

One of the most outstanding authors of this movement was **Jacques Roumain.** In his fictional works, there are not only literal representations of voudu practices and ceremonies but also characters whose very temperaments exemplify various *loa,* or spirits, of the voudu pantheon. His novel *Gouverneurs de la rosée* (1944) is considered the best example of the peasant novel. The movement also encouraged the use of Kreyòl as the nation's language. *See also Ainsi Parla l'* *Oncle;* Créolité; Haitian Literature in Kreyòl; Indianismo; Nègritude; Vodou in Literature.

Further Reading

Antoine, Jacques C. *Jean Price-Mars and Haiti.* Washington, DC and Colorado: Three Continents Press and Lynne Rienner Publishers, 1981.

Price-Mars, Jean. *Ainsi Parla l'Oncle.* Paris: Imp. De Compiègne, 1928.

—*D. H. Figueredo*

Insularismo

This term comes from a collection of essays titled *Insularismo; Ensayos de inter-* *pretación puertorriqueña* written in 1934 by Puerto Rican author **Antonio S. Pedreira,** who believed that the island's dependence on the United States as well as four hundred years as a Spanish colony robbed Puerto Ricans of their identity and made them docile. Pedreira favored Spanish heritage and dismissed the black presence on the island.

Other writers who displayed a preoccupation with a Puerto Rican identity include dramatist **René Marqués** and short-story author and dramatist **Emilio S. Belaval.** Recent Puerto Rican scholars in Puerto Rico and in the United States denounce the ideology as somewhat racist.

Further Reading

López-Baralt, Mercedes. *Sobre "ínsulas extrañas": el clásico de Pedreira/anotado por Tomás Blanco.* San Juan: Editorial De La Universidad De Puerto Rico, 2000.

—*D. H. Figueredo*

In the Castle of My Skin (1953)

The first novel by Barbadian writer **George Lamming** was considered a masterpiece of Caribbean literature the moment it was published. An autobiographical exercise, a trend in Caribbean literature at the time, the title refers to a line from the poem "Letter to Margaret" by **Derek Walcott.** In the novel, Lamming employs a poetic interpretation of arts, an "ars poetica," to describe three distinct worlds for the writer: (1) the private world—in the castle of my skin—that is only known to others when the author reveals it; (2) the world with other men; (3) the world with other communities. Lamming believes that the writer must find meaning for his or her destiny and that the writer is judged by the authenticity of his or her written expressions and his or her honest interpretations of social relations.

The novel, consisting of fourteen chapters, tells the story of a boy, identified only by the initial "G," and his childhood in a poor village of Barbados from 1936 to 1946. In the narrative, the author describes the experiences of childhood—anxiety of separation, memories kindled by objects—and the depiction of everyday events. But to these events, Lamming assigns symbolic significance: the fear that one day the child will lose a sense of history and identity. *In the Castle of My Skin* also illuminates the nature of colonialism: the absent rulers who have no attachment to the colony. As an illustration of this sentiment, Lamming presents a character, the director of the school that G attends, who has no shadow. Contrary to this detachment is a married couple named Ma and Pa, the oldest couple on the island. The couple represents popular wisdom, the collective consciousness, and African heritage.

This realistic novel is highlighted by the use of dialect; the narrative is propelled through the use of dialogues. *See also* Postcolonialism.

Further Reading

Cooke, Michael G. "The Strains of Apocalypse: Lamming's Castle and Brodber's Jane and Louisa." *Journal of West Indian Literature* 4, no. 1 (1990): 28–40.

Lamming, George. *In the Castle of My Skin.* London: Michael Joseph, 1953.

Rodríguez, Emilio Jorge. "*En el castillo de mi piel*: context sociohistórico y literario." In *Literatura caribeña; bojeo y cuaderno de bitácora.* la Habana: Editorial Letras Cubanas, 1989.

—*Emilio Jorge Rodríguez*

J

Jamaican Literature, History of

The scholarly tendency has been to date the beginning of Jamaican literature to the early the twentieth century, but the literary seeds were planted in the mid-eighteenth century. In the 1750s, a free black Jamaican named **Francis Williams** wrote odes in Latin. Sent to study in England by the duke of Montague—as an experiment to prove or disprove that black people were able to learn—Williams studied the Greek and Latin classics and foreign languages at Cambridge University. Upon his return to Jamaica, he set up a school and wrote poetry. In 1759, he penned Latin elegiacs to welcome a new governor to the island. He also wrote a ballad, "Welcome, Welcome, Brother Debtor," that became popular in London.

Williams was imitating the style used by British writers of the period. This was a practice common enough throughout the Caribbean, where the colonized imitated the art of the colonists. Sometimes it was a way of mastering literary techniques; sometimes it was way of proving to white Europeans that the people in the Caribbean could think and express themselves just like anyone else.

In such style and with such purpose, there were a series of novels written from the 1800s to the 1860s by authors born or in raised in Jamaica. Possibly the earliest entry is *Hamel, The Obeah Man*, written anonymously and published in London in 1827, a story of a Jamaican obeah man who aborts the plans of a missionary who is enticing rebellion against England in order to satisfy his own romantic and sexual needs—he lusts after the daughter of a plantation owner. An early depiction of oppression and the brutality of slavery appear in the novel *Busha's Mistress*—written in 1855, serialized in the newspaper *Daily Gleaner* in 1910, and finally released as a book in 2003. Its author was Cyrus Perkins, the son of a white doctor who lived in Jamaica. In 1862, Myane Reid published *The Maroon*, a Victorian narrative about an obeah man seeking revenge—a novelty, for the hero was not a British colonist. During the same year, *Captain Clutterbuck's Champagne* was published. Written by William G. Hamley, it was an antislavery novel.

Also during this period one of the best-known works of the century appeared. It was an autobiography written by a Jamaican nurse who served in the Crimean War: *The Wonderful Adventures of Mary Seacole*, the narrative served as a travelogue—for **Mary Seacole** traveled from Jamaica to Colombia and Panama before sailing for England—as well as an action story that tells how Seacole set up an hospital near the battlefront to treat wounded British soldiers. The autobiography was also

412

a pioneering feminist text, as it demonstrated Seacole's gentle rebellion against British society: she did what she wanted to do and went wherever she wanted to go despite objections by British authorities. For example, not allowed to enlist as a nurse in the British army because she was black, she nevertheless journeyed to Crimea. Seacole, however, tended to identify more with Great Britain than with Jamaica.

It is not until the early 1900s that a sense of Jamaica, that a national identity, began to appear. The writings of **Tom Redcam**—his collections of stories *Becka's Buckra Baby* (1903), the book of poetry *Collections of Orange Valley and Other Poems*, and the play *Santa Gloria*—glorified the natural beauty of the island and revealed the author's preference for Jamaica over Great Britain, a rarity at the time. A romantic, Redcam was a popular writer, and many of his poems were recited by generations of schoolchildren. In Redcam's footsteps came **J. E. Clare McFarlane**, the founder of the **Poetry League of Jamaica**, the editor of the first anthology of Jamaican poetry–*From Overseas* (1924)—and the first to write a critical history of Jamaican literature, *A Literature in the Making* (1930). Neither of these writers, however, drew international attention.

The first Jamaican novelist to achieve recognition in Europe was **Herbert George de Lisser**, the influential editor of the equally influential newspaper the *Daily Gleaner*. He wrote over a dozen novels set in Jamaica and peopled by Jamaican characters. His two most famous works are *Jane's Career* (1914), about black Jamaican woman's odyssey from poverty to middle class, and *The White Witch of Rosehall* (1929), a story about supernatural events that take place on a plantation. The first to achieve international critical acclaim was **Claude McKay**, who saw his black heritage as a source of energy and creativity. Leaving Jamaica in 1912 for the United States, he is both claimed as one of their own by American and Jamaican readers and scholars. His best-known works are *Home to Harlem* and *Banjo*, both published in 1928.

In the 1930s, one of the most influential figures in Jamaican literature appeared. Her name was **Una Marson**, and she was a feminist—called Britain's first feminist—a poet, a playwright, and a literary mentor. She was the first Anglophone Caribbean to seek self-exile in England—leading what would become a migration pattern after World War II—and the creator of **Caribbean Voices**, the radio program that would launch dozens of West Indian writers onto the world scenes, including Nobel Prize winners **V. S. Naipul** and **Derek Walcott**. In her works, Marson explored religious practices—in the play *Pocomania* (1938)—and promoted black consciousness in such poems as "Kinky Hair," where she criticizes the imposed Western Europeans' standard of beauty.

The 1940s was a decade of excitement: stirrings of nationalism, the movement toward independence, and the appearance of a group writers who invigorated Jamaican literature. The writers were associated with the journal *Focus*, which was directed and edited by artist and literary mentor, **Edna Manley**, the mother of would-be prime minister Michael Manley (1924–97). Manley believed that the journal needed to promote social and cultural changes and a growth toward a true Jamaican identity. Many writers responded to her call, but two altered the literary landscape, writing works that were truly unique to the Jamaican experience: **Victor Reid** and **Roger Mais**. Reid was the author of *New Day* (1949), the first nationalist novel of Jamaica and the first to incorporate the Jamaican dialect into the narrative. Mais wrote *The Hills Were Joyful Together* (1953), the first novel to depict exclusively the slums, or barrack yards, of Jamaica. The novel studied social disadvantages on the island, advocating for political change, even revolution.

Before dying of cancer, Roger Mais had spent some time in England, where he had gone to look for better publishing opportunities. It was not a trajectory he had undertaken by himself: with him there were dozens of writers who had left Jamaica. Some of these writers, like **John Hearne,** eventually returned, others, like **Andrew Salkey,** did not. A trend was established, and since the end of World War II, most Jamaican writers have—either for a short or long time—lived either in England or in Canada, with a few settling in the United States. Some of these writers include the novelist and academician **Orlando H. Patterson,** poet and children's writer **James Berry,**novelist and essayist **Sylvia Wynter,** and dub poet **Linton Kwesi Johnson.** Their lives in exile helped to globalize Jamaican literature as they became known at home and abroad.

But if Jamaican literature in the 1950s and 1960s was the province of men, women writers began to make their presence felt in the 1970s. Two women in particular achieved the status of celebrities: **Louise Bennett** and **Jean Binta Breeze.** Bennett is a versatile poet and performer, reciting her works while impersonating different characters and persona. Her use of Jamaican dialect has made her accessible to all audiences throughout the island. Likewise, Breeze uses the jargon of the streets to write poems of social protest and criticism of a male-driven society. Both Bennett and Breeze have become representative of **dub** and **performance poetry,** a type of poetry that is meant to be heard, sometimes to the beat of music, and not written on paper.

Women's presence continued into the end of the twentieth century and the beginning of the twenty-first. An area of growth was that of criticism, in which where feminists such as **Barbara Lalla** have questioned masculine dominance in creative writings and the ongoing presence of feminine stereotypes in the works of Jamaican writers. Children's and young-adult literature has also gained popularity with the publication of works by the likes of **Jean D'Costa.**

Jamaican literature will continue to grow. One outcome is clear: it will be both a literary expression of Jamaicans on the island and Jamaicans abroad. *See also* Children's Literature in the English-speaking Caribbean; Literary Journals.

Further Reading

Dance, Daryl Cumber, ed. *Fifty Caribbean Writers: A Bio-Bibliographical-Critical Sourcebook*. Westport, CT: Greenwood Press, 1986.

Dathorne, O. R. *Caribbean Narrative: An Anthology of West Indian Writing*. London: Heinemann Educational Books, 1966, 1973.

Gilkes, Michael. *The West Indian Novel*. Boston: Twayne, 1981.

Lalla, Barbara. *Defining Jamaican Fiction: Marronage and the Discourse of Survival*. Tuscaloosa: The University of Alabama Press, 1996.

Ramchand, Kenneth. *An Introduction to the Study of West Indian Literature*. Kenya and Jamaica: Nelson Caribbean, 1976.

—Ian H. Marshall and D. H. Figueredo

James, CRL (1901–89)

Cyril Lionel Robert James is considered one of the greatest writers and thinkers of the twentieth century. His work includes short stories and a novel, as well as significant contributions in the field of cricket, literary criticism, Caribbean history, Pan-African politics, and Marxist theory. So great has been his impact on the literary, political, and philosophical world that an Institute—the CLR James Institute—has been founded in his name to collect, document, and disseminate information on James. His work spans over six decades and several countries, including Trinidad, Great Britain, the United States, and Ghana.

CLR James was born in Port-of-Spain, Trinidad, in 1901, and grew up in Tunapuna, a small town east of Port-of-Spain. After graduating from secondary school, he became a teacher and also a prominent intellectual figure in the country at that time. His literary pursuits began in the 1920s when he coedited two literary magazines *Trinidad*, and *The Beacon*. These magazines encouraged aspiring writers in Trinidad, and it was in these magazines that James published his short stories— "Triumph," "La Divina Pastora," and "Turner's Prosperity," which, like his novel *Minty Alley* (1936), deal with ordinary men and women.

In 1932, James migrated to England with the intention of becoming a writer. On his arrival, he wrote his reflections on life in London, which he sent to the *Port-of-Spain Gazette* in Trinidad. Some of these pieces were published in 2003 in a book entitled *Letters from London: Seven Essays by CLR James*, edited by Nicolas Laughlin. He also became a cricket correspondent for the *Manchester Guardian* and later for *The Glasgow Herald*. In 1936, he published his only novel, *Minty Alley*, a highly acclaimed work that portrays barrack-yard living in Trinidad. However, James soon abandoned the idea of becoming a writer of fiction. As he told his assistant, Anna Grimshaw, "The world went political; and so did I." He joined the social democratic Independent Labour Party, became involved in the Pan-African movement, and became a student of Marxism.

In 1938 James completed his major work, *The Black Jacobins: Toussaint L'Ouverture and the San Domingo Revolution*, which is an historical account of the successful slave revolts in Haiti in 1791 to 1803. To date, it is the best book published on the subject. *A History of Negro Revolt* was also published in 1938. In that year, James migrated to the United States, where he spent his time lecturing, writing, and getting involved in social and political issues. He joined the Socialist Workers Party—a Trotskyite movement that was concerned with racism and the black struggle. In addition to other activities, he published a pamphlet titled *The Revolutionary Answer to the Negro Problem in the United States* (1948). In 1953, he was deported from the United States for alleged passport violations.

After his sojourn in the United States, James returned to England for a while and continued his political involvement and his writing. One of his important works was a literary criticism and discussion of Shakespeare's works entitled *Preface to Criticism* (1955). In 1958, he returned to Trinidad, where he became a leading intellectual figure in the national independence movement. He continued to lecture and to write and produced *Party Politics in the West Indies* (1962), which deals with the move toward independence by colonial states. He also published his second-best-known book, *Beyond a Boundary* (1963). This book, although partially biographical and also deals with cricket, has deeper social and political meanings. Actively involved in local politics, James formed the Workers and Farmers Party in 1966 to contest the general elections. This proved to be disastrous, and James, disillusioned, returned to England.

Back in England, he once more continued to write and lecture, becoming interested in the politics of Africa and the decolonization process. He visited Africa, and his interest in African politics inspired him to write *Nkrumah and the Ghana Revolution* (1977), which is an analysis of the triumph and failure of Africa's independence movement. In his later years, James was able to return to the United States and spend his time lecturing at colleges there; he also traveled to Europe, where he lectured at many universities. He returned permanently to London in 1981, passing away in 1989.

CLR James produced a large and interesting body of work. As a writer, his contribution cannot be overlooked, as he contributed enormously to the understanding of a wide range of subjects, including literature, criticism, cricket, cultural studies, political theory, history, and philosophy.

Further Reading

Buhle, P. *CLR James: The Artist as Revolutionary*. London: Verso, 1982.

Cudjoe, S. R. and W. E. Cain. *CLR James: His Intellectual Legacies*. Amherst: University of Massachusetts Press, 1995.

Grimshaw, A., ed. *The CLR James Reader*. Oxford, UK: Blackwell, 1992.

—*Janet Fullerton-Rawlins*

Janvier, Louis-Joseph (1855–1911)

A writer who foresaw the end of Haiti as a rich, agricultural nation and who feared that the Catholic Church would rob Haitians of their African heritage, Janvier was a political philosopher and a novelist. He was one of the first writers from the Caribbean to spend more time away in Europe than in his country, a pattern that would characterize the fate of scores of authors and political figures in the nineteenth and twentieth centuries.

The son of a Protestant family, Janvier was born on May 7, 1855, in Port-au-Prince. As a child he attended a Wesleyan Primary School before going on to the Lycée Pétion for his secondary education. Upon graduation, he went to Paris to study medicine with a scholarship from the Haitian government. Remaining in France for nearly thirty years, he socialized with French writers and intellectuals of the era, studied at several schools, including the Sorbonne, and began to write articles that he submitted to journals.

During the 1880s, he published several books *La Républic d'Haïti et ses visiteurs* (1883), *Haïti aux haitiens* (1884) and *L'Egalité des races* (1884). He then published two novels, *Le Vieux Piquet* (1888) and *La Chercheuse* (1889). In these works, he defended Haiti and its leaders, claiming that if patriots like Jean-Jacques Dessalines (1758–1806) were dictatorial, it was to defend the sovereignty of the emerging nation; he also reminded readers that Europe had had its share of tyrants. Another theme was the role of the Catholic Church in Haiti: Janvier opposed the state's support of the Church, which was administered by priests from France. And a third concern was the potential for political instability to affect agriculture negatively, reducing the relative wealth of Haitian farmers, a development that finally occurred in the twentieth century.

In 1905, Janvier returned to Haiti, but not for long: after losing his candidacy for mayor of Port-au-Prince, he sailed back to Europe, living first in London and then Paris. He passed away in France in 1911.

Further Reading

Berrou, Raphaël, and Pradel Pompilus. *Histoire de la littérature haïtienne*. Tome 1. Port-au Prince, Haiti: Editions Caraïbes, 1975.

Pompilus, Pradel. *Louis Joseph Janvier par lui-même: le patriote et le champion de la négritude*. Port-au-Prince, Haïti: La Presse évangélique, 1995.

—*D. H. Figueredo*

Jesús Castro, Tomás de (1902–70)

Jesús Castro was a Puerto Rican essayist and journalist. A labor and political leader, he edited and published several journals.

A native of Carolina, Puerto Rico, Jesús Castro was active in the socialist movement on the island during his youth. When he was in his twenties, he joined the Socialist Party and wrote articles and columns for the socialist publication *Unión Obrera*. His skills as a writer were sought by such newspapers as *El Mundo*, *El Imparcial*, and *Alma Latina*. He also wrote articles for a Venezuela daily, *El Universal*.

In 1937, he founded his own magazine, *Revista*. Many of the political essays he wrote during this period were published in 1941 in the volume, *Aldea y urbe*. In the 1940s, he matriculated at the Universidad de Puerto Rico. In 1947, he earned a law degree. A year later, he was appointed editorial director of *Ahora*, a position he maintained for five years. In the 1950s, he practiced literary criticism, publishing the volume *Esbozos* (1947–59).

Further Reading

Toro-Sugrañes, Jose A. *Nueva enciclopedia de Puerto Rico*. Vol. 4, Biografias: Hato Rey, Puerto Rico: Editorial Lecture, 1994.

—*D. H. Figueredo*

Jin, Meiling (1956–)

A British Guyanese Chinese writer, Meiling Jin explores her Chinese heritage in her poems and short stories.

Meiling was born in Guyana but was raised in Great Britain. While attending school in London, she and her sister were discriminated by her classmates. To find escape, Jin secluded herself in a nearby public library, where she read the British classics, from Joseph Conrad (1857–1924) to George Bernard Shaw (1856–1950). Later on, she discovered such American Caribbean writers as **Audre Lorde**.

In 1981, Jin traveled to China. Upon her return, she contemplated the idea of writing about her experiences. The result was *Gifts from My Grandmother* (1986), poems that explore her Chinese Guyanese heritage; the volume was published by Sheba, an independent press committed to literature written by women. In 1996, she published a collection of short stories, *Song of the Boatwoman*. In between the dates of two publications, she worked as a radio broadcaster.

A shy and reclusive writer, Jin lives in London.

Further Reading

"Mieling Jin." http://www.peepalpress.com.author (accessed 8/31/05).

—*D. H. Figueredo*

Joglar Cacho, Manuel (1898–1994)

Joglar Cacho was a Puerto Rican poet who after initial neglect became a favorite of the reading public. His poems were inspired by Puerto Rico and by his compatriots.

Born on March 20, 1898, in Morovis, Joglar Cacho went to live with his grandparents in Manatí when he was six years old. When he was in the eighth grade, his father, a Spanish merchant, died, and Joglar Cacho had to leave school to help support the family. In 1925, he and an uncle set up a retailing business, but Joglar Cacho made it a point of regularly attending literature conferences at the **Ateneo Puertorriqueño**, the island's cultural center. At the Ateneo, he befriended writers and intellectuals and the stimulus resulted in the publication of his first book of poetry, *Góndolas de nácar* in 1925. The book was not well received by the critics, and disappointed, Joglar Cacho invested his energy in his business.

When he was mid-forties, he published a book of poems he had written as a young man, titled *En voz baja*, which again was ignored by the critics. Joglar Cacho did not publish another collection until a decade letter, *Faena íntima* (1955). This time, however, the book received an award from a cultural association, Círculo Cultural Yaucano. Encouraged, Joglar Cach began to write in earnest, publishing *Soliloquios de Lázaro* (1956), which received a literary prize from the Instituto de Literatura Puertorriqueña. From then on, his reputation as a poet grew.

Through the 1960s and 1970s, he published dozens of volumes, including *La sed del agua* (1965), *La canción que no va contigo* (1967), *Vuela un pájaro* (1975), *Donde cae y no cae la noche* (1978). In the 1980s and 90s, numerous conferences were prepared to honor his work. Many of his poems appeared in popular journals.

When Joglar Cacho passed away on November 8, 1994, he was still writing poetry and enjoying his compatriots' appreciation. The ease of his rhyme, the clarity of his diction, and the depth of the sentiments he expressed made him a popular poet. Observes critic Jorge María Ruscalleda Bercedóniz, in *La poesía de Manuel Joglar Cacho* (1998): "Joglar Cacho was a poet rooted to the soil. . . . The architecture of his words is rural material . . . a manifestation of his country" (28).

Further Reading

Figueroa, Javier. "Diccionario: Diccionario Histórico-Biográfico." In *La gran enciclopedia de Puerto Rico,* edited by Vicente Báez, 176. San Juan: Puerto Rico en La Mano and La Gran Enciclopedia de Puerto Rico, 1980.

Ruscalleda Bercedóniz, Jorge María. *La poesía de Manuel Joglar Cacho.* San Juan: Editorial Lea, 1998.

—*D. H. Figueredo*

John, Errol (1924–88)

A playwright and actor from Trinidad, Errol John, with dramatist **Errol Hill**, changed the dramatic landscape of his country by invigorating the national literature with his performances as an actor and the writing of the drama *Moon on a Rainbow Shawl*. He was also a screenwriter.

Born in Tobago on December 20, 1924, John was the son of a legendary cricket player, George John, whom **CRL James** glorified in his history of the sport, *Beyond a Boundary* (1963). John was raised in Port of Spain, Trinidad, where his writing ability impressed the likes of CRL James. John worked as a journalist but soon embraced the theater, achieving regional fame as an actor. When intellectuals lamented the absence of plays written by Trinidadian writers, John took up the challenge and wrote two one-act plays, *How Then Tomorrow and Brittle* and *The City Fathers*. The plays were staged in 1947 to great acclaim.

Errol John believed there would be better opportunities for him as a writer and actor in England. Like many of his contemporaries, such as **Jan Carew** and **Andrew Salkey**, in 1951, John left for England. He performed in theatrical productions and wrote radio dramas, including *For the Children* (1952), an adaptation of *Emperor Jones* (1954) by Eugene O'Neill (1888–1953), and *Small Island Moon* (1958), all of them produced by the BBC. In 1955, he turned to his recollections of Trinidad and began to write his most famous play, *Moon on a Rainbow Shall*. The realistic drama, set in a barrack yard, a Caribbean tenement built around a courtyard with a well, a community bathroom, and a kitchen, told the story of an ambitious young man, who, like the author, feels trapped in Trinidad and longs to go to England.

The play also depicted the tragic fate of a once great cricket player who is now a thief and drunkard. *Moon on a Rainbow Shall* was performed in England, the United States, and Trinidad. A classic example of the genre known as **barrack yard literature**, the play is regularly staged throughout the Caribbean and especially in Trinidad.

In 1963, Errol John portrayed Othello in an Old Vic production in Bristol, England. During this period, he wrote several television dramas for the BBC and published, in 1967, the anthology *Force Majeure, The Dispossessed, Hasta Luego: Three Screenplays*. In 1970, John traveled to Mexico to rest from his stage work and to write. As he grew older, he grew increasingly frustrated with the roles assigned to him as actor, roles that were all based on his skin color.

John was not able to write another play as successful as *Moon on a Rainbow Shawl*. In the 1980s, he felt alone and underappreciated. When he passed away on July 10, 1988, no one noticed his absence until his landlady found his body in his apartment. *See also* Trinidadian and Tobagonian Literature, History of.

Further Reading

"Errol John." *Dictionary of Literary Biography*. http://www.galenet.galegroup.com (accessed 10/5/05).

Morris, Davina. "Black people in British theater." *The Voice*, no. 1135 (October 11–17, 2004): 3.

—D. H. Figueredo

Johnson, Linton Kwesi (1952–)

One of the most popular Dub poets in England, Linton Kwesi Johnson, also known as JLK, belongs to a generation of Jamaican poets who opted to create poetry that was meant to be performed by the poet rather than read on paper. But his poems, exploring racism, are as effective on the written page as in a stage reading.

Born in Chapeltown, Jamaica, Johnson moved to London in 1963. In 1967, he joined the Black Panthers League of Britain, the radical group that had originated in the United States. In 1973, he graduated from University of London with a degree in sociology. He was inspired to write poetry after a reading of the classic *The Souls of Black Folks*, by WEB Du Bois (1868–1963), deciding to become a performance poet to reach a wider and younger audience. He became well known for delivering passionate poetry in a voice that was calm and controlled but with an edge of anger and rage, as illustrated in the line: "Madness tight on the heads of the rebels / the bitterness erupts like a hot-blast" from the collection of poetry *Dread Beat an Blood* (1974).

Johnson uses poetry to protest social conditions and bigotry in England. In 1981, he wrote "New Cross Massahkah," condemning the demise of thirteen black militants who were burned to death in a house in London. His collection of poems *Inglan Is a Bitch* (1980) is an angry indictment of racism. The poems in *Tings an' Times* (1991), on the other hand, are of a more personal and pensive nature. In later works, Johnson started to write phonetic poetry, abandoning grammar as well, as demonstrated in the volume *Mi revalueshanry fren: Selected Poems* (2002). Johnson's poetry is influenced by reggae and calypso music as well as the Jamaican vernacular.

In 1977, Johnson was awarded the Johnson C. Day Lewis Fellowship. He has his own recording company and has recorded four albums, including *Poets and the Roots* (1977), and *Dread Beat an' Blood* (1978). Young audiences in England consider Johnson the equivalent of a super star in the music industry. *See also* Dub Poetry; Performance Poetry.

Further Reading

Hoyles, Asher, and Martin Hoyles. *Moving Voices: Black Performance Poetry*. London: Hansib Publication Limited, 2002.

—*D. H. Figueredo*

Joven Poesía Dominicana

This term refers to a group of writers from the Dominican Republic who, responding to the 1965 civil war and the subsequent American intervention, wrote stories and poems celebrating and encouraging opposition to American forces, reaffirming nationalism and a commitment to social change. Included in this group of writers were **Mateo Morrison**, Enrique Eusebio, Soledad Álvarez Alexis Gómez Rosa, **Andres L. Mateo**, Norberto James Rawlings, Wilfredo Lozano, **Enriquillo Sánchez**, Tony Raful, **Luis Manuel Ledesma**, and José Molinaza. These writers attempted to create a literary national consciousness that promoted political change. They preferred to work in small groups—cells—with names such as La Isla, La Mascara, and El Puño.

Further Reading

Enciclopedia ilustrada de la República Dominicana. Volume 6: Lengua, literatura y arte. Santo Domingo: Eduprogreso, 2003.

—*D. H. Figueredo*

Juliana, Elis (1927–)

Award-winning poet, ethnologist, sculptor, and musician from Curaçao, Juliana is one of the most important exponents of Papiamentu, the native language used in the Dutch Caribbean. A fundamental characteristic of his work is the preeminent presence of values and traditions rooted in an African heritage, which the author employs as a way of rescuing with honor the past of Caribbean countries.

Born in Curaçao on August 8, 1927, Juliana began writing in Spanish, submitting his works to Spanish newspapers in the region—such as *La Prensa*, from Cuba—and using the pseudonym Micha Rodalfa. As a young man, he also wrote in Dutch, but it was his writings in Papiamentu that brought him recognition.

From 1950 to 1951, he wrote for the journal *Simadan*, the first publication published completely in Papiamentu. This serial advocated a literature in the local vernacular, a literature that was evocative of the flora and fauna of the Caribbean as well as its peculiarities: a longing for the past coupled with social criticism. In the 1950s, Juliana, with the German Catholic priest Paul Brenneker, collected native songs, expressions, and folkloric traditions from Curaçao. His essay "Origen di baile di tambú na Kòrsou," published in the journal *Kristòf* (vol. 6, no. 4), reflected his research on folklore.

In 1955, the poet **Pierre Lauffer** published the anthology *Kumba*, the first collection of poems in Papiamentu. To this effort, Juliana added several collections, *Canta clara* (1955), *Flor di tatu* (1956), *Dama di anochi* (1959), and *Flor di anglo* (1961). In these volumes, Juliana expanded the rhythmic potential of the Papiamentu language, which Lauffer had first developed. The same artistic expansion of the language occurred with the narratives Juliana published in the 1960s, *Mata taka* (1961) and *Wazo riba rondu* (1967).

Juliana's poems and stories flow from his assimilation and incorporation of the rich creativity found in the oral tradition, be it in storytelling or in folkloric music. His works established a balance between the celebration of Afro-Caribbean heritage and criticism of local customs, using humor as a reflective tool. Irony in his writings substituted the didacticism—meant to be exemplary and with obvious allusions—that characterized the Catholic-influenced Papiamentu literature before World War II.

Throughout his long life, Juliana has published in scores of journals, including *Culturele Kroniek*, *Cadushi*, *Anittaanse Cahier*, *Social y Cultural*, *Pueto*, *Voz Antillano*, *De Klok*, and *Preludium*. Critics consider the four volumes of *Organizashon Planifikashon Independensia* (1979, 1980, 1983, 1988) his best work.

Juliana has received some of the highest honors awarded in the Dutch Caribbean: the Cola Debrot Award (1979), and the Bienal Pierre Lauffer Prize (1986). In 1990, a bronze bust of his likeness was unveiled at the central Public Library of Willemnstad, Curaçao's capital.

Further Reading

Broek, Aart G. *Pa sak kara, tomo I; Historia di literatura papiamentu*. Willemstad: Fundashon Pierre Lauffer, 1998.

Clemencia, Joceline A. *Het grote camouflagespel van de OPI*. Leiden, Nederlands: KITLV-Caraf, 1989.

Rutgers, Wim. *Beneden en bowen de wind; Literatuur van de Nederlandse Antillen in Aruba*. Amsterdam, Nederlands: De Beziege Bij, 1996.

—*Emilio Jorge Rodríguez*

K

Kanellos, Nicolás (1945–)

Author, publisher, and scholar, Nicolás Kanellos is a promoter of Latino culture and writers who has devoted his professional life to the unearthing of literary works written by writers from Latin America and Spain who lived in the United States before the twentieth century. Kanellos has also mentored and launched the careers of such distinguished writers as the Chicanas Sandra Cisneros and Denise Chavez, Cuban American **Virgil Suárez**, and Puerto Rican **Tato Laviera**.

Born in New York City of a Puerto Rican mother and a Greek father, as a child he noticed how the New York press during the 1950s and early 1960s constantly depicted a negative image of the Puerto Rican community. He experienced discrimination in public schools and in college realized that many professors preferred European civilization over Latin American culture, which they deemed inferior. He observed that Latino students interested in literature were encouraged to study the North American

Anthologist, editor, and literary mentor, Nicolás Kanellos has discovered and promoted numerous young authors such as Tato Laviera and Virgil Suárez. *Courtesy of Nicolás Kanellos.*

or European canon. Such bigotry prompted him to demonstrate to his colleagues the wealth and richness of Latino and Latin American cultures.

After graduating from Fairleigh Dickinson University, in New Jersey, in 1966, and earning a doctorate from the University of Texas, he founded in 1972, with $500 from the head of the Latin American Studies at Indiana University, in Bloomington, where he was teaching, and his own funds, the journal *Revista Chicano-Riqueña*, the first national Latino publication to include contributions by Cuban

423

Americans, Chicanos, and Puerto Ricans, not a common practice at the time when each group preferred contributions that mirrored their national and political interests. Seven years later, he founded Arte Público Press with the intention of creating a national press that promoted Latino talent.

Within a decade, Arte Público Press had published thirty titles and had beckoned the interest of foundations such as Andrew W. Mellon and the Rockefeller Foundation. In 1992, these foundations supported the Recovering the U.S. Hispanic Literary Heritage Project, which documented literary activity in Spanish from colonial times to the early twentieth century. Researching archives and manuscript collections, Kanellos and his associates were able to uncover the first Latino novel written in the United States, *Jicótencal* (1826), probably written by Cuban author **Félix Varela,** and to introduce to a new audience the writings of pioneer Puerto Rican activist **Jesús Colón,** who wrote in New York City during the 1940s and 50s.

Kanellos is the author and editor of several reference volumes and anthologies, including *Los Tejanos: A Texas-Mexican Anthology* (1980), *The Literature of Puerto Ricans, Cuban Americans, and Other Hispanic Writers* (1985), *Nuevos Pasos: Chicano and Puerto Rican Drama* (1989), *History of Hispanic Theatre in the United States* (1990), *The Hispanic Almanac: From Columbus to Corporate America* (1994), *Chronology of Hispanic-American History: From Pre-Columbian Times to the Present* (1995), *Hispanic Firsts: 500 Years of Extraordinary Achievement* (1997), *Herencia: The Anthology of Hispanic Literature of the United States* (2002). He has received numerous awards including in 1988 the White House Hispanic Heritage Award for Literature. *See also* Cuban American Literature; Literary Journals; Nuyorican Literature.

Further Reading

Figueredo, Danilo H. "Love's Labour Not Lost: Latino Publishing." *Multicultural Review* 7, no. 3 (September 1998): 24–33.

Kanellos, Nicolás. *Curriculum Vitae.* April 25, 2005.

—*D. H. Figueredo*

Kempadoo, Peter Lauchmonen (1926–)

The author of *Guyana Boy* (1960), one of the first novels to depict the lives of East Indians working on a sugar plantation, Kempadoo is a novelist from Guyana.

Kempadoo was born on a sugar estate in Guyana, the son of sugarcane workers. He was expected to follow in his parents' footsteps but managed to attend school. As a young man, he worked in a sugar factory, taught at a school, and eventually became a reporter. In the early 1950s, he left for London, where he worked for the BBC's World Services and spent hours at the library reading British literature.

In 1960, he wrote *Guyana Boy*, an autobiographical novel that depicted a great deal of the daily toils of the East Indians who lived and worked on a sugar plantation. In 1965, he published his second book, *Old Thorn's Harvest*. He traveled extensively throughout the Caribbean, Asia, and Africa, helping the United Nations establish rural community programs. In the 1980s, after his wife's death, he visited South Africa and eventually settled in Zimbabwe, where he teaches construction. He spends part of the year in Great Britain. Kempadoo regards himself as more of a rural activist than a writer.

Further Reading

"Mr. Peter and His Principles." *Unesco Learning Resources*, no. 98. February 1998. http://www.unesco.org/education/educprog (accessed 4/15/05).

—*D. H. Figueredo*

Kennedy, Elena. See Ortea, Virginia Elena.

Khan, Ismith (1925–2002)

Trinidadian novelist who explored the conflicts experienced by East Indians in the Caribbean as well as the racial diversity that characterizes the region. A brilliant storyteller, he created memorable characters through whom the sights and cadences of Trinidad will forever live.

Ismith Khan was born in Trinidad on March 16, 1925, to Muslim parents who were Pathan Indians. After attending the prestigious Queen's Royal College in Port of Spain, Khan worked as a reporter for the *Trinidad Guardian*. He later moved to the United States and studied at Michigan State University. He then went on to earn a BA in social sciences from the New School for Social Research in New York and an MA in Writing at Johns Hopkins University. Between 1955 and 1970, he taught at the New School and Johns Hopkins. From 1970 to 1982 he taught at various universities in California, including Berkeley, the University of California–San Diego, the University of Southern California, and California State College–Long Beach. He moved back to New York in 1982, where he wrestled with depression following the end of his third marriage. Though he often thought of returning to Trinidad for good, he remained in New York, declaring to Sasenarine Persaud in the online journal *Indo Caribbean World*, "I am one of the homeless of the homeless. . . . I feel homeless in New York [but] I feel more comfortable in New York than I feel anywhere else in the world." There he continued to devote his time to his writing and served as an adjunct lecturer at Medgar Evers College.

Khan frequently spoke of writing something set in the United States, but his published work invariably treats the emptiness and violence of Trinidad, where his characters try to find some meaning in their lives, or as one puts it, "What de ass to do wid meself" in *Crucifixion* (17). Death is his constant and recurring subject; Christ imagery pervades his work; self-righteousness is the ultimate sin: "A man ain't have no right playin' God" (*Crucifixion*, 121).

His first novel, *The Jumbie Bird* (1961), treats the dilemma of three genera-tions of East Indians in Trinidad, including those such as his grandfather Kale Khan, who still remembers India and who longs to return. Kale Khan, however, stands out as a leader among his people and a hero to his grandson Jamini because he did "not come here like the rest of these low-class coolies in bond" (3). The nov-elist told me that Kale Khan is the only character in this highly autobiographical work who is a direct portrait, "name and all." In reading this novel or in talking to the author, it is clear that this complex, contradictory, and flawed grandfather had the greatest influence on his life.

His second novel, *The Obeah Man* (1964), moves away from the focus on the East Indian community to emphasize the racial mixtures that are Trinidad: Zampi, the Obeah man, had " the eyes of the East Indian, the build of the Negro, the skin of the Chinese, and some of the colour of all" (11); indeed all of the characters rep-resent, like Massahood, the stickman, "the same question mark of lost races and cultures" (32). In this work, Khan creates in Zampi one of his most memorable and admirable characters. Though Zampi at first simply "played" the role of an Obeah man, he proceeds to seek to learn as much about himself and about Obeah as he can. His journey is one that results in greater knowledge, greater spiritual power, greater service to others, and even fulfillment in love. He achieves a kind of self-re-alization and wholeness that escapes Khan's other frustrated heroes and in the process leaves the reader with unique visions of Carnival and a perceptive and real-istic exploration of Obeah.

The Crucifixion, written as the author's master's thesis, was not published until 1987. Here the significantly named Manko is also on a quest for knowledge. As we are constantly reminded in the Creole voice of this novel that alternates between standard English and Creole: "*He want to learn some damn t'ing.*" However, Manko, certain that God has called him and that others must listen to him to be saved, constantly persecutes and destroys in his efforts to save and resurrect. His agony, fury, and frustrations in life are relieved only by his temporary refuge in a bar and his constant pilgrimages to the cross on Calvary Hill, where he finds the peace of seeing himself as a crucified Christ. In 1994, *A Day in the Country*, a col-lection of short stories, was published. *Day* brings together some of Khan's previ-ously anthologized stories and a few of those unpublished ones that he feared, when I interviewed him in 1981, "somebody will find . . . tucked away back there . . . when I am dead and gone." Fortunately, he saw them published and witnessed the positive reception the collection received. *See also* Grandparents in Caribbean Literature.

Further Reading

Brown, Stewart. Introduction. "*The Jumbie Bird.*" London: Longman, 1985.

Cobham, Rhonda. "*The Jumbie Bird* by Ismith Khan: A New Assessment." *The Journal of Commonwealth Literature* 21, no. 1 (1986): 240–49.

Dance, Daryl Cumber. "Conversation with Ismith Khan." *New World Adams: Conversa-tions with Contemporary West Indian Writers.* Leeds: Peepal Tree Books, 1992.

Drayton, Arthur. "Ismith Khan." *Fifty Caribbean Writers: A Bio-Bibliographical Critical Sourcebook*, edited by Daryl Cumber Dance, 246–54. Westport, CT: Greenwood Press, 1986.

Persaud, Sasenarine. "Why Port of Spain Comes Alive in *The Jumbie Bird.*" *Indo Caribbean World.* May 3, 2004. http://www.peepaltreepress.com/review (accessed 9/7/05).

—Daryl Cumber Dance

Kincaid, Jamaica (1949–)

■

Kincaid is an internationally acclaimed writer who is originally from Antigua and whose novels depict the complex psychological relationships between mothers and daughters. Her sensitive portraits of adolescence and racial and social conflicts have made her works popular on college campuses, where students can readily identify with Kincaid's heroines.

Born Elaine Potter Richardson on May 25, 1949, Jamaica Kincaid was reared by a well-meaning but strong-willed mother in St. Johns, Antigua. She suffered from the ongoing disputes with her mother, who wanted her daughter to behave properly and ladylike but believed she would not. This conflict, together with the stifling colonial ambiance of Antigua prompted Kincaid to leave her home at the age of seventeen. In her first novel, *Annie John* (1985), she described her bitter-sweet departure:

> . . . I remembered that it was customary to stand on deck and wave to your rela-tives . . . I could see my mother facing the ship, her eyes searching to pick me out. I removed from my bag a red cotton handkerchief that she had earlier given me for this purpose. . . . Recognizing me immediately, she waved back just as wildly, and we continued to do this until she became just a dot. (147–48)

After arriving in New York City, Kincaid worked as an au pair. She finished high school and then went on to study photography at the New School for Social Re-search, transferring to Franconia College. A friend encouraged Kincaid to submit a story to *The New Yorker*; she did, and the submission turned into a position as a staff writer from 1976 to 1995. In 1983, she published her first collection of short stories, *At the Bottom of the River*. Critics, writing in such important publications as the *New York Times* and the *Village Voice*, praised her well-developed characters, her rhythmic prose, and her repetitive, musical style. The volume won the Morten Dauwen Zabel Award from the American Academy and Institute of Arts and Letters.

Equally well received was Kincaid's second book, the autobiographical *Annie John*. In 1990, she published *Lucy*, an account of her first year in New York City. In 1996, she published *The Autobiography of My Mother*, an attempt at under-standing her mother. A year later, *My Brother* was published, a memoir about her brother who died of AIDS. As if to take a respite from such analytical and emotion-ally draining works, Kincaid then wrote two books on gardening: *My Favorite Plant* (1998) and *My Garden* (1999). In 2002, she returned to fiction with the book *Mr. Potter*, about the life of a chauffeur in Antigua. That same year she wrote the lyrics to a symphonic work composed by her husband, Allen Shaw, *And in the Air These Sounds*.

Kincaid has been praised for writing in a "mesmerizing poetic style," as scholar Lucy Melbourne phrases it in the 2003 volume *Women in Literature* (15). Though her novels are based on true events, Kincaid prefers fiction over nonfiction. She explained in *Backtalk* (1993): "Writing exactly what happened had a limited amount of power. To say exactly what happened was less than what I knew happened. . . . I wanted something more than that" (129).

Kincaid has received numerous honors, including the Lila Wallace-*Reader's Digest* Fund Writer's Award (1992), the Boston Book Review Fisk Fiction Prize (1997), and a National Book Award nomination (1997) for *My Brother*.

Further Reading

Kincaid, Jamaica. *Annie John*. New York: Plume Book, 1983.

Melbourne, Lucy. "'Young Lady' or 'Slut': Identity and Voice in Jamaican Kincaid's *Annie John*." In *Women In Literature: Reading Through the Lens of Gender*, edited by Jerilyn Fisher and Ellen S. Silber, 1, 5–17. Westport, CT: Greenwood Press, 2003.

Perry, Donna. *Backtalk: Women Writers Speak Out*. New Brunswick, NJ: Rutgers University Press, 1993.

—Angela Conrad and D. H. Figueredo

Klang, Gary (1941–)

A Haitian Canadian writer, Klang is a novelist, a dramatist, and a poet. Like many Caribbean authors who are published outside their native countries, such as **Cristina García** from Cuba, his work is better known in Canada than in Haiti.

Klang was born on December 28, 1941, in Port-au-Prince. He attended primary and secondary schools in Haiti, then went to Paris to pursue his college education, earning a PhD in literature from the Sorbonne. From Paris he emigrated to Montreal, where he worked as an editor and proofreader at Éditions La Presse and taught at the University of Montreal. In 1976, he published his first book, a work of nonfiction, *La méditation transcendantale*, which became a best-seller in Canada. In 1979, he wrote the drama *L'immigrant*, which was staged on television.

During the 1980s and 90s, he alternated between poetry and fiction, writing the books of poems *Ex-île* (1985), *Je veux chanter la mer* (1993), and *Moi natif natal, suivi De Le Temps du vide* (1995), and the novels *Haïti! Haïti!*—in collaboration with **Anthony Phelps** (1985), *L'île aux deux visagesvisages* (1997), and *L'adolescent qui regardait passer la vie* (1998). While the novels explore political conditions in Haiti—with plots often characterized by violence—the poetry exposes a more sentimental and universal expression about the condition of exile and the longing for a person's native country.

In the 1990s, Klang became involved with different writers groups, specifically the Canadian PEN club and the Société des écrivains canadiens. In 2000, he was the guest of honor for the festival l'Union Française à Montréal. His other works include *La terre est vide comme une étoile* (2000), *La vraie vie est absente* (2002), both works of poetry, and *Kafka m'a dit* (2004), a collection of stories. Despite his prolific output and newspaper articles on his works, Klang awaits scholarly study.

Further Reading

"Gary Klang." http://www.lehman.cuny.edu/ile.en.ile/paroles/klang.html (accessed 9/8/05).

Klang, Gary. *Callaloo* 15, no. 3 (Summer 1992): 595.

—*D. H. Figueredo*

Kom, Anton de (1898–1945)

■

Kom was a Surinamese political activist who wrote poetry and chronicled the history of his country. He was a victim of Nazism, dying in a concentration camp during World War II.

Cornelis Gerard Anton de Kom was born on February 22, 1898, in Paramaribo, Suriname. He studied at the school Paulusschool, in Paramaribo, from where he obtained a degree in accounting. He also mastered several languages: English, French, German, Negerengels, and Papiamentu. From 1916 to 1920, he worked at the firm Balata-Compagnie. In 1920, he visited Haiti and worked there for two months before resuming his trip to Holland where he earned his living as accountant's assistant. In 1926, he married a Dutch woman, Petronella Catherina Borboom, with whom he had four sons.

His knowledge of the political activism of Indonesian students and Mohammed Hatta, one of the founders of Perhimpuan Indonesia, who were arrested in 1927 for antigovernment activities, fostered his nationalism. During this period, de Kom developed a reputation as an orator and contributor of articles to leftist publications, including the review *Links Richten*. In this journal, de Kom published excerpts from the history of Suriname he was writing, based on his research at the Royal Library of Holland.

In 1931, De Kom was fired from his job at Reusen and Smulders, due to the company's reorganization but also because of his interest in politics. Unemployed, on December 20, 1932, he and his family sailed to Paramaribo. His political reputation preceded him and upon arrival at Suriname on January 4, 1933, hundreds of sympathizers welcomed him home. In the crowd were three policemen who monitored de Kom constantly.

By now, de Kom's objectives were to create a multiracial political party that would oppose the colonial authorities. For that purpose, he set up in his home a headquarters where his compatriots could meet and report the government's abuses. However, repressive agents blocked de Kom from organizing any political manifestation. Later on, after being involved in a few disturbances, de Kom was arrested. When that occurred, about four thousand compatriots marched to the judge's office to demand de Kom's release but were forced back by police armed with bayonets. The judge promised de Kom's release but instead sent him to prison,

Casa de Reclusion Preventiva. When demonstrators took to the streets again, the police fired on them, killing two and wounding twenty-two protesters. As a result of the unrest, on May 10, 1933, de Kom was deported to Holland.

In Holland, de Kom completed the manuscript *Wij slaven van Suriname*, in which he reports his recent experiences in Suriname. He found a publisher in 1934, but the authorities censored the sections about his arrest. The volume consisted of a social history of Suriname, emphasizing the slavery years and the social struggles of the twentieth century. De Kom analyzed the consequences of colonialism, which he blamed for unemployment, poverty, poor medical services, and racial discrimination. He also proposed a solution for the national reconstruction of Suriname through the creation of well-equipped and modernized companies managed by Suriname workers. He expressed a desire for solidarity with all ethnic groups; from this union would sprout the seed of a new country.

De Kom continued publishing articles and lecturing on conditions in Suriname. When the Nazis occupied Holland, he published his articles and poems in the underground press—in 1969, many of these poems would be published posthumously in the book *Strijden ga ik*. On August 7, 1944, the Nazis arrested de Kom and sent him to the Neuengamme concentration camp, where he perished the following year.

In 1960, his remains were found in a common grave: he was recognized by his teeth and the scar from a lesion he had on his head in his youth. His body was transferred to Holland, and from there to Suriname. In May 1983, half a century after his deportation to Holland, an exhibit about his work and life was inaugurated in Suriname. Numerous honors and acknowledgments were bestowed upon his memory, including the renaming of the national university as Anto de Kom University.

Further Reading

Phaf-Rheinberger, Ineke. "Conclusions." In *A History of Literature in the Caribbean. Vol. 2: English-Dutch-Speaking Regions*, edited by A. James Arnold, 651–57. Philadelphia: John Benjamins Publishing Co., 2001.

—*Emilio Jorge Rodríguez*

Kreyòl. See Haitian Literature in Kreyòl.

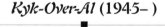

Kyk-Over-Al (1945–)

A Guyanese literary journal that published the early works of such important writers as **Derek Walcott** and **Wilson Harris**, *Kyk*, as it was often called, was founded by poet **A. J. Seymour**. Like his counterpart **Frank Collymore**, the editor of the Trinidadian journal *Bim*, with whom he corresponded, Seymour was a tireless promoter of Guyana and West Indian literature.

Published annually, Kyk's objective was to create a national literature by giving voice to Guyanese writers, regardless of residence, though writers from other Anglophone islands were included. The preference was for literature rather than political topics, but poets such as **Martin Carter** included politics in their poetry. A. J. Seymour managed and edited the journal for sixteen years. In 1984, **Ian McDonald** took over the directorship of the journal. In 1990, there was a joint edition of *Kyk* and *Bim*. In 1995, *Kyk* celebrated its fiftieth anniversary. In 2000, the journal dedicated its pages to honor the memory of Guyana's greatest poet, Martin Carter, who had passed away three years before.

Further Reading

McDonald, Ian. *AJS at 70: A Celebration on His 70th Birthday of the Life, Work, and Art of A. J. Seymour*. Georgetown, Guyana: Autoprint, 1984.

—*D. H. Figueredo*

L

Labrador Ruiz, Enrique (1902–91)

In the 1930s, this Cuban novelist developed a unique literary style that heralded the innovative techniques used decades later by other writers from Latin America, including Julio Cortázar (1914–84), from Argentina. Dubbed by Labrador Ruiz "novelas gaseiformes," novels formed by gas, the stories have no clear beginnings and endings; in fact, the reader can begin the books anywhere he or she chooses.

Labrador Ruiz began his writing career as a self-taught journalist, and during the 1920s, he worked for the best-known Cuban newspapers of the time—*El Mundo, El País, Prensa Libre*—as well as numerous popular magazines, such as *Bohemia, Chic,* and *Social.* In 1951, he was awarded the Juan Gualberto Gómez prize for journalism.

What really interested him, though, was literature, and in 1933 he wrote the psychological novel *El laberinto de si mismo,* in which the main character gets lost in a world of words. In 1936, he wrote *Cresival* and in 1940, *Anteo*; the structure of these novels resembles the broken shards of a mirror, in which each piece provides a different element of the story. In 1950, Labrador Ruiz wrote a novel in a more traditional style. Titled *La sangre hambrienta,* it earned him the national award for fiction from the Ministry of Education.

With the triumph of the Cuban Revolution in 1959, Labrador Ruiz worked for the publishing house Editorial Nacional and traveled throughout the former Soviet Union and China. In the 1970s, he sought exile in the United States, settling in Miami but visiting the New York area quite often, where he lectured at universities and public libraries. Regarded as a writer's writer, Labrador Ruiz's works have yet to receive the scholarly attention they deserve.

Further Reading

Henríquez Ureña, Max. *Panorama histórico de la literatura cubana, Tomo II.* Habana: Editorial Arte y Literatura, 1979.

Sánchez, Reinaldo, ed. *Homenaje a Enrique Labrador Ruiz: textos críticos sobre su obra.* Montevideo, Uruguay: Editorial Ciencias, 1981.

—*D. H. Figueredo*

Lacrosil, Michèle (1915–)

Author of the well-known plantation novel *Demain Jab-Herma* (1967), Lacrosil is an early feminist novelist and short-story writer from Guadeloupe who studied the psychological effects of colonialism and racism. In her novels, according to Beverly Ormerod, in *Center of Remembrance* (2002), she "dramatized the fate of unhappy protagonists neurotically obsessed by a conviction of their own unworthiness" (23).

Reclusive and shy, Lacrosil was born in Guadeloupe in 1915 and left the island for Paris, where she became a French professor. In 1960, she published *Sapotille et le serin d'argile*, followed a year later by *Cajou*. Each of these first-person novels tells the story of a mulatto woman who faces discrimination in Guadeloupe because of the color of her skin. Sapotille's diary recounts the racism she suffers at a boarding school and her later oppression in her personal relationships with men. Cajou, too, relates the pain of being dominated by a sadistic white lover. These novels provoked a negative reaction among Guadeloupean readers, who felt the author had unfairly portrayed racial conflicts on that island.

In 1967, Lacrosil's third novel, *Demain Jab-Herma*, produced further sharp criticism. Set in 1952, as the end of plantation farms and the end of the power of the great plantation owners was coming to a close, the novel focuses on a protagonist who sets out to assess the estate's viability and to solve a series of crimes taking place there.

Since this work, Lacrosil has not published any other books. Yet, because of her importance in the field of Caribbean studies, her life and her writings deserve more study. *See also* Mulata in Caribbean Literature; Plantation Society in Caribbean Literature, The.

Further Reading

Gros, Isabelle. "Michèle Lacrosil: La Libération par l'écriture ou comment vômir le dégoût de soi." *Elles écrivent les Antilles*, edited by Susanne Rinner and Joëlle Vitiello, 123–32. Paris: L'Harmattan, 1997.

Ormerod, Beverly. *Center of Remembrance: Memory and Caribbean Women's Literature.* London: Mango Publishing, 2002.

Praeger, Michèle. *The Imaginary Caribbean and Caribbean Imaginary.* Lincoln: University of Nebraska Press, 2003.

—*Jayne R. Boisvert and D. H. Figueredo*

Ladoo, Harold Sonny (1945–73)

Harold Sonny Ladoo was a Trinidadian writer whose novels explored and documented the experiences of East Indian immigrants in the Caribbean.

Harold Sonny Ladoo was born in 1945 in Mc Bean Village Couva. He was a descendant of East Indian indentured servants, whose grim lives he explored fictionally in *No Pain Like This Body* (1972) and *Yesterdays* (1974). As if in tragic fulfillment of the murderous ethos that he wrote about, Ladoo met a violent death at age twenty-eight, when he returned to Trinidad from Canada to mediate in a land dispute that had dispossessed his mother. Although the official cause of death is hit-and-run, to this day suspicions of foul play clings to his untimely passing.

A mature student at Erindale College, University of Toronto, Ladoo, an avid reader and writer, painstakingly completed his university degree while writing fiction intensely and prolifically and working sporadically as a short-order cook. His publication success became an inspiration of the potential of ordinary immigrants for noteworthy accomplishments. Brilliant and essentially self-schooled, Ladoo, according to his mentor Peter Such, demonstrated a habit of "getting into novels through his short stories" because "the canvas was really too small for the vastness of his conceptions, and the long creative input a novel demands was more to his liking."

His first full-length novel, *No Pain Like This Body*, has been termed the most horrific evocation of Indian family violence to date. The historical novel is set in 1905 in an Indian settlement on the periphery of the bound Coolie estate. It speaks of a displaced family and community in crisis as a result of transnational flow of labor under the indentureship scheme to service the demands of the colonial sugar industry. These are former indentees who have served their fiveyear term and remain in Trinidad to build a life. They scrape a poor living through rice farming and animal husbandry. Caught in a liminal space between a rich ancestral tradition and the anomie of plantation culture, their task is to craft a mode of being, pattern of family interaction and community dynamic that can root and empower them.

The text frames its bitter domestic battles within the parameters of cosmic disorder. A manifestation of an inimical world is persistent rain, not in its beneficent form to cause the earth to produce, but a pouring of rain without end, which promises to engulf the world in a deluge. The constant outpouring disrupts crappo fish (tadpoles), excites poisonous snakes, and dislodges scorpions from leaky roofs, attacking sick children who are sleeping. The operations of the sky and watery foundations of a cosmos threaten life.

The novel is tied together by a complex lineage of imagery, which binds hostile and inimical cosmic aberrations to near inconceivable family violence. The mother, who retains the faith that her children would mature and flourish in "dis here Tola," loses her mind when the father's brutality causes her eight-year-old son's death. The remaining children—Balraj, twelve, Sunaree, ten, and the surviving twin, Panday, eight—in response to a totally disruptive and brutal experiential reality, lose hold on the objective world and take recourse in an imagined evil that sums up their childlike attempts to confront their deepest fear. The cosmic, paternal, and family violence in this narrative is alleviated only by the presence of maternal grandparents Nanny and Nanna, who retain faith in a benevolent God.

Yesterdays is an equally complex novel about a family who would like to send their son to Canada to establish Hindu mission and the conflict that arises over whether to mortgage their home to finance the trip. Each member of the family has a different motive for either supporting or opposing the mission trip.

Ladoo's work is a significant exploration of the impact of indenture ship and the violence that deterritorialization, displacement, and loss of faith can engender within families and communities. He was working on a third novel when he died.

Further Reading

Salick, Roydon. "The Bittersweet Comedy of Sonny Ladoo: A Reading of 'Yesterdays.'" *Ariel* 22, no.3 (July 1991): 75.

—*Paula Morgan*

Laferrière, Dany (1953–)

Novelist and journalist who achieved fame with the publication of two erotic novels, Laferrière was born in Port-au-Prince and was baptized as Windsor Kléber Laferrière fils. His father, Windsor Kléber Laferrière Sr., the youngest mayor in the history of Port-au-Prince, was posted abroad in 1959 for criticizing the government of **François Duvalier**. Later on, Laferrière Sr. went into hiding in New York City, where he died in 1986, refusing to see his son. Under the regime of Jean-Claude Duvalier (1951–) Dany was forced to flee for his life in 1976, following the murder of a journalist friend. Laferrière landed in Montreal alone and almost penniless. After surviving by working at odd jobs, he began to appear as the weatherman for a Montreal television station and became widely known for his humorous, unconventional presentation of weather changes.

Dany Laferrière is a Haitian novelist whose erotic novels are actually an exploration of political oppression in Haiti. *Source: Americas Society. Courtesy of Elsa M. Ruiz.*

Laferrière achieved international fame with the publication of his first novel, *Comment faire l'amour avec un Nègre sans se fatiguer* (How to Make Love with a Black Man without Getting Tired) (1985). He has acknowledged that the sensational title helped provoke the amused or indignant reaction of a broad public. Interviews with this intriguing Haitian—who unabashedly spoke of erotic adventures with eager white women—many of them conducted by female journalists and television talk-show hosts, numbered in the hundreds. This was followed by a second erotic novel, *Éroshima* (1987).

Laferrière surprised readers with a third novel, *L'odeur du café* (1991), in which the scene abruptly shifts to nostalgic, highly poetic reminiscences of his childhood, spent living with his grandmother in Petit-Goâve, just west of Port-au-Prince. *Le goût des jeunes filles* (1992) continues the adventures, still autobiographical, of Laferrière at age eighteen. Fearing for his life at the hands of Duvalier's police, he hides with a female acquaintance in the apartment of a group of adolescent girls who live exuberantly in the luxury provided by Duvalier's hired killers. Vieux Os, the nickname given Dany by his grandmother, is paralyzed at once by desire, surrounded with these uninhibited young women, and by fear of being recognized and killed.

At some point Laferrière realized that he was writing an account of his life in the Americas and political changes he had witnessed. "American Autobiography" (*Une autobiographie américaine*) was the title that he finally gave to the entire series of ten novels. In retrospect, the novels of the "Autobiography" can be grouped into three categories by the chronology of the principal scene of each work: (1) the novels of childhood and adolescence—1963–76: *L'odeur du café, Le charme des après-midi sans fin, Le goût des jeunes filles, La chair du maître* (a collection of twenty-four highly varied short stories), and *Le cri des oiseaux fous*; (2) the novels of exile in North America—beginning in 1976: *Chronique de la dérive douce, Comment faire l'amour . . . , Éroshima, Cette grenade dans la main du jeune nègre est-elle une arme ou un fruit?*; and (3) *Pays sans chapeau* (1996), in which Laferrière evokes his first return to Haiti after twenty years in exile.

While he appears constantly young and mischievous, Laferrière has gone in several directions since publishing the tenth volume of the "Autobiography." After living some ten years in Miami, he has returned to live in Montreal, where he has written a weekly cultural chronicle for *La Presse*. He published a book-length interview with Bernard Magnier, *J'écris comme je vis* (2000), followed by a diverse collection of autobiographical reflections as *Je suis fatigué* (2001). These books are highly revealing of Laferrière's life, favorite authors, pet peeves, and attitudes toward sex and racism. Laferrière has undertaken to rewrite, with significant additions, certain volumes of the "Autobiography." He places an intriguing, augmented version of *Cette grenade dans la main du jeune Nègre . . .* (Montréal/Paris, 2002) under the patronage of Walt Whitman, his "traveling companion." He has foreseen a revision of *Le goût des jeunes filles*. Unhappy with a film version of *Comment faire l'amour . . .* , Laferrière has collaborated on other film scenarios and now has in progress a film version of *Le goût des jeunes filles*.

Laferrière's first seven novels have been translated by David Homel and published in Toronto by Coach House Press under the titles of *How to Make Love to a Negro, Eroshima, An Aroma of Coffee, Dining with the Dictator*, and *Why Must a Black Writer Write About Sex*. Douglas & McIntyre published *A Drifting Year* and *Down Among the Dead Men*. Several short stories from *La chair du maître* have been translated by Carrol F. Coates and published in journals: "A Country Wedding" (*Callaloo*, Fall 1999); "Nice Girls Do It Too" (*Review: Latin-American Literature and Arts*, Spring 1999) and "A Little House on the Slope of That Blue Mountain" (*Review: Latin-American Literature and Arts*, 2004). *See also* Grandparents in Caribbean Literature.

Further Reading

Braziel, Jana Evans. "From Port-au-Prince to Montréal to Miami. Trans-American Nomads in Dany Laferrière's Migratory Texts." *Callaloo* 26, no. 1 (2003): 235–51.

Coates, Carrol F. "In the Father's Shadow: Dany Laferrière and Magloire Saint-Aude." *Journal of Haitian Studies* 8, no. 1 (2002): 40–55.

Essar, Dennis F. "Time and Space in Dany Laferrière's Autobiographical Haitian Novels." *Callaloo* 22, no. 4 (1999): 930–46.

—*Carrol F. Coates*

Laforest, Edmund (1876–1915)

∎

To protest against the **American occupation of Haiti** in 1915, Laforest committed suicide. He was found with a copy of the Larousse dictionary hanging from his neck; the dictionary of the French language symbolized this poet's affirmation of his country's French origins and his rejection of American intervention.

Laforest was born in Jérémie on June 20, 1876, into a Protestant family. His father was a teacher and his cousin was the poet **Etzer Vilaire**. Laforest studied with his father and uncle and became interested in poetry at an early age. He also studied music and French art.

Laforest worked as a teacher in his hometown, and at the turn of the twentieth century served as the administrator of the Department of Finances in Jérémie. In 1911, President Cincinnatus Leconte (1854–1912) appointed him chief of the Department of the Interior. A brilliant conversationalist, he soon befriended the intellectuals and members of the high society in Port-au-Prince. He submitted essays to the local publications and in 1914 became a collaborator of the journal *La Plume*, in which he wrote about the initial conflicts of World War I as well as on Haitian literature.

In 1910, Laforest published *Sonnets-medaillons dud ix-neuvieme siecle*. This was followed, in 1912, by the collection *Cendres et Flammes*. His poetry expressed preoccupation with themes such as love, nature, and religion. But, according to scholar Naomi M. Garret, in *The Renaissance of Haitian Poetry* (1963), the dominant sentiment was that of an obsession with death and the macabre: "In an almost constant state of morbidity, Laforest is obsessed with the idea of the macabre; but instead of fearing death, he seems fascinated by it" (30).

When the U.S. Marines landed in Haiti, Laforest rallied against their presence. But he also criticized Haitian politicians and the members of the ruling families, whom he deemed responsible for creating the political situation—the assassination of President Vilbrun Guillaume Sam (1835–1915)—that resulted in the intervention. Proud of his country—the second to achieve independence in the Americas and to defeat Napoleon Bonaparte's forces during the Haitian revolution—Laforest could not stand what he saw as a national humiliation. He ended his own life on October 17, 1915. His other works include *L'Évolution* (1901), *Poèmes mélancoliques, 1894–1900* (1901), *La darnière fée* (1909).

Further Reading

Garret, Naomi M. *The Renaissance of Haitian Poetry*. Paris: Présence africaine, 1963.

Trouillot, Hénock. "Edmond Laforest, un évadé des tropiques." *Le Nouveau Monde*, 8. (Janvier 1982).

—*D. H. Figueredo*

Laguerre, Enrique (1906–2005)

■

One of Puerto Rico's most important and prolific novelists, Laguerre has written extensively about social and historical changes in Puerto Rico while also attempting to construct a narrative that mirrors and is reflective of the island's major transformations in the twentieth century, particularly in relation to the different political and cultural stages of American influence. His best-known novel, *La llamarada* (1935), is still considered a classic of Latin American literature and a prototype of the rural or Telluric and **peasant novel**. Laguerre was also a journalist, an essayist, and a radio commentator.

Enrique Arturo Laguerre Vélez was born on May 3, 1906, in Municipio de Moca, Puerto Rico, the child of a family of coffee plantation owners. His exposure to nature and the lifestyles of peasants and farmers served as the setting for many of the dramas articulated in his early novels. He attended a rural elementary school that was miles away from his home and later on went to high school in a nearby town; at the high school, he wrote short stories while also becoming interested in teaching. During his last year in secondary school, he took a course in pedagogy. After graduation in 1924, he worked as a rural teacher. Four years later, he relocated to San Juan, enrolling at the University of Puerto Rico, earning a BA and a master's in education. In 1951, he earned a doctorate from Columbia University. As a professor he taught at the University of Puerto Rico, was director of Hispanic Studies at the Catholic University of Ponce, and visiting professor at many institutions in the United States, including City University of New York.

Laguerre coupled his passion for teaching—he was a teacher for over six decades—with writing. At the age of twenty-five, he wrote his first novel, *La llamarada*. It is the powerfully symbolic story of an idealistic young man, a recent graduate with a degree in agriculture, whose reformist strategies to better the conditions of the peasants and improve productivity succumb to indifference and graft, converting him into a corrupt plantation overseer. The character, according to **Rosario Ferré**, writing in *Latin American Writers* (1989), symbolizes "the weakness which Laguerre considers endemic to some Puerto Ricans in his indecisiveness, his inability to act according to his conscience, his selling out to corporation interests, and his betrayal of the . . . labor movement" (1051). In 1941, he wrote his second novel, *Solar Montoya*, about a coffee plantation owned by Puerto Ricans who are ruined by changes in the market once the island becomes part of the United States. With his third novel, *El 30 de febrero* (1943), Laguerre begins to center his texts on street life in the urban setting, particularly the university city of Río Piedras, and the poor slums around the metropolitan area, with the adjacent theme of crime. In addition, his narrative not only focuses on man's existential and psychological quests but reflects also the tremendous political, social and economic transformations of an island that was moving from an agrarian society to an industrialized one, that was trying a new form of government—the Commonwealth—that was pursuing land and social reform, and was coping with an emerging new middle class.

Most critics agree that the publication of *La resaca* (1949) signaled the beginning of the construction of a total Puerto Rican saga, covering historically the last three decades of the nineteenth century to contemporary times. While *La resaca* privileged the subservient position under Spanish domination of the Puerto Rican Creole class before the arrogant and classy Spanish captains, in *Los dedos de la mano*, Laguerre explores the issues of social ambition of a woman of poor origins who aspires to get an education against the background of the post–World War I years, where in Puerto Rico there were many contradictory positions with regard to the labor efforts to secure better conditions for the workers. *La ceiba en el tiesto* (1956) and *El Laberinto* (1959) deal with Puerto Rican nationalism, racial profiling, and especially with the immigration of Puerto Ricans to New York. *Cauce sin rio* (1962), subtitled "*Diary of My Generation,*" depicts the psychological and social struggle of the affluent protagonist between the existential and cultural emptiness he felt and the decision to go back to his rural and authentic moral and cultural values. His next two novels, *El fuego y su aire* (1970) and *Los amos benévoles* (1976), dwell on the national and collective panorama of the new alienated Puerto Rican caught in the struggle for a national identity; these texts, in terms of structure and discourse, parallel the techniques popularized by the novelists of the **Latin American Boom** of the 1960s and 1970s.

More recently, Laguerre published *Infiernos privados* (1986), *Por boca de caracoles* (1990), *Los gemelos* (1992), *Proa libre sobre mar gruesa* (1996) and *Residuos de los tiempos* (2000). Laguerre also wrote essays on Puerto Rican literature and culture—*El jíbaro de Puerto Rico: símbolo y figura*, with Esther M. Melón *(1968)* and *La poesía modernista en Puerto Rico (1969),* a seminal study on **Modernismo**—as well as a drama—*La resentida* (1960).

Though his oeuvre is vast and diverse in themes—political corruption, influences of materialism, cultural displacement, and so forth—as Estelle Irizarry has stated in *Enrique A. Laguerre*, "Laguerre's most significant accomplishment is that of creating in his fiction a saga of a land and its people, but at the same time his vision transcends geographical contexts and projects his novels into the timeless and universal relevance of all great art" (30).

Further Reading

Ferré, Rosario. "Enrique A. Laguerre." In *Latin American Writers*, vol. 3, edited by Carlos A. Solé and María Isabel Abreu, 1049–55. New York: Scribner's 1989.

Irizarry, Estelle. *Enrique A. Laguerre*. Boston: Twayne Series, 1982. *Ortega-Vélez, Ruth E. La educación como niveladora social a través de la obra de Enrique A. Laguerre*. Santurce, Puerto Rico Ediciones Situm, 1995.

—*Asela R. Laguna*

Lagun, Chadi. See Debrot, Cola.

Lahens, Yanick (1953–)

∎

Haitian essayist, novelist, and short-story writer, Lahens belongs to a generation of Haitian women writers, such as **Marie Chauvet** and **Jan J. Dominique**, who achieved maturity during the latter year of the Duvaliers'—father and son—dictatorship, which lasted from 1957 to 1986.

Lahens was born on December 22, 1953, in Port-au-Prince, Haiti, and was raised in that city. She went to France to complete her secondary studies, subsequently graduating from the Sorbonne with a degree in literature. She returned to Haiti, where she taught comparative literature at École Normale Supérieure until 1995. A participant in both political and cultural activities, she served in the Ministry of Culture during the mid-1990s, was one of the founders of the l'Association des écrivains haïtiens, and moderated a radio show for Radio Haiti International with Jan J. Dominique.

After producing numerous scholarly articles in Haiti and in the Caribbean, Lahens published in 1990, *L'exil, entre l'ancrage et la fuite: l'écrivain haitien*, which contains a series of critical essays about Haitian writers in exile. In 1994, she published her first work of fiction with the collection of short stories *Tante Résia et les dieux*. These tales deal with the everyday reality of Haitian life, treating themes such as fear, joy, love, life, and death. In 1999, she collected some of the stories she had printed in literary reviews into the volume *La petite corrupcion*. The topics covered in this collection include poverty, political oppression in Haiti, sexual abuse, and the difficulties exiled Haitians face in the United States. The positive critical reception the stories received encouraged Lahens to produce a novel, *Dans la maison du père* (2000). This coming-of-age novel, set in the 1940s, depicts the life of a young girl from the Haitian elite who learns about popular culture from her maid and her uncle.

Lahens serves on the board of directors of the prestigious Conseil International d'Études Francophones (CIEF). She is currently preparing two literary works: a collection of short stories and another of critical essays. *See also* Duvalier, François; Exile Literature.

Further Reading

Susanne, Rinne, and Joëlle Vitiello, eds. *Elles écrivent des Antilles: Haïti, Guadeloupe, Martinique*. Paris: L'Harmattan, 1997.

Zimra, Clarisse. "Haitian Literature after Duvalier. An Interview with Yanick Lahens." *Callaloo* 16, no. 1 (1993): 77–93.

—*Jayne R. Boisvert*

Lair, Clara (1895–1973)

∎

A poet who caused controversy in Puerto Rico during the early twentieth century because of her liberal and feminist views, as well as her criticism of cultural life on the island, Lair wrote a poetry that, according to critics Margot Arce de Vázquez, Laura Gallego, and **Luis de Arrigoitia** in *Lecturas puertorriqueñas* (1968), was nevertheless "dramatically tropical . . . with an acute sense of diction and rhythm." She was the niece of the poet and politician **Luis Muñoz Marín**.

Lair's actual name was Mercedes Negrón Muñoz. In 1918, she left her hometown of Barranquitas to travel to New York City, where she wrote the book of poems *Un amor en Nueva York*. After returning to the island, in 1937 she published the collection *A ras del cristal*. However, it was in 1950 that her volume *Trópico amargo* brought her recognition and notoriety. One of the poems in this collection, "Angustia," angered many of her compatriots for her negative depiction of Puerto Rican men:

> Y el hombre de la esquina
> . . . que no mira a mis ojos y que mira a mi seno,
> que masculla entre sus dientes una lasciva
> cuando paso a su lado . . .

(And the man in the corner / . . . who does not look at my eyes but at stares at my breasts / who murmurs between teeth a lascivious comment / when I walk past him . . .).

Lair would often stop her poetic activities to work as the personal secretary of her uncle Muñoz Marín, who served as governor of Puerto Rico from 1949 to 1965. In 1961, the Instituto de Literatura Puertorriqueña published a monograph that includes some of her poetry and fragments of the memoir *Memorias de una isleña*.

Lair passed away on August 26, 1973, in San Juan. In 2000, a street in the colonial section of the city was named to honor her memory.

Further Reading

Arce de Vázquez, Margot. *Lecturas puertorriqueñas: poesía*. Sharon, CT: Troutman, 1968.

Lair, Clara. *De la herida a la gloria: la poesía completa de Clara Lair / estudio preliminar de Mercedes López-Baralt*. Carolina, Puerto Rico: Terranova, 2003.

—D. H. Figueredo

Laleau, León (1892–1979)

One of Haiti's most popular writers, Laleau could be described as a man with three personalities. One personality was that of the professional diplomat. A second was that of the conservative poet who imitated French writers. And a third personality was that of the nationalist novelist who wrote one of the first anti-American novels about the occupation of Haiti published in that country.

Laleau was a diplomat, posted at cities such as Lima, London, Rome, and Santiago, Chile. When he wasn't at his official posts, he traveled extensively, finding poetic inspiration in the landscapes of such countries as France and Italy, and was also involved in such cultural institutions as l'Academie Ronsard. In Europe, he contributed regularly to numerous journals, including the *Paris-Revue* and *Figaro*. His knowledge of European literature, and the French classics in particular, the works of Victor Hugo (1802–85) for example, influenced his poetry. In rhyme, style, and vocabulary, he imitated French models, so much so that his contemporaries, according to Naomi Garret in *The Renaissance of Haitian Poetry* (1963), described him as "poete francais." Yet underneath the controlled and stylized poems, an image of Haiti, a nostalgia for his homeland, and a black consciousness emerged, as evidenced in such poems as "Mal du pays" (1934). His most famous book of poetry, *Musique negre* (1931), is composed of images from Haiti and Haitians. Lines such as "On certain nights I hear within the screeching of the horn / that called my forebears to the mountain long ago"—from the poem *Legacies*—hint at his recognition of his African ancestry.

While his work as a poet brought him international recognition, in Haiti he was known as the author of the novel *Le choc* (1932), a chronicle of the American occupation of his country. When the intervention occurred in 1915, Laleau was criticized for not responding to the political situation. His answer was the novel *Le choc*, which he wrote in 1915 but published two decades later. The novel is still being studied in Haiti as an affirmation of nationalism and as a condemnation of American influence. His poetry has made him one of the most popular poets in Haiti.

Laleau's most active period as a writer was during the 1930s. When he left the Foreign Service, he retired to Haiti. He passed away Petionville, Haiti. *See also* American Occupation of Haiti, Literature of the.

Further Reading

Garret, Naomi M. *The Renaissance of Haitian Poetry*. Paris: Présence africaine, 1963.

—*D. H. Figueredo*

Lalla, Barbara (1949–)

A novelist, critic, and scholar, Lalla is a professor of language and literature in the Department of Liberal Arts, the University of the West Indies (UWI), St. Augustine, Trinidad-Tobago. Born in Jamaica, Lalla has also taught at the University of the West Indies–Mona, and at the Oral Roberts University, in Tulsa, Oklahoma. She is the UWI St. Augustine Campus Orator, Co-Chair, Cultural Studies Initiative for the St. Augustine Campus, and past president of the Society for Caribbean Linguistics.

Lalla's publications include *Language in Exile* (1990) and *Voices in Exile* (1989), both coauthored with **Jean D'Costa**, *Defining Jamaican Fiction* (1996), *English for Academic Purposes* (1997), and *Arch of Fire* (1998), a novel, also translated into German as *Flammedes Land* (2000), as well as articles on language history and literary discourse.

Arch of Fire is a fictional reconstruction of the histories of the groups that constitute contemporary Jamaican society. Pivotal to the present time of the narrative—and to the period in which the author was actually writing—is the mass exodus of the middle classes from a society toppling into a chaotic heap. The present time of *Arch of Fire* tells the story of Catherine Donalds, a dogla—person of mixed African and Indian origin—of the prosperous and aspiring middle class who falls prey to the sexual advances of a Creole landowner and bears a child out of wedlock. This family unit is at the focal point of the narrative and is the point of interface for all other families in the complex interwoven narrative—the Castries, O'Reillys, Stollmeiers, Hayneses, Cohons, Lions.

In Lalla's grand saga, all families are traced back to the earliest arrivants on the island. As the novel weaves backward and forward through time, the personal histories symbolize the histories of collectivities and ethnicities—Jews, Scots, Irish, Spaniards, Africans, Indians, and Amerindians.

Arch of Fire flirts with and ultimately extends beyond the generic constraints of the **historical novel**, the plantation novel, the family saga, the psychological thriller, the novel of suspense, and supernatural novel. This historical saga of five hundred pages is based on scribal and oral narratives, which Lalla collected over decades. The popular genres invite broad-based readership. While affirming Jamaican roots and heritage, the novel has gained Lalla an audience beyond the Caribbean. *See also* Jamaican Literature, History of; Plantation Society in Caribbean Literature, The.

Further Reading

Morgan, Paula. "Historicizing Islands in the Sun: Nation and Beyond in Lalla's *Arch of Fire* and Brodber's *Jane and Louis*." In *Swinging Her Breasts at History*, edited by Joan Anim-Addo and Moria Inghilleri. London: Mango Publishing, forthcoming.

—Paula Morgan

Lamming, George (1927–)

∎

Considered one of the most important novelists from the Anglophone Caribbean, Lamming was the first writer from the region to explore the relationship between the colonialist and the colonized from a realistic sociological and psychological perspective. His autobiography, *The Pleasures of Exile* (1960), is a seminal study of the African diaspora, exile, and colonialism.

George Lamming was born in Carrington, Barbados, in 1927. His family was poor, but he was able to study beyond elementary school as a result of scholarships. Attending Combermere College, he was mentored by poet and editor **Frank A. Collymore**, who encouraged young authors to write about the Caribbean. Lamming began to publish his poetry in the journal *Bim*, edited by Collymore, in 1946. That same year, he relocated to Trinidad, where he taught at a private school for students from Venezuela. In Trinidad, he befriended the Guyanese novelist **Edgar Mittelhölzer** and the Trinidadian writer **Samuel Selvon** and became a distributing agent for *Bim*. In that capacity, he also solicited writings from numerous authors from Trinidad-Tobago, including Ernest Carr, Cecil L. Herbert, Clifford Sealy, and Harold M. Telemaque. In 1950, Lamming traveled to England with Samuel Selvon, following Edgar Mittlelhozler, who had already settled in Europe, partaking of an exodus of Caribbean authors who were relocating to London in search of better economic and publishing opportunities. In 1951, after working in several factories, he started to read poetry texts, written by him and other Caribbean authors, in a radio program produced by the BBC; eventually, he became the editor of a weekly show that featured book and film reviews.

In 1953, he published his first novel, *In the Castle of My Skin*, which was immediately considered a milestone of Anglophone Caribbean literature. In 1954, Lamming published the novel *The Emigrants*, which told of the sea crossing from the Caribbean to England and of the dreams and aspirations of several of the emigrants aboard the ship. Once they reached England, disappointment was an experience that united all West Indian emigrants and made them conscious of a Caribbean identity. Later on, in his autobiography, *The Pleasures of Exile*, Lamming phrased it thusly: "It was only when the Barbadian childhood corresponded with the Grenadian or the Guianese childhood in important details of folk-lore, that the wider identification was arrived at. In this sense, most West Indians of my generation were born in England. The category West Indian, formerly understood as a geographical term, now assumes cultural significance" (214).

In 1954, Lamming was awarded a Guggenheim scholarship that enabled him to travel to the United States. In 1956, he returned to the Caribbean for the first time, hired by *Holiday* magazine to write an article about the region, from Haiti to Guyana; the magazine, however, was not happy with the end result, and the article was never published. Nonetheless, Haiti proved a catalyst—just as it had been for Cuban writer **Alejo Carpentier**—for Lamming, helping him to develop concepts about the relationship between colonialism and society. In 1958, he published the novel *Of Age and Innocence*, which takes place on a fictitious island named San Cristobal, the setting for his subsequent novels. This work offers an imaginative compendium of the colonial history of the Anglophone Caribbean: the social and ethnic conflicts are depicted through three generation of characters, from colonization to independence. The major themes of the novel were political rivalries and the need for solidarity.

After touring West Africa from 1958 to 1959, Lamming returned to the fictional San Cristobal with the novel *Season of Adventure* (1960), in which he searched, through the protagonist, for the African origins of voudouism and the music of steel bands. In this novel, everyday acts became symbolic manifestations of the conflict between African culture and European traditions. The same year, Lamming published his autobiography, *The Pleasures of Exile*, in which he wove his creative processes with the social reality, the customs and the magic and religions of the Caribbean. After a ten year absence, Lamming published the novels *Water with Berries* (1971) and *Natives of My Person* (1972). The title of the first novel alludes to a line from William Shakespeare's *Tempest* and explored the relationship between Prospero, whom Lamming saw as a colonialist, and **Caliban,** the colonized. The latter novel examined the ills brought to the New World by European colonialists.

George Lamming has received numerous honors, including the Somerset Maugham Award (1958), Canadian Council Scholarship (1962), Writer in Residence at the University of West Indies (1967–68), and an honorary doctorate from the same university (2003). He has been visiting professor at such prestigious institutions as Cornell University (1973), Nairobi University (1975), and University of Puerto Rico (1984). *See also* Exile Literature; Immigrant Literature; Anglophone Caribbean Literature, History of; Vodou in Literature.

Further Reading

Lamming, George. *Conversations: Essays, Addresses, and Interviews 1953–1990.* Ann Arbor: University of Michigan Press, 2000.

———. *The Pleasures of Exile.* London: Michael Joseph, 1960.

Nair, Supriya. *Caliban's Curse: George Lamming and the Revisioning of History.* Ann Arbor: University of Michigan Press, 1996.

Rodríguez, Emilio Jorge. "*En el castillo de mi piel*: contexto sociohistórico y literario." In *Literatura caribeña; Bojeo y cuaderno de bitácora,* 106–34. Habana: Editorial Letras Cubanas, 1989.

—*Emilio Jorge Rodríguez*

Larak, Pòl. See Laraque, Paul.

Laraque, Paul (1920–)

∎

A Haitian writer of socially engaged literature, Paul Laraque, Pòl Larak in **Kreyòl**, was the first author from the francophone Caribbean to win the **Casa de las Américas**—from Cuba—literary prize. In his poetry—rhythmic, direct, accessible—Laraque lashes out at the United States and at such dictators as **François Duvalier**. He writes both in French and in Kreyòl.

Laraque was born on September 21, 1920. He attended Haiti's military academy in 1939, graduating as an officer two years later. While pursuing a career in the military, he was also attracted to literature, and under the pen name of Jacques Lenoir submitted his poetry to the journal *Optique*. In 1964, he was deprived of his citizenship by the Duvalier regime and spent two decades in exile in Spain and in the United States, where he attended Fordham University, in New York City, earning a graduate degree in literature. When the Jean-Claude Duvalier dictatorship ended in 1986—Jean-Claude (1951–), the son of François Duvalier—Laraque returned to Haiti. He was exiled again in 1991 when president Jean-Bertrand Aristide (1953–) was overthrown. That same year, Laraque's brother, the poet and essayist Guy F. Laraque, was murdered.

Laraque won the Casa de las Américas literary award in 1979 for *Les armes quotidiennes / Poésie quotidienne*. The poem MADIGRA/MARDI GRASS (2001), written in Kreyòl, is representative of his style and message:

> tankou Kiba Vyetnam Angola
> Ayiti va pran chemen geriya
> Ayiti va pran chemen

(Like Cuba Vietnam Angola / Haiti's taking the path of the guerrilla / Haiti's taking the road to liberty).

His works in French include *Ce qui demeure* (1973), *Le vieux nègre et l'exil* (1988), and *Oeuvres incomplètes* (1998). In Kreyòl, he is the author of *Fistibal* (1974), *Sòlda mawon / Soldat marron* (1987), and *Lespwa* (2001). His poetry has been translated into English, Italian, and Spanish.

Further Reading

Hirschman, Jack, and Paul Laraque, eds. *Open Gate: An Anthology of Haitian Creole Poetry.* Willimantic, CT: Curbstone Press, 2001.

—*D. H. Figueredo*

Las Casas, Bartolomé de (1474–1566)

Born in Spain but claimed by the Dominican Republic as one of its first writers and celebrated in Cuba and Puerto Rico as a hero, Las Casas was the first priest ordained in the Americas and one of the first to protest against the abuses inflected on the Amerindians by Spanish colonists. His best known work, *Brevísima relación de la destrucción de las Indias* (1552), was one of the earliest books that attempted to bring about social changes in the Caribbean.

Las Casas was born in August 1474—some sources say 1484—as Bartolomé Casuas in Seville, Spain, the descendant of Jews who had converted to Christianity, and was related to several men who participated in the exploration and conquest of the Americas, beginning with his father, who partook of Columbus's second journey to the Caribbean in 1493. Las Casas studied in a school that belonged to the local cathedral and was probably tutored by several priests. In 1502, he sailed for Hispaniola, participating in the suppression of Amerindian uprisings. For his effort, he was awarded an "encomienda," a grant of indigenous labor for working either in the fields or in the mines.

In 1510, Las Casas was ordained into the priesthood and in 1513 went to Cuba to participate in the conquest of that island, being rewarded there once again with lands and Amerindians. But the abuses he witnessed and the poverty and servitude subjected upon the Amerindians made him remorseful of his participation in the conquest. Deciding to dedicate his life to protect the indigenous population, he handed out his "encomiendas" to Cuba's governor and returned to Hispaniola. From that island, he traveled to Spain, where he pleaded for the Amerindians' cause before the royal court. In 1516, he was named "Protector of the Indians."

During the next three decades he traveled throughout Latin America and sailed back and forth to Spain. He also devoted time to collecting materials that would become part of his books later on and summarized part of Christopher Columbus's diary—the only document in existence now that tells of the explorer's journeys. In 1550, Las Casas confronted the Spanish historian Juan Ginés de Sepulveda (1490–1573), who believed Amerindians were barbarians and natural slaves, whereas Las Casas advocated for the peaceful religious conversion of Amerindians. The debate, which lasted several months, was published as *Una disputa o controversia entre Bartholome de las Casas y el doctors Ginés de Sepulveda* (1550).

Remaining in Spain, Las Casas devoted his time to writing. In 1552, he published *Brevísima relación de la destrucción de las Indias*. His other two major works were *Apologética historia sumaria*, in which he demonstrated the humanity and rationality of the Amerindians, and *Historia de las Indias*, his account of the discovery and conquest of the New World from 1492 to 1520, neither of which were published during his lifetime.

Las Casas passed away on July 18, 1566. His volume on the destruction of the West Indies was widely circulated and translated, appearing in several languages, including Dutch, English, and French, between the years 1578 and 1597. Though the Spanish kings accepted Las Casas's supplication for the better treatment of the Amerindians, the conquistadores sided with Ginés de Sepulveda, which resulted in genocide.

Further Reading

Castañeda Salamanca, Felipe. *El indio, entre el bárbaro y el cristiano: ensayos sobre filosofía de la conquista en Las Casas, Sepúlveda y Acosta*. Bogotá, Colombia: Ediciones Uniandes, Departamento de Filosofía: Alfaomega Colombiana, 2002.

Malagón, Javier. "Bartolomé de las Casas." In *Latin American Writers*, vol. 1, edited by Carlos A. Solé and María Isabel Abreu, 1–9. New York: Scribner's, 1989.

—*D. H. Figueredo*

Lataillade, Robert (1910–31)

A young Haitian poet who died at an early age, Lataillade wrote personal poetry that contemplated the themes of mortality and the need for artistic creation.

Native of Jérémie, Haiti, Lataillade attended elementary school in his hometown and was a childhood friend of poet **Jean Brierre**. Lataillade was the nephew of the poet **Edmund Laforest**. At the age of seventeen he attended an agricultural college in the town of Damiens. He was a sickly child and the work weakened him, thus he returned home infirm. A sense of early death prompted him to write poetry as fast as he could. At a time when Haitian writers were exploring social issues and their reactions to the American occupation of their country, Lataillade was writing personal poetry about passionate love and his own melancholia.

Lataillade died at the age of twenty-one. His friend Brierre selected the poems that make up the collection, *L'urne close* (1933); the volume itself was funded by a group of friends who founded the committee Le Comité des Amis de Robert Lataillade. The poems in *L'urne close* follow a traditional format of four rhyming lines. Over all, the poems express the poet's sorrow. Naomi M. Garret observes, in *The Renaissance of Haitian Poetry* (1963), "Lataillade's suffering rendered him pessimistic, but it developed in him a greater understanding of the man in the face of death. His poems are the result of his analysis of the drama of his soul" (163). *See also* American Occupation of Haiti, Literature of the (1915–34).

Further Reading

Garret, Naomi M. *The Renaissance of Haitian Poetry*. Paris: Présence africaine, 1963.

—D. H. Figueredo

Lauffer, Pierre A. (1920–81)

Lauffer was the first poet and novelist to publish an anthology written solely in Papiamentu, the language of the people of Curaçao. He devoted his life to the promotion of this language as an acceptable vehicle for the creation of a national literature.

Pierre Antoine Lauffer was born on August 22, 1920, in Curaçao. Writing under the pen names of José Antonio Martis and Carlos M. Fernandes, Lauffer published the novels *Carmen Molina* and *Martirio di amor*, both in 1942. The first novel, which told of a love affair between a young man and a prostitute, was banned in Curaçao and placed in the "Index" of forbidden works.

In 1943, Lauffer and two other writers, Jules De Palm and Rene de Rooy, published a song book entitled *Cancionero Papiamento No. 1* with the objective of deterring the influence and diffusion of songs written on the island in the languages of Dutch, English, and Spanish. The volume, which the three authors released under the name of Julio Perrenal, also aimed at encouraging the use of Papiamentu for the creative arts. A year later, Lauffer published the book of poems *Patria*. Divided into four parts—"The Earth," "The Sun," "Men" and "Cactus Flower"—the first poem, entitled "Kórsou," defined Curaçao, rather than Holland as the poet's mother country, an uncommon practice at the time.

Lauffer was a member of the Cultureel Centrum Curaçao, created in 1949, and a founder, with Rene de Rooy and Nicolas Pina, of the journal *Simadan* (1950–51), the first periodical published entirely in Papiamentu. The journal proposed the use of the island's vernacular to create literature, evoke nature, and describe the island's characteristics. The journal longed for a pre-European past and was a tool for social criticism. These positions had a tremendous positive impact on the people of the island.

In 1953, Lauffer became editor of the journal *Antillano*, pursuing therein the same objectives as in his previous periodical. However, interest in his cause—the promotion of the language of Papamientu—did not really solidify until the publication of his book of poetry *Kumbu* (1955), supported by the Cultureel Centrum Curaçao. The volume, the work of a matured poet, demonstrated a preoccupation with social concerns, as can be observed in the poems "Kehy di Katibu," about slavery, and "Mi tera," about Curaçao.

Lauffer's literary production, coming of age after the onset of World War II, values the Afro-Caribbean heritage of Curaçao, identifying with the black community, the poorest, and keeping a distance from the Catholic traditions prevalent in the island's literature written before the war. His works present, often with autobiographical touches, the suffering and the pleasures of the people in a realistic vein. Many of his poems incorporate puns and Afro-Caribbean musicality and rhythm; humor and irony are always present.

Lauffer's writings constitute an attempt at bringing dignity to Papiamentu as a language of cultural expression. In that spirit, in 1971, Lauffer published the first anthology ever in Papiamentu, *Di nos*. In 1974, he prepared several texts on Papiamentu for scholars, including *Mangasina* and *Sukuchi*. Throughout his life, Lauffer collaborated with numerous journals, the likes of *Stoep*, *Culturele Kroniek*, *de Passt*, *Branding*, and *La Cruz*, among others. He was awarded some of the Dutch Caribbean's highest honors: the Cultureel Centrum Curaçao prize for his book *Kantika pa bjentu* (1963), the Premio Cola Debrot from the Insular Government, the first individual to receive such recognition (1969), and the Premio Sticusz, the first also to receive it (1975).

A few weeks after his death, on June 14, 1981, the Fundashon Pierre Lauffer was created to disseminate knowledge of the Papiamentu language and to honor and keep his memory alive. This foundation assumed the task of preparing the reedition of all his works and the publication of the three volumes *Pa saka kara* (1998). The foundation established a literary prize called, Chapi di plata.

Further Reading

Broek, Aart G. *Pa saka toro, tomo I; Historia di literature papiamentu*. Willemstad: Fundashon Pierre Lauffer, 1998.

Habibe, Henry. *Un herida bida ta. Een verkenning van het poëtisch ouevre va Pierre Lauffer*.Willemstad: Kòrsou, 1994.

Palm, Jules De and Juian Coco. *Julio Perrenal: Dichters van het Pariamente lied*.Ámsterdam: De Bezige Bij, 1979.

Rutgers, Wim. *Beneden en bowen de wind: Literatuur van de Nederlandse Antillen en Araba*. Ámsterdam: De Bezige Bij, 1996.

—*Emilio Jorge Rodríguez*

Lauture, Denizé (1946–)

A children's writer, Lauture is inspired by his native Haiti. His depiction of loving relationships between fathers and sons and his evocative portrayal of Haiti have won him a wide readership in schools. He is also a college professor at St. Thomas Aquinas College, New York.

Born in Haiti, Lauture migrated to New York in 1968. Without a high school diploma and only a limited knowledge of English, Lauture worked as a welder. As his English improved, he started to take courses at City College of New York, graduating in 1977 with a BA in sociology. He was attracted to the field of education, and four years later he earned a masters in bilingual education from the same school.

While his first book of poems was written in **Kreyòl**, *Boula Pou Yon Metamòfoz Zèklè* (1987), it was his work in English that brought him recognition in his adopted country. In 1989, he published *When the Denizen Weeps*. In 2000, his second children's book, *Running the Road to ABC*, was praised for its lyrical language and ability to evoke Haiti.

Lauture was awarded the 1993 National Association for the Advancement of Colored People Image Awards, and in 1997, the New York Public Library selected *Running the Road to ABC*, as one the best books of the year

Further Reading

"Poetry—Father and Son by Denize Lauture." *The Horn Book Magazine*, no. 5 (September 1993): 614–16.

—*D. H. Figueredo*

Laviera, Jesús Abraham "Tato" (1950–)

The first Latino author to win the American Book Award of the Before Columbus Foundation, which recognizes and promotes multicultural literature, Laviera is the best-selling Latino poets in the United States and bears the distinction of still having all of his books in print.

Born September 5, 1950, in Santurce, Puerto Rico, he migrated with his family to New York City at the age of ten and settled in a poor area of the Lower East Side. After finding himself in an alien society and speaking little English, Laviera eventually graduated from high school as an honor student. Despite having no other degrees, his intelligence, aggressiveness, and thorough knowledge of his community led to a career in the administration of social service agencies.

After the publication of his first book, *La Carreta Made a U-Turn* (1979), Laviera gave up administrative work to dedicate his time to writing. Aside from writing, Laviera has toured the United States as a performer of his poetry, has directed his own plays, and has produced cultural events. In 1980, he was received by President Jimmy Carter at the White House Gathering of American Poets. In 1981 his second book, *Enclave*, was the recipient of the American book Award. Tato Laviera has said, "I am the grandson of slaves transplanted from Africa to the Caribbean, a man of the New World come to dominate and revitalize two old world languages."

Laviera is the inheritor of the Spanish oral tradition, with all of its classical formulas, and the African oral tradition, with its wedding to music and spirituality; in his works he brings both the Spanish and English languages together as well as the islands of Puerto Rico and Manhattan—a constant duality that is always just in the background. His first book, *La Carreta Made a U-Turn* uses **René Marqués's** classic drama *La Carreta* (1952) as a point of departure and redirects it back to the heart of New York instead of Puerto Rico, as Marqués had desired; Laviera is stating that Puerto Rico can be found here, too. His second book, *Enclave* (1981), is a celebration of diverse heroic personalities, both real and imagined: **Luis Palés Matos** and salsa composers, the neighborhood gossip and John Lennon (1940–80), Miriam Makeba (1932–), and Tito Madera Smith, the latter being a fictional, hip offspring of a Puerto Rican and a Southern American black. *AmeRícan* (1986) and *Mainstream Ethics* (1988) are surveys of the lives of the poor and marginalized in the United States and a challenge for the country to live up to its promises of equality and democracy. *See also* Code Switching; Kanellos, Nicolás; Nuyorican Literature; Performance Poetry.

Further Reading

Luis, William. *Dance Between Two Cultures: Latino Caribbean Literature in the United States*. Nashville: Vanderbilt University Press, 1997.

Rivero Marín, Rosanna. *Janus Identities and Forked Tongues: Two Caribbean Writers in the United States*. New York: Lang, 2004.

—*Nicolás Kanellos*

Laviera, Tato. See Laviera, Jesús Abraham "Tato."

Leante, César (1928–)

■

Cuban novelist, short-story writer, and essayist, César Leante has written much about the Cuban Revolution, both as an admirer and a critical observer.

Born on February 11, 1928, Leante was a television and radio writer before 1959. After Fidel Castro came to power, he secured a position as a journalist for the newspaper *Revolución* and collaborated in the influential weekly supplement *Lunes de Revolución*. He also worked for Prensa Latina, the Ministry of Foreign Affairs in Paris, the **Unión de Escritores y Artistas de Cuba**, and the Ministry of Culture.

In 1962, Leante published a journalistic account of Castro's militia, *Con las milicias*. Two years later, he wrote *El perseguido*, about the 1957 attack on the presidential palace where dictator Fulgencio Batista (1901–73) worked. In 1975, Leante won a literary award from UNEAC, the Union of Cuban Writers and Artists, for his novel Los *guerrilleros negros*.

Leante sought exile in Spain in 1981. Out of Cuba, he has written essays critical of the Cuban government and of Fidel Castro, including *Calembour* (1988), *Fidel Castro: el fin de un mito* (1991), and *Hemingway y la revolución cubana* (1993). He has continued writing novels and short stories and is the editor of the publishing house Pliegos. Leante lives in Madrid. *See also* Anti-Castro Literature.

Further Reading

Luis, William. "Myth and Reality in César Leante's *Muelle de Caballería*." *Latin American Literary Review* 8, no. 16 (1980): 246–57.

———. "La novelística de César Leante." *Cuadernos Americanos* 244, no. 5 (1982): 226–36.

—William Luis

Lenoir, Jacques. See Laraque, Paul.

Lergier, Clara (1919–)

Clara Lergier is a Puerto Rican poet who was the director of the library of the **Ateneo Puertorriqueño**, the prestigious and influential cultural society based in San Juan, Puerto Rico.

A native of Lares, Clara Luz S. de Lergier studied pedagogy at the Universidad Interamericana de San Germán during the 1940s. Later on, she pursued a library degree at the Universidad de Puerto Rico. Not much is written about her during this period, but in 1970 she was appointed library director of the Ateneo where she was one of the organizers of the annual prize Premio de Honor del Ateneo, established in 1972 to honor the cultural contribution of Puerto Rican writers and intellectuals.

Lergier began her own writing career just as she arrived at the Ateneo, publishing poems and stories in journals. She is the author of the volumes *Con los ojos del alma* (1969) and *¡Vibracio—!* (1982), meditative poems written in a romantic vein. In 2000, the Universidad Interamericana honored Lergier with a merit certificate for her contribution to Puerto Rican culture.

Further Reading

Enciclopedia puertorriqueña: Siglo XXI. Vol. 6. Santurce: Cariber Grolier, 1998.

—D. H. Figueredo

Lespès, Anthony (1907–78)

Lespès is a Haitian novelist and literary critic who wrote about the massacre of Haitian workers by Rafael Leónidas Trujillo in 1937. He spent much of his life working as an agronomist. His experience with Haitian farmers informed much of his writing.

Born in Cayes, Haiti, on February 7, 1907, Lespès studied agriculture at the School of Agriculture in Damien, earning a degree in 1927. Specializing in soil conservation, he was appointed agricultural agent and toured Haiti in that capacity. In 1938, he served as manager of an agriculture colony, and the experience there served as the basis for his *Les semences de la colère,* a **peasant novel** set during the infamous massacre of Haitian workers by Dominican forces in 1937. After the novel's publication in 1949, Lespès cultivated poetry. In 1955, he published *Quelques poèmes.*

After his retirement, Lespès wrote numerous essays promoting Haitian culture and literature. In 1974, he published "La voie tracée par Jacques Roumain," a tribute to the great Haitian writer. The essay was included in the collection *En Avant.* *See also* **Compère Général Soleil.**

Further Reading

Herdeck, Donald E. *Caribbean Writers. A Bio-Bibliographical-Critical Encyclopedia.* Washington, DC: Three Continents Press, 1979.

—*D. H. Figueredo*

Lezama Lima, José (1910–76)

■

A central figure in twentieth-century Cuban culture, poet, novelist, and essayist Lezama Lima fostered a resurgence of Cuban poetry with the founding of the journal *Orígenes* and the group Orígines, a grouping of Cuban writers of which he was the leading member.

Lezama Lima was born on a Cuban army base in Havana on December 19, 1910. His father died when he was nine years old, and he and his mother moved in with his maternal grandmother. In 1929, he enrolled at the Universidad de la Habana, earning a doctorate in law nine years later. He worked as an attorney until 1945, when he was appointed to an administrative post in the Ministry of Education.

Pillar and lifeblood of Cuban culture of his day, Lezama Lima founded four influential journals. The first was *Verbum* (1937), followed by *Espuela de Plata* (1939–41), *Nadie Parecía* (1942–44), and finally, *Orígenes* (1944), the best known of the group. In 1937, Lezama Lima published one of his most famous poems, "La muerte de Narciso," in which the description of a donkey falling off a side of a mountain allows for the author's contemplation of eternity and the significance of life and creativity. His poetic production of the 1940s is followed by several books of essays, including *Analecta del reloj* (1953), *La expresión Americana* (1957) and *Tratados en La Habana* (1958). In 1966, he wrote the novel *Paradiso* (1966), considered his masterpiece and one of the first works in Latin America to portray a complex and likable homosexual character.

Lezama Lima redefined the baroque literary style, which he perceived as sensuous, colorful, full of life, and playfully intellectual rather than academic and abstruse. Like **Wilson Harris,** from Guyana, Lezama Lima enriched his writings with the diverse and numerous texts he had read throughout his life, often alluding to seminal works from Western European literature but including references to Latin American history and mythology.

Lezama Lima was marginalized by Cuba's revolutionary government. From 1969 to 1976, he lived in virtual isolation, and though invited to lecture abroad, he was never given exit visas. Government officials, however, later on reevaluated his work, considered it appropriate, and reprinted limited editions during the 1970s and 1980s. Lezama Lima left an unfinished manuscript, *Oppiano Licario*, which was published in 1971. His works have been widely translated, and his fame has grown since his death. Some of his other works include *Cantidad hechizada* (1970), *Las eras imaginarias* (1971), *Esferaimagén* (1976), and *Fragmentos de un imán* (1977).

Further Reading

Cella, Susana. *El saber poético: la poesía de José Lezama Lima*. Buenos Aires: Nueva Generación, Facultad de Filosofía y Letras, 2003.

Gutiérrez Richaud, Cristina. *Las fronteras del erotismo y otros ensayos*. Guadalajara, Jalisco, México: Dirección General, Patrimonio Cultural, Secretaría de Cultura, Gobierno de Jalisco, 2000.

—*Pamela María Smorkaloff*

Lhérisson, Justin (1873–1907)

In 1903, Justin Lhérisson, a Haitian journalist and lawyer who had been a member of the "Société du Centenaire"—the society of the Centenary—since 1893, submitted a poem of five stanzas and four-syllable lines to the jury for the selection of a national anthem. The poem was titled "**La Dessalinienne**," and the members of the jury, which included novelist **Fernand Hibbert**, poet Arsène Chevry, and journalists Sténio Vincent and Solon Ménos, selected it as Haiti's national anthem.

The poem, set to music by Nicolas Geffrard (1871–1930), was first performed at the "Autel de la Patrie"—Altar of the Fatherland—in Saint-Marc on October 17, 1903, when a bust of patriot Jacques Dessalines (1758–1806) was unveiled. In 1919, Haiti's State Council voted the law of August 5, 1919, declaring "La Dessalinienne" the "Chant National Haïtien."

The author of Haiti's national anthem was born in Port-au-Prince, February 10, 1873. In the early 1890s, he cultivated poetry, publishing three volumes: *Myrtha* (1892), *Les chants de l'aurore* (1893), and *Passe-Temps* (1893). In 1894, he founded the review *Jeune Haïti* and in 1898 established the newspaper *Le Soir*, where he wrote a series of whimsical articles on Haitian society and politics. In 1905, he used the sense of irony and of the ridicule that he had first essayed in his articles on his first novel: *La Famille des Pitite-Caille* about a young man whose political ambitions lead to tragedy. The novel, capturing Haitian speeches and the nuances of **Kreyòl**, proved very popular and soon became a work familiar to all literate Haitians. In 1906, he published a second novel, *Zoune chez sa ninnaine*. In the novels, Lhérisson created a unique style: the storyline was presented through a series of conversations held during a literary salon.

Lhérisson was influential in the development of modern Haitian literature. His ability to combine the French language with Kreyòl, though initially criticized by some reviewers, was imitated decades later by **Jacques Roumain** in his classic novel *Gouverneurs de la rosée* (1944). *See also* Tertulias/Cénacles/Literary Salons.

Further Reading

Joassaint, Erick. *Haïti, Golimin et les autres: une lecture de Justin Lhérisson*. Port-au-Prince, Haiti: Presses de l'Impr. Nouvelle, 1986.

—Carrol F. Coates and D. H. Figueredo

Linden Lane Magazine (1982–)

■

A literary journal founded in the United States by Cuban poets **Belkis Cuza Malé** and **Heberto Padilla,**who were married to each other, with the objective of publishing works by Latin American authors living in exile and who were not published in publications edited by pro-Castro intellectuals. The journal was named after the street where the couple lived in Princeton, New Jersey; the title was Cuza Males's suggestion who liked the romantic connation of the street's name and the fact that there was a Linden tree in full bloom on the front yard.

Cuza Malé edited and directed the publication with suggestions and ideas from her husband. She also hired novelist **Reinaldo Arenas**, who as special editor was responsible for soliciting manuscripts from other writers. Modeled after the American literary journal *The New York Review of Books*, *Linden Lane* published only works written in Spanish. Published four times a year, the journal was funded by Cuza Malé and subscriptions. Since 1982, the journal has been published in four different locations: New Jersey, Florida, Texas, and even Spain. In 2003, the journal appeared in electronic format: www.lacasaazul.org/Linden_ Lane_Magazine. *See also* Literary Journals.

Further Reading

Cuza Malé, Belkis. *El destino de Linden Lane*. http://www.lajiribilla.cu./2001/n10_julio/elgranzoo.html (accessed 9/9/05).

—Belkis Cuza Malé

Literary Journals

■

Literary journals provide writers and critics an important opportunity to present new works and ideas within a publishing format that allows for many contributions of varying length. These journals document the debates surrounding political, social, and aesthetic questions of the day, thereby extending the readership and potential impact on society well beyond the limited circle of contributing authors. Most editors are major intellectual or literary figures, with similar individuals on the editorial board. Generally the board's membership is of national compatriots, although a few exceptions exist in the cases of francophone journals published in Paris and some titles from the Anglophone Caribbean. Over the course of a century, these journals attest to the evolution of thinking about race—especially Afro-Caribbean identity and consciousness—nationalism, sovereignty, connections with Europe and the United States, language, translation, gender issues, and creolization. Many journals fostered young writers and allowed the best to transition from local acknowledgment to international acclaim. Today most of the former colonies and territories are independent, and part of this history of self-determination appears in contributions ranging from essays to fiction to poetry.

The small reading public forced many journals to appeal beyond the strict boundaries of literature, but even then, press runs were small and circulation limited. Some important titles existed for only a few issues and today are rarely found in libraries. Fortunately reprints and microfilm enable many titles to be accessible.

The linguistic and political divisions within the Caribbean demarcate journals. Cuba, the area's largest publisher, ignored the writings from non-Hispanic authorship until 1959, when the revolutionary government commenced a strong support of culture and interest in authors beyond its borders. Nevertheless, most Caribbean journals remain parochial and often favor European or American contributors. As Caribbean migration accelerated throughout the twentieth century, intellectual and political forces arose to encourage translation and access to the ideas and expressions of neighboring peoples. In certain quarters the linguistic barriers responsible for keeping states alienated from each other gave way to discussions about Creoleness and localized languages, along with debates about Americanness and its evolution into Caribbeanness through the forces of history and migration.

The Caribbean diaspora contributed to the **Négritude** movement and later black nationalism. Both have their reflection in journals published in the Caribbean and Europe. The black internationalism with its strong cultural component addressed issues of racial subordination and inequality, along with racial solidarity, creolization, and the fragmented culture experienced by many Caribbean peoples. These discussions and concrete realities anticipated the mixed races and integration of cultures characteristic of the late twentieth century.

Anglophone

Barbados, Guyana, Jamaica, and Trinidad and Tobago account for the principal journals. Often more than literature appeared because the limited readership sought opinion and information on events and personalities shaping their local realities. These journals introduced nearly all the area's major writers and served to encourage, if not unite, writers from various colonies. Ideally a forum for creative dialogue existed, thereby reducing the isolation between lands, but never to the exclusion of the United Kingdom for authorship and publication.

Bim (St. Michael, Barbados, 1942–92), under the editorship of its founder **Frank Collymore**, encouraged new forms of creative writing and was a major source for short fiction, poetry, and articles on literary language. Promotion of West Indian literature in general extended to reviews of theater, books, and art. In *Focus* (Kingston, Jamaica, 1943–60, 1983), editor **Edna Manley** promoted unpublished prose fiction and poetry mainly by Jamaicans. *Pepperpot* (Kingston, Jamaica, 1951–79), begun by Elsie Benjamin Barsoe, reflected the transition from colony to independence through poetry, fiction, reviews of theater and books, along with major parts concerning the practical concerns of life such as agriculture, economy, women, and sports. *Jamaica Journal* (Kingston, Jamaica, 1967–98) provided substantial coverage of culture, music, history, language and literature, especially poetry, and short stories and plays. Topics covered include Black Power, Négritude, and race. *The New Voices* (Diego Martin, Trinidad and Tobago, 1973–) promotes creative writing as well as criticism for the islands and other parts of the Anglophone Caribbean. *Kyk-Over-Al* (Georgetown, Guyana, 1945–95) initially focused on Guyanese fiction and poetry and later branched to include other West Indians. The racial mix with black and East Indians predominating makes this journal an early one to treat multicultural topics, including racial cooperation, emigration, and exile.

Dutch

From their origin in the sixteenth century, the Dutch-speaking territories had multiracial populations, with whites coming from different countries and religions. As elsewhere in the Caribbean, separate worlds for the nonwhite populations evolved into multiculturalism that recently has come to be recognized as a sociopolitical reality in the United States and Europe. Dutch-speaking territories used *Christoffel* (Curaçao, 1955–59) and *Vox Guyanae* (Paramaribo, Suriname, 1954–59) to grapple with racial and linguistic issues, and emigration.

Francophone

Haiti, Guadeloupe, and Martinique contribute the core of journals published locally or in Paris. Issues of race, the effects of colonialism, and the role of a black intelligentsia figure prominently. *La Revue du monde noir* (Paris, France, 1931–32) addressed the creation of new races as a result of colonialism. Many articles advanced ideas concerning racism, equality, and democracy. *Tropiques* (Paris, France, 1941–45), edited by **Aimé Césaire**, flourished through its connecting literary and cultural currents of the metropole with the harsh realities of Martinique. *Revue indigène* (Port-au-Prince, Haiti, 1927–28) arose partially in response to the United States' occupation of Haiti along with the national elite's infatuation with France. Its pages advanced an African-derived culture and sponsored an opening to various literary styles as well as discussion of such topics as voudou and peasant culture. *Conjonction. Bulletin de l'Institut Français* (Port-au-Prince, Haiti, 1946–) advances the intellectual expression of Haitians and a collaborative partnership in the expansion of Haitian culture. Featuring contemporary poets, novelists and essayists, the journal also endeavors to treat issues of interest within the Caribbean through reviews of exhibitions, summaries of new publication, and notice of conferences. France and French intellectuals serve as both inspiration and point of departure for much of the content. The Société Haïtenne d'Histoire, de Géographie et de Géologie's *Revue* (Port-au-Prince, Haiti, 1925–) carries the intellectual imprint of **Jean Price-Mars**, Hénock Trouillot, and Catts Pressoir. Many articles treat language, culture, religion, ethnicity, and social history.

Hispanic

By virtue of its land mass, wealth, and historical experiences Cuba produced far more significant literary journals than did the Dominican Republic or Puerto Rico. From the nineteenth century forward, reference and respect for Spain's literary traditions and authors are evident. Although the United States held greater economic and political significance, its literature receives far less attention. With the triumph of the Cuban Revolution, a bold experiment of state support for culture began but soon devolved into state domination and control of the creative process and publication. Until 1990 it was difficult and politically risky to publish abroad without official permission, but with the Special Period's shortage of resources, more authors successfully gained access to foreign journals and publishers. In the Dominican Republic long periods of political instability and dictatorship inhibited authorship and publishing. Puerto Rico's shift from Spanish to American control brought economic stability, but it also fostered a yearning among many authors for independence. These general themes came to characterize the journals in all three countries.

In the nineteenth century, Cubans created and supported a variety of cultural and literary journals or included sections devoted to those themes in journals dedicated to history, geography, and politics. The most important was the *Revista bimestre cubana* (Habana, Cuba, 1831–34, 1910–59, 1994–). After independence, a number of major journals recorded debates and creativity; among them were *Cuba contemporánea* (Habana, Cuba, 1913–27), **Revista de avance** (Habana, Cuba, 1927–30), and *Revista cubana* (Habana, Cuba, 1935–57). Significant contributions appeared in the journals associated with **José Lezama Lima**: *Verbum* (Habana, Cuba, 1937), *Espuela de plata* (Habana, Cuba, 1939–41), *Nadie parecía* (Habana, Cuba, 1942–44), and **Orígenes** (Habana, Cuba, 1944–56). After 1960, state-supported journals flourished, thereby encouraging the writing and reading of various forms of literature. Often journals endeavored to connect with Caribbean and Latin American cultural movements and figures. The most successful along these lines is the **Casa de las Américas** (Habana, Cuba, 1960–). Cuban writers also rely upon *Unión* (Habana, Cuba, 1962–), which depending on political considerations has carried the original works of many writers. *Gaceta de Cuba* (Habana, Cuba, 1962–) endeavors to more closely associate the Revolution with literature and the arts. *RC, revolución y cultura* (Habana, Cuba, 1967–) appeals to a broader audience, with coverage of the arts and literature, and since the 1990s has become far more sophisticated, with broader cultural coverage and focus on Latin America. *Revista de literatura cubana* (Habana, Cuba, 1982–97) provided literary criticism on contemporary Cuban authors along with a bibliography of current works. *Letras cubanas* (Habana, Cuba, 1986–94) focused on Cuban contemporary fiction, essay, and testimony. The remarkable emergence of *Trazado de Azoteas* (Habana, Cuba, 2001–) under Reina María Rodríguez brings the best authorship and includes writers increasingly published abroad.

Puerto Ricans parallel the experience elsewhere in the Hispanic Caribbean, with most journals being the effort of a single person or small group, and the publication itself being subject to economic and political pressures, of which assimilation into the United States sphere predominates. *Asomante* (San Juan, Puerto Rico, 1945–70) emphasized the distinctiveness of Puerto Rican cultural traditions and language as its contribution in the creation of a national conscience. More focused on Spain than other Caribbean islands, *Asomante's* articles and literary criticism address Puerto Rico's intellectual isolation. *La Torre* (Río Piedras, Puerto Rico, 1953–) offers broad coverage, including criticism and essays by major Puerto Ricans. *Sin nombre* (San Juan, Puerto Rico, 1970–84), under the direction of **Nilita Vientós Gastón**, provided excellent coverage of Puerto Rican writers because her intent was to enable citizens to access the writings of local authors. Content includes Latin Americans and translations into Spanish.

Few exclusively literary journals exist for the Dominican Republic. *Cuadernos dominicanos de cultura* (Ciudad Trujillo, Dominican Republic, 1943–52) combined original fiction, especially poetry, along with literary criticism and scholarly articles on history, art, and music. *Helios* (Santo Domingo, Dominican Republic, 1973–) concerns itself broadly with advancing culture through articles and literature.

Caribbean Area

Nieuwe West-Indische gids ('s-Gravenhage, The Netherlands, 1919–) is an excellent source for the highest levels of scholarship. **Caribbean Quarterly** (Mona, Jamaica, 1949–) captures the West Indies through history, culture, and literature, often with thematic issues addressing language and literature. Major writers consistently appear here. *New World Quarterly* (Kingston, Jamaica, 1964–72) brought together West Indian and Hispanic interests through critiques of colonialism, neocolonialism, decolonization, and their influences on culture and politics. *Savacou* (Kingston, Jamaica, 1970–80) attempted to address the whole Caribbean area as a cultural entity through articles on literary criticism and history and with essays, poetry, and fiction. Cuba bridges the divides within the Caribbean through *Anales del Caribe del Centro de Estudios del Caribe* (Habana, Cuba, 1981–) and *Del Caribe* (Santiago de Cuba, Cuba, 1983–). The editors and authors recognize the balkanization of the area due to colonialism and later imperialism, and hence they encourage contributions addressing slavery, religion, and culture as shared histories.

Today Caribbean content no longer suffers from isolation. Most major journals carry during the course of a year or two some works by Caribbean authors, and these are readily identified through bibliographic databases such as the *Handbook of Latin American Studies*, *Hispanic American Periodicals Index*, and the *MLA International Bibliography*. Of the trans-Caribbean journals especially worthwhile are *Wadabagei* (Brooklyn, NY, 1998–) for its thematic issues, *Callaloo* (Baltimore, Maryland, 1976–) for its Afro-Caribbean coverage, and *Calabash: A Journal of*

Caribbean Arts and Letters (New York, 2000–) with its original fiction and poetry. *See also Notas y Letras; semanario de literatura y bellas artes.*

Further Reading

Barquet, Jesús J. *Consagración de La Habana (Las peculiaridades del Grupo Orígenes en el proceso cultural cubano).* Miami: Iberian Studies Institute, North-South Center, University of Miami, 1992.

Esquenazi-Mayo, Roberto. *A Survey of Cuban Revistas, 1902–1958.* Washington, DC: Library of Congress, 1993.

Haïti à la une: une anthologie de las presses haïtienne de 1724 à 1934. Compiled by Jean Desquiron. Port-au-Prince: privately printed, 1993.

Jiménez Benítez, Adolfo E. *Historia de las revistas literarias puertorriqueñas.* San Juan, Puerto Rico: Ediciones Zoe, 1998.

Olivera, Otto. *La literatura en periódicos y revistas de Puerto Rico (siglo XIX).* Río Piedras, Puerto Rico: Editorial de la Universidad de Puerto Rico, 1987.

—Peter T. Johnson

Literatura Comprometida/Socially Engaged Literature

■

The closest equivalent to "literatura comprometida" in English is not actually English at all but French: "engage," meaning engaged or committed to a political viewpoint. It may be either the artist or the art form that is "engagé," that is, willing to take sides and allow social commitment to make itself manifest in the work. This is the polar opposite, in theory, of "art for art's sake." In the end, however, there may be no such thing as an art devoid of any or all social engagement; like absolute objectivity, it is an ideal that one can strive for though not necessarily attain. Jean-Paul Sartre (1905–80) may be found at the center of the debate surrounding literature and commitment in twentieth-century Europe. In Latin America and the Caribbean, however, the debate dates back to the turn of the last century, and José Enrique Rodó's (1872–1917) essay "Ariel." Inspired by Shakespeare's characters in the The *Tempest*, a drama of colonialists and colonized, Rodó offers his own meditation on the interaction of the arts and society in the young Latin American republics as well as the role of the artist and the intellectual. Leading figures in Latin American and Caribbean arts and letters responded critically to Rodó's appeal to an "art for art's sake." Cuban **José Martí**'s manifesto "Our America" may be read as a counterpoint to Rodó. Martinican **Aimé Césaire**, of the **Négritude** movement, wrote an adaptation of *The Tempest* for Afro-Caribbean theater, which poses a challenge to the assumptions of Rodó's Ariel. In the charged anti-imperialist, anticolonialist climate of the 1960s, Latin American and Caribbean artists and intellectuals were being asked to question tradition, to step away from Europe, to side with **Caliban**, Shakespeare's feisty indigenous inhabitant of a Caribbean island in the process of being colonized by Europeans. The Cuban Revolution, and particularly **Fidel Castro**'s 1961 speech "Words to the Intellectuals," with its famous phrase "**within the Revolution everything, outside the Revolution nothing,**" has had a similarly polarizing effect among artists and writers.

Further Reading

Césaire, Aimé. *Une tempête; d'après "La tempête" de Shakespeare. Adaptation pour un théâtre nègre*. Paris: Éditions du Seuil, 1969.

Fernández Retamar, Roberto. *Calibán y otros ensayos: nuestra América y el mundo*. Habana, Cuba: Editorial Arte y Literatura, 1979.

—*Pamela María Smorkaloff*

Literature of Local Color. See Costumbrismo.

LKJ. See Johnson, Linton Kwesi.

Llanes, Manuel (1899–1976)

∎

A poet from the Dominican Republic whose fame is based on one volume of poetry, entitled *Fuego* (1953), Llanes was a member of the group known as the **Poesía Sorprendida**, writers who rejected **costumbrismo**—regional writing or writing of local color—and realistic poetry, advocating for experimental literature instead. Because of his enigmatic nature, Llanes was dubbed "El Buda," the Buddha.

Not much is written about Llanes's personal life except that he worked as a teacher from 1914 to 1944. When he first started to write poetry, he was attracted to the writers associated with the **Postumismo** movement, which cultivated nationalistic poetry, but he soon befriended the writers connected with the Poesía Sorprendida and wrote for the journal of the same title. Llanes also submitted his poetry to the newspapers *El Caribe* and *Listín Diario*.

His poetry tended to be of a religious nature, with numerous allusions to biblical characters and incidents. The poems also revealed a sense of loneliness and sadness. Though he didn't seem interested in publishing his poetry, he often read his poems to his students and friends. He passed away on May 4, 1976.

Further Reading

Cabral, Manuel del. *10 poetas dominicanos: tres poetas con vida y siete desenterrados*. Republica Dominicana: Publicaciones América, S.A., 1980.

"Manuel Llanes." http.//www.escritoresdominicanos.com (accessed 9/10/05).

—*D. H. Figueredo*

Llerena, Cristóbal de (1540–1610?)

Considered the first playwright born in the Americas, Llerena was a cleric and a professor who hailed from the Dominican Republic. He was also one of the first writers in the Caribbean to experience the government's censorship and censure.

Llerena taught grammar at the Colegio de la Paz. As a Catholic teacher, he was expected to write religious drama with the objective of illustrating Church theory and demonstrating proper Christian behavior, but Llerena also wrote comedies and historical pieces. The plays were staged twice a year, with Llerena's students as the actors, usually to celebrate the arrival of a Spanish personage or a religious event. It is believed that many of Llerena's plays were performed, but the only surviving text is a drama entitled *Entremés*, a one act-play performed in Santo Domingo in 1588. The play depicted the sack of the capital by Francis Drake (1540–96) in 1586. But the play also revealed the political rivalry between government officials in Santo Domingo. His negative depiction of the officials led colonial authorities to question his loyalty, but the Church protected Llerena from further criticism and persecution. *See also* Dominican Republic Literature, History of.

Further Reading

Atehortúa Atehortúa, Arbey. "Antigüedad clásica y literatura colonial latinoamericana." *Revista de Ciencias Humana,* no. 21. www.utp.edu.co/~chumanas/revistas/revistas/rev21/atehortua.htm (accessed 9/10/05).

Cortés, Eladio, and Mirta Barrea-Marlys. *Encyclopedia of Latin American Theater.* Westport, CT: Greenwood Press, 2003.

Veloz Maggiolo, Marcio. *Cultura, teatro y relatos in Santo Domingo.* Santiago de los Caballeros, Republica Dominicana: Universidad Católica Madre y Maestra, 1972.

—*D. H. Figueredo*

Llorens Torres, Luis (1876–1944)

Considered Puerto Rico's national poet, Llorens Torres evolved from costumbrista literature, a literature of local color, to contemplative works about the nature and identity of Puerto Rican culture. He also sought and promoted solidarity with Cuba and the Dominican Republic.

Born in Juana Díaz, Puerto Rico, on May 14, 1876, Llorens Torres's parents were owners of a coffee plantation. As a child, Llorens Torres spent hours roaming through the fields and the countryside. His appreciation of Puerto Rico's natural beauty fostered his love of the island and his nationalism, becoming years later a central theme of his poetry.

Llorens Torres attended elementary and secondary schools in the towns of Mayaqüez and Maricao. Traveling to Spain in the mid-1890s, he studied law at the

Universidad de Barcelona and obtained a PhD in philosophy and literature from the University of Granada. He toured Spain and in 1899, influenced by **romanticismo**, wrote the book of poems *Al pie de la Alhambra*.

When he returned to Puerto Rico in 1901, he established a law office with the writers **Nemesio Canales** and **José de Jesús Esteves**. Upset over American presence on the island at the end of the Spanish-Cuban-American War of 1898, he wrote a poem of protest entitled *El Patito Feo*; he also began to promote independence for Puerto Rico.

In 1908, he was elected to the Puerto Rican House of Representatives. In 1913, he cofounded, with Nemesio Canales, the journal *La Revista de Las Antillas*. In 1914, he published *Sonetos sinfónicos* and, in 1929, *La canción de las Antillas y otros poemas*. Of these poems, critics **Margot Arce de Vázquez**, Laura Gallego, and **Luis de Arrigoitia** comment in *Lecturas puertorriqueñas: poesía* (1968): "Llorens describes the beauty of [Puerto Rico], our types and customs, our folklore, expressing the sentiments and attitudes held by Puerto Ricans" (160). In 1940, Llorens Torres published *Alturas de Américas*, where he again celebrated the love of his island but also manifested his love for the Caribbean. He also wrote a historic drama, *El grito de Lares* (1916), about a nineteenth-century insurrection against Spain. As a poet, Llorens Torres described his philosophy as "Pancalismo," meaning everything is beautiful, and insisted there was no such thing as prose, since all writing was poetry.

He died on June 16, 1944. In his honor, an avenue was named after him in San Juan, and a statue of his likeness was erected in a park in his hometown.

Further Reading

Arce de Vázquez, Margot et al. *Lecturas puertorriqueñas: poesía*. Sharon, CT: Troutman Press, 1968.

Cabrera de Ibarra, Palmira. *Luis Lloréns Torres: ante el paisaje*. San Juan, Puerto Rico: Editorial Yaurel, 1990.

—*D. H. Figueredo*

Lluch Mora, Francisco (1924–)

Lluch Mora is a Puerto Rican poet and professor. His poetry is known for expressing sentiments of a personal and philosophical nature while also celebrating the island's heritage and culture. Two collections exemplifying these characteristics are *Cartapacio del amor* (1961) and *Canto a Eugenio María de Hostos* (1956)

A native of Yauco, Lluch Mora studied pedagogy at the Universidad de Puerto Rico, earning a teacher's certificate in 1946. He taught at different schools throughout the island and was also active in promoting Puerto Rican culture. In 1950, he published his first book of poems, *Del asedio y la clausura*. The volume revealed a dominant theme in all his poetry: the conflict between what an individual can actually achieve versus what that individual aspires to achieve.

In 1955, Lluch Mora was hired by the Universidad de Puerto Rico as a literature professor. The following year, he left for Spain, where he enrolled at the Universidad de Barcelona, concentrating on literature. He returned to Puerto Rico and in 1961 earned an MA in Hispanic studies from the Universidad de Puerto Rico. His poetry appeared in prestigious journals, such as *Alma Latina*, **Asomante**, and *Revista del Instituto de Cultura Puertorriqueña*. He also published several collections of poetry, including *Cartapacio de amor, Poemas sin nombre* (1963), and *Canto de despedida a Juan Ramón Jimenez* (1965). Critic **Arce de Vázquez**—with Laura Gallego and **Luis de Arrigoitia**—in *Lecturas puertorriqueñas: poesía* (1968) describes his poetry as "well rounded and sonorous, expressing a sentimental soul susceptible to beauty" (396).

As a critic, Lluch Mora published major studies on some of his compatriots, *La naturaleza en La charca de Manuel Zeno Gandia* (1960), and *Palabras sobre dos libros de Cesáreo Rosa-Nieves* (1960), as well as on international literature, *La huella de cuatro poetas del cancionero en las coplas de Jorge Manrique* (1964). In 2001, the Puerto Rican Senate passed a proclamation honoring Lluch's contribution to Puerto Rican culture, describing him as "a dedicated student of our history, a salient figure in our poetry and intellect. . . . His life has been consecrated by his investigative labor, his creativity, and his teachings, all from the perspective of someone with a profound love for his country." His other work includes *Momento de la alegría: 1955–1956* (1959), *Decimario primero* (1976), *Canto a Yauco* (1980), *La huella del latido: decimario: 1947–1985* (1994).

Further Reading

Arce de Vázquez et al. *Lecturas puertorriqueñas: poesía*. Sharon, CT: Troutman Press, 1968.

Cautiño Jordán, Eduardo. *La personalidad literaria de Francisco Lluch Mora*. San Juan, Puerto Rico. Ateneo Puertorriqueño, Ediciones Mairena, 1994.

Senado de Puerto Rico. *Resolución*, Nov. 1, 2001. http://www.pucpr.edu/alianzas/ateneodeponce (accessed 5/15/05).

—*D. H. Figueredo*

Lochard, Paul (1835–1919)

An early religious poet, Lochard introduced a philosophical vein to Haiti's national literature. His poetry, however, also revealed a preoccupation with the political and economic situation in Haiti.

Lochard was born in Petit-Goave, Haiti, in 1835. A professor and director of Customs, Lochard was a pastor as well. In 1878, he published his first book of poetry, *Chants du soir*. These religious poems explored the relationship between man and God. Nearly twenty years later, he published his second volume of poetry *Les feuilles de Chêne* (1907). From this second volume come some of his best-known poems, "La Creation," "Lucifer," and La Vie." Again, religious meditation is the dominant theme, though some of the poems also address patriotism.

Scholar Naomi Garret describes Lochard as melancholic thinker resigned to divine intervention; Lochard also believed there was little he could do to change the political and economic situation in his country. He is representative of the somberness and resignation that appeared in the writings of many Haitian poets during the end of the nineteenth century.

Further Reading

Garret, Naomi. *The Renaissance of Haitian Poetry*. Paris: Présence africaine, 1963.

—D. H. Figueredo

Logan, Mark. See Nicholson, Christopher R.

López, César (1933–)

López is a Cuban writer and diplomat who won the 1999 National Literature Award in Cuba. He has translated into Spanish the works of the Anglo-Irish writer Lawrence Durrel (1912–90).

López was born in Santiago de Cuba on December 12, 1933. During the 1950s, he joined the underground in the fight against the dictatorship of Fulgencio Batista (1901–73). Exiled to Spain, he earned a medical degree from the Universidad de Salamanca in 1959. From 1960 to 1962 he served as Cuban consul in Scotland. When he returned to Cuba, he worked in the ministry of foreign affairs, coordinated the literature section of the **Unión de Escritores y Artistas Cubanos**, and taught literature at the Instituto Preuniversitario "Raúl Cepero Bonilla."

In 1966, he won honorable mention in the **Casa de las Américas** literary contest with his book of poetry *Primer libro de la ciudad*. However, his ambivalent stance toward the Cuban Revolution brought him isolation and censorship as a result of the Padilla affair, when poet **Heberto Padilla** was arrested in 1970 for writing anti-revolutionary poetry. In 1991, López's work was reevaluated, and he then published *Doble espejo para muerte denigrante*. Since then, his works have been reissued in Cuba. His other works include *La busca de su signo (1971), Segundo libro de la ciudad (1971), Quiebra de la perfección (1983), Ceremonias y ceremoniales (1988), Consideraciones, algunas elegías (1990), Seis canciones ligeramente ingenuas (1992), y Tercer libro de la ciudad (1996). See also* "Within the Revolution Everything. . . ."

Further Reading

Reynaldo, Andrés. "Notas sobre el fascismo corriente." *El Nuevo Herald*, April 19, 2003.

—D. H. Figueredo

López Baralt, Luce. See López Baralt Sisters.

López Baralt, Mercedes. See López Baralt Sisters.

López Baralt Sisters

■

These two sisters, Luce and Mercedes, are major intellectual and cultural figures from Puerto Rico. They are internationally recognized for their individual accomplishments in Arabic and Amerindian studies.

López Baralt, Luce (1944–). López Baralt is an eminent Puerto Rican scholar and essayist known for her research on Arabic influences in the Spanish language and literature.

A native of San Juan, López Baralt attended primary and secondary schools in that city. In 1966, she earned a BA in Hispanic studies from the Universidad de Puerto Rico. Two years later, she received an MA from New York University in Hispanic literature. In the 1980s, she was awarded a PhD from Harvard University. In 1985, she published *San Juan de la Cruz y el Islam: Estudio de la filiación semítica de su poesía mística,*beginning her fascination with the role the Arabic language played on the evolution of Spanish literature. Her research on the linguistic exchange between Arabic and Spanish has made her the Caribbean's foremost expert on the subject. In 1993, she published the first work to examine the Kama Sutra and Hispanic literature, *Un Kama Sutra español.* López Baralt's scholarly style is elegant and highly readable, as a critic, in writing in the *Hispanic Review* (1995), points out, "López-Baralt's strengths . . . are meticulous research, eloquent expression, and imaginative sympathy with her subject."

López Baralt's numerous essays have been published in such influential and prestigious periodicals as **Sin Nombre**, *El Mundo*, *Insula*, and *Hispanic Review*. An international scholar, she is a frequent presenter at conferences in France, Italy, Spain, and Mexico. A visiting professor at Harvard University, Yale University, and el Colegio de España in Malaga, she is a member of the *Asociación Internacional de Hispanista*, *Asociación International de Cervantistas*, and the **Ateneo Puertorriqueño**. In 1998, she and her sister Mercedes edited their great-grandfather's (Esteban López Giménez) account of an episode in Puerto Rico during the Spanish-Cuban-American War, *Crónica del 98. El testimonio de un médico puertorriqueño*. Her writings include *Huellas del Islam en la literatura española: de Juan Ruiz a Juan Goytisolo* (1985), *Entre libélulas y ríos de estrellas: José Hierro y el lenguaje de lo imposible* (2002), and *El viaje maravilloso de Buluqiya a los confines del universo* (2004).

López Baralt, Mercedes (1942–). A Puerto Rican scholar and essayist, López Baralt has dedicated her life to the research of pre-Columbian and colonial literature and arts as well as reinterpreting from a Freudian and Jungian perspective the writing of classic Spanish works by such authors as Benito Pérez Galdós (1843–1920). An expert on modern interpretation of Andean art, she is one of Latin America's leading intellectuals.

López Baralt was born in San Juan. In 1966, she graduated from the Universidad de Puerto Rico with a BA in Hispanic studies. She researched Taínos, the island's Amerindians, and their culture before the Spanish conquest, publishing *El mito taino: raíz y proyecciones de la Amazonia continental* (1977). A year after this publication, she received her MA in Hispanic studies from her alma mater and continued her writings on Amerindians: *Taínos: El mito taíno: Levy-Strausss en las Antillas*.

In 1980, she was awarded a PhD in anthropology from Cornell University. She wrote for numerous journals, including *La Revista del Centro de Estudios Avanzados de Puerto Rico y el Caribe, Cuadernos Americanos*, and ***Sin nombre***, and taught at her alma mater, Cornell University, and Emory University. She expanded her research on the Amerindians and colonial literature to a study on the works of her compatriots **Luis Pales Matos**—*Luis Pales Matos: La poesía de Luis Pales Matos* (1993)—and **Clara Lair**—*De la herida a la gloria: la poesía completa de Clara Lair* (2003). Her other work includes *El retorno del inca rey: mito y profecía en el mundo andino* (1989), *Icono y conquista: Guamán Poma de Ayala* (1992), and *Insularismo: ensayos de interpretación puertorriqueña* (2001).

Further Reading

Enciclopedia puertorriqueña. Siglo XXI. Tomo 4. Santurce: Caribe Grolier, Inc. 1998.

López-Morillas, Consuelo. *Hispanic Review* 63, no. 1 (Winter 1995): 98.

Mejias López, William, ed. *Morada de la palabra: homenaje a Luce y Mercedes López Baralt*. San Juan, Puerto Rico: Editorial de la Universidad de Puerto Rico, 2002.

—D. H. Figueredo

López Nieves, Luis (1950–)

∎

Luis López Nieves is one of the most eclectic contemporary Puerto Rican writers. A college professor of literature and communications, he has worked also as translator, scriptwriter, and literary journalist at various dailies such as *Claridad, El Mundo, Momento,* and *The San Juan Star*. He received his PhD in Comparative Literature from the State University of New York–Stony Brook, where he was the first student allowed to fulfill his dissertation requirements with a novel, *La felicidad excesiva del Alejandro Príncipe* (1980, still unpublished). In the cultural world, he has been founding member of several of the most important innovative literary publications, namely *Penélope* (1972), *Talleres* (1983), and *Cupey* (1983–84).

López Nieves has written few books, but each one has received favorable reviews and acceptance by the reading public. Furthermore, they all have brought new insights, new constructions, and new readings of Puerto Rican history and society. *Seva: historias de la primera invasión noteamericana de la isla de Puerto Rico ocurrida en mayo de 1898*, his first novel, which appeared in the Socialist newspaper *Claridad* on December 23, 1983, without any introduction or caution about its fictional character, was an immediate success, and many took it as a historical new finding and not as a literary fabrication. The novella centers on the mysterious disappearance of a university professor who decides to investigate a new reference about an American invasion of Puerto Rico in a month other than the one historically recorded—in May rather than in July 1898. As in a detective story, he goes to the archives of one of General Miles's granddaughters, Peggy, in Virginia, where he unveils new documentation in the form of diaries about an unknown invasion on the east coast, where the inhabitants bravely died defending their land. The few survivors are then exterminated by the invaders. Ancillary documentation—maps, Miles's letters, affidavits, photos—support the professor's findings of a conspiracy at the American Roosevelt Roads Base at Ceiba to conceal the savagery of the massacre. A powerful and convincing short novel, *Seva* stands among the first-rate narration that shows the multiple postmodern literary strategies of reinventing or debunking "official" history.

He also has published a book of short stories, *Escribir para Rafa*, (1987), and an anthology, *Te traigo un cuento* (1997). His last text, another historical novel, *La verdadera muerte de Juan Ponce de León* (2000), was awarded the Premio Nacional de Literatura and Primer Premio del Instituto de Literatura Puertorriqueña. Like in *Seva*, López Nieves resorts to the historical past as a source and excuse for his subversive literary writing, but this time, he reinvents not a story about the 1898 American invasion but of the historically painful beginnings of Puerto Rico as a Western society in 1493 and the sixteenth century. López Nieves brings alive historical figures—Christopher Columbus (1451–1506), Ponce de León (1460–1521), Governor Nicolás de Ovando (1460–1518)—or fictional ones—Rodrigo de las Nieves and Fray Juan de Borbón—to fictionally populate the streets and ports of the Old San Juan in a masterful intermingling of history and inventiveness.

Further Reading

Martínez-Fernández, Luis. "Puerto Rico in the Whirlwind of 1898: Conflict, continuity, and change." *Magazine of History* 12, no. 3 (Spring 1998): 24–30.

—*Asela R. Laguna*

López Suria, Violeta (1926–)

López Suria is Puerto Rican poet. A cerebral writer, her poems often portray the conflict between benign dreams and a hard world, between creation and destruction.

Born in Santurce, Puerto Rico, on May 19, 1926—some sources say 1929—her literary productivity began in the 1950s and subsided in the 1970s. Her poetry reveals a fascination with death and portrays a world that is detached from individuals. Yet her approach is more intellectual than emotional. Many of her early poems appeared in such influential journals as **Asomante**. In 1953, she published two books of poetry, *Gotas en mayo* and *Elegía*, which were well received by the critics.

During the 1960s, she explored love poetry, *Amorosamente* (1961), and poems that celebrated the beauty of Puerto Rico, *Poemas a la Cáncora* (1963), as well as Negrista poetry, poems celebrating black culture and traditions. In 1969, she published one of her most famous volumes *Obsesión de Heliotropo*, which consisted of essays and short stories. Her other work includes *La piel pegada al alma* (1962), *Me va la vida* (1965), and *Antología poética* (1970). Her life and work have yet to be studied outside Puerto Rico. *See also* Negrista Literature.

Further Reading

Arce de Vázquez, Margot, et al. *Lecturas puertorriqueñas: poesía*. Sharon, CT: Troutman Press, 1968.

Arrillaga, María. *Concierto de voces insurgentes: tres autoras puertorriqueñas, Edelmira González Maldonado, Violeta López Suria y Anagilda Garrastegui*. Río Piedras, San Juan, Puerto Rico: Decanto de Estudios Graduados e Investigación, Recinto de Río Piedras, Universidad de Puerto Rico; San Juan, Puerto Rico: Isla Negra Editores, 1998.

—*D. H. Figueredo*

Lorde, Audre (1934–92)

Of Caribbean parents but born in the United States—like **Oscar Hijuelos** and **Paule Marshall**—Lorde was a prolific poet and novelist who explored political and sexual repression in her writings. She is often regarded as a major contributor to the development of contemporary African American literature.

Lorde's parents migrated to New York City from Grenada with the hopes of a return that never happened. Lorde was born on February 18, 1934, in New York City. She developed a love of reading and writing poetry in her youth, publishing her first poem in the popular magazine *Seventeen* when she was in high school. She graduated from Hunter College at the age of twenty-five and went on to earn a master's in library science from Columbia University in 1961. As an educator, her career had two phases: from 1961 to 1968, she worked as a librarian; from 1968 until her death, she was a college professor and lecturer.

In the 1960s, Lorde submitted her poems to journals and anthologies. These early poems were of a romantic and exploratory nature as she tried to understand her love for her family—she had two children—her marriage and her lesbianism. In 1968, she received a National Endowment for the Arts grant and became a poet in residence at Tougaloo College, a small black college, where she flourished as a poet. As her recognition increased, in 1976, W. W. Norton and Company published her volume *Coal*, which consisted of earlier poems she had published in two small presses: *The First Cities* (1978) and *Cables to Rage* (1970).

The recognition from a major publisher accelerated her career as a writer. Her poems, which affirmed her blackness, criticized sexual repression within the black community, and advocated for a woman's identity neither defined nor imposed by a patriarchal society, became popular with feminist readers; her works were soon studied in literary journals and college campuses.

In 1978, she published her masterpiece, *Black Unicorn*. In one of the poems in this volume, she wrote

> I have been woman
> for a long time
> beware my smile
> I am treacherous with old magic . . .

In 1980, there was another change in Lorde's life: she was diagnosed with breast cancer. Her suffering inspired her to write a chronicle of the disease, *The Cancer Journals*. She followed this work with a novel, *Zami: A New Spelling of My Name* (1982), and several works of fiction. Awareness of her mortality was now a present theme in her poetry. Though she battled cancer for the next decade, she continued to teach, write, and promote sexual equality. In the 1980s, she founded a press dedicated to publishing the works of black feminists, Kitchen Table: Women of Color Press.

Lorde passed away on November 17, 1992. Her many awards include Creative Artists Public Service grants (1972, 1976), American Book Award Before Columbus Foundation (1989), and poet laureate of New York (1991). *See also* Feminist Literature.

Further Reading

De Veaux, Alexis. *Warrior Poet: A Biography of Audre Lorde*. New York : W. W. Norton, 2004.

Lorde, Audre. *The New York Head Shop and Museum*. Detroit, MI: Broadside Press, 1974.

Upton, Elaine Marie. "Audre Lorde." In *Contemporary Lesbian Writers of the United States*, edited by Sandra Pollock and Denise D. Knight, 316–24. Westport, CT: Greenwood Press, 1993.

—*D. H. Figueredo*

Lo Real Maravilloso. See Magical Realism.

Loro, Moncho. See Ramos, Juan Antonio.

Loveira, Carlos (1881–1928)

■

Cuba's foremost exponent of the literary movement known as **naturalismo**, naturalism, Carlos Loveira was an internationally recognized labor leader, journalist, and novelist. His masterpiece, *Juan Criollo*, published in 1927, reflects the political and social pessimism that many Cubans experienced when independence from Spain and the establishment of the republic in 1902 didn't translate into equality for all.

The life of Carlos Loveira reads as if it were a novel. Born on March 21, 1881, in the province of Las Villas, in Cuba, he was orphaned by the age of three. His widowed mother found work as a cook with a middle-class family but died before Loveira was ten years old. The family that had hired his mother relocated to New

York City, taking with them the young boy. In Manhattan, Loveira worked as a busboy and street vendor. When revolutionary war broke out against Spain in 1895, Loveira returned to Cuba to join the insurgents. He proved himself a brave fighter and was promoted to lieutenant. At the end of the war, he found employment as a railroad worker. Concerned over social and labor issues, he founded La Liga Cubana de Empleados de Ferrocarriles, the first labor union for railroad employees established in Cuba. After the union was disbanded by the Cuban government, Loveira left for Mexico, where he worked in the government's labor department. Throughout the late 1910s and the early 1920s, he traveled extensively for the Mexican government and participated in dozens of labor-oriented conferences and seminars. He was appointed secretary of the American Federation of Labor and worked alongside its first president Samuel Gompers (1850–1924) in Washington, D.C.

Despite his world traveling and union activism, Loveira managed to write articles and fiction. According to critic **Max Henríquez Ureña,** in *Panorama histórico de la literatura cubana*, one day in 1919, Loveira walked into a newly established publishing house in Havana and handed the clerk at the office a manuscript. It was his first novel, *Los inmorales*. This work was followed by other novels: *Generales y doctores* (1920), *Los ciegos* (1922), *La última lección* (1924), and *Juan Criollo* (1927).

Juan Criollo is Loveira's most representative work. Autobiographical, it tells the story of an orphaned boy who grows up into a labor leader. The world Juan Criollo sees around is one of exploitation, abuses, and materialism, a world where only the wealthy get ahead. From Loveira's naturalist perspective, there is no hope for the underclass: individuals are puppets for the powerful to use for entertainment.

Loveira also wrote a book of essays on labor issues and journalism. His ability to duplicate Cuban vernacular in his novels and his demonstrated knowledge of the Spanish language earned him membership in the prestigious Real Academia Española de la Lengua. He passed away in Havana in 1928. *See also* Realismo/ Realism.

Further Reading

Henríquez Ureña, Max. *Panorama histórico de la literatura cubana. Tomo II.* Habana: Editorial Arte y Literatura, 1979.

Molina, Sintia. *El Naturalismo en la novela cubana.* Lanham, MD: University Press of America, 2001.

—*Sintia Molina and D. H. Figueredo*

Lovelace, Earl (1935–)

■

Earl Lovelace is considered one of the major twentieth-century Caribbean writers. He is a novelist, playwright, short-story writer, and essayist. His major awards include the British Petroleum Literary Award for the manuscript of *While Gods Are Falling*, in 1964; the Pegasus Literary Award for outstanding contribution to the

Arts in Trinidad and Tobago, in 1966; a Guggenheim Fellowship in 1980; and the Commonwealth Writers Best Book Prize in 1997 for his widely acclaimed novel *Salt*. In recognition of his contribution to literature and culture he was awarded the Chaconia Medal (Gold) by the Government of Trinidad and Tobago in 1988 and an honorary doctor of letters from the University of the West Indies, St. Augustine Campus, Trinidad and Tobago in 2002.

A major twentieth-century Caribbean novelist, Earl Lovelace addresses colonialism, racism, and urban poverty in his novels, short stories, and essays. *Courtesy of Janet Fullerton-Rawlins.*

Born July 13, 1935, in Toco, Trinidad, Lovelace, unlike most of the writers of his generation, chose to live and work in Trinidad instead of migrating. He did, however, spend some time in the United States studying and lecturing at various universities. His decision to stay at home has, as he told the *Trinidad Guardian* in 1987, helped him "to address themes in the society with much more confidence and depth; to present a Caribbean perspective on the world."

His work deals with themes such as colonialism, urban versus rural conflict, politics, racism, sense of community, search for personhood, affirmation of self, building a new society, and reparation. His work also shows a love of his country, its language and its people. He writes about the "ordinary people" who, according to him, inspired his work. His characters are folk people, stick-fighters, and Spiritual Baptists whose existence and history he has chosen to celebrate in his work. Rich descriptions of the landscape come from his own observation and experience, as he worked as an agricultural officer and as a forest ranger for many years and lived in rural communities in Trinidad.

His published works include the novels *While Gods Are Falling* (1964), *The Schoolmaster* (1986), *The Dragon Can't Dance* (1979), *The Wine of Astonishment* (1982), and *Salt* (1997); a collection of plays—*Jestina's Calypso And Other Plays* (1984); a collection of short stories—*A Brief Conversion and Other Stories* (1988); and *Growing in the Dark (Selected Essays)* (2003).

From the politics and quest for meaning of life in *While Gods Are Falling* to the urban and rural conflict in *The Schoolmaster*, to the search for personhood and community building in *The Dragon Can't Dance* to the survival of religion and folk culture of the 'ordinary people' in *The Wine of Astonishment*, he has moved to his most serious concern—the question of colonialism and building a new society in the aftermath of colonialism in *Salt*.

His book of selected essays gives great insight into Lovelace the man, the writer, and the thinker. These essays show his concern for his society, its politics, the survival and preservation of the folk culture, and the creation of a new world society. The essays mirror the themes in his novels, plays and short stories, and provide his raison d'être as a writer in an emerging society. In one of his essays, "From de I Lands" (1983), he says "I recognized that the central theme of people's existence was resistance to enslavement and colonialism and their efforts were for visibility and affirmation of self." Culture, he says, is a means of self-affirmation. Although Lovelace touches on universal themes in his work, he deals mainly with themes unique to his society, born out of colonialism, enslavement and indentureship.

Further Reading

Cary, N. R. "Salvation, self, and solidarity in the work of Earl Lovelace." *World Literature in English* 28, no. 1 (1988): 103–14.

Lovelace, E. *Growing in the Dark (Selected Essays)*. Edited by Funso Aiyejina. San Juan, Trinidad: LEXICON Trinidad Ltd., 2003.

Rahim, J. "The 'Limbo Imagination' and New World Reformation in Earl Lovelace's *Salt.*" *Small Axe* 5 (1999): 151–60.

Thorpe, M. "In Search of the West Indian Hero: Earl Lovelace's Fiction." In E. Smilowitz and R. Knowles, eds, *Selected Papers from West Indian Literature Conference 1981–1983*, 90–100. Parkesburg, IA: Caribbean Books, 1984.

—*Janet Fullerton-Rawlins*

Loynaz, Dulce María (1902–97)
■

Poet and novelist Dulce María Loynaz was born in Havana to an illustrious and wealthy family that provided her and her siblings with a classical education at home. She always spoke with pride of her patrician ancestors, some of whom were military officers in the separatist armies that fought for Cuba's independence from Spain. In 1927, she graduated with a law degree from the Universidad de la Habana but never practiced as a lawyer. She married her cousin Enrique de Quesada y Loynaz in 1938, but they divorced in 1943. In 1946, she married the journalist Pablo Álvarez de Canas.

Loynaz began writing at an early age, publishing *Versos 1920–1938*, her first book of poetry, in 1938. Three other books of poetry followed: *Juegos de agua* (1947), *Poemas sin nombre* (1953), and *Últimos días de una casa* (1958). She also wrote prose and, in 1951, caused a literary stir with her experimental novel *Jardín*, where she rejects plot, characterization, and sequential time. During the first decade of her marriage to Álvarez de Canas, she became active in literary circles in Havana, cultivated friendships with such celebrated literary figures as the Chilean poet Gabriela Mistral (1889–1957), and traveled extensively throughout the Spanish-speaking world.

The Cuban revolution of 1959 brought a dramatic change to Cuban society, and to Loynaz. After 1959, she claimed to have lost inspiration and did not publish except for the narrative *La novia de Lazaro*. She secluded herself in her palatial home in the Havana neighborhood called El Vedado, venturing out only to attend meetings of the Cuban Academy of Language, which she hosted. It might be concluded that she detested the new order in Cuba, but Loynaz never made signs of wanting to leave revolutionary Cuba, and at one point she said that the daughter of a hero of Cuba's wars of independence would not leave her fatherland.

Cuban poets of the generation that came of age in the 1980s rediscovered her work. In 1984, a compilation of her poetry was published in Havana, and in 1991, *La novia de Lazaro* was published in Madrid. In 1992 she received the prestigious Cervantes Literature Prize, which led to a reappreciation of her work. In 1993, her collection *Poemas sin nombre* was translated into English and published in Havana as *Poems Without a Name*. In 1992, Loynaz broke her seclusion to travel to Madrid to receive the Cervantes Prize. Upon her return, she published two collections of poems, *Poemas náufragos* and *Bestiarium*, both in 1992, and the anthology of literary essays *Ensayos literarios*, published 1993. She died in Havana in 1997.

Loynaz's inward, insightful style, and the preciseness, measure, and passion of her expression as a writer distinguished her from other Cuban authors of her generation. Critics have called attention to the grasp of the mundane and the elusive found in her poetry alongside with expressions of depth and insight. Intellectual **Cintio Vitier** pronounced her one Cuba's best poets.

Further Reading

Loynaz, Dulce María. *Antología lírica*. Madrid: Espasa Calpe, 1993.

Simón, Pedro. *Dulce María Loynaz: valoración múltiple*. Habana: Ediciones Casa de las América y Editorial Letras Cubanas, 1991.

Vitier, Cintio. *Cincuenta años de poesía pura cubana (1902–1952)*. Habana: Dirección de Cultura del Ministerio de Educación. Ediciones del Cincuentenario, 1952.

—*Rafael E. Tarrago*

Lugo Filippi, Carmen (1940–)

A Puerto Rican short-story writer who explores the frustrations experienced by affluent women who are assigned stereotypical roles by a male-driven society, Lugo Filippi is an essayist and a French-language professor. In Puerto Rico, she developed experimental approaches to the teaching of a foreign language as well as designing the French curriculum for higher education.

Lugo Filippi was born in Ponce, Puerto Rico, on May 25, 1940. Her father owned a general store and her mother was a natural storyteller. An avid radio listener—to soap operas and adventures—Lugo Filippi's imagination was influenced by these soap operas, her mother's stories, and the activities at her father's business. While a teenager, she began to write stories imitative of the radio dramas popular of the era.

In 1957, she graduated from high school and began to study French at the Universidad de Puerto Rico. After obtaining her BA in French, she was awarded a scholarship to study at Columbia University. In 1962, she returned to the island, where she worked for the Department of Education and taught in several provincial schools. In the 1960s, she befriended the writer **Ana Lydia Vega**, a friendship that would result in several creative and academic partnerships: designing French courses and writing books together. In 1974, she met and married the Puerto Rican writer **Pedro Juan Soto** and traveled to France to pursue doctoral stories at the University of Toulouse. She received her PhD two years later.

During this period, Lugo Filippi was writing short stories and submitting them to local competitions. In 1976, the influential journal *Sin Nombre* awarded her the first prize for the story, "Pilar, tus rizos." The following year, she again received the first prize for another short story. Some of these stories were compiled for the volume *Virgenes y mártires* (1981). The collection also included stories by her friend Ana Lydia Vega. The two cowrote one short story, "Cuatro selecciones por una peseta," which received the literary prize **Nemesio Canales** in 1980. The story drew a satirical sketch of middle-class life. In 1981, she published the college text, *Le français vécu*, which for many years was used to teach French in Puerto Rico.

Her creative impulses were curtailed by the murder of her stepson, Carlos Soto Arrive, a victim to police overreaction to a supposedly terrorist plot, and the many years of investigation conducted by her husband and the subsequent trial—the officers were found guilty. During the 1980s, she cultivated the essay, publishing *El trama ancla* (1988) and *Los cuentistas y el cuento: encuesta entre cultivadores* (1991). She also devoted much of her time to researching the life of the nineteenth-century patriot and poet **Ramón Emeterio Betances**. In 1998, she published *Los dos indios: episodios de la conquista de Borinquen*, which included her literary analysis of Betance's poetry. She retired from teaching in 1996. In 1999, she published the novel *Narromaniando con Mirta*.

Further Reading

Torres, Víctor Federico. *Narradores Puertorriqueños del 70*. Guía biobliográfica. San Juan: Plaza Mayor, 2001.

Vega, José Luis. *Reunión de espejos*. Río Piedras: Editorial Cultural, 1983.

—*D. H. Figueredo*

Luis, William (1948–)

∎

A literary critic who is one of the first to study and document Caribbean American literature as a whole rather than the separate expression of Cuban American, Puerto Rican, and Dominican writers, William Luis is the author of several histories of Spanish Caribbean literature and the seminal study *Dance Between Two Cultures: Latino Caribbean Literature Written in the United States*, which examines the relations between Caribbean and North American writings.

An Afro-Cuban-Chinese, William Luis was born on July 12, 1948, in New York City. He earned a BA from the State University of New York–Binghamton, an MA from the University of Wisconsin–Madison, a second MA and a PhD from Cornell University. Luis is a full professor at Vanderbilt University and has been a visiting scholar to such prestigious institutions as Washington University and Yale University.

Determined to explore new areas of scholarly studies, in 1981 Luis edited, with controversial Cuban novelist **Edmundo Desnoes**, the anthology *Los dispositivos en la flor*, which placed for the first time in one volume writings by Cubans in Cuba and in exile. In 1997, he published *Dance Between Two Cultures*, which explores the similarities and differences in the writings of authors from Cuba, the Dominican Republic, and Puerto Rico, a novel approach at the time. During the decades between these books, Luis wrote, edited, and coedited several

William Luis is a Cuban American literary critic who was one of the first to study Cuban American, Dominican American, and Nuyorican literature as a regional expression rather than as separate national interests. *Courtesy of William Luis.*

books, including *Voices from Under: Black Narrative in Latin America and the Caribbean* (1984), *Literary Bondage: Slavery in Cuban Narrative* (1990), *Translating Latin America: Culture as Text* (1991*), Modern Latin American Fiction Writers, First Series* (1992) and *Second Series* (1994). He also wrote *Culture and Customs of Cuba* (2001) and *Lunes de Revolución: Literatura y cultura en los primeros años de la Revolución Cubana* (2003).

In his studies, Luis doesn't approach literature as an isolated expression of a group but as the product of numerous experiences, such as historical and sociological events and the role of popular culture and ethnicity, often bringing together disciplines that are usually separated, such as literature and music. He has said, in an interview in the *Multicultural Review*, that Latino "literature and studies represent a different way of envisioning our traditional disciplines, one that questions boundaries."

Further Reading

Figueredo, Danilo H. "Of Salsa and Sonnets, Stories and Soul: A Conversation with Cuban-American Literary Critic William Luis." *Multicultural Review* 9, no. 4 (December 2000): 34–37, 56–58.

—*D. H. Figueredo*

Lunes de Revolución (1959–61)

■

A weekly supplement of the newspaper *Revolución, Lunes de Revolución* was the most important Cuban, and probably Latin American, literary journal of its time, reaching a circulation of 250,000. The journal's director was novelist **Guillermo Cabrera Infante**, who would become a member of the **Boom** writers.

Lunes attempted to provide a direction for the unfolding literature and culture of the Cuban Revolution. The supplement was anti-imperialistic and critical of the United States government, but it supported a wide definition of culture, publishing writers who were not necessarily supportive of the revolutionary regime. The supplement accepted submissions from such a variety of contributors as Jorge Luis Borges (1899–1986), Jean-Paul Sartre (1905–80), and **Fidel Castro** himself.

The journal became a threat as Castro began to align himself with Cuba's Communist Party. When *Lunes de Revolución* opted to support a documentary—titled *P. M.*, about nightlife in Cuba—censored by the government, the journal was closed down. The closing of *Lunes de Revolución* signaled an end to a period of plurality and openness in Cuban society and culture. *See also* Cuza Malé, Belkis; Literary Journals; Padilla, Heberto; "Within the Revolution Everything. . . ."

Further Reading

Luis, William. *Lunes de Revolución: Literatura y cultura en los primeros años de la Revolución Cubana*. Madrid: Verbum, 2003.

—*William Luis*

Luz y Caballero, José de la (1800–62)

José de la Luz y Caballero was a Cuban philosopher who through his school lectures, newspaper articles, and a collection of sayings, proverbs, and ideas dubbed "aforismos"—gathered and published as *Aforismos y apuntaciones* in 1945—promoted the formation of a Cuban character as a separate identity from Spaniards. One of his better known statements is "He who can not master himself can not master anything."

Born in Havana, as a young man he traveled extensively throughout Europe and the United States, where he befriended such major literary figures as Sir Walter Scott (1771–1832), Johann Wolfgang Goethe (1749–1832), and Henry W. Longfellow (1807–1882). Back in Cuba in the 1830s, he became a lawyer and was director of the school Colegio de San Cristóbal, where he taught philosophy. In 1848, he established his own school, El Salvador; there he promulgated his ideas on politics, philosophy, and education, and advocated for the end of colonial rule on the island. He was accused of participating in La Conspiración de la Escalera—the Conspiracy of the Ladder—, a supposedly abolitionist plot, along with poet **Gabriel de Concepción Valdés "Plácido,"** but was acquitted.

Luz y Caballero wrote for the periodicals *Revista Bimestre Cubana* and *Diario de la Habana*. His pedagogical text *Libro de lectura por el método explicativo* (1833) promoted participatory education and explanations rather than memorization. His liberal ideas influenced the Cuban leaders of the 1868 rebellion known as The Ten Years' War.

Further Reading

Cartaya Cotta, Perla. *José de la Luz y Caballero y la pedagogía de su época*. Habana: Editorial de Ciencias Sociales, 1989.

Chávez Rodríguez, Justo A. *Del ideario pedagógico de José de la Luz y Caballero (1800–1862)*. Habana: Editorial Pueblo y Educación, 1992.

—*D. H. Figueredo*